77442

KF
8841
.B47
2007

Bergman, Paul, 1943-

W9-CUP-479

...urt

Make the law as simple as
possible, saving you time,
money and headaches.

DATE DUE

WITHDRAWN

GAYLORD   PRINTED IN U.S.A.

...ion

ALWAYS UP TO DATE

Sign up for NOLO'S
LEGAL UPDATER

Old law is bad law. We'll
email you when we publish
an updated edition of this
book—sign up for this
free service at **nolo.com/
legalupdater**.

*Find the latest updates
at* NOLO.COM

Recognizing that the law
can change even before you
use this book, we post legal
updates during the life of this
edition at **nolo.com/updates**.

Is this edition the newest?
ASK US!

To make sure that this is
the most recent edition
available, just give us a call
at **800-728-3555**.

(Please note that we
cannot offer legal advice.)

...Will, as well as online forms for LLC formation,
incorporation, divorce, name change—and
many more! Check it out at **http://nolonow.
nolo.com**.

NOLO'S LAWYER DIRECTORY

Meet your new attorney

If you want advice from a qualified attorney,
turn to Nolo's Lawyer Directory—the only
directory that lets you see hundreds of in-depth
attorney profiles so you can pick the one that's
right for you. Find it at http://lawyers.nolo.com.

FASKEN LEARNING RESOURCE CENTER

9000077442

Please note

We believe accurate, plain-English legal information should help you solve many of your own legal problems. But this text is not a substitute for personalized advice from a knowledgeable lawyer. If you want the help of a trained professional—and we'll always point out situations in which we think that's a good idea—consult an attorney licensed to practice in your state.

NOLO

77442

6th edition

Represent Yourself in Court

How to Prepare & Try a Winning Case

by Attorneys Paul Bergman & Sara J. Berman-Barrett

Cartoons by Mike Twohy

Sixth Edition	JANUARY 2008
Editor	EMILY DOSKOW
Cover Design	SUSAN PUTNEY
Cartoons	MIKE TWOHY
Book Design	TERRI HEARSH
Proofreading	MARK NIGARA
Index	BAYSIDE INDEXING SERVICE
Printing	CONSOLIDATED PRINTERS, INC.

Bergman, Paul, 1943-
  Represent yourself in court : how to prepare and try a winning case / by Paul
Bergman & Sara J. Berman-Barrett ; cartoons by Mike Twohy. -- 6th ed.
     p. cm.
  Includes bibliographical references and index.
  ISBN-13: 978-1-4133-0710-8 (pbk. : alk. paper)
  ISBN-10: 1-4133-0710-8 (pbk. : alk. paper)
  1. Trial practice--United States--Popular works. 2. Pro se representation--
United States--Popular works. I. Berman-Barrett, Sara J., 1964- II. Title.
  KF8841.B47 2007
  347.73'504--dc22

                                          2007018039

Copyright © 1997, 2000, 2003, 2005, and 2008 by Paul Bergman and
Sara J. Berman-Barrett.
ALL RIGHTS RESERVED. PRINTED IN THE U.S.A.

No part of this publication may be reproduced, stored in a retrieval system, or
transmitted in any form or by any means, electronic, mechanical, photocopying,
recording, or otherwise without the prior written permission of the publisher and
the authors. Reproduction prohibitions do not apply to the forms contained in this
product when reproduced for personal use.

Quantity sales: For information on bulk purchases or corporate premium sales,
please contact the Special Sales department. For academic sales or textbook
adoptions, ask for Academic Sales. Call 800-955-4775 or write to Nolo at 950 Parker
St., Berkeley, CA, 94710.

77442

Dedications

To Andrea, Daniel, and Julia, and to all our readers whose active and knowledgeable participation in courtrooms across the country will improve the American system of justice.

Acknowledgments

Our continuing gratitude to Jake Warner and Steve Elias. In a field dominated by texts devoted to specific types of legal problems, Jake and Steve saw a need for a book cutting across the entire spectrum of civil cases, and urged us to produce a book that could help all pro se litigants achieve justice while helping litigants represented by lawyers achieve effective representation by becoming "educated clients." Our thanks also to Mary Randolph for carrying on Nolo's tradition of excellence and caring. We have done our best to fulfill all of their visions by trying to demystify the entire civil justice process.

Over the course of six editions, we have been assisted by an array of fine editors and other creative members of the Nolo staff. We have also benefited immensely from research assistance provided by a number of attorneys as well as by UCLA law students and law librarians. All of your contributions continue to be reflected in this edition and we thank you again for them.

Finally, for this sixth edition we gratefully recognize the wonderful editorial assistance provided by Emily Doskow. To the extent that we have been able to produce a new edition that is not only up to date but also more complete and helpful than its predecessors, we must give much of the credit to Emily, her years of litigation experience, and her careful reading of the entire text.

Illustration Credits

Cartoons

All cartoons in this book were drawn by Mike Twohy. The following cartoons are being reprinted with permission from the artist:

Page 8, © 1981 Mike Twohy, originally appearing in *Criminal Defense*.

Page 24, © 1987 Mike Twohy, originally appearing in *The National Law Journal*.

Page 143, © 1987 Mike Twohy, originally appearing in *The Wall Street Journal*.

Page 216, © 1991 Mike Twohy, originally appearing in *The National Law Journal*.

Page 232, © 1979 Mike Twohy.

Page 270, © 1981 Mike Twohy.

Page 296, © 1991 Mike Twohy, originally appearing in *Trial Diplomacy Journal*.

Page 398, © 1981 Mike Twohy, originally appearing in *Medical Economics*.

Page 465, © 1984 Mike Twohy, originally appearing in *The National Law Journal*.

Computer Drawn Illustrations

All computer drawn illustrations were done by Terri Hearsh.

Table of Contents

Going It Alone in Court

This book provides the information you need to prepare for trial and represent yourself in court.

Understanding the procedures and techniques described in the book will help you present a persuasive, legally proper case whether you are a plaintiff (meaning that you have filed a lawsuit yourself) or a defendant (meaning that you have been sued). Illustrated with sample forms, pleadings, and courtroom dialogues, the book will take you through the litigation process step by step, from deciding whether you have a valid legal claim or defense to preparing an appeal if you lose.

If you had your druthers, you might prefer to turn your case over to a trial attorney (often called a "litigator"), who is trained to gather and present evidence in court. But in many common situations, it doesn't make economic sense to hire a lawyer. Perhaps you find yourself in a situation like one of the following:

- You injured your back when you slipped on loose carpeting in an office building you were visiting.
- You own a small manufacturing business and have sued a supplier for delivering faulty raw material.
- Your landlord has sued to evict you from your apartment, and you claim that the eviction is unlawful.
- You have filed a claim against your ex-spouse seeking increased child support.
- You are a building contractor who has been sued by a homeowner for using building materials other than those specified in a remodeling contract, and you claim that the homeowner asked you to modify the contract after work was begun.

- Money that was left to you in trust by your parents has been depleted by improper investments made by the trust company that controls the trust assets.

In any of these instances—and countless more—if you can't resolve your dispute in a friendly way, you may have to go to court to protect your rights.

Unfortunately, with fees charged by lawyers commonly running in excess of $150 an hour, it may not make economic sense—or even be financially possible—for you to hire a lawyer. Even if you win and are able to collect what the other side owes you, the lawyer's fees may devour much of your gain. As a result, representing yourself in court or dropping your claim or defense altogether may be your only realistic alternatives.

The Scope of This Book

This book explains rules and techniques for preparing and trying a civil case, including how to handle a case in family court or bankruptcy court. It does not cover criminal cases. See "Civil and Criminal Cases," below. You will learn how to figure out what evidence you need to present a legally solid case, whether you are a plaintiff or a defendant. Among other things, you will also learn:

- how to prepare the initial pleadings (usually called a "complaint" or an "answer") that get a civil case underway (see Chapter 3)
- how to comply with the important "pretrial procedures" and activities that typically take place after the initial pleadings but before trial (see Chapter 4)

- how to investigate your case and gather evidence, using both informal methods and formal "discovery" (see Chapter 5)
- how to try to settle your case without going to trial (see Chapter 6)
- how to select a jury if you are involved in a jury trial (see Chapter 10)
- how to present your own testimony and conduct direct examination of your witnesses and cross-examination of your adversary's witnesses (see Chapters 12 and 13)
- how to apply rules of evidence so that a judge will accept your admissible evidence and exclude your adversary's improper evidence (see Chapter 16)
- how to locate, hire, and effectively use expert witnesses (see Chapter 19)
- how to present a persuasive opening statement and closing argument (see Chapters 11 and 14), and
- how to comply with courtroom procedural rules, such as where and when to sit and stand (see Chapter 2), how to handle exhibits (tangible objects like photographs and receipts) (see Chapter 15), and how to address the judge and opposing counsel (see Chapters 2 and 17).

The book guides you, step by step, through every phase of a civil trial.

Unless you are in court regularly, you may not know how a case proceeds from initial filing through trial. Therefore, this book also provides you with background information about what you will see—and what you need to do—when you enter the courtroom where your case will be heard.

Why Do People Represent Themselves?

The National Center for State Courts recently conducted a study to find out why more and more people are representing themselves in court instead of hiring an attorney. The study found that those who represent themselves believe that:

- lawyers are too expensive
- courts and lawyers do not deliver quality services, and
- their cases are simple enough to handle themselves.

Analysts of civil court systems provide additional reasons for the growth in self-representation, including:

- people want to be in control of their cases
- lawyers often lack good "bedside manners," inadequately explaining to clients what is happening with their cases
- many people distrust lawyers, both because of negative personal experiences and because of the negative images of lawyers often portrayed on TV, in books, and in the movies, and
- legal assistance is available from other sources, such as the Internet, computer software, and paralegal or other legal document providers.

(Source: M. Tebo, "Self-Serve Legal Aid," *ABA Journal*, August 2002.)

Civil and Criminal Cases

This book covers only civil cases, which arise when private citizens (including corporations and other associations) sue each other. Criminal trials, by contrast, occur when a state or the federal government seeks to punish someone for violating a criminal law. The major differences are:

- **The result.** Civil cases typically end with money paid by one party to the other; criminal cases may result in fines paid to the government and imprisonment.
- **The burden of proof.** In most civil cases, a plaintiff wins by convincing a judge or jury by a "preponderance of evidence" that its claim is true. In criminal cases the prosecution must prove a defendant's guilt "beyond a reasonable doubt."
- **The right to a jury trial.** You are entitled to a jury in all criminal cases but not in all civil cases. For example, you are entitled to a jury trial in personal injury cases but not in child custody and spousal support cases. Also, most states require unanimous jury verdicts in criminal trials but agreement by only three-fourths of the jurors in a civil case.
- **The right to counsel.** Defendants facing criminal charges have the right to an appointed lawyer, at the government's expense, in almost all cases. In civil cases, plaintiffs and defendants have to pay for their own lawyers or represent themselves.

We have written another book that can be of great help if you or someone you know has been arrested or accused of a crime and is facing possible criminal charges. It's called *The Criminal Law Handbook: Know Your Rights, Survive the System* (Nolo). While that handbook does not recommend self-representation in criminal cases, it can be a tremendous resource at a time you need solid, trustworthy information.

You will learn where to file your court papers; how to subpoena witnesses (order witnesses to come to court and testify); the functions of a courthouse Clerk's Office and a courtroom clerk; and the powers and duties of all the personnel who typically carry out courthouse business, including bailiffs, court reporters, interpreters, attorneys, jurors, and judges.

Finally, the book devotes separate chapters to two types of specialized court proceedings. Chapter 21 provides information about hearings in divorce and related family law matters, such as spousal abuse, child custody, child support, and spousal support. Chapter 22 provides information for debtors and creditors about contested hearings that often occur in bankruptcy cases.

Family law and bankruptcy matters merit separate chapters for a number of reasons. Each involves specialized hearings that you don't find in other types of civil cases. Also, judges usually decide these disputes alone, without juries. And litigants frequently represent themselves in both family law and bankruptcy cases. This is especially true in divorce court, where at least one of the parties is self-represented in 80% of cases.

Can You Really Represent Yourself?

Unless your case is unusually complex, you really can represent yourself. You may not have all the legal training of a lawyer, but you do not need to go to law school to have common sense, to learn how to ask intelligent questions, or to recognize what makes people and information believable. In the words of Oliver Wendell Holmes, one of the country's most revered U.S. Supreme Court justices, "The life of the law has not been logic, it has been experience." As these words suggest, your everyday life experience is the foundation of most of what you need to know to present a coherent, convincing case. Besides, as former Supreme Court Chief Justice Warren Burger was fond of pointing out, many lawyers are not such hotshots; they often come to court ill-prepared and lacking professional skills.

Nor do you need to be intimidated by the difficulty of the law or legal reasoning. Your trial will probably be concerned with facts, not abstract legal issues. For the most part, you can look up the law you need to know. (See Chapter 23 for information on how to do this.) Legal reasoning is not so different from everyday rational thinking. Forget the silly notion that you have to act or sound like an experienced lawyer to be successful in court. Both lawyers and nonlawyers with extremely varied personal styles can succeed in court. The advice to "be yourself" is as appropriate inside the courtroom as outside.

No matter how many times you read this book and how carefully you prepare, you will probably feel anxious when you represent yourself in court, especially if your opponent has a lawyer. Perhaps it will help you to realize that you aren't alone. Many professionals feel anxiety—particularly before a first performance—whether they are lawyers about to begin a trial, teachers about to teach a class, or actors about to perform on stage. So take a deep breath and gather up your courage. As long as you combine your common sense with the principles and techniques described in this book, and are not afraid to ask a court clerk, a law librarian, an attorney, or even the judge for help if you become confused, you should be able to represent yourself competently and effectively.

To represent yourself successfully, especially if your adversary has a lawyer, you must be prepared to invest substantial amounts of time in your case—and particularly in the many pretrial procedures and maneuvers that can mean the difference between winning and losing. To nonlawyers, the legal system seems to center on the outcomes of trials. After all, that's the dramatic part—and the focus of so many movies and TV shows. If you believe these portrayals, you might think you just have to file a few papers, tell your story to a judge, and claim victory. (This was the belief of Vinny, who represents two defendants charged with murder in the wonderful courtroom comedy film, *My Cousin Vinny*. Vinny shows up for an arraignment and tries to explain to the judge that the police made a mistake. Vinny is shocked when the judge advises him that he's not going to set aside all of his state's procedures just because Vinny finds himself "in the unique position of representing clients who say they didn't do it.")

For lawyers, in contrast, the legal system is an array of procedures that begin long before trial (and often continue long afterwards). In fact, few cases ever actually make it to trial—they settle out of court—or are dismissed—because of these pretrial procedures. Although individually justifiable, collectively these procedures create the potential for adversaries to engage in lengthy "paper wars" that you might find harrowing. Many lawyers are fair and reasonable and will not try to "paper you to death." Nevertheless, you have to realize from the outset that representing yourself effectively is likely to require a substantial commitment of time—even if your case never goes to trial.

Coping with Being a Stranger in a Strange Land

Courts are public institutions belonging to the people, and you have the right to represent yourself there. However, courts are also bureaucratic institutions with very heavy case-loads. Historically, filing clerks, courtroom clerks, court reporters, and even judges have usually preferred to deal with lawyers rather than with people who represent themselves. (When you represent yourself, you may find yourself referred to as a "pro per" or "pro se" litigant, Latin abbreviations favored by judges and lawyers.) Although the increasing number of people representing themselves is beginning to change these attitudes in some places, many court personnel believe (often

mistakenly) that they can do their work more quickly and easily when they work with lawyers than when they work with people who are representing themselves.

So even if it seems highly unfair, do not be surprised if you encounter initial hostility from court personnel. In your eyes, you are an individual seeking justice and doing what you have a right to do. But to the people who work in courthouses every day, you may be perceived as someone who will make their jobs more difficult. Instead of helping you, they may even attempt to put obstacles in your path, hoping that you will get discouraged and go away.

Knowing ahead of time that you may encounter a hostile attitude is the best weapon against it. Read and study this book and other legal resources, many of which are available free online or in your local library. Learn how to prepare and present a persuasive case and follow the proper procedures for the Clerk's Office and the courtroom. If you believe that court personnel at any level are being rude to you, be courteous and professional in return, even as you insist upon fair treatment. By knowing and following court rules and courtroom techniques, you can often earn the respect of the judge and the others who work in the courtroom. As a result, you may well find that they will go out of their way to help you.

Realize too that even those lawyers who are in their comfort zone in the court system often get yelled at and harassed by other lawyers, judges, and court personnel. For many lawyers, hassles like these go with the job, and they tend to develop a thick skin. To survive as a stranger in this strange land, your skin probably has to be even thicker.

The Changing Face of Civil Court

In the years since this book first appeared, the number of people representing themselves in civil court cases has continued to grow. We can't give you exact statistics because few courts track the percentage of self-represented parties. However, one study in Idaho shows that during a seven-year period 87% of civil defendants in that state were self-represented. (Patrick D. Costello, Courthouse Assistance Offices, 42-JUN *Advocate* (Idaho) 13 (1999).) Other research indicates that at least one party was self-represented in more than two-thirds of domestic relations cases in California and in nearly 90% of divorce cases in Phoenix, Arizona, and Washington, DC. (See Jona Goldschmidt et al., *Meeting the Needs of Pro Se Litigation* (1998).) A Consumer Based Approach.) These studies are substantiated by many civil court administrators and judges, who estimate that the number of self-represented parties has increased by at least 50% over the past five years.

Politicians and judges have started to respond to the growth in self-representation. For example, some courts have created fill-in-the-blank court forms tailored to the types of documents a self-represented party is most likely to need. In other courts, "pro se advisors" are available in the courthouse to give free advice to people representing themselves. As a result, while you may still feel like a stranger in a strange land, you will not be alone—and the land won't be as strange as it was just a few years ago.

Finding a Legal Coach

Even if it does not make economic sense for you to turn your entire case over to an attorney, you may want or need to seek occasional legal advice during the proceedings. A legal coach—someone you can turn to on an as-needed basis—might help you in a number of areas. For example, your legal coach might prepare documents, shorten the time you spend on legal research by suggesting helpful sources, suggest evidence that might help you establish a legal claim, advise you of filing deadlines, and inform you of rules and customs peculiar to your local courts (and, therefore, beyond the reach of this book). Throughout the book, we point out the specific stages of a lawsuit when it might be wise to seek help from a legal coach.

An experienced civil litigator (an attorney who primarily works on civil lawsuits) who is willing to work with you on a part-time basis is generally the best choice for a legal coach. However, you may have difficulty finding an attorney who will agree to such an arrangement. Traditionally, almost all litigators took cases on an all-or-nothing basis. That is, they assumed complete responsibility for a case or declined representation altogether. In part, litigators' reluctance to help self-represented parties is probably attributable to fears about violating lawyers' ethical codes or committing legal malpractice for giving advice based on incomplete knowledge. Reluctance also stems, at least to some extent, from professional bias; many attorneys believe that only lawyers are competent enough to deal with America's courts.

Fortunately, many lawyers' attitudes toward serving as a legal coach are changing. The American Bar Association's Standing Committee on the Delivery of Legal Services has sponsored conferences on "unbundling," which refers to providing legal advice and services on a piecemeal basis to consumers who are representing themselves. The benefits of unbundling are further promoted in the book *Unbundling Legal Services* by attorney Forrest Mosten (ABA). (Consider asking an attorney of good will who is nevertheless hesitant to act as a legal coach to read that book!)

Many states allow attorneys to offer unbundled services, sometimes referred to as "limited representation" or "limited scope representation." A lawyer's services may include providing advice, preparing documents, and even making court appearances. The scope of the lawyer's services should be clearly explained in a written agreement. Limited scope representation should also be reasonable under the circumstances. For example, lawyers should be reluctant to serve as a legal coach when legal issues are very complex or a client has a serious disability or has suffered horrific injuries.

Some lawyers may not be familiar with the term "legal coach." When you are looking for a legal coach, explain to the attorneys you interview that you are looking for coaching or limited scope representation, or ask them whether they're willing to do the specific tasks you need, such as reviewing documents or helping you prepare for a court hearing or trial.

You may also be able to hire someone other than a lawyer to be your legal coach.

Some states now allow licensed paralegals (attorney assistants) to perform some tasks that formerly were the exclusive domain of lawyers. For instance, in California and Florida, paralegals are allowed to prepare many types of documents for self-represented parties to file. If you are considering hiring a legal coach, therefore, check to see whether paralegals are available in your area and what services they are allowed to provide. (We the People is the name of one business that provides paralegal services directly to consumers in some states.)

Legal websites may provide another source of legal coaching. While websites such as www.nolo.com offer loads of high-quality legal information and tools to create many simple forms, very few Internet companies provide case-specific legal advice and comprehensive document preparation services to people who represent themselves. Here are a few websites that may be able to provide legal information, form preparation, or advice:

- www.lawguru.com
- www.AllLaw.com
- www.legalzoom.com
- www.findlaw.com, and
- www.courtinfo.ca.gov/programs/equalaccess/ethiss.htm#limited

(prepared by the California Judicial Council. This website has extensive articles and information on unbundling).

Before consulting a legal coach, read through this book and your local court rules. (Court rules are discussed and explained in the next section of this chapter.) You may find answers to questions that you would otherwise pay a legal coach to answer. (For more detailed advice about hiring and working with an attorney as a legal coach, see Chapter 23.)

Be Cautious When Getting Advice from Nonlawyers or the Internet

When lawyers provide substandard representation, dissatisfied clients can get help from state disciplinary authorities and file legal malpractice claims in court. By contrast, while it may be cheaper and easier to get help from a nonlawyer, the services they can provide are limited—and it may be much more difficult to seek redress for their mistakes. For example, paralegals or websites may help you prepare a document, but they can't give you legal advice as to whether that document is best suited to your situation. Also, you are ultimately responsible if a document provider fills out a form incorrectly; a clerk or judge is unlikely to correct any mistakes.

And, of course, charlatans may be waiting to take advantage of you. An article in the August 2002 issue of the *ABA Journal* describes one such ploy: A nonlawyer who provides legal assistance may promise a self-represented party,

"I can go to court with you." However, the party may understand this to mean that the nonlawyer can provide representation in court, which of course the nonlawyer cannot do. (M. Tebo, "Self-Service Legal Aid.")

Finally, be aware that the concept of legal advice on the Internet is still new. Shakeouts in the industry are likely; some websites may disappear only to be replaced by others. Also, remember that the risk of inaccuracy and miscommunication may be greater when you communicate over the Internet than when you seek legal assistance face to face.

For all these reasons, you should always be a cautious consumer when seeking assistance from nonlawyers. Seek references and ask about the nonlawyer's background, training, and experience. Just as important, do some research yourself so that you have a basis for evaluating the nonlawyer's work.

> ## Working With an Attorney Who Is Representing You
>
> This book can be of assistance to you even if you are represented by an attorney in the traditional fashion. Your case belongs to you, not to your lawyer. A good lawyer will be able to do a better job of representing you if you are informed and knowledgeable about the litigation process and can participate in making critical decisions. For detailed advice and information on working with your lawyer through every stage of a civil lawsuit, see *The Lawsuit Survival Guide: A Client's Companion to Litigation,* by Joseph Matthews (Nolo) and *How to Win (& Survive) a Lawsuit,* by Robert M. Dawson (Arbor Books).

ticular chapter immediately, begin preparing to represent yourself by reading through the book as a whole. As you become familiar with the litigation process, you will understand the significance of procedures and techniques that may initially seem peculiar or unnecessary.

> ## Learning the Lingo
>
> There's no way to avoid it: If you represent yourself in court, you're going to run into a lot of unfamiliar legal terminology. This book tries to translate the most common jargon into plain English. For quick reference, check the glossary at the back of the book. You can find more plain language definitions in Nolo's online legal glossary, available for free at www.nolo.com.

Using This Book

This book is very different from other books written for nonlawyers. It does not focus on any single area of the law or type of legal problem but serves as a guide to courtroom self-representation in any kind of case. Because of the book's unique nature, you may find the following comments and suggestions helpful.

If Time Permits, Read Through the Entire Book

This book is designed both to increase your overall understanding of the litigation process and to provide detailed advice about each stage of trial. Unless you are already in the midst of trial and need to refer to a par-

Use This Book in Conjunction With Local Court Rules

This book can guide you through nearly every kind of trial in every court system (state or federal) because the litigation process is remarkably uniform throughout all of them. In part, this is because federal courts and most state courts share a "common law" heritage—a way of trying cases that came over from England and developed along with the country. And, in part, it is because many local procedures are consistent with national legal codes (sets of rules and regulations).

For example, the Federal Rules of Evidence (often referred to as the FRE) govern the introduction of evidence in federal court trials. But about 40 states also use the FRE in their state court trials. And even those states that have not formally adopted the FRE have evidence rules that are remarkably similar to them. This means that, for the most part, trials are conducted in the same way nationwide. Another set of federal rules, the Federal Rules of Civil Procedure (or FRCP) apply similarly to govern procedural (rather than evidentiary) rules. Because of this basic uniformity, the book frequently refers you to specific rules that, even if they differ somewhat from your state's rules, should help you understand the basic procedures that will apply to your case.

However, this book cannot serve as a complete guide to all the rules you need to know. For one thing, the exact rule in your court system may be somewhat different from the example we give. In that event, knowing about another similar rule—either a federal rule or another state's rule—can help you locate the rule in your state. (See Chapter 23 for information on doing your own legal research.) Also, each court system has its own procedural rules that, though important, cannot be covered in this book. For example, local court rules set time limits for filing various kinds of documents and page limits on the length of those documents. You will have to learn and comply with these local requirements.

Whenever you are concerned about a specific rule of evidence or procedure, you should always read your court system's specific provision. In general, the rule books you will need to have handy are these:

- **Your state's "Rules of Evidence."** These rules define the evidence you and your adversary are allowed to introduce for a judge or jury to consider. Evidence rules may be collected in an "Evidence Code" or a particular "chapter" or "title" of your state's laws, or they may be included in a larger collection of laws called "Rules of Civil Procedure."

- **Your state's "Rules of Court."** These are rules that set the procedures and deadlines that the courts in a state must follow. Generally, states have separate sets of rules for different kinds of courts. For example, a state may have one set of rules for its municipal courts (courts that try cases involving limited amounts of money), another for its superior courts (courts that try cases involving higher amounts of money), and still others for its appellate courts (courts that review the decisions of municipal and superior courts). All the rules may, however, be published in a single book. Some states also have separate sets of rules for specialized courts, such as family law courts, which hear cases involving divorce, child custody, and child support; or probate courts, which hear cases involving wills and trusts.

- **Your court's "Local Rules."** These are the rules for a specific courthouse or set of courthouses in one county that generally allocate business between different courtrooms, specify where to file documents, set rules of courtroom behavior, and the like.

States Organize Their Trial Courts Differently

Some states have just one kind of trial court, which hears all sorts of cases. In Illinois, for example, circuit courts hear all kinds of disputes. In other states, by contrast, cases that involve less than a certain dollar amount may be tried in one type of court (municipal, city, or justice court, for example), while larger cases go to another type of court (superior, county, or circuit court, for example).

Books containing all of these rules should be available in a public law library. You may also want to purchase these books separately from the Clerk's Office in the courthouse in which your case is filed, or from a legal bookstore, so that you can have them close at hand for reference as you read through this book and go to court. You can also find most court rules on the Internet. The information in Chapter 23 will help you start your search.

 CAUTION

You must follow court rules. Even though you are not a lawyer, judges will expect you to know and follow all court rules. If you miss a deadline, use the wrong kind of paper, or violate some other rule, you will suffer the consequences even though you are representing yourself.

For instance, assume that you want to ask for a jury trial and that your local rule requires a jury trial request to be made 30 days after the initial pleadings are filed. If you miss that deadline, you will not have a jury trial unless you go through a laborious process to request an extension of time to file your demand and the judge is willing to make an exception (but don't count on it!).

Make a Trial Notebook

We strongly recommend that you prepare a trial notebook. A trial notebook is a series of outlines covering matters such as what you must prove (or, if you are a defendant, disprove); the evidence you will use to prove (or disprove) those matters; the topics you intend to cover on direct and cross-examination; a list of the names, addresses, and telephone numbers of your witnesses; and the exhibits you plan to introduce into evidence. The notebook serves as your courtroom manager. You can refer to it to make sure that you do not overlook evidence you planned to offer or an argument you intended to make.

As you read through the chapters describing the various stages of a trial, you will find specific sections on how to prepare related outlines for your trial notebook. Chapter 18 pulls together suggestions from earlier chapters and describes how to organize a trial notebook.

Trying to Settle Your Case

Over 90% of all lawsuits are resolved without a trial. If you and your adversary can arrive at a fair resolution without going to trial, you can save yourself time and money. By showing you how to prove and disprove legal claims, this book can help you arrive at a fair resolution of your dispute using settlement procedures. For a complete discussion of settlement, see Chapter 6.

Alternatives to Trial

There are many popular alternatives to trials that still require you to organize and make your case—such as hearings, arbitrations, and mediation. If you become involved in one or more of them, you can still use this book to understand and prepare your arguments.

Here are the typical situations aside from a trial in which you may also be representing yourself.

Court Hearings

Depending on the kind of dispute you're facing, you may find yourself in a hearing rather than a trial. For example, you'll probably have a hearing if you are seeking an increase or a decrease in spousal or child support following your divorce or if you need to prove how much money you are entitled to after a defendant has failed to respond to your claims. A court hearing is usually a short and narrowly defined proceeding in which you are not entitled to a jury. A judge conducts the hearing and makes a ruling. The other party to the dispute may not even show up. This book's advice is as pertinent to hearings as it is to trials. Many of the courtroom procedures and rules of evidence are exactly the same in a hearing as in a trial. And you still must offer evidence in a way that persuades the judge or hearing officer to rule in your favor.

Arbitration

Arbitration is an alternative to trial that is often perceived to be quicker and less costly. In arbitration, a privately agreed-to arbitrator, not a judge, rules on the case. There is no jury, procedures before the hearing are more informal, and the arbitrator is not strictly bound by rules of evidence. Arbitrators generally charge by either the full or half day; you and your adversary split the arbitrator's fee.

If you have a legal dispute, you may well find yourself involved in an arbitration rather than a trial. One reason is that in many states, judges have the power to order you and your adversary to arbitrate certain kinds of disputes. Or you may have signed an agreement that provides for binding arbitration of all disputes arising under the agreement. For example, if you are an investor who believes a brokerage house violated securities laws while handling your account, a condominium owner who has filed suit against your condominium association for unreasonably restricting your right to remodel your unit, or a business-person who wants to sue for breach of a written contract, you may have agreed in writing (in the broker's agreement, the condominium association's set of rules, or the business contract) to arbitrate all disputes.

Though arbitration proceedings are generally less formal than trials, most of the principles described in this book also apply to arbitration. As in a trial, you and your adversary present evidence to the arbitrator through your own testimony and the testimony of witnesses. Like a judge, an arbitrator evaluates the credibility and legal significance of evidence to decide whether you win or lose the case.

Also, because most arbitrators are lawyers or retired judges, their actions tend to be strongly influenced by their legal training. The rules and procedures they follow generally closely resemble those used by judges in trials.

RESOURCE

Resouces on Arbitration. *Settle It Out of Court: How to Resolve Business and Personal Disputes Using Mediation, Arbitration, and Negotiation*, by Thomas Crowley (John Wiley & Sons), is a comprehensive guide that includes strategies for selecting arbitrators and mediators.

Alternative Dispute Resolution: Panacea or Anathema, by Harry T. Edwards, 99 *Harvard Law Review* 668 (1986), is an analysis of the advantages and disadvantages of arbitration and other dispute resolution procedures.

Dispute Resolution: Negotiation, Mediation, and Other Processes, by Stephan B. Goldberg et al. (Aspen Publishers), is a textbook that sets forth arbitration principles and methods.

Mediation

Another popular method of resolving disputes outside of court is mediation, which is generally less formal and less costly than arbitration. Mediation is a voluntary process in which you meet with your adversary in the company of a neutral third person, the mediator. The mediator has no power to impose a solution; rather, the mediator's role is to facilitate settlement by clarifying each party's position, encouraging cooperation, and suggesting possible solutions. Professional mediators charge for their services, typically by the hour. Normally, the parties split the mediator's fee.

Even though mediation is informal, to reach a successful result you will need to show your adversary that you have strong evidence to support your legal position—evidence that is admissible in court should mediation fail. Otherwise, your adversary may not be willing to settle the case on terms you think are fair. This book will help you represent your position effectively during mediation.

RESOURCE

Resources on Mediation. *Mediate, Don't Litigate* by Peter Lovenheim & Lisa Guerin (Nolo), available as an electronic book at www.nolo.com.

Mediation: A Comprehensive Guide to Resolving Conflicts Without Litigation by Jay Folberg & Alison Taylor (Jossey-Bass).

Mediation Process: Practical Strategies for Resolving Conflict by Christopher Moore (Jossey-Bass).

A Student's Guide to Mediation and the Law by Nancy H. Rogers and Richard A. (Matthew Bender).

Divorce Without Court: A Guide to Mediation & Collaborative Divorce, by Katherine E. Stoner (Nolo).

Negotiation

The most ancient way to settle a dispute is negotiation, in which you sit down with your adversary and try to resolve your differences. Whether or not your case goes to trial, you will almost certainly find yourself negotiating some or all of the issues that are important to you.

Against this background, it doesn't normally make sense to interpret your adversary's offer to "talk settlement" as a sign of weakness. Nor should you be reluctant to be the one to suggest a negotiated settlement. In fact, judges, arbitrators, and mediators routinely urge adversaries to explore settlement even if previous attempts have failed. It's a wise person who never closes the door to a reasonable settlement.

RESOURCE

Resources on Negotiation. *Effective Legal Negotiation and Settlement* by Charles Craver (Matthew Bender).

Effective Approaches to Settlement: A Handbook for Lawyers and Judges by Wayne Brazel (Prentice Hall).

Getting to Yes: Negotiating Agreement Without Giving In by Roger Fisher et al. (Houghton Mifflin) (considered to be the bible on positional bargaining).

Joy of Settlement: The Family Lawyer's Guide to Effective Negotiation and Settlement Strategies by Gregg Herman (ABA).

Administrative Agency Hearings

Administrative hearings rather than trials typically result when individuals contest decisions made by government agencies, or when government agencies refuse to act favorably on individuals' requests. Thanks in part to movies and TV, a popular notion is that in the U.S., trials are the most common method of resolving civil disputes. In fact, across the country many more administrative hearings than trials occur.

Examples of the numerous kinds of situations in which you will participate in an administrative agency hearing rather than a trial include the following:

- After you were fired from a job your claim for government unemployment insurance benefits was denied, and you ask for a hearing to establish that you are entitled to benefits.

- You seek to establish that you are totally disabled after the Social Security Administration reduces your disability payments.
- You are a licensed building contractor or liquor store owner and challenge the licensing agency's decision to suspend or revoke your license.
- You request a hearing to challenge the notice from your state's Department of Motor Vehicles that your driving privileges have been suspended.
- The Internal Revenue Service claims back taxes based on its determination that you took improper deductions, and you ask for a hearing to establish that the deductions were proper.

Administrative law judges (often called "ALJs") preside over administrative hearings. ALJs are typically appointed based on their expertise concerning the work of a particular agency. Most ALJs are not in fact judges; some may not even be lawyers. Moreover, administrative hearings typically take place in small officelike hearing rooms rather than in courtrooms, and no juries are present. Usually, individuals involved in administrative hearings represent themselves. However, whereas only lawyers can represent people in court, agency rules usually allow nonlawyers called "lay representatives" to appear on behalf of individuals in administrative agency hearings. If you will participate in an administrative hearing, you may want to prepare for it by at least conferring with a lay representative before the hearing takes place.

If you represent yourself in an administrative hearing you should be as respectful to the ALJ as you would be to a judge, even though the former wears a suit and the latter a robe. Moreover, whether you address your arguments to a judge or an ALJ, you have the same need to present a clear and persuasive case. Make sure you understand the basis of an agency's action, or what evidence you need to produce to uphold your claim. Also, any witnesses you rely on should attend the hearing, and you should be ready to support your claim with documents and records.

If the ALJ rules against you, you typically can appeal within the agency. If the agency's decision is still unfavorable, you have "exhausted your administrative remedies" and can go to court and file a pleading asking a judge to overturn it. However, the judge who reviews the case will decide it based on the information you provided at the hearing. You won't be able to present new evidence in court.

Every agency tends to make its own rules and follow its own unique set of procedures. Many agencies describe their procedures on a website. In addition, an agency will furnish you with its rules as soon as you indicate that you want to file a claim. Be sure to contact the agency, ask for a copy of its rules before initiating a hearing, and follow them. The federal government and every state have an Administrative Procedure Act that provides basic protections in administrative hearings. You should read the applicable law and make sure the agency follows it. You can get information about these laws from a convenient database maintained by Florida State University at www.law.fsu.edu/library/admin.

While practices vary widely from state to state and even among different agencies within the same state, here are a few characteristics that administrative hearings tend to have in common:

- Formal "discovery" (see Chapter 5) is unavailable. You can examine an agency's records, but you cannot depose agency officials nor submit written questions that they have to answer under oath.
- ALJs do not normally have to follow the rules of evidence that govern courtroom trials. For example, you can offer hearsay evidence.
- You may be the only person other than the ALJ who is present at a hearing. In Social Security hearings, for example, ALJs typically question claimants, review any information they submit, and make decisions, all without any representative appearing for the agency.
- While ALJs are, of course, supposed to be fair and impartial, the ALJ who hears your case will probably be employed by the agency involved in your case. ●

The Courthouse and the Courtroom

Representing yourself in court can be like traveling to a different country. Courtrooms, like nations, have unique rules and customs and even a somewhat different language. Just as with traveling, a successful courtroom experience depends on knowing where you want to go, what the rules are during your journey, and what to expect when you get to your destination.

If you think of this book as your "travel guide" to the world of lawsuits, this chapter is the part that explains the duties and functions of the various people you will encounter, the "lay of the land," customs and etiquette of the "natives," and tips for dealing with them.

An Overview of Different Courts

Federal courts decide two kind of cases: cases involving federal laws or the U.S. Constitution, and cases where the parties are from different states and the amount of money in dispute is more than $75,000.

In the federal system, there are three levels of courts:

- district courts, where most trials occur
- courts of appeal, which hear appeals from the district courts, and
- the U.S. Supreme Court (the highest of the federal courts), which hears appeals in a few cases of its choosing.

There are also some specialized courts within the federal court system, such as tax and bankruptcy courts.

State Courts

State courts decide all the matters that are not covered in federal courts. State courts handle disputes involving state constitutions and state laws covering a wide variety of subjects, such as contracts, personal injuries, and family law. In some situations, either a state or a federal court can hear a case.

State court systems have a variety of different names for their courts. Many (but not all) states have two or more kinds of trial courts. The lowest-level courts are often called small claims, municipal, city, justice, or traffic court—all of which have fairly tight limits on the types of cases they can hear. The next level of trial courts, often called "superior" courts, typically handles larger civil cases, serious criminal cases, and most divorce and other domestic cases. In addition, some states have separate courts that handle only very specialized types of cases, such as juvenile or probate courts; these may be divisions of the general trial court. Trial courts are where most court cases begin and end.

The next level of court, in most states, is the court of appeal, which can review trial court decisions. And last is the highest state court, often called the supreme court (in New York, however, it's called the "Appellate Division"). State supreme courts, like the U.S. Supreme Court, generally choose which cases they will hear from among the many requests they receive. They choose cases that deal with important legal issues, such as those that affect large numbers of people, those that deal with new or conflicted areas of law, and those that test the constitutionality of laws.

To "appeal" a case means to go to an appellate court and ask it to review and overturn the lower court's decision. Usually, you can appeal only if you think the trial court made a mistake about the law that affected the outcome of your case. You cannot appeal just because you don't think a judge or a jury made the correct decision. A trial court is often called the "finder of fact," and an appellate court almost always has to accept the trial court's factual conclusions as true. (See Chapter 20 for more on appeals.)

This book only deals with court cases. See "Civil and Criminal Cases," in Chapter 1.

RESOURCE

Resources on Courts. For more information, you may want to look at a book on the U.S. legal system, such as *Law and the Courts: A Handbook About United States Law and Court Procedures* (ABA).

A Typical Courthouse

Before looking inside a courtroom, let's consider the courthouse as a whole. A courthouse is, in essence, a public office building for judges and their support personnel. Different courts are often located in different buildings—for example, the criminal court may be in a different building than the civil court.

Inside the main entrance to a courthouse, you will often find a directory that lists particular courtrooms or offices. To locate the room you need, however, you may have to ask a guard, because courthouse directories tend not to be user-friendly. They usually don't list helpful information such as where you must go to file legal papers or get information, and they often don't say where places such as the cafeteria or law library are located. Court personnel assume that lawyers—the courthouse's main clientele—know such things already.

Beefed-Up Security

As you enter some courthouses or courtrooms, especially in larger metropolitan communities, you may have to pass through a metal detector. Like airports, courthouses are now concerned about people bringing weapons into the buildings. There may also be a guard on duty.

Because of the metal detectors, there may be long lines to get into the courthouse—especially between 8 a.m. and 9 a.m. when courts tend to start their business hours. So, leave plenty of time. And leave behind any metal or electronic objects you do not need. Cell phones are banned in many courthouses, but you may be allowed to carry a cell phone so long as it's turned off.

You may feel a little lost or intimidated, especially on your first trip to court. The corridors—full of busy lawyers dragging huge briefcases, jurors roaming in bunches, and the occasional armed guard standing by—can be rather imposing. It may help to know that you are not the only one who feels out of place. Because little effort is expended to orient the newcomer, new lawyers often get lost too. Of course, this lack of even minimal hospitality tends to hit self-represented parties a bit harder.

It may help to remember the foreign country analogy; think of this as a very strange land where the people have a different culture and language. Learn their ways by putting aside any shyness you feel and asking for help as soon as you need it. If you don't understand the answers, just keep asking. The courthouse is a public building, supported by your tax dollars; you have the right not only to be there but also to ask as many questions as you want.

Try not to get frustrated or angry. At times, court personnel can appear hostile even when they don't mean to be, simply because they are busy and usually overworked. Also, too often they assume that everyone who appears in court is experienced, and they don't take the little bit of extra time necessary to orient people who are representing themselves. With some patience, you will learn your way around the courthouse, and soon enough you may look so much like you know where you are going that people start asking you for help!

The Clerk's Office

One of the most important offices in the courthouse is the Clerk's Office. It's often located on the first or main floor. Typically, the Clerk's Office is where documents relating to all the cases pending or decided in a courthouse are filed and stored. If one building houses two or more courts, such as a small claims and a civil court, or a federal district and a bankruptcy court, each court will have its own Clerk's Office. That's because each court has its own filing and record-keeping procedures. You'll have to locate the Clerk's Office for the court hearing your case.

Waiting in Line at the Clerk's Office

At many Clerk's Offices, as at the post office or bank, you'll probably file papers and talk to clerks over a counter or through a window. And, also as at the post office, there may be bureaucratic details like rigid hours and different windows for different services. For example, even if you've been waiting patiently in line, the Clerk's Office may close at lunchtime, or you may belatedly learn that you waited in the criminal instead of the civil clerk's line. To avoid such problems, call ahead for information about hours and the specific procedures you must follow to file papers for your civil case.

Once you get to the front of the line, be sure to be polite. The Clerk's Office personnel can help or hinder you, so it pays to try to get them on your side. Understand, however, that some clerks are prejudiced against self-represented parties. (A few even post signs warning you not to ask questions because they don't practice law.) So if you run into someone who is hostile, you must remain firm and not become intimidated. You are entitled to the procedural information you need, provided in language that you can understand. If you don't get it, ask to see the supervising clerk.

> (!) **CAUTION**
>
> **Don't confuse the Clerk's Office and a judge's clerk.** Each judge (or courtroom) usually has an assistant called a clerk. And that clerk may even have an office. But that is not the same as the central Clerk's Office in the courthouse, where documents are filed and stored. You will likely have to consult both the general Clerk's Office and your judge's clerk as your case progresses. The duties of a judge's clerk are discussed in "The Courtroom Players," below.

You will need to go to the Clerk's Office when you file legal papers for your case. You may also deal with the Clerk's Office to check court rules and procedures throughout your case. For example, you will go to the Clerk's Office if you need to file documents such as a pretrial motion (a request for a court order, discussed in Chapter 7) or to get a subpoena (a court order to appear in court). You can also review documents in in your own court file—a master file that typically includes all documents filed by you or your opponent or is issued by the judge.

The Law Library

Many courthouses contain law libraries that are open to the public. The first day you go to the courthouse, it may be a good idea to locate the law library, find out its hours, and walk through to take a look. You will learn more about using the law library in Chapter 23, but the more comfortable you are there, the easier it will be to use.

Often, several courthouses rely on one central library, and a few states don't provide courthouse libraries at all. If you need to consult some legal research materials and your courthouse doesn't have a public law library, ask someone at the Clerk's Office or an attorney you pass in the hallway where the nearest public law library is located. It may, for example, be at a nearby law school.

Courtrooms

The most important part of the courthouse is its courtrooms. We'll explore the inside of a typical courtroom in detail in "The Courtroom and Its Physical Layout," below, but first a few words about the outside. Judges usually have their own regular courtrooms, where they hold trials and other public hearings, and the judge's name and a number are usually posted on or next to the courtroom door.

Most courts prepare a calendar each day, listing the scheduled court hearings, and post it on or near the front door of the courtroom. And calendars for all courtrooms are usually posted in or near the Clerk's Office. A judge may be assigned to different courtrooms on different days, and other calendaring changes may occur, so it is good practice to verify the time and place of your court hearing both at the Clerk's Office and at the courtroom.

> **TIP**
>
> **A courtroom by another name is still courtroom.** The word "courtroom" may not appear on either posted calendars or the courtroom doors. Some courts use other words, such as "department." For example, you may see a sign like this outside a courtroom: "DEPARTMENT 1 – JUDGE SUZANNE KAY. "

Almost all trials are public, so unless there is a sign to the contrary, it's fine to walk into a courtroom, sit in the spectator section, and observe. Always enter quietly so as not to disturb ongoing court proceedings.

Other Offices

Courthouses contain offices for court personnel, from judges to secretaries. They may also house the offices of local officials, such as the city or county attorney and public defender, and law enforcement officers, such as the sheriff or marshal. Courthouses sometimes contain office space for legal newspapers (newspapers that feature articles about current cases and advertisements for lawyers, legal secretaries, court reporters, and other legal services). You may not need to deal with any of these offices personally.

TIP

Don't forget to eat. It's hard to function on an empty stomach, so you may want to find out whether the courthouse has a snack bar or cafeteria. Many do, but the location is often so obscure that you wouldn't find it on your own.

The Courtroom Players

You need to know the identities and roles of typical courtroom players, if only to know whom to approach for advice when you have questions.

The Judge

The judge is the man or woman, usually wearing a black robe, who sits on a raised platform at the front of the courtroom and presides over pretrial hearings and trials. As their principal duties, judges:

- conduct hearings and make rulings on pretrial motions and discovery disputes
- preside over pretrial conferences and facilitate settlement conferences
- control the trial of your case, subject to legal rules of evidence and procedure
- make legal rulings, such as deciding whether a particular piece of evidence can be presented in court or whether it must be kept out of the case
- when there is no jury, decide who wins and loses and how much the loser must pay in damages, and
- when there is a jury, instruct the jury as to the law it must follow in rendering its verdict.

TIP

A judge by any other name is still a judge. The words "court," "bench," "magistrate," "commissioner," and "justice" are sometimes interchanged with the word "judge." ("Justice" typically refers to a judge on an appeals court or on the U.S. Supreme Court.) So if the judge asks you to "approach the bench," that means the judge wants you to step up close so he or she can talk to you and your opponent privately. You'll refer to the judge as "Your Honor" or "the court." For example, you might say, "I ask that the court [meaning the judge] instruct Ms. Loretta Charles, a witness the Defendant intends to have testify later on today, to leave the courtroom immediately."

Some judges hear criminal matters; others conduct only civil (noncriminal) proceedings; still others hear only cases involving

juveniles. Judges' powers depend on the courts in which they preside. For instance, judges in small claims courts usually have power only to grant a limited sum of money damages, often between $2,500 and $10,000.

Judges in appeals courts do not conduct trials at all, but review decisions of trial courts. (See Chapter 20 for more on appeals.) In large communities, where there are many judges, some judges may conduct hearings on pretrial concerns but not the trials themselves. (See Chapter 7.) It follows that a different judge may be assigned to your case during different parts of the litigation process. For example, one judge may rule on your opponent's pretrial motion to dismiss the case, another may conduct settlement negotiations, and still another may preside over the trial.

Cases are also sometimes decided by someone known as a "judge pro tem" (short for the Latin, "judge pro tempore"). Generally, a judge pro tem is a practicing lawyer who is appointed to serve as a temporary judge. You almost always have a right not to accept a judge pro tem and to insist on a regular judge. However, if you exercise this right, your case may be delayed. If you agree to have your case heard by a judge pro tem, the pro tem has all the powers of a regularly appointed judge.

In some courtrooms, the judge is called a "commissioner" or "magistrate." A commissioner or magistrate, typically an employee of the court system, is appointed to act as a judge and hear cases relating to a particular subject matter or in a particular court, such as city, municipal, small claims, or traffic court. Magistrates are appointed by judges of federal district courts (federal trial courts); they hear pretrial matters in civil and criminal cases and conduct some trials. Sometimes the magistrate will hear a case (if the parties agree) and make a recommendation to the district court for a particular ruling. The district court judge must then approve and sign the actual court order.

The Judge's Court Clerk

The judge's clerk (also called the court clerk or the judge's court clerk) is a member of the court clerk's staff who works for a particular judge. The judge's clerk has many duties, including preparing and maintaining the judge's calendar (often called the "docket"), which, like an appointment calendar, lists the dates and times for trials and other matters. The judge's clerk normally sits at a desk in front of or next to the judge's bench. You will typically have to check in with either the clerk or the bailiff (see "The Bailiff," below) when you arrive in the courtroom.

The judge's clerk also retrieves court or case files which are maintained and stored centrally in the main Clerk's Office. Your case file consists of the papers, briefs, pleadings, and other documents relating to your case that have been filed—that is, delivered to the court's custody to be stored as permanent public records.

During trial, the judge's clerk keeps custody of exhibits; administers oaths to witnesses, jurors, and interpreters; and generally helps the judge move cases along. If there are papers you must present to the judge during a court proceeding, you may be directed to hand them to the court clerk (or sometimes the bailiff), who will then pass them on to the judge or file them in the court file. For example, you may need to show the clerk a copy of a subpoena that you served on a witness who did not appear.

When a judge makes a final decision or issues an interim order (a decision on an issue that arises before the close of the case), the judge's clerk typically prepares the order for the judge to sign, although some judges ask the attorneys or self-represented parties to prepare the orders.

Law Clerks

Many judges, especially in federal and higher-level state courts, have law clerks. While the judge's court clerk helps with scheduling and administration of the judge's courtroom, the judge's law clerk helps with the legal substance of the cases that come before the judge. Law clerks are often recent law school graduates. To assist their judge, law clerks:

- research the legal issues presented by the parties
- assist the judge with legal questions that arise before and during trials, and
- help draft the written orders or opinions that judges sometimes produce to explain their rulings.

Getting Advice From Clerks

Generally, you are not supposed to discuss the merits of your case with any court personnel without the other side present (if you do, it's called an "ex parte" contact). And clerks cannot give legal advice. However, you may ask commonplace procedural questions of the judge's clerk or law clerk, such as how you might get an extension (continuance) for a court deadline you will not be able to meet. The judge's clerks (both the court clerk and law clerk) can also be a very valuable resource for routine questions about local court rules and special procedures unique to your judge. For example, a judge may want an extra copy (called a courtesy copy) of pleadings you file with the main Clerk's Office to be sent directly to the judge's courtroom.

If you are concerned that your question may be improper, try explaining the general idea of what you want to ask before you proceed with the full question. The most important thing to remember is to be especially polite to the judge's clerk and law clerk. They work with the judge on a daily basis, and they will not hesitate to tell the judge when someone has been rude to them.

The Bailiff

The bailiff, often classified as a peace officer and commonly uniformed and armed, is an official of the court. As part of a wide range of duties, the bailiff:

- maintains order and decorum in the courtroom—for example, by removing disruptive spectators from the courtroom and ordering people to silence their cell phones (and possibly confiscating them)
- takes charge of juries—for example, brings them into and out of the jury box and deliberation room
- escorts witnesses into and out of the courtroom, and
- hands exhibits to witnesses who are testifying (if the court clerk does not).

The Court Reporter

In most courts, a person called a court reporter records every word that is said during any official (on the record) proceeding in the courtroom. During the proceeding, the reporter may read back testimony of a witness or a statement by a lawyer or self-represented party, upon request of the judge. If you want something read back for your own or the jury's benefit, you must ask the judge for permission to have the court reporter read it back.

In a few courts, such as small claims and some lower-level state trial courts, a court reporter is used only if the parties request one. And some courts now record proceedings with tape recorders. Someone (often a clerk) still runs the tape recorder, so that statements can be played back at the judge's request.

TIP

Speak clearly for court reporters and tape recorders. When you're in court, stand tall and speak up so that a tape recorder or court reporter can correctly record your statements. Speak slowly and directly into the microphone if one is provided. Have your witnesses speak up too. And avoid interrupting, except when it is essential, such as when you need to make objections. (See Chapter 17.) It's difficult for a court reporter, and sometimes for a judge or jury, to sort out what's said when two or more people talk at once.

Court reporters will prepare a transcript booklet of what was said at a particular court session, upon the request of a party or the judge. It is often necessary to get a transcript if you plan to file an appeal. (See Chapter 20.) Court reporters typically charge by the page to prepare transcripts. Depending on the length of the hearing, they can be costly—several hundred dollars for just a few hours of court time.

At the end of the court hearing or other proceeding, ask the court reporter (or a clerk or bailiff in the courtroom) for information on how you can contact the court reporter to obtain a transcript. Or, leave your own phone number and email address with the clerk with a note indicating that you want to buy a copy of the transcript and would like to be notified when it is ready.

Interpreters

Interpreters translate for witnesses and parties who have difficulty speaking or understanding English. Interpreters are sworn to interpret accurately. Parties typically pay for interpreters in civil cases—a one-day trial may cost between $150 and $300 for a common language such as Spanish and as much as three or four times that for a less common language. In most cases, you cannot bring in just anyone (such as a friend or relative), even if that person would be well qualified to interpret. If you or a witness need an interpreter, ask the Clerk's Office, your judge's court clerk, or your legal coach how to arrange for a court-certified interpreter.

Jurors

Jurors evaluate evidence and render verdicts in both criminal and civil cases. They are drawn from the geographic region in which the court is located. Typically called to be available for a couple of weeks at a time, potential jurors may never actually serve on a trial, either because they are never needed or because the judge or a party dismisses them.

When jurors do serve on civil trials, their job is to decide whether claims are factually valid and, if money is awarded, how much the winning party should receive. In limited situations, judges can overturn a jury's verdict or modify the amount of damages the jury awarded. (See Chapter 20.)

In typical civil jury trials, there are between six and 12 jurors and a few alternates, in case a juror gets sick or is unable to finish the trial. In contrast to criminal cases, which often require a unanimous jury, most states allow civil cases to be decided when three-fourths of the jurors agree.

Many cases do not come before juries; they are handled by judges alone. In a few situations, you are not allowed a jury; for example, judges alone handle many family law, bankruptcy, and pretrial matters. In other types of cases in which having a jury trial is an option, it's possible that neither you nor your adversary may want to have a jury. Chapter 10 has tips on deciding whether to try your case before a jury.

Parties

"Parties" are the people or organizations (such as businesses or nonprofit groups) in whose names a case is brought (usually called plaintiffs) or defended (usually called defendants). Cases can involve multiple defendants and sometimes multiple plaintiffs. As a party who is representing yourself, you may be called a "pro per" or "pro se" party.

Witnesses

Two kinds of witnesses may appear at a trial: ordinary witnesses and expert witnesses.

Ordinary Witnesses

Most witnesses testify under oath to information they know through personal knowledge. In the language of the courtroom, they may testify only to things they have perceived with their own senses—meaning what they have personally seen, heard, smelled, tasted, or touched. For example, a bystander at a car accident may come into court and, when asked what he or she saw, say, "I saw the red car go through the stop sign and hit the blue car." However, if the owner of the blue car went home after the accident and told his neighbor (who did not witness the accident) all about it, the neighbor could not testify about how the accident actually occurred. The reason is that the neighbor did not perceive the accident with his or her own senses.

Except for reimbursement of the costs of coming to court (a limited allowance for things like mileage to and from the courthouse), ordinary witnesses cannot be paid to testify. You can obtain a subpoena (court order) to compel a witness to come to court and testify, but typically only if the witness lives or works relatively near the courthouse—in some courts, within 100 miles. (For more details on subpoenas, see Chapter 12.)

Expert Witnesses

Witnesses who have specialized knowledge that is relevant to the case can testify as expert witnesses. A judge must rule that a witness is qualified as an expert before that person can testify based on special knowledge or training. Experts are not just medical doctors or rocket scientists but also people such as auto mechanics, building contractors, and computer programmers.

Experts can testify under oath about what they have personally seen or heard (like ordinary witnesses). More commonly, however, experts give their opinions about what conclusions can be drawn from testimony given by nonexpert witnesses.

Unlike other witnesses, experts are almost always paid for the time they spend preparing for and giving testimony, and they are reimbursed for their costs of coming to court. (See Chapter 19 for more on expert witnesses.)

Attorneys

Attorneys—also called counsel, counselors, or lawyers—speak and act on behalf of parties. Attorneys generally handle most aspects of a case for the parties they represent. For example, during trial, attorneys may do the following:

- question witnesses to bring out testimony that helps the client's case or refutes the opposing party's evidence (see Chapters 12 and 13)
- object to improper testimony, exhibits, or arguments of the opposing party (see Chapter 17), and
- argue to the judge or jury how the facts and law show that the attorney's client should win the case (see Chapter 14).

Attorneys also perform many functions outside the courtroom, such as conducting legal research, advising clients on strategy, drafting legal documents, and negotiating settlements on behalf of their clients. Attorneys also sign and arrange for documents to be filed with the court and served on (delivered to) the other party and witnesses on behalf of their clients.

In some courts, attorneys may be asked to draft court orders after a judge has made a ruling. This may be the judge's final decision or an interim decision, such as a ruling to exclude a certain document from being admitted into evidence.

As a party representing yourself, you will perform many of the functions that a lawyer does for a client. If your opponent is represented by a lawyer, you are expected to deal with only the lawyer and not directly with your adversary. This means you should make phone calls to the attorney, not your opponent, and when you serve legal papers on your opponent, you should deliver them to the attorney. Attorneys are forbidden by ethical rules from contacting someone represented by an attorney directly. However, because you are not a lawyer, there may be an exceptional situation in which, if the opportunity arises, you will want to bypass the lawyer and talk to your opponent directly—for example, in an effort to settle the case.

Another ethical rule requires lawyers to communicate certain important information to their clients. For example, if you make an offer of settlement to the attorney, the attorney must communicate it to the client, even if the attorney thinks it's a bad proposal (see Chapter 6 on settlement). So you need not be concerned that your opponent is not getting information from his or her lawyer.

Even when you represent yourself in court, you may want to hire a lawyer as a coach to help you find the applicable law and advise you on particular questions as your case progresses. (See Chapter 23 for more on legal coaches.)

Spectators

Most court proceedings are open to the public, so family members, friends, and even total strangers may watch hearings and trials. You may find it helpful to enlist supportive friends to come to court with you and perhaps assist by carrying things and taking notes for you.

Spectators must usually sit in the back of the courtroom behind what is called "the bar"—actually a low partition or gate—that divides the area immediately surrounding the judge and jury from the rest of the room. In some courts, and especially in cases of spousal battering or sexual harassment, judges may grant permission for nonlawyer supporters to sit next to you at counsel's table (the place at the front of the courtroom where lawyers and parties sit while presenting

their cases, discussed in the next section), to provide moral (though usually not verbal) support. If this is something you feel will help you present your case more effectively, ask the judge for permission.

The Courtroom and Its Physical Layout

Even though, as a self-represented party, you are not expected to understand court rules and legal principles perfectly, you should know where you will sit and stand and where everyone else belongs when you go to court. The more familiar you are with the lay of the land, the more easily you will find your way around—and the more confident you will look and feel doing so. This section describes a typical courtroom layout.

Spectator Area

The spectator area is usually in the back of the courtroom, often separated from the rest of the courtroom by a bar or low partition. Members of the public sit in this area, as you will if you visit a courtroom. Upon arriving in the courtroom, attorneys, parties, and witnesses usually check in with the clerk and then sit in this public area until the names of their cases are called (announced) by the judge or clerk.

Jury Box

The jury box is where jurors sit during the jury selection and throughout trial. Traditionally it seats 12 jurors, although many states now use smaller juries in civil actions. The jury box area remains empty when there is no jury or the jury is out of the courtroom.

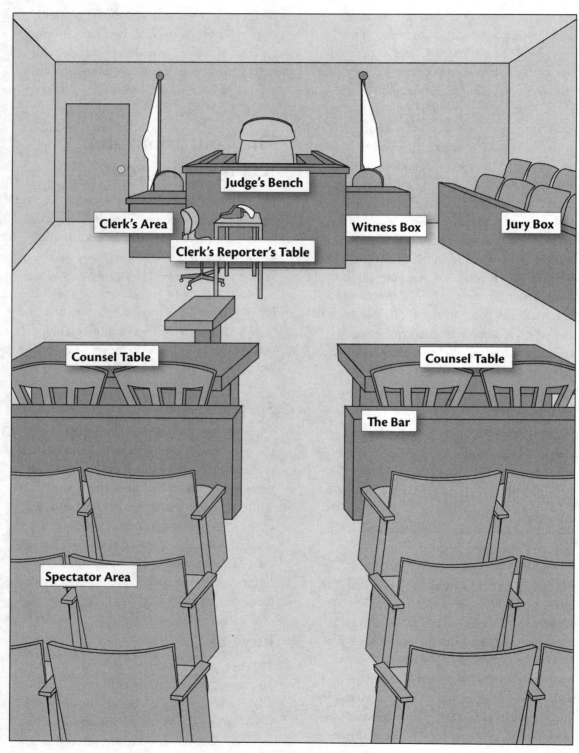

Courtroom

Jury Room

The jury room is separate from and often behind or adjacent to the courtroom itself. During jury trials, this is where jurors go to evaluate the evidence, deliberate, and decide on their verdict.

Witness Box

This boxlike area, also called the witness stand or the stand, is located to the left or the right of the judge's bench, on the same side of the courtroom as the jury box. Witnesses sit here when they testify. Before they are asked to testify, witnesses either sit in the spectator area or wait in the corridor outside the courtroom (if the judge has excluded them from the courtroom until they are called to the stand).

It is fairly routine for witnesses to be excluded (kept out of the courtroom until it is their turn to testify) so that their testimony is not influenced by what other witnesses say, but you may have to ask the judge to direct the witness to wait outside. Let your witnesses know ahead of time that they may be excluded so that they won't feel that the judge is somehow biased against them if they are asked to leave. You might suggest that they bring a book to read while they wait.

Judge's Bench

The judge's bench is the raised wooden desk or podium at the front of the courtroom where the judge sits. No attorneys or parties may go near the bench except upon the judge's request or by asking the judge for permission to approach the bench. During a jury trial, it's fairly common for the judge or a lawyer or self-represented party to request a short meeting at the bench (sometimes referred to as a sidebar conference) to discuss some point outside of the jury's earshot.

Judge's Chambers

The chambers are the judge's private offices, often a room adjacent to or behind the courtroom. Judges may ask you to have a conference in chambers during a trial or other proceeding, if they want to go "off the record" and have a quiet place to confer. Judges use such conferences for various reasons—for example, to admonish one or both sides for inappropriate conduct in a jury trial or to urge one or both sides to settle. (See Chapter 6 for more on settlement conferences.)

If you are asked to go into chambers and are uncomfortable with whatever is said, you may request that the conference be put on the record. That means the court reporter will come in or you will all go back into the courtroom, so the reporter can record what is said.

Clerk's Area

The court clerk usually sits on the side of the judge's bench opposite from the witness box. The clerk is usually present during the court's proceedings.

Counsel Table

This area, which includes a table or two, chairs, and sometimes a podium and microphone, is where attorneys and parties sit during trials and hearings on their cases. In most courtrooms, you make arguments and question witnesses while standing at the podium or microphone, though some judges may allow you to remain at the counsel table or stand closer to the witnesses.

You'll take your place at a counsel table when your case is called. If the counsel tables are labeled for plaintiff or defendant, sit at the appropriate table. If they are not, the plaintiff usually sits on the side that is closer to the jury box.

The Well

The well is the space between the counsel table and the judge's bench. The court clerk and the court reporter may sit in the well area. Don't go into the well area, unless the courtroom is so small or the architecture is such that you must pass through it to take your seat at the counsel table. You may also have to go into the well very briefly, when you first arrive in court to check in.

Courtroom Rules, Customs, and Etiquette

In representing yourself, you may feel a bit insecure, especially before you have had a chance to observe other courtroom sessions. This is normal. You are not trained and experienced in conducting trials, and you may have been treated with hostility or heard stories about other self-represented parties being treated that way.

Again, just as if you were traveling to a distant land, you will have a more pleasant and productive trip if you follow local customs (in this case courtroom etiquette) and are as polite as possible. This section explains some of those customs.

Dress in Business Attire

Generally, in court you should dress as if you were going to a job interview or a professional job—suits for men and suits or other professional-looking clothing for women. Better to overdress than to under-dress. Federal courts tend to be more formal than state courts.

In lower courts, such as traffic, municipal, or justice courts, however, it's appropriate to dress as you normally dress for your work—particularly if you come to court directly from your job. For example, if you are a contractor, nurse, or security guard and are coming from work, you don't need to change into a suit.

Be Courteous to Everyone, Especially Court Personnel

Of course, it's always good to be courteous to others. But it's particularly important in court, where you are likely to need a bit of helpful advice from time to time. You may also need small favors, such as a five-minute recess or for the clerk to notify you if your case is called and you need to be out of the courtroom for a minute to use the restroom or make a phone call. And you will have questions—even the most experienced attorneys do—such as how to label exhibits or file legal papers. Simply put, court personnel are much more apt to grant your requests and help you out if you are polite.

Check In When You Enter the Courtroom

When you enter the courtroom, check in with the court clerk. Give your name and case number, ask whether the court is on schedule, and ask when the clerk believes your case will be called (heard by the judge). If court is in session when you enter the room, wait until the judge takes a break or pauses long enough after a proceeding is finished so that you can discreetly hand the clerk a note with your name and case number, saying you want to check in.

Stay Close Until Your Case Is Called

Clerks usually have a good handle on the judge's schedule, but sometimes things go faster than anticipated because other parties aren't ready or a case is settled at the last minute. Or the judge may call cases out of order. Also, some courts schedule hearings in blocks, so that several matters are all set for the same time. In these courts, judges often take the routine or quick matters first and the cases or hearings they feel will take up more time after all the routine items are finished. Sometimes, judges put cases on "first call" or "second call," meaning earlier or later in the time block, and the lawyers or self-represented parties can request that their case be heard earlier or later, depending on their schedules.

For all these reasons, if you need to leave the courtroom, even for a minute, it's best to let the clerk know where you are in case the judge is ready for your case sooner than expected. Often, the judge won't wait.

When the judge is ready to hear your case, the clerk or the judge will call out your name and the names of the other parties in your case. You will stand and say that you are present and ready to proceed. When the judge or clerk motions for you or tells you to

come forward, you will take your seat at the counsel table.

Master Calendar Systems

In some courts, the first judge you are assigned to go see is not the judge who will be presiding over your trial, but the master calendar judge. The master calendar judge is a bit like a tour organizer who takes a bunch of tourists into one central office first and then assigns them to particular tour guides according to what sights they will see, what language they speak, or how big the group is. The master calendar judge evaluates a whole slew of cases to determine how long they will take and how complicated they will be. Sometimes, he or she tries to help the parties with settlement negotiations. Then, based on the cases and on the availability of particular courtrooms, the master calendar judge assigns those cases that are ready for trial out to other courtrooms.

In assigning the case, the judge might say something like, "*Nolo v. Klotchman* to Department 2, trailing." This means that your case will be heard by the judge in Courtroom 2, but that it will trail (follow) one or more other cases. The Clerk's Office should be able to tell you whether your court uses a master calendar system and, if so, how it works.

Speak to the Judge Respectfully

As a general rule, you should always stand when addressing the judge. Only if you see that attorneys routinely talk to the judge while seated at the counsel table, as is the practice in some state courts, should you sit while you speak to the judge. Even then, it might be worth showing the courtesy of standing until the judge says you may be seated. If you are unable to stand for medical reasons, tell the judge that at the outset of the proceedings.

Always call the judge "Your Honor" when you speak to him or her. Do not say "Sir" and especially not "Ma'am." In court, by long-running tradition, "Your Honor" is the neutral, respectful term used by all. You are not giving anything up by using it, and are, in fact, expected to use it.

Even if the judge appears to be "barking" a bit at you, continue to be calm and polite and do not raise your voice or bark back.

Don't Speak Directly to Opposing Counsel

When your case is being heard, always address the opposing attorney or self-represented party through the judge, not directly. For example, say, "Your Honor, this morning Ms. Ellis stated here in court that she would not be calling any other witnesses. Now she has stated that she intends to call two additional witnesses. I ask that they not be allowed to testify." Do not turn to Ms. Ellis directly and say, "You said you wouldn't call any other witnesses."

Always address or refer to attorneys, parties, and witnesses by last names—for example, Mr. Neustadt or Ms. Doherty. Even if you have talked a lot on the phone and the person has told you to call him or her by first name, use last names in court. This maintains the formal, respectful courtroom tone.

Find Out About Special Procedures

All judges follow the same broad procedural rules discussed in this book. Nevertheless, some judges have their own preferences as to the details, and, if you can learn these, you will be well served. One good way to start is by watching your judge in action before your day in court; another is by talking with the clerk or a lawyer who has appeared before your judge. (For more information on researching your judge's background and style, see Chapter 10.)

Don't Speak to the Judge About the Case Without Opposing Counsel Present

Legal rules prevent ex parte (one-sided) contacts with the judge. You wouldn't want the other lawyer to talk to the judge out of your presence; you should follow the same rules. Normally, if a judge or one party suggests a meeting either at the judge's bench (a sidebar conference) or in the judge's chambers (office), both sides must be represented. Sometimes it will be up to you to help arrange a mutually convenient time for such a meeting.

Never Speak to Jurors About the Case Before the Verdict

If you are conducting a jury trial and happen to pass one of the jurors in your case in the hallway, a nod, smile, or "hello" is permissible. But it's very important that you do not enter into any discussion with a juror or comment on your case within earshot of a juror.

Be Discreet

Do not discuss your case with witnesses, family members, or anyone else in any public place where you can be overheard, such as the elevators, restrooms, or cafeteria. The lawyer for your opponent is likely to know many people in the courthouse, and your words may quickly be passed along.

Ask for Help If You Are Treated Badly

Once a trial starts, it is normally too late to request a different judge. (See Chapter 10 for information on challenging a judge before trial.) This does not mean, however, that you are helpless if you are treated in a demeaning or hostile way. For example, if you ask a simple question and are given a stern lecture that, for example, only idiots appear in court representing themselves and that you should immediately hire a lawyer, it's pretty clear that you are facing a steep uphill battle. In such a case, you can try any of the following approaches:

- **Ask to speak to the judge privately.** If the judge agrees, tell the judge that you are doing your best to follow the rules and point out politely that you have the right to represent yourself and to be treated respectfully.
- **Write a letter to the presiding judge (head or chief judge) of the court.** The Clerk's Office can tell you who this is. Describe the specific instances in which you feel you were treated unfairly and ask that another judge be assigned to your case.

- **File a written complaint with a state agency that has the power to discipline judges.** Most states have such an agency—it may be called the Commission on Judicial Performance or something similar. Such agencies have the power to investigate complaints against judges and even to remove them from the bench for serious or repeated violations of rules and judicial decorum.
- **If all else fails, consider filing a written motion with the court requesting a mistrial.** The judge can be disqualified on the grounds that the judge's bias (prejudice) against self-represented parties is making it impossible for you to have a full and fair trial.

If the judge's clerks or law clerks treat you unfairly or rudely, follow similar guidelines. First try speaking with them in a polite but firm way. If they do not improve, write a note to the judge (or presiding judge if you don't get anywhere with your judge) about the problem.

All this said, although extreme rudeness should be addressed, it is an unfortunate part of the process that you must expect some amount of rude and abrupt behavior, and you must develop a thick skin. Lawyers are used to being "combatants" of sorts, and discourse between lawyers is often less than civil and courteous. People in this sort of "battle mode" can forget common politeness. Therefore, do not rush to assume that anyone is out to get you personally. Just take the steps outlined here to address concerns that the behavior of someone else in your case is affecting or will affect your case. ●

Starting Your Case

Almost nobody wants to go to court. People usually attempt to resolve disputes out of court, informally, before filing a lawsuit. For example, if someone owes you money from a contract, you will most likely ask the person for the money before suing. If your request is denied, you may try another phone call, a written request for payment (called a demand letter), or perhaps a face-to-face negotiation session. Assuming enough money is at stake, your next step might be to show you mean business by hiring a lawyer to call or to write on your behalf. If you still haven't gotten paid, you might suggest a formal mediation or arbitration proceeding. (See Chapters 1 and 6 for more on these out-of-court processes, called alternative dispute resolution, or ADR).

Eventually, however, if the person who owes you money continues to refuse to pay, you have a choice to make: You can either bring a lawsuit or write off the money.

> ! **CAUTION**
>
> **Can you sue?** These days, many companies, such as banks, realtors, and insurance companies, include mandatory arbitration or mediation clauses in the contracts you sign to do business with them. These provisions require you to resolve any dispute you have with the company through one of these out-of-court dispute resolution methods. By signing a contract that includes such a mandatory clause, you give up your right to bring a lawsuit in court.

This chapter describes the process by which lawsuits typically get underway. The most important rules that come into play at this preliminary stage concern how much time the plaintiff has after the event happens or the conflict arises to file a lawsuit, called a "statute of limitations," and which court has power to hear a case, called "jurisdiction." Next, plaintiffs and defendants set the stage for trial by filing "pleadings"—documents that assert and contest legal claims. A plaintiff's initial pleading is usually called a "complaint." A complaint asserts one or more legal claims against a defendant and asks a court to take some action—to award money damages, for example. A defendant's initial pleading is often called an "answer." An answer disputes either all or key portions of a complaint. In an answer, a defendant may also ask for legal relief against the plaintiff (money damages, for example) or even against a third party.

Many years ago, pleading rules were extremely technical and rigid, designed to weed out what the law regarded as unmeritorious claims at the earliest possible stage. As a result, many lawsuits never made it past this initial pleading stage. Modern pleading rules are somewhat more relaxed. Complaints and answers determine a case's general boundaries, but usually they don't need to be long-winded or contain technical language. (As a result, the weeding-out function performed by pleading rules in earlier days now falls to other procedures, such as summary judgment motions. (See Chapter 7.) Court systems in some states even use official "check the boxes and fill in the blanks" pleading forms for many common kinds of cases. If such a form is available for your kind of case, you can often download it or simply obtain it from a courthouse clerk. If not, look for "pleading requirements" in your local court's procedural rules. Then, to find the correct language and format for your case, refer to one of the commercially published attorney "form books" or "pleading guides," available at any law library. There's much more about this in Chapter 23.

CAUTION

Read the rules for your local court. As you might expect, the legal system has not completely escaped its picky past. Judges still occasionally use violations of pleading rules as an excuse to get rid of cases before the cases cross the threshold of a courtroom. You can often find picky detailed rules in sets of "local rules" that govern the practices and procedures in a specific court jurisdiction. For more information on finding local rules, see Chapter 23. For instance, except when official fill-in-the-blanks forms are available, you are still likely to encounter pleading rules governing such matters as what kind of paper you must use and where to put the staples. You can usually obtain a copy of your local court rules and your particular judge's rules, if any, from the main Clerk's Office in your courthouse. Follow them carefully to make sure that a clerk does not reject your pleading.

RESOURCE

Resources on procedural rules. To locate resources that can help you learn the necessary procedural rules involved in civil lawsuits, see Chapter 23. For a quick summary, try *Civil Procedure in a Nutshell* by Mary Kay Kane (West Publishing Co.). For more detailed information, we recommend the following:

- *Civil Procedure* by Jack Friedenthal, Mary K. Kane, and Arthur Miller (West Publishing Co.).

- *Moore's Federal Practice* by James W. Moore (Matthew Bender).
- *Federal Procedural Forms*, Lawyer's Edition (West Group).
- *Fundamentals of Litigation for Paralegals* by Marlene Maerowitz (Aspen Publishers).

Do You Have a Good Case?

Before you decide to file a lawsuit, you should do at least enough research and investigation to make sure that the facts and law on your side support a legally valid claim. For example, the fact that your adversary gave you a menacing look is not a legally valid claim, unless the look was accompanied by some threatening action. Similarly, if a car lightly touched your fender but did not damage your car or hurt you in any way, you don't have a solid legal claim.

But some of the disputes and injuries that occur in our daily lives do give rise to legally valid claims. For example, you may want to sue if you suffered broken bones, pain, and a damaged car due to an auto accident, or if a roofer breached a contract by using materials that caused your new roof to leak.

Even if you seem to have a valid legal claim, you should assess the strength of your case before you file a lawsuit. If a lawsuit has been filed against you, you won't have the luxury of thinking about whether to go to court. However, you need to estimate the chance of a successful defense and assess the potential advantages of settling. The following considerations will help you make a reasonable assessment.

Your evidence. Consider not only *what* happened, but what you can *prove* happened in court. Do you need witnesses to support your story, and if so, are the ones you have credible? Will they be available to testify when the case goes to trial? Do you have all the paper documents and electronic records that you need? If not, do you know how to get them? (See Chapter 5.) Are the documents and records admissible under the rules of evidence? (See Chapters 15 and 16.)

Your adversary's story. Examine your story from your adversary's perspective. Do you know what story your adversary will present? Assuming that the stories conflict, can you tell a judge or jury why your story should be believed?

What you must prove. Do you know what elements or material facts you have to prove, and do you have evidence to support each element? For example, if you are thinking about whether to file a claim for wrongful termination of employment, do you know whether the law requires you to "mitigate damages" by trying to find a new job? If so, do you have evidence of your job search? To succeed as a plaintiff you have to convince a judge or jury (usually by a preponderance of the evidence) that you have proved each element of a claim. By contrast, a defendant can succeed by preventing proof of any single element. (See Chapters 8 and 9.)

What you can collect. Will you be able to collect a judgment if you win? It won't be worth your while to bring a lawsuit if your adversary has no money or assets, because you will not be able to collect any money if you win. So before you go to court, be sure to read about collecting judgments. (See Chapter 20.)

TIP

Damage control. If you have been sued for behavior or conditions that might result in harm to others, you might want to practice damage control by eliminating the problem as soon as you can. For example, if you are an employer who has been sued for sexual harassment based on a supervisor's misconduct, consider how to prevent the supervisor from harassing other employees by terminating the supervisor, providing the supervisor with appropriate training, or transferring the supervisor to a different department. Proactive measures like this can limit future liability, and under Federal Rule of Evidence 407 the plaintiff cannot offer those measures into evidence to prove that you were at fault for not having taken them sooner. (See Chapter 16.)

Before filing a lawsuit, you should also think about all the people or businesses who might be legally responsible for the harm you have suffered. This means that you should not focus only on the driver who struck you, the doctor who mistreated you, or the building contractor who added on the room whose roof collapsed. The more parties you can legitimately name as defendants in your lawsuit, the better your chances both of achieving a favorable settlement and of collecting a judgment should you prevail at trial. Here are a few examples to illustrate this point:

- In an auto accident case, you plan to sue the driver of a car that struck you. If you do some investigation and find out that faulty brakes may have contributed to the accident, think about adding the brake manufacturer and the auto repair shop that recently worked on the brakes as defendants in your lawsuit. Perhaps after you name them as defendants in your lawsuit, the brake manufacturer and repair shop may be so anxious to avoid bad publicity, legal expenses, or the risk of a large adverse judgment that they will make quick settlement offers.

- In the case of a doctor who may have mistreated you, your inquiries may indicate that the insurance company that included the doctor in its company's health plan negligently allowed the doctor to practice medicine in areas in which the doctor was not qualified. If so, you might name the insurance company as well as the doctor as defendants in the lawsuit.
- In the case of a building contractor who did a substandard room addition, you may learn that part of the reason for the roof's collapse is that the contractor was itself supplied with substandard roofing materials by a roofing supply company. If so, you might name both the manufacturer and the seller of the roofing materials as defendants in the lawsuit.

Unless you have expertise in the subject matter of the lawsuit, you may not immediately be able to identify all individuals or businesses that could be legally responsible for the harm you have suffered. And even when you can identify additional legally responsible parties, you must balance the likelihood of collecting from them against the fact that naming additional defendants increases the scope and cost of case investigation and adds to the overall complexity of your lawsuit.

Jurisdictional rules that determine which court has power to hear a case may also make it hard to include all defendants in a single lawsuit. (See "Which Court Has the Power to Hear Your Case," below.) In short, you may want to consult a legal coach before filing a lawsuit to talk about whether the possible financial benefits of adding defendants outweighs the additional time, money, and energy you will have to invest in your case.

 CAUTION

Don't file a frivolous lawsuit. Investigate before you sue. To reduce the possibility that the parties you sue will claim that you filed a groundless lawsuit simply to harass them—and perhaps sue you for "abuse of process" or "malicious prosecution"—make sure that you have what Federal Rule of Civil Procedure 11 refers to as "evidentiary support" for the claims in your complaint. You may have to do some legwork or even hire an expert in the particular field before deciding whether you are legally justified in filing the complaint. Occasionally, you may even encounter rules that require you to demonstrate that a complaint is justified. For example, in many states, if you want to sue a doctor for medical malpractice, you will have to attach to your complaint a physician's certificate attesting to the legitimacy of your claims.

Is Your Lawsuit Timely?

You may have a great case, but if you wait too long to sue, the defendant can quickly get the case dismissed (thrown out of court). Statutes of limitations protect defendants from being hit with stale legal claims by strictly limiting how long a plaintiff has to file a lawsuit. As a plaintiff, you have to be careful not to spend so much time negotiating with an adversary or debating whether to file a lawsuit that you miss this deadline.

How Much Time Do You Have in Which to File?

How long do you have in which to file a lawsuit? It depends on your state's law and your legal claims. Every state has its own time limits, and even within a state the period you have to file a lawsuit varies according to the type of claim. For example, rules in one state may allow plaintiffs with personal injury claims (for instance, a broken leg suffered in an auto accident) one year from the date of the injury to file a lawsuit, but those same rules give plaintiffs who sue for breach of a written contract (for example, failure to make good on a promissory note) four years from the date of the breach to sue. In another state, personal injury plaintiffs may have two years to sue, and plaintiffs with breach of written contract claims may have five years.

TIP

Forget about statutes of limitations if you file suit within a year. Except for when you sue a government agency (see "Shorter time limits apply to claims against government agencies," below), you almost always have at least one year from the date of harm to file a lawsuit, no matter what type of claim you have or which state you call home. So, if you sue within this one-year period, you should be fine.

EXAMPLE: Henry is injured in an auto accident on February 1. On March 1 of the same year, a lawyer whom Henry hires for a couple of hours of advice recommends that he seek compensation for his injuries from the driver of the other car. Henry spends months trying to settle with the other driver's insurance company. Finally, on September 1 of the same year, the insurance company writes to Henry and offers to settle the case for $1,000. Henry concludes that the offer is grossly inadequate and decides to sue the other driver. If Henry isn't sure of his state's statute of limitations for personal injury cases, he should be sure to file the suit by February 1 of the next year. If Henry doesn't wait more than a year, his lawsuit will be timely.

CAUTION

Shorter time limits apply to claims against government agencies. Often you cannot sue a government agency unless you first file an administrative claim with the city, county, or state of which the agency is a part. Check your state's rules quickly after you suffer harm—you may have only 60 days to submit an administrative claim. If (as often happens) the government denies your claim, the denial letter will tell you how long you have to file a lawsuit in court.

Statutes of limitations only set deadlines for filing a lawsuit, not for how long it takes for the case to conclude. However, most states do have separate "diligent prosecution" statutes that require you to move your case to trial within a certain amount of time or you could face a dismissal.

Defendants Must Alert the Court to a Statute of Limitations Violation

If you are a defendant who thinks that the plaintiff may have waited too long to sue, you'll also need to check the applicable state or federal limitations period to determine whether the lawsuit is timely. Judges rarely throw out late claims on their own. To be sure that a judge dismisses an untimely case, you will probably have to include an "affirmative defense" in your answer, alleging that the plaintiff's complaint is untimely (see "Defendant's Response," below). As an alternative to filing an answer, some courts allow you to file a Motion to Dismiss asking a judge to throw out an untimely complaint.

When Does the Clock Start Ticking?

Once you have learned what statute of limitations applies to your case, your next step is to determine when the clock starts ticking. As mentioned above, in most situations the time starts to run on the "date of harm." However, there is a huge exception to this general rule to protect plaintiffs in situations where they may not be aware for months or even years that they have been harmed. In such situations, statutes of limitations may begin the clock ticking either on the "date of discovery" of the harm, or the date on which the plaintiff "should have discovered" the harm. In short, for some types of legal actions the statute of limitations clock can start ticking at any of three different times:

- At the earliest, the date on which the harm occurred.
- If not, then later—the date on which the plaintiff reasonably should have discovered the harm. This refers to the date when a judge considers it fair to say that the plaintiff should have known about the harm, even if the plaintiff did not actually know about it.
- At the latest, the date on which the plaintiff actually discovered the harm.

EXAMPLE 1: On February 1, a doctor performs a gallbladder operation on Phoebe, but mistakenly removes Phoebe's spleen. The doctor tells Phoebe of the mistake as soon as she wakes up. Phoebe's time period for suing the doctor begins to run on February 1, because the harm occurred on that date and Phoebe actually knew it. If a two-year statute of limitations for medical malpractice applies to Phoebe's case, she'd have two years from February 1 to file a lawsuit against the doctor.

EXAMPLE 2: The same case as above, except the doctor tells Phoebe nothing of the surgical mistake. Phoebe is in constant pain following the February 1 surgery. A month later, on March 1, Phoebe talks to another doctor, who tells her that she should not be in pain and that she should immediately come in to have it checked out. Phoebe delays going to the doctor until July 1 of the same year, at which time she finds out that her spleen had been removed mistakenly on February 1. In this situation, Phoebe's time period for suing the doctor probably begins to run on or shortly after March 1, because the pain coupled with the second doctor's advice determines when Phoebe should reasonably have discovered the harm.

EXAMPLE 3: The same case as above, except that Phoebe suffers no unusual aftereffects following the February 1 surgery. Phoebe is unaware that anything went wrong with the surgery until July 1 of the same year, when an X-ray during a routine medical checkup reveals that her spleen was removed. In this situation, because Phoebe did not discover and could not reasonably have discovered the harm until July 1, most states would start counting Phoebe's time to sue on July 1.

EXAMPLE 4: After Andre was convicted of murder, the conviction was set aside by an appellate court because Andre's arrest was illegal. After the charges were dropped, Andre sued the

---

If You Don't Know the Names of All Potential Defendants, Protect the Statute of Limitations by Suing John Doe

If you think that a person or organization whose identity you don't yet know has contributed to your damages, consider naming "Doe Defendants" in addition to the defendant or defendants you are able to name. Doe defendants (so called because, like John or Jane Doe, their identities are unknown) act as placeholders in the complaint. If and when you discover the actual identity of one of these anonymous troublemakers, you can amend your complaint to substitute the actual name for one of the Doe defendants.

For example, assume that you are a homeowner who intends to sue Bill Jones for vandalizing and destroying expensive plants. You have information that at least two others participated in the vandalism, but you don't know who they are. If so, your complaint might name "Bill Jones and Does 1 through 5" as defendants. The complaint should allege that "Bill Jones and other persons acting in concert with him" vandalized your plants. If you later find out that Mary Smith was one of the other participants, you could amend the original complaint to substitute Mary Smith for Doe 1.

The primary reason to name Doe defendants is to overcome a potential problem with a statute of limitations. For example, assume that your state's relevant statute of limitations requires you to file a vandalism lawsuit within one year after the vandalism incident. By the time you learn Mary Smith's identity, more than a year may have passed. If you don't name Doe defendants, and then more than a year later try to amend your complaint to add Mary as a defendant, Mary could have the complaint dismissed against her because the statute of limitations has expired. However, if you substitute Mary Smith for Doe 1, the substitution dates back to the date when the complaint was originally filed, before the statute of limitations expired. Thus, Mary could not have the complaint dismissed as untimely.

arresting officers and the city for false arrest. Andre argued that the statute of limitations did not begin to run until the murder charges were dropped. However, because false arrest consists of "detention without legal process," the statute of limitations on Andre's lawsuit began to run much earlier, on the date that he was taken to court and charged with murder. (*Wallace v. Kato*, U.S. Sup. Ct. 2007)

Plaintiffs who are minors when they suffer harm generally have longer than the usual periods within which to file suit. In general, statutes of limitations don't start running (in legalese, they are "tolled") until a minor reaches age 18, no matter how old the minor was when the harm occurred.

EXAMPLE: Mack Awley, age 12, had been the adorable child star of a hit TV show for seven years when the show went off the air. At that time an accountant told Mack's family that during its entire seven-year run, the show's producer had paid Mack only half of what was due under Mack's written contract. Most states would start counting Mack's time to sue from the date of his 18th birthday. And because states generally have either four-year or five-year statutes of limitations for disputes based on breaches of written contracts, Mack might be able to wait until he was 22 years of age to file suit— or 10 years after the date of discovery of the underpayments and 17 years after the earliest underpayment! (Of course, Mack's parents or guardians would be wise to file suit on Mack's behalf while Mack is still a minor. A stale case is generally harder to prove, and after years of delay, Mack might well be less adorable than he is now.)

Sample Statutes of Limitations Periods

The list below sets forth California's statutes of limitations for many common types of lawsuits. Different time periods may apply in your state, so be sure to check your state's rules carefully. However, the California rules are fairly typical and should give you a good idea of what you're likely to find when you read your state's rules. (See Chapter 23 for information about how to look up state laws.)

- **Medical malpractice:** three years from the date of injury or one year from the date of discovery of the injury, whichever occurs first.
- **Breach of an oral contract:** two years.
- **Breach of a written contract:** four years.
- **Child sexual abuse:** eight years from the victim's 18th birthday or three years after the victim realizes that physical or psychological injury has resulted from the abuse, no matter what the victim's age.
- **Suits for libel or slander:** one year.
- **Personal injury claims based on negligence:** one year.
- **Suits for injuries resulting from domestic violence:** three years from the last act of domestic violence.

Which Court Has the Power to Hear Your Case?

The U.S. and state constitutions, as well as federal and state laws, establish and limit courts' "jurisdiction." Jurisdiction simply means the power to hear and decide a case. To make a legally valid decision, a court must have both "subject matter jurisdiction" (power to hear the kind of case a lawsuit involves) and "personal jurisdiction" (power over the parties involved in the lawsuit).

This is important because in addition to filing a case on time, a plaintiff has to file it in the proper court. If you mistakenly file a case in the wrong court, a defendant may get the case moved (perhaps to a court that's less convenient or favorable to you than if you had chosen the proper court), or even get the case dismissed altogether by filing a Motion to Dismiss for Lack of Jurisdiction. If your case is dismissed for lack of jurisdiction, you may be able to refile the lawsuit in the proper court. But if the statute of limitations runs out before you can do this, your mistake in selecting a court may mean that the defendant can have your lawsuit thrown out permanently.

For almost every type of case, the rules we talk about below make it pretty simple to figure out in which court you should file your complaint. Be aware, however, that jurisdiction issues can occasionally become extremely complex when they involve such fundamental questions as whether a case should be heard in federal or state court or whether a state has the power to require residents or businesses from a different state to appear in its courts.

Honoring Other Court Cases

Under what is known as the "Full Faith and Credit Clause" of the U.S. Constitution, every state has to honor cases legally decided in other states. This means that if the court in which you file a lawsuit has proper jurisdiction, meaning the legal right to decide the case, you can enforce the judgment anywhere in the country. (You may have to register your judgment in another state before you can collect in that state.)

Federal Court Jurisdiction

In general, you file a case that involves state law in a state court. Because the overwhelming majority of cases (such as those involving personal injury claims, divorce, landlord-tenant problems, consumer claims, probate matters, and contract disputes) arise under state law, it is fairly easy to separate out the few types of cases that must (or can) be filed in a federal trial (district) court. Each state has at least one federal district court, and populous states contain as many as four different federal districts.

You may file a case in federal district court only if the court has what lawyers call "subject matter jurisdiction." Federal courts have subject matter jurisdiction in two kinds of cases:

Cases that arise under a federal law (called "federal question" cases). Federal district courts have subject matter jurisdiction if your case is based on (arises under) any federal law. Examples include:

- You sue a police officer who wrongfully arrested you under a federal civil rights statute that allows people who are arrested unlawfully to file civil lawsuits seeking damages.
- You sue an individual under federal patent law for manufacturing an item that violates your patent.
- As an owner of a small business, you sue a large company for violating federal antitrust laws.
- Under a federal law aimed at eliminating discrimination by businesses, a civil rights organization sues a restaurant chain for policies that discourage patronage by members of ethnic minority groups.
- Pursuant to a federal law called ERISA, you sue the insurance company that has denied your claim for mental health benefits.

Diversity of citizenship cases. Federal district courts also have subject matter jurisdiction if you are suing a citizen of a different state (or a foreign national), and you are asking for at least $75,000 in money damages. (This monetary floor may be responsible for the old saying, "Don't make a federal case out of it.") Don't be fooled by the "subject matter jurisdiction" label: If a federal court has jurisdiction based on diversity of citizenship, the subject matter of the case doesn't matter. Examples of federal diversity jurisdiction include:

- As a citizen of New York injured in a traffic accident, you sue the New Jersey citizen who was driving the car that struck you for $90,000 in damages. (You could file the complaint in a federal court in either New York or New Jersey.)

Citizenship

For diversity jurisdiction purposes, individuals can be a citizen of only one state at a time and are generally citizens of the state in which they maintain a principal residence. A corporation can be a citizen of two states: the state in which it is incorporated and the state in which it maintains its principal place of business. Federal courts have diversity jurisdiction only if complete diversity exists between all of the plaintiffs and all of the defendants (that is, if every plaintiff is a citizen of a different state than every defendant).

EXAMPLE 1: Cobb, a Georgia citizen, wants to sue Peachy Corp., a Delaware corporation with its principal place of business in Atlanta. Diversity jurisdiction does not exist, because Cobb and Peachy are both Georgia citizens.

EXAMPLE 2: Cobb, a Georgia citizen, wants to sue Ruth, a Maryland citizen, and Wagner, a Georgia citizen. Diversity jurisdiction does not exist, because Cobb and one of the defendants are citizens of the same state.

- As a businessperson who is a citizen of Florida, you sue a citizen of Great Britain for breaching a contract and causing you to lose $100,000.
- Bluegrass Corp., a corporation whose headquarters are in Kentucky, sues Seedling Corp., a company headquartered in Washington, for $300,000 for breach of contract based on Seedling's supplying the wrong kind of grass seed. (You could file the complaint in a federal court in either Kentucky or Washington.)
- A company headquartered in Tennessee sues a Texas Internet news service provider for $125,000 for publishing false information about the company's business operations. (You could file the complaint in a federal court in either Tennessee or Texas.)

Dual Jurisdiction

Most lawsuits that can be filed in federal district court can also be filed in state court. Federal courts have "exclusive jurisdiction" only in very few kinds of federal question cases, such as lawsuits involving copyright violations, patent infringement, and federal tax claims. This means that plaintiffs in all diversity jurisdiction cases and nearly all federal question cases have a choice of suing in federal or state court. Lawyers call the process of deciding which court is best for a plaintiff's case "forum shopping." A plaintiff who has a choice of courts may consider such factors as:

- Which courthouse is closer to the plaintiff's place of work and business? For example, a plaintiff may choose to file in a state court simply because the nearest federal court is 250 miles away.
- Which court has a longer statute of limitations? A plaintiff whose case is untimely under state law would surely choose to file suit in federal district court in a federal question case if federal law provided a longer statute of limitations. (Federal courts use a state's statute of limitations in diversity jurisdiction cases.)
- Differences in the judges. For instance, a plaintiff may think that local state court judges have a judicial philosophy that makes them more likely to sympathize with the plaintiff's claim.
- Differences in the jury panel. State and federal courts may have different boundaries for jury selection purposes. A plaintiff may, for example, file suit in federal court because it selects jurors from a wider geographic area.

SEE AN EXPERT

Consult a legal coach for advice on forum shopping. When you try to choose the court that will be most favorable for your case, many subtle factors come into play. If you have a choice of courts, it would be wise to consult with a lawyer who has experience in both federal and state courts. See "Finding a Legal Coach" in Chapter 1.

State Court Jurisdiction

State courts almost always have the power to hear cases involving events that took place in that state. They can also hear cases in which the defendants reside in or are served with the relevant court papers (usually a summons and complaint) in that state. Unless your lawsuit is one of the few types of cases over which federal courts have exclusive jurisdiction (see above), the state court in the state where you live will probably have jurisdiction to hear your case, whether you're seeking an adoption, guardianship, or divorce; suing a landlord, a tenant, a contractor, or a repair shop; taking someone to small claims court; probating a will; or getting involved in one of the vast variety of other kinds of legal disputes. If you're reading this book and are or will be involved in a lawsuit, the odds are overwhelming that you'll be in state court.

EXAMPLE 1: Dobbs, a Michigan resident, buys a used car from Rick's Used Cars, a Michigan business. A few weeks later the car breaks down, and Dobbs learns that it needs a new engine. Dobbs sues Rick's Used Cars for fraud and breach of contract in Michigan, which has jurisdiction because Rick's is a Michigan business.

EXAMPLE 2: Allnut lives in Arizona and is involved in a traffic accident in Arizona with Marlowe, a Texas resident. Allnut could file a lawsuit in Arizona state court, which would have jurisdiction because the accident took place there. (Every state has a "motorist" law that confers jurisdiction on its state courts to hear cases involving all traffic accidents occurring in that state.) Allnut could also file suit in Texas, where Marlowe resides, because state courts almost always have jurisdiction to hear cases filed against defendants who live

in that state. (However, Allnut could not file the lawsuit in California or Florida in an effort to combine a vacation with legal business. Neither state is the site where the traffic accident occurred or the defendant lives.) Finally, this case is an example of dual or "concurrent" jurisdiction, and Allnut could file in federal court if he wished.

EXAMPLE 3: Elaine, a New York citizen, sues Officer Kramer, also a New York citizen, for violating her civil rights by falsely arresting her. Elaine bases the suit on a federal statute (42 United States Code § 1983) and asks for damages of $10,000. A New York federal court has the power to hear Elaine's case. Because the case is based on (arises under) a federal statute, the New York federal court has jurisdiction even though Elaine and Officer Kramer are citizens of the same state and Elaine seeks less than $75,000. Alternatively, Elaine could file the lawsuit in New York state court, which would have the power to hear the case because the arrest occurred in New York and both Elaine and Officer Kramer live there. The state court has "concurrent jurisdiction" with the federal court and can enforce the federal law as it would a state law. Elaine can choose between federal and state courts in New York.

Even after you determine that the state court in which you plan to file your lawsuit has proper subject matter jurisdiction, your search for the correct court is not finished. You must next consider the following issues:

- whether the state has a specialized court to hear your type of case (because most states divide up their trial courts' business according to the plaintiff's desired relief and the case's subject matter), and

- which county or city court within a state is the proper place for your case (called determining "venue").

These issues are discussed briefly below.

State Courts That Specialize According to the Plaintiff's Desired Relief

When states divide up their trial courts' business according to what the plaintiff is asking for (also known as "relief"), they typically consider the amount of money and the type of remedy a plaintiff seeks. For example, a court may only have the power to award monetary damages up to $5,000 or may not have the power to issue a nonmonetary (extraordinary) remedy, such as an injunction (an order that a defendant do something other than pay money, like tearing down a fence that encroaches on the plaintiff's property).

States use somewhat varied formulas when allocating business to trial courts according to a plaintiff's desired relief. However, the following three divisions are typical:

- small claims courts, which hear cases involving up to a certain amount (usually between $5,000 and $10,000) in damages
- courts for medium-sized claims, perhaps limited to cases involving up to $25,000, and
- courts for all cases involving higher amounts or involving requests for injunctions or other nonmonetary remedies.

Terminology for different court divisions varies from one state to another. For example,

a few states refer to their highest-level trial courts as "supreme courts," while other states refer to them as "superior," "district," or "county" courts. Check your state's court rules if you don't know which court has the power to hear your case.

 TIP

Check your state's latest rules on courts' monetary limits. States often amend the dollar divisions between different trial courts. For example, a few states that now limit small claims courts to cases involving up to $5,000 are considering raising the amount to $7,500 or even $10,000.

State Courts That Specialize According to the Case's Subject Matter

Just as many restaurants have a limited menu, many courts only hear certain types of cases—regardless of the dollar amount of the case or the type of relief the plaintiff seeks. Specialization by subject matter allows judges and other court personnel to build expertise and handle a certain type of case quickly. For example, a particular state may have specialized family law courts (hearing divorce, child support, and related matters), probate or surrogate courts (hearing guardianship cases, determining the validity of wills and trusts, and distributing the property of deceased persons), and even landlord-tenant courts. If a state has set up a specialized court to hear your type of case, that is the court to which you will be assigned regardless of how much money you seek or whether you seek a nonmonetary remedy.

Sample State Trial Court Structures

Here are the general trial court structures for seven states, based on the courts' monetary limits. To determine the current court structure for other states, consult your state's court rules or the *Directory of State and Federal Courts, Judges, and Clerks*, published annually by the Bureau of National Affairs (BNA).

California

Small Claims Court—Claims up to $7,500 for individuals, up to $5,000 for corporate plaintiffs

Superior Court—Claims in any amount

Colorado

Small Claims Court—Claims up to $7,500

County Court—Claims up to $15,000

District Court—Claims in any amount

Illinois

Small Claims Court—Claims up to $2,500

Circuit Court—Claims above $2,500

Michigan

Municipal Court—Small Claims Court up to $1,750; other cases up to $15,000

District Court—Small Claims Court up to $3,000; other cases up to $25,000

Circuit Court—Claims above $25,000

New York

Town and Village Justice Court—Small Claims Court up to $3,000

City Court—Small Claims Court up to $3,000; other claims up to $15,000

District Court—Small Claims Court up to $3,000; other claims up to $15,000

County Court—Claims up to $25,000

Supreme Court—Claims above $25,000

Pennsylvania

Philadelphia Municipal Court—Small Claims Court up to $10,000

District Justice Court—Claims up to $8,000

Court of Common Pleas—Claims above $8,000

Texas

Justice of the Peace Court—Small Claims Court up to $5,000

County Court—Claims from $200 to $5,000

District Court—Claims above $200

Venue

Once you've determined which type or level of state court has the power to hear your case, you must pick the proper "venue"—choose which county in the state is the correct location for the lawsuit. Venue rules limit the counties in which a case can be filed in order to spare defendants the needless inconvenience of fighting a case far from where the defendant lives or where relevant events took place. For venue purposes, the correct county may be the county where:

- the defendant resides or does business
- a contract was signed
- a contract was to be carried out
- an auto accident took place, or
- other events leading up to the lawsuit transpired.

Because more than one county can be the correct venue for a lawsuit, often a plaintiff can compare courts (often called forum shopping) when deciding in which county to file a lawsuit.

> **EXAMPLE:** George and Jerry are both citizens of Texas. George lives in North County, near Oklahoma, and Jerry lives 600 miles away in South County, near Mexico. One day George drives south and Jerry drives north, and they collide in the middle of Texas, in Deep in the Heart of Texas County. George wants to sue Jerry. Venue rules probably require George to sue Jerry either in South County (where Jerry resides) or in Deep in the Heart of Texas County (where the collision occurred). George's home base, North County, is not a proper venue for the lawsuit, so Jerry is spared the inconvenience of having to defend himself there.

Moving to a More Convenient Court

The doctrine of "forum non conveniens" allows a defendant to ask a court to transfer a case to a court that is more convenient to the defendant and has a greater connection to events involved in the lawsuit. For example, diversity jurisdiction rules would allow Dan (a California citizen) to sue Raquelle (a Maine citizen) in California for $100,000 for a traffic accident that occurred in Maine. Almost certainly, the witnesses and all the physical evidence will be in Maine. Raquelle could file a motion asking the California court to exercise its forum non conveniens discretion and transfer the case to a federal court in Maine, and the court should grant her request.

> **TIP**
>
> **Venue made easy.** The venue is almost always proper if you file a lawsuit in the court closest to the place in which the defendant resides or does business. If you are in doubt about venue and don't want to wade through the rules and exceptions, file the lawsuit there.

Personal Jurisdiction

To obtain an enforceable judgment in either a federal or state court, the court must have power over the particular defendant (individual or business) you are suing. Lawyers refer to this as "personal jurisdiction." Subject matter jurisdiction rules determine where a plaintiff can file a case; personal jurisdiction rules determine whether a court has power over a particular defendant.

TIP

Personal jurisdiction rules are usually the same in state and federal courts. With a few exceptions beyond the scope of this book, federal courts have the same personal jurisdiction as the state courts located in the same state. (Federal courts do have greater jurisdiction than state courts when a defendant is not a resident of any state but has enough contacts with the "United States as a whole" to justify a federal court exercising jurisdiction. See FRCP 4 (k)(2). This is a very unusual situation that you almost surely won't have to deal with.)

Defendant Resides or Does Business in the State

The nearly universal rule is that the courts in a state have personal jurisdiction over all people or businesses that are citizens of or do business in that state. For example:

- You sue an Illinois citizen in an Illinois state court for breach of contract. It doesn't matter where you live or where the events leading up to the lawsuit took place because an Illinois state court has personal jurisdiction over all citizens of Illinois.
- You sue an Illinois citizen in an Illinois federal court for breach of contract. Just like an Illinois state court, an Illinois federal court has

personal jurisdiction over all citizens of Illinois. However, to establish that the Illinois federal court also has subject matter jurisdiction, you'd need to be a citizen of some state other than Illinois and ask for damages in excess of $75,000, or the case would have to arise under federal law.

Other Ways to Get Personal Jurisdiction

Personal jurisdiction rules can be a bit stickier when you file the suit in a state other than the one in which the defendant is a citizen or does business. To protect a defendant from being sued in a "hostile," possibly distant location, personal jurisdiction rules require that it be fair for a court to exercise power over a noncitizen, based on the facts of the case.

EXAMPLE: Debbie is a Texas citizen vacationing in Florida. While in Florida, Debbie buys what she is told are two brand new "fully loaded" computer systems at Kevin's Computer Shop. Debbie later learns that the computers are loaded with reused parts and won't perform the tasks that Kevin claimed. Debbie cannot sue Kevin in her home state of Texas. Texas has no personal jurisdiction over Kevin because Kevin doesn't reside or do business in Texas (and he hasn't been served with the court papers—usually a summons and complaint—in Texas, as described below).

Nevertheless, courts can and often do have personal jurisdiction over citizens of and businesses in other states in a variety of circumstances. Here are standard situations in which courts have personal jurisdiction over noncitizens in their state:

- The defendant enters the state in which you filed suit after the case is filed, even if only for a short visit, and you serve the defendant with the court papers (normally a summons and complaint) in the state. (As in the children's game of "tag," you have to find and "tag" the defendant with the papers while the defendant is in the state.)

EXAMPLE: You sue Herb, an Ohio citizen, for breach of contract in a court in Minnesota, where you live. After the suit is filed, your process server sees Herb drive into Minnesota for lunch and serves Herb with the summons and complaint in Minnesota. (Of course, the Minnesota court would also need subject matter jurisdiction. A Minnesota state court has subject matter jurisdiction because Herb was served in Minnesota. A Minnesota federal court would have subject matter jurisdiction if you and Herb were citizens of different states and the complaint asked for more than $75,000 in damages or if the complaint was based on federal law.)

- The defendant caused a traffic accident in the state in which you've filed a lawsuit based on the traffic accident. Remember, all states have "motorist" statutes giving their courts power to decide cases growing out of accidents on their highways, regardless of the parties' citizenship. You could serve the defendant with the lawsuit anywhere, not just in the state where the lawsuit was filed.

- The defendant (individual or business) has engaged in at least a small but significant amount of activity that constitutes "minimum contacts" in the state in which you've filed a lawsuit based on that activity. The minimum contacts requirement generally means that a defendant (person or business) who is a citizen of a different state must have enough connection to the state where a case has been filed for a judge to conclude that it's fair for the state to exercise power over the defendant. While it's risky to overgeneralize in these situations, a judge would probably conclude that minimum contacts exist in the following situations:

  - A business with its headquarters in another state maintains a branch office, store, or warehouse in the state in which the suit is filed.

  - A business with its headquarters in another state sends mail order catalogs into the state in which the suit is filed.

  - An individual who is a citizen of another state solicits business by making phone calls to customers or publishing advertisements in the state in which the suit is filed.

  - An Internet service provider that is a citizen of another state does business with paid subscribers or takes online orders from customers in the state in which the case is filed.

EXAMPLE: While on vacation in Vermont, Aura, an Ohio citizen, visits Fred's Vermont Antiques and sees what is labeled as a packet of "ancient Etruscan coins." Fred tells her they are rare and worth much more than the $5,000 he is asking for them. When Aura returns home to Ohio, she calls Fred and buys the coins. She then discovers the coins are actually worth only a few hundred dollars and wants to sue Fred. If Fred neither advertises nor does business online or by telephone in Ohio, Aura will have to file the lawsuit in Vermont. Because Aura made the phone call to Fred rather than the other way around, Fred does not have enough minimum contacts with Ohio to allow an Ohio court to exercise power over him.

TIP

A minimum contacts claim is stronger when the claim relates to the purpose of the contacts. Assume that you want to sue an out-of-state business, Abel Co., in your state. You believe the court has jurisdiction because Abel maintains a bicycle warehouse in your state. If your claim relates to a bicycle that you picked up at the warehouse, a judge is likely to conclude that it's fair to exercise personal jurisdiction over Abel Co. and allow your suit to proceed. But if your claim against Abel Co. grows out of a totally separate problem that has nothing to do with bicycles, the judge may conclude that Abel Co. does not have enough minimum contacts and dismiss your case at Abel Co.'s request.

Jurisdiction Based on Real Property Ownership

A state has limited jurisdiction (which lawyers call "in rem jurisdiction") over a noncitizen person or business that owns real property in the state. Jurisdiction in this situation is limited in two ways:

- Jurisdiction extends only to the fair market value of the real property. This means that if you sue a noncitizen who owns an apartment house worth $500,000 in the state in which you file the lawsuit, the most your judgment can be worth is $500,000.
- In addition, the claim probably has to relate to the property. For example, you could get jurisdiction over the noncitizen owner of an apartment house if you slipped and fell on the property. But you could probably not get jurisdiction over the noncitizen owner if the lawsuit grows out of an entirely separate problem that has nothing to do with the apartment house.

Beginning a Lawsuit

In the beginning of a lawsuit, the parties must file several documents with the court.

Plaintiff's Complaint

The complaint is the document that starts a lawsuit. It sets forth the facts underlying the dispute, the legal claims, and the damages or other relief the plaintiff (person bringing the lawsuit) seeks from the defendant (person or business being sued).

TIP

The names may change, but pleadings are essentially the same. A complaint or initial pleading is called a "petition" in some courts or for some types of cases. When the term "petition" is used, the person suing is called the "petitioner," and the person responding is called the "respondent."

For example, someone hurt in a car accident may sue the other driver. In the complaint, the plaintiff may ask the court to order the defendant to pay monetary damages to compensate the plaintiff for bodily injuries and damage to the car from the accident. Translated into everyday language, that complaint may say something like:

"The Defendant hit my car. He hit my car because he carelessly ran a red light, which is against the law. I suffered damages in the amount of $100,000 because of his carelessness— $10,000 for the car repairs, $50,000 for medical bills, $20,000 in wages I lost since I couldn't work because of the injuries, and $20,000 for the tremendous pain suffered. Therefore, I want the court to order the Defendant to pay me $100,000."

To draft (write up) your complaint in the pro per format, you should first determine whether your court requires you to use a court-approved form. Ask at the Clerk's Office and read the court rules. If you don't have to use a specific court-approved form, follow the example of many lawyers and consult a legal form book in the law library. As the name implies, form books are collections of legal documents written in a fill-in-the-blank style. (See Chapter 23 for more on legal form books.)

CAUTION

Sample forms are illustrations, not models. Throughout this book, you will find examples of legal documents that you are likely to encounter. We include these samples only to give you an idea of what the documents may look like. Because rules differ in different court systems, the actual documents used in your case may vary greatly from the samples. (Chapter 23 will help you find forms that meet specific requirements in your court.)

Subject to local variations, complaints commonly include:

1. **Identifying information.** Your name, address, and phone number go in the upper left-hand corner of the first page. As an option, you may also include a fax number and an email address. This information enables court personnel and the defendant to contact and mail documents to you.

2. **A caption.** A caption identifies the court in which you've filed the case, the parties (such as "John Doe, Plaintiff" versus "Jane Doe, Defendant"), the case number (issued by a court clerk at the time of filing), and sometimes the type of case. For example, a caption may mention that the complaint is for "Breach of Contract" or "Negligence."

3. **Jurisdictional facts—federal court cases.** To establish a federal district court's power to hear a case (see "Which Court Has the Power to Hear Your Case?," above), the plaintiff must include in a complaint information establishing the court's subject matter jurisdiction. (See FRCP 8-(a).) For example, in a federal court

Sample Complaint (State Court)

```
 1    Nolo Pedestrian          ①
      [Street Address]
 2    [City, State, Zip Code]
      [Phone number]
 3
 4    Plaintiff in Pro Per

 5

 6

 7            THE _____ COURT OF _____ COUNTY

 8                  STATE OF _____

 9

10    Nolo Pedestrian,                    )
                                          )
11                      Plaintiff,        )
                                          )
12    ②        v.                         )    Case No. _____
                                          )
13    Sarah Adams,                        )    COMPLAINT
                                          )
14                      Defendant.        )    JURY TRIAL DEMANDED
                                          )
15    _____    )

16

17        1. On approximately January 1, 20XX, at 3 p.m., while Plaintiff Nolo Pedestrian was crossing Main    ③

18    Street at Elm Street in the City of _____, County of _____,    ④

19    Defendant Sarah Adams drove her truck through the crosswalk, negligently failing to stop for Plaintiff,

20 ⑤ and thereby injuring Plaintiff.

21        2. As result of Defendant's negligent driving, Plaintiff's leg was broken, causing substantial pain and

22    suffering, medical expenses, and lost income.

23 ⑥     WHEREFORE, Plaintiff prays for judgment against Defendant in the sum of $100,000 plus costs and

24    interest.

25

26    ⑦  *Nolo Pedestrian* _____
          Nolo Pedestrian, Plaintiff in Pro Per

27    ⑧  Plaintiff demands trial by jury

28
```

diversity jurisdiction case, the complaint must refer to the different states of which the parties are citizens and request damages in excess of $75,000. In a federal question case (a case that arises under federal law), the complaint must refer to the federal law on which the case is based. (See Appendix of Forms to FRCP, Form 2.) Facts showing a federal district court's personal jurisdiction need not be specially mentioned; it's up to the defendant to raise a problem of personal jurisdiction if one exists.

④ Jurisdictional facts—state court cases. Stating jurisdictional facts is ordinarily not necessary in state court cases. However, it's usually necessary that the complaint establish venue by identifying the county in which events giving rise to the dispute took place or in which the defendant resides or does business.

⑤ Factual assertions. In plain English, you should briefly recite the facts (allegations) that make up your legal claim. You do not have to set forth all the evidence on which you rely. A short summary of what happened is usually good enough. (Legal form books, discussed in Chapter 23, have very helpful examples of allegations for common types of legal claims, such as negligence and breach of contract.)

TIP

Don't just recite your desired result. Though your complaint doesn't have to state all the background facts involved in your claim in detail, you do have to do more than make a vague, conclusory statement such as, "The

Defendant owes me money, and I want the court to order him to give it to me." Instead, refer to the key facts giving rise to the debt. For example, if you are suing to recover money someone owes you on a written promissory note, refer to the contents of the note and attach it as an exhibit to your complaint.

TIP

A few states insist on more detailed complaints. Several states (including California and New York) are what lawyers often refer to as "code pleading" or "fact pleading" states. These states require that complaints include facts that support each "element" of your legal claim (though you don't have to specifically refer to the elements by name or include voluminous details in the complaint). For a discussion of how to identify the elements of a legal claim, see Chapter 8.

⑥ The "prayer for relief." Your complaint has to tell the court what you want by way of legal relief. (The term "prayer" means "request" and is a throwback to times when the church heavily influenced the courts.) Most often you'll ask only for money damages. However, you might also ask the court to order the defendant to do something, such as tear down a fence that encroaches on your property or stop circulating a defamatory letter. In some states, the prayer may also ask for a jury trial if you want one. A prayer for relief comes at the end of a complaint. (See below for more about damages.)

⑦ Your signature. Normally, your last task is to follow the prayer for relief with your signature, identifying you as the person making the legal claims. In many states you can "verify" your complaint by including, above the signature line or on a separate page a verifying statement such as, "I declare under penalty of perjury that the allegations in the complaint are true." (Look at your state's rules for the exact language.) When you verify a complaint, you force the defendant to file a verified and more detailed answer. In some instances, such as petitions for marital dissolution (divorce), a state's law may require that your initial pleading be verified.

(8) **Jury trial demand.** This part of the complaint tells your adversary and the court that you want a jury trial. But be aware that pretrial rules in your court may also require you to file a separate jury demand document and pay jury fees to preserve your right to a jury trial. Be sure to check your state's rules.

> **CAUTION**
>
> **You may have to attach an "exhibit" to your complaint.** Many states require plaintiffs to attach documents called "exhibits" to complaints in certain types of cases. For example, if a plaintiff's suit is based on a written contract, the plaintiff may have to attach the contract to the complaint (unless the plaintiff can explain why the contract is unavailable). Similarly, if a plaintiff sues a doctor for medical malpractice, the plaintiff may have to attach a "Good Cause Affidavit" from another doctor, stating that the plaintiff has a reasonable basis for filing the complaint.
>
> If exhibits are required, the complaint should state that the necessary exhibit is attached.

For example, a complaint may state: "A copy of the Licensing Agreement is attached hereto as Exhibit 1."

> **CAUTION**
>
> **Be scrupulously accurate when you verify a complaint.** Your representation that all statements in your complaint are made under penalty of perjury will ordinarily be taken very seriously by judges. For example, if what you say under oath later in the case—perhaps in an affidavit you submit to the court, during a deposition, or when testifying at trial—varies from what you say in a verified complaint, your opponent may offer the contradictory complaint language into evidence to cast doubt on your credibility. This will not happen if your complaint is unverified.

> **CAUTION**
>
> **Check your local court rules before you try to file anything.** In many courts, it is customary, and may be required by court rule, to submit papers on "pleading paper," which is just paper (8.5" by 11") with line numbers running down the left side of each page. You can get a supply of this paper at a stationery store. If you use a computer to type your documents, check to see whether your word processing program offers it as a built-in option.
>
> Some courts impose other rules on how papers must be presented. A court may, for example, require two holes to be punched at the top of the page so that papers can be inserted directly into the court's file folder. Or it may require you to attach what's sometimes called a "blue-back"—a stiff piece of blue paper—to the back of your pleadings. And some courts require a cover sheet with your initial complaint.

TIP

You can amend your complaint. Pleadings such as the complaint can normally be amended (changed) after they are filed. For example, assume you are Nolo Pedestrian, the plaintiff suing Ms. Adams in the car accident example just above. After you have already filed a complaint against her, you determine that the companies that manufactured the car and the brakes may also be legally liable, and you want to add these companies as defendants.

Typically, if the defendant has not yet responded by filing an answer, you do not need permission from the court to amend. But you do need permission from the judge if the defendant has already answered your complaint. In that case, you will have to file another paper with the court—a request for "leave" (permission) to amend your complaint—in which you state the reasons for the changes.

You May Have to Complain to a Governmental Agency First

Lawyers and self-represented parties alike may find the legal system exhausting, but that isn't what lawyers mean when they talk about "exhaustion of remedies." This legal principle is designed to save judges the trouble of having to decide cases that could be resolved in a different forum, through noncourt procedures. Plaintiffs are often required to "exhaust," or take advantage of, administrative complaint processes before going to court.

For example, assume that a shipping company thinks that a new state trucking regulation is unfair and illegal. Before suing to overturn the regulation in court, the shipping company might have to challenge it before the state agency that drafted the regulation. Only if the agency upholds the regulation after all administrative processes have been completed can the shipping company challenge the regulation in court. Similarly, assume that a property owner seeks a variance from a zoning ordinance before a city's zoning board. If the zoning board turns down the request for a variance, the property owner may have to appeal the decision to the city's zoning appeals board before going to court.

However, plaintiffs are required to "exhaust remedies" only if the remedies they seek are actually available. For example, a judge will require a property owner to appeal an adverse zoning decision only if a city's administrative procedures provide for an appeal process.

When a judge upholds a defendant's objection to a complaint that the plaintiff failed to exhaust other remedies, the judge normally issues a "stay" of the complaint. As a result, the complaint is not dismissed (thrown out of court). Instead, the complaint remains on file in the court system, and the plaintiff may resume court proceedings if the noncourt proceedings are unsatisfactory. This insures that a plaintiff won't miss the statute of limitations deadline while exhausting other potential remedies, as long as the complaint was filed on time in the first place.

Sample Factual Language Necessary for Some Common Legal Claims

Though modern pleading rules allow for much flexibility, here are examples of acceptable "short summary" factual statements for common types of legal claims:

Negligence:

1. On September 22, 20XX, Plaintiff Kebo was driving westbound and Defendant Jackson was driving eastbound on Olympic Boulevard.
2. Defendant negligently made a left-hand turn to go north on Main Street, colliding with Plaintiff's car.
3. As a result of Defendant's negligence, Plaintiff suffered loss of income and personal injuries that required hospitalization. Plaintiff will require additional medical treatment and will lose additional income in the future. Plaintiff's car was also damaged beyond repair.

Breach of Contract:

1. On March 12, 20XX, Plaintiff Knaplund and Defendant Edelstein entered into a contract for certain repairs to Edelstein's house. A copy of the contract is attached to this Complaint as Exhibit A.
2. Plaintiff made all the repairs called for by the contract and has fully performed all obligations required by the contract.
3. Defendant has refused to pay, and continues to refuse to pay, $17,000 that is due and owing under the terms of the contract.

Fraud:

1. On March 31, 20XX, Plaintiff Even and Defendant Strauss entered into a written contract in which Plaintiff agreed to purchase from Defendant a vacant lot located in Milwaukee County, Wisconsin. The price agreed upon was $125,000. A copy of the contract is attached to this Complaint as Exhibit A.
2. Under the terms of the contract, Defendant stated that the lot was suitable for building a home.
3. This representation was false and fraudulent, because Defendant had used the lot for many years for dumping brewery residue, rendering the land clearly unsuitable for human habitation. Defendant knew that the representation was false and made it for the purpose of inducing Plaintiff to enter into the contract.
4. Plaintiff relied on Defendant's representation when purchasing the lot and was damaged as a result.

Promissory Note:

1. On or about February 14, 20XX, Plaintiff Martinez loaned Defendant Chung the sum of $10,000. Defendant signed a promissory note (a copy of which is attached as Exhibit A) agreeing to repay this amount in its entirety to Plaintiff along with interest at the rate of 10% per year on October 14, 20XX.
2. Defendant did not pay the amount due under the promissory note, and the entire amount plus interest is now due and owing to Plaintiff.

More About Damages and the "Prayer for Relief"

A prayer for relief doesn't necessarily have to specify an exact amount of damages. For example, in a personal injury action the prayer for relief may simply ask for "damages according to proof." Specific amounts aside, a prayer for relief may ask for compensation of various types, such as:

- **General damages** (also called **compensatory damages** and **actual damages**) are damages that are directly attributable to the defendant's wrongful act. Common examples of general damages include lost wages and medical bills.

- **Pain and suffering** is a form of general damages by which defendants have to compensate those they injure for the pain and inability to carry on everyday activities that the injuries produce. Because the amount of damages for pain and suffering depends on judges' and jurors' subjective feelings, some states put "caps" (limits) on the amount of damages for pain and suffering that they can award.

- **Special damages**, sometimes called **consequential damages**, are indirect harms that flow from wrongful acts. For example, a business owner's claim for compensation for the loss of reputation caused by the defendant's wrongful act is a claim for special damages. To allow defendants to fairly assess the scope of the potential damages they may be ordered to pay, many jurisdictions require plaintiffs to specify special damages (if any) in their complaints.

- **Punitive damages**, sometimes called **exemplary damages**, are a form of punishment of defendants whose actions have not only been wrongful, but malicious and egregious. For example, a jury may order a cigarette manufacturer to pay punitive damages if it concludes that the manufacturer intentionally added ingredients increasing the addictiveness of its cigarettes. Plaintiffs must be entitled to general damages before punitive damages are even a possibility. In most states, punitive damages are not even a possibility in breach of contract actions. And even if a defendant's reprehensible conduct has caused damages to thousands of people, a punitive damages award can reflect only the harm done to the parties to a specific lawsuit. (*Philip Morris USA vs. Williams*, U.S. Sup. Ct. 2007)

- **Liquidated damages** are the amount of damages that parties agree to in advance, typically in a written contract. For example, an employment agreement may state that if the employer fires the employee before the agreement expires, the employee's damages are limited to $50,000. Courts typically enforce liquidated damages clauses only if they were reasonable at the time they went into effect.

Summons

After a complaint is filed with the Clerk's Office (along with the required filing fee), the court usually issues a paper called a "summons." The purpose of a summons is to advise the defendant about the lawsuit and to provide a number of important facts about the case, including the names of the plaintiff and defendant (called the "parties"); the name, address, and phone number of the plaintiff's lawyer (if any); the case number (assigned by the Clerk's Office); and the dates by which the next pleading (normally a response by the defendant) must be filed.

Generally, after the summon is issued the plaintiff arranges for the summons and complaint to be served on (physically delivered to) the defendant. Rules about how these and other legal documents must be served (called "service of process") must be strictly followed. If they are not, sometimes the lawsuit cannot go forward. Service of process is governed by Federal Rule of Civil Procedure (FRCP) 4 in federal courts; you can usually find local service rules in your state statutes, usually in the volumes on "Civil Procedure." (See Chapter 23 for more information on finding legal rules and reference books.) Here are some rules about service of process that apply in many court systems:

- Normally, as a party to the lawsuit, you may not personally serve your own complaint and summons (if you are the plaintiff) or your own answer (if you are the defendant). You also cannot serve your own motions (requests for a court order) or subpoenas (court orders compelling someone to come to court). Another person must serve these pleadings for you. In some states, legal documents must be served by a law enforcement officer (sheriff, marshal, or constable) or a licensed private process server; in other states, any adult not connected with the lawsuit can serve legal papers.

- A complaint must be served on the defendant within a certain time after it is filed. For example, a complaint and summons must be served within 120 days after filing in federal courts (FRCP 4(j)) and within 60 days under certain state rules.

- To serve legal documents on a business—for example, when your adversary is a company rather than an individual—you usually don't have to serve them personally. In most cases, it's enough to have the document delivered to the business and have a copy of the document mailed to the same address.

- Some courts don't require personal delivery at all in certain circumstances; they allow service by regular U.S. mail.

- Courts require proof of service, usually in the form of a signed document that states when, how, and on whom the complaint and summons were served (see "Sample Proof of Service," below). Often, you must file a proof of service whenever you file any type of pleading with the court (FRCP 4(g)). There's usually a deadline for filing. For example, a proof of service must be filed within 90 days of filing the complaint in some court systems.

Sample Proof of Service

1   Nolo Pedestrian
     [Street Address]
2   [City, State, Zip Code]
     [Phone number]
3

4   Plaintiff in Pro Per

5

6

7   THE _____ COURT OF _____ COUNTY

8   STATE OF _____

9

10   Nolo Pedestrian   )
)
11   Plaintiff,   )
)   Case No. 12345
12   v.   )
)   DECLARATION OF SERVICE BY MAIL
13   Sarah Adams,   )
)
14   Defendant.   )
15   )

16

17   Ms. Dana Lauren, the undersigned, hereby declares:

18   I am a citizen of the United States. I am over the age of 18 years and not a party to within action.

19   On February 28, 20XX, at the direction of Nolo Pedestrian, Plaintiff in Pro Per, I served the within

20   COMPLAINT FOR NEGLIGENCE AND SUMMONS on the following interested party by mailing, with

21   postage thereon fully prepaid, a true copy of thereof to:

22   Greta Charles, Esq., Attorney for Sarah Adams, Defendant

23   [Street Address]

24   [City, State, Zip Code]

25   I declare under penalty of perjury that the foregoing is true and correct.

26   Executed at [City, State] on February 28, 20XX.

27   *Dana Lauren* _____
                                 Dana Lauren
28

TIP

You can be reimbursed for filing fees. The filing fee that the plaintiff pays when the complaint is filed with the Clerk's Office is considered one of the "fees and costs of suit." That means that if the plaintiff wins the lawsuit, the court may order the defendant to reimburse the plaintiff for the filing fee. U.S. courts typically do not, however, order the losing party to pay the winner's attorneys' fees.

Defendant's Response

A properly served defendant must respond to a complaint within a short period of time, typically 30 days. Under Federal Rule of Civil Procedure 12(a), the defendant has to serve an answer within 20 days after the complaint and summons is served.

If a defendant fails to respond in time, the plaintiff can apply for what's known as a "default judgment." A default judgment is a court order granting a judgment against the defendant to pay the amount requested in the complaint, based on the defendant's failure to answer or defend against the lawsuit after having been given proper notice. In some courts, the plaintiff simply files a Request for Default Judgment with the Clerk's Office. In other courts, the plaintiff must appear in court to show the judge that the threshold requirements for a valid claim have been met (this is sometimes called a "prove up" hearing).

Once a default judgment is entered (filed and written into the official court records), it has the status of any other judgment. It is as if the plaintiff had conducted and won a full trial. A defendant may, however, move very quickly to have it set aside (undone

and taken off the record). Some judges will set aside a default judgment only if the defendant was not served properly, or if the defendant's failure to answer the complaint or show up in court is excusable. For instance, if the defendant was in the hospital at the time the papers were served, or the defendant's attorney neglected to respond on behalf of the defendant, the judge might set aside a default judgment. Other judges are more lenient towards defendants and will set aside a default more readily. (For reference, default judgments in federal courts are governed by FRCP 55, and reasons for setting them aside by FRCP 60(b).)

Assuming that as a defendant you are unwilling to let the plaintiff win by default, you generally have to respond to a plaintiff's complaint in writing within 20 to 30 days after you were served. (The summons accompanying the complaint will specify exactly how much time you have.) If you need additional time (for example, you are just about to leave town for two weeks), contact the person (usually an attorney) whose name and phone number are in the upper left-hand corner of the complaint and ask for additional time to respond. Confirm an extension of time to respond with a letter.

CAUTION

Confirming extensions with the court. If your adversary agrees to extend your time to respond, you still may have to file a short notice with the court confirming that the time for response has been extended. Check your local court rules or ask the court clerk to see whether your state imposes this requirement.

If the opposing party does not agree to extend the time for response, you can go to court with a Motion for Extension of Time to Respond. If you don't have time to do that, file any kind of answer that contests the complaint to prevent the plaintiff from entering a default judgment against you before you return home. You can always amend your answer later when you have more time.

> ! CAUTION
>
> **Don't file a frivolous response.** Like plaintiffs, defendants can be subject to monetary penalties if they make false claims or factual claims that are not supported by any evidence. (See FRCP 11(b)(4).)

You can respond to the plaintiff's complaint in two general ways:

- **Answer on the merits.** This more common method of response typically requires filing a pleading known as an "answer," which challenges a complaint's factual accuracy, makes claims against the plaintiff, and even brings new parties into the lawsuit. It may also assert affirmative defenses.
- **Raise technical defects.** Typically, this means filing a legal document called a "motion." Motions focus on procedural issues instead of a complaint's factual accuracy. For example, if you are not a citizen of the state in which you are sued, you may have a basis for filing a motion challenging a court's personal jurisdiction. (You've always heard of "winning on a technicality." This may be your chance!) If the judge dismisses your technical objection and upholds the complaint, you can still file an answer challenging the merits.

Let's look briefly at each type of response.

Answer on the Merits

A defendant's answer somewhat resembles a plaintiff's complaint. Like a complaint, your answer will include:

1. **Identifying information** in the upper left-hand corner of the first page.

2. **A caption**, which, of course, will say "Answer" instead of "Complaint."

3. **Factual assertions** denying the claims the plaintiff made in the complaint. The simplest way to do this is through a "general denial," which states that "Defendant denies each and every allegation of the Complaint." Assuming that you are eligible to file a general denial, it's fine to do this even if you recognize that some of the plaintiff's allegations are accurate. A general denial simply lets everyone know that the defendant will force the plaintiff to "prove it."

In some cases, you are not eligible to make a general denial. Either local court rules (get a copy pronto from the courthouse Clerk's Office) or the fact that the complaint is "verified" (signed under penalty of perjury) may prevent you from making a general denial. In this situation, you will be required to respond separately to each numbered paragraph of the plaintiff's complaint. In doing so, it will probably be necessary to concede the accuracy of certain allegations while denying others. For example, assume that you are sued for negligence and that paragraph 3 of the

Sample Answer

1 Sarah Adams, President
   [Street Address]
2 [City, State, Zip Code]
   [Phone number]
3 Defendant in Pro Per

4

5

6

7 THE _____ COURT OF _____ COUNTY

8 STATE OF _____

9

10 Nolo Pedestrian   )
)
11   Plaintiff,   )
)   Case No. 12345
12   v.   )
)   DEFENDANT'S ANSWER TO PLAINTIFF'S
13 Sarah Adams,   )   CIVIL ACTION FOR NEGLIGENCE
)
14   Defendant.   )
)
15 _____   )

16

17 Defendant Adams Answers the Complaint as follows:

18   1. Defendant admits that on January 1, 20XX, she was driving in the vicinity of Elm and Main

19 Streets, but Defendant denies each and every other allegation in paragraph 1.

20   2. Defendant denies each and every allegation in paragraph 2.

21 Defendant asserts the following affirmative defense:

22 Plaintiff barred from pursuing the cause of action stated in Plaintiff's Complaint under the State

23 of _____'s applicable statute of limitations for negligence actions as it

24 occurred more than two years before the Complaint was filed.

25 WHEREFORE Defendant prays that Plaintiff take nothing and that Defendant be awarded all fees

26 and costs of suit.

27   *Sarah Adams*
        _____
28   Sarah Adams, Defendant in Pro Per

complaint states that you negligently made a left-hand turn while driving on Olympic Boulevard and struck the plaintiff's car. Your answer may state that "I admit that I was driving eastbound on Olympic Boulevard on June 3, but I deny each and every other allegation of paragraph 3 of the Complaint."

If you do not know whether an allegation in a complaint is true, you may deny "based on information and belief." (FRCP 8-(b).) For example, if a verified complaint alleges in paragraph 6 that the plaintiff suffered a broken leg, and you have no way of knowing whether that is really true, your answer may state that "Defendant has no information or belief regarding the allegation of paragraph 6, and based on such lack of information and belief denies the allegation in paragraph 6."

CAUTION

How to avoid the "negative pregnant." Back in the days when pleading rules were incredibly picky, the "negative pregnant" became one of the legal system's most colorful traps for an unwary defendant. A negative pregnant consisted of a defendant's denial that a sum of money is owed, phrased in such a way that a judge treats it as an admission that some other sum of money is owed. For example, if an answer stated that "Defendant denies owing $50,000," a judge could interpret this as a negative pregnant in which the defendant admits owing $49,999! Fortunately, the negative pregnant has been largely consigned to the scrap heap of legal history. However, to protect yourself against a judge who decides to make an example of

you, play it safe and state that you "deny owing $50,000 or any other sum."

④ **A prayer for relief,** which typically requests that "the Plaintiff take nothing" and that the court award court costs to you. If your answer includes claims against the plaintiff (called a counterclaim; see below) or a third party (called a cross-complaint or cross-claim; see below), the prayer for relief will also ask for money damages in a specified amount or "according to proof," just like the prayer for relief in a complaint.

⑤ **Your signature,** which follows the prayer for relief. If the complaint is verified, you'll probably be required to verify your answer. This means that you'll have to include a statement, such as "I declare under penalty of perjury that the allegations in the Answer are true," immediately above your signature or on a separate page. (Check your state's law or a legal form book for the wording required in your state.)

In addition to denying all or some of a complaint's allegations, your answer may also include affirmative defenses, counterclaims and cross-complaints. Let's briefly look at each of these.

Affirmative Defenses

Affirmative defenses consist of new factual allegations that under legal rules defeat all or a portion of a plaintiff's claim. As the defendant, you have the obligation to raise any affirmative defenses on which you hope to rely, and at trial you'll have the burden of proving their truth. Common affirmative defenses are listed in FRCP 8(c).

They include:

- The Statute of Limitations, an allegation that the plaintiff failed to file the complaint within the time required by law (see "Is Your Lawsuit Timely," above).

TIP

If the court lacks jurisdiction over you, say it here. Normally, your answer will not dispute the court's power to hear the case (jurisdiction), because the plaintiff probably filed the lawsuit in the proper court. In the unusual case in which the court's power to hear the case is an issue, you may include that as an affirmative defense or, in the alternative, file a pre-answer motion raising lack of jurisdiction as a technical defect. (See "Raise Technical Defects," below.)

- In a negligence case:
  - the plaintiff's own carelessness (often called "contributory negligence") was the cause of all or some of the plaintiff's injuries, or
  - the plaintiff "assumed the risk" of injury by voluntarily engaging in a dangerous activity, such as rock climbing, playing in a football match, or walking next to a building where thousands of pigeons roosted.
- In a contract action:
  - a particular oral contract is invalid because by law (called the "Statute of Frauds") the agreement was required to be in writing—or at

least referred to in a document—to be enforceable

  - the defendant was a minor at the time the contract was made, or
  - the contract was a product of duress, because the plaintiff threatened the defendant with physical harm if the defendant refused to sign the contract.
- Accord and satisfaction, meaning that you and the plaintiff have already settled the dispute.

CAUTION

Be sure that your answer states all possible affirmative defenses. If you do not include an affirmative defense in an answer (or get a judge's permission to add an affirmative defense later), you will not be able to offer evidence to support an affirmative defense at trial. A legal coach can help you determine whether any affirmative defenses are available to you. See "Finding a Legal Coach" in Chapters 1 and 23.

Some states have preprinted "check box" forms that you can use. You can find them at a law library.

Counterclaims

Counterclaims (governed in federal courts by FRCP 13) are a way for a defendant to make claims against, and seek money damages or other legal relief from, a plaintiff. A counterclaim is particularly appropriate if you planned to sue the plaintiff before plaintiff won the race to the courthouse door and sued you first. A counterclaim allows you to use an answer not only to deny a plaintiff's allegations but also to go on the offensive against the plaintiff. A counterclaim says, in effect, "The plaintiff says I owe money to him? No way—it's the plaintiff who broke the contract and as a result owes me the money I lost." A defendant who wants a judgment against a plaintiff has to include a counterclaim in an answer (rather than filing a separate lawsuit) if the defendant's claim is based on the same series of events as the plaintiff's (lawyers call these "compulsory counterclaims").

If a defendant has a compulsory counterclaim but doesn't include it in the answer, the defendant won't be allowed to bring that claim later.

EXAMPLE: You've been sued for negligence. The plaintiff's complaint states that you carelessly made a left-hand turn and collided with the plaintiff's oncoming car. Your answer may set forth a counterclaim in which you allege that it was the plaintiff who carelessly drove into the road from a driveway after you had begun to turn, colliding with you and causing you to suffer personal injuries that required hospitalization, continuing medical treatments, lost future income, and severe damage to your car. If you don't include this counterclaim in your answer, you'll give up the right to seek damages from the plaintiff caused by the accident.

"We'll see your hundred thou and countersue you a million."

(Again, legal form books—discussed in Chapter 23—set forth sample counter-claims for different kinds of cases.)

Cross-Complaints or Cross-Claims

More rarely, you may also want to use your answer to bring a new party into the case by including a "cross-complaint" in your answer. (See FRCP 13g).) A cross-complaint in essence blames a new third party for any harm the plaintiff suffered. For example, if you are a defendant in an auto accident case, you may include a cross-complaint against the company that repaired the brakes on your car, claiming that the improper brake repair (and not your carelessness) caused your brakes to fail and your car to collide with the plaintiff's.

Raise Technical Defects

Before filing an answer (or sometimes as part of an answer), you might respond to a complaint by filing a Motion to Dismiss, claiming that the case cannot proceed because the plaintiff has violated one or more procedural requirements. (See FRCP 12.) A judge may dismiss a case for serious procedural violations, and if the statute of limitations expires before the plaintiff can refile it, the procedural error may spell the end of the lawsuit. More likely, your valid procedural objections will disrupt the case by forcing the plaintiff to start over with a new complaint or even in a new court. If nothing else, the ensuing fuss and delay may convince the plaintiff that winning the case won't be easy and lead to an offer to settle.

Common technical defects you can raise include:

- The court lacks power to hear the case (jurisdiction), either over the defendant personally or over the subject matter of the case. For example, perhaps the plaintiff has filed the case in federal court, even though the claim does not arise under federal law and the plaintiff and defendant are citizens of the same state. (See "Which Court Has the Power to Hear Your Case," above.)

- Improper service of the summons and complaint. For example, instead of handing you the papers personally, the plaintiff's process server simply discarded them but claimed to have served you.

- The complaint is vague and ambiguous. This response is not usually successful, because modern pleading rules allow each side to postpone providing the details of the case until disclosure and discovery (see Chapter 5). However, if a complaint is so vague that you are not sure of what you are supposed to have done wrong, you can make a Motion for a More Definite Statement, which—if successful—can force the plaintiff to prepare and serve a more factually detailed complaint.

- The complaint fails to state a claim for relief. Essentially, this response asserts that even if everything the plaintiff alleges is true, there is no valid legal claim. For instance, a complaint would not state a valid claim if it alleged that "I bought a stock recommended by my stockbroker and it went down in value." Just because your stockbroker recommended a stock that lost value does not give you legal grounds on which to sue the broker. (By contrast, the claim might have been valid if it alleged that the stockbroker recommended a stock without disclosing that it was a speculative stock, and you had previously told the stockbroker that you wanted only conservative investments. This might be grounds for a lawsuit.)

RESOURCE

American Jurisprudence Pleading and Practice Forms Annotated (Lawyers Cooperative Publishing Co.) is a comprehensive, multivolume guide with numerous forms and examples.

Basics of Legal Document Preparation, by Robert Cummins (Delmar), contains numerous examples of state and federal pleadings.

Plain Language Pleadings, by Carol Ann Wilson (Prentice Hall), is an attorney assistant's guide to preparing pleadings. ●

Pretrial Procedures

This chapter provides an overview of the procedures that commonly take place between the conclusion of the initial paperwork stage of a lawsuit (see Chapter 3) and the time that a case either settles or goes to trial. Despite what we have all seen in movies and TV shows, most cases don't go straight from initial papers to trial (with perhaps a few commercials in between). Like most civil litigation professionals (lawyers and paralegals), you will probably spend most of the time you devote to your case not in court but instead engaged in the pretrial activities outlined in this chapter and described in more detail throughout the book.

Pretrial tasks include preparing and gathering documents, exchanging them with your adversary, and participating in the process of fact investigation called "discovery." And, at least the first few times you go to the courthouse, it likely will not be to conduct your trial but to participate in a pretrial conference with your opponent (and often a judge) or to ask the judge to decide some preliminary dispute (called "arguing a pretrial motion").

Especially if you represent yourself and are unfamiliar with litigation, it is important to understand at the outset that the pretrial stage of your case is likely to be time-consuming. Rules governing pretrial activities tend to be technical and exacting. This is the "inside stuff" of the law generally familiar only to experienced attorneys and paralegals, and often changed by legislators and judges in response to attorneys' maneuverings. Moreover, while some processes will be dictated by state law and followed in all of a particular state's courthouses, others may be a product of local court rules and even unwritten customs that operate only in the courthouses of a single county. Thus, while we can outline common pretrial procedures, we can't anticipate all of the local rules and practices that may occur in your case. Your court may follow a practice not touched on below, may refer to a similar procedure by a different name, or may follow similar procedures but in a different order. Also, if your case involves less than $50,000 and doesn't present complex legal issues, it may be put on an expedited "short cause" calendar. In these cases, many of the processes described in this chapter don't apply or are streamlined.

To find out which procedures will apply to your specific case, you'll have to consult your state and local rules carefully (and talk to your legal coach, if you have one). Courthouses often provide procedural guides, and the latest versions of court rules are generally available in public libraries and online. For more information about how to do legal research, including websites where you'll find court rules and legal forms, see Chapter 23.

Know and Follow Pretrial Deadlines

The substantial roster of pretrial procedures outlined in this chapter typically unfolds according to a fast-paced schedule that is, at least in theory, subject to rigorous oversight by judges. In many areas of the country, the swift pace of pretrial activities (often called "fast track" or "rocket docket" procedures) has reduced the long case backlogs that were common just a few years ago, when parties themselves had the power to dictate the pace of litigation, subject only to very loose statutory controls. If you're serious about representing yourself in court, be prepared to meet a number of pretrial deadlines for filing documents in court, exchanging documents with your adversary, conducting discovery, and attending conferences with your opponent and possibly the judge.

 CAUTION

Pro se litigants must follow the rules. Most judges won't cut you any slack simply because you're representing yourself and doing your best to negotiate a minefield of unfamiliar procedures. Miss a deadline, and you may have to pay a penalty to your opponent or lose a right that you might otherwise have had—for example, to ask for a jury trial or to take a particular witness's deposition. Miss deadlines frequently, and a judge may even dismiss your complaint or answer.

Pretrial Conferences

If your case goes all the way to trial (or even if it settles the day before), you probably will participate in a number of meetings along the way, often with both your adversary and a judge present. These pretrial conferences go by different names in different courts, sometimes depending on when in the pretrial process a conference takes place. For example, a pretrial conference might be called a "scheduling conference," an "arbitration status conference," a "status conference," a "trial setting conference," or a "settlement conference." And while a

particular state's court rules may require only attorneys (not parties) to attend some types of pretrial conferences, if you're self-represented, you will have to attend all of them.

Court rules often require conferences in nearly every case. In addition, Federal Rule of Civil Procedure 16(a) and similar rules in most states grant judges discretion to order attorneys and self-represented parties to attend additional pretrial conferences to discuss such matters as settlement and discovery or to whittle down the number of disputed issues in the case. (For a more complete list of subjects that are commonly discussed during pretrial conferences, see FRCP 16(c).)

Court-Ordered Mediation and Arbitration

In addition to slogging through a succession of pretrial activities, in many states a judge may order you to attempt to settle your case through mediation or arbitration, sometimes both. Broad rules designed to promote settlement authorize judges to "sidetrack" certain types of cases—for example, child custody cases and cases involving less than $50,000—by ordering the parties to take their disputes through some form of alternative dispute resolution (ADR). Usually this means mediation or arbitration.

In mediation, a neutral third party (the mediator) gets the parties together and tries to informally facilitate resolution of a dispute. However, the mediator has no power to impose a settlement. If the mediation fails, the case typically comes back "on track" and proceeds to trial (or settlement) as though the mediation had not occurred.

Arbitration is more formal than mediation. It resembles a trial in that, like a judge, a neutral third party (the arbitrator) hears testimony, examines documents, and issues a decision, usually called an "award." In some states, an arbitrator's decision has the same finality as if it were issued by a judge or jury. But in others—especially if you didn't agree in advance to be bound by the arbitrator's decision—you have the right to reject it, which means your case will be returned to the court system. However, if you reject an arbitration award that turns out to be more favorable to you than the outcome of trial, you may be ordered to pay your adversary's court costs.

For more information about court-ordered mediation and arbitration, and tips for representing yourself effectively in both types of proceedings, see Chapter 6.

Initial Pretrial Procedures: Setting Ground Rules

This section examines pretrial activities that commonly take place shortly after the initial pleading (paperwork) stage is complete. These early procedures can be critical because decisions made at this time often determine the scope and timing of the pretrial activities to follow.

Filing a "Proof of Service" and an "At Issue Memorandum"

In most states, the service of a complaint and answer is not sufficient to start your lawsuit rolling toward settlement or trial. If you are a plaintiff, you also have to "start the clock" by filing a paper called a Proof of Service that notifies the court that your complaint has been served on the defendant. (FRCP 4(l); see Chapter 3.) In addition, you may need to file a separate document, sometimes called an At Issue Memorandum, that indicates that the defendant has filed an answer. If you want a jury trial but didn't make a jury trial request in your complaint or answer, you may do so in the memorandum. Alternatively, court rules may require that you make a jury request in a separate document.

Attending an Early Meeting of Parties and Preparing a Report

FRCP 26(f) and similar rules in many states require you to meet with your adversary "as soon as practicable" after a complaint and answer have been filed. This meeting typically must take place before the judge conducts what is often called a "scheduling conference" and issues a Scheduling Order. (See "Attending a Scheduling Conference," below.) You and your adversary generally have to arrange the meeting yourselves; you might not get a notice from the court ordering you to meet. The issues that you and your opponent are expected to discuss in good faith during this meeting include the following:

- Your competing claims, with an eye to a possible quick settlement.
- The timing of the disclosures that you and your adversary must provide to each other under FRCP 26(a)(3). (Federal and many state courts provide that very soon after the "early meeting of parties," the parties must exchange basic information such as the names,

addresses, and telephone numbers of potential witnesses and the identity and whereabouts of relevant documents. For more information on what has to be disclosed under FRCP 26(a)(3), see Chapter 5.)

- The formation of a discovery plan, which often includes the issues on which each party will seek discovery and the timing of each party's depositions and other discovery requests. (For a description and analysis of discovery methods, see Chapter 5.)
- An estimate of how long the trial will take.

Under FRCP 26(f) and similar rules in many states, you and your adversary are required to prepare a single Joint Report of Early Meeting (or some similarly named document that outlines the agreements reached during your early meeting). You must submit the report to the court within ten days after the meeting. If you are representing yourself and your adversary is represented by an attorney, the attorney may offer to prepare and submit the report. If so, make sure that the attorney sends you a draft before submitting the report to the judge so that you can carefully check to see that it reflects the agreements you made. A sample joint report is included below.

CAUTION

Beware of slanted reports. Whoever drafts any court document has many subtle—and sometimes not-so-subtle—opportunities to slant it in the drafter's direction. Always read drafts of reports and other documents prepared by your adversary promptly. If they don't reflect

what you agreed to, rewrite the misstatements and mail, fax, or email the document back to your adversary. You may have to exchange several drafts before you reach consensus. With a document such as a Joint Report of Early Meeting, bring your final draft to the conference with the judge in case it differs from the version your adversary presents. Sometimes you'll agree to include each party's version of some element of the report.

Attending a Scheduling Conference

The "scheduling conference" described in Federal Rule of Civil Procedure 16(b) is likely to be the first pretrial conference with the judge that you'll attend. A scheduling conference may take place in the judge's office (often called "chambers"), with you, your adversary, and the judge all present in person. However, the conference may also take place via telephone or by electronic means.

Rule 16(b) puts the judge in the role of case manager. Normally, after reviewing the early meeting report (discussed above) and hearing from both parties at the scheduling conference, the judge will issue an order (often called a Scheduling Order) that sets time limits for filing any pretrial motions, completing discovery, conducting other pretrial conferences, and starting trial. As a self-represented party, you may find it difficult to predict how much discovery you'll need to do and how long it will take. One option is to consult a legal coach before attending the scheduling conference. (See "Finding a Legal Coach" in Chapter 1.) Also, ask the judge to give you leeway when

Sample Joint Report of Early Meeting

1 Fred Nolo
[Street Address]
2 [City, State, Zip Code]
[Phone Number]
3
4 Plaintiff in Pro Per
5
6
7 THE _____ COURT OF _____ COUNTY
8 STATE OF _____
9 Fred Nolo,)
)
10 Plaintiff,)
) Case No. 12-3-456789-1
11 v.)
)
12 Austin Tayshuss,) JOINT REPORT OF EARLY MEETING
)
13 Defendant.)
14 _____)
15
16
17 Plaintiff Fred Nolo and Counsel for Defendant Austin Tayshuss submit the following Joint Report
18 of Early Meeting.
19 1. No later than March 1, 20XX, the parties will make the following disclosures under the terms of
20 F.R.C.P. 26(a)(3): [*include a list of what will be disclosed, such as descriptions of documents and witness*
21 *information*].
22 2. Plaintiff Nolo will depose Defendant Tayshuss no later than March 12, 20XX.
23 3. Following the completion of Defendant Tayshuss's deposition, Defendant Tayshuss will depose
24 Plaintiff Nolo no later than March 31, 20XX.
25 4. No other depositions will be taken.
26 5. No pretrial motions are contemplated at this time.
27 6. No other parties will be brought into the case.
28

-1-

Sample Joint Report of Early Meeting (continued)

1   7. The estimated time for trial is one day.

2   8. The parties attempted in good faith to resolve their dispute and settle the case but were

3 unable to do so. The parties intend to conduct further settlement discussions following the

4 completion of the depositions.

5

6

7 Date: _____   _____

    Attorney for Defendant

8   Austin Tayshuss

9

10

11

12

13

14

15

16

17

18

19

20

21

22

23

24

25

26

27

28

setting deadlines. For example, a portion of your scheduling conference may go as follows:

1 **Judge:**

It seems to me that all depositions can be finished by March 31.

2 **You:**

Your Honor, I'll do my best to do that. But I need the medical records from Mercy Hospital before I take my opponent's deposition, and to do that I'll need to serve the hospital with a Subpoena Duces Tecum. Not only that, the supervisor of records at Mercy told me they are temporarily short of staff, so they may be delayed in sending out the records. In view of all this, I'd ask that I have until the end of April to depose my opponent. I don't think the extra month will affect the trial date that you've given us.

3 **Judge:**

Well, you've done your homework and know what you have to do, so I'll grant the request and give both parties until the end of April to complete all depositions.

As in the example above, a judge will probably be more inclined to grant your request for more time if you indicate the reasons why you need it and demonstrate familiarity with pretrial procedures. You must have a good reason to obtain a flexible Scheduling Order: Under Rule 16(b), a judge will consider your request for a change in the order only if you can demonstrate "good cause" for needing more time.

Though the judge formally makes the Scheduling Order, you and your adversary will likely be expected to prepare a Proposed Order for the judge's signature. (You won't have to go very far in the pretrial process before you realize that most orders issued by judges are in fact prepared by one of the parties for the judge's signature.) The Proposed Order may simply be tacked on to the end of the Joint Report of Early Meeting. A Proposed Order may resemble the sample below.

Making a Demand for Jury Trial

If you want your case tried by a jury rather than a judge, you'll probably have to submit a written demand for a jury trial (along with payment of jury fees) long before trial takes place. For example, FRCP 38 requires jury trial demands to be served and filed "no later than 10 days after the service of the last pleading" (typically, the defendant's answer). For further discussion of jury demands and the jury selection process, see Chapter 10. (In some courts, you may make a jury trial request in the complaint or answer, or in the At Issue Memorandum discussed above.)

Intermediate Pretrial Procedures: Discovery and Motions

Once the ground rules are laid out, most cases move into an intermediate phase in which the main activities center on the methods of fact investigation (discovery) that are discussed in Chapter 5. Parties are supposed to carry out discovery on their own, without active participation by the judge. However, if a dispute arises or if you or your adversary want the judge to make legal rulings as to the scope or the merits of

1	PROPOSED SCHEDULING ORDER
2	
3	The parties propose that the Court issue the following Scheduling Order:
4	1. The pretrial disclosures set forth in the Joint Report of Early Meeting are to be made no later
5	than March 1, 20XX.
6	2. Plaintiff Nolo will first depose Defendant Tayshuss no later than March 12, 20XX.
7	3. Defendant Tayshuss will next depose Plaintiff Nolo no later than March 31, 20XX.
8	4. No other depositions other than those referred to above will be taken.
9	5. Following the taking of depositions, the parties are ordered to meet for good faith discussion
10	of settlement. Before the meeting takes place, the parties will read the brochure entitled "Central
11	District Dispute Resolution Procedures" and consider the use of the alternative dispute resolution
12	procedures discussed therein.
13	The Court hereby adopts the Proposed Order as its Scheduling Order.
14	
15	
16	Date: _____ _____
17	United States District Judge
18	
19	
20	
21	
22	
23	
24	
25	
26	
27	
28	

the case, you may also make or respond to motions (written requests for court rulings on legal issues).

Discovery

Most civil litigators spend the bulk of their professional lives engaged in the process of fact investigation. When you represent yourself, you too will participate in the fact-investigation process with an eye toward accomplishing two primary goals:

- developing credible evidence that supports your own legal claims, and
- uncovering and trying to undermine the supporting evidence your adversary is likely to put forward.

As discussed in Chapter 5, some fact investigation may be informal. For example, you might interview a witness privately or ask a government agency to send you a report that pertains to your case. But informal investigation may not yield all the information you need to achieve the two goals mentioned above. For one thing, you can't make anyone turn over information unless you use a formal discovery method. And information you do get through informal investigation may not be in a form that is admissible at trial.

Formal discovery methods, by contrast, allow you to compel disclosure (force the sharing of information) of many types of relevant information from adversaries, private companies, government agencies, and witnesses who aren't parties to the case. Moreover, as the information you'll get by using a formal discovery method is provided under oath, on the record, and subject to discovery rules, it is more likely to be admissible as evidence at trial.

As set out in Chapter 5, the discovery processes you are most likely to encounter are depositions, written interrogatories, requests for production of documents, and requests for admissions. Each of these discovery methods resembles the children's card game of "Go Fish." That is, you may be legally entitled to the information you seek, but only if you ask for it properly. To curtail the more obnoxious gimmicks that attorneys may use to hide information during discovery, many jurisdictions have enacted rules requiring "initial disclosures." Initial disclosure rules require parties to voluntarily (without waiting for the adversary to ask) reveal such information as the names, addresses, and telephone numbers of potential witnesses; documents containing information pertinent to the case; and the basis of demands for damages. (Information subject to initial disclosure is often set forth in the Joint Report of Early Meeting; see "Initial Pretrial Procedures: Setting Ground Rules," above.) For more information on initial disclosure and discovery tools, including evaluation of the comparative advantages and disadvantages of the different methods of fact investigation, see Chapter 5.

Motions

A motion is a formal request asking the judge to rule on a legal or procedural issue. While judges' rulings on some types of motions concern pretrial procedures, rulings on other types of motions can determine which party wins and which party loses.

To file a motion, a party must prepare the appropriate "moving papers," serve them on an adversary by mail, file them in the court in which the case is pending, and appear personally before a judge to argue why the judge should grant the moving party's request. The moving party may also have to try to resolve the dispute informally with the opposing party before asking the court to step in. Chapter 7 explains motion procedures in more detail.

Motions usually relate to issues that arise during the pretrial phase of litigation. Some common pretrial motions are:

- **Motion for a Continuance.** This motion usually asks a judge to postpone the date of a court hearing or to extend a deadline for filing a pleading or providing an adversary with information. (You'll only file a motion like this if you've already asked your adversary to agree to the postponement without success.

- **Motion for Dismissal.** This motion is normally filed by a defendant to obtain a ruling that a plaintiff's complaint fails to state a valid legal claim and therefore should be dismissed (thrown out of court), either in whole or in part.

- **Motion to Compel Answers.** This motion is made in connection with discovery procedures, usually to seek a ruling that an adversary has to turn over information that it has improperly refused to provide.

- **Motion for Sanctions.** This motion asks a judge to punish a party for ignoring previous court orders or failing to comply with court rules—for example, for conducting discovery in such a way as to cause "annoyance, embarrassment, oppression, or undue burden or expense." (See FRCP 26(c)).

- **Motion for Summary Judgment.** In this very crucial motion, the moving party asks the judge to decide the entire lawsuit in its favor, without ever having a trial. To win a summary judgment motion, the moving party must show, in essence, that a jury could not possibly decide the case in favor of the other party. Judges decide summary judgment motions by reading written affidavits rather than by listening to witnesses, so preparing the paperwork that supports or opposes these motions is a very painstaking task. For more information about summary judgment motions, see Chapter 7.

Though most motions are made before trial begins, parties can also make motions as part of the trial process itself. For example, a Motion in Limine is made at the beginning of a trial and asks a judge to decide whether certain evidence will be allowed (admissable) during the trial. Motions may also concern issues that arise after trial. For example, a Motion for Judgment Notwithstanding the Verdict (or JNOV) asks a judge to overturn a jury's unfavorable decision. (See Chapter 20 for more on a JNOV motion.)

For further discussion of motions, examples of common motions, and suggestions about how to handle yourself during a court hearing on a motion, see Chapter 7.

Final Pretrial Procedures: Trial Preparation

During the 30 to 60 days before your case is supposed to go to trial, the judge may schedule additional pretrial conferences so that you and your adversary can continue to explore settlement. (Judges know from experience that many cases do settle "in the shadow of the courtroom." For further discussion of settlement strategies at a pretrial conference, see Chapter 6.) Although the judge hopes your case will settle, the judge will also expect you and your opponent to cooperatively develop a "blueprint" for the trial that will ensure it is conducted in an orderly and time-efficient manner. As a result, you'll probably have to identify in advance such matters as the legal theories you'll present, the witnesses you plan to call, and the evidence you plan to introduce at trial.

Preparing a Joint Pretrial Memorandum

You and your adversary should prepare a Joint Pretrial Memorandum (or some similarly named document) and submit it to the judge before the final pretrial conference. The subsections below identify information commonly included in such a pretrial memorandum.

Pretrial Disclosures

FRCP 26(a)(2)(3) and similar state rules require parties to make "pretrial disclosures" that provide information about the evidence each plans to offer at trial. Under FRCP 26(a)(3), you and your adversary must serve each other with these disclosures at least 30 days before trial. The information you are required to disclose in writing under FRCP 26(a)(3) includes:

- The name, address, and telephone number of each key witness you expect to call, including expert witnesses and yourself, if you will testify. If you plan to use an expert witness at trial, FRCP 26(a)(2) also requires you to provide your adversary with a report describing the expert's testimony. This report is due at least 90 days before the trial date.

- The name, address, and telephone number of each witness you may call "if the need arises." These are secondary witnesses—people you plan to call only if you are in an unexpectedly tight spot. For example, you may not know whether one of your primary witnesses will be able to come to the trial or will be able to remember enough details to be a credible witness. In either event, if you have a "backup" witness, you should list that person as a witness you may call if you need to.

- Evidence you plan to offer in the form of deposition testimony. If a witness whose deposition has been taken is unavailable to testify in person at trial, you might be able to introduce the deposition testimony that you consider helpful at trial. FRCP 26(a)(3) requires you to disclose in advance your intention to offer deposition testimony instead of a witness. If the deposition was videotaped rather than recorded in a deposition booklet, you must also include a transcript of the deposition testimony you plan to offer.

Sample Joint Pretrial Memorandum

1   JOINT PRETRIAL MEMORANDUM

2   Plaintiff Fred Nolo and Defendant Austin Tayshuss submit the following Joint Pretrial

3 Memorandum:

4 Jurisdiction

5   The Court has jurisdiction based on diversity of citizenship under 28 U.S.C. 1332. Plaintiff is a

6 citizen of the state of Washington and Defendant is a citizen of the state of Florida, and the amount in

7 controversy exceeds $75,000 exclusive of interest and costs.

8 Uncontested Facts

9   Plaintiff and Defendant were involved in a vehicle collision on September 22, 20XX. The

10 collision occurred in the intersection of Crock and Gator Avenues in the city of Miami, Florida, at

11 approximately 1:00 A.M. At the time of the collision, Plaintiff was driving a two-year-old Ford four-

12 door sedan and going south on Crock; Defendant was driving a three-year-old Toyota two-door

13 sports car. The intersection is controlled by traffic lights. At the time of the collision, the Plaintiff was

14 employed as a pastry chef in the Wet Noodle Restaurant in Seattle, Washington. Plaintiff missed a

15 month of work as a result of the accident, accruing lost wages of approximately $5,000. Plaintiff also

16 suffered permanent injuries to the left hand that required reconstructive surgery and will impair

17 Plaintiff's ability to work as a pastry chef in the future. Plaintiff's medical bills totaled $26,000, and the

18 cost of repairing Plaintiff's vehicle was $8,500.

19 Disputed Issues of Fact and Law

20   1. Did the Defendant run a red light?

21   2. Was the Defendant driving under the influence of alcohol at the time of the collision?

22   3. Was the Defendant driving negligently at the time of the collision?

23   4. What were the extent of the Plaintiff's injuries resulting from the collision?

24   5. What are the Plaintiff's reasonable damages?

25 ///

26 ///

27 ///

28 ///

Sample Joint Pretrial Memorandum (continued)

Plaintiff's Exhibit List

No. of Exhibit	Description	Defendant's Objections, if any
2	Photo of Plaintiff's vehicle	None
5	Emergency room admitting form	None
8	Hospital bill	None
11	Officer Krupke's accident report	Hearsay

List of Witnesses

Plaintiff's Witnesses

1. Plaintiff
2. Dr. Hans Offe

Defendant's Witnesses

1. Defendant
2. Dr. E. K. Gee
3. Minnie Ola

Respectfully Submitted,

Date: _____

_____
Fred Nolo, Plaintiff in Pro Per

_____
Attorney for Defendant, Austin Tayshuss

CAUTION

Familiarize yourself with deposition rules. If you plan to offer deposition testimony as evidence at trial, or if your adversary intends to do so, read FRCP 32. FRCP 32 explains when a witness is legally considered "unavailable to testify"—meaning that you can introduce the witness's deposition testimony at trial instead— and describes how to offer deposition testimony into evidence. Also, be aware that the rules of evidence at depositions are much broader and less strict than they are at trial, so testimony that was allowed at a deposition will not necessarily be admissible at trial. If you or your adversary intends to offer important evidence from a deposition, you should probably consult a legal coach or a resource such as *Nolo's Deposition Handbook*, by Paul Bergman and Albert Moore (Nolo). Chapter 5 also provides information about deposition.

- Identifying information about any document or other exhibit you expect to offer (or may offer if the need arises), including a summary of its contents.

After the parties have served each other with reports containing the information described above and filed these reports with the court, FRCP 26(a)(3) gives you and your adversary 14 days to object to the admissibility of deposition testimony or to any documents or exhibits that the opposing party identified in the reports. If you don't make an objection before trial, you waive your right to do so unless the trial judge concludes that you had "good cause" for failing to object earlier. Though these provisions may help trials proceed more quickly, they mean that you can't wait until trial to decide whether deposition testimony

or a document that your adversary plans to offer at trial is admissible. You have just 14 days after getting the pretrial disclosures to object—and if you don't object, you probably won't be able to do so at trial.

Jurisdictional Statement

Under the U.S. Constitution, federal courts have power to decide only certain types of cases. (See Chapter 3 for a discussion of federal jurisdiction.) In legal lingo, they are called courts of "limited jurisdiction." There- fore, a plaintiff must be ready to establish that a federal court has jurisdiction over a case—and the Joint Pretrial Memorandum in a federal court case should clearly state the basis of the court's power. For example, the jurisdictional statement in a pretrial memo- randum might indicate that "this Court has jurisdiction because the parties are residents of different states and the amount in dispute exceeds $75,000." Most state trial courts are courts of "general jurisdiction," so you usually won't need to include the basis of state court jurisdiction in a pretrial memoran- dum for state court.

Legal Contentions

Complaints and answers often set forth many possible legal theories. By the time trial is near, discovery has often clarified many facts and reality has begun to set in. As a result, each party often decides to rely on one or a least a very limited number of key legal theories and let the rest go. The theories that the parties will try to prove at trial should be identified in the Joint Pretrial Memorandum.

For example, assume that you're a plaintiff in a personal injury case, and your complaint alleges that the defendant is liable for injuries you suffered both because the defendant was negligent (unreasonably careless, perhaps driving too fast) and because the defendant's conduct was in violation of a legal rule (ran a red light). Though you include both of these theories in the complaint, make sure you also set them out in the pretrial memorandum and in the judge's pretrial order. Legal theories can be relied on at trial only if they are part of such an order.

On the other hand, assume that your Complaint in the same case asks for damages for the personal injuries you suffered in an auto accident, and for the earnings you lost for the time you were off work recovering from the injuries. By the time of trial, the defendant has compensated you for the lost wages and the only remaining dispute is the extent of your injuries. In this situation you could drop the claim for lost wages by not mentioning that claim in the pretrial memorandum or order.

Factual Contentions

To set limits on the scope of the evidence that will be presented at trial, the judge may require you and your adversary to identify your factual contentions. For example, you might provide a summary narrative of events that you claim constitute a basis for relief (if you are a plaintiff) or a legal defense (if you are a defendant). The Joint Pretrial Memorandum should identify any facts on which you and your adversary agree (these are called "undisputed facts"). The judge's pretrial order will probably state that the parties have stipulated (agreed in writing) that these facts are accurate, and, in a jury

trial, the judge will simply read those facts to the jury to save time.

The adversarial feeling of litigation may make you reluctant to agree to your adversary's request to admit that certain facts are true. However, admissions are a good idea if you don't genuinely dispute a fact's accuracy, or if the fact is obviously not important. As a practical matter, a shorter, simpler trial is in your interests. And if you refuse to agree, your adversary can serve you with a set of Requests for Admissions. (See Chapter 5.) If you continue to refuse to admit to the accuracy of facts that are later proved to be true at trial, the judge will almost certainly order you to pay your adversary the cost of proving those facts at trial.

Handling Other Pretrial Documents

In addition to the Joint Pretrial Memorandum, you may be required to prepare or respond to a variety of other trial-related documents. The subsections below briefly describe these additional documents.

Jury Instructions

In jury trials, jurors are given information about the law that relates to the facts of the case. This information is presented to jurors in the form of jury instructions. Traditionally, judges read the jury instructions to the jurors, sometimes at the outset of a trial and sometimes at a trial's conclusion. Prior to the final pretrial conference, the judge may ask you and your adversary to serve each other with proposed jury instructions and to make any objections you have to the other's proposed instructions. For a list of resources that provide "pattern" or "model" jury instructions for use in common types of trials, see Chapter 23. A sample cover sheet is shown below.

Voir Dire Questions

Voir dire (pronounced "vwar-deer") questioning probes potential jurors' experiences and beliefs to determine their fitness to serve as jurors in your case. In most courts, judges do all or part of the voir dire questioning. Parties can often submit, with the Joint Pretrial Memorandum, any questions that they want the judges to ask prospective jurors. For further information on voir dire questioning, see Chapter 10.

Trial Briefs

"Briefs" are written arguments whose length often belies their name. Before trial, parties may submit briefs to try to convince the judge to make a ruling in their favor. For example, a trial brief may argue that an important item of evidence is or is not admissible (in which case, especially if a jury is involved, it may also be called a Motion in Limine, discussed below) or that a particular legal principle is or is not applicable. If you are an inexperienced party representing yourself, you may find it difficult to prepare a trial brief or respond to one filed by your adversary's lawyer. Before you can prepare a trial brief arguing the admissibility of evidence or the validity of a new legal principle, you'll probably need to do legal research or consult with a legal coach. (For further information on finding and working with a legal coach, see Chapter 23.)

Motions in Limine

The typical purpose of a Motion in Limine (literally, a motion made "at the threshold" of trial) is to seek a judge's ruling that evidence that the moving party's adversary plans to offer at trial is inadmissible. For example, a defendant's Motion in Limine in an auto accident case might ask a judge to rule that evidence that the defendant was insured at the time of the mishap is irrelevant and unduly prejudicial—and therefore inadmissible. A Motion in Limine is an alternative to the more common (and simpler) strategy of objecting to evidence when it's offered into evidence during trial. Some of the advantages of such a motion are:

- The motion is usually in writing, so it may carry more weight than an oral objection made during trial.
- The motion will probably be accompanied by a Memorandum of Points and Authorities (laws, court rules, and case decisions that back up the party's legal position), which the judge will have more time to consider before trial than in the heat of trial.
- If the judge denies or postpones ruling on the motion, the party can (and should) renew the objection when the evidence is offered during trial. In that event, arguments made at the time of the hearing on the Motion in Limine may add to the force of the objection at trial.
- The motion is made and considered before the jury is seated, so the jurors can't be influenced by any statements made by the judge or attorneys in connection with the motion.

Sample Proposed Jury Instructions

1	Fred Nolo [Street Address]
2	[City, State, Zip Code] [Phone Number]
3	
	Plaintiff in Pro Per
4	
5	
6	
7	THE _____ COURT OF _____ COUNTY
8	STATE OF _____
9	Fred Nolo,)
10	) Plaintiff,)
11	) v.) Case No. 12-3-456789-1
12	) Austin Tayshuss) PROPOSED JURY INSTRUCTIONS
13	) Defendant.)
14	_____)
15	
16	Proposed Jury Instructions
17	Plaintiff's and Defendant's proposed jury instructions are attached.
18	1. The parties jointly agree to the instructions numbered 1 through 11, 14, 16, and 19.
19	2. Plaintiff objects to Defendant's requested instructions numbered 12 and 13 for the reasons set
20	forth in the attached Memorandum of Points and Authorities.
21	3. Defendant objects to Plaintiff's requested instructions numbered 15, 17, and 18 for the reasons
22	set forth in the attached Memorandum of Points and Authorities.
23	
24	Date: _____ _____
25	Fred Nolo, Plaintiff in Pro Per
26	_____ Attorney for Defendant Austin Tayshuss
27	
28	

If your adversary submits a Motion in Limine, you will probably have a chance to oppose it both in writing and during an oral pretrial hearing. If you want to oppose the motion but are unfamiliar with evidence rules, you'll probably have to do some legal research or consult a legal coach. Chapter 16 may also provide helpful information. (For more about Motions in Limine, including a sample form, see Chapter 17.)

Attending a Final Pretrial Conference and Obtaining a Pretrial Order

FRCP 16(d) and similar rules in many states provide for a final pretrial conference to be held "as close to the time of trial as reasonable under the circumstances." During a final pretrial conference, you can expect the judge to focus on a plan for trial. For example, the judge will probably want you and your adversary to agree on the legal issues that have to be decided at trial (and agree to the nondisputed issues), the witnesses to be called, and the order in which they will be called.

If you will have a jury trial and you or your adversary has filed a Motion in Limine, the judge may also rule in advance on the admissibility of some types of evidence. For example, the judge may rule that a police report that your adversary wants to submit as evidence at trial is "hearsay" and therefore inadmissible. (See Chapter 16 for more on hearsay.) Many of the decisions arrived at during the final pretrial conference will be based on information in the Joint Pretrial Memorandum.

After the pretrial conference, the judge is likely to enter a pretrial order reflecting the agreements made in the Joint Pretrial Memorandum and decisions made at the pretrial conference. (See FRCP 16 (c); most states have similar rules.) The contents of the pretrial order are extremely important— more than any other document, the order serves as a road map for trial. The pretrial order supplants the initial pleadings and determines the legal theories that you and your adversary can rely on at trial. For instance, if you're a defendant and you've claimed (alleged) in your answer that the plaintiff's claim has been filed too late and is therefore barred by the statute of limitations (see Chapter 3), you can raise your statute of limitations issue in the courtroom only if the pretrial order identifies it as a defense. Consequently, you must make sure that any witness you want to call, any document or exhibit you want to introduce into evidence, and any legal theory you want to rely on at trial is included in the pretrial memorandum and order.

Attending a Mandatory Settlement Conference

Most state courts require parties to meet with a judge shortly before trial specifically for the purpose of "talking settlement." If a mandatory settlement conference is scheduled in your case, the judge might require you to specify the terms on which you are willing to settle your case. The judge who presides over your settlement conference may be a "settlement specialist" whose main task is to settle cases rather than try them. Judges who specialize in settlement are often the most experienced, capable, and persuasive judges in the courthouse.

During a settlement conference, a judge may talk to you and your adversary (both lawyer and client) separately several times, trying to winnow down the areas of disagreement and promote what the judge considers a realistic assessment of the trial's outcome. Such a judge can be your best friend, saving you the time and rigors of a courtroom battle and persuading your adversary to settle on terms that are acceptable to you.

> **CAUTION**
>
> **Just say yes.** Whether you are a plaintiff seeking money or a defendant trying to avoid paying it, be grateful for a judge who can get you two-thirds or even half of the "loaf" from a contentious adversary. As you are almost surely inexperienced, it is almost always in your best interest to accept a reasonable settlement in order to avoid a trial. To put it bluntly, if a deal is even half good, you should say yes. ●

Investigating Your Case

Once the initial pleadings are filed (see Chapter 3), the parties to a lawsuit typically begin gathering evidence to prove that their claims are true and that their adversary's are not. This phase of a lawsuit is often called "case investigation," "fact investigation," or "discovery." Think of it this way: Although you may personally know exactly what happened, now that you are in the formal legal system you will have to prove it to a judge or jurors who know nothing about you or your lawsuit. And to make your task more difficult, your opponent will probably present a very different version of events. The upshot is that you should approach case investigation with two main questions in mind:

- What evidence can I find that is legally admissible in court and will back up my claims?
- How can I best present my evidence to a judge or jury to convince them that I should win at trial?

Case investigation takes two forms: informal investigation and formal "discovery." Informal investigation includes all information gathering that you can do on your own, working with cooperative people or organizations both before and after a lawsuit is filed. Informal investigation encompasses such activities as:

- conducting interviews
- collecting documents
- taking photographs (of damaged property, accident sites, or other pertinent objects or locales), and
- finding out about an adversary's insurance coverage.

By contrast, formal discovery is a legal process that kicks in after a case has been filed. Formal discovery encompasses a number of investigatory tools, including:

- document requests—written requests to your adversary to turn over certain documents
- interrogatories—written questions to your adversary that the adversary must answer in writing, under oath
- depositions—oral questions that the adversary or another person must answer in person, under oath, and
- requests for admission—written requests that your adversary admit that certain facts are true or that certain documents are genuine.

One big disadvantage of formal discovery is that it can be expensive. A major advantage, however, is that it doesn't depend on anyone's voluntary cooperation. That is, you can use formal discovery tools to compel an adversary or witness to provide you with information and documents.

Informal Investigation

Informal investigation consists primarily of gathering information and documents from people who will voluntarily cooperate with you. You can informally question or seek documents from anyone, including eyewitnesses, public agencies, and police officers. If you are not an attorney, you can also seek information directly from your adversary, even if the adversary is represented by a lawyer. (Lawyers can talk only to an adversary's lawyer.) Obtaining information informally obviously saves the time and expense of formal discovery methods. Like many lawyers, you may

be able to gather all the evidence you need to prove your claims (or disprove your adversary's claims) through informal investigation.

CAUTION

Be aware of "unauthorized investigation" laws. Some states have "unauthorized investigation" laws that make it a misdemeanor to investigate without a license. If your state has this kind of law, it almost surely does not apply to you if you are self-represented and investigating your own case. However, the law may prevent you from asking a nonlicensed friend to question witnesses or perform other investigatory tasks on your behalf.

As an example of how informal investigation might work, assume that you are involved in an auto accident in which an uninsured driver ran into your car. Because you do not have uninsured motorist coverage, you file a lawsuit on your own. You may do any of the following types of information gathering:

- Obtain a copy of the report prepared by the police officer who came to the scene of the accident by going to the local police station and paying a small fee. This accident report may include statements made by the other driver that will help you prove that the other driver was at fault. The report may also give the names and phone numbers of bystanders (including the police officer) whom you can try to question informally.

- Interview eyewitnesses and, if their information is helpful, serve them with subpoenas requiring them to appear in court once you have a trial date. Among the ways of finding eyewitnesses in an auto accident case are getting their names from a police report, talking to bystanders right after an accident, posting notices in the vicinity of an accident that ask eyewitnesses to contact you, and even putting a notice in the classified section of a local newspaper.

TIP

Gather evidence promptly. Memories fade and scenes change. If you intend to photograph a scene or interview witnesses, do so as soon as possible after an accident or other event that may become the subject of a lawsuit. Any substantial delay may result in your questioning a person who no longer remembers key events. Similarly, physical changes in a location, road, or piece of equipment may occur over time, perhaps depriving you of evidence that would have been useful at trial.

- Prepare audiotapes or written statements at the conclusion of interviews. Be sure that the witness signs a written statement or states on an audiotape that you are recording the conversation with the witness's consent. An audiotape or written statement should refer to the important facts supporting your version of events and should indicate the date when it was created. While audiotapes or written statements usually are not admissible in evidence at trial, they can nevertheless be extremely valuable during a trial when used to refresh an uncertain witness's recollection or cross-examine witnesses who change their stories. Also, prompt preparation of an audiotape or written statement setting forth facts favorable to you may discourage a witness from later changing a story to favor the other party.

TIP

Use written statements and audiotapes to improve your negotiating posture. Written or orally recorded statements can help you negotiate a favorable settlement with your adversary or an insurance company (if the adversary has insurance). Once an adversary or insurance company realizes that you have witnesses to back up your claims, your settlement proposals will be taken more seriously.

- Take photos of your injuries, the damage to your car, and the scene of the accident. (Use a camera that automatically superimposes dates on photos or write the date that a photo was taken on the back promptly after you develop the photo.) Either you or a friend can take the photos, but no matter who wields the camera, anyone with personal knowledge of what a photo depicts can lay the groundwork for the photo to go into evidence at trial. (See Chapter 15 for more information on how to get photos into evidence.)

- Obtain from your doctor a copy of a medical report describing your injuries, course of treatment, and the likelihood of future physical problems.

- Secure receipts for all medical treatment, psychological counseling, physical rehabilitation, and any other out-of-pocket expenses resulting from the accident. Sometimes you can recover these fees from the defendant even if your insurance company has already paid them. In addition, these expenses document the extent of your injuries and add to any damages you might claim for "pain and suffering."

- If the defendant claims that some other person or business is responsible for the harm you suffered ("The auto repair shop put defective brakes in my car"), ask the defendant for supporting documentation (copies of the brake repair records and any records relating to brake inspections). If the information supports the defendant's claim, you may decide to name the repair shop as an additional defendant in the lawsuit.

- Examine a county's land records to see whether the defendant owns real estate in the county. Also check court records to see whether the defendant is involved in any other litigation. This information may help you decide whether the defendant has assets from which you can collect a judgment.

TIP

Ensure that evidence is admissible at trial. Gathering information serves little purpose (beyond possibly helping foster a settlement) if you can't use it at trial. Because most documents and objects won't waltz into evidence by themselves, you or another witness will have to "sponsor" them with appropriate testimony showing a judge that they are authentic and in good condition. In other words, you will need to produce at trial the favorable witnesses you've talked to informally. The suggestions below will make it easier for you to offer the fruits of your investigative labor into evidence should your case go to trial.

- Keep originals of all documents in a safe place for court. Make copies to show to witnesses or to attach to pleadings—do not use the originals.
- Do not add writing or punch holes in original documents.
- During an interview, ask witnesses for the names and phone numbers of friends or relatives who will know the witnesses' whereabouts should they move before your case goes to trial.
- If you know your trial date when you interview a favorable witness, serve the witness with a subpoena at the time of the interview. (A subpoena is a court order requiring a person to come to court. You can

How to Document Property Loss Claims

You can often use informal investigation to gather the documents you'll need to prove the value of damaged property, such as a car or a stereo. The general rule is that you are entitled to compensation for the fair market value of repairing or replacing damaged property. For example, if your car had a fair market value of $3,000 before an accident totaled it, you will be awarded only that amount, even if you have to spend $5,000 to replace it. To informally gather documents you'll need in court to support your claim for the value of a car, you might:

- Consult the *Kelley Blue Book* (available in a library or online at www.kbb.com) to prove the value of a totaled car. At trial, judges generally take "judicial notice" of a car's *Kelley Blue Book* value, meaning that the book itself provides evidence of the car's value. You don't need to hire an expert to testify.
- Obtain receipts from car mechanics and similar repairpersons. At trial, to overcome a possible objection that a receipt is inadmissible hearsay (see Chapter 16), you can testify that you paid (or will pay) the amount stated on the receipt.
- Look in your personal papers for photos that show an item's condition before it was damaged and for any appraisals done by an insurance company or expert. "Before and after" photos are a great way to document the harm you've suffered.

pick up subpoenas at a courthouse. For more information, see "Requests for Production of Documents and Subpoenas," below.) This will save you the trouble of finding the witness a second time to serve a subpoena. If you want the witness to bring documents or other evidence to court as well, you will need to serve a "Subpoena Duces Tecum." (See "How to Fill Out a Subpoena Duces Tecum," below.)

How to Fill Out a Subpoena Duces Tecum

A Subpoena Duces Tecum is an official court form available at a courthouse Clerk's Office or online. To complete this form, identify the documents you want a witness to bring to court, fill in the name of the person who has custody of them (if you are serving a business or government agency, you may simply refer to the "custodian of records"), and state the relevance of the documents to your case. For example, assume that you want to prove that you had just installed an expensive CD player system in your car, which was subsequently totaled. You might serve a Subpoena Duces Tecum on the bookkeeper of the company that performed the installation, asking the bookkeeper to bring to court copies of all records pertaining to the installation of the CD player and stating that you need the records to prove your property damage in a car accident case.

- Keep any tangible objects you want to offer into evidence (for example, a damaged stereo) in a place where friends and family members cannot meddle with them, preferably under lock and key. This precaution will usually enable you to defeat an adversary's possible claim that an object should not be allowed into evidence at trial because it could have been altered or tampered with.

- Take photographs of the damaged item, especially if it is too large to bring to court or if its condition is likely to change before the date of trial. You can offer photos into evidence through your own testimony or that of any other witness who has seen the damaged item and can testify that the photo accurately depicts the item's condition. (See Chapter 15 for more on introducing photos into evidence.)

When requesting copies of documents, you can encourage voluntary cooperation by being very specific about the information you seek. For example, assume that you sue the Chicken Feed Restaurant after coming down with what you believe was food poisoning. It is important to know whether records in your local county health office can help you prove that the Chicken Feed was responsible for your illness. If you ask for "all records pertaining to the Chicken Feed Restaurant," a health office employee facing hours of hunting for documents, many of which may not be germane to your case, may reply, "Sorry, you'll need a court order." But if your request is easier to deal with (for example, "I'd like a copy of records of any sickness reports made by patrons of the Chicken

Feed Restaurant during last July and a list of the restaurant's health code violations for the past two years"), you may get the information promptly without a court order.

Some sources may initially be reluctant to disclose information, perhaps fearing that they can be sued for violating a person's privacy. However, don't give up without trying a bit of persuasion. Explain:

- that the information the person has pertains to a case that has already been filed in court, and

- that cooperation is easier for everyone, because if you can't get the information voluntarily, you may have to take the person's deposition or serve a subpoena that will require the person to turn over the documents you seek.

Finding evidence and witnesses may take a bit of ingenuity, perseverance, and maybe even a little help from your friends. Here are some tips to get you started.

- Do your own field investigation. In one case, law students represented a woman who was seeking to collect unemployment benefits after she was fired by a casino. The casino claimed that the woman was not entitled to benefits because she had carelessly allowed a stack of gambling chips to be stolen by leaving them on a counter to which the public had access. To investigate whether the casino's own carelessness could have led to the theft, the law students went to the casino and noticed that a metal grate had recently been installed in front of the counter where the theft occurred. They took a photo of the grate. The photo convinced the hearing officer that the

absence of a grate and not the woman's carelessness led to the theft of the chips, and the woman was awarded unemployment benefits.

- If you are trying to contact a witness for whom you have a name but no other identifying information, check with government agencies, such as a motor vehicle department, or a utility company. If these agencies are uncooperative (a real possibility), and if a witness is important enough and the amount of money in dispute justifies it, consider hiring a private investigator to locate the witness. Or try using an Internet search engine to hunt for an address and phone number.

- If you are suing a former employer for firing you illegally, consider talking to former employees about their experiences and knowledge of company policies.

- If you are suing a moving company for damaging and losing your personal property, collect insurance records, purchase receipts, photographs, and the like to prove ownership and condition of the lost or damaged items.

- If you are suing a government agency, look in your local public library for reports and relevant statistics concerning the agency's operations.

 TIP

Large businesses and institutions often insist on subpoenas. Parties to court cases often want records from large organizations, such as hospitals and telephone companies. Such organizations tend to protect themselves from "invasion of privacy" claims by the person whose records you seek by releasing records only after being served with a subpoena. You may find an employee willing to talk to you off the record, but to secure evidence admissible in court you'll probably need a subpoena.

RESOURCE

Resource on informal investigation techniques. *How to Find Almost Anyone, Anywhere,* by Norma Mott Tillman (Thomas Nelson), is a private investigator's how-to book of techniques for searching for missing persons, with an emphasis on tracing relatives.

Formal Discovery

The word "discovery" refers to a number of evidence-gathering tools that the legal system makes available to you to compel your adversary, witnesses, and others with information about your dispute to answer questions and produce documents before your case goes to trial.

Under Federal Rule of Civil Procedure (FRCP) Rule 26 (b), you and your adversary may seek any information that is relevant to the claims made in the pleadings. This includes identifying people who have the information and how to contact them, as well as descriptions of records, documents, and other tangible items. Amendments to FRCP 26 that took effect in 2006 extend discovery to electronically stored information, such as email messages and computer files, even if you have never printed them out. Under FRCP 26(e), parties may have to supplement responses they've already given that later turn out to be incomplete or incorrect.

In general, the three goals of formal discovery are:

- to uncover evidence that favors your story
- to uncover the evidence that your adversary is likely to offer against you if the case goes to trial, and
- to lock the adversary into a story before trial, so that you can attack the credibility of witnesses who testify at trial to different stories or facts.

One of the primary limitations on discovery is that you cannot ask about "privileged" information (for example, private conversations between your adversary and the adversary's lawyer). Another limitation is that you normally cannot obtain information about your adversary's trial preparation work and materials (often called "work product"). For example, you can't ask your adversary, "How does your lawyer plan to cross examine me and my witnesses?" Finally, judges have the power to limit or forbid discovery if requests are "unreasonably cumulative" or if a court order is needed to "protect a party or person from annoyance, embarrassment, oppression, or undue burden or expense."

Laws setting up formal discovery methods were first enacted in the 1930s by legal reformers who believed the information exchange would promote justice by fostering settlement and cutting back on the "surprise" aspect of trials. Reformers also hoped to conserve judicial resources by leaving the discovery process largely in the hands of the litigants themselves, involving judges only if litigants were unable to resolve discovery disputes.

Unfortunately, over the years lawyers have found ways to move battles that formerly took place in the courtroom into pretrial discovery, so that the reformers' hopes have been only partly realized. For example, some lawyers try to avoid complying with discovery requests by claiming ambiguities in questions that any two-year-old would understand. Other lawyers (often representing big corporations) may drive up the cost of litigation (both to their own clients and to their adversaries) by swamping individuals and small businesses with burdensome discovery requests in order to coerce them into giving up or settling cheap.

As a result, many state and federal courts have streamlined their discovery rules in an effort to combat such abuses. For example, many states have a "disclosure" rule similar to FRCP 26(a). This procedure requires parties to disclose key information voluntarily, without waiting for their adversaries to request it. The data that parties are supposed to disclose include the identity of expert and nonexpert witnesses, relevant documents, tangible objects, and insurance agreements that might cover all or part of a judgment. If the source of a disclosure consists of electronically stored information (such as information in email messages, a mobile telephone, or a PDA), under Rules 26(f), the disclosure should identify the electronic source.

FRCP 26(a)(3) requires additional voluntary disclosures in advance of trial. At least a month before trial is scheduled to begin, each party must disclose to the other the names and telephone numbers of their witnesses, and identify any deposition testimony and all documents that the party plans to offer into evidence. The purpose of requiring these pretrial disclosures is to prevent surprise at trial and help the trial proceed smoothly.

In addition to requiring voluntary disclosure, local discovery rules may also limit the number of questions that parties can ask and may set strict time limits for completing discovery. In addition, parties often have a responsibility to "meet and confer" to set up a mutually acceptable discovery plan (see FRCP 26(f)) and to sort out any disputes before dragging each other into court. When parties disagree over whether information is "discoverable," judges often speed up the process by conducting discovery hearings by phone.

Judges are increasingly willing to impose sanctions (ranging from monetary penalties to dismissal of cases) on parties who abuse discovery rules. Judges will expect you to follow discovery rules even if you are self-represented, so seek the advice of a legal coach if you are uncertain of your discovery obligations.

TIP

Which is better: informal investigation or discovery? Self-represented litigants, in small cases especially, should attempt to get necessary information by first using informal investigation techniques—particularly to gather information that supports their own legal claims. Formal discovery tends to be so expensive and complex that even attorneys often forgo it unless a substantial amount of money is in dispute. If your case is a good-sized one, or if you plan to use formal discovery methods for some other reason, follow these general guidelines:

- take a deposition (a formal discovery method, discussed below) to preserve helpful testimony from a witness who may not be available when the case goes to

Sample Initial Disclosures

1	Fred Nolo
	[Street Address]
2	[City, State, Zip Code]
	[Phone Number]
3	
	Plaintiff in Pro Per
4	
5	
6	
7	THE _____ COURT OF _____ COUNTY
8	STATE OF _____
9	Fred Nolo)
10	)
Plaintiff,   ) Case No. 12-3-45689-1
	)
11	v.) PLAINTIFF NOLO'S INITIAL DISCLOSURES
	)
12	Austin Tayshuss,) (FRCP 26(A)(1))
	)
13	Defendant.)
14	_____)
15	
16	Plaintiff Nolo's Initial Disclosures (FRCP 26(a)(1))
17	Plaintiff Nolo makes the following initial disclosures to Defendant:
18	1. Persons Who Are Likely to Have Information About Disputed Facts
19	a. Fred Nolo—Plaintiff, will testify to events and conversations that took place before, during, and
20	after the collision.
21	b. Benny Diction—Eyewitness, saw Defendant in a bar and talked to Defendant approximately
22	one hour prior to the collision.
23	c. Dr. Jill Jacks—Emergency room physician, observed nature and extent of Plaintiff's injuries
24	following the collision.
25	d. Sy Attica—Licensed physical therapist treated plaintiff after the accident.
26	2. Documents and Tangible Things
27	a. Photographs of accident scene
28	

-1-

Sample Initial Disclosures (continued)

1   b. Photographs of Plaintiff and Defendant's cars following collision

2   c. Photographs of Plaintiff's car prior to collision

3   d. OMH Hospital emergency room records

4   e. Officer Krupke's accident report

5   3. Computation of Damages

6   a. OMH Hospital bill—$3,600

7   b. Dr. Jacks's bill—$2,600

8   c. Walt Green Pharmacy bills—$330

9   d. Lost wages, Hans Ohrt Bike Shop payroll records—$1,600

10   e. Pain and suffering—$15,000

11

12

13   Date: _____   _____

                                       Fred Nolo, Plaintiff in Pro Per

14

15

16

17

18

19

20

21

22

23

24

25

26

27

28

trial (perhaps because the witness is ill or about to move to another state)

- consider preparing "requests for admissions" (another formal discovery device, discussed below) to force your adversary to admit quickly that some of your factual claims are accurate, and

- use formal interrogatories and possibly depositions to find out about your adversary's case only if informal methods don't work.

Even if you don't choose to use formal discovery methods, your opponent might. The rest of this chapter explains how formal discovery works. We briefly examine the four primary tools of formal discovery:

- depositions
- written interrogatories
- requests for production of documents, and
- requests for admissions.

 TIP

Pay attention to discovery deadlines. Judges and court rules often set and enforce strict discovery schedules and time limits. For example, a judge may order that "all depositions are to be completed within 30 days" or that "no discovery is to take place within 30 days of the trial date." Mark such deadlines on a calendar and plan to abide by them strictly. If an unexpected delay arises or an adversary's misconduct prevents you from meeting a deadline, you may have to request extra time from a judge by filing a Motion for Extension of Time to Complete Discovery (or some similarly named document) in court. A simpler alternative is to ask your adversary to stipulate (agree) to an extension of time. However,

this will probably not work if your adversary has intentionally caused the delay or if your local court follows a "fast track" pretrial system that aims to reduce court backlogs by setting short time limits and giving only judges the power to extend them.

Depositions

Depositions normally consist of face-to-face questioning in an office setting. (FRCP 27 through 32 outline deposition procedures in federal court cases; most states have similar procedures.) You can depose anyone you have reason to think has information relevant to your case. This includes your adversary, an expert witness hired by your adversary, or a potential witness for you or your adversary.

In style, depositions resemble courtroom testimony. A court reporter places a witness (colorfully called a "deponent") under oath and records the testimony (and may videotape or audiotape it as well if the party taking the deposition requests it). The court reporter later produces a written deposition transcript. The deponent is supposed to look over the transcript, change answers if necessary, and sign the transcript. (But if a deponent does significantly change an answer, you can try to undermine the deponent's credibility at trial by offering evidence of the change to the judge or jury. What happens to a transcript after a deponent signs it varies from state to state. In many states, transcripts are filed in court once they are signed. In other states, the party taking the deposition keeps signed transcripts, filing them in court only if the party intends and is legally entitled to read from the transcript at trial.

Although you always hope to uncover evidence helpful to your case, a deposition's main purpose is to help you assess the strength of your opponent's case by learning in advance how much harm an adverse witness may cause you if the case goes to trial. For this reason, you gain nothing by trying to avoid harmful testimony at a deposition. If a witness has bad things to say, better to find out about it as early as possible than to be surprised by harmful testimony in the middle of trial. During a deposition you also have a chance to observe a deponent's demeanor, allowing you to estimate whether a judge or jury is likely to believe the deponent.

A recent report issued by the Federal Judicial Center demonstrates the importance of depositions in civil cases. Based on information from more than 1,100 attorneys, the report indicates that attorneys take one or more depositions in about two-thirds of all cases. The report cautions that depositions are by far the most costly aspect of pretrial discovery procedures. You can read this report—a comprehensive snapshot of current discovery practices and problems—on the Federal Judicial Center's website, at www.fjc.gov. Choose the Publications & Videos link and look for "Discovery and Disclosure Practice, Problems, and Proposals for Change."

Advantages and Disadvantages of Taking Depositions

The four main formal discovery tools often work best in combination. For instance, you may send out a set of written interrogatories to uncover witnesses your adversary knows about, take depositions of those witnesses, and finally send your adversary a request to admit that a fact testified to by a witness in a deposition is true. However, because formal discovery can be expensive and time consuming, you should be aware of the general advantages and disadvantages of each discovery tool.

Advantages

Depositions generally have the following advantages:

- **Reach unavailable witnesses.** You can offer a deposition transcript into evidence at trial if the deponent is unavailable to give live testimony. This rule explains why you might consider deposing a helpful witne`ss who may not be available to testify at the time of trial. (By contrast, the hearsay rule would probably bar you from offering an informal written statement or audiotape into evidence. See Chapter 16.)

- **Use for impeachment.** If an adversary's witness whose deposition you have taken testifies significantly differently at trial than at the deposition, you can read the inconsistent deposition testimony into the trial record to impeach (attack) the deponent's credibility. By contrast, impeachment is not nearly as effective if a judge or jury hears only your testimony that a witness told you something different informally.

EXAMPLE: You have sued your former employer for violating state law by firing you for missing work because you served on a jury in a lengthy trial. Before trial you take the deposition of your former supervisor, Paul Chepick. At the deposition, Chepick testified that your work performance had been satisfactory before you were called for jury duty. At trial, Chepick testifies that you were fired not because of your jury service but because of a number of work-related problems. Because Chepick's deposition testimony contradicts his trial testimony, you could read the deposition testimony into the record at trial to call his credibility (how honest and believable he is) into question. (For more on using deposition testimony to attack a witness's credibility at trial, see Chapter 13.)

- **Flexibility in questioning.** As compared to conducting discovery by asking written questions (interrogatories), depositions allow for more flexibility in questioning because you hear a deponent's answer before you ask the next question. For example, assume that a deponent unexpectedly refers to an important business meeting that you didn't know about. In a deposition, you can immediately follow up the remark with questions about what took place during this meeting. By contrast, you have to prepare all of your written inter-rogatory questions ahead of time, before you know any of the witness's answers. Sending out a second set of interrogatories is a possible option when a first set turns up unexpected information, but this is unwieldy and often requires a judge's permission.

- **Reach all witnesses—not just your opponent's.** You can take anyone's deposition. You can depose your adversary, an employee who works for your adversary, or an ordinary or expert witness hired by your opponent—even your opponent's attorney! For an expert, you'll probably have to pay an hourly fee, which can be quite high (see Chapter 19), but an ordinary witness is usually reimbursed only for travel expenses to attend the deposition. By contrast, you can send written questions (interrogatories) only to your opponent, not to an ordinary or expert witness.

- **Get witness—not attorney—answers.** You elicit the testimony of an individual deponent. Though your adversary's lawyer will probably attend the deposition and can consult with the deponent during recesses (breaks during the deposition), it is the deponent who has to answer the questions. By contrast, attorneys often play a major role in preparing the answers to written interrogatories and usually help their clients answer them in a way that provides you with as little information as possible.

- **Obtain documents.** You can use a deposition to learn about and get copies of documents (or other tangible items) by simply using a Notice of Deposition (for your opponent) or a Subpoena Duces Tecum (for a nonparty witness) to list documents you want the deponent to bring to the deposition.

Sample Notice of Deposition

1   Nolo Pedestrian
  [Street Address]
2   [City, State, Zip Code]
  [Phone Number]
3

4   Plaintiff in Pro Per

5

6

7   THE _____ COURT OF _____ COUNTY

8   STATE OF _____

9   Nolo Pedestrian,   )

10   Plaintiff,   )
)

11   v.   )   Case No. 12345

12   )
  Austin Tayshuss,   )   NOTICE OF DEPOSITION

13   )
         Defendant.   )

14   _____)

15

16

17   TO EACH PARTY AND TO EACH ATTORNEY OF RECORD IN THIS ACTION:

18   YOU ARE HEREBY NOTIFIED THAT THE DEPOSITION OF_____

19   will be taken at _____ [location] _____,

20   on _____ [date] _____, commencing at _____ [time] _____.

21   YOU ARE FURTHER NOTIFIED THAT: (check and fill in appropriate boxes)

22   [ ] Nonparty deponent: The deponent is not a party to this action. So far as is known to the

23   deposing party, the deponent's address and telephone number are as follows:

24   The deponent has been served with a Deposition Subpoena.

25   A COPY OF THE DEPOSITION SUBPOENA IS ATTACHED HERETO AND SERVED HEREWITH.

26   [ ] Deponent is a corporation or other entity: The deponent is not a natural person. The matters

27   on which the deponent will be examined are as follows: (describe in detail so that corporation will

28   produce the "most qualified" person to testify)

-1-

Sample Notice of Deposition (continued)

1   [ ] <u>Items to be produced by deponent-party</u>: The deponent, who is a party to this action, is

2   required to produce the following documents, records, or other materials at this deposition:

3   (describe materials or categories of materials in detail)

4   [ ] <u>Recording proceedings</u>: The deposing party intends to cause the proceedings to be recorded

5   both stenographically and by (audio/video) tape.

6   [ ] <u>Expert witness video</u>: The deponent is an expert witness or a treating or consulting physician.

7   The deposing party intends to make a videotape recording of the proceedings and reserves the right

8   to use this videotape recording at trial in lieu of live testimony from the deponent.

9

10

11

12   *Nolo Pedestrian*
      Nolo Pedestrian, Plaintiff in Pro Per

13

14

15

16

17

18

19

20

21

22

23

24

25

26

27

28

- **Size up your opponent.** A deposition gives you a chance to observe your adversary's lawyer. The lawyer's behavior at deposition is some indication of how he or she may behave in court. And having already dealt with the lawyer at a deposition can reduce the chances that you will be intimidated in the courtroom.

Disadvantages

Unfortunately, deposing an adversary or a witness who supports your adversary also has considerable disadvantages. Weigh these considerations very carefully before you decide to take a deposition:

- **Cost.** Depositions are the most expensive of the discovery tools. Even if you are representing yourself (and therefore not paying an attorney to take or attend a deposition), you must pay a court reporter to transcribe the testimony and prepare a written transcript. While costs vary somewhat by locality, it's not unusual for a court reporter to charge up to $5 per page of transcript. A day of deposition testimony fills up about 150 pages, meaning that a day-long deposition may cost you around $750. You probably won't have to purchase a transcript if you simply attend a deposition taken by your adversary. (If you want and have the legal right to use at trial a transcript that you haven't purchased, you might have to send the adversary a subpoena to make sure the adversary brings the transcript to trial.) If you lose the case, however, a judge might order you to pay your adversary's deposition expenses. (By the same token, if you win, ask the judge to order your adversary to pay your deposition costs.)

- **Witness may lack knowledge.** If you haven't investigated a case thoroughly enough to know which witnesses are most likely to have important information, you may end up paying dearly to depose a witness whose main answers are "I don't know." (By contrast, written interrogatories give you access to "corporate knowledge." When you send interrogatories to an adversary that is a business or other entity, the business must answer the questions with information known to the company as a whole—which means the business is responsible for figuring out who has the answers.)

EXAMPLE: You have sued a record company for releasing a song that you believe violates your copyright. You take the deposition of Jan Winter, a record company executive who you think was in charge of releasing the song and therefore knows all about the decision to publish it. However, at the deposition, Jan testifies repeatedly that she had nothing to do with the song because she worked in a different division of the company until after it was released. You've spent lots of money and learned nothing. (By contrast, if you had first sent interrogatories to the record company asking for the names of people in charge of releasing the song, you might have been able to target the most knowledgeable deponent.)

TIP

Ask your adversary to designate a deponent. When your opponent is an organization and you are not sure whom to depose, consider asking the adversary to identify and bring to the deposition the most knowledgeable employee. For example, in the record company case, your Notice of Deposition might have directed the company to "produce for deposition the employee who is most knowledgeable about the process by which the song was developed and published." (See FRCP 30(b)(6).) If the adversary tries to give you a hard time by producing someone who knows nothing about the song, you could go to court and ask a judge to order the adversary to pay your wasted deposition expenses.

- **Difficult to do well.** Effective deposition questioning is a difficult skill, even for many attorneys. You have to pose questions carefully to figure out how adverse witnesses will testify at trial. If your questions are vague or you forget to cover a topic, you won't be prepared for your opponent's evidence at trial or be able to show that a witness has changed a story and therefore should not be believed.
- **Opposing attorney's presence.** Your adversary's lawyer will probably be present at a deposition. The attorney may throw you off track by objecting to your questions. An adversary's attorney can also help witnesses "refresh their recollections" during recesses. Seeing you in action will allow the attorney to evaluate your credibility—and by listening to your questions, the attorney might learn more about your case than you learn about the adversary's. However, the same goes for you. Paying attention to how the other side answers and what the other side's lawyer does or does not say might help you anticipate their behavior in court. You may also find yourself much less intimidated in the courtroom after you have faced your opponent and survived the deposition.
- **Help the other side.** If you depose an adverse witness who becomes unavailable for trial, you enable the adversary to offer the deposition transcript into evidence at trial.

Taking a Deposition

Once you've decided to take a deposition, you've got some preparation to do.

Noticing and Preparing for a Deposition

First, check your local court rules. Pay particular attention to when you can take depositions and how to notify a person whose deposition you want to take. You'll need to select a date and location for the deposition, arrange and pay for a court reporter's presence (check the phone book), and give the deponent and opposing counsel (or your self-represented adversary) at least ten days' written notice. Even better, as a courtesy, talk to all the necessary people ahead of time and arrange a mutually convenient date and location.

Written notice procedures tend to differ depending on whether the deponent is the adverse party or some other person. In most states, you set up a deposition of your adversary by using a document called a Notice of Deposition. In some states, if you want the adversary to bring documents to the deposition (so that you can examine them and ask questions), you can simply list those documents in the notice. However, in states that follow FRCP 30(b)(5), you'll have to request documents by sending out a separate form called a Request for Production of Documents. (See "Requests for Production of Documents and Subpoenas," below, for more on such requests.

If you want to depose a "nonparty witness" (someone other than your adversary), you'll probably have to serve the witness with an official court form called a Subpoena re Deposition. If you want the nonparty witness to bring documents to the deposition, use instead a form carrying the fancy title Subpoena Duces Tecum re Deposition. (These forms should be available from a court clerk.) List the documents you want the witness to bring along, and state briefly how they pertain to the case. Legal form books, discussed further in Chapter 23, contain sample language that you can adapt to your situation.

Lawyers usually take depositions in their offices, but any office will do. If you have a convenient office or can borrow one, use it. You'll probably feel more comfortable on familiar turf! Otherwise, you may arrange to use either your adversary's or the court reporter's office.

TIP

Videotaped depositions. Rules in many courts allow for videotaping of depositions, usually in addition to having a court reporter present. While this procedure is optional and adds to a deposition's cost, a videotape can be particularly desirable if you want to preserve favorable testimony from a witness who may not be available to testify in person at trial. Showing a videotape of an unavailable witness's deposition testimony to a judge or jury is likely to be more impressive than reading a transcript of the testimony.

TIP

How to prepare to take an effective deposition. Follow these tips to learn as much information as you can at a deposition:

- Prepare a list of questions before you take a witness's deposition. You need not slavishly follow the list, but having one should prevent you from forgetting important topics.
- Bring (or subpoena) copies of any written statements about the case that the deponent has previously given. For example, bring the police report if the witness gave a statement to a police officer, or the witness's own affidavit (written statement signed under oath), if one was attached to a pleading filed in court. Ask the deponent about the events to which the statement refers, then check to see if the deponent in any way contradicts the prior statement. If so, you might ask the witness to repeat the contradictory statement during the deposition. That way, if you impeach (attack the credibility of) the witness at trial, the witness cannot easily wriggle out of your trap by saying, "I made a careless mistake during my deposition."
- Bring copies of any other documents you want to question the witness about, regardless of whether the witness wrote

the document or has any connection to it. For example, you may want to know whether the witness ever saw a document, the date on which the witness saw it, or whether the witness is aware of the information in the document.

- Review and bring along all paperwork relating to the case organized chronologically, including the complaint, the answer, and any motions or court rulings. These documents can help if an adversary challenges the relevance of your questions.

For much more information and advice on taking depositions, see *Nolo's Deposition Handbook* by Paul Bergman and Albert Moore (Nolo).

Deposition Questions

So after noticing and preparing for the deposition, what do you do when it's time to start? Before getting into the facts of a case, it's a good idea to begin with what lawyers call a "deposition preamble" or "admonitions." This consists of a series of questions lawyers often ask to try to prevent deponents from discounting or weaseling out of their own deposition testimony at trial. Routine preamble questions include:

- "Are you currently under the influence of any medication?"
- "Have you had a chance to review any previous statements you've given to your lawyer or anyone else in connection with this case before coming here?"
- "Have you looked at any documents in preparation for your deposition?" (If the answer is "yes," you may then ask, "Can you please tell me what documents you looked at?")
- "Have you had a chance to meet and discuss the case with your lawyer before coming here today?" (This is a fairly innocuous question. However, if you are deposing your opponent, your opponent's attorney may object and instruct your opponent not to answer on the ground that your question "calls for privileged information"—that is, that answering the question would require the deponent to reveal what was said in a conversation with his or her attorney. This is probably an invalid objection, because your question asks only whether a meeting took place, not what was said. Nevertheless, you can't force an answer, so if your opponent refuses to answer, just go on to your next question. A "privilege" objection is completely improper if you are deposing a nonparty witness. There's no privilege for anything said between attorneys and witnesses who are not their clients.)
- "If you don't understand a question, will you tell me so that I can rephrase it?"
- "Do you realize that you are under oath, just as if we were in a court of law?"
- "Is there any reason you can't give your best testimony today?"

The purpose of these preliminary questions is to undermine any explanation a deponent may come up with to excuse a change in the deponent's testimony at trial. For example, a witness who doesn't raise a fuss during the preamble and then contradicts testimony given at the deposition will have a tough time making an excuse such as "I couldn't concentrate at the time of my deposition because I was really feeling ill" or "I hadn't had a chance to review the facts of the case with my attorney at the time of the deposition."

Once past the preliminary questions, you can ask questions seeking case-related information. The scope of questions you can ask at a deposition is very broad, far wider than at trial. For example, you can ask witnesses about rumors they have heard or opinions they have formed, even though these questions would probably be out of bounds at trial, so long as the answers might "reasonably lead to the discovery of admissible evidence." While each case is factually unique, the following general guidelines may help you think of questions to ask in your case:

- Ask questions that take a deponent through a story chronologically rather than by topic. Following a chronological format helps you understand the deponent's story and question more thoroughly. For example, ask questions such as: "After the June meeting, what's the next thing that happened?" or "Before you heard what you referred to as a squeal of brakes, did anything else happen?"
- Ask "wrap-up" questions before leaving one topic to move to another. Wrap-up questions give deponents an opportunity to search their memories for details that you haven't brought up. For example, before moving on from questioning a deponent

about a meeting that occurred on June 1, conclude by asking, "Is there anything else you can recall that took place during the June 1 meeting?" The answer may be an unexpected windfall. But even if, as is usually the case, the deponent responds, "I don't recall anything else," the answer can be very valuable. If at trial the deponent suddenly remembers additional information that helps the other side, the answer allows you to cast doubt on the witness's believability by reading the contradictory deposition testimony to the judge or jury.

- Use a combination of open and narrow questions. Open questions may elicit information you would not have thought to ask about and may encourage witnesses to describe events in their own words: "Please tell me everything that you can recall about the June 1 meeting." Narrow questions allow you to probe for precise information: "Did Johnson say anything about upgrading computers during the June 1 meeting?"
- Refer directly to the allegations of the complaint or the answer when questioning your adversary. For example:
  - "Your answer alleges that my own negligence caused the accident. Please tell me what I did that you think was negligent."
  - "Your complaint alleges that I was driving carelessly. Do you know of any witnesses to my alleged careless driving?"

- "Your complaint asks for economic losses you suffered due to my alleged breach of contract. Please specify the losses to which the complaint refers."

- Show documents and tangible objects to a deponent and ask about their contents. To do this, you may use materials that you brought with you or that you asked the deponent to bring along. (Be sure to take the time to read documents carefully and study objects closely that a deponent brings in before you ask questions.) For example: "Your statement to the police officer indicates that you had left your eye doctor moments before you saw the accident. Please tell me why you went to see the eye doctor."

TIP

Marking exhibits. When you plan to refer to a document during deposition questioning, have a copy available and ask the court reporter to "mark the copy as an exhibit." For example, if you've questioned a deponent about a letter that the deponent wrote to Aunt Sally, ask the court reporter to "mark this copy of the letter to Aunt Sally as Exhibit A." The exhibit will accompany the deposition, and you can refer to the document as well as the deposition testimony if you have a reason to use the deposition at trial. (See Chapter 15.)

- Use documents to refresh a deponent's recollection. For example: A construction worker says that he cannot recall what grade of wood was used on the exterior of your house. You may respond, "Please look over the construction agreement that's been marked as Exhibit A and see if that refreshes your recollection."

- Ask if the deponent knows of any other person or document that might have information pertaining to your case. For example:
  - "You testified that the subject of computer upgrades was discussed during the June 1 meeting. Are you aware of any document, memo, or report that supports your testimony? Have you talked to anyone who has told you that he or she recalls this subject being discussed at that meeting?"
  - "Following the accident, did you talk to anyone who said that they saw any part of it?" If the answer is yes: "Please give me the names, addresses, phone numbers, and any other information you have that would help me to contact the persons you talked to."

- Don't be afraid to ask for details of unfavorable evidence: Remember that a deposition is your chance to find out how bad the case against you will be if you go to trial. A deposition is not the place to argue your side. As best you can, try to pretend you're representing someone else and trying to find out how the witness can hurt this "other" person."

  For example, if a deponent testifies to seeing you having drinks in a bar shortly before you drove off in your car, you might continue with open questions to encourage the deponent to describe events in the deponent's own words:

- "You testified that you saw me drinking in a bar on the night of the accident. Please tell me everything you can remember about my activities that night."
- "Can you recall anything about my physical condition that night?"
- "You said that I seemed a bit tipsy. Please explain what you mean."
- "Anything else you can recall?"

Then move on to narrow questions asking for details:

- "Over what period of time did you see me in the bar?"
- "You testified that you saw me holding a drink. Did you see how many drinks I had?"
- "Could you tell in any way what I was drinking?"

- Ask questions concerning a deponent's general background. The information may suggest new topics for questioning and may allow you to estimate the deponent's general credibility. For instance, you may ask about a deponent's:
  - family background (including marital status)
  - education
  - employment history
  - membership in various organizations
  - relationship to your adversary, the adversary's lawyer, or other witnesses
  - financial interest in the case (this topic is particularly appropriate for an expert witness, because the size

of the expert's fee may suggest a motive for the expert to bend an opinion in your adversary's favor), and

- criminal convictions, if any.

How a Deposition Background Question Paid Off Big Time

In the mid-1980s, a group of families sued two Woburn, Massachusetts, businesses for poisoning groundwater and causing town residents to suffer leukemia deaths and other physical injuries. During the deposition of a doctor who had important information that helped the plaintiffs, a defense lawyer asked about the doctor's marital status. The doctor mentioned an ex-wife, who, after being tracked down by the defense, provided negative information about the doctor's personal background. The plaintiffs' lawyer, fearing that the jury might learn this information, decided not to have the doctor testify at trial. (*A Civil Action*, by Jonathan Harr, Vintage Books, p. 190.) So the plaintiffs lost a valuable witness, based on the answer to a routine background question at a deposition.

- Probe a deponent's credibility by questioning the deponent's ability to observe and recollect. For example, you may ask whether a deponent has any special reason to be able to recall what happened months or years earlier. And you might ask whether the deponent has any physical limitations. Finally, you might also ask about any external conditions (weather, darkness, background noise) that may have interfered with the deponent's ability to see or hear what happened. Questions you may ask along these lines include:

- "Is there any special reason why you remember what took place during the June 1 meeting?"
- "Please describe your activities on the day that the accident took place, up until the time you heard the screech of brakes."
- "Do you ordinarily wear glasses?" If the answer is yes: "Were you wearing them at the time of the accident?"

• Deponents can often be hard to pin down, especially when you try to elicit information they'd rather not provide. One good approach is to watch out for "weasel words" and qualifiers and insist on definite responses. For example, a deponent testifies, "I might have left my glasses at home." Because "might have" are clearly weasel words, you will want to follow up by asking, "Please answer yes or no. Did you leave your glasses at home?"

• Look in a law library for lawyer "practice guides" that suggest areas of deposition questioning for specific types of cases. For example, a practice guide might suggest topics that you should probe in a breach of contract or an auto accident case. One well-known and quite comprehensive source is *Bender's Forms of Discovery*, a ten-volume treatise updated regularly.

After you've finished questioning the deponent, your opponent's lawyer can also question the deponent. Often, opposing counsel will ask no or a very few questions. This makes sense. The deponent is probably on your opponent's side, which means that your opponent can get any additional information from the witness through informal questioning—and outside of your presence.

 CAUTION

Watch the clock! FRCP 30(d)(2) and similar rules in many states generally say that a deposition may last no longer than "one day of seven hours." This rule allows you to call a halt to a deposition that your adversary takes once time expires. If you are taking a deposition, make sure to ask all your important questions before time runs out. No matter which side is taking the deposition, you can agree to longer or shorter time limits with your adversary. Also, if your adversary's obstructionist tactics prevent you from completing a deposition within the time limit, you can file a motion asking a judge for additional time. If you do, be sure that your motion indicates what information you seek and why it is important. You can also ask the judge to sanction (penalize) your adversary for your inconvenience in having to prepare and argue the motion. (In some jurisdictions a court officer might be available by telephone to resolve a dispute over time limits immediately.)

Defending a Deposition

As a party to a lawsuit, you have a right to be present at every deposition your adversary takes. Lawyers call this "defending a deposition." (Lawyers occasionally save their clients money by skipping the deposition and ordering a transcript instead.) If you are a self-represented party, you automatically defend your own deposition. Below are suggestions that can help you or a deponent who supports your side of the case (and is willing to meet with you beforehand) to testify as completely, accurately, and credibly as possible. This is important because solid depositions strengthen your bargaining position. Moreover, following this approach should prevent you or another deponent from having to explain to a judge or jury why you or the deponent have changed your deposition story or can suddenly remember details at trial that were not mentioned months earlier at the deposition.

CAUTION

Your adversary can ask about any predeposition discussions you have with a witness. Your adversary's lawyer can ask a witness what you said to the witness before the deposition started. Or as lawyers put it, your predeposition discussions are not "privileged." Therefore, don't say anything that would embarrass you or hurt your credibility if the witness were to repeat it during the deposition.

The following tips can help you or your witness testify fully and accurately at a deposition:

- Just as you would do if you were getting ready to take a deposition, prepare in advance to defend a deposition. To do this, review the pleadings and any case-related written statements you or your witness made, such as demand letters sent to your adversary, affidavits attached to a pleading or motion (for example, as part of a summary judgment motion; see Chapter 7), or even letters written to a newspaper about the incident giving rise to the lawsuit. Similarly, review all pertinent documents that constitute the "paper trail" leading to litigation. For example, in a breach of contract case, this would include any memos that you or a witness might have written before signing a contract and the contract itself.

- Don't volunteer information. Listen carefully to questions and answer only what you are asked. You or a witness may be tempted to defend your position with long, rambling answers, but such answers almost inevitably provide an opponent with useful information. (If you really want a witness to elaborate on an answer, wait until the end when you will have a chance to ask questions.)

- If you don't understand a question, or if a question is confusing because it has several parts, ask the questioner to rephrase it.

- Ask for a recess if you become mentally fatigued, need a bathroom break, or just need time to think. During this time, you can continue to refresh your recollection with notes or other documents.

- Object if you think that a question is improper. However, you should then go on to answer it unless a question is totally irrelevant or asks about legally privileged information—for example, conversations you've had with your legal coach.

• Tell the truth.

Deposition Objections

During a trial, lawyers and self-represented parties can object to each other's questions during depositions. (See FRCP 30(d)(1).) See also Chapter 17 for a discussion of common objections and objection procedures.) But because judges are not present at depositions, it is not possible to get an immediate ruling on your objection's validity. Typically, a judge rules on a deposition objection only if the side taking the deposition wants to read the objected-to testimony into the record at trial (and has a legal basis for doing so). If the trial judge determines that the objection was proper, the judge will probably not permit the testimony to be read at trial.

Again, because judges are not present at depositions, a deponent normally answers an objected-to question just as if no objection had been made. The fact that you (or your adversary's attorney) made an objection comes up later, if one of you seeks to admit that portion of the testimony into evidence at trial, at which point the judge will rule on the objection. For example, an attorney defending a deposition may object that a question calls for hearsay, but then tell the deponent to "go ahead and answer the question." The big exception to this practice occurs when the basis of an objection is that a "question is improper because it calls for privileged information." ("Privileged Information," below, explains why.)

CAUTION

An attorney may try to take advantage of you. If you defend a deposition as a self-represented litigant, an attorney might try to take advantage of you (and the absence of a judge) by bullying you or your witness. Bullying tactics include asking rapid-fire repetitive questions, raising his or her voice, arguing with you, asking questions so far afield that they are outside even the broad scope of discovery, or—if defending a deposition—objecting constantly. You can object to an attorney's questions just as you can at trial, which has the effect of preserving your objection for trial (as explained above). But if you're asking the questions, don't stop just because an attorney repeatedly objects to your questions—the attorney may just be trying to rattle you. Persevere with your questions no matter how obstreperous the attorney is. However, in an extreme situation in which an attorney is repeatedly insulting or excessive, it may be appropriate to terminate a deposition and promptly file a motion in court, using the transcript as a basis to request a judge to impose sanctions (penalties) on the attorney. A middle ground between stopping the deposition altogether and ignoring the bullying is to ask for a break—and insist on it if necessary. Even a five-minute bathroom break can interrupt the nasty momentum and give you a chance to catch your breath and regain your confidence.

RESOURCE

Resources on depositions. *Nolo's Deposition Handbook*, by Paul Bergman and Albert Moore (Nolo), explores deposition rules and strategies for self-represented parties, as well as information for nonparty witnesses (including experts) who face being deposed.

Privileged Information

As you've seen, deponents are normally expected to answer questions that may be legally objectionable, leaving it to a judge to rule on whether the answers can be used at trial later if an effort is made to introduce the information into the trial record. The big exception to this practice occurs when a question seeks "privileged information." In all states, and subject to various exceptions, legal privileges exist for confidential communications between attorneys and clients, spouses, physicians and patients, and ministers and congregants. Depending on a state's law, privileges may also exist in some other situations, such as between psychotherapists and clients. A privilege also exists for an attorney's "work product," meaning an attorney's strategic papers and files. (For a good general discussion of privileges, see *Introduction to the Law of Evidence*, by Graham C. Lilly (West Group).)

When a legal privilege exists, the protection of privacy in the privileged relationship (for example, between doctors and patients) has been deemed more important than the need to get the information in any one case. Neither you nor any other witness has to reveal privileged matter, whether at a deposition or a trial. For example, you do not have to reveal the case-related private conversations you've had with your legal coach or a personal conversation you had with your spouse following a car accident or the making of a contract. Nor can you ask your adversary for a copy of the adversary lawyer's "trial strategy memo," because that represents the lawyer's privileged work product.

EXAMPLE 1: You ask your adversary, "Please tell me what you and your attorney talked about before we started the deposition." The question calls for privileged information, and the deponent does not have to answer it.

EXAMPLE 2: Amanda Nolo, a self-represented litigant, discusses her case with a friendly witness before the adversary takes the witness's deposition. The adversary's lawyer asks, "What did you and Nolo talk about before the deposition?" The question is proper. Because Amanda Nolo is not a lawyer, no privilege exists for conversations between her and the witness.

Deponents who are unaware of the protection for privileged material may unwittingly disclose it during a deposition, in which case the privilege is waived. That is why a lawyer who represents a deponent usually instructs the deponent not to answer a question that seeks legally privileged information. If you are self-represented, you don't have the right to instruct a deponent to refuse to answer a question that calls for privileged information. However, you can interrupt a deposition to advise a friendly deponent that a question calls for privileged matter, and leave it to the deponent to decide whether or not to answer it.

- *American Jurisprudence Pleading and Practice Forms* (Lawyers Cooperative Publishing Co.) is a multivolume treatise that includes numerous examples of deposition forms.
- *Basics of Legal Document Preparation*, by Robert Cummins (Delmar), reviews the fundamentals of various discovery tools and contains many examples and sample forms.
- *The Effective Deposition: Techniques and Strategies That Work*, by David M. Malone and Peter T. Hoffman (National Institute for Trial Advocacy), is a comprehensive guide to deposition rules and techniques, based on the Federal Rules of Civil Procedure.

All is not necessarily lost if you neglect to object to an improper question or answer during a deposition. You might be allowed to make the objection for the first time at trial should your opponent seek to read improper deposition testimony into the record. However, the safest course is to become familiar with grounds for objection and to make objections for the record whenever you are uncertain. You especially need to object if your objection concerns the form of a question or answer (for example, a question is leading or vague). You cannot make a "form" objection at trial if you failed to make it during the deposition. (See FRCP 32(d)(3)(B).)

Written Interrogatories

Written interrogatories are questions that you or your adversary must answer in writing, under oath. (See FRCP 33; most states follow

similar procedures.) Court rules usually give the answering party—called a respondent—30 days to answer. However, because answering interrogatories often requires searching records and gathering documents, judges usually grant a party's Motion for Additional Time to Answer. Realizing this, parties usually informally stipulate (agree) to a request by their opponents for a reasonable extension of time to answer.

Advantages and Disadvantages of Sending Interrogatories

Compared to depositions, written interrogatories provide the following advantages:

- **Lower cost.** Your only interrogatory expense is the time it takes you to prepare them. You don't have to pay a court reporter or arrange for videotaping or set a date and location. You simply prepare the questions at your convenience and serve them on your adversary by mail.

TIP

Save time and money by sending out interrogatories before taking depositions. Interrogatory answers can pinpoint the witnesses who are likely to have important information, reveal documents that you can use when questioning witnesses, and supply background information that you would otherwise have to ask about during a deposition. As a result, your deposition questioning can target key witnesses and issues and, therefore, be shorter and more efficient.

- **Broad scope.** The scope of your questions can be very broad. Whether you

take a deposition or send out interrogatories, you can seek information
"reasonably calculated to lead to the
discovery of admissible evidence."

- **Get corporate knowledge.** When you
send interrogatories to an organization, you are entitled to "corporate
knowledge," or the collective memory
of all employees and representatives,
not merely the single witness whose
deposition you are taking. A typical
preface to interrogatory questions
instructs the recipient to "furnish all
information known by or in possession of yourself, your agents, and
your attorneys, or appearing in your
records."

EXAMPLE: You have sued a hospital
for negligently allowing Doctor Rex
to perform a medical procedure for
which you claim that Doctor Rex
was not qualified. You ask, "Please
describe the process you followed to
investigate Doctor Rex's qualifications to
perform the above-mentioned medical
procedure." An individual deponent
might be able to testify only about a
small part of the investigation. The
interrogatory, by contrast, should reveal
the combined investigation activities of
various individuals.

However, just like depositions, interrogatories have a number of downsides that often
limit their utility. (Remember, we advised you
to rely on informal investigation to the extent
that it is possible!) These include:

- **Limited number of questions.** Court
rules are likely to limit the number
of interrogatories you can ask. FRCP

33(a) allows 25 questions (including
a reasonable number of subparts),
unless a judge gives you permission
to ask more. Few states allow more
than 50.

- **Lack of flexibility in questioning.** Court
rules often limit you to a single set
of interrogatories. Even if this isn't
true (or a judge makes an exception
in your case and allows a second
set), you have to prepare and send
out a whole set of interrogatories
before you receive any responses.
This means that you often don't have
the information (the answer to your
first question) that might allow you to
make more pointed inquiries (follow-
up questions), as you normally would
at a deposition.

- **You can reach only the opponent.** You
may pose interrogatories only to the
opposing party. You cannot send them
to witnesses or other third persons.

- **Lawyers write the answers.** Interrogatory
answers are frequently prepared with
strong input from lawyers. Lawyers
tend to provide narrow answers that
conceal rather than reveal helpful
information, and they avoid answers
entirely by claiming that questions are
ambiguous, vague, unduly burdensome, seek impermissible legal
conclusions, or violate the attorney-
client privilege. (These types of
responses are especially likely if you
represent yourself and your opponent
has a lawyer.) Though you can file a
motion asking a judge to compel your
adversary to answer your question,
this process can be time-consuming
and frustrating.

EXAMPLE 1: In a personal injury case, your interrogatory asks, "Please identify the witnesses you have talked to or taken statements from, and attach those statements (or summaries) to your answers." The probable response: "Objection—the question asks for the attorney's work product and is protected from disclosure under Federal Rule of Civil Procedure 26(b)(3)." To avoid this objection, ask only for the names and addresses of witnesses, not for the attorney's decisions about which witnesses are worth talking to or taking statements from. (For example, a proper interrogatory might be: "State the full name and address of each person known to you who witnessed or claims to have witnessed the collision between Plaintiff and Defendant's cars on May 4, 20XX.") If you want to know what the witnesses saw or heard, you'll have to interview them informally or take their depositions.

EXAMPLE 2: You are the plaintiff in a breach of contract case, and your interrogatory says, "Please identify all documents in your possession that pertain to the case." The probable response: "Objection—the question is vague and overbroad." To avoid this objection, narrow your requests. For example, a more acceptable interrogatory would be: "Please identify any documents in your possession pertaining to conversations between Sam Spade and Plaintiff relating to the contract described in Plaintiff's Complaint."

- **Summary responses.** Lawyers rarely provide, and judges rarely insist that they provide, lengthy answers to broadly worded interrogatories. The legal culture generally allows for summary responses to open-style interrogatories, perhaps out of a sense that information should not be too available "on the cheap." If you want to elicit a full story, you'll probably have to take a deposition.

EXAMPLE: You ask, "Please describe the process leading to the hospital's hiring of Doctor Rex." Instead of a lengthy, fully detailed answer, you're likely to get something closer to, "Thorough review of past employment and numerous committee discussions and analyses."

Drafting Interrogatories

Without experience, you'll probably find it hard to draft clear, unambiguous interrogatories. One way around this problem is to consult a legal treatise such as *Bender's Forms of Discovery*, which has predrafted questions for specific kinds of cases. (Unfortunately, *Bender's* won't be of much help if it doesn't have sample interrogatories for a case with facts similar to yours.) Another possibility is to have your proposed interrogatories reviewed by your legal coach, if you have one. The coach can probably provide quick suggestions for tightening up your questions. (See Chapters 1 and 23 for more about legal coaches.)

Seven Tips for Drafting Good Interrogatories

The following suggestions should help you draft more effective interrogatories.

1. If court rules in your jurisdiction require parties to voluntarily disclose pertinent documents and witnesses, do not begin to prepare interrogatories until your adversary has completed disclosure and you've had a discovery-planning meeting with the adversary's lawyer. That way you'll have background information that can help you pinpoint specific topics for interrogatories.

2. Because you can submit only a limited number of interrogatories, use sub-questions to reduce the number of interrogatories you use to cover a single topic. Remember, however, that subparts must be reasonable in number. A judge won't allow you to evade limits on the number of interrogatories by adding 20 to 30 subparts to a question.

EXAMPLE 1: "Please state whether you wear prescription corrective lenses. If the answer is 'yes,' please also state the vision problem for which you have a prescription and the prescription."

EXAMPLE 2: "During the past five years, have you suffered any other personal injuries? If your answer is 'yes,' please state for each injury:
   a. the date of the injury;
   b. where you were at the time of the injury;
   c. how the injury took place;
   d. the nature and extent of the injury;
   e. the name and address of each medical facility or office in which you received treatment for the injury;
   f. whether and from whom you sought compensation for that injury."

3. If you are going to ask a series of interrogatories about a single event or document, define the event or topic in a "Definitions" section that comes before the questions. This way you don't have to describe the defined event or topic every time you refer to it in an interrogatory.

EXAMPLE 1: "Definitions. The following term used in these interrogatories has the following meaning: The term 'September 22 contract' refers to the contract signed by Plaintiff and Defendant on September 22 and attached as Exhibit A to these interrogatories."

EXAMPLE 2: "Definitions. A request for any 'document' refers to all writings of any kind, including but not limited to correspondence, memoranda, notes, pamphlets, books, computer printouts, fax documents, graphs, photographs, videotapes, and electronically stored records, whether stored on tapes, cassettes, computers, or other similar devices." (Whew! You wouldn't want to say this more than once!)

4. When you ask for information, also ask if your opponent has any document or record reflecting that information, and, if so, ask

Seven Tips for Drafting Good Interrogatories (continued)

that they include a copy of the document with the answers. This saves you from having to seek the document in a separate Request for Production of Documents form.

> **EXAMPLE:** "Do you contend that you shipped the widgets to Plaintiff on March 12? If so, please state whether you have in your possession or control any document or record indicating that such a shipment was made, and attach a copy of any such document or record to your answers to these interrogatories."

5. Ask your adversary to set forth the facts on which his or her legal claims are based.

> **EXAMPLE:** You are the defendant in a personal injury action; the plaintiff's complaint asks for "damages of no less than $100,000." You might submit an interrogatory such as, "Please identify separately each element of harm (economic, physical, psychological, or otherwise) for which you seek damages, the dollar amount you seek for each element of harm, and the facts constituting each element of harm."

6. When serving interrogatories on an entity such as a corporation, ask for "the identity of each person who participated in preparing the answers to these interrogatories, and of each document that was consulted in the course of preparing answers to these interrogatories." The answers can help you decide who to depose and what documents to request.

7. Make use of "form" interrogatories. Legal form books and attorney practice guides are available at any good-sized law library. Such guides typically contain sample interrogatories for use in specific types of cases. For example, a form book may have a set of plaintiff's interrogatories in a case about breach of a shopping center lease. Consult form books for your type of case before preparing a set of interrogatories. (See Chapter 23 for tips on using form books.)

RESOURCE

Resources on interrogatories.
Bender's Forms of Discovery (Matthew Bender) is a ten-volume treatise with sample interrogatories for numerous kinds of cases, including product liability, employment discrimination, slip and fall, and building construction.

American Jurisprudence Pleading and Practice Forms Annotated and *Basics of Legal Document Preparation* (See citations under "Resources on Depositions," above.)

Requests for Production of Documents and Subpoenas

We have so far discussed several ways of obtaining or inspecting and copying documents (or other objects), including:

- making informal requests to cooperative witnesses or businesses
- asking for voluntary disclosure from your adversary
- using a Notice of Deposition or a Subpoena Duces Tecum re Deposition to order a deponent to bring documents to a deposition, and
- asking a party to attach documents to its answers to written interrogatories.

There are several additional methods for gaining access to written materials, including:

- sending your opponent a Request for Production of Documents (see FRCP 34; most states have similar rules), and
- serving a nonparty with a subpoena ordering the recipient to allow you to inspect and copy designated materials. (See FRCP 45; many, but not all, states provide for this option.)

Amendments to the FRCP adopted in 2006 provide that "electronically stored information" is subject to discovery on the same basis as tangible written documents. By submitting a Request for Production, you can obtain email messages that your adversary has sent or received, and information in your adversary's computer files. You may obtain this information even if the email messages or computer files have never been printed out. Of course, your adversary may obtain the same information from you.

Generally, you should produce electronic information in the form in which you ordinarily maintain it. For example, if you store data that you have to turn over to your adversary in a Word file, you can provide your adversary with that file; you don't have to convert the file to another form.

CAUTION

Don't destroy electronic evidence.
Just as you cannot destroy written documents in order to prevent an adversary from obtaining them, you cannot destroy email messages or other electronic files to prevent their disclosure. If your adversary seeks relevant information that is stored electronically in a computer, you have a duty to provide it unless the information is privileged, constitutes your "work product" (legal theories and other work you've done on the case), or unless the adversary's request is "unreasonably cumulative" or unduly burdensome. For example, your adversary can't force you to spend money to retrieve information that is stored on a very old backup tape that you no longer use and that no modern computer can read.

At the same time, just as many individuals and companies routinely shred paper records, they may also regularly destroy or purge electronically stored information. If you do adhere to such a practice, you don't have to change what you do simply because a document or an email message may at some uncertain time become relevant to a dispute. So long as you act in what lawyers call "good faith," and don't destroy electronically stored information that you are aware pertains to a dispute, you can follow a routine practice of cleaning up your files and records.

A request for a document must be precise enough that the recipient can reasonably determine what you want. For example, a request to "produce every document that has anything to do with this case" is likely to be objected to as vague. The requirement that your request be specific often means that you have to delay sending out a Request for Production of Documents until you know enough about the case to identify the documents you're after. (On the other hand, a recipient can't avoid furnishing a document because, for example, your request failed to mention the weight of the paper on which it was printed.)

TIP

It's proper to request documents you can't identify. You do not necessarily have to know a document's exact title, or even that it actually exists, to send a Request for Production of Documents to your opponent or issue a Subpoena for Production of Documents to a third party. For example, you might serve a subpoena on a hospital, asking the hospital to send you copies of (or to allow you to inspect and copy) "all

records, reports, notations, charts, X-rays, results of medical tests, or any other document (as defined above) pertaining to General Hospital's treatment and care of Penny Sillen on February 13–15, 20XX." The obvious advantage of wording a subpoena this broadly is that it may well produce documents that you don't know about.

A recipient has to allow you to inspect or copy a document as long as it's in the recipient's "possession or control." The "or control" language is important. It means that a scummy recipient can't play "hot potato" with a document, giving it to an attorney or friend and then responding, "I'd love to give it to you but I can't; it's not in my possession."

EXAMPLE: Assume you are the plaintiff in an auto accident personal injury case. You might serve the following Request for Production of Documents on the defendant. (Your reasoning is in italics at the end of each request.)

Plaintiff Les Ismore requests that defendant produce the following documents for inspection and copying at Ismore's business office at 950 Campion Way, Leamington, OH, between the hours of 2:00 p.m. and 4:00 p.m. on March 31, 20XX:

1. The document of title (pink slip) to Defendant's Ford Explorer. *(This can help you prove that the Defendant owned the car and is therefore legally responsible for your injuries.)*

2. The Defendant's automobile insurance policy that provides insurance coverage for Defendant's

Sample Request for Production of Documents

Nolo Pedestrian
[Street Address]
[City, State, Zip Code]
[Phone Number]

Plaintiff in Pro Per

THE _____ COURT OF _____ COUNTY

STATE OF _____

Nolo Pedestrian,	)
Plaintiff,	)
	) Case No. 12345
v.	)
	)
Sarah Adams,	) REQUEST TO DEFENDANT ADAMS FOR
	) PRODUCTION OF DOCUMENTS
Defendant.	)
	)

Plaintiff Nolo Pedestrian requests, pursuant to Federal Rule of Civil Procedure 34, which our state has adopted, that Defendant Sarah Adams produce the following documents by delivering them to the office of Plaintiff located at _____ *[address]* _____ within 30 days from the date of service of this Request.

1. Registration and proof of ownership of the truck driven by Defendant that struck Plaintiff on January 1, 20XX.

2. Receipts and records showing all maintenance and repairs to the truck referred to in Request 1 above, during the one-year period before January 1, 20XX.

3. Copies of Defendant's business records reflecting Defendant's appointments on January 1, 20XX, the day of the accident in question in this lawsuit.

Nolo Pedestrian
_____
Nolo Pedestrian, Plaintiff in Pro Per

Ford Explorer. *(This can help you decide whether you are likely to be able to collect a judgment in your favor.)*

3. Any other insurance policy (including "umbrella insurance") that insures the Defendant against liability growing out of an automobile accident. *(This serves the same purpose as Request No. 2, above.)*

4. Receipts for and records of any repairs or servicing done on Defendant's Ford Explorer during the one-year period immediately preceding the date of the accident that is the subject matter of this lawsuit. *(This can help you decide if the Defendant failed to make necessary repairs or whether a repair shop or parts manufacturer might also be liable for your injuries.)*

5. Defendant's appointment book for the date of the accident. *(This may help you prove that the Defendant could have been distracted at the time of the accident, as might be the case if the Defendant was late for a critically important meeting or had just received disturbing medical news.)*

RESOURCE

American Jurisprudence Pleading and Practice Forms Annotated and *Basics of Legal Document Preparation*. (See citations under "Resources on Depositions," above.)

Requests to Examine Objects or Inspect Land or Buildings

Discovery rules generally also allow you to request production of "things" and to request entry on an opponent's land to make an inspection. For example, if you claim that you were injured by a piece of poorly designed automotive equipment, you may request that "Defendant produce the Sherr 9000 tire inflator for inspection and testing at the offices of Burridge Testing Labs at 30 Clifton Avenue, Coventry, MD, on June 3, 20XX." Or, if you claim that a ditch dug by your next-door neighbor is improper because it causes flooding on your property, you may "request that Defendant permit Plaintiff and Plaintiff's engineering expert to enter Defendant's property located at 229 Elm Drive on March 27, 20XX at 2:00 p.m. for the purpose of inspecting and photographing the property."

You or your adversary may respond to a Request for Production of Documents in a variety of ways, depending on such factors as convenience, the way records are kept, and the number of records. Standard alternative ways of responding include any of the following:

- Mailing copies of the documents to the requesting party, with the sender bearing the copying costs.
- Bringing the originals to the requesting party and letting that party pay to make copies.
- When the records are voluminous, making them available at the place where they are usually stored and

allowing the requesting party to inspect and copy them. (However, the recipient of a request to produce cannot, for example, ship documents to the North Pole and tell the other side to go there to inspect them!)

- Objecting. Common objections are that a request is "unduly burdensome" (too much trouble, given the amount of money in dispute) or "vague and overbroad."

- Replying that "there are no documents in the possession or control of Defendant that correspond to Plaintiff's Request."

Requests for Admissions

Requests for Admissions are written statements or assertions that you prepare and serve on an adversary to secure the adversary's admission that facts are true or that documents are genuine. (See FRCP 36; most states have similar rules.) Requests for Admissions are not designed to "discover" information from an adversary but to make life easier at trial. That's because once you or an adversary admit that a fact is true or that a document is genuine, the admission can be offered as evidence at trial and cannot be disputed.

> **EXAMPLE:** In an auto accident case, you serve the following Requests for Admission on the Defendant:
>
> - "Admit that the following fact is true: 'On February 29, Defendant Sarah Adams consumed two martinis between the hours of 9 a.m. and 10 a.m.'"

- "Admit that the following document is genuine: A letter dated March 1 and signed by Sarah Adams."

If these requests are admitted (either because the defendant answers them affirmatively or fails to deny them within the time set by law, often 30 days), you can offer the requests into evidence to prove that Sarah Adams consumed two martinis and wrote the March 1 letter. Moreover, the Defendant cannot try to contradict this evidence.

As a self-represented litigant, you must be especially alert if you are served with Requests for Admissions. First, you must respond in writing within 30 days, or everything in the request is "deemed admitted." Second, you cannot automatically deny every request, figuring that "I can't lose by denying." To the contrary, if your case goes to trial, and your opponent proves a fact to be true or a document to be genuine after you denied it in a Request for Admissions, the trial judge can force you to pay whatever it cost your opponent to make the proof—including attorneys' fees! (See FRCP 37(c).)

If you don't have a document or are uncertain as to how to answer a Request for Admissions, often the safest course is to respond by saying that "I neither admit nor deny the requested fact because I do not have sufficient information to do so." This will usually protect you against having to pay your adversary's expenses for proving that the fact is true, unless a judge concludes that you answered in bad faith or could have readily found out whether a fact was true or a document genuine.

Requests for Admissions are usually served near the end of the formal discovery

Sample Request for Admissions

1 Nolo Pedestrian
   [Street Address]
2 [City, State, Zip Code]
   [Phone Number]
3
   Plaintiff in Pro Per
4

5

6

7   THE _____ COURT OF _____ COUNTY

8   STATE OF _____

9   Nolo Pedestrian,   )
10   )
                   Plaintiff,   )   Case No. 12345
11   )
      v.   )   REQUEST FOR ADMISSIONS
12   )   SET NUMBER: ONE
    Sarah Adams,   )   PROPOUNDING PARTY: NOLO PEDESTRIAN
13   )   RESPONDING PARTY: SARAH ADAMS
                   Defendant.   )
14 _____

15   PLAINTIFF NOLO PEDESTRIAN HEREBY REQUESTS THAT DEFENDANT SARAH ADAMS ADMIT

16 the truthfulness of each of the facts set forth below; and the genuineness of each document a copy of

17 which is attached to this Request.

18   EACH OF THE FOLLOWING IS TRUE:

19   1. Defendant Adams was talking on a mobile phone at the time that defendant Jones's car collided

20 with the car driven by the plaintiff.

21   2. Defendant Adams had learned that her request for a job promotion had been denied approximately

22 15 minutes before the car that Adams was driving collided with the car driven by the plaintiff.

23   EACH OF THE FOLLOWING DESCRIBED DOCUMENTS, COPIES OF WHICH ARE ATTACHED TO

24 THIS REQUEST, IS GENUINE:

25   1. Bill's Auto Body Repair Statement dated July 1, 20XX.

26   2. Six photographs marked A through F depicting the plaintiff's and defendant's cars after they

27 collided on June 21, 20XX.

28 Date: _____   _____
                                          Nolo Pedestrian, Plaintiff in Pro Per

period. If you serve requests on an opponent before the opponent has had a reasonable opportunity to investigate the case, your opponent will almost certainly deny them or answer by citing "lack of sufficient information." And a judge is unlikely to penalize the opponent for failure to make admissions at this early stage, even if you prove at trial that a fact is true or a document is genuine. Similarly, it is not usually until case investigation is nearly done that you can identify the facts and documents that you want to include in a Request for Admissions. ●

Settlement

Salmon swimming upstream to spawn in an obstacle-filled river have a far better chance of accomplishing their goal than a case has of making it all the way to trial. Informal estimates are that around 90% of cases filed in court wind up being settled rather than resolved by the verdict of a judge or jury. This conventional wisdom is reinforced by a recent study led by Jonathan Hyman for the New Jersey Administrative Office of the Courts. Not only did just 10% of all the cases in the New Jersey sample go to trial but 12% of these cases settled after a trial had started. Thus, the Hyman study also confirmed another basic truth about litigation: It's never too late to settle.

Settlement is a popular option for a number of reasons:

- As a plaintiff, you can take advantage of the time value of money. The dollar you get by settling now could be more valuable than the two dollars you may get years down the road.
- If you are self-represented, no matter whether you are a plaintiff or a defendant, the biggest benefit of settlement can be extricating yourself from a complex and often alien and hostile legal system. Also, you can save yourself the hundreds of hours you may otherwise have to spend doing legal research, talking to witnesses, gathering documents, engaging in numerous other case-related activities, and ultimately going to court.
- Settlement affords both plaintiffs and defendants the certainty of a known result. By comparison, the outcome of a trial is always in doubt. (Lawyers are fond of referring to trial as a "crapshoot.") Even the most solid case can occasionally succumb to such factors as lost exhibits, disappearing or forgetful witnesses, a hostile judge, or a rogue jury.
- Settling often allows both sides to tailor the outcome to meet their specific needs. For example, if a business dispute goes to trial, a judge may be limited to awarding the plaintiff money damages that the defendant cannot pay. By settling, the parties might structure future dealings in such a way that the plaintiff is paid off over time or is guaranteed future contracts that more than make up for the money the plaintiff lost.

EXAMPLE: Daniel and Julia see an orange on the sidewalk. When both lunge for it, a nasty argument ensues. In court, a judge would probably have to award the entire orange to Daniel or Julia according to a legal rule—perhaps to the one who saw it first. However, in settlement discussions the parties might realize that Daniel wants the orange to use its peel in a recipe, while Julia wants it only for the pulp to make orange juice. In short, the orange can be divided so that both parties get what they want. In this way, a settlement can produce a mutually satisfactory "win-win" outcome that the legal system could not.

For these and many other reasons, settlement is often in your best interests—even though it almost always means that you have to back off from an earlier hard-line position. Or, as Sir Winston Churchill put it, better to "jaw, jaw, jaw" than wage "war, war, war."

Because every case that settles is one fewer that the formal legal system has to find time and room for, legislators and judges think that settlement is also in the best interests of the legal system. After a complaint and answer are filed and before a case goes to trial, you will inevitably encounter judges, backed by court rules and procedures, encouraging you to consider settlement. Accordingly, this chapter provides a guide to the postfiling settlement procedures you are likely to encounter and offers suggestions for dealing with them effectively.

One way to achieve a fair and effective settlement before going to (or being dragged into) court is to employ techniques known collectively as "alternative dispute resolution," or "ADR." Prominent among these techniques are negotiation (trying to resolve a dispute by talking to another person face to face) and mediation (trying to resolve a dispute with the help of a neutral third-party mediator). While you have undoubtedly engaged in negotiations and even informal mediations your entire life, these activities are more likely to result in fair and satisfactory outcomes if you learn and use the best information on these techniques. There are many good resources you can consult to increase your knowledge and skill in negotiation and mediation.

Try Settling Before Litigating

Waiting to try to resolve a dispute until after court papers have been filed ordinarily makes little sense. People should—and most probably do—attempt to settle their arguments before going to court. In fact, filing and serving a complaint is often proof that these early settlement efforts have failed. Paradoxically, a complaint itself can often serve as a settlement device in the sense that it represents one side telling the other, "I mean business, and you'd better be willing to compromise if you want to avoid a long and nasty fight."

There's no real downside to trying to settle, either. Your adversary isn't allowed to present evidence at trial about any compromise offers you make during settlement negotiations.

RESOURCE

Settle It Out of Court: How to Resolve Business and Personal Disputes Using Mediation, Arbitration, and Negotiation, by Thomas Crowley (Wiley and Sons), contains information on the wise and effective selection of arbitrators and mediators, as well as how to craft workable settlement strategies.

Getting to Yes: Negotiating Agreement Without Giving In, by Roger Fisher & et al. (Houghton Mifflin), is considered to be the "bible" on how to promote settlement by focusing on underlying needs and objective positions rather than personalities.

Mediate, Don't Litigate: Strategies for Successful Mediation, by Peter Lovenheim and Lisa Guerin (Nolo), is an excellent guide to the mediation process, including how to prepare for a mediation and what happens during mediation. Available by download at www.nolo.com.

The Pocket Lawyer: Solve Your Own Legal Disputes, by Marilyn Sullivan (Venture), written for nonlawyers, reviews the major ADR techniques.

In addition, there are numerous websites where you can learn more about ADR, including www.adr.org (the American Arbitration Association's website), www.jamsadr.com, and www.mediate.com.

Court-Ordered Mediation

Mediation is a descendant of dispute resolution methods used by village or tribal elders in ancient times. In mediation, you discuss a dispute with your opponent and a neutral, usually professionally trained, third person called a mediator. The mediator's role is to facilitate discussion, help the parties focus on concrete issues, help parties create and evaluate settlement proposals, and, if the process gets that far, help the parties craft a written settlement agreement. A mediator has no power to impose a solution. Because mediations so often produce settlements, courts in many localities require parties in some kinds of cases to go through mediation before their cases can proceed towards trial. (This is often called "judicial" mediation.)

Every state sponsors low-cost, voluntary, community-based mediation programs in specific fields, usually including neighbor disputes, consumer problems, landlord-tenant problems, and child custody and visitation disputes. In addition, many mediators who specialize in divorce and business disputes practice privately. The upshot is that mediation is so widely available that, one way or the other, you may well have voluntarily participated in a mediation before going (or being taken) to court. Whether or not this is true, if you find yourself in small claims court, in a child custody dispute, or in a case involving a "small" amount of money (often, $50,000 or less), a judge is likely to suggest strongly or even order you and your opponent to try mediation. Of course, if mediation does not produce a settlement, your case continues on through the court system.

The American Arbitration Association (online at www.adr.org), to which many mediators belong, states that "in most cases mediation results in a settlement." Other mediation groups generally concur. Because it is quite likely that you will resolve your dispute with a mediated settlement and not a court judgment, you'll obviously want to guard against a disadvantageous result by preparing carefully for mediation. The following tips should help you achieve a satisfactory mediated settlement:

- **Understand the process.** You will be attempting to resolve the case with your opponent personally, even if your opponent is represented by a lawyer. (Lawyers sometimes attend mediations, but only to counsel clients and facilitate the discussion.) However, recognize that a representative of a business or other large organization is likely to have prior mediation experience, will be savvy about and at ease with the process, and may be a lawyer to boot. To gain something of an equal footing, you should learn exactly how mediation works by reading a book such as Peter Lovenheim and Lisa Guerin's

Mediate, Don't Litigate: Strategies for Successful Mediation (Nolo), available by download at www.nolo.com.

- **Think in advance about what outcomes you would find acceptable.** Though a mediator may suggest ideas you haven't considered, getting a head start on your thinking can help you evaluate new proposals. While you want to keep an open mind, it is particularly important that you think in advance about an acceptable bottom-line compromise position so that you don't find yourself conceding too much.

- **Bring documents and other exhibits supporting your legal claim.** Even though no judge or jury is present to declare a winner or loser, tangible objects lend force to your points and provide you with psychological support.

- **Remember the goal.** The idea behind mediation is not to produce winners and losers but to find solutions—often creative ones beyond the power of a judge to order—that meet both parties' real needs (but not always their fondest wants or expectations).

Though specifics vary somewhat from state to state, there are similarities in how you are likely to encounter mediation as part of the formal legal system. A judge often has the power to order mediation of any civil lawsuit involving less than $50,000 and of all child custody and visitation disputes. The parties usually have a chance to agree on a mediator of their choosing, but in some instances the judge simply appoints one from a panel of available mediators. When a judge orders the parties to mediate, the mediator's fees are paid by the court. And mediations are more informal than trials; they take place in office settings, not in courtrooms, and operate without regard to evidence rules. Disputants are therefore free to say whatever they want and to back it up with whatever information they consider important.

TIP

Mediation of a single issue. A judge can stop a hearing and send the parties to mediate a single issue and then return to the courtroom. Some courthouses have mediators on site who are available on an "on-call" basis to handle such matters. You will not get to choose the mediator, and the mediation will not cover the whole case—just the single issue that is hanging things up. You will not have to pay for the mediator. Typically, the mediator is either paid by the court or is a volunteer.

EXAMPLE: Hilary has invested $20,000 to become a partner in a bagel/flower shop business started by Skye. Hilary asks for her money back after becoming convinced that Skye seriously understated the level of competition in their locality. When Skye refuses, Hilary sues Skye for fraud and breach of contract; Skye denies Hilary's allegations. At an early stage of the litigation a judge orders the parties to try mediation. During mediation, Hilary refers to "reliable rumors I've heard about a national bagel chain's plan to open a couple of nearby outlets in the next few months." In a trial, a judge would probably rule that Hilary's reference to rumors (no matter how "reliable") is inadmissible on the grounds of vagueness and hearsay (see Chapter 16). However, Hilary is entirely free to talk about rumors in mediation, and her statements have as much force as Skye and the mediator are willing to give them.

If mediation doesn't produce a settlement—and remember that neither a mediator nor a judge can force you to accept a mediated solution—your case proceeds to trial. Nothing you or anybody else says during mediation is admissible as evidence at trial. For example, your opponent can't testify that during the mediation you admitted that "I might have been driving a few miles over the speed limit." (See below.)

To help you understand how mediation works, consider how the mediation in Hilary's and Skye's dispute might unfold. (*Mediate, Don't Litigate: Strategies for Successful Mediation,* by Peter Lovenheim and Lisa Guerin (Nolo, available by download at www.nolo.com), describes six stages of a typical mediation. The discussion below tracks those stages.) Depending on the complexity of a dispute and the attitudes of the parties, the stages described below may be completed in an hour or two, or they may continue over several days. But no matter how long it lasts, the mediation is likely to proceed as follows:

- **Stage 1:** The mediator reviews the goals and rules of mediation and encourages the parties to work cooperatively towards a settlement. For instance, a mediator might tell Hilary and Skye, "I encourage each of you to be honest with the other and to make your best effort at reaching

an agreement. I won't take sides, and I'll keep everything you say confidential."

- **Stage 2:** Each side has an uninterrupted chance to describe that party's view of what the argument is all about and to offer possible solutions. For example, Hilary and Skye in turn could describe their understanding of the events, documents, and conversations leading up to the agreement. They could then each discuss their perceptions of the level of competition the new business will face. Finally, both could say how they want to resolve the dispute. Initially, for instance, Hilary might demand "my money back right now," while Skye might say, "I want to keep Hilary's money in the business for at least one year, but I am willing to sign a note promising to pay her back in a year with interest."

- **Stage 3:** The mediator tries to get the parties to identify and agree on the issues that must be dealt with to resolve the dispute. In this case, the mediator might identify "level of expected competition" and "duration of the partnership agreement" as issues that Hilary and Skye absolutely must discuss.

- **Stage 4:** The mediator meets privately (called "caucusing") with each side to discuss the strengths and weaknesses of each person's position and try to refine settlement ideas. In a private caucus with Hilary, for example, the mediator might want to discuss her ability to prove Skye's alleged misrep-

Statements Made During Mediation Are Confidential

Generally, settlement offers and statements made during mediation are "privileged," meaning that they are not admissible as evidence at trial. This is to promote frank discussion during settlement talks to encourage settlement. For example, assume that during mediation you say, "Look, I'm willing to settle this if you pay me $5,000. I was a little bit at fault, too." However, your adversary refuses to settle and the case goes to trial, where you ask for $13,000 in damages. Your adversary cannot testify either to your offer to settle for $5,000 or your statement that you were partly at fault. Mediation agreements and mediators' own ethical rules also generally provide that mediators cannot be called as witnesses at trial, and mediators' statements and recommended outcomes are likewise inadmissible.

However, you still need to watch what you say during mediation because your adversary might take advantage of your statements in other ways. For example, your adversary might embarrass you by repeating what you said to friends or business associates. Or, your adversary might use what you say as a lead to locate evidence that can be used against you at trial. For example, assume that during mediation you say, "Lucky for me you never found out about Ed Jones. His information is really damaging to me." If the mediation effort fails and the case goes to trial, confidentiality rules won't prevent your adversary from calling Ed Jones as a witness.

To avoid this problem, you and your adversary might sign a "confidentiality agreement" before entering into mediation. The agreement can provide that neither of you will disclose anything said by anyone during mediation to any other person, whether in or out of court. The agreement can also provide that neither of you will offer evidence against the other at trial if the source of the evidence is information that was disclosed during mediation. In other words, evidence can be admissible at trial (subject to other evidence rules, of course) only if the offering party learned about the information other than during mediation. A confidentiality agreement with provisions such as these gives you added protection against disclosure or use of what you reveal during mediation. If your adversary violates the agreement, you would be able to sue for breach of contract if the violation causes you economic harm.

resentations and what information she might consider relevant to a decision to keep the partnership going.

- **Stage 5:** The mediator and the parties again meet all together to continue working towards a solution. Sometimes the parties might find it best to agree to adjourn the mediation for a week or two so that they can seek out additional information. When the mediation continues, all three will meet to see if settlement is a realistic possibility.

- **Stage 6:** Mediation ends with a resolution that is summarized in writing, or with a joint decision to return to the court system because agreement cannot be reached and further efforts to mediate would be futile. In this case, one possible settlement would consist of Skye agreeing to increase Hilary's interest in the partnership by 5% or 10% to compensate her for the unanticipated risk presented by additional competition. Another possibility would be for the two parties to agree to change their merchandise mix to avoid head-to-head competition. If an agreement is reached, the mediator would help the parties put it in writing, report back to the court, and file papers dismissing the case.

The stages described above unfold when a mediator is thorough and the parties are relatively cooperative. In a court-ordered mediation, when time may be short and one or both parties may not want to mediate, the process may be quite different—but an agreement may well result anyway.

Court-Ordered Arbitration

Many states give judges a second way to resolve "smaller" cases (generally those involving $50,000 or less) without going to trial: court-ordered or "judicial" arbitration, a kind of informal trial. In states that authorize both court-ordered mediation and court-ordered arbitration, you'll need to check your local court rules to find out whether you can have any input into which procedure a judge orders you to follow. If you and your opponent agree, it might even be possible for a judge to order that both procedures occur. That is, if court-ordered mediation fails to produce an agreement, you might ask the judge to order the case to arbitration.

Like mediation, arbitration is designed to be a less expensive alternative to resolving a dispute in court. However, arbitration is more like a trial than mediation is. That's because in an arbitration you and your adversary present oral testimony, documents, and other tangible exhibits to a neutral third party (an arbitrator) who is empowered to make a decision, usually called an "award." Arbitrators are professionally trained in arbitration procedures and are usually lawyers or retired judges. Most courts maintain panels of arbitrators; a judge will appoint one for your case. The arbitrator's fee (often around $100 per case or hearing day) is paid by the court. (In some localities, parties whose cases involve too much money to be covered by court-ordered arbitration can request voluntary arbitration, in which case they pay the arbitrator's fees themselves.)

Arbitrations typically take place in the arbitrator's conference room, and the arbitrator need not strictly abide by rules of evidence. Moreover, an arbitrator can try to fashion an outcome that is fair, even if the outcome is different from what might happen in court. After both parties have presented their evidence, the arbitrator will issue a written award deciding the case.

The arbitrator can make an award regardless of whether the parties agree with it, unlike in mediation. However, an award resulting from court-ordered arbitration is ordinarily nonbinding. That is, if you are not happy with the outcome of court-ordered arbitration, you can reject an arbitrator's award and insist that your case be returned to the court system. When your case goes back to the court system, you are eligible for a trial (which lawyers often call a "trial de novo"), just as if the arbitration never took place. (However, in many states you can be saddled with court costs if you reject an arbitration award and don't achieve a better outcome at trial than you did in the arbitration.) If neither you nor your opponent asks for a trial de novo, the arbitrator's award becomes the court's judgment and is generally enforceable to the same extent as a court judgment.

> **EXAMPLE:** Assume that a judge orders Hilary and Skye's bagel/flower shop dispute to arbitration. After hearing evidence, the arbitrator decides that Hilary is entitled to dissolve the partnership and that Skye must return the $20,000 Hilary invested in the business. However, Skye rejects the award and goes to trial in an effort to uphold the partnership agreement and keep Hilary's money in the business. Unless a judge or jury holds that the partnership agreement is valid, Skye will probably have to reimburse the county for the arbitrator's fee and pay Hilary's trial costs (though probably not her attorneys' fees).

CAUTION

Mandatory arbitration. The court-ordered arbitration system we describe here is just one type of arbitration. Another form is nonjudicial "binding" arbitration, in which the arbitrator has the power to issue an award with which you must comply. Without realizing it, you may have entered into a contract that provides for binding arbitration in the event of a dispute— and just about eliminates your ability to go to court. For example, if you have an account with a stock brokerage, are a member of a health care plan, or live in a condominium, you have probably signed a document that provides that any dispute will be resolved exclusively through arbitration rather than through the court system. Courts generally uphold provisions for binding and exclusive arbitration, and they do not overturn arbitrators' awards so long as the procedures were followed fairly.

Because arbitration procedures closely resemble trials, and arbitrators are almost always lawyers or retired judges, you should prepare for an arbitration in much the same way you would for trial. For instance, you should figure out what you have to prove (see Chapters 8 and 9), gather the documents you'll need, and present any witnesses who can back up your contentions after working with them carefully to be sure that their testimony covers the key points. Nevertheless, you should find it easier to represent yourself in an arbitration because evidence rules are relaxed, and the proceedings are likely to be less formal than a trial.

Offers of Judgment

An offer of judgment (sometimes called a "statutory offer") is a written offer a defendant makes to a plaintiff proposing to settle a case on specified terms. (See FRCP 68; most states have similar provisions.) If you receive an offer of settlement this way and it's even marginally reasonable, consider it seriously before saying "no." If you refuse the offer of judgment and you wind up losing at trial—or winning less than the defendant offered to settle the case—the judge may order you to pay any court costs the defendant incurs after you turn down the offer, such as witness fees and court reporter fees. However, you won't generally have to pay the defendant's attorneys' fees.

An offer of judgment can unfairly pressure you into a quick decision if you receive it early in the case, before you've had a chance to evaluate the strength of your and your adversary's cases. If you receive an offer of judgment before you've had a chance to engage in informal investigation or formal discovery (see Chapter 5), consider these responses:

- Ask your adversary to extend your time to reply. An offer may give you as few as ten days to reply, and a request for a month or even longer is reasonable if the offer is made before you've had a chance to investigate.

- If the adversary refuses to extend your time to respond and later asks the judge to order you to pay costs (under FRCP 68 or something similar), explain to the judge that such an order would be unfair because the offer was made at a time when you could not reasonably have been prepared to accept it. (Your argument will be stronger if you can show the judge that you asked for an extension of time to respond to a statutory offer and your adversary refused the request.)

Sample Offer of Judgment

Offer of Judgment

To: Plaintiff Nelly Nolo, in pro per.

Defendant Really Big Corporation offers to allow judgment to be entered against it and in favor of Plaintiff Nelly Nolo in the sum of ten thousand dollars ($10,000) plus costs of suit incurred by Plaintiff to the date of this offer.

This settlement offer is made pursuant to Rule 68 of the Federal Rules of Civil Procedure and Rule 408 of the Federal Rules of Evidence, and is not to be taken as an admission of any liability or wrongdoing on the part of Defendant Really Big Corporation.

This offer shall remain open for ten days after service of the offer on Plaintiff Nolo.

Date: _____

_____
Attorney for Defendant

Pretrial Settlement Conferences

Part of what happens between the time of filing initial pleadings and the start of the trial is that a judge will conduct one or more "pretrial conferences." (See, for example, FRCP 16.) During a pretrial conference (which doesn't usually take place until after you've had a chance to gather documents and evidence), a judge will meet with you and your adversary's lawyer for any of a variety of purposes. For example, a judge may use a pretrial conference to schedule hearings on motions or try to shorten the trial by getting you and your adversary to stipulate (agree) to particular facts. However, probably the main reason that judges schedule pretrial conferences is to facilitate settlements. Rules such as FRCP 16(a) authorize judges to order the attendance (either in person or by telephone) of parties who have the power and authority to settle the case.

The style that judges use to conduct pretrial settlement conferences varies widely. Some judges act much like mediators, trying to facilitate discussion and help the parties arrive at their own settlements. Others take a more active role, sizing up "what a case is worth" and trying to cajole or occasionally even browbeat the parties into a settlement (sometimes by caucusing with each side individually, as mediators often do). Some judges require parties to prepare confidential (not shown to the adversary) "settlement memoranda" justifying their settlement demands or offers. Finally, judges sometimes even ask lawyers to cut their fees to facilitate a settlement.

If you are a self-represented party, obviously you'd like to know in advance what to expect from your judge during a settlement conference. Unfortunately, because these conferences usually take place in judges' private offices (often called chambers), you won't have a chance to watch your judge in action in another case. However, you can consult with your legal coach, who may have experience with the judge or know someone who does. You could also ask a judge's clerk or secretary about a judge's preferred method of conducting a settlement conference.

When thinking about what sort of settlement you would accept, it is important to be realistic about what is likely to happen if your case goes to trial. If you are a plaintiff, ask yourself questions such as:

- "What are my chances of winning?"

"Why don't you fellows go outside and settle this in the parking lot?"

- "How much money am I likely to receive?"
- "How much time and energy will it take to prepare for trial, and how will that affect my business or other activities?"
- "How long will the trial take, and to what extent will it disrupt my life?"
- "Will I have a hard time collecting the judgment if I win?"

If you are a defendant, ask yourself questions such as:

- "What are my chances of winning?"
- "How much time and energy will it take to prepare for trial, and how will that affect my business or other activities?"
- "How long will the trial take, and to what extent will it disrupt my life?"
- "What's the possibility that a judge or jury will order me to pay much more than I could settle for now?"
- "Can the publicity of a lawsuit hurt my reputation or business?"

TIP

If you have limited experience with the court system, get help before going into a settlement conference. As a self-representing party, you may not have enough experience with the legal system to feel that you can answer the above questions with any degree of accuracy. You might ask a legal coach to help you craft a reasonable settlement offer or evaluate the other side's offer.

At a pretrial conference it is easy to feel like an outsider, especially if your adversary is represented by a lawyer. You might even feel as if the judge and your adversary's attorney are ganging up to force you to accept a bad settlement. On the other hand, a judge's experience can help guide you to a settlement outcome that is at least as good as you are likely to achieve at trial. While it's important not to be buffaloed into saying "yes" to a bad settlement, you'll also want to avoid being so angry at your adversary or so emotionally invested in your case that you pass up a chance for a reasonable compromise. Again, a discussion with your legal coach before a settlement conference can guide you toward a realistic settlement outcome.

Pressure to Settle: The Consequences of Saying "No" to a Judge

If you are self-represented, you may be concerned that refusing a settlement a judge is urging you to accept will turn the judge against you at trial. Start by understanding that in many localities the judge who presides over a settlement conference is not the same judge who will preside at trial. In any event, most judges' court rulings will not be affected by your refusal to settle. However, if a judge's behavior or statements during a settlement conference indicate that the judge may have already arrived at an unfair conclusion about your case, the laws of most states allow you to file a Motion to Disqualify, asking that another judge be assigned to preside over your trial. (Attorneys' practice guides, available in a law library, will probably have a sample Motion to Disqualify.)

Post-Settlement Documents

Settlements are typically accompanied by a number of documents. (This is the legal system, after all!) The terms of the settlement may be set forth in a written settlement contract called a Release or a Stipulation for Dismissal. If your adversary's lawyer prepares the contract, it is critical that you read it over carefully and perhaps ask for modifications before signing. A settlement contract is enforceable in court, just like any other kind of contract. And if you later claim that the adversary is not living up to the settlement, then only the written contract, not the oral discussions leading up to it, will establish your rights and obligations.

The language of a release (sometimes also called a General Release or a Release of All Claims) is often quite broad, typically terminating all of plaintiff's claims, existing and unknown, against all existing and potential defendants. Your state may have a law providing that releases do not extend to claims that you don't know about; if so, you'll probably have to waive (give up) that protection in the release agreement.

For example, if you receive $10,000 to settle your personal injury claim, you will probably be asked to sign a release not only on your behalf, but also on behalf of your "heirs, agents, and assigns." In addition, the release will probably state that the settlement covers every possible type of injury, including "personal injuries, property damage, physical disabilities, medical expenses, lost income, loss of consortium, and all other claims that have been or could

have been brought, whether now known or that might become known in the future." It may seem unfair for you to be asked to settle possible claims that you aren't even aware of, but courts routinely uphold this type of broad release language and rely on it to justify barring future lawsuits growing out of the events referred to in the release. Before signing a release, you should be certain of the full extent of your property losses and personal injuries.

EXAMPLE 1: You slip and fall outside a department store, which you then sue for improperly maintaining the sidewalk in front of the store. You agree to drop the suit in exchange for a payment of $5,000 to compensate you for medical expenses of $1,500, lost wages, and "pain and suffering." You sign a broadly worded General Release of All Claims under which you agree to dismiss the lawsuit and irrevocably release the department store from any future claim growing out of your fall. A month later, your doctor tells you that your injuries are not responding as well to treatment as the doctor expected, so you'll need around six months of additional therapy, costing an additional $2,000. You cannot refile the case or seek additional money from the department store. The release terminated all your claims, both known and unknown.

EXAMPLE 2: In the same case, the department store offers to settle your case by paying you $5,000 if you'll dismiss the case and sign a General Release of All Claims. Trying to decide whether to accept the offer, you check with your doctor, who tells you, "At this point I can't be certain how much more treatment you need. Normally, you'd be looking at a few months of therapy costing around $1,500. But you've been a little slow to respond to treatment, so you could be looking at expenses of twice that or even more." In this situation, you should probably ask for additional time to accept or reject the settlement offer, until you have a firmer sense of the extent of your medical bills. If you accept the offer and sign the release, you'll have no recourse if your medical expenses turn out to be greater than you thought.

A Stipulation for Dismissal, when filed with the court, means the case will be terminated, usually "with prejudice." The term "with prejudice" indicates that the case

cannot later be reopened or refiled as a separate action.

Secret Settlements

It is common for a release to require that you keep confidential the amount of money you receive in settlement. For example, a release may state, "This settlement is confidential, and neither party shall disclose the terms of the settlement to anyone, whether orally or in writing. Failure to maintain confidentiality voids the settlement." Such language is especially popular with businesses that fear that public disclosure of settlement terms will encourage litigation. If you want to settle, you'll probably have to agree to confidentiality.

Pretrial Motions

Pretrial motions are written requests for court orders (rulings by a judge) on legal issues. Often, pretrial motions result from disagreements between parties concerning issues that arise in the course of the pretrial investigation (discovery) process. For example, the parties to a lawsuit may disagree about whether certain deposition questions one of the parties seeks to ask are proper. If so, the deposing party may file a motion asking the judge to order that the questions be answered, or the adversary may file a motion asking the judge to rule that the deposition questions are improper and therefore need not be answered.

Parties also commonly file pretrial motions to attack their adversaries' legal claims, often seeking to winnow down legal issues or even to end a case entirely before it goes to trial. For example, either party's Motion for Summary Judgment may ask a judge to make a final ruling on the merits of a case based entirely on evidence provided in written affidavits (statements by parties and witnesses under penalty of perjury) and other documents.

This chapter discusses general motion procedures, common types of pretrial motions, and tips for effectively arguing a motion in a court hearing. As is true for other aspects of pretrial procedures, making and responding to motions (which lawyers and judges typically call "motion practice") can be frustrating and time-consuming. Don't let it daunt you. If your adversary serves you with a pretrial motion, you'll usually have a chance to respond both in writing and orally in a hearing before a judge. And, of course, you may want to file your own motions. In either event, the procedures explained in this chapter will serve as a general guide to motion practice. However, specific procedures vary from one court to another, so check your local rules carefully before making or responding to a motion. (See Chapter 23 for a list of websites that provide court rules.) Finally, be sure to consult a legal coach if you have questions—some motions can dramatically affect the outcome of your case.

Overview of Pretrial Motion Practice

This section provides a brief introduction to motion practice. (For additional background information, see Chapter 4.)

When Do You Make a Motion?

Depending on what you're asking the court to do, a party can make a motion before, during, or after trial. Some motions are made orally and others are made in writing, depending on the rules of court and the type of decision you are asking the judge to make. For example, during trial, parties make oral motions to strike (delete improper testimony from the record). This chapter focuses mainly on motions that arise before trial, most of which must be made in writing. Check the rules in your court to be sure.

Who Can Make a Motion?

Only a named party to the case, such as you or your adversary, may file a motion. Witnesses or other third parties may not make motions.

The Basic Motion Process

Although motion procedures vary from one courthouse or judge to another, the process generally involves these six steps:

1. **Meet and Confer.** Before filing certain types of motions (especially those relating to discovery disputes), court rules may require parties to try to resolve the dispute themselves without involving the court. These rules are generally referred to as "meet and confer" requirements, even though most courts won't require you to actually sit down face to face with your opponent—you can usually "meet" by phone or in correspondence. If you are required to meet and confer, try hard to work something out informally even if it means bending over backwards to be reasonable. Many judges quickly grow frustrated when parties are unable to resolve what seem like trivial procedural disputes. Remember that, as a self-represented party, you are an easy target for a judge's anger, even if you are technically correct.

2. **File and Serve a Notice of Motion.** The moving party (the one making the request, called "Party A" for purposes of this example) serves a written document called a Notice of Motion on the opposing party ("Party B"). At the same time, Party A files a copy of this same notice with the court.

3. **Determine the Contents of the Notice of Motion.** Check your local rules to find out what you need to include in your Notice of Motion (or "the moving papers.") Typically, a Notice of Motion will include:

- A statement of the legal issue that Party A wants the judge to address. For example, in a discovery dispute, the notice may state "Party B refuses to respond to my written interrogatories."
- The ruling that Party A wants the judge to make. For instance, the notice may ask the judge to "Order Party B to answer the interrogatories and also order Party B to pay me for the time and trouble it took me to prepare this motion."
- The date, time, and location when the parties can appear in court to argue the motion orally. Party B would generally be entitled to at least ten days' advance notice of the court hearing, but be sure to check with your local court rules about notice requirements. The parties may also forgo oral argument or conduct the hearing by phone, if the judge agrees.
- Affidavits (sometimes called "declarations"), which are written, factual statements made under oath. Affidavits are essentially "paper testimony"—they consist of information that the "affiant" (the person who signs the affidavit) could testify to in court. The affiant must swear that the facts in the affidavit are true and correct and those facts must concern information that is within the affiant's personal knowledge, such as what the affiant saw or heard. (See Chapter 12 for more information about personal knowledge to be sure you understand

what types of facts may properly be included in an affidavit. See also the sample affidavits set forth later in this chapter.)

- A Memorandum of Points and Authorities, which typically sets forth the statutes (laws), court rules, and possibly cases (appellate court decisions) that constitute the legal justification or authority for the rulings that the moving party wants the judge to make.

4. **File and Serve an Opposition to the Motion.** After being served with Party A's moving papers, Party B (called the "responding party") may then serve and file a written Opposition to the Motion. An opposition typically presents the reasons the judge should not grant Party A's motion. For example, in the discovery dispute example above, Party B may argue that the discovery questions Party A wants answered are improper or that Party B has already sufficiently responded to those questions. Like Party A, Party B may also submit affidavits and a Memorandum of Points and Authorities.

5. **Attend a Court Hearing.** The court may decide the motion without a hearing if the other party doesn't oppose the motion or if the judge feels that the issue is fairly straightforward. If a hearing is scheduled, it is likely to be a relatively short court appearance (often less than 30 minutes) and will be before a judge alone (no jury). A hearing gives you the chance to amplify what you've said in your papers and respond to any questions

the judge may have—so if you have the option of scheduling a hearing, you may want to take that opportunity rather than rely solely on the papers. When you get to the courtroom, ask the court clerk whether the judge has issued a "tentative ruling." A tentative ruling is an informal decision that lets the parties know which way the judge is leaning after reading both sides' written papers, before the hearing starts. Though judges have the power to change their tentative rulings, they don't do so very often. If you have an argument that you want the judge to seriously consider, be sure that you put it in your written papers.

TIP

Be succinct. When judges are deciding motions, they tend to move fairly quickly. After all, the judge has probably already faced these issues before in other cases and may have a long list of motions to decide on the day of your argument. Don't simply repeat—or worse yet, read from—the statements you made in your papers. Instead, make your strongest argument or two, respond briefly to any issues your opponent has raised, and offer to answer any questions the judge might have.

6. **Get the Judge's Ruling.** The judge will issue a ruling granting, modifying, or denying the motion. The judge may rule from the bench as soon as a hearing concludes, or you may receive notice of the ruling by mail some time after the hearing.

Motions Made During and After Trial

These motions can be made during and after trial:

- **Motion in Limine.** A request for a court order excluding irrelevant or prejudicial evidence, typically made at the outset of a jury trial. (See Chapter 17.)
- **Motion to Strike.** A request that the judge delete improper testimony from the trial record. It's usually made after the judge has ruled that particular testimony is not admissible. (See Chapter 17.)
- **Motion for a Directed Verdict.** A request that the judge rule against the plaintiff without letting the matter go to the jury, typically made in a jury trial after the plaintiff has presented evidence. The usual reason is that the plaintiff has not established the legal claims as a matter of law. (See Chapter 20.)
- **Motion for Judgment Notwithstanding the Verdict (JNOV).** A request by one party for the judge to rule against the other party, after the jury has already decided in the other party's favor. This motion effectively asks the judge to overrule the jury's verdict. (See Chapter 20.)

Frivolous Motions

A party must have a valid legal basis for filing a motion.

Some people use motions for reasons other than what they state in their papers—for example, to delay proceedings or to increase their adversary's costs, perhaps in an effort to force their adversary to drop the case or settle cheaply and quickly. Do not do this. Make sure any motion you bring is truthful and that your request is legitimate.

Judges have begun to crack down on frivolous motions (those without a valid legal basis). A party who can show that the other side has filed a frivolous motion may request sanctions (punishment—usually a fine) against both that party and the attorney. If one side files a series of frivolous motions, the judge may even rule that the other side wins the case.

If your adversary has acted outrageously, in a way that prejudices your case, you can make a Motion for Sanctions. For example, you may ask for sanctions if your adversary has asked for repeated continuances seemingly for the purposes of delay or harassment. You might also ask for sanctions if your adversary refused to stipulate and forced you to go to court for a continuance even though you gave an excellent reason (such as your being in the hospital) why the earlier date was not suitable.

Like other motions, a Motion for Sanctions should state what you want and why, and it should include supporting documentation describing what happened, such as a declaration or affidavit, discussed in "What Goes Into a Motion," below. For example, if your adversary repeatedly forces you to come to court on frivolous motions, you may ask the court to order the adversary to pay your expenses for preparing and attending those hearings.

> **CAUTION**
>
> **Don't ask for sanctions unless your adversary's conduct is outrageous.** Sanctions are serious business, and most judges do not impose sanctions unless a party's conduct is fairly outrageous. It makes sense to ask for sanctions only in extreme cases and to be sure of the facts before you make accusations.

Is a Motion Necessary?

Before making a written motion or responding to one made by your adversary, try to informally reach an agreement. For example, if you need to postpone a deadline, you might ask your adversary to agree to a "continuance." If the other side agrees, you can prepare a document called a "Stipulation to Continue [insert name of what's been continued]." Ask the court clerk and check the rules in your court for any special procedures for preparing and filing one. Typically, both you and your adversary must sign the stipulation and file it with the court. If both sides agree, the court will probably grant the continuance without requiring either you or your adversary to appear in court. The clerk will then schedule the matter for a later date, as agreed, and notify the parties of the new date and time.

A sample of a stipulation to continue a hearing on a Motion for Summary Judgment is shown on the following page.

What Goes Into a Motion?

Your motion must tell the court exactly what you want and why you want it. Unfortunately, because legal proceedings are rarely that simple, you must put your request and reasoning in the form the court requires and expects. (Federal Rule of Civil Procedure (FRCP) 7(b) governs the form of motions in federal courts.) This section discusses documents you typically must prepare in order to make a motion.

The Notice of Motion

A legal document called a Notice of Motion gives notice to (informs) your adversary that you are bringing the motion, so that the other side has time to prepare for the court hearing and possibly respond in writing. Your Notice of Motion should tell the other party:

- when the motion will be heard (the date, time, and place of the court hearing)
- the grounds (reasons) for your motion, and
- the supporting documents you will be referring to in your request to the judge, such as "points and authorities" (written legal arguments that support the reasons for your motion with citations to relevant laws), declarations, or affidavits (sworn factual statements).

The Motion

The "motion" itself is your request to the judge for a specific court order. It states what you want and why you are entitled to that particular order. To justify your request, sometimes it's enough to include a short reference to the rule of law that entitles you to the order, especially for routine matters. (See the sample Motion for a Continuance in "Common Pretrial Motions," below.) Other

Sample Stipulation

```
1    SARAH ADAMS
     [Street Address]
2    [City, State, Zip Code]
     [Phone Number]
3
4    Defendant in Pro Per

5

6

7              THE _____ COURT OF _____ COUNTY

8                    STATE OF _____

9

10   Nolo Pedestrian,                    )    Case No. 12345
                                         )
11                        Plaintiff,     )    STIPULATION TO CONTINUE HEARING ON
                                         )    PLAINTIFF'S SUMMARY JUDGMENT MOTION
12        v.                             )
                                         )    Date:  April 15, 20XX
13   Sarah Adams,                        )    Time:  10 a.m.
                                         )    Place: [Court Address]
14                        Defendant.     )           [City, State, Zip Code]
                                         )           [Courtroom 10]
15   _____ )

16

17

18        Defendant Sarah Adams and Plaintiff Nolo Pedestrian agree to the following:

19        The parties jointly request that Plaintiff's Motion for Summary Judgment, set for hearing before

20   this Court on April 15, 20XX, be continued to a date and time convenient to the Court, on or after

21   June 15, 20XX.

22

23

24   Date: March 8, 20XX_____          Sarah Adams_____
                                          Sarah Adams, Defendant in Pro Per
25

26   Date: March 1, 20XX_____         Nolo Pedestrian_____
                                          Nolo Pedestrian, Plaintiff in Pro Per
27

28
```

times, however, especially in more complex motions, you may need to list (cite) other relevant legal authorities, such as court cases, and explain how those authorities support your position. This type of explanation and citation is called a Memorandum of Points and Authorities. (You can find a sample below. But you should consult a legal form book or your legal coach for more on how to prepare this type of document. See Chapter 23.)

Supporting Documentation

As supporting documentation, you may need to include statements of facts in the form of a declaration or affidavit (see sample below). You may also include copies of other relevant documents as exhibits (attachments).

Scheduling a Court Hearing on a Pretrial Motion

Some motions are made, responded to, and ruled on by the judge in writing—all without a court hearing. In some courts, motions can be argued on telephone conference calls. But many times, a party bringing a motion must obtain a court hearing date for the judge to consider and rule on a motion. The court clerk can tell you how to obtain a hearing date in your court. In many places, you schedule a date by phoning the court. The clerk will assign you a hearing time and enter your case on the court docket (calendar) for that day.

When you phone the clerk, be prepared to give your case name and number, the type of motion, and an approximate time you want to schedule the hearing (if you

have a choice). For example, you might say: "Yes, this is Sarah Adams, the defendant in *Pedestrian v. Adams*, Case No. 12345. I would like a court date, if possible in about six weeks, for a Motion for Summary Judgment."

Sometimes courts have a particular time or day of the week devoted solely to hearing motions ("law and motion" day) or special "law and motion" judges (different from the judge who will conduct your trial). When you call, ask the clerk when motions are heard.

CAUTION

Double-check the judge's calendar. Court schedules sometimes change at the last minute. For example, judges sometimes try to clear their calendars (hear routine or uncontested matters first, then move on to disputed and complex proceedings) or otherwise change their calendars around. It is good practice to check with the judge's clerk the day before just to verify the time of your hearing and find out how early you should be there. This may have an extra advantage, too, of showing the clerk that you respect the courtroom routine and appreciate the clerk's help.

Serving and Filing Your Documents

To give your adversary adequate notice, you must often have the papers served at least ten to 15 days before the motion is due to be heard in court. FRCP 6(d) requires notice of at least five days for most types of motions; local rules often extend that time period.

Most courts allow you to serve (deliver) your Notice of Motion, Motion, and related documents by mail. (FRCP 5(a),(b),(c), and your state's equivalent govern how service must be made.) The papers you serve should include a copy of your Proof of Service, which is a signed document stating when, how, and on whom the notice was served. Keep a second copy of the Proof of Service for your records and file the original with the court, as required by your court's rules.

> **TIP**
>
> **You may ask the court for more time to respond to a motion.** If your adversary schedules a motion and gives you less than one week's notice of the hearing date and time, you may want to let the judge know. The judge may reschedule the hearing or reprimand your adversary—especially if you have not had time to respond or prepare. To protect yourself, always note the date you receive documents from your adversary or the court.

Typically, you are not allowed to serve your own documents; check the rules in your court. Often you must have an adult who is not a party to the lawsuit mail or deliver your documents. The person who actually serves your motion for you is the one who should sign the Proof of Service.

In addition, you must typically file originals with the court. (See FRCP 5(d), (e), and the rule in your state that governs filing papers with the court.) You can file legal papers in person at the courthouse Clerk's Office (where you filed your complaint or answer), or you may be able to file documents by mail. Check your local rules and talk to a clerk (or your legal coach) for other rules, such as the number of copies you must file. You should always take an extra copy to the court and ask the clerk to "conform" (stamp the document as filed on the date received) and give it back to you for your files. If you file your documents in person, you can wait for your conformed copy. If you mail the documents, you may need to send an extra copy clearly marked "Please conform and return to [your name and address]" with a self-addressed, stamped envelope.

Court Hearings on Motions

Before a judge grants or denies a written motion, the judge may hold a brief court hearing. There are no jurors and normally no witnesses, although sometimes a judge will want to hear testimony in connection with a complex motion. But, typically, any factual information from you, your adversary, or a witness is presented in the form of a declaration or affidavit—a statement of facts personally observed, which is dated and signed under penalty of perjury.

Some judges issue a tentative ruling, based on the papers you and your adversary have filed, a day or two before the hearing. This ruling will indicate whether the judge is inclined to rule for or against the motion, and might state the reasons for the judge's decision. Ask the court clerk and check the court's local rules to find out whether your judge makes tentative rulings—and to find out any procedures you have to follow to contest the judge's decision.

> ! **CAUTION**
>
> **Find out the rules on tentative rulings.** Some courts, particularly those in busy metropolitan areas, require parties to request a hearing if they want to fight the tentative ruling. These courts may have a hotline you can call to hear a recorded message of the court's tentative rulings, or you may have to call the judge's clerk to find out how the judge has ruled. If the tentative ruling doesn't go your way, you can still show up at the hearing and argue your case—but only if you notify your adversary (and sometimes the court) that you plan to contest the ruling. If you don't give the proper notice, the court will not allow you to present any arguments and will simply adopt its tentative ruling as the final decision on the motion.

On the day of your hearing, the clerk will call out the name of your case when it's your turn. You and your adversary will go to the counsel tables to argue the motion. Whoever brought the motion (called the movant or moving party) will usually argue first. After the movant, the respondent (party responding to the motion) argues. Both sides make points based on the law and the facts, showing why the judge should or should not grant the request. Because the judge already has documents setting out the parties' positions, it is usually unwise to repeat exactly what is in the papers. The whole hearing typically lasts no more than ten to 15 minutes.

Don't be too surprised if the judge has not have read any of the papers you or the other side filed prior to the hearing; just fill in information where it's needed. And, while you may feel pressure to get your points in quickly, make sure you take the time to direct the judge's attention to the most important points or pieces of documentation.

> 💡 **TIP**
>
> **Watch a motion hearing before arguing one.** A good way to get a feel for how to argue a motion is to watch a motion in the court where you will argue before your hearing. Note where people sit and stand, where the microphones are, how much time the judge seems to spend with people, and what types of questions the judge asks. Also, use any time you have before your hearing begins to review your own notes and observe carefully what the judge seems to expect from others arguing before you.

Though a hearing is not a trial, you should observe the same formalities when arguing a motion. Stand when you make your presentation and address the judge as "Your Honor." Don't talk directly to or argue with your adversary (or the adversary's lawyer). (See Chapter 2.)

At the end of the hearing, the judge will often make a final decision, either orally or in writing. Other times the judge may decide to take the matter "under submission." That means the judge will think about it and let you know the ruling later, in writing.

If the judge makes an oral ruling, take detailed notes to be sure you know its exact terms. Also make sure you know who is in charge of writing up the order and notifying all interested parties (people who are affected by the ruling). Sometimes the clerk prepares the order for the judge to sign; other times the judge asks the winning party to draft the order for the judge's signature and notify other parties of the court's ruling. If you are asked to draft an order, refer to your notes and check with the clerk as to exactly what form the notice should take. One good approach is to ask the clerk for a sample and a list of everyone who must be notified.

Who Must Be Notified

In many cases, the notice list (names and addresses of the interested parties who should be notified about court decisions in the case) is relatively short: your adversary and the court. However, a notice list can be quite long. For example, even in the most routine bankruptcy matters, notice of motions must often be given to all creditors (people owed money).

Because notice can be defective (invalid) if the necessary people are not included, find out who must be "noticed" (notified) of specific decisions that arise in your case. Do this by checking your state and local rules about notice (or federal and local rules if you are in federal court). Also, if the judge asks you to draft an order, ask the judge's clerk directly who must be given notice.

 CAUTION

Don't rely on these sample motions. The sample motions in this chapter are illustrations only. To draft (write) a motion in your case and be certain you are using the format and

language required by your court, refer to your local court rules and a legal form book. Form books, often used by lawyers to prepare motions, also contain helpful explanations of the relevant legal references and factual information (called "points and authorities") you may need to include to support the arguments you are making in your motion. (Chapter 23 discusses form books.)

Common Pretrial Motions

This section focuses on four of the most common pretrial motions: motions relating to dismissals, continuances, discovery issues, and summary judgment. It contains sample motion papers and dialogues from court hearings to give you an idea of what may come up when you bring or respond to a motion.

Motion to Dismiss

If a defendant thinks the plaintiff's claims are not legally valid, the defendant can ask the judge to dismiss the complaint before trial. Essentially, the defendant is saying, "Even if everything the plaintiff says in the complaint is true, the plaintiff isn't entitled to anything from me." The defendant makes this request by filing a Motion to Dismiss a Complaint for Failure to State a Claim (in some courts this is called a demurrer, pronounced "de-murr-er").

For example, say the plaintiff's complaint asserts a legal claim of assault, alleging that you gave the plaintiff a menacing look. A look, though perhaps frightening and even rude, does not, by itself, amount to an act for which the plaintiff can bring a valid lawsuit.

Only if you had also taken some threatening action, such as swinging your fist, would the plaintiff have a legally valid claim of assault.

If the motion is denied and the judge finds that the complaint is valid, the defendant will have a short time (often another 30 days) to answer the complaint. If the motion is granted and the complaint is dismissed, the judge may allow the plaintiff a chance to amend (fix), refile, and re-serve the complaint and summons on the defendant.

Motion for a Continuance

The purpose of a Motion for a Continuance is to delay the date of a hearing, settlement conference, deposition, or even the trial itself. For example, if you will be hospitalized for surgery when a motion is supposed to be heard, or if a witness will be out of the country on the date set for trial, you can ask for a continuance.

Some courts routinely grant one continuance, especially if the other side does not object; others want to see a good reason for the delay before they grant a continuance. This may be especially true in courts that have adopted "fast track" or expedited procedures—streamlined systems to move cases along at a faster pace than in traditional systems. You may be granted a continuance if a scheduled surgery causes you to be hospitalized, but denied a continuance if you are simply going on vacation.

If you cannot reach an agreement with your adversary about a postponement, you will need to tell the judge, in your moving papers, why the current date is bad. Next,

point out that you and the other side have discussed the problem. The judge will likely appreciate your efforts to handle the matter in a friendly way.

If you oppose a continuance, emphasize in your opposition papers why a delay would prejudice (hurt) you. For example, you may point out that an important witness will not be available if trial is delayed. Or you may argue that the other side appears to be requesting repeated continuances in an effort to stall or force you to settle.

For example, assume you are Sarah Adams, a building contractor whose truck struck a pedestrian, Nolo Pedestrian, as he crossed Elm and Main Streets. Mr. Pedestrian has sued you; you are the defendant and are representing yourself. You had barely sent your answer (reply to Pedestrian's complaint) when Pedestrian's attorney sent you a Notice of Motion for Summary Judgment (request for the judge to resolve the case without going to trial because the facts are not in dispute).

You believe that Pedestrian's attorney is bringing the motion thinking that you will be easily intimidated as a self-represented party and won't know how to respond. You think the attorney is hoping to get a quick court judgment or advantageous settlement by moving fast, before you get a chance to prepare. All you know for sure is that you were not driving carelessly and that you dispute the plaintiff's claim that you were negligent. In addition, you believe that investigation may reveal that the plaintiff's injuries did not come from your truck, but from some preexisting injury. To oppose the motion, you will need to show that there is a factual dispute that should go to trial. But you need additional time to gather evidence about what really happened. So far, you have not had a chance to conduct any discovery or other investigation.

You should first contact the other side and ask them to agree to continue the hearing to a later date. When you do, they refuse. (Keep records of your request and their refusal.) You are left with two choices:

1. Oppose the summary judgment at its scheduled date and time, with little evidence to back up your legal position.

2. File a Motion for a Continuance of the Summary Judgment Motion, so you have time to find at least enough evidence to show that there is a genuine dispute of facts.

You decide to file the continuance motion. First, you will need to contact the clerk to schedule a hearing date for your motion (see "Scheduling a Court Hearing on a Pretrial Motion," above). Next, you'll need to draft and file several documents and send copies to your adversary.

You will probably have to file with the court (and serve on your opponent) a Notice of Motion and Motion for Continuance. The purpose of these documents is to tell your opponent (in this example the plaintiff, Nolo Pedestrian) that, on the date specified, you will formally ask the judge to delay the date on which the plaintiff's Motion for Summary Judgment will be considered and to extend your deadline for responding to that motion.

You will also need to support your Motion for Continuance with a legal brief (sometimes called a Legal Memorandum or Memorandum of Points and Authorities) that tells the court why you believe you deserve the continuance and what legal rules give the court the authority to grant your request. A sample draft Memorandum of Points and Authorities follows the sample Notice of Motion and Motion, below.

In this case, you will also need to attach a declaration (a sworn, factual statement) that tells the judge why you do not yet have the evidence you need to oppose Plaintiff's Motion for Summary Judgment. Pedestrian is asking the judge to decide the case as a matter of law and is claiming that you both agree on the key facts. In your declaration, you will have to identify facts that you believe are in dispute and indicate what steps you plan to take to gather evidence that will help you prove it. For example, in the sample declaration of Sarah Adams, below, you (Sarah Adams) state that you intend to send interrogatories to the plaintiff and to take a deposition of witness Cynthia White.

After the sample declaration of Sarah Adams, you will find a Proof of Service by Mail, which proves that the defendant sent copies of these documents to the plaintiff's lawyer.

Following these sample papers, you will find samples of the documents that Plaintiff Pedestrian might file in opposition to the motion for a continuance.

Sample Defendant's Notice of Motion and Motion for Continuance

1   SARAH ADAMS
    [Street Address]
2   [City, State, Zip Code]
    [Phone Number]
3
4   Defendant in Pro Per

5

6

7   THE _____ COURT OF _____ COUNTY

8   STATE OF _____

9

10 Nolo Pedestrian,   )   Case No. 12345
)   NOTICE OF DEFENDANT'S MOTION AND
11   Plaintiff,   )   MOTION REQUESTING CONTINUANCE OF
)   PLAINTIFF'S SUMMARY JUDGMENT MOTION:
12   v.   )   MEMORANDUM OF POINTS
)   AND AUTHORITIES
13 Sarah Adams,   )   DECLARATION OF SARAH ADAMS
)
14   Defendant.   )   Date: March 17, 20XX
)   Time: 10 a.m.
15   )   Place: [Court Address]
)   [City, State, Zip Code]
16   )   [Courtroom 10]
    _____)
17

18

19   TO PLAINTIFF AND HIS ATTORNEY(S) OF RECORD:

20   You are notified that on March 17 at 10:00 a.m. in courtroom 10, Defendant Adams will bring a

21 motion to continue Plaintiff's Summary Judgment Motion. Plaintiff's Summary Judgment Motion was

22 originally scheduled for April 15, 20XX. Defendant will move the Court to continue that date at least

23 60 days so that Defendant has adequate time to conduct discovery and respond to Plaintiff's Motion.

24   This Motion is based on the Notice of Motion, the Motion itself, and the attached Declaration of

25 Defendant Adams. Any responses to this Motion must be served not later than March 12, 20XX.

26

27 Date: _March 6, 20XX_____   _Sarah Adams_____
                                        Sarah Adams, Defendant in Pro Per
28

Sample Motion for Continuance

1	<u>MOTION REQUESTING CONTINUANCE OF</u>
2	<u>PLAINTIFF'S SUMMARY JUDGMENT MOTION</u>
3	
4	Defendant Adams moves this Court for an order continuing the hearing on Plaintiff's Summary
5	Judgment Motion, currently scheduled for April 15, 20XX, to a date not less than 60 days after April
6	15, 20XX. In support of this Motion, Defendant asserts:
7	1. Defendant was served on February 28, 20XX, with Plaintiff's Summons and Complaint.
8	2. Defendant was served on March 5, 20XX, with Plaintiff's Notice of Hearing on Summary
9	Judgment Motion scheduled for April 15, 20XX.
10	3. Because Defendant has not had adequate time to conduct discovery, Defendant cannot
11	adequately respond at this time to Plaintiff's Motion.
12	4. Under Federal Rule of Civil Procedure 56(f), and based on the attached Memorandum of Points
13	and Authorities and Supporting Declaration, this Court has discretion to extend the time period in
14	which Defendant must respond to Plaintiff's Motion for Summary Judgment and to continue the
15	hearing date for Plaintiff's Motion.
16	WHEREFORE, Defendant requests that this Court continue the hearing date of Plaintiff's Motion
17	to a date not earlier than 60 days after April 15, 20XX, and extend the amount of time within which
18	Defendant must respond to that Motion accordingly.
19	
20	
21	Date: *March 6, 20XX* *Sarah Adams*
	Sarah Adams, Defendant in Pro Per
22	
23	
24	
25	
26	
27	
28	

Sample Memorandum of Points and Authorities in Support of Motion for Continuance

```
 1   SARAH ADAMS
     [Street Address]
 2   [City, State, Zip Code]
     [Phone Number]
 3
     Defendant in Pro Per
 4

 5

 6

 7                    THE _____ COURT OF _____ COUNTY

 8                       STATE OF _____

 9

10   Nolo Pedestrian,                    )
                                         )   Case No. 12345
11                        Plaintiff,     )
                                         )   MEMORANDUM OF
12        v.                             )   POINTS AND AUTHORITIES
                                         )
13   Sarah Adams,                        )
                                         )
14                        Defendant.     )
     _____ )
15

16

17        LEGAL MEMORANDUM IN SUPPORT OF MOTION REQUESTING CONTINUANCE

18

19                            STATEMENT OF FACTS

20      Plaintiff Nolo Pedestrian has filed a Motion for Summary Judgment, which is now scheduled to be

21   heard on April 15, 20XX. Defendant Sarah Adams has filed this Motion for Continuance asking that

22   this Court postpone the hearing on the Summary Judgment Motion for at least 60 days.

23

24                        STATEMENT OF LEGAL AUTHORITY

25      For cause shown in the Declaration of Sarah Adams attached hereto, and under the authority of

26   Federal Rule of Civil Procedure 56(f), this Court has the power and discretion to extend Defendant's

27   time to respond to Plaintiff's Motion for Summary Judgment and to continue the hearing date for

28   Plaintiff's Motion.
```

Sample Memorandum of Points and Authorities (continued)

1   <u>ARGUMENT IN SUPPORT OF MOTION REQUESTING CONTINUANCE</u>

2   A postponement of the hearing on Plaintiff's Motion for Summary Judgment is appropriate and

3 necessary because Defendant needs to have an opportunity to conduct discovery in order to develop

4 evidence with which to oppose the Motion. Plaintiff filed the Summary Judgment Motion before

5 Defendant had a chance to send out written interrogatories or conduct any other investigation.

6

7   <u>CONCLUSION</u>

8   For the reasons and based on the law set forth above, Defendant is entitled to a continuance of the

9 hearing on Plaintiff's Motion for Summary Judgment to a date that is not less than 60 days after April

10 15, 20XX.

11   Respectfully submitted:

12

13 Date: _March 6, 20XX_____   _Sarah Adams_____

14   Sarah Adams, Defendant in Pro Per

15

16

17

18

19

20

21

22

23

24

25

26

27

28

Sample Declaration of Defendant in Support of Motion for Continuance

<u>DECLARATION OF SARAH ADAMS</u>

I, Sarah Adams, declare under penalty of perjury:

1. I am the Defendant in the case of Pedestrian v. Adams (Case No. 12345) currently pending in the

_____ Court of _____ County

in the State of _____, and I am acting as my own attorney.

2. On February 28, 20XX, I received Plaintiff's Summons and Complaint.

3. On March 5, 20XX, I received notice of Plaintiff's Summary Judgment Motion, originally

scheduled for April 15, 20XX.

4. As of March 5, 20XX, when I received the notice, I had not yet had time to take any discovery to

obtain information I need to adequately defend myself in the pending case.

5. I intend to send at least one set of interrogatories to Plaintiff. I also plan to depose Cynthia

White, a witness at the scene of the accident.

6. On March 5, I phoned Plaintiff's lawyer and explained to her that I need additional time

to conduct and complete this discovery so that I can adequately respond to Plaintiff's Summary

Judgment Motion. Plaintiff's lawyer refused to agree to a continuance.

7. After Plaintiff refused my request to continue the Summary Judgment Motion, I prepared this

Motion for Continuance and had it set for the earliest available court date, March 17, 20XX.

I declare under penalty of perjury that the foregoing is true and correct.

Date: *March 6, 20XX*

Sarah Adams
Sarah Adams, Defendant in Pro Per

Sample Proof of Service by Mail

1	SARAH ADAMS [Street Address]
2	[City, State, Zip Code] [Phone Number]
3	
4	Defendant in Pro Per
5	
6	
7	THE _____ COURT OF _____ COUNTY
8	STATE OF _____
9	
10	Nolo Pedestrian,)
11	Plaintiff,) Case No. 12345
12	v.) DECLARATION OF SERVICE BY MAIL
13	Sarah Adams,)
14	Defendant.)
15	
16	
17	Ms. Dana Lauren, the undersigned, declares:
18	I am a citizen of the United States. I am over the age of 18 years and not a party to this action. On
19	March 6, 20XX, at the direction of Sarah Adams, Defendant in Pro Per, I served the within NOTICE OF
20	DEFENDANT'S MOTION AND MOTION REQUESTING CONTINUANCE OF PLAINTIFF'S SUMMARY
21	JUDGMENT MOTION; DECLARATION OF SARAH ADAMS on the following interested party by
22	mailing, with postage thereon fully prepaid, a true copy thereof to: Loretta Charles, Esq.
23	Attorney for Nolo Pedestrian [Street Address]
24	[City, State, Zip Code]
25	I declare under penalty of perjury that the foregoing is true and correct.
26	Executed at [City, State] on the 6th day of March 20XX.
27	*Dana Lauren*
28	Dana Lauren

Sample Plaintiff's Opposition to Motion for Continuance

1 LORETTA CHARLES, Esq.
   [Street Address]
2 [City, State, Zip Code]
   [Phone Number]
3
4 Attorney for Nolo Pedestrian, Plaintiff
5
6
7 THE _____ COURT OF _____ COUNTY
8 STATE OF _____
9
10 Nolo Pedestrian,   ) Case No. 12345
)
11   Plaintiff,   ) NOTICE OF OPPOSITION TO DEFENDANTS
) MOTION REQUESTING CONTINUANCE OF
12   v.   ) PLAINTIFF'S SUMMARY JUDGMENT MOTION
)
13 Sarah Adams,   ) Date: March 17, 20XX
) Time: 10 a.m.
14   Defendant.   ) Place: [Court Address]
)   [City, State, Zip Code]
15   )   [Courtroom 10]
)
16 _____   )
17
18 TO DEFENDANT ADAMS, IN PRO PER:
19   Plaintiff objects to Defendant's Motion to Continue Plaintiff's Summary Judgment Motion
20 originally scheduled for April 15, 20XX. Defendant has had ample time to investigate. The facts are
21 clear and not in dispute, and the Court's and parties' time would be greatly economized by going
22 forward with the motion on the date and time scheduled. This Notice of Opposition to Defendant's
23 Motion is based on the Notice itself and the attached Declaration of Plaintiff Pedestrian.
24
25
26 Date: *March 9, 20xx*   *Loretta Charles*
                                             Attorney for Plaintiff Nolo Pedestrian
27
28

Sample Declaration of Plaintiff in Opposition to Motion for Continuance

<u>DECLARATION OF NOLO PEDESTRIAN</u>

I, Nolo Pedestrian, declare under penalty of perjury:

1. I am the Plaintiff in the case of Pedestrian v. Adams (Case No. 12345) currently pending in the

_____ Court of _____ County

in the State of _____.

2. On or about February 28, 20XX, I caused Defendant Sarah Adams to be served with a Complaint and Summons.

3. On or about March 5, 20XX, I caused Defendant Sarah Adams to be served with a Notice of Motion and Motion for Summary Judgment.

4. Defendant has had approximately 10 days from the date she received the Complaint, and nearly two years since the accident occurred, to investigate this case.

5. The facts are clear and undisputed in this simple negligence action. They are set out in the Summary Judgment Motion and the declarations supporting the motion, which were filed with this Court on or about March 5, 20XX.

The above is true and correct to the best of my knowledge.

Date: _March 8, 20XX_   _Nolo Pedestrian_____
                                       Nolo Pedestrian, Plaintiff

The date for the hearing on the continuance motion arrives. You arrive in court a few minutes early, dressed in business attire. You check in with the clerk, giving your name and the case name and number. You then wait until your case is called. Finally, you hear the clerk or judge say "Nolo Pedestrian v. Sarah Adams. Are the parties present?" If you and your adversary have both checked in, the clerk may tell the judge that you are here. You both stand to signify your presence. When the judge calls or motions for you to approach, you take your places at your respective counsel tables.

In this instance, you are the moving party (the one making the motion), so you will likely be called on first. Typically the judge will ask what you have to say. Here's what might follow:

1 **You (Moving Party):**
Good morning, Your Honor. I am Sarah Adams, the defendant in this matter. I am a building contractor here in [city], and I am representing myself. The reason I am requesting a continuance is simple. The plaintiff scheduled a summary judgment motion two weeks after my answer was filed. I have not had time to thoroughly investigate the case. I plan to serve interrogatories on the plaintiff. I will also probably take one or more depositions. I feel strongly that once I have investigated more thoroughly, I will be able to demonstrate that I was not careless.

2 **Judge:**
This is not trial, and I don't want to hear arguments or testimony.

3 **You:**
Your Honor, I was merely trying to say that I think I will be able to show very soon that there are significant factual disputes, but I need more time. This summary judgment motion is premature. And having to go forward with one now would unfairly prejudice my right to a fair hearing in this case.

As you see by the judge's comment, the judge may interrupt to ask questions or steer you toward the proper issues. Here the judge may continue with questions about the discovery you plan to take, the facts as you know them right now, or whether you have tried to get the opposing party to stipulate to a continuance. The judge may also turn to your adversary.

4 **Judge:**
What are your objections to such a continuance?

5 **Your adversary (Responding Party):**
Your Honor, as stated in our papers, we feel the defendant has had ample time to conduct discovery. We have not been served with any interrogatories or received notice about any depositions. We don't believe the defendant really intends to conduct any discovery. The defendant just wants to try to keep this matter pending as long as possible to force a settlement. My client is injured….

6 **Judge:**
Do you have any response?

7 **You:**
Well, yes, Your Honor. That is simply not true. I have no hidden agenda of

forcing a settlement. I just want to be treated fairly and to have sufficient time to prepare. My adversary is represented by counsel, but I am not a lawyer and I am not as familiar with all of the legal proceedings. I have been working on interrogatory questions and will get them out as soon as I possibly can. Just 60 more days, which can't possibly hurt them, would be most helpful for me to get the facts straight and know how to respond to the summary judgment motion.

8 Judge:

Motion granted. Defendant will have an additional 60 days to respond to the plaintiff's summary judgment motion.

If the judge rules your way, don't allow your elation to get in the way of your need to clarify some key information. You need to record the exact date and time to which the hearing is continued and find out whether, as the victorious party, you will be responsible for preparing the court order (the document, signed by the judge, that officially changes the date of the hearing).

Discovery Motions

If problems arise during discovery, you or your adversary may need to go to the judge with a motion asking the court to order the other side to comply with discovery requests. If you send interrogatories, for example, and your adversary refuses to answer one or more of them, you can file a motion asking that the judge compel an answer—a Motion to Compel. If a party that is ordered to answer still refuses to do so, the judge can impose sanctions (a fine) or hold that party in contempt of court. "Contempt of court" usually means imposing a fine or even a short jail sentence on the party that continues to refuse to comply with a court order.

The flip side of a Motion to Compel is called a Motion for a Protective Order—an order allowing you not to answer certain questions. (In federal courts, these orders are allowed under FRCP 26(c) and 30(d).) A party can seek a Protective Order if the other side's discovery request causes undue annoyance, embarrassment, oppression, or expense, or if the other side is seeking privileged or otherwise confidential information.

 TIP

Try to get your adversary to agree before you file a motion. Before filing a motion to either compel a response to discovery or to get a protective order (to avoid having to respond to discovery), try to reach an agreement with your adversary. For example, if your adversary doesn't respond adequately to your interrogatories, don't rush into court. Instead, try to work out the problem—perhaps by rephrasing the questions. You might even write a formal letter setting forth why you believe you have a right to the information (if they are objecting) or why you feel you should not have to reveal the information (if you are objecting to your adversary's discovery requests).

A persuasive letter indicates that you mean business and are not willing to drop the issue, and it may resolve the dispute. And if your negotiations ultimately fail and you eventually bring a motion, the letter (which you can attach as an exhibit to the motion) shows the judge that you attempted to resolve the matter without costing the court time and money, but that the other side simply refused to cooperate.

You may want to consult your legal coach before answering questions to see if they are improper. But it is generally improper to ask questions that do any of the following:

- Force someone to reveal a confidential, privileged communication, such as a statement made to a lawyer during a lawyer-client consultation, to a doctor during a medical examination, or to a spouse.

- Require an enormous amount of time, money, or other resources to comply with. For example, if you are a small business owner asked to produce every piece of paper you signed having to do with your employees for the past three years, you could ask your adversary to confine the request to a shorter, more relevant time period or otherwise narrow it.

- Harass your adversary rather than discover some admissible evidence—for example, a question about sexual history or a possible past criminal record.

- Ask for information that's not relevant to the case. Although the standard for relevance in discovery is much looser than in the trial itself, neither you nor your adversary can seek information about matters that are totally unrelated to the case.

(FRCP 37 and your state's equivalents govern discovery disputes.)

If the court finds you have shown good cause for a Protective Order, the judge can help you out in a variety of ways, from blocking your adversary's entire discovery request to limiting the people who must attend a deposition, sealing (keeping confidential, out of the public record) the discovery, or otherwise narrowing the request.

TIP

Resolve discovery disputes with a phone call if you can. Because discovery problems are frequent, and going to court to resolve them is expensive and wasteful, many courts have established a phone-conference procedure so that a judge can quickly resolve such disputes. Check with the court clerk or your judge's clerk to see if such a procedure is available in your case.

If you are initiating a Motion to Compel, you probably need the information and believe your request is reasonable. Your papers must tell the judge why this is true. Usually this means explaining that the request will lead you to relevant evidence in your case and that it will not hurt or unfairly prejudice your adversary to reveal it.

If you are opposing your adversary's motion, you need to give the judge a good reason why you should not have to turn over the information requested—for example, on the contrary to the arguments above, the information is totally irrelevant, privileged, or unfairly prejudicial to your case.

For example, say a request asks you to describe each and every conversation you've had with your business partner, Edwin, during the past ten years. Especially if you and Edwin do business on a daily basis, putting together the description requested would be nearly impossible. In this case, you will at least want to have the request narrowed down.

Here's an example of oral arguments in the case of the auto accident at Elm and Main, Nolo Pedestrian v. Sarah Adams. This time, assume that you are the plaintiff. You were crossing the street when the defendant's truck hit you. You are trying to prove that the defendant, a building contractor, had gotten a phone call reporting a missed job site inspection just before the accident occurred. At trial, you plan to argue that the call caused her to be distracted and drive carelessly. As part of your discovery, you have requested these documents:

- records pertaining to all other traffic accidents in which she has been involved, to see whether she has had other similar accidents
- business books and records from her business, to determine how common missed inspections are, and how much money is at stake because of a missed inspection, and
- her phone bill for that month, to verify the exact time the inspection phone call was received.

You served Defendant with a Request for Production of Documents asking for driving and business records. She refused to produce these documents because she is represented by a lawyer who is trying to bully you. You get the feeling they think that if they refuse your discovery requests, you won't know what to do and may just give up without fighting. But you have confidence

in yourself (and you have this book), so you fight back. You bring a Motion to Compel the production of the requested documents.

Before you can go to court, of course, you have to get a hearing date and draft, file, and serve your Motion to Compel, as described above.) When your hearing date arrives, after you check in and wait for your case, your hearing may proceed as follows:

1 Judge:

Mr. Pedestrian, I have read your papers, and you have undoubtedly seen my tentative ruling. I am inclined to grant your request as to the business records and phone bill and order Ms. Adams to produce them immediately. But I am going to deny the driving record request. Do you wish to add to your written arguments?

2 You (Plaintiff Pedestrian):

Yes, Your Honor. I would ask that the court also order the respondent to produce the driving records. It is essential to my case to see how many other people have suffered from her negligence in the past.

3 Judge (turning to the Respondent/ Defendant):

Do you have any response?

4 Ms. Miller, Defendant's attorney (Respondent):

Yes. As Your Honor knows, such evidence, even if it existed, would be inadmissible evidence of prior acts —not to mention irrelevant to what happened on the day of the accident in question. We should not be required to produce that driving record now or ever, and we strongly urge

*that your tentative ruling be made final
as to that issue.*

[For more on why such evidence would
not be admissible in court, see Chapter 16.]

5 Judge:

*So ordered. Ms. Adams does not have
to produce her driving records. Now,
as to the business records and phone
bill. Respondent, do you have any good
reason why the movant should not be
allowed to inspect these?*

6 Ms. Miller:

*Again Your Honor, these records
are irrelevant to the case. My client's
business had nothing to do with the
accident. The plaintiff ran in front of my
client's truck, she tried to swerve, but…*

7 Judge:

*This is not the trial. I am not going to
hear evidence today. Your client has her
version, and the plaintiff has his. Unless
you can tell me why he should not be
allowed to fully investigate his theory,
which includes reviewing your business
records, I will order you to produce them.*

8 Ms. Miller:

*Your Honor, even if you were to believe
my client's business records are relevant,
which we contend they are not, the
plaintiff's request is too broad. He has
asked for all my client's business records
from the past five years. If he is really
just concerned about the cost of missed
inspections, then at least we would
ask that you limit the request to those
inspections we missed during the month
of the accident only. Otherwise, their
request will put my client out of business.*

*She'll have to spend all her time going
through back records and will lose many
new projects because of it.*

9 Judge (turning to you):

Any response?

10 You:

*Nothing I haven't written in my papers,
Your Honor. The defendant's business
records are essential for me to prove
how much the fact that she missed an
inspection that day distracted her and
caused her to be careless. We must look
at one year's worth of figures, at the very
least, to make an accurate….*

11 Judge:

*Okay, I will allow the request but limit it
to the six months before the accident and
to only those documents directly related
to missed site inspections. Movant, will
you draft the order and give notice?*

12 You:

Yes, Your Honor, I will prepare the order.

To follow up on exactly how the order
should read, you might say something like
this:

13 You

*Your Honor, could you please review
your exact order and possibly have your
clerk give me a sample? I have never
prepared an order, and I want to be sure
it is correct.*

14 Judge:

*The clerk can assist you as to the
format and, again, my order was that
your request for the driving records is
denied. The request for the phone bill
was granted, and the request for the*

business records was granted in part. Defendant is ordered to produce all business records pertaining to missed inspections in the past six months and the phone bill in questions. Next matter on calendar, Jack v. Jill.

Motion for Summary Judgment

One of the primary functions of a trial is for a judge or jury to decide which party's account of the events leading up to a lawsuit is accurate. If you can show that the important facts are undisputed and that those facts entitle you to a judgment in your favor, you may want to file a Motion for Summary Judgment. A summary judgment motion asks a judge to decide the case in your favor based on the information contained in your motion. If the judge grants your motion, you win the case "on the papers," without it ever going to trial. The judge's decision carries the same weight as a verdict following a full-blown trial. In other words, summary judgment happens instead of trial: If a judge decides the case in your favor on summary judgment, you win the case right then and there. If the judge denies your motion, the case continues on to trial unless it settles first.

By the same token, if your adversary files a Motion for Summary Judgment, you may have to oppose it to avoid losing without having the opportunity to go to trial. You can appeal a judge's granting of your opponent's summary judgment motion, just as you can appeal an adverse judgment following a trial. (For more information about the appeal process, see Chapter 20.)

TIP

Try to settle the case before filing a summary judgment motion. Before going to court on a Motion for Summary Judgment, you should try to settle. Especially if you and your adversary agree on the most important facts, this may be a good time to try to resolve the case without either of you having to spend the time or money it takes to go to court.

You may also consider filing a Motion for Summary Judgment if you can show that the adversary's evidence, even if believed, is insufficient to support one or more of the essential elements of a legal claim. (See FRCP 56(c), which provides for summary judgment when "there is no genuine issue as to any material fact and … the moving party is entitled to judgment as a matter of law.")

For instance, assume that Mary sues you for breach of contract. You are a wholesaler, and Mary claims that you failed to deliver merchandise that she planned to sell at retail. Though you disagree with Mary's claim that you and she had finalized a contract, you have learned through discovery that Mary was able to get the same merchandise from another wholesaler at the price and on the schedule that she claims you agreed to. Because Mary has the burden of proving "damages," and you can show that any failure on your part to deliver merchandise did not harm her business in any way, you should file a Motion for Summary Judgment asking the judge to decide the case in your favor. (See Chapter 8 for more information about essential elements of legal claims.)

Pros and Cons of Filing a Summary Judgment Motion

Like most things in life, filing a Motion for Summary Judgment has benefits and disadvantages. Consider these pros and cons carefully before you decide to file.

Potential benefits

- Your dispute may be completely or partially resolved long before a trial would take place, thus saving you time and money.
- Helpful witnesses may be unavailable by the time your case goes to trial. But if they are willing to sign a declaration that you attach to your summary judgment motion, you can present their testimony to the judge in written form.
- If your witnesses are likely to be nervous when testifying orally in court, the evidence that they provide may seem more impressive in a written affidavit than if they were to testify at trial.

- Even if a judge refuses to grant your motion, the motion may emphasize weaknesses in your opponent's case, which may in turn lead to a more agreeable offer of settlement.

Potential drawbacks

- A Motion for Summary Judgment takes time to prepare and can be complex, because you have to include not only declarations but also legal arguments in a supporting Memorandum of Points and Authorities (or Legal Memorandum).
- You and your witnesses' declarations may reveal information that your adversary doesn't know about, thus giving your adversary time to prepare to oppose it if your motion is denied and the case goes to trial. Also, if a witness's trial testimony differs from what the witness said in a declaration, your adversary can offer the declaration into evidence at trial to cast doubt on the witness's testimony.

CAUTION

! **Lawyers may file summary judgment motions to intimidate self-represented parties.** For instance, your opponent's lawyer may claim that no facts are in dispute when plenty really are. Don't fall for this. Assess the facts on both sides and, if you continue to believe that you have a genuine dispute about what happened, fight the motion by filing an Opposition to the Motion for Summary Judgment. Include in your opposition a written description of the factual disputes that you believe exist, supported with as much evidence as you can muster in written affidavits or declarations. You may want to stress the legal policy favoring a party's right to go to trial, clearly explaining why a trial is needed to resolve the factual disputes. For example, let the judge know that a trial is necessary because a witness whose affidavit your adversary counts on is biased and has made conflicting statements about what happened.

Summary judgment can be an especially cost-effective and useful tool if your dispute centers around a written document, such as a lawsuit for breach of a written contract. The judge can review the written contract, assess both parties' written affidavits and arguments, and make a decision. Cases that may not be as well suited to summary judgment are those in which a judge or jury needs to decide what someone's intentions were or whether to believe an important witness. It may be harder to make a fair and accurate decision "on the papers" in such a situation because the judge has no opportunity to observe witnesses and evaluate their demeanor and credibility.

Partial Summary Judgment

If you and your adversary don't agree about everything that happened but agree on the key facts relating to a specific legal claim, that claim may be decided on a Motion for Partial Summary Judgment. If the judge grants partial summary judgment, that claim is resolved, and only the remaining claims would be decided at trial. For example, assume that your adversary sues you for breach of contract and defamation. If appropriate, you might file a Motion for Partial Summary Judgment asking the judge to decide the defamation claim in your favor. If the judge grants your motion, only the claim for breach of contract would remain to be tried. Partial summary judgment can save both time and money because any trial you do have will be shorter. Moreover, partial summary judgment often pushes adversaries towards settlement.

Like the other motions discussed in this chapter, a Motion for Summary Judgment typically includes a Notice of Motion and Motion, a Memorandum of Points and Authorities, affidavits or declarations (sworn statements providing relevant information based on firsthand knowledge), and contracts or other exhibits (such as helpful answers in a deposition transcript or responses to written interrogatories). You will have no opportunity to put on or cross-examine live witnesses.

Some jurisdictions also require parties to submit a Statement of Uncontroverted Facts—a document that lists each important fact that the parties agree on as well as the exact source of evidence that proves that fact (such as the page and line number of a deposition transcript in which a witness testified to the fact). You will probably have to attach copies of any documents or testimony that you rely on to prove these facts. For example, if you state that your opponent admitted a crucial fact in deposition, attach the page(s) of the deposition transcript containing the admission. Be sure to check your court's local rules to find out exactly what must be included in either a Motion for Summary Judgment or in an Opposition to the Motion for Summary Judgment. Courts are very fussy about these motions and it's important to follow the procedural rules.

If you want to go to trial and do not want the judge to make a final decision based on the papers alone, you will be the party opposing summary judgment. To oppose your adversary's summary judgment motion, you must show that one or more important facts are disputed, or that a court hearing is required to evaluate crucial evidence. For instance, if you contend that a fair decision in the case depends on whose version of events the court believes, you will want to stress that the credibility (believability) of particular witnesses is important and that the only way to properly determine who to believe is to see and hear the witnesses in person.

If you are opposing a Motion for Summary Judgment, your most important job will be preparing an opposition to your adversary's Statement of Uncontroverted Facts. Generally, you should go through your adversary's statement fact by fact, admitting those that are not in dispute and contesting those that are. For example, if your adversary says "The defendant was driving a white Ford Pinto on Main Street, at approximately 3 p.m. on May 5th, 20XX. Defendant ran a red light at the corner of Main Street and Avenue A," you might admit that you were driving the car at that time and place, but dispute that you ran the red light. Include evidence to back up your version of any facts you dispute. In the above example, you might refer to your own affidavit, in which you state that you did not run the red light, or you might refer to the deposition of a witness who testified that you appeared to have the green light when you crossed the intersection.

CAUTION

It depends what the meaning of "is" is. When you draft declarations or affidavits, write your facts in a convincing manner, but be very careful not to shade the truth. Declarations are "paper testimony." In other words, just as at trial, declarations are made under penalty of perjury, and they must be based on personal knowledge. If you submit a declaration that includes a statement not based on your personal knowledge, the judge will probably just disregard that statement. But if you submit declarations that contain false or misleading statements, you risk sanctions or worse. And, if you have to try the case before the same judge who decides your motion, you will be digging yourself out of a very deep hole for your lack of candor. (Before trying to draft a declaration, you may want to refer to the sample declarations in this chapter and study the material on personal knowledge in Chapter 12 of this book.)

If you refer to information contained in a different document, be sure to attach a copy of the relevant portion of the document so that the judge can quickly and easily find the source of your information. (For example, in the sample declaration of Sarah Adams below, Adams attaches a document that supports a statement she makes in her declaration.)

Below are sample motion papers and declarations that parties might file in support of and in opposition to a request for summary judgment. The sample forms are accompanied by a transcript of the courtroom hearing that might take place in conjunction with the summary judgment request. The sample forms and hearing transcript relate to the plaintiff seeking summary judgment in the sample case discussed earlier, the car accident in which a pedestrian was allegedly injured after being struck by the truck of the defendant, contractor Sarah Adams. In the sample dialogue that follows, Sarah Adams, who is representing herself, is opposing the plaintiff's motion.

Sample Plaintiff's Notice of Motion and Motion for Summary Judgment

1	LORETTA CHARLES, Esq.
	[Street Address]
2	[City, State, Zip Code]
	[Phone Number]
3	
4	Attorney for Nolo Pedestrian, Plaintiff
5	
6	
7	THE _____ COURT OF _____ COUNTY
8	STATE OF _____
9	
10	Nolo Pedestrian,) Case No. 12345
11	) NOTICE OF MOTION AND MOTION BY
	Plaintiff,) PLAINTIFF FOR SUMMARY JUDGMENT;
12	v.) MEMORANDUM OF POINTS AND AUTHORITIES;
	) DECLARATION OF NOLO PEDESTRIAN
13	Sarah Adams,)
	) Date: March 17, 20XX
14	Defendant.) Time: 10 a.m.
	) Place: [Court Address]
15	) [City, State, Zip Code]
	) [Courtroom 10]
16	_____)
17	
18	TO DEFENDANT SARAH ADAMS IN PRO PER:
19	NOTICE IS HEREBY GIVEN that on April 15 at 10 a.m., or as soon thereafter as the matter can be
20	heard, in courtroom 10 of the Court, located at [*address of court*], Plaintiff Nolo Pedestrian will and
21	hereby does move for an Order Granting Summary Judgment in favor of Plaintiff.
22	The motion is made on the grounds that there is no triable issue of fact as to liability, and therefore
23	the moving party is entitled to judgment on the issue of liability as a matter of law. The motion will be
24	based on the Notice, the attached Declaration of Nolo Pedestrian, and the attached Memorandum of
25	Points and Authorities.
26	
27	Date: *March 5, 20xx* *Loretta Charles*
28	Loretta Charles, Esq.
	Attorney for Plaintiff Nolo Pedestrian

Sample Memorandum of Points and Authorities

<u>MEMORANDUM OF POINTS AND AUTHORITIES</u>

<u>IN SUPPORT OF PLAINTIFF'S MOTION FOR SUMMARY JUDGMENT</u>

Plaintiff Nolo Pedestrian submits the following legal authorities in support of his Motion for Summary Judgment:

1. A plaintiff may seek summary judgment at any time after 20 days from the time a lawsuit commenced. Federal Rules of Civil Procedures, Rule 56(a).

2. The Court has the power to grant summary judgment to Plaintiff on the issue of liability and leave open the issue of the damages that will be awarded to Plaintiff. Federal Rules of Civil Procedure, Rule 56(c).

3. The Court shall render a partial judgment in Plaintiff's favor if there is no genuine issue as to any material fact and Plaintiff is entitled to judgment as a matter of law. Federal Rules of Civil Procedure, Rule 56(c).

Date: _March 5, 20xx_

Respectfully submitted,

Loretta Charles
Loretta Charles, Esq.
Attorney for Plaintiff Nolo Pedestrian

Sample Declaration of Plaintiff in Support of Summary Judgment

DECLARATION OF NOLO PEDESTRIAN

I, Nolo Pedestrian, declare under penalty of perjury:

1. I am the Plaintiff in the case of Pedestrian v. Adams (Case No. 12345) currently pending in the

_____ Court of _____ County in the State of _____.

2. On March 31, 20XX, at about 3:00 p.m., I began to cross Elm Street at its intersection with Main Street.

3. There is a marked crosswalk on the southern side of Main Street at the Elm Street intersection, and I was in the crosswalk when I began to cross Elm Street.

4. While I was crossing Elm Street in the crosswalk, I was struck by a truck driven by Defendant Sarah Adams.

5. Just before I was struck by the truck, I saw Defendant Sarah Adams talking on a cellular telephone while she was driving.

6. I am familiar with Main Street, and I know that the posted speed limit along Main Street is 25 m.p.h.

7. I saw the truck that Defendant Sarah Adams was driving for a few seconds before it hit me. I estimate that the defendant was driving the truck at a speed of at least 35 m.p.h. at the time she slammed on the brakes.

I declare under penalty of perjury that the foregoing is true and correct.

Date: *March 5, 20XX*   Signed: *Nolo Pedestrian*
                                        Nolo Pedestrian, Plaintiff

Sample Declaration of Defendant in Opposition to Plaintiff's Summary Judgment Motion

<u>DECLARATION OF SARAH ADAMS</u>

I, Sarah Adams, declare under penalty of perjury:

1. I am the Defendant in the case of Pedestrian v. Adams (Case No. 12345) currently pending in the _____ Court of _____ County in the State of _____ .

2. I oppose Plaintiff's Motion for Summary Judgment because I disagree with Plaintiff Nolo Pedestrian's claims as to how the accident occurred.

3. On March 31, 20XX, at about 3 p.m., I was driving my truck near the intersection of Main and Elm Streets.

4. At around 3 p.m. I received a cell phone call, which I answered, engaging in a routine business conversation that lasted two minutes. (See phone bill from my cell phone provider, a copy of which is attached to this Declaration as "Exhibit A," which states the time and duration of the phone call in question.) (*Note to Readers: Exhibit A is not included in this illustration.*)

5. The phone call did not distract or upset me. I watched the road carefully while I talked on the phone, and I obeyed all traffic laws.

6. Within moments after my cell phone call ended, I saw Plaintiff dart out into the street from between two parked cars.

7. The moment I saw Plaintiff, I put on my brakes and stopped the truck as fast as possible, but not fast enough to avoid hitting Plaintiff.

8. I immediately got out of my truck to check on Plaintiff's condition. I then ran back into my truck to phone the police and notify them of the accident.

9. I then got out of my truck again and stayed with Plaintiff until the police arrived.

I declare under penalty of perjury that the foregoing is true and correct.

Date: *March 15, 20XX*   Signed: *Sarah Adams*
                                              Sarah Adams, Defendant in Pro Per

1   Judge:

I have the plaintiff's summary judgment motion and the defendant's opposition to that motion here. Unless you, Ms. Adams, can tell me why I should not, I intend to grant the plaintiff's motion and decide this case as a matter of law based on the facts presented to me. It seems to me that the facts are not disputed and that it is in the interests of efficiency and all parties involved for me to decide the legal questions now, without proceeding to trial.

2   Adams:

Your Honor, it is true there is some evidence we both agree to. We both agree that my truck hit the plaintiff at Elm and Main. But there are several other very important facts about which we don't agree.

First, the plaintiff was injured only slightly by my truck. According to Dr. Even's affidavit, which I've included in my opposition papers, the plaintiff's serious injury, the one he really wants money for, was a preexisting injury. The plaintiff's declaration states that injury was caused by my truck hitting him. We clearly have a fact dispute, and Your Honor [or the jury, if you will have one] must listen to all the evidence and decide who is right.

Second, the plaintiff contends that I was distracted and not paying attention to the road at the time of the accident. But, as I submitted in my sworn declaration, this is not true. I was driving especially carefully at the time, because I had expensive kitchen cabinets in my truck. My statement shows that I

was only going 15 m.p.h. Then, without warning, the plaintiff dashed out from between two parked cars. These are crucial questions of fact, and they need to be decided in trial.

3   Plaintiff's attorney, Ms. Charles:

By way of response, Your Honor, you have all the facts necessary to make a fair, full, and final determination of law in this case. The plaintiff's declaration states he was crossing the street at Elm and Main. No one disagrees. It further states that as he entered the street, the defendant's truck hit him. No one disagrees. The facts are clear. The only thing left to do is determine whether or not the defendant was negligent—an issue of law, Your Honor. Both sides have put forth detailed evidence in the declarations attached to our motions, the arguments have been set forth, and it would be a clear waste of time and money for the court and everyone involved to start dragging witnesses into court for each and every point in the case.

4   Adams:

Your Honor, I should not be deprived of the right to cross-examine the plaintiff and his witnesses. My affidavit indicates that he ran out in front of my truck, and that I was watching the road carefully. The plaintiff wants you to decide the matter on the papers so his story will not be exposed to cross-examination. But my right to a fair trial will be denied if you grant this motion, Your Honor. I renew my request that you deny the motion and that a trial date be selected.

5 **Judge:**

In light of Ms. Adams's arguments this morning, and given that it appears there are significant issues of fact and credibility, I have decided to deny the plaintiff's motion, and the matter of Pedestrian v. Adams will proceed to trial. The clerk will notify you when a trial date has been selected.

RESOURCE

Resources on pretrial motions. *American Jurisprudence, Pleading and Practice Forms Annotated* (Lawyers Cooperative Publishing) is a comprehensive multivolume treatise with discussion and examples of many different kinds of pretrial motions.

Pretrial by Thomas Mauet (Aspen Law & Business); Chapter 7 describes the motions process and has sample forms. ●

Proving Your Case at Trial: The Plaintiff's Perspective

Once your case gets to trial, you must prove that the claims you made in your complaint are accurate. To do this, you'll have to prove specific facts. This chapter explains how to figure out exactly what facts you have to prove to win your claim.

It also explains how to organize a legal claim outline that will identify the elements you have to prove, the facts you will use to prove them, and the evidence you will offer at trial to prove these facts.

The Elements of a Legal Claim

Any legal claim you make almost certainly consists of separate elements. It's a little like a beam of light passed through a glass prism: What at first looks like a unitary beam of light in fact consists of separately colored bands. In the same manner, what looks like a unitary legal claim based on negligence, breach of contract, breach of warranty, or almost any other type of legal theory in fact consists of separate legal elements. To win a claim, you must prove each and every one of its elements at trial.

To demonstrate how this works, let's examine three common legal claims.

Negligence Claim

Negligence occurs when one person's carelessness causes harm to another. How does the law define how careful we must be? Lawyers often describe it this way: We must all exercise "ordinary and reasonable care." If we don't, we are negligent—and if our negligence causes harm, we are legally

responsible to pay for it. Here are some common examples of negligence:

- A driver drives carelessly, causing a traffic accident.
- A store employee neglects to mop up a wet spot on the floor, causing a customer to fall.
- A road is poorly designed, resulting in a car sailing over an embankment.
- A bank fails to provide adequate safety mechanisms at an automated teller machine (ATM), resulting in the robbery of a customer.

Here's where the concept of legal elements comes in. Start by understanding that you cannot win at trial just by showing that a defendant behaved carelessly. You have to prove each of the legally required elements of a claim for negligence, which (in most states) are:

1. **Duty:** The defendant owed you a legal duty of care.
2. **Breach of Duty (Carelessness):** The defendant acted unreasonably.
3. **Causation:** The defendant's carelessness directly caused you harm.

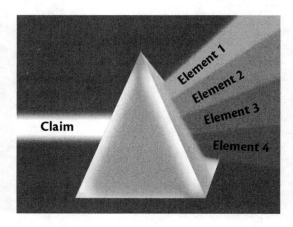

4. **Damages:** You suffered economic losses, property damage, personal injuries, or psychological distress.

Understanding Causation

In some books describing negligence, as well as in some standard (form) complaints for negligence, you may see a reference to an element called "proximate cause" or "legal cause." These terms are just another way of saying that a defendant is liable for negligence only if the defendant's carelessness directly causes you harm.

For example, assume that a defendant carelessly hits you with a car and breaks your right leg. While recovering from surgery to your right leg and walking with the aid of a cane, you slip on ice and break your left leg. You sue the defendant for both injuries. The defendant will probably be liable (legally responsible) for damages attributable to the injury to your right leg because the accident directly caused the injury. But the defendant probably would not be liable for your broken left leg; a judge would not regard the defendant's negligence as a direct (proximate) cause of that injury.

Difficult issues can arise over whether a defendant's negligence is the direct cause of your injuries. If you are in doubt about whether you can prove causation, contact a legal coach with experience in personal injury cases as long before trial as possible.

Breach of Contract Claim

A breach of contract occurs when a person violates the terms of a legally valid contract.

Here are some typical breach of contract situations:

- A seller refuses to honor an oral agreement to sell a consumer a car at the agreed-upon price.
- A manufacturer ships defective products to a retailer.
- A borrower fails to repay a loan.
- A company refuses to pay agreed-upon compensation to an independent contractor.

Like a negligence claim, a claim for breach of contract consists of individual elements, and to win at trial you must prove all of them. The elements you have to prove are:

1. **Formation:** You and the defendant had a legally binding contract.
2. **Performance:** You did everything you were required to do under the contract.
3. **Breach:** The defendant failed to do what was required by the contract.
4. **Damages:** The defendant's breach caused you actual financial loss.

 TIP

Oral contracts are often valid. Many people think that a court will enforce contracts only if they are in writing. However, oral agreements are often enforceable, though you may have more difficulty proving their terms. A law known as the Statute of Frauds (so named by the English in 1677, which gives you some idea of the pace of change in legal terminology) will tell you whether yours is one of the relatively few types of contracts that must be in writing to be enforced. To find your state's Statute of Frauds, look in an index to your state's civil laws or ask a law librarian for help.

Legal Malpractice Claim

Legal malpractice occurs when an attorney fails to use at least ordinary legal skill when representing a client. Generally, the elements necessary to establish a legal malpractice claim are:

1. **Duty:** The defendant attorney owed you a duty to use at least ordinary legal skill.
2. **Breach of Duty (Carelessness):** The defendant attorney failed to use at least ordinary legal skill in carrying out a task.
3. **Causation:** The defendant attorney's carelessness directly caused harm to you.
4. **Damages:** The harm you suffered resulted in actual economic loss to you.

> **TIP**
>
> **There is a higher standard of care for professionals.** If you compare the elements of an ordinary negligence claim with the elements of a legal malpractice claim, you will see that they are largely identical. The difference is that a professional (for example, an attorney, doctor, or architect) cannot avoid liability by showing that the professional simply acted reasonably. An attorney, for example, must act with the care and knowledge of a competent attorney. For further information on professional malpractice, consult a torts (civil wrongs) treatise in your law library. (Chapter 23, discusses how to use treatises.)

Finding the Elements of Your Claim

You may have to do a bit of legal research to figure out the elements of your claim. The complaint that you used to initiate your lawsuit may not identify your claim's elements, because many court systems do not insist that complaints do so. If your claim is based on your adversary's violation of a statute, the text of the statute may not identify the separate elements that you have to prove. In fact, the elements of a claim may be buried in appellate court opinions, which can be difficult to find.

Here are some places to look for the elements of your claim:

- Your state's book of standard jury instructions. Jury instructions often identify the elements of claims to let the jury know exactly what you must prove to win.
- Books called legal outlines, written as quick refreshers for law students on subjects such as torts and contracts, typically list the elements of common claims. They are generally available in law bookstores near law schools.

If you need more help, consult your legal coach or a law librarian. (See Chapter 23 for additional suggestions on doing your own legal research.)

> **TRIAL NOTEBOOK**
>
> Once you identify the elements of your claim, list them in the "Legal Claim Outline" section of your trial notebook. (See Chapter 18.)

Legal Claims

Most small lawsuits involve breach of contract or negligence claims, which are discussed above. But there are hundreds of other legal claims. A few of the more common ones are defined below.

This list is for general background information only. Each state has its own rules on the specific elements required to prove these legal claims, and you must know those elements before trying to bring or defend against a lawsuit. Chapter 23 explains how to find your state's list of the elements of a legal claim.

Assault. The plaintiff has a reasonable fear or concern that the defendant is about to commit an immediate battery. (Assault can also be a criminal offense.)

> **EXAMPLE:** Someone threatens you with a knife.

Battery. The defendant deliberately and offensively (that is, in a way the plaintiff would not permit) touches the plaintiff. (Battery can also be a criminal offense.)

> **EXAMPLE:** Someone hits you.

Breach of fiduciary duty. A fiduciary (someone who occupies a position of trust) fails to live up to that duty of trust, and as a result the person to whom the fiduciary owes the duty of trust suffers loss.

> **EXAMPLE:** A trustee (someone who is in charge of the property in a trust) spends trust money for personal purposes instead of using it for the trust's beneficiary.

Conversion. The defendant intentionally converts to his own use some property of the plaintiff.

> **EXAMPLE:** You lend your stereo to a friend, who later sells it without your permission and keeps the money.

Defamation (libel and slander). The defendant makes to third persons (or causes to be made to third persons) a false statement about the plaintiff, and the statement harms the plaintiff's reputation.

> **EXAMPLE:** A newspaper prints statements that falsely claim that a teacher had been convicted of a crime.

False imprisonment. The defendant intentionally and unlawfully restrains the plaintiff's freedom of movement.

> **EXAMPLE:** A salesperson refuses to let a shopper leave a store when there's no legitimate reason to think the shopper was trying to steal anything.

Fraud (intentional misrepresentation). The defendant knowingly makes a statement that misrepresents a fact, with the intention of inducing the plaintiff to rely on that statement, and the plaintiff justifiably relies on that statement and suffers loss.

Legal Claims (continued)

EXAMPLE: A salesperson tells a prospective buyer that a water-purification system will make water safe when the salesperson knows that it won't. The buyer, relying on the statement, buys the system and as a result loses the money spent on it.

Private nuisance. The defendant prevents or disrupts the plaintiff's use and enjoyment of the plaintiff's property.

EXAMPLE: Your neighbor lets his dogs bark at all hours of the day and night, making it impossible for you to use your backyard.

Public nuisance. The defendant causes a health or safety hazard to the residents of a particular area.

EXAMPLE: A chemical plant lets toxic fumes drift onto neighboring property, posing a health threat to the residents.

Wrongful termination. An employer fires an employee for an illegal reason.

EXAMPLE: A car manufacturer fires an assembly line worker for notifying a government safety agency that the manufacturer was using defective parts.

Proving Each Element

As the plaintiff, you must prove each element of a claim. If you don't, you will lose the case. To illustrate this critical point, let's focus briefly on a typical attorney malpractice claim. Assume that you wish to file a lawsuit against your former attorney, Jean Blue. About two years earlier, you went to see Blue after you were injured on your neighbor's property. Blue agreed to handle your case but neglected to pursue it. When she finally filed a lawsuit on your behalf against your neighbor, the legal time limit in which the suit could have been filed (the statute of limitations) had expired, and your suit was thrown out of court.

In assessing whether you can win a malpractice suit against Blue, start with two obvious points: Blue had a duty to represent you competently, and her failure to file suit before the statute of limitations expired is carelessness that constitutes a breach of that duty. So the first two elements are satisfied.

But as you can see from the list of elements, you must also show that you suffered actual economic loss as a result of the breach. Logically, to do this you must be able to convince the judge or jury that you would have won the suit against your neighbor had Blue filed it on time. Put another way, if the judge or jury decides that you would have lost the case against your neighbor, Blue's breach of duty didn't actually harm you, and you would lose the malpractice case.

Your Burden of Proof

As the plaintiff, you carry the "burden of proof." This means that to win at trial, you must convince a judge or jury that *each element* of your legal claim is true. If you fail to prove even one element, you will lose.

But how convincing does your proof have to be? In most civil cases, your burden of proof is to prove your case by "a preponderance of the evidence." In other words, even if a judge or jury thinks that the probability that you have proved an element is only slightly better than 50%, you have successfully carried your burden of proof as to that element.

However, a higher burden of proof is occasionally required. In a few types of civil cases, such as those involving claims for fraud or for breach of an oral agreement to make a will, you may have to prove the truth of each element by "clear and convincing evidence." Although no precise mathematical difference

separates "clear and convincing evidence" from "a preponderance of the evidence," your evidence generally has to be stronger to win a claim requiring this higher burden of proof.

When preparing for trial, be sure you know what burden of proof you have to meet. The best sources of this information are jury instructions for your type of claim, a legal treatise that discusses the elements of your type of claim, or your legal coach. (See Chapter 23.)

TIP

Explain the burden of proof to a jury. To illustrate the civil burden of proof during closing arguments, many plaintiff's attorneys like to hold their arms out to either side in imitation of a scales of justice. They then tilt very slightly to one side to indicate that if the plaintiff's evidence has moved the judge or jury even slightly in the plaintiff's direction, the plaintiff has met the burden of proof.

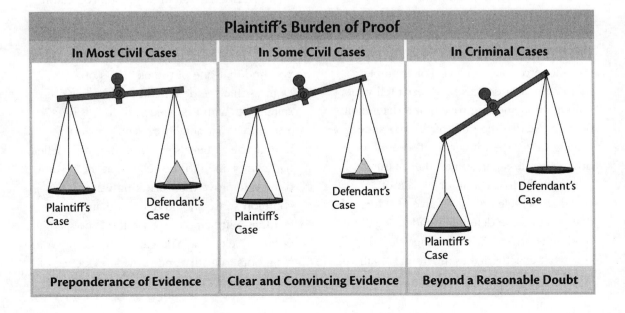

Plaintiff's Burden of Proof

In Most Civil Cases	In Some Civil Cases	In Criminal Cases
Plaintiff's Case / Defendant's Case	Plaintiff's Case / Defendant's Case	Plaintiff's Case / Defendant's Case
Preponderance of Evidence	**Clear and Convincing Evidence**	**Beyond a Reasonable Doubt**

You may not want to be so theatrical at trial. But you will want to let the jury know that you don't need to prove any element of your legal claim beyond a reasonable doubt, as a prosecutor must do in criminal cases; convincing the jury by 50.01% is good enough. (See Chapter 14 for more on closing arguments.)

Identifying Facts to Prove the Elements of Your Claim

You might reasonably think that once you've identified the elements of your claim, you will know exactly what facts you have to prove to win at trial.

Unfortunately, it's not so simple. As you can see from reading the lists of elements in "The Elements of a Legal Claim," above, legal elements are abstract concepts. The abstract language of legal elements is no accident; elements have to be stated in broad terms if they are to apply to a wide variety of possible conduct.

For example, let's look more closely at the second element of a negligence claim: that the "defendant breached the duty of care." This language doesn't refer to any specific, provable conduct. For example, in an auto accident case it doesn't tell you whether you should prove that a defendant driver breached the duty of care by speeding, driving under the influence of alcohol, or driving carelessly in some other manner.

Similarly, in a claim for breach of contract, one element you have to prove is that you and the defendant had a "legally binding contract." This language doesn't tell you what exactly makes a contract legally binding.

The abstract language of legal elements would not be a problem if you or a witness could go into court and simply testify that, "While driving on June 3, the defendant breached the duty of care," or that "The contract was legally binding." But testimony must refer to what witnesses actually saw and heard—what was said in conversations, what people did, and how events unfolded. You and your witnesses must testify about facts and events *in your specific case* that satisfy the legal elements. After hearing about the competing versions of what actually took place, it is up to a judge or jury to decide whether a duty of care was breached, whether a contract was legally binding, or whether any other legal element has been satisfied.

There is no magic way to identify the facts that will satisfy each element in your case. For the most part, it works just fine to rely on your everyday experience and common sense. For example, assume that you are suing a door-to-door seller of a water-purifying system for fraud. You claim that the salesperson induced (tricked) you to purchase the system by making false claims about it. After doing some research, you find that one of the elements of a fraud claim is that the defendant made a false statement "with knowledge of its falsity." You know that neighbors who previously bought the same system from the same seller had complained to the seller that the system did not improve their drinking water. Your common sense should tell you that this is a fact that will help you prove the "knowledge of falsity" element. You can then line up your neighbors to testify and provide evidence of this fact.

Common sense won't always suffice, however. For example, in a breach of contract case, you may find that to prove the element that there was a "legally binding contract," you must prove "consideration." But "consideration" is another abstract term, and you may not know its meaning in a legal context. In such situations, an easy method of making sure you know what you have to prove is to consult a law dictionary. (By the way, "consideration" refers to the profit or other benefit that each party to the contract was to receive.)

RESOURCE

Resources to help you identify and understand the elements of your claim. A reference book that may help you identify facts that satisfy legal elements is *American Jurisprudence Proof of Facts* by Clarence Taber (Lawyers' Cooperative Publishing Co.). This is a multivolume treatise that discusses how to prove hundreds of legal claims. Though the facts you will have to prove in your case will undoubtedly be different from the facts discussed in the treatise, the treatise may help you understand what you have to prove.

For a list of good law dictionaries, see Chapter 23.

To illustrate how to identify facts that satisfy abstract elements, this section provides examples for three kinds of lawsuits—negligence, breach of contract, and attorney malpractice—the three legal claims described in "The Elements of a Legal Claim," above. Even if your claim falls into one of these categories, the facts you will have to prove in your case will, of course,

be different. But the process you will go through to identify facts will be very similar.

CAUTION

Identifying facts is crucial. We cannot overstate the importance of making sure that you know before trial what facts you will try to prove to satisfy each element of your claim. Otherwise, you may lose at trial not because your witnesses were not credible or because your claim was an improper one, but because you neglected to prove facts to satisfy each element of your claim.

A good way to organize your thoughts as you go through this process is to make an outline of each element, the facts you will need to prove it, and the evidence you will use to prove the facts. (Samples are shown below.) It will let you know, at a glance, whether you have identified facts to prove each element, and it will also be a good reference for you during your trial. Depending on the type of claim you have made, your outline may have as many as four, five, or six elements. Devote a separate page to each grouping of element, fact, and evidence to organize your case as clearly as possible. (If the same item of evidence is relevant to more than one fact, simply include it on more than one page.)

TIP

A fact by any other name is still a fact. In the course of your legal research, you may run across the terms "material facts" or "ultimate facts." This is simply more legal jargon, which refers to facts that satisfy legal elements. All the facts set forth below are material facts or ultimate facts.

Claim for Negligence

Your story: About 3 p.m. on March 31, you were standing on the corner of Elm and Main Streets, waiting to cross the street. When the light in your direction turned green, you stepped off the curb into the crosswalk. You had gotten about one-third of the way across the street when you suddenly saw a truck driven by the defendant, Sarah Adams, bearing down on you. You tried to get out of the way, but the truck struck you. You suffered a broken leg, which took four months to heal and left you with a permanent limp. An eyewitness will testify that you were in the crosswalk when the truck made a left turn and struck you.

Adams is a building contractor. During her deposition, she admitted that her truck struck you, that just moments before the accident she had gotten a call on her cell phone telling her about a missed inspection on a big job she was working on, and that she turned left to visit that job site. Adams denies that she drove carelessly.

You file a complaint against Adams for negligence and find the list of elements you must prove. Now you're ready to write down a specific fact that satisfies each element. Do not worry about your exact words—this process is only for your benefit. Neither the judge nor the defendant will ever see your list.

Element 1:

The defendant owed me a legal duty of care.

Fact:

At the time of the accident, Adams was driving a truck in the immediate vicinity of where I was a pedestrian crossing the street.

TIP

You may not need to prove the duty of care. As a general rule, a defendant has a duty of care towards anyone who is likely to be harmed by the defendant's careless conduct. Because Adams admits striking you, you would probably not need evidence to prove this fact.

Element 2:

The defendant acted unreasonably.

Fact:

Adams made a left turn when she was thinking about a job problem and not paying attention to pedestrians in the road.

Element 3:

The defendant's carelessness directly harmed me.

Fact:

Being hit by Adams's truck broke my leg and left me with a limp.

 TIP

Watch out for the "preexisting injury" defense. In many personal injury cases, a defendant will try to deny causing your injuries by offering evidence that an injury you say resulted from the defendant's conduct actually existed before that conduct took place.

Element 4:

I suffered economic losses, personal injuries, and psychological distress.

Fact:

My broken leg had to be operated on. I lost two weeks of work, was on crutches for four months, was in constant pain during that period, and had medical expenses of $50,000. Also, I was left with an embarrassing permanent limp, soreness, and stiffness.

Claim for Breach of Contract

Your story: On February 14, you hired the defendant, Von Jarrett, a contractor, to build an addition of 600 square feet onto your house. The price was $75,000. The written contract called for a down payment of $5,000, then for periodic payments tied to defined completion stages until the job was finished. The contract called for the addition to be completed by June 14.

Jarrett stopped working around the beginning of April and demanded an additional $20,000 over and above the $75,000 to finish the job. Because you had properly made all due interim payments and because Jarrett breached the contract by refusing to continue working, you refused to pay the additional money and hired another contractor to complete the work. After you hired the new contractor, you learned that Jarrett had used substandard materials, which had to be replaced. Your total cost for the addition (including replacing the substandard materials) ended up being $110,000. You also had to pay $3,000 extra to stay in a hotel two months longer than you anticipated.

Element 1:

We had a legally binding contract.

Fact:

On Feb. 14, Jarrett made a written promise to build a 600-square-foot addition onto my house, and I promised in writing to pay a total of $75,000 by the time the job was completed.

TIP

Exchange of promises is sufficient.
In a contract case, one party's promise is adequate "consideration" for another party's promise. Stripped of legal jargon, this means that if each party promises to do something of value to the other (such as pay money, deliver a product, or build an addition to your house), a contract is formed unless the judge regards the transaction as a gift from one party to the other.

Element 2:

I did everything I was required to do under the contract.

Facts:

I paid Jarrett a down payment of $5,000 and an additional $15,000 when the first and only stage of the work was completed by Jarrett. In addition, I provided Jarrett with complete access to my property to do the work. That's all the contract required me to do.

Element 3:

Jarrett failed to fulfill his side of the contract.

Facts:

Jarrett stopped working on the addition in early April, when the addition was only partially complete. Jarrett also refused to complete the addition unless I promised to increase the total contract by $20,000, even though I had made all payments due under the contract. Also, Jarrett did not use the quality of materials called for by the contract.

Element 4:

Jarrett's breach produced actual economic losses.

Facts:

Because of Jarrett's refusal to complete the job for the contract price and his substandard work, I had to hire another contractor to complete the addition according to plan, for a total cost of $110,000. My damages include the $35,000 that I had to pay in excess of the $75,000 contract price for the addition, as well as $3,000 in additional living expenses because I couldn't live in the house for two extra months while the addition was completed.

Claim for Legal Malpractice

Your story: A number of years ago your stepmother hired an attorney to draft a will leaving her entire estate to you. After she signed the will, your stepmother gave birth to a son. Sometime later, she wanted to make sure that the son would get no part of her property. Your stepmother called the same attorney, who assured her that no change in the will was necessary—all of the stepmother's property would still go to you under the will. After your stepmother's death, you discovered that under your state's law, which was in effect when your stepmother called the attorney, the son was automatically entitled to half ($60,000) of your stepmother's estate despite the terms of the will. Your state's law, known as a "pretermitted heir statute," states that a child born after a will is made takes half of the estate no matter what the will says, unless the child is specifically disinherited.

Element 1:

The lawyer owed me a duty of professional care.

Fact:

Defendant is a licensed attorney who was hired by my stepmother to prepare a will leaving all her property to me.

CAUTION

State laws vary as to a lawyer's duty to a will beneficiary. Your claim against the lawyer can succeed only if the lawyer's duty of professional care extends to you, the beneficiary under the will. In some states, a lawyer has no duty toward will beneficiaries, but only to a client (here, your stepmother). If your case arises in one of these states, the claim would not succeed even though the lawyer was careless.

Element 2:

The lawyer failed to use at least ordinary legal skills.

Fact:

After the lawyer drafted a will for my stepmother that made no reference to a child, my stepmother told the lawyer that she had given birth to a son and asked if she had to change her will to make sure her entire estate went to me. The lawyer mistakenly told her that she did not have to change her will to disinherit the son.

Element 3:

The lawyer's carelessness was the direct cause of harm to me.

Fact:

Because of the lawyer's advice, my stepmother failed to change her will to disinherit her son.

Element 4:

I suffered actual economic losses.

Fact:

I lost $60,000 that I would have received had the will been changed to disinherit the son.

CAUTION

Disinheritance laws in your state may be different. If you are involved in a dispute involving children omitted from a will, check your state's "probate" or "wills" laws very carefully. In most states, a child omitted from a will is entitled to a share of a parent's estate only if the child was born after the will was signed. But in a few states, a child omitted from a will may receive a share of a parent's estate even if the child was born before the will was signed.

Looking Ahead to Trial: Organizing Your Evidence

Once you have an outline of the facts satisfying each element of your claim, you can add greatly to its usefulness by taking the next step: listing under each fact the most important evidence you will introduce to prove it.

TIP

If your opponent agrees, you don't have to prove everything. A stipulation is an agreement between you and your adversary. You can stipulate to many things, including the truth of a fact. To arrange for a stipulation, before trial simply ask your adversary to agree to certain facts. For example, you might say, "Are you willing to stipulate that you are a licensed attorney and that my stepmother hired you to prepare her will?" If necessary, support your request for a stipulation with reasons, saying something like, "The stipulation will save us both time, because I won't have to present evidence. And you don't really dispute this fact anyway." Once you and your adversary reach an agreement, write out its terms, sign it, and ask your adversary to sign it as well. That way you will prevent your adversary from suddenly denying the existence of a stipulation at trial and leaving you unprepared to offer evidence. (For a sample stipulation, see Chapter 15.)

For example, look back at Element 1 in the legal malpractice case. The fact that satisfies the element of duty is that the defendant was a licensed attorney who was hired by your stepmother to prepare a will leaving all her estate to you. Under this fact, list the evidence you will offer to prove it. For example, the will may be bound in a cover that has the defendant's name and address on it, and you may have a canceled check showing payment by the stepmother to the defendant for the will. You could also produce evidence by demanding that the defendant bring to court the file showing that your stepmother had been a client. Finally, the defendant may stipulate (agree) that he is an attorney and that your stepmother

hired him to prepare her will. If the attorney stipulates to this fact, you needn't prove it at trial. In that event, your outline of facts and evidence for Element 1 will look like the one shown below.

Claim: Legal Malpractice
Element 1:
The lawyer owed me a duty of professional care.
Fact satisfying Element 1:
Defendant is a licensed attorney who was hired by my stepmother to prepare a will leaving all her estate to me.
Evidence to prove fact:
a. Defendant has agreed to stipulate that he is a licensed attorney who prepared my stepmother's will.
b. The will names me as sole beneficiary.

You can use this same procedure for each element that you have to prove. For a somewhat more complex example, look back at Element 2 in the same legal malpractice case. To satisfy this element, you have to introduce evidence that after the lawyer drafted the will, your stepmother told the lawyer that she had given birth to a son and asked if she had to change her will to make sure all of her estate went to you, and that the lawyer told her that she did not have to change her will to disinherit the son.

As you can see, one thing you have to prove is that the will that the attorney drafted made no reference to a son. The will itself is evidence of this fact, and you should include a reminder in your outline to introduce the will into evidence. (See Chapter 15.)

Offering evidence of what your stepmother told the attorney, and what she was told in return, may be more difficult. Your stepmother, your most obvious source of evidence, is deceased.

Of course, the defendant may admit the conversation—but you would hardly be going to trial if the defendant admitted this fact. Perhaps you or another relative or friend heard your stepmother talking to the defendant, or at least heard her say that she was going to find out from the attorney if she needed to change her will. In addition, you may have to call another estate planning attorney as an "expert witness" to testify that the defendant's failure to advise your stepmother to change her will was legal malpractice. An expert's testimony may be necessary because the average judge or jury is unlikely to know what "competent legal skills" are in this context. (See Chapter 19.)

Moving on to Elements 3 and 4, briefly, to prove that the lawyer's advice was the direct cause of your stepmother's failure to change her will, you may offer evidence (from you, a relative, or a friend) that your stepmother said that she was not going to change her will because her lawyer said that she didn't have to. And to prove that you lost $60,000, you may offer evidence of the will itself (which demonstrates that your stepmother wanted you to inherit her entire estate), testimony from the son that he received $60,000 of your stepmother's estate, or receipts and records from your stepmother's estate proving that $60,000 of the estate was paid to the son.

Claim: Legal Malpractice
Element 2:
The lawyer failed to use at least ordinary legal skills.
Facts satisfying Element 2:
After the lawyer drafted a will for my step-mother that made no reference to a child, my stepmother told the lawyer that she had given birth to a son and asked if she had to change her will to make sure all her estate went to me. The lawyer mistakenly told her that she did not need to change her will.
Evidence to prove fact:
a. My stepmother's good friend James went with her to the attorney's office and heard the lawyer tell my stepmother she didn't need to change her will to leave me everything.
b. Expert witness will testify that the lawyer's mistaken advice was legal malpractice.

TRIAL NOTEBOOK

After you complete the outline of the facts and evidence necessary to prove each element of your claim, put it in your trial notebook. The outline will be a big help in guiding your presentation of evidence at trial. (See Chapter 18.)

Learning About Your Adversary's Case

Even though you're a plaintiff, you should read Chapter 9, which discusses trial preparation from the defendant's perspective. Understanding how the defendant is likely to attack your case at trial gives you a chance to prepare a response.

RESOURCE

Resources on Specific Legal Claims.
American Bar Association Guide to Consumer Law: Everything You Need to Know About Buying, Selling, Contracts, and Guarantees (Times Books) covers consumer disputes, including basic contract law; residential leases; warranties; automobile sales, leases, and repairs; consumer credit; buying and selling a home; and insurance.

American Bar Association Guide to Family Law: The Complete and Easy Guide to the Laws of Marriage, Parenthood, Separation, and Divorce (Times Books) covers claims involving cohabitation and premarital agreements, divorce, alimony, child support and custody, and domestic violence.

Every Tenant's Legal Guide, by Janet Portman and Marcia Stewart (Nolo), covers eviction

defense, housing discrimination, and housing repairs and maintenance. It comes with blank forms you can tear out and use.

How to Win Your Personal Injury Claim, by Joseph L. Matthews (Nolo), covers auto accident disputes.

Your Rights in the Workplace, by Barbara Kate Repa (Nolo), covers employee rights, workers' compensation, and unemployment benefits.

The Employer's Legal Handbook, by Fred Steingold (Nolo), covers claims regarding hiring, paying, and discharging workers.

Neighbor Law: Fences, Trees, Boundaries & Noise, by Cora Jordan and Emily Doskow (Nolo), covers boundary and personal disputes.

Patent, Copyright & Trademark: An Intellectual Property Desk Reference, by Richard Stim (Nolo), covers trade secrets, copyrights, patents, and trademarks.

The Rights of People Who Are HIV Positive, by William Rubenstein, Ruth Eisenberg, and Lawrence O. Gostin (Southern Illinois University Press) covers the rights of people with HIV and AIDS (ACLU guide).

Solve Your Money Troubles: Get Debt Collectors Off Your Back and Regain Financial Freedom, by Robin Leonard and John Lamb (Nolo), covers sales fraud, credit cards, car loans, collection agencies, and credit discrimination. ●

Proving Your Case at Trial: The Defendant's Perspective

As a defendant, you prepare your case in much the same way as a plaintiff does: by figuring out exactly what you want to prove at trial and deciding what evidence you'll present to prove it. Begin by following these three steps:

1. List each legal claim (for example, breach of contract, fraud, or both) that the plaintiff made in the complaint.

2. List the elements of each claim—that is, what the plaintiff must prove to win on the claim. (See Chapter 8.)

3. Identify the facts with which the plaintiff is likely to try to satisfy each element.

Once you have finished Step 3, you then do one or both of the following:

a. Identify evidence you can offer to disprove the facts listed in Step 3.

b. Identify your own facts that contradict the facts listed in Step 3, and identify evidence you can offer to prove your own facts.

You'll end up with an outline that looks like the one shown below.

Depending on the type of claim the plaintiff has made, your outline may have as many as four, five, or six elements.

Now let's go through these steps and see how following them can help you win at trial.

Legal Claim:

Element 1:

Plaintiff's fact for Element 1:

Evidence disproving this fact:

a.

b.

c. (etc.)

My contradictory fact:

Evidence proving my fact:

a.

b.

c. (etc.)

Element 2:

Plaintiff's fact for Element 2:

Evidence disproving this fact:

a.

b.

c. (etc.)

My contradictory fact:

Evidence proving my fact:

a.

b.

c. (etc.)

Identifying the Elements of the Plaintiff's Legal Claim

Legal claims consist of discrete elements, and a plaintiff must prove every element to win on that claim. Chapter 8 explains how to identify the elements of common claims, such as negligence or breach of contract. It is imperative that you read this material because you need to build your defense around those same elements. Using the instructions in that chapter, list the elements of each claim the plaintiff made in the complaint.

 TIP

Don't rely on the plaintiff's complaint. The plaintiff's complaint will state whether you have been sued for negligence, breach of contract, fraud, or some other legal claim. However, the complaint probably will not list the elements of the legal claim, because court rules in most states do not require it.

Identifying the Plaintiff's Facts

As Chapter 8 also explains, all legal elements are written in the abstract so as to apply to any such case. Therefore, knowing what legal elements the plaintiff must prove does not tell you the specific facts the plaintiff will try to prove at trial. For example, knowing that one element of a plaintiff's negligence claim is that you acted carelessly doesn't tell you specifically what the plaintiff will try to prove to show that you were careless. The

plaintiff must try to prove specific facts at trial for each of a claim's elements, and you must try to anticipate what those facts will be.

Fortunately, figuring out the facts a plaintiff will try to prove to satisfy each legal element usually does not require technical legal knowledge on your part. Using common sense, you can usually identify the plaintiff's facts by matching what you know about the plaintiff's case to the elements the plaintiff has to prove.

For example, from Chapter 8, you know that there are four elements of a negligence claim:

1. **Duty:** You owed the plaintiff a legal duty of care.
2. **Breach of duty:** You acted unreasonably.
3. **Causation:** Your carelessness caused the plaintiff harm.
4. **Damages:** The plaintiff suffered economic or other loss.

Now assume that you are a defendant in a negligence case based on an automobile accident. You know from your settlement discussions with the plaintiff's lawyer that the plaintiff claims that you were exceeding the speed limit, and that the plaintiff suffered a broken arm, incurred medical bills of $10,000, and lost a week's wages at work. Common sense tells you that the fact the plaintiff will try to prove to satisfy the element of "breach of duty of care" is that you were speeding, and that to prove "damages" the plaintiff will try to prove that he had his arm broken, he had medical expenses of $10,000, and he lost a week's wages. You can begin organizing this information in outline form, like the one shown below.

Legal Claim: Negligence
Element 1:
Duty of care
Fact Plaintiff will try to prove:
Plaintiff was in an area where he was likely
to be harmed if I drove carelessly.
Element 2:
Breach of duty
Fact Plaintiff will try to prove:
I was speeding when the accident occurred.
Element 3:
Causation
Fact Plaintiff will try to prove:
My speeding caused Plaintiff to suffer a
broken arm.
Element 4:
Damages
Fact Plaintiff will try to prove:
As a result of his broken arm, Plaintiff had
medical bills of $10,000 and lost a week's
wages.

Usually, you can find out all you need to know about the plaintiff's case through informal discussions and standard pretrial contacts. Some of these opportunities include:

- **Your personal dealings with the plaintiff and the plaintiff's associates.** You almost certainly will have had a variety of contacts with the plaintiff, employees or other business associates of the plaintiff, as well as the plaintiff's lawyer leading up to the filing of the lawsuit. Most lawsuits are preceded by oral discussions and written demands that provide information about the plaintiff's legal position.

- **Negotiation and settlement discussions.** Even after the lawsuit is filed, you and the plaintiff (or the plaintiff's lawyer) will probably discuss the possibility of settling your dispute, either informally or in a pretrial conference conducted by a judge. (See Chapter 7.) During these discussions, you should be able to find out most of what you need to know about the plaintiff's case. In trying to convince you to agree to a certain settlement figure, the plaintiff will probably refer to the facts he is prepared to prove at trial and much of the evidence he will rely on to prove them.

 TIP

Settlement offers and statements can't be admitted at trial. The law encourages litigants to settle disputes before trial. To promote frank discussion during settlement talks (whether conducted by a judge or between the parties informally), neither the Federal Rules of Evidence (FRE) nor any court system allows offers to settle or statements made during settlement discussions to be admitted as evidence. (See, for example, FRE 408.) So while you will learn information about the plaintiff's case during settlement discussions, you cannot offer evidence that the plaintiff offered to settle the case or evidence of any statements made by the plaintiff during those discussions.

- **Direct inquiry.** Don't overlook that favorite information-seeking device of generations of parents and teachers: Ask! Most people are socialized to respond to direct questions, and they are likely to follow that habit during pretrial discussions. For example, you know that in a negligence case the plaintiff has to prove that you behaved carelessly. If you are unsure about what the plaintiff claims you did that was negligent, you may ask, "In what way do you claim that I was careless?"

- **Formal discovery.** As a nonlawyer, you may be reluctant to initiate formal discovery, such as depositions, interrogatories, and requests for admissions. But if informal methods of finding out what facts the plaintiff will try to prove have not worked, discovery may be worth a try. For instance, in a negligence case, you can send an interrogatory to the plaintiff saying, "Please state each and every fact you rely on that demonstrates that I was careless." Similarly, to find out about the plaintiff's claimed damages, during a deposition you can say to the plaintiff, "Please tell me all the personal injuries you claim you suffered as a result of the accident." In both instances, the plaintiff must respond to your questions under oath.

Although it's more expensive than informal methods of learning about facts, formal discovery does have a big advantage: the way you use it at trial. For example, an admission made in response to your request for admission is binding on the plaintiff if you present it at trial. That means, for example, that if the plaintiff admits in response to your request for admission that

"the car was blue," the plaintiff can't argue the point at trial.

Similarly, if the plaintiff (or a witness for the plaintiff) gives a different answer while testifying at trial than he or she gave at an earlier deposition, you can impeach (attack the credibility of) the witness by bringing up the inconsistent deposition answer. For instance, assume that at trial the plaintiff testifies that "the light turned green when I was about 50 feet away from the intersection." During a pretrial deposition, however, the plaintiff testified that "the light turned green when I was about ten feet from the intersection." You can impeach the plaintiff's testimony at trial by introducing the conflicting deposition testimony to show that the plaintiff's story has changed. If you can successfully impeach the plaintiff or the plaintiff's witnesses on one or two important points, the judge or jury may doubt the credibility of the plaintiff's entire case. (Impeachment techniques are discussed below and in Chapter 13.)

Defeating Any One Element of a Claim

To win at trial, the plaintiff must prove each and every element of a claim. In most civil cases the plaintiff's burden is to convince a judge or jury that facts are true by a "preponderance of the evidence," which means that the plaintiff must establish that the chances are at least slightly better than 50% that the plaintiff's facts are true.

But as the defendant, you have one big advantage over the plaintiff. To win on a claim, you need only disprove—or prevent the plaintiff from proving—one element of that claim. Because the plaintiff has the burden of proof—and not you—you do not have to prove that the plaintiff's evidence is untrue. You only have to raise enough doubt in the judge's or jury's mind about any one element to prevent the plaintiff from winning.

For example, assume that you are sued for negligence. At trial, the plaintiff succeeds in proving three of the four elements of negligence by a preponderance of the evidence. That is, the plaintiff persuades a judge or jury that (1) you acted carelessly, (2) your careless actions were the direct cause of the plaintiff's loss, and (3) your careless actions produced actual damages. However, the plaintiff is unable to convince the judge or jury by a preponderance of the evidence as to the remaining element: that you had a duty towards the plaintiff to act carefully. You win! The plaintiff met the burden of proof for three of the four elements of negligence, but not for the fourth.

This kind of scenario is very plausible. For example, in one recent case, a number of investors sued an accounting firm for conducting an audit negligently. Relying on the audit, the investors had invested money in a company and lost money when the company turned out to be in far worse financial condition than the audit suggested. The court decided that the accounting firm was negligent and that its negligence directly caused economic damages to the investors. However, the court also decided that the accounting firm had no duty toward the investors because the firm had no idea who the investors might be. The result: The accounting firm won the case.

Disproving the Plaintiff's Facts by Impeaching Witnesses

Once you have a good idea of the facts the plaintiff will offer to satisfy each element of a claim, you should next identify any evidence you can offer to disprove those facts. Remember, if you can prevent the plaintiff from proving any one element, you win. One way to disprove the plaintiff's facts is to come up with evidence that casts doubt on the credibility of the plaintiff's evidence. If the judge or jury simply doesn't believe the plaintiff's key testimony on some fact, chances are the judge or jury will conclude that the plaintiff has not met the burden of proving that fact. Damaging a witness's credibility is called "impeaching the witness."

If you are going to impeach an adverse witness during trial, normally you have to identify evidence casting doubt on the witness's credibility before trial. To help you look for such evidence when you are talking informally to potential witnesses or perhaps even taking a deposition, here are some common ways to attack a witness's credibility. Most of them should be familiar to you from everyday life.

Bias

If you have evidence suggesting that a witness has a financial or emotional interest in the outcome of a case, you can offer it at trial to show that the witness is biased. For example, assume that the lawsuit against you is based on negligence, and the fact the plaintiff is trying to prove is that you were driving too fast. (This fact satisfies one of the elements of negligence, "breach of duty of care.") To support this claim, the plaintiff plans to call a witness to testify that you were driving 50 m.p.h. in a residential area. If you can get the witness to admit to having made disparaging remarks about a group to which you belong, to being a close friend or relative of the plaintiff, or to standing to gain financially if the plaintiff wins, the judge or jury may conclude that the witness has a bias that casts doubt on the believability of the witness's testimony. Similarly, you can argue that a doctor called as an expert witness by the plaintiff to testify to the severity of the plaintiff's injuries is biased if you can show that the doctor has received a large payment to examine and testify for the plaintiff.

Impaired Ability to Observe

Evidence indicating that a witness did not have a good opportunity to see what the witness claims to have seen can also be very helpful to your case. For example, in the same negligence case, if you can show that the witness saw you driving for only a split second, has terrible eyesight, saw you from a long distance, or had consumed three martinis a half hour before seeing the accident, you can attack the witness's believability based on his or her impaired ability to observe.

Prior Inconsistent Statements

Evidence that, before the trial, a witness made statements that conflict with the witness's trial testimony can make for a devastating attack on credibility. For instance, if at trial a witness testifies that you were driving 50 m.p.h., and you then introduce a

sworn deposition or even an oral statement by the same witness saying you were going 40 m.p.h., or saying that the witness couldn't tell how fast you were going, you can cast serious doubt on the witness's credibility.

If you can offer evidence to impeach the plaintiff's version of events, include it in your outline. For example, if you have evidence that a witness for the plaintiff, Johnson, made two oral statements that are inconsistent with his expected testimony, you would update Element 2 in your outline as follows:

Legal Claim: Negligence
Element 2:
Carelessness (breach of duty)
Fact Plaintiff will try to prove:
I was going about 50 m.p.h. when the accident occurred.
Evidence disproving this fact:
a. Johnson told a police officer after the accident that he didn't get a very good look at my car before the accident.
b. Johnson told me on the telephone that he didn't think I was going more than 40 m.p.h.

Proving Your Version of Events

As a defendant, you are not limited to trying to disprove what the plaintiff claims are facts. You may also testify and call witnesses in support of your own version of events. And remember that to prevail, you needn't convince the judge or juror that your version is correct; you simply need to offer enough evidence to lead the judge or juror to doubt that the plaintiff has met the required burden of proof as to any single element. This approach is the legal equivalent of the sports saying, "The best defense is a good offense."

To prepare to offer your own version of events, rely on your common sense and the information you gather before trial. Look at the list of elements and identify for any or all elements a contradictory fact that you can prove. For example, assume that you have been sued for breach of contract. The plaintiff, Andrea, claims that after a series of negotiations you orally agreed on September 22 to buy her stamp collection for $15,000. After checking the elements necessary to prove a breach of contract claim, you see that one of the elements that Andrea must try to prove is that a binding contract was formed. In this case, the fact that she will use to prove that element is that on September 22, she agreed to sell and you agreed to buy her stamp collection.

But you deny agreeing to buy the stamp collection. Your version of the September 22 conversation is that you agreed to buy Andrea's stamp collection for $15,000, but only if she also threw in her coin collection. Andrea said that she would think about your proposal and get back to you. That's the last you heard from her until you were sued. So at trial you will try to prove a contradictory fact for the element of "binding agreement." To show that there was no binding agreement, you will try to prove that you offered to buy Andrea's stamp and coin collection for $15,000 and that Andrea never accepted your offer. In your outline, you will list this information as shown below.

Legal Claim: Breach of Contract

Element 1:

There was a legally binding contract.

Fact Plaintiff will try to prove:

On September 22, I agreed to buy her stamp collection for $15,000.

Evidence disproving this fact:

My contradictory fact:

On September 22, I offered to buy her stamp and coin collections for $15,000, but she never agreed to my proposal.

Evidence for my contradictory fact:

a. My testimony that this is what happened on September 22.

b. Testimony of dealer Jim Pelowski, who says that on September 24, Plaintiff offered to sell her stamp collection to him for $15,000. This shows that she didn't think she had an agreement with me.

Putting Defense Strategies Together

Let's put the two defense approaches you've just read about together in a single example to help you understand how you can use both to defend yourself at trial. We'll use the negligence claim introduced in Chapter 8; put yourself in the position of the defendant, Sarah Adams.

PLAINTIFF'S STORY: The plaintiff contends that at about 3 p.m. on March 31 he was standing on the corner of Elm and Main Streets, waiting to cross the street. When the light in his direction turned green, he stepped off the curb into the crosswalk. He had gotten about one-third of the way across the street when he saw your truck bearing down on him. He tried to get out of the way but failed, and your truck struck him. As a result, he had to undergo an operation for a broken leg that took four months to heal, had medical expenses of $20,000, and was left with a permanent limp. The plaintiff will offer evidence that you are a building contractor and that just before the accident you received a call on your cell phone from your office informing you of a missed inspection on one of your big remodeling jobs. He will argue that the call distracted you and that you carelessly neglected to see him in the crosswalk. He will produce a witness who claims to have seen you looking out the driver's side window of your truck instead of straight ahead.

YOUR STORY: You agree with the plaintiff that at about 3 p.m. you were driving a pickup truck approaching the intersection of Main and Elm and that you had just gotten the call from your office about the missed inspection. But you will offer evidence that missed inspections are fairly common and that the phone call in no way distracted you. Also, you were driving with expensive kitchen cabinets in the back of your truck, so you were driving especially carefully. After waiting for traffic coming the other way to clear, you made a left turn onto Elm. As you did so, your eyes were on the road. You plan to offer evidence that the plaintiff's witness, who will say that she saw you looking out your driver's side window, is the plaintiff's fiancee, and so is biased. In addition, you will impeach her with her statement to a police officer at the scene of the accident that she was not paying close attention to your truck before it struck the plaintiff.

Your version of what happened next is that as you straightened out and started driving at a normal rate of speed on Elm, the plaintiff suddenly ran out from between two parked cars directly into the path of your truck. You braked, but could not avoid hitting the plaintiff. Nevertheless you were not going much more than 5 to 10 m.p.h. when you struck the plaintiff, and you do not believe that you broke his leg. Indeed, an orthopedic doctor who examined the plaintiff's X-rays and other medical records at your request is prepared to testify for you that the plaintiff's leg problem was an old injury that was not caused by your hitting him.

Based on the information above, at trial you can attack the credibility of at least one of the plaintiff's facts. That is, you can impeach the plaintiff's witness based on her possible bias and the inconsistent statement she made to a police officer. You can also try to prove two facts of your own contradictory to the plaintiff's version based on your evidence: that you were driving carefully, and that you did not cause the plaintiff to break his leg. Based on this information, your outline will look like the one below.

Legal Claim: Negligence

Element 1:

I had a legal duty of care towards Plaintiff.

Fact Plaintiff will try to prove:

At the time of the accident, I was driving a truck in the immediate vicinity of where Plaintiff was a pedestrian crossing the street.

Evidence disproving this fact:

None. [*You might as well stipulate (agree) to the truth of this fact. You will not contest this fact. As a matter of law, you had a duty to the plaintiff to drive safely. Whether the plaintiff was in the crosswalk, running out from between two cars, or standing on his head and barking for a fish, the plaintiff was in the vicinity of your truck.*]

Element 2:

I breached the duty by acting carelessly.

Fact Plaintiff will try to prove:

I drove carelessly by making a left turn while not paying attention to pedestrians in the road.

Evidence disproving this fact:

Plaintiff's witness is not credible—as his fiancee, she is biased. Also, she has made inconsistent statements about her ability to observe. She now says that she saw me looking out the driver's side window, but right after the accident she told a police officer that she wasn't paying close attention to my truck before the accident.

My contradictory fact:

I was driving carefully with my eyes on the road.

Evidence proving my fact:

Nothing was distracting me; phone calls about missed inspections are routine. Also, I was driving especially carefully because I had expensive kitchen cabinets in the back of my truck that I was going to deliver to another job.

Element 3:

My careless driving directly caused harm to Plaintiff.

Fact Plaintiff will try to prove:

Being hit by my truck directly caused Plaintiff's leg to be broken.

Evidence disproving this fact:

I have no information to impeach Plaintiff.

My contradictory fact:

I did not break Plaintiff's leg; any leg problem that he had was due to an old injury not caused by my truck.

Evidence proving my fact:

Dr. Even will testify based on examining Plaintiff's medical records that Plaintiff's leg problem was caused by an old injury.

Element 4:

Plaintiff suffered economic losses and personal injuries.

Fact Plaintiff will try to prove:

Plaintiff's broken leg had to be operated on. He was on crutches for four months, was in pain during that period, and has a permanent limp. His medical expenses were $20,000.

Evidence disproving this fact:

None. All these things may be true, but I wasn't the cause of them and I wasn't careless.

TRIAL NOTEBOOK

Once you have completed it, place your outline in the "Legal Claim Outline" section of your trial notebook. Devote a separate page of your notebook to each element you plan to contest. That way, you will not get confused in the heat of trial about which evidence pertains to which fact. If the same evidence pertains to more than one element, simply include it on more than one page. ●

Selecting the Decision Maker

Trial by jury is one of the traditions of the American legal system. But many cases, especially civil cases, are decided by a judge sitting without a jury. Some kinds of cases never have a jury. Usually, however, the parties themselves decide whether a case is tried in front of a jury. In most court systems, judges decide cases unless one of the litigants makes a timely pretrial request for a jury trial and posts (deposits) jury fees.

This chapter discusses your role in choosing who will rule on your case. You'll learn how to find out whether you are entitled to a jury trial. And you'll see that even if you are, as a self-represented party, you are almost always better off choosing a judge trial. However, yours may be the unusual case that should be tried to a jury, or your adversary may put in a jury trial request. Therefore, this chapter also explains the entire jury selection process.

Are You Eligible for a Jury Trial?

A jury trial may not be available for your case. For example, you are not entitled to a jury trial if you are not seeking money but instead an order that your adversary do (or stop doing) something —called "injunctive relief"—such as tear down (or stop building) a building that encroaches on your property. Also, in most states you cannot have a jury trial in cases involving child support and child custody. In most other cases, such as those involving personal injury, breach of contract, professional malpractice, libel, or slander, you are entitled to a jury trial.

And You Thought We Won Our Independence

The reason that jury trials are not available in all kinds of cases is that many of our legal procedures trace their roots to England, where in centuries past there were two kinds of courts: law courts and equity courts. Each handled different matters. Jury trials were available in courts of law but not in courts of equity. Today, even though these ancient distinctions between courts have largely disappeared, your right to a jury trial often depends on whether English courts would have dealt with your case in the law or equity courts. Ironically, England, which started the whole mess in the first place, has nearly eliminated jury trials in civil cases altogether.

TIP

Check out your options. If you are considering requesting a jury trial, first check with the court clerk to make sure that you are entitled to one. If the clerk cannot tell you, seek the advice of an experienced trial lawyer.

Are You Better Off With a Judge or a Jury?

When representing yourself, you are generally better off trying your case to a judge than to a jury. By not going before a jury, you eliminate a number of procedural hassles. For example, you do not have to worry about:

- meeting the deadline to make a jury request
- depositing jury fees with the court, and
- preparing jury instructions. (Chapter 14 discusses jury instructions.)

In addition, a judge trial is likely to be more informal and easier for you to conduct than a jury trial. For example, in the absence of a jury, your judge may not insist on strict adherence to courtroom procedural rules and rules of evidence. And you can reasonably expect a judge to ignore inflammatory, irrelevant, or other inadmissible evidence from your adversary that slips by you because of your unfamiliarity with evidence rules. Jurors, however, may well be influenced by the evidence even if the judge tells them to disregard it. (See Chapters 16 and 17 for more on evidence and objections.)

Despite the additional complexities a jury trial brings, you may prefer one because you think that a jury will be more sympathetic to your case than a judge. But whether a judge or a jury trial is more likely to produce a favorable result is a complicated question, one that many experienced lawyers readily acknowledge rarely has an easy answer. Lawyer "folk wisdom" often points to choosing a jury if a case has emotional appeal and choosing a judge if a case is complex and based on technical legal questions. However, even lawyers are wary of such broad stereotypes. Your knowledge of the attitudes and values of the people in your community is probably more relevant than general folk wisdom.

For example, assume that you have sued two police officers for using excessive force when mistakenly arresting you. If the trial will take place in a conservative law-and-order community where likely jurors regularly back the police, but several local judges have a reputation for being highly independent of local politics, you may want to choose a judge trial. By contrast, if many of the people in the community have themselves been victimized by overzealous police officers, and local judges have close ties with police officer associations, you may be better off with a jury trial.

As a rough guide to juror attitudes, talk to acquaintances who seem representative of the people who are likely to become jurors. How do they react to your case? Even allowing for feelings of personal friendship, do they seem sympathetic to your position? Or do they have a negative reaction, perhaps because your case seems to depend on legal technicalities? Such discussions can help you decide whether to opt for a jury trial.

Your Opponent's Right to a Jury Trial

You may end up with a jury trial even if you prefer a judge trial. This is because your adversary has an independent right to request a jury trial. Unfortunately, if your adversary requests a jury trial, you will have one, whether you want it or not.

Disqualifying a Judge

Judges wield much power, even in jury trials. A judge, not a jury, decides what evidence may be admitted and (subject to broad guidelines) how other important procedural rules will be applied. A judge even has the power to overturn a jury verdict and either enter a different verdict or order a new trial. (See Chapter 20 for more on these procedures.)

If you are unhappy with the background or the attitudes of the judge who has been assigned to preside over your case, consider disqualifying the judge, whether or not you plan to have a jury trial.

Automatic Disqualification

Some states' civil procedure rules give you the right to automatically disqualify your assigned judge, even if a jury will decide your case. For example, in California you can disqualify a judge by filing a form called an Affidavit of Prejudice. (See California Code of Civil Procedure § 170.6) You needn't actually prove that the judge is prejudiced against you or your legal claim; your statement of belief is sufficient.

After you file the Affidavit of Prejudice, a second judge is automatically assigned to preside over the trial. However, this automatic disqualification is almost always a one-shot opportunity. (That's why such rules are sometimes referred to as "one free bite" rules.) You'll have to accept the second judge unless you can prove that the second judge is actually biased against you or your legal claim or has an obvious conflict of interest (for example, before becoming a judge, the judge represented your adversary).

Federal courts do not have a "one free bite" rule. In federal courts, a party seeking to remove a judge on the ground of bias or prejudice normally has to demonstrate that the judge is actually biased or prejudiced against the party. Under 28 United States Code. § 144, a party has to file an affidavit that states "facts and the reasons for the belief that bias or prejudice exists." The statute doesn't establish a procedure for deciding whether a judge is biased: Strangely enough, in actual practice, the very judge whom a party is seeking to disqualify usually decides whether the assertions in an affidavit are sufficient to establish actual bias or prejudice.

> **CAUTION**
>
> **Watch your deadlines.** Your right to disqualify a judge is likely to be subject to strict time deadlines. You may have as few as ten days after a judge has been assigned to preside over your trial to disqualify the judge. If you don't find out which judge will preside over your trial until the day that your case is assigned for trial, you may have as little as ten minutes to seek to disqualify the judge! Check your local rules carefully for deadlines for disqualifying a judge, and for the name of any form that you have to file in connection with your disqualification request.

Who Will Be Your Judge?

Some court systems use "all-purpose judges," meaning that the judge assigned to your case the moment it is filed will preside over all court proceedings, from pretrial motions to trial. If your case is assigned to an all-purpose judge, you may have plenty of time to check out and consider disqualifying him or her.

But in other court systems, you may not learn who will preside over your case until the day it is set for trial. If you find yourself in this kind of court system (and you can easily find out by asking the court clerk when you file a complaint or answer), you will have to check into the backgrounds of the various judges to whom your case may be assigned. Armed with that knowledge, you can disqualify a judge within the time allowed if you decide to do so.

TIP

Beware of pro tem judges. Because what are called "pro tem judges" don't have independent status (they serve at the pleasure of the court), they may be less likely to make a controversial ruling than a regular judge for fear of not being rehired. Even more important, because many pro tems do not conduct trials as frequently as judges and do not attend judges' training and continuing education sessions, they may not be as familiar with the law that affects your case. Nolo regularly receives complaints about inadequate pro tem judges.

Investigating a Judge

Your right to disqualify a judge won't do you much good unless you know enough about the judge's background and attitudes to make an informed judgment about how fair your judge is likely to be. Here are some of the ways to investigate a judge:

- **Check with lawyers, especially your legal coach if you have one, about the judge's reputation.** Ask what kinds of cases the judge handled before going on the bench, whether the judge is generally plaintiff- or defendant-oriented, how the judge might react to your type of case, and what the judge's attitude towards a self-represented party is likely to be.

- **If you live in an area that has a newspaper directed toward lawyers, find out if it publishes biographies of judges.** Many legal newspapers publish judicial profiles for lawyers that describe judges' law practice backgrounds, their attitudes towards litigation, and the community organizations to which they belong. Often, judicial profiles also contain capsule "reviews" by attorneys who have appeared in a judge's court. (In California, these biographies are compiled in a regularly updated book called *Judicial Profiles*, which is available to the public in law libraries.)

- **If you have time, sit in the courtroom while the judge who is assigned to your case presides over a different trial.** Observe the judge's attitude, listen to the rulings the judge makes, and watch how the judge works with parties, lawyers, and witnesses. Though you cannot make definitive judgments based on a short observation, you may gain some insight as to whether the judge will be fair-minded in your case.

Making a Timely Request for a Jury Trial

Even if your case is eligible for trial by jury, in most court systems it will be tried by a judge alone unless you or your adversary requests a jury trial. Jury requests must usually be made in writing well in advance of trial and even before a trial date is set. For example, if your case is in federal court, your "demand" for a jury trial must be served on your adversary no later than ten days after service of the last pleading, often the defendant's answer. (FRCP 38.) And, in California, a party wanting a jury trial must make a written Notice of Motion for a jury trial within five days after an At Issue Memorandum has been filed. (Rule 377 of the California Pretrial and Trial Rules.) (An At Issue Memorandum is simply a document indicating that all parties have been served and estimating the likely amount of time required for trial. Your court system may well require the filing of a similar document, though it may not go by the same name. See "Initial Pretrial Procedures" in Chapter 4.) If you miss the request deadline, you waive your right to a jury trial.

If you want a jury trial, check your court's rules carefully to find out the deadline for making the request. Rules about deadlines for jury trial requests are often found in a book of civil procedure rules or local court rules. If you have difficulty finding the rule for your court system, ask a court clerk or a law librarian or check with your legal coach.

> **CAUTION**
>
> **Pay jury fees on time.** People selected as jurors receive a small amount of money for each day they serve, and, in civil cases, the parties themselves have to pay this money. In most court systems, whoever requests a jury usually has to pay a deposit of one day's jury fees (often $50–$150) before trial. You can lose your right to a jury trial if you fail to post jury fees on time.

TIP

You can recover jury fees from your adversary if you win. Jury fees are a "cost of trial," which ordinarily means the loser of a trial must reimburse the winner. If the jury decides the case in your favor, be sure to ask the judge to order your adversary to reimburse you for any jury fees you paid.

The Jury Selection Process

The exact procedures for selecting a jury vary from one court system to another, but they are similar in all courts. On the day your case goes to trial, a group of prospective jurors is selected at random from a large pool of possible jurors. If the jury will consist of the traditional 12 jurors, about 30 prospective jurors will be called. If civil juries in your court system consist of only six or eight jurors, the jury pool is likely to be correspondingly smaller.

The pool of prospective jurors is bought into the courtroom, and a smaller group of 12 (or fewer) jurors is chosen at random and seated in the jury box. After they are seated, jurors are often referred to by number, with "Juror No. 1" typically occupying the seat in the upper left-hand corner of the jury box. This group is the initial jury panel. The other prospective jurors remain in the courtroom, ready to replace any prospective jurors who are excused (dismissed) from serving on the jury.

Once the prospective jurors are seated in the jury box, the judge (or the judge and the parties) ask them questions. The goal of this questioning process, which goes by the old French term "voir dire," is to select a fair and impartial jury. (By the way, don't

Who Questions the Prospective Jurors?

Traditionally, lawyers did almost all of the voir dire questioning. However, over the years, many judges have come to believe that lawyers take too much time to question prospective jurors and use the process to try to persuade jurors of the merits of their case rather than to simply select a group of impartial jurors. For example, a defense lawyer in a negligence case may ask, "Ms. Johnson, just because Ms. Nolo happened to get hurt when she came uninvited to my client's house, you don't think that she should automatically recover any damages, do you?" By asking dozens of questions such as these, some lawyers have managed to make jury selection take longer than the trial itself! As a result, today many judges conduct most or all of the voir dire questioning.

If your case will be tried to a jury, find out ahead of time how the judge who will preside over your trial handles voir dire. You will probably have to ask the judge's court clerk, because local court rules may leave the procedure up to the judge. Here are the likely alternatives:

- Your judge may ask only a few background questions and leave most of the questioning to you and your adversary.
- The judge may conduct most of the voir dire but allow you and your adversary a limited amount of time to ask questions afterwards.
- The judge may conduct all of the voir dire but invite you and your adversary to submit written questions that the judge may choose to ask.

worry about the exact pronunciation of voir dire. Like recipes for Caesar salad dressing, everyone's is different. For what it's worth, we pronounce it "vwar-deer.")

Initially, jurors are usually questioned by the judge about their general personal backgrounds, such as their marital status, occupations, and previous jury service. Then either the judge or you and your adversary will question them further, searching for biases that might prevent them from being fair and impartial. These questions typically relate directly to the evidence that will be offered in the upcoming trial. For example, say you're suing an attorney for legal malpractice for giving erroneous advice about a will, as a result of which you didn't get an inheritance. It makes sense for you (or the judge) to question the prospective jurors both as to their experiences with or biases for or against attorneys. In addition, you may ask them if they have ever received property through a will or failed to receive property when they expected to.

Similarly, if you are involved in a negligence case and there is a claim that you or your adversary had been drinking before an accident, you (or the judge) will probably question the prospective jurors about their attitudes towards and experiences with alcohol. For instance, they will probably be asked whether or not they drink, what they think about people who drink, and whether they think it's possible for a person to drink alcohol without becoming drunk.

Many voir dire questions are asked of the jury panel as a whole. For example, you may ask, "Have any of you personally hired an attorney in connection with a will?" Other questions are put to individual prospective jurors. For instance, assume that a prospective juror named Mike Asimow raised his hand in response to your question about having hired an attorney in connection with a will. You may then ask a question such as, "Mr. Asimow [or "Juror No. 3"], please tell me about your experience with the attorney."

After the panel of jurors has been questioned, you and your adversary are allowed to excuse prospective jurors in a process called "challenging jurors." (See "Your Right to Challenge Jurors," below, for more on this process.) Prospective jurors are challenged and excused one at a time, with the plaintiff usually getting to exercise the first challenge. For example, a plaintiff may say, "I wish to excuse Juror No. 5." (In some courts, the parties send notes to the judge indicating which prospective jurors they want to excuse. The judge then does the actual excusing, so that the remaining jurors cannot blame either party if a friend is dismissed from the panel.)

If the judge allows the challenge, the challenged juror will be sent back to the jury room and a new prospective juror will be selected at random from the original jury pool. The new Juror No. 5 will be questioned, then the defendant will have a turn to challenge a juror. The defendant can then challenge any one of the original prospective jurors or the new Juror No. 5. Or, the defendant can temporarily pass, meaning that the right to challenge goes back to the plaintiff.

The question-and-challenge process continues until both sides accept the same group of jurors or until both sides have challenged as many prospective jurors as they are allowed by local court rules. At that point the court clerk officially swears in the jury, and the trial—mercifully—begins.

TRIAL NOTEBOOK

Keep track of jurors. If you will have a jury trial, devote a section of your trial notebook to jury selection. You can include in that section a box chart that, for a 12-person jury, looks like the one shown below.

As each potential juror takes a seat, write the juror's name in the numbered space corresponding to his or her seat in the jury box. If that juror is removed, cross out the name and write in the new one. In the remaining space, take notes on the jurors' answers during voir dire questioning so that you can ask follow-up questions (if you are able to) and exercise challenges.

Juror 1	Juror 2	Juror 3	Juror 4	Juror 5	Juror 6
Juror 7	Juror 8	Juror 9	Juror 10	Juror 11	Juror 12

Your Right to Challenge Jurors

Because part of the jury selection process entails challenging and excusing prospective jurors, you need to understand the two kinds of juror challenges and the important distinctions between them.

Challenges for Cause

A challenge "for cause" asks a judge to excuse a person as a prospective juror on the ground that a legal impediment to that person's service as a juror exists. Normally, the impediment is something in a person's background or answers to questions indicating that the person is not fair and impartial. You and your adversary are allowed an unlimited number of challenges for cause, because you are both entitled to jurors who are fair.

Sometimes the basis of a challenge for cause is so obvious that the judge will excuse a juror him- or herself as soon as it becomes apparent. For example, assume that in response to the judge's initial background questioning, a prospective juror states that he or she is personally acquainted with you or your opponent. That juror will probably be excused by the judge at once on the ground that it is almost impossible for a person who knows one of the parties to decide a case fairly based on the evidence presented in court. Likewise, a judge will immediately excuse a prospective juror who has a job that will inevitably bias the juror's attitudes towards you or your adversary. For example, assume that you are suing a lawyer for legal malpractice. The judge will probably excuse for cause any prospective jurors who are lawyers or who work for insurance companies that write legal malpractice insurance. Finally, the judge will probably excuse for cause any prospective jurors who appear to be ill or infirm or unable to serve for the length of time your trial is likely to last.

Usually, however, judges do not excuse jurors on their own. It is up to you to ask the judge to excuse a juror for cause on the ground that the juror's personal background or voir dire answers demonstrate bias against you. Your request will be granted if the judge agrees that a prospective juror is biased.

To persuade a judge to grant your challenge for cause, you may have to convince the judge that a prospective juror is biased. Your adversary can also get into the act and may well try to persuade the judge that the juror has not demonstrated bias. After all, the same answers that prompt you to think that a prospective juror may be biased against you will probably lead your adversary to want that person to serve on the jury.

Let's illustrate briefly how an argument over a challenge for cause might proceed. Assume that you are the plaintiff in a negligence lawsuit. You know that there will be evidence that you drank a beer one hour before the accident and you know that the defendant will argue that because you had

been drinking, the accident was your fault. During voir dire, Juror No. 3, Ms. Morrow, said that she does not drink, that she does not serve liquor of any type in her house, and that, in her opinion, people would be far better off if they never drank alcohol. At the same time, she said that she could be fair to you and would not decide the case against you simply because you had taken a drink. However, you do not trust Juror No. 3 to decide the case fairly; based on what she said and how she said it, you think she is likely to be biased against you because you had a drink. Here is how you might try to persuade the judge to excuse Juror No. 3 for cause:

1 **Judge:**
Ms. Nolo, it is your turn to challenge.

2 **You:**
Your Honor, I challenge Juror No. 3 for cause.

3 **Judge:**
What is the basis of your challenge?

4 **You:**
Your Honor, she said that she is a lifelong teetotaler. She never drinks, she does not associate with people who drink, and she thinks that nobody should drink. She is entitled to that belief, but I don't think that someone who has those beliefs can give me a fair trial. There will be some evidence that I had a beer, and from what she said, it's clear that she'd be biased against me because of that.

5 **Judge:**
Mr. Scott [opposing counsel], *any response?*

6 **Mr. Scott:**

Yes, Your Honor. We oppose the request and ask that you deny the challenge for cause. Ms. Morrow described her beliefs, which many people share, but she said that she will be fair, that she will listen to the evidence for both sides, and that she will base her decision strictly on the evidence and not on her personal beliefs. I see no basis for a challenge for cause.

7 **Judge:**

Well, based on what I heard, she said she could be fair and has in no way prejudged the case. If we kicked everybody off the jury who doesn't drink or thinks drinking is a social problem, we'd have trouble putting juries together. I don't think there's enough here to sustain a challenge for cause. I'm going to deny the request.

Losing a request to dismiss a juror for cause is not uncommon. As long as a prospective juror claims to have an open mind and promises to base a decision strictly on the evidence, many judges feel that a challenge for cause should not be granted. But having lost the argument, you may still be able to remove Juror No. 3 by exercising a peremptory challenge, discussed below.

Peremptory Challenges

A "peremptory challenge" is one that you can exercise for any reason whatsoever. Unlike a challenge for cause, you don't have to explain or justify your challenge to the judge. For example, perhaps you want to excuse Juror No. 8 because she has an occupation that suggests to you that she will not give you a fair shot, because she smiled at your adversary but not at you, or because she dresses in a way that you do not like. Or maybe your intuition tells you, "This is not a person who I want making a very important decision that affects my future." The point is that you have a right to excuse any prospective juror with a peremptory challenge by simply telling the judge that you wish to "thank and excuse Juror No. 8."

If all this sounds too good to be true, be aware of a major restriction on peremptory challenges: You get only a few. This makes sense—if the number of peremptory challenges were unlimited, you or your adversary could excuse all the jurors in the pool. The exact number of allowed peremptory challenges varies from one court system to another. For example, in federal civil trials, each party gets only three peremptory challenges. (28 U.S.C. § 1870.) In California, each party gets six peremptory challenges, while Arizona allows four peremptories each. (Cal. Civ. Proc. Code § 231; Arizona Rule of Civil Procedure 47(e).)

Before trial, read your state statutes and court rules very carefully and talk to the court clerk so that you know how many peremptory challenges you will be allowed. You do not want to use up your last peremptory challenge on a whim, only to have the next prospective juror be someone you really do not like. Remember, your adversary has the same number of peremptory challenges as you and, unfortunately, may use them to excuse jurors whom you really want to have on the jury.

TIP

Make a challenge for cause rather than a peremptory challenge whenever possible. If you think that a prospective juror's background or responses to voir dire questioning demonstrate bias against you, always try to convince a judge to excuse a juror for cause before you exercise a peremptory challenge (assuming that you have a peremptory left). Because excusing a juror for cause does not cost you one of your precious, limited number of peremptory challenges, you are much better off convincing a judge to grant your challenge for cause than exercising a peremptory challenge.

But if you have no peremptory challenges left, do not challenge a juror for cause unless you are confident your challenge will be granted. It's almost always a bad idea to have a juror on the panel whom you have unsuccessfully challenged for cause. If the juror you tried to dismiss for cause did not think ill of you before you argued that he or she was biased, think of how that juror is likely to feel toward you after you have pointed out in public why he or she is likely to be unfair!

What Jurors Should You Challenge?

Just reading about the jury voir dire process may convince you that you are generally better off with a judge than a jury trial. Deciding who is likely to be fair and who may be biased can be a difficult task. However, the fact that you are not an attorney does not put you at a big disadvantage. For example, in a recent nationally reported case, a judge granted a defense attorney's request to excuse a juror in the middle of a trial, on the ground that the juror appeared to be biased against the attorney's client. After he was excused, the juror told reporters he was in fact very sympathetic towards the lawyer's client! Most trial attorneys admit that selecting jurors is based as much on intuition and common sense as on anything else and that your most crucial tasks are to listen and observe carefully. If you pay close attention to what prospective jurors say and how they say it, there is no reason why you cannot do as good a job of selecting jurors as an attorney.

Perhaps no area of the law has been as dominated by lawyer folk wisdom as the selection of jurors. Traditionally, lawyers have drawn upon broad stereotypes when deciding whether to exercise peremptory challenges. For example, people who belonged to certain groups were said to be either good plaintiffs' jurors or good defense jurors, based on stereotypes about those groups. Today, in our multicultural and complex society, broad stereotypes tend to be of little value. You are probably better off learning as much as you can about each prospective juror's personal background and evaluating how someone with that background is likely to react to your evidence.

For example, if you are 25 years old and were injured in a traffic accident when going from one party to another at 2 a.m., you may not want an 80-year-old person who never goes out at night to sit on your jury. If you claim that you were illegally fired from your position as an executive earning $200,000 a year, you may not want a person who works for minimum wage sitting on your jury. And if you are a tenant seeking the right to remain in your apartment by fighting what you claim is an unlawful eviction notice, you may not want a landlord on your jury. Admittedly, such decisions also rest on stereotypes: that an 80-year-old shut-in might have no sympathy for a young "party animal," that a person who works for minimum wages might be unable to identify with a corporate executive, and that one landlord will sympathize with another. But at least these assumptions rest on specific, relevant factors in your case rather than on broad categories that may very well be untrue.

What Should You Ask Prospective Jurors?

Whether or not you are allowed to question jurors yourself (remember, some judges only let you submit questions for the judge to ask), think carefully about what information will help you decide whether a person can be fair and impartial in your case.

Word your questions in a way that encourages prospective jurors to talk about their experiences and attitudes, rather than giving yes or no answers. For example, compare these two ways of asking about the same information:

WRONG: *Will you be biased against me just because I had one beer to drink an hour before the accident?*

RIGHT: *How do you feel about someone who drinks one beer and then drives a car an hour later?*

A prospective juror can answer the first question yes or no. But even a juror

who says no may harbor attitudes that would prevent the juror from being fair and impartial toward you. The second question, by contrast, encourages the juror to talk. The answer may give you a better gauge for deciding whether to exercise a challenge. Remember that a prospective juror's "body language" and how you and a juror relate to each other as people are probably at least as important as any specific response the juror gives.

TIP

You don't have to play the voir dire game. As an alternative to the approach of questioning and challenging prospective jurors, at least one authority, California Superior Court Judge Rod Duncan, suggests that a self-represented litigant may be better off simply standing up and saying something like, "These look like good and honest people to me. I'm not a lawyer and neither are they, and I trust them to apply the law fairly. No questions." Or, you might make the same type of statement and ask only, "Will any of you hold it against me because I'm not a lawyer and I may make a few mistakes trying to represent myself?"

An advantage of this approach is that you show from the outset that you are not going to try to pretend you are a lawyer. Particularly if your adversary is represented by counsel, the jurors may empathize with your "little guy vs. big guy" approach. On the other hand, to fully carry out this alternative approach, you have to be willing to forgo all challenges. You should, however, be able to rely on your judge to excuse any prospective juror who demonstrates an obvious bias against you.

TRIAL NOTEBOOK

List the topics you plan to cover during voir dire. In the jury selection section of your trial notebook, write down the topics you plan to ask about during voir dire. You won't need to ask general background questions; the judge will ask those. Instead, focus on the facts of your case.

Unless your judge allows you only to submit written questions, do not write out specific questions. If you do, you may keep your face buried in your notes rather than maintaining eye contact with the juror you are questioning and talking as one person to another.

Here's an example of how to prepare for and conduct voir dire questioning. Say you're the plaintiff in a breach of contract case, suing a building contractor for doing shoddy work and then stopping work on a 600-square-foot room addition to your home. Before trial, you made a note in your trial notebook to ask prospective jurors about their previous contacts with building contractors, whether they had any problems and, if so, how the contractor handled them, and whether they were especially sympathetic toward contractors.

1 You:

Ms. Sossin, I believe you said that you had some work done by a building contractor, is that right?

2 Juror:

Yes, we did.

3 You:

When was that?

4 Juror:

Let's see, I guess a little over four years ago.

5 You:

What did the work involve?

6 Juror:

It was just after my husband and I moved into our house. We loved it, but the den was very small. I have a large collection of Beatles albums, posters, and other memorabilia, and I wanted a larger den to display them in. So we knocked out the back wall and extended the den by about 10 feet. Altogether, we added about 150 square feet to the room.

7 You:

Did you hire a contractor to do the work?

8 Juror:

Yes.

9 You:

How did you go about finding a contractor?

10 Juror:

Well, we called on a couple of ads and asked friends for some recommendations. I think we got about three or four estimates and went with one that was not the cheapest, but that seemed like he'd do a good job.

11 You:

How did the job turn out?

12 Juror:

Very well. No major problems, maybe a couple of the usual little ones.

13 You:

What do you mean by "little ones"?

14 Juror:

I remember one problem was the ceiling. I know I asked for a smooth ceiling, but he sprayed that cheaper stuff that looks like cottage cheese up there. When I said that wasn't what we wanted, he said there must have been a misunderstanding, that the price he had quoted was for the ceiling he had sprayed. It turned out that's what the contract said; we knew we had asked for a smooth ceiling and didn't notice that the contract said something different. We worked it out—we paid a little more and got our smooth ceiling.

15 You:

Were you happy with how the contractor worked that problem out?

16 Juror:

Yes, I'd say so. The remodel cost a little more than we thought it would, but he said that he charged us less for a smooth ceiling than he would have if it had been in the contract in the first place.

17 You:

Any other problems that you remember?

18 Juror:

No.

19 You:

As you know, in this case I'm suing a building contractor for doing substandard work and refusing to finish my job. Is there anything about the experience you had with your contractor that might make you lean towards one side or the other in this case?

20 Juror:

Not at all.

21 You:

As you sit there now, what is your attitude about building contractors, based on your own personal experience and any other things you've heard about?

22 Juror:

I'd say that the person we dealt with was very professional, but I've heard that not all contractors are that way. I guess they're like people in any other line of work—some good ones, some not so good.

23 You:

Do you think you can give both sides a fair trial in this case?

24 Juror:

Oh, yes.

25 You:

You wouldn't pay more attention to what the defendant says just because you were satisfied with the contractor you worked with?

26 Juror:

Not at all.

27 You:

Would you have any special sympathy for the defendant just because he's a building contractor?

28 Juror:

No.

29 You:

All right, thank you Ms. Sossin; I appreciate your candor. Now, Mr. McCalla, I believe that you also raised your hand ….

These questions do a good job of getting the prospective juror to discuss her experiences with a building contractor. Although you ask directly whether she has any special sympathy towards contractors (No. 27), you mostly ask her to talk about those experiences. No matter how she answers No. 27, you may decide to exercise a peremptory challenge if you think that her other answers and manner of speaking suggest that she is likely to feel favoritism toward your adversary.

Your entry for this juror in the jury selection box chart of your trial notebook might look like the following:

Juror 3
• Hilary Sossin
• Mid-20s
• Graphic artist
• Married - no kids
• Never served on jury
• Had work done by contractor
Satisfied, only "little problems"
Doesn't seem particularly pro or
anti building contractors

TIP

Ask voir dire questions in a conversational manner. Studies suggest that many prospective jurors resent attorneys' voir dire questioning, feeling that they have somehow been placed on trial. They may be even more resentful of questions coming from a self-represented party, especially if you try to come off sounding like Perry Mason. So when you ask voir dire questions, always be polite, avoid lawyer imitations, and err on the side of brevity. Try to ask questions "person to person," apologize if you ask a question that even you cannot understand, and try to smile when appropriate.

Keep this respectful attitude even if you plan to exercise a peremptory challenge against a juror. Jurors often empathize with each other, and you don't want a juror on the panel who is angry at you for excusing a fellow juror in an unkind way.

Alternate Jurors

If the judge thinks that your trial will last more than a few days, the judge may seat (impanel) a regular jury panel of 12 (or fewer) jurors as well as one or two alternates. The alternate jurors sit next to the regular jurors and listen to all of the testimony but do not take part in the deliberations or the decision unless one of the regular jurors drops out. That way, the trial doesn't have to start all over again if a juror becomes ill or for some other reason must cease acting as a juror during the trial.

If no alternates have been selected and a juror drops out before the conclusion of your trial, or if more jurors drop out than there are alternates to replace them, one possibility is to start the trial all over again. That may involve relocating witnesses, missing additional days of work, and incurring additional expenses. Another possibility is to ask your adversary to stipulate (agree) to proceeding with the remaining jurors. If you both agree, a judge will almost always allow you to proceed with fewer than the regular number of jurors. Obviously, you are more likely to prefer this latter possibility if you think the trial has gone well. If the trial has not gone well, the former possibility gives you a chance to present a stronger case to a new jury. And don't overlook the possibility that your threat to insist on a whole new trial may strengthen your bargaining position if you and your adversary decide to reopen settlement discussions.

RESOURCE

Resources on Jury Selection. *Jury Selection*, by Walter Jordan (Shepard's/McGraw-Hill), is a single-volume treatise that describes common legal grounds for exercising challenges for cause and provides sample voir dire questions for plaintiffs and defendants in a variety of civil cases. An appendix lists how many peremptory challenges are allowed in each state.

Fundamentals of Trial Techniques by Thomas Mauet (Little, Brown & Co.); Chapter 2 contains a short overview of jury selection procedures and sample questions.

Jury Selection: An Attorney's Guide to Jury Law and Methods, by V. Hale Starr and Mark McCormick (Little, Brown & Co.), provides sample voir dire questions for a variety of cases and reviews some of the psychological literature on nonverbal communication. It also has a lengthy review of a simulated voir dire exercise, complete with pictures and backgrounds of prospective jurors. ●

Opening Statement

The opening statement is your first opportunity to outline the evidence you plan to offer the judge or jury. Like a good map, your opening statement should guide the judge or jury through the testimony they will hear and the documents they will see.

Giving an overview—the big picture of your case—is important. Oral testimony is normally presented during trial by a number of different witnesses in a question-and-answer format, and it can be difficult for the judge or jury to follow. They can easily get lost in the details and miss your overall story. Also, if a particular part of your witnesses' testimony is crucial to your case, you can flag it in your opening statement, so the judge or jury will pay special attention to it during the trial.

It's important to keep in mind, though, that in your opening statement you are allowed to provide only a preview of your case. It is not the time to argue how the evidence proves you should win—that comes much later, at closing argument. (See Chapter 14.)

Should You Make an Opening Statement?

Opening statements are optional, and lawyers sometimes choose not to make them. (In legal jargon, this is called "waiving" the opening statement.) Sometimes, in relatively uncomplicated cases, they figure the judge will pick up all the necessary information soon enough. Or, the judge may already have a good idea what the case is about from the pretrial conference. (See Chapter 7.) In fact, it is for this reason—to avoid repetition—that many lawyers waive their opening statements when trying a case to a judge alone.

You may not even be given the chance to make an opening statement. Your judge may consider an opening statement a waste of time, especially if there is no jury, and may not let you make an opening statement. If this happens, you may have to just proceed with the case. But you can try to assure the judge, diplomatically, that your statement will be brief. Also, you can tell the judge that you believe an opening statement will clarify an important point.

If you are the plaintiff, you should rarely, if ever, voluntarily forgo your opening statement. You want to make the most of this opportunity to tell the judge or jury about your case. After all, the burden of proof is on you, so it is an excellent idea to get the first words in.

If you are the defendant, you likely will want to give an opening statement on the theory that the best defense is a good offense. But you may decide not to make an opening statement or to make a very brief one, if your defense rests primarily on undermining the plaintiff's evidence.

For example, if your strongest theory is that the plaintiff has insufficient evidence to prove one of the elements of the claims, you may not need to outline your own evidence. Your opening statement may be quite effective if it merely states that, as the defendant, you are not obligated to prove anything, that the burden of proof requires the plaintiff to prove every element of the claims by a preponderance of the evidence, and that the evidence will clearly be insufficient for the plaintiff to meet that burden. (See Chapters 8 and 9 for more information about burdens of proof.)

TIP

Don't dwell on the burden of proof in the opening statement. You may not argue during the opening statement. (See "What Not to Say During Your Opening Statement," below.) Because the judge may regard comments about the burden of proof and the insufficiency of the evidence as argument, keep them brief.

How a Trial Proceeds

1. *Jury Selection**

2. Opening Statements
   - Plaintiff's Opening Statement
   - Defendant's Opening Statement****

3. Plaintiff's Case
   - Plaintiff's Direct Examination of Plaintiff's Witnesses
   - Defendant's Cross-Examination of Plaintiff's Witnesses

4. Defendant's Case
   - Defendant's Direct Examination of Defendant's Witnesses
   - Plaintiff's Cross-Examination of Defendant's Witnesses

5. Closing Arguments
   - Plaintiff's Closing Argument
   - Defendant's Closing Argument

6. *Jury Instructions*

7. *Jury Deliberation*

8. Verdict/Judgment

* Italicized stages occur only in jury trials.

** Defendant may choose to postpone making an opening statement until just before presenting his or her own case.

When to Make Your Opening Statement

As the term suggests, opening statements are made at the very start of a case. In a jury trial, opening statements are made after the jury has been selected and sworn in. In a judge trial, the time for opening statements occurs right after the court clerk or judge calls (announces) the case for trial.

The judge will probably ask you, if you're the plaintiff, whether you want to make an opening statement. But because some plaintiffs trying a case before a judge alone choose not to make an opening statement, the judge may assume you wish to skip your statement and start the trial by asking you to call your first witness. If this occurs, ask the judge for permission to make your opening statement.

Defendants have a choice about when to make an opening statement. The defendant who wants to make one can either:

- make an opening statement immediately after the plaintiff's opening statement, or
- wait until after the plaintiff has presented all the evidence and the defendant has cross-examined all the plaintiff's witnesses, but before the defendant calls the witnesses (called "reserving" opening statement).

If you are the defendant, there are at least a couple of advantages to making your opening statement right after the plaintiff's. Perhaps the most important is that you immediately show the judge or jury that there are two sides to the story. If you don't deliver your opening then, you take a risk that the plaintiff's story will become fixed in the judge or jury's mind before you get to present your evidence.

However, there also can be advantages to reserving your opening statement until after the plaintiff has finished presenting witnesses and you have had a chance to cross-examine those witnesses. You not only may avoid revealing evidence that the plaintiff doesn't know about, but you also have a chance to tailor your statement to the plaintiff's evidence. Finally, your opening will be fresh in the minds of jurors or the judge when you present your evidence. This allows your statement to serve as a more effective road map through your own evidence.

Pick whichever order seems best in your case, but don't be overly concerned about your decision. There is no one right way.

Putting Together Your Opening Statement

In some cases, opening statements explain legal principles, trial procedures, and other information, but the main objective is always to preview or outline the evidence. When representing yourself, your best bet is almost always to make a brief opening statement, probably no more than five or ten minutes, and stick to the essentials discussed below. It is even more important to avoid giving a long opening statement in a judge trial than in a jury trial. Judges, unlike jurors, are used to following along with testimony and figuring out what is essential to a case.

"Mornin' folks"

Introduce Yourself and Your Main Witnesses

If the judge who presides over your trial is new to you, introduce yourself. As a short and sweet introduction, you may say:

Good morning, Your Honor. I am David Martinez. I am a homeowner, and I am representing myself today in this case for breach of contract against the defendant, Ira Isaacs, the building contractor who repaired my roof.

During a jury trial you may omit this if you already introduced yourself during jury selection. If, however, the judge conducted all the jury questioning and you never got to mention your name, go ahead and introduce yourself to the jury now.

You can also introduce the various witnesses—perhaps previewing a bit of what they will testify about during trial. As the defendant in a negligence case, for instance, you can say:

Good afternoon, Your Honor. I am the defendant in this case, Sarah Adams. I am a building contractor here in town, and I am representing myself in this case brought by the plaintiff, Mr. Pedestrian. Both Mr. Pedestrian and myself will testify in this trial, as will three other main witnesses. Ms. Cynthia White will be testifying about how Mr. Pedestrian crossed in the middle of the street, darting out between several parked cars, and about how difficult it was to see him. Kevin Reback, a college student and part-time salesperson, will testify that I was driving at a safe, normal speed. And Dr. Even will testify about Mr. Pedestrian's preexisting injury to the leg he claims was hurt in the accident.

Explain the Purpose of Your Opening Statement

After you introduce yourself, briefly tell the judge or jury what's coming in your opening statement. For example, in a jury trial you might say:

Ladies and gentlemen, I will briefly tell you about the testimony you will hear and the documents I am going to introduce into evidence in this case. You will hear detailed accounts from witnesses later, so for now I will just summarize the main points.

If your case is before a judge alone, you might say:

Your Honor, as you know, I am representing myself today. I will do my best to present all of my evidence as clearly as I can and follow the court's rules to the best of my ability. So, very briefly, I will go over the witnesses you will hear from and the documents I plan on introducing into evidence to give you an idea of what this case is about in a nutshell.

Don't be surprised if the judge cuts you off at this point, especially if this same judge handled your pretrial conference. If you feel strongly that your opening statement will be helpful, ask the court to allow you just one minute to make a certain point. Otherwise, proceed, as the judge will likely direct you, to call your first witness.

Summarize Your Evidence

If you are the plaintiff, during trial you must prove facts supporting each element of your legal claims. (See Chapter 8.) Accordingly, in your opening statement, you will want to mention at least some of the evidence that you will offer to provide that proof.

Let's look at an example based on a legal malpractice case. Assume that you are suing your deceased stepmother's attorney for legal malpractice because the attorney failed to advise your stepmother, in response to her request, that she needed to change her will to disinherit a child born after the will was signed. Even though the will says you are to receive everything, because of the attorney's neglect, you are now being forced to share your stepmother's estate with the child. You may say:

The defendant admits he is a licensed attorney in this state. The evidence will show that my stepmother called the defendant and asked whether it was necessary to change her will after having a new child whom she did not want to take any of her property. You will hear from my stepmother's best friend that she heard my stepmother say she wanted all her property to go to me and not to her son. My stepmother did not want him to have her money because she knew he had problems, and she believed he would waste the money. She also knew I had two children to support. You will also see proof in letters she wrote me through the years saying that she wanted me to have all her property. But because the defendant negligently advised her, the son she wanted to disinherit will get half her property, and some $60,000 that my family and I need desperately will now go to him—just what my stepmother wanted to prevent.

Although it's unlikely, a case can be dismissed if the plaintiff's opening statement is deficient. A defendant can ask the judge to dismiss the lawsuit (this is called "declaring a nonsuit") if the plaintiff's opening statement shows that the plaintiff does not have evidence to prove each of the required elements of his or her legal claims. So, if you are the plaintiff, when summarizing the evidence be sure to at least touch on some facts that help prove each element of your legal claims. (See Chapter 8.)

If you are the defendant, however, it's best not to ask the judge to dismiss the lawsuit for this reason. Judges usually allow plaintiffs some—often a great deal of—leeway. And by saying what evidence the plaintiff has failed to prove so early in the case, you may end up helping the plaintiff fix the defects and present sufficient evidence on all the right points during the trial.

Tell the Judge or Jury What You Want

Ask explicitly, at the outset, for the ultimate result you want. This sometimes gets lost in the many details presented during trial. Make it easy for the judge or jury to know what you want from them. For example:

Your Honor, after hearing all the evidence, I hope you will rule that the defendant breached our contract to repair my roof and order that he pay me the $20,000 I had to pay to get it repaired properly.

What Not to Say During Your Opening Statement

There are two important pitfalls to avoid when you make your opening statement: Do not discuss evidence that may not become part of the court record, and do not argue.

Don't Refer to Evidence That May Not Be Presented

If you are not sure how a witness will testify, don't tell the judge or jury what you think the witness will say. There are two good reasons for this. First, if your speculation turns out to be wrong, your opponent (or even the judge) may point out your misrepresentation during closing arguments. This can make you look bad. Second, if you distort key testimony or misrepresent a crucial fact, and it becomes clear that your opening prejudiced your opponent's case, your adversary can ask the judge for a mistrial.

Declaring a mistrial means the judge will stop the trial and set a new one. A mistrial is granted when something jeopardizes a party's right to a fair trial. For example, assume you hope the defendant will testify that she had three martinis before she got in her truck and that she was not watching the road when she hit you, but you are not sure exactly what she will say. If you tell the jury that the defendant consumed the three drinks before the accident, and it turns out that no evidence is admitted to support your assertions, you may have seriously damaged the defendant's chances of getting a fair trial. And you'll raise the chances of the judge declaring a mistrial.

> **TIP**
>
> **Use "the evidence will show" in your statement.** It can be helpful to introduce some of your comments with the phrase, "The evidence will show …." This forces you to stick to evidence you can and will prove during trial and not shift into argument. Even if you omit the phrase when you actually speak in court, writing it in a draft statement before trial may serve as a reminder to summarize only evidence you know will be presented.

Similarly, do not refer to documents or other exhibits that you are not certain will be admitted into evidence. For example, do not refer to a business record you hope to introduce unless you are certain you can lay a foundation showing it is trustworthy. (See Chapter 15 for more on exhibits.)

How do you know what evidence you can refer to so that you can make a legally bulletproof opening statement? There are a number of ways to be sure you are on safe ground. It's safe to mention evidence if:

- you can testify about that evidence from your own personal knowledge
- it involves a fact that was referred to in a letter, business or government record, or other admissible exhibit that you will present in evidence (see Chapter 15)
- your opponent or a witnesses corroborated the information in pretrial discovery (for example, your adversary made the statement in interrogatories or requests for admission or a witness or your opponent said so in a deposition), or
- one of your witnesses, whom you have interviewed many times, has stated this information very clearly each time you talked. (While there is always some risk, if you have interviewed the person thoroughly before trial and you trust the person, you can probably feel comfortable that the evidence will not suddenly change at trial.)

Don't Argue

You are not allowed to argue during your opening statement. In addition to the usual meaning of "argument"—raising your voice or demeaning your adversary—in this context, argument also means going beyond just stating what you will prove and how you will prove it. Demonstrating why the facts and law compel the judge or jury to arrive at a particular result is considered argument. Think of it this way: Your opening statement should be a preview, not an analysis.

Unfortunately, the line between merely presenting evidence and arguing about or analyzing that evidence is not always clear. To help you stay on proper footing, let's look at some of the verbal techniques that are generally considered argument, so that you can avoid them in your opening statement.

Don't Discuss Credibility

The credibility (believability) of each witness is important—often critical—to the resolution of a case. The judge or jury will likely accept evidence from someone they believe, but discredit what they have difficulty believing. You will strive to bring out both positive and negative credibility issues in your direct and cross-examinations, as well as in your closing argument. But during opening statement, you are not allowed to say why the judge or jury should believe you or your witnesses or why they should discount the testimony of your opponent's witnesses.

Let's look again at an example using the attorney malpractice case about the will dispute. Your stepmother's best friend, Lori Van Lowe, a clinical psychologist by profession, will testify on your behalf. She is not to receive anything under the will and doesn't stand to gain anything from the case. The only reason she is testifying is that, as a close friend and confidante of your stepmother, she likely knew better than anyone else what your stepmother wanted.

This background may show that Ms. Van Lowe is a credible witness. And in your closing argument, you will be allowed to tell the judge or jury exactly how the information demonstrates her credibility. (See Chapter 14 for more on closing arguments.) During your opening statement, however, you must confine yourself to simply stating the evidence or else you may slide over the line into impermissible argument. For example, it is acceptable to say:

Ladies and gentlemen, a woman named Lori Van Lowe will be one of the chief witnesses in this trial. She was a close friend and confidante of my stepmother, so she knew better than anyone else what my stepmother wanted. Ms. Van Lowe, a clinical psychologist by profession, will not receive anything under my stepmother's will—no matter who wins this case.

By contrast, it is *impermissible* argument to say:

Ms. Van Lowe is believable. She has nothing to gain from saying that I was to take everything under the will. She knows about human nature because she's a psychologist. And she is far more believable than the lawyer, whose professional reputation is at stake.

Don't Draw Inferences From Evidence

Another no-no during opening statement (though an essential part of your closing argument) is drawing inferences from evidence. Drawing an inference means linking the evidence to the facts you are trying to prove or disprove.

For example, let's look at an item of evidence in a breach of contract case. Assume that you are the plaintiff who hired a builder to put a new roof on your home. After the roof was completed, a storm hit, and the neighbor's tree fell onto your home. The roof caved in immediately. An inspection showed the builder used ultrathin plywood instead of the stronger product you contracted for.

In your opening, you can properly say:

As the contract that will be put into evidence in this case shows, on January 4 I hired the builder Corrie Kaufman to put a new roof on my house. After the roof was completed, a storm hit and the neighbor's tree fell on our home. The roof caved in immediately. We then hired Danica Bradley, a building inspector who will be testifying, who found that the builder used quarter-inch plywood instead of the half-inch plywood we contracted for.

But you cannot ask the jury to make an inference about the facts. For instance you may *not* say:

After the roof was completed, a storm hit, and the neighbor's tree fell on our home. The roof caved in immediately. It's obvious that the builder used inferior quality wood because he was trying to earn extra profits at my expense.

In the first (proper) example, you have evidence from the inspector that the builder actually used quarter-inch plywood, a breach of the contract term that required using a thicker grade of wood. But in the second (improper) example, you are asking the jury to make an inference that the roofer used thin plywood to make extra profits. Without specific evidence to support this assertion, you must wait until closing argument to ask the judge or jury to draw this inference.

Let's take a look at another example. Assume that you are the plaintiff in a car accident case. You sued the defendant, Sarah Adams, for negligence because her truck hit you at Elm and Main Streets. To help prove that the defendant was speeding, you will offer evidence that just before the accident she got a call on her cell phone telling her about a problem on one of her jobs, and she changed course to drive to the job site.

It would be proper to say:

Ladies and Gentlemen, you will hear evidence that just before the accident, Ms. Adams got a call on her cell phone telling her about a problem on one of her job sites, and she changed direction at once to go to that job site.

It would be improper to add to the above remarks:

Ms. Adams must have been very upset by the phone call and in a hurry to get to the job site. That's why she was speeding.

In the proper example, you refer only to the evidence that will be presented. In the second example, you improperly tell the jury what inference to draw from the evidence. The second example is, however, perfectly proper for your closing argument (see Chapter 14).

Don't Personally Attack Your Adversary

It is clearly inappropriate to attack your opponent personally. Don't, for instance, add to your comments above by saying:

And besides, it's clear that this slimy builder [pointing and making a face at the defendant] *was trying to make a quick buck. He screwed me because he knew I didn't have the time to stand there and watch every minute of work he did.*

The judge may sharply reprimand you for such attacks, and if you are trying your case to a jury, you will not impress and may greatly offend them. In rare instances, a judge may feel you so violated the rules and prejudiced your opponent as to merit a mistrial. So stick to the evidence and be respectful, even if your adversary *is* slimy.

If your adversary personally attacks you, take the high road. Don't fall into the trap and argue back. The judge or jury may find your opponent's comments just as distasteful as you do, causing them to lean in your favor. If the comments get too offensive, either object (that the comments are not within the proper scope of opening statement) or ask to speak to the judge at the bench. Then tell the judge that you feel your opponent's comments are inappropriate and prejudicial. Request that the judge admonish (reprimand and warn) your opponent to stop making them.

Rehearsing and Presenting Your Opening Statement

Most of these suggestions apply any time you speak in court, and they are especially helpful for a strong opening statement.

Use an Outline, Don't Read a Speech

After deciding what you want to say, write out your opening statement. Then practice saying it, both alone in front of a mirror and with a trusted friend, to hear how it flows and to get comfortable with it. Also, you may ask your legal coach to briefly review it and make suggestions for improvement or warn of any impermissible material you have inadvertently included.

In court, however, do not read the full opening statement. Reading word-for-word makes you sound stilted and boring, and it keeps you from making important eye contact with the judge or jurors. Instead, outline your key points on a sheet of paper. Keep the outline in your trial notebook, which you will take to court with you. (See Chapter 18.) Take a quick look at your outline before you go up to speak, and then refer to it as needed during your opening statement. You can look down briefly and verify that you are on track as you pause between sentences or thoughts. Remember, the outline is just a guide. You can still do a fine job if your actual statement varies from it.

A completed sample outline is included below. The general format for your outline may look like the one shown below.

Remember, this is your case. You know the facts. You don't have to memorize details, just say what happened. And if you go to court with a good outline, you can use it as a checklist of points. That way you can relax and be assured you won't forget important items.

> **Opening Statement Outline**
>
> 1. Introduce Yourself and Your Main Witnesses
>
> Me: I'm not an attorney, but I'll try my best
>
> Witness #1:
>
> Witness #2:
>
> 2. Road Map (what you plan to cover in your statement and what they can expect in trial)
>
> Summary now; details about testimony and exhibits later, during trial.
>
> First you will hear evidence, then you will decide case. Judge will instruct you on law.
>
> 3. Summarize Evidence
>
>   (element by element for your claims)
>
>   a. Element 1:
>
>   (evidence supporting Element 1)
>
>   b. Element 2:
>
>   (evidence supporting Element 2)
>
>   c. Element 3:
>
>   (evidence supporting Element 3)
>
>   d. Element 4:
>
>   (evidence supporting Element 4)
>
> 4. Bottom Line:
>
> Rule in My Favor; Order

Speak Slowly and Strongly

Speak a bit more slowly than you do in normal conversation. This allows you to think clearly as you talk and helps the judge or jury follow your points. Also, speaking slowly makes it less obvious when you pause to find something in your notes or to think about how to phrase a particular point. (Use this same technique later in the trial, when you are asking questions of witnesses or making arguments to the judge or jury.)

Practice speaking slowly. Many people speed up without even realizing it because they are nervous in court. You may find it rather difficult to slow down if you are used to speaking rapidly.

Also, you must speak up. The judge or court reporter will likely tell you if you can't be heard, but jurors may not feel comfortable doing this. You don't want jurors deciding against you because they didn't hear something you said.

Stand at the Lectern

Standing is proper whenever you speak in court. It is a sign of respect. Standing gives you an air of authority and control. It also helps you project your voice. In most courtrooms, there will be a lectern for you to use, but if one isn't available, stand behind the counsel table.

Sample Opening Statement and Outline

Let's look at a completed opening statement in a case where you are a pedestrian suing a building contractor named Sarah Adams for negligence. Adams's truck hit you as you walked across Elm Street, at the corner of Elm and Main Streets. In your jury trial, your opening statement might proceed as follows:

1   *Good morning. My name is Nolo Pedestrian. I am representing myself in this action against the defendant, Ms. Adams. I am not an attorney, and I don't know all the technical rules of trial, but I will do my best.*

2 *The evidence you will hear today will show that at about 3:00 on the afternoon of March 31, I was crossing the street at Elm and Main. I was in the crosswalk when the defendant's truck hit me.*

3 *You will hear me and others testify under oath about the details of the accident. So for now, let me just give you an overview, to help you follow along.*

4 *First, I will testify. I will tell you when I saw her truck coming at me. Then I'll explain how I tried to get out of the way. I'll tell you how she hit me and broke my leg. I'll explain how it took four full months for my leg to heal, and I'll show you the doctor bills that back it up.*

5 *Then you will hear from a witness, Cynthia White, a stranger to me at the time, who saw the whole accident. She will confirm just how the defendant hit me.*

6 *Then evidence will be presented showing that just moments before she struck me, the defendant got a call on her cell phone telling her about a missed job inspection.*

7 *You will hear all this testimony. And I'll show you some photos and doctor bills.*

8 *Then, after the judge gives some important instructions on how you should weigh the evidence, it will be up to you to deliberate earnestly and make the right decision. I hope that decision will be to hold the defendant responsible for the pain and loss of income she caused, and to award me the $100,000 I need and deserve to recover from this injury. Thank you."*

Transcript Analysis: In No. 1, you set the tone as a respectful person representing yourself and trying your best. And in No. 2, you properly use "the evidence will show" technique to give a nice preview of the facts of the case, being sure to stay on the right side of the line between reviewing evidence and impermissibly arguing your case. Next, in No. 3, you signal that you are just giving the judge and jury a road map and not every detail.

In No. 4, you preview your own testimony and the exhibits you will introduce. You are properly careful not to present too much detail in your opening statement, lest you bore the judge or jury and risk their not listening carefully during trial. You appropriately avoid saying why they should believe you over the defendant.

No. 5 illustrates the dangers of stating what you expect another witness will say. If Cynthia White doesn't testify as you promised, your opponent may point out the contradiction to the judge or jury, making you look foolish. And if the misrepresentation is severe, your adversary can ask for a mistrial.

What you have promised here is that Ms. White will "confirm just how the defendant hit" you. So long as you are reasonably certain she will confirm this (you have interviewed her many times and know that she saw things the same way you did), you are probably fairly safe with this statement, especially since you did not put specific words in her mouth.

In No. 6, you refer to evidence from the defendant. You normally should not discuss the defendant's testimony or evidence you think the defendant will present. There is too much risk of getting it wrong. But in this example you are on fairly safe ground mentioning the defendant's phone call, especially if you have other evidence of the call, such as her phone bill (if she called out), a note on an inspection form that she had the conversation, her own admission that she got the call, or a witness who saw her holding the phone to her ear. That way, if she denies being on the cell phone before the accident, you can introduce your other evidence.

You properly do not ask the jury to draw the inference that the reason the defendant hit you was because the call distracted her and she wasn't paying attention to the road. That would be an impermissible argument, well beyond the scope of your opening statement previewing the facts. You will have a chance to tie the evidence to the facts you need to prove and convince the judge or jury they stack up in your favor during your closing argument. (See Chapter 14.)

Last, in No. 8, you properly ask for a ruling in your favor. That alone is not considered argument. It can be helpful to let the jury or judge know from the outset what you want and may bring you one step closer to winning.

Though it may be helpful for you to write out your full opening statement in order to practice it, you will want to summarize it in an outline form to actually use as you speak. That way, you will not read word for word, but you also won't forget important points. An outline for the sample opening statement above appears on the following page. Yours may look different, but as long as you hit the main points you want to mention, it should be helpful for you.

Introduction

I'm not an attorney, but I'll try my best.

The evidence will show… (basic facts, e.g., Adams driving on public streets, Elm and Main—hit me in crosswalk.)

(This covers Element 1—duty to drive with care)

Road Map

- This opening statement is a "road map."

- I will summarize testimony and exhibits now, give details later, and tell you a little bit about the order in which things will proceed.

Summary of Evidence

I will testify, White will testify, and Adams's records show that:

- She was distracted when driving, she was looking down and talking on the cell phone rather than paying attention to the road. Adams's business records show this (This covers Element 2—breach of duty, Adams driving carelessly)

- White will testify: she saw Adams's truck hit me. (This covers Element 3—causation, her carelessness caused my injury)

I will testify:

- I paid money in doctor bills, lost money from being out of work for four months, and have suffered tremendous pain. (This covers Element 4—damages)

Bottom Line

- After you hear all the evidence, the judge will instruct you and you will decide.

- Rule in my favor; order that defendant pay $100,000 for my pain, doctor bills, and lost wages.

RESOURCE

Resources on opening statements.
For more detail on preparing effective opening statements, you may look for a continuing education or lawyer practice guide in your state on "Opening Statement." You can also consult these resources.

Trial Advocacy in a Nutshell, by Paul Bergman (West Publishing Co.), is an easy-to-read, helpful, and inexpensive paperback about effective and persuasive trial techniques. Chapter 5 covers opening statements.

The Trial Process: Law, Tactics, and Ethics, by J. Alexander Tanford (Lexis/Matthew Bender), a textbook on trial practice, includes excerpts from many other leading books and dialogues of trial scenarios.

Fundamentals of Trial Techniques by Thomas Mauet (Little, Brown & Co.).

Trying Cases to Win: Voir Dire and Opening Argument, by Herbert Stern (Aspen Publishers), includes sample opening statements. ●

Direct Examination

irect examination is your primary chance to explain your version of events to the judge or jury and to undercut your adversary's version. It consists of your own testimony and the testimony of your witnesses in response to your questions.

Despite the dramatic images presented in movies and television, you are unlikely to either uncover significant helpful information when you cross-examine your adversary's witnesses or to change a judge or jury's mind with a stirring closing argument. Direct examination is your best chance to tell your side of the story to the judge or jury, and well-organized and credible direct examinations are the key to success at trial. This chapter will help you plan and carry out persuasive direct examinations.

! CAUTION

Know exactly what you need to prove or disprove. Direct examination testimony should be built around the legal claim or claims set out in the plaintiff's complaint. If you are the plaintiff, you must prove facts that satisfy each element of a claim. If you are the defendant, it is your job to disprove one or more of your adversary's facts. If you are uncertain of a claim's elements and the facts you are trying to prove or disprove, reread Chapters 8 and 9.

Direct Examination as Storytelling

This chapter will help you with many of the technical aspects of direct examination, including the kinds of questions you are allowed to ask and how to comply with the requirement that a witness's testimony be based on personal knowledge.

Leaving aside the mechanics for a moment, it's important that you understand that presenting an effective direct examination is very similar to telling an absorbing story in an ordinary social situation. You'll want to focus a judge or juror's attention on the events that are the most important to your claim or defense by spending more time on the details of those events and moving more quickly through less important events. And you'll want to make sure each of your witnesses tells a clear, easy-to-follow story that dramatically builds to the main events by drawing out evidence in chronological order. Have your witnesses testify as much as possible in their own words, so it sounds like they are telling the story, not you. And, if you have photographs or any other records to back up your witnesses' testimony, introduce them into evidence as the witness testifies to convince the judge or jury that the stories are accurate. (Chapter 15 explains how to do this.)

Overview of Direct Examination Procedures

Direct examination begins after opening statements. The plaintiff begins by conducting direct examination of the first witness on the plaintiff's side. This may be the plaintiff him- or herself. The defendant then has a chance to cross-examine that witness. The plaintiff then puts on the next plaintiff's witness, and again the defendant has the opportunity to cross-examine. Only after the plaintiff finishes presenting all witnesses ("rests," as in "I rest my case") does the defendant begin conducting direct examination of the defense witnesses. After each one of the defendant's witnesses testifies, the plaintiff similarly has an opportunity to cross-examine that witness.

TIP

Direct examination controls the scope of cross-examination. Cross-examination questions must relate to the topics covered during direct examination. For example, if you call a witness only to testify to your whereabouts at 8 a.m., your adversary cannot cross-examine that witness about a series of events having nothing to do with where you were at 8 a.m. The adversary could of course elicit the desired testimony by re-calling the same witness for direct examination when it is the adversary's turn to present evidence.

After the direct and cross-examination of each witness, the judge normally excuses the witness from further testimony. This means that neither you nor your adversary can ask any more questions of the witness unless you get the judge's permission to question the witness further. This questioning is called "redirect examination." If you want to ask your witness more questions following your adversary's cross-examination, say something like, "Your Honor, before you excuse the witness I'd like to ask a few more questions on redirect examination." Redirect is limited to the scope of cross-examination, meaning that you may only ask questions pertaining to the subjects that your adversary went into on cross-examination. You cannot rehash all

of a witness's direct examination testimony on redirect; the purpose of redirect is to offer evidence in response to testimony your adversary brought out during cross-examination.

After your redirect, a judge may also allow your adversary to conduct brief "recross," limited to the scope of your redirect. After that, the witness will definitely be excused, and your next witness will be called. Then the cycle of direct, cross, and perhaps redirect and recross repeats itself until you have called all of your witnesses.

As you can see, at each successive stage of testimony, the scope of questions is limited to what was covered during the preceding stage. This means that each phase of testimony is narrower than the one that came before. This funnel effect can be a problem if you conclude a witness's direct examination without asking about an important subject, because the scope rule would seem to forbid you from going back and opening up a new subject after your adversary cross-examines. Happily, a possible solution exists as long as a witness has not been excused. You can ask the judge for permission to "reopen" the witness's direct examination when it is your turn to conduct redirect. Say something like, "Your Honor, I know that this is redirect, but I ask permission to reopen the direct examination to ask just a few questions." Your request to reopen tells the judge, "Oops, I forgot something. As long as the witness is still right here, it's only fair to give me a chance to ask about it now." Usually, the judge will (especially in nonjury trials) grant your request, so you aren't unfairly punished for forgetting to ask some questions.

> ## The Jurors May Have a Few Questions as Well
>
> Traditionally, jurors have to sit passively by as spectators at the trial until they begin deliberations to reach a verdict. However, a number of states have recently adopted "active juror rules," which allow jurors to question witnesses during trial. (See, for example, New Jersey court rule 1:8-8(c).) These rules are intended to make sure that jurors understand witness testimony and to improve juror morale.

Preparing for Direct Examination

Just like a play in a theater, an effective direct examination is usually the result of careful planning. Here are the important steps you should take before trial to present your strongest possible case.

Subpoena Your Witnesses

A subpoena (sometimes spelled "subpena") is a court order requiring a witness to come to court. A properly subpoenaed witness who fails to show up at the time and date specified is subject to arrest.

Once you are assigned a trial date, ask the court clerk to issue a subpoena for each of your witnesses. Subpoenas are free and are usually issued in blank. You can easily fill in the name of the case, the witness's name, the time and date the witness must appear, and other necessary information. In some court systems, you can personally serve a subpoena on a witness, but in many others you must get a marshal, a licensed process server, or an adult friend to serve your subpoenas.

You should subpoena all of your witnesses, even friendly ones who are eager to testify for you. This is not a sign of distrust. Unless you have subpoenaed a witness, your judge may deny your request for a continuance (postponement) of the trial if an emergency or illness prevents the witness from coming to court on the day of trial. The witness can also show the subpoena to be excused from work to attend the trial.

All court systems impose limits on who you can subpoena, when the subpoena must be served, and how much you must pay witnesses for their attendance at trial. (See, for example, FRCP 45.) Though these rules vary somewhat from one court to another, here are some typical requirements.

- **Territorial limits.** Most courts' subpoenas are legally valid only if served on a witness who lives or works within a limited geographical area, often around 100 to 150 miles from the courthouse. A subpoena served on a person outside these limits is ineffective, and the person does not have to obey it.
- **Witness fees.** In most court systems, you must tender (offer) to the witness, in advance, the court attendance and mileage fees set by your local statute—typically about $30 to $60 per day.

TIP

You can recover witness fees if you win. After trial, the judge has the power to award "costs of suit," including witness fees, to the winning party. So if you win the trial, ask the judge to order your adversary to pay your witness fees.

- **Time limits.** Your subpoena must be served on a witness long enough before trial to give the witness reasonable notice of when he or she is to come to court. For a witness whom you have already informed of the trial date and who has no conflicting demands, serving a subpoena the day before trial may be reasonable. For other witnesses, you may have to serve a subpoena weeks in advance of trial.

TIP

Find out about "on-call" procedures. Ask the court clerk if the court rules in your state have an "on-call" procedure. With an on-call procedure, a subpoenaed witness does not have to report to the courtroom until you need the witness's testimony. The witness agrees to come to court when you telephone and say it's time, but need not waste hours sitting idly in the courthouse corridor.

- **Subpoena Duces Tecum.** If you want a witness to bring receipts, records, notices, or other documents and articles to court, ask the clerk to issue a Subpoena Duces Tecum. A Subpoena Duces Tecum has space for describing the documents you want a witness to bring to court. Fill it out, identifying exactly what documents the witness is to bring. Then have the Subpoena Duces Tecum served on the witness. (For information on how to

fill out a Subpoena Duces Tecum, see Chapter 5.)

Outline Your Direct Examination

You must know what you're going to ask before you're standing in the courtroom and the judge tells you to call your first witness. To organize your questioning, it's helpful to make an outline for each direct examination you plan to conduct. A sample is shown below.

TRIAL NOTEBOOK

In the direct examination section of your trial notebook, include an outline of your testimony and one for each witness whose direct examination you plan to conduct. (See Chapter 18.)

Some attorneys outline all the evidence they plan to elicit during a witness's direct examination and the questions they plan to ask. While writing out a few important questions and answers makes sense, don't write down too much detail. Direct examinations rarely proceed exactly according to plan, and a predetermined list of dozens of questions may end up confusing you more than it helps.

An outline is usually adequate if it refers to the main points in a witness's story and includes a few questions you want to be sure to ask. If you plan to offer any exhibits (such as business records or photographs) into evidence during a witness's testimony, your outline should refer to those exhibits and the "foundational" evidence you have to introduce to make the exhibits admissible. (See Chapter 15 for more information on exhibits.)

<u>**Direct Examination Outline**</u>

<u>Witness:</u>

<u>Background Information:</u>

<u>Important Evidence:</u>

<u>Important Questions:</u>

<u>Exhibits to Introduce Into Evidence:</u>

TIP

Make sure your outline is user-friendly. You'll want to use your direct examination outline for each witness when you ask questions. So as you make it, think of the little details that can affect your questioning. For example, if you have sight problems, write extra big or copy your typed outline on a photocopy machine that enlarges. You may also find it useful to use a fluorescent marker to highlight the most important testimony.

Rehearse Each Witness's Testimony

Even though you may have talked to a witness several times already, always have a final meeting with the witness to rehearse your questions and the witness's answers. You want the witness to know what evidence you are after and the kinds of questions you will ask. You don't need to script every word of your direct examination, but the rehearsal will help your witnesses testify completely and confidently. You may wish to follow the lead of many attorneys and actually run through a practice direct examination. And if you know or strongly suspect the types of questions your adversary is likely to ask on cross-examination, it's a good idea to ask them yourself during rehearsal to give your witness practice responding to them.

Before rehearsing testimony, consider returning with the witness to the scene of important events, assuming that its appearance has not changed radically. The visit may lead the witness to remember details that add credibility to the witness's testimony.

Some witnesses think that it is improper to rehearse testimony before trial. But it's both proper and routine, and your witness should know that. Also, remind your witness that the purpose of the rehearsal is not to influence the witness's testimony; all you want is the truth. That way, if your adversary asks on cross-examination whether you coached your witness to make up a story, your witness can answer honestly, "No. Mr. Pedestrian and I talked about what he was going to ask me, but he just told me to tell the truth."

If you are going to ask a witness to identify a document or a photograph or to draw a diagram as part of direct examination, make sure you rehearse this. You don't want a somewhat nervous witness suddenly becoming unable to identify an important exhibit in the middle of trial! (See Chapter 15 for information on how to admit exhibits into evidence.)

For example, say your case involves an auto accident in an intersection. During the rehearsal, you and the witness can draw the intersection, including fixed landmarks such as traffic signals and crosswalks. At trial, you may begin the witness's testimony about the diagram by asking the witness what has already been drawn and then asking the witness to make further markings—for example, paths of cars—as the direct testimony unfolds. (Chapter 15 gives an example of how to do this.)

> **TIP**
>
> **Practice your questioning.** An unexpected answer or objection may throw you off stride and cause you to ask leading or other improper questions. The best way to prevent this is to practice your questioning, both during rehearsal with each witness and in your own mind.
>
> Mentally formulate different questions for eliciting the same evidence in response to different answers a witness may give and then think about which of the possible questions will be proper and which will not. If necessary, write out specific questions that you have difficulty phrasing properly and include them in your outline to give you the comfort of a written backup. This pretrial practice will prepare you for the unexpected developments that almost always occur during trial.

When you rehearse with your witnesses, you can also offer a few suggestions that may enhance the credibility of their testimony:

- Remind a witness to make occasional eye contact with the judge or jury while testifying. People often come across as more credible when they look listeners right in the eye. Tell the witness something like, "I'll say, 'Please tell the jury what happened after the chicken crossed the road.' Then you should look at the jury when you answer."
- Ask a witness to dress in business attire. A witness need not wear a suit or expensive clothes but should dress in a manner that indicates respect for the court.

> **TIP**
>
> **Familiarize yourself with your judge's direct examination procedures.** Before trial, visit the courtroom where your trial will take place. Ask the clerk whether your judge has any general rules about direct examination. For example, one judge may insist that you stand at a podium when asking questions; another may allow you to sit at the counsel table. Most judges, however, will not let you stand next to the witness or wander about the courtroom when asking questions. Also, if you plan on showing an exhibit to a witness, find out whether your judge will allow you to personally hand the exhibit to the witness or whether you should give it to the bailiff to hand to the witness.
>
> Violating such rules will not make or break your trial. But following these rules lets your judge know that you have prepared thoroughly and seriously, frees you to concentrate on your witness's testimony, and allows your witnesses to relax and present convincing testimony.

Presenting Your Own Testimony on Direct Examination

As you undoubtedly know from watching movies and TV, direct examination usually unfolds in a question-and-answer format: An attorney asks questions and a witness answers them. But what happens when you are a self-represented party serving both as attorney and witness?

A humorous answer was provided by the movie *Bananas*. In one of the most well-loved courtroom scenes, Woody Allen is representing himself in a trial. When it comes time for him to testify, he asks a question from the counsel table, runs up to the witness stand to answer it, then runs back to the counsel table to ask another question, and so forth.

Luckily, the procedure in real courtrooms is not nearly so strenuous. Normally, when it is your turn to testify, tell the judge something like, "Your Honor, I'm now going to testify in my own behalf." Then walk to the witness box, remain standing, and swear or affirm to tell the truth. Then sit in the witness chair and give your evidence as you would tell a story. Because most judges are used to the question-and-answer procedure, however, you may find that the judge occasionally stops your narrative to ask questions.

TIP

You can look at notes to refresh your recollection. If you think you have forgotten to say something while testifying, ask the judge for permission to review your notes. Say something like, "Your Honor, I think I've forgotten something here. May I have permission to return to the counsel table for a moment to review my notes?" Just like any other witness, you may review any document to refresh your recollection. (See "Questioning Witnesses," below.) Once your memory is refreshed, return to the witness box and carry on with your testimony.

However, note that Federal Rule of Evidence 612 and similar rules in each state give your adversary the right to examine any documents you use to refresh your recollection. Those rules also allow your adversary to offer into evidence not only the portion of a document that you use to refresh your recollection but also any other portion concerning the same subject matter—even if it wouldn't otherwise be admissible! Thus, be very careful that the document you use to refresh your recollection doesn't contain information that might embarrass you or damage your case.

For example, assume that you are a tenant, and your landlord is suing you for not paying your rent. You are testifying on your own behalf, trying to prove that you legally refused to pay because the landlord failed to maintain your apartment in a habitable condition. (Many states have a law requiring landlords to keep rental units livable.) Your testimony about the leaky ceiling problem in your apartment might look like this:

1 **You:**

The worst time I remember was on March 12. I came home from work and saw about five separate leaks in the living room. There were more in the bedroom and the kitchen. A couple of leaks I couldn't even put a bucket under because the water was just dripping down the walls.

2 Judge:

Excuse me, Mr. Nolo. The water dripping down the walls, are you referring to leaks in the living room?

3 You:

Yes, Your Honor.

4 Judge:

So three of the leaks were away from the walls and you put buckets under those, but the other two you couldn't?

5 You:

That's right.

6 Judge:

All right, please continue.

7 You:

Well, I got right on the phone and called the landlord and told him about the leaks. He said that he'd get around to it when he had a chance, but that a lot of his tenants were complaining, so I'd just have to wait my turn. Well, two weeks went by ….

Transcript Analysis: Here, you present your testimony largely in story form. As is common, however, the judge interrupts to ask questions. When the judge does so, you stop your narrative to answer the questions and then continue telling your story.

> **TIP**
>
> **Testify first or last.** Whether you are the plaintiff or the defendant, you may call your witnesses and testify personally in whatever order you choose. However, you are generally better off testifying either first or last.

The usual advantage of testifying first is that you give an overview of your whole case and have a chance to capture a judge or jury's immediate attention. By testifying last you lose this chance to frame your case but gain the opportunity to address problems that arose during the testimony of your other witnesses and make a strong final impression. If you or your adversary request it, the judge is likely to order all witnesses to remain out of the courtroom until after they testify. As a party to the case, however, you can be present throughout the trial. Thus, you may be the only witness for your side who is personally aware of problems that came up during other witnesses' direct examinations.

Questioning Witnesses

When it's your turn to question a witness, you may not know where to start. This section gives you a structure that will let you plan an effective direct examination.

> **CAUTION**
>
> **Do not make speeches.** A frequent complaint of judges is that self-represented litigants often violate the orderly process of trial by making argumentative speeches during direct examination instead of presenting evidence through testimony and questions. The time to make a speech summing up your case is closing argument, not direct examination.

For example, assume that your landlord is trying to evict you from your apartment for making excessive noise in violation of a lease provision that requires tenants not to disturb the neighbors. You call Bernie Rhodes as a witness to testify that there was no excessive noise on the two nights that, according to a landlord's witness, your stereo was blaring. Examine this sample testimony:

1 You:

Now Mr. Rhodes, tell us about June 3 and 4.

2 Your Witness:

Mr. Nolo, those were the nights that you and I were working on the Keck proposal. It was due on June 5, and we were working pretty much all night in your apartment on both those nights.

3 You:

Did we play the stereo in the apartment on those nights?

4 Your Witness:

I remember that we played it a little one of the nights when we stopped to have a pizza, but I know it wasn't real loud.

5 You:

Do you remember if anyone knocked at the door asking us to turn down the volume?

6 Your Witness:

No, I'm sure that didn't happen.

7 You:

Your Honor, this proves what I've been saying all along. Mr. Rhodes was inside the apartment with me on both nights, and as he told you there was no loud music. We were working on a very important proposal that had to be finished, and there's no way we'd mess ourselves up by blasting a stereo.

Transcript Analysis: Your outburst in No. 7 is an improper speech. When conducting

direct examination of a witness, you are limited to asking questions. It is improper for you to argue about the credibility and significance of evidence until closing argument.

Begin With Background Questions

Direct examination begins when you call a witness (yourself or someone else) to the stand. The witness then takes an oath to tell the truth (administered by the court clerk). At that point the judge will turn to you and say something like, "You may proceed."

After taking a deep breath, you may want to start right in on the witness's story. But before you do, ask a few questions about the witness's personal background. Witnesses who are not used to giving testimony or being in court often gain confidence (and therefore look more credible) when they can begin their testimony by talking about their own background. At the same time, the personal background testimony tends to humanize witnesses in the eyes of a judge or a jury.

For example, here is how you might begin the direct examination of your witness, Ilene Johnson:

1 You:

Ms. Johnson, are you employed?

2 Your Witness:

Yes. I'm the assistant manager of the Brentwood branch of First Savings and Loan.

3 You:

How long have you been employed at the bank?

4 Your Witness:

Just about eight years now. I started out as a teller and then went through a management training program. I became an assistant manager a little over three years ago.

5 You:

Could you briefly tell us what you do as an assistant manager?

6 Your Witness:

I'm basically responsible for hiring and training the teller staff.

7 You:

All right. Now, turning your attention to the afternoon of March 12 …

If a witness is not employed, consider other possible background topics. For example, if a witness is in college, ask the name of the college and the witness's course of study. Or if a witness is a parent, ask the names and ages of the witness's children. Obviously, you want to emphasize information that makes the witness appear to be someone the judge or jury can rely on. So if your witness is serving a life sentence for murder or if your witness's only interests are TV talk shows and soap operas, you may want to skip personal background questioning altogether!

No matter what theme you choose to pursue, your background questioning should not generally be much longer than the sample above, because technically the information is not relevant to the meatier testimony the witness will give. But if you are brief, judges normally allow background questions so that the witness can relax and

the judge or jury can learn a little bit about the person.

Background Questioning of Expert Witnesses

Background questioning of witnesses must usually be brief because the information you elicit has nothing to do with whether a witness's testimony is accurate. This is not so with an expert witness, who, by definition, is a person whose special skill or knowledge enables him or her to interpret evidence that is beyond the understanding of the average judge or juror. Before an expert witness testifies, you have to demonstrate to the judge that the witness has special knowledge, skill, or experience. This ordinarily requires extensive background questioning about the witness's qualifications. (See Chapter 19 for more on questioning experts.)

 TIP

Don't nominate your witness for the Nobel Prize. Most judges will not allow you to ask about honors and achievements a witness may have received or good deeds a witness may have performed. For example, a witness may be the employee of the month, the citizen of the year, a volunteer in the pediatrics ward of a hospital, or the Little League president. Judges typically think of this kind of information as going beyond personal background and into a witness's moral character, and evidence of moral character is rarely admitted in civil trials.

Ask Legally Permissible Questions

After you conclude background questioning, you are ready to ask questions to elicit a witness's story. All questions fall into one of four broad categories:

- narrative questions
- open questions
- closed questions, or
- leading questions.

Rigidly classifying a question in one category or another is not important. What is essential is that you become familiar enough with these different types of questions to know which types you are usually allowed to ask at different stages of a trial and which you are not. During direct and redirect examination you are primarily limited to asking open and closed questions.

In addition, familiarity with the different types of questions allows you to adjust your questioning technique according to whether you want a witness to tell a story in his or her own words (for which you should ask open questions) or to testify to specific information (use closed questions).

Narrative Questions

Narrative questions are broad and open ended. They ask a witness to describe an entire series of events. Here are some examples:

- "Please tell us everything that happened on February 14."
- "Describe the events leading up to the signing of the contract."

Because narrative questions allow witnesses to describe events in their own words, they have the advantage of avoiding any suggestion that you are telling a witness what to say. However, many judges believe that if questions are too open ended, witnesses (especially nonexpert witnesses) will refer to legally improper evidence and waste time with irrelevant digressions. Your judge may not allow you to ask narrative questions or may severely restrict your use of them.

Open Questions

Like narrative questions, open questions invite witnesses to testify in their own words. But typically an open question limits a witness to a description of a specific event or condition. Open questions are one of your principal direct examination tools because most witnesses make their best impressions on a judge or jury when they are allowed to be themselves and tell a story in their own words.

Here are some open questions:

- "Can you describe the condition of the car after the accident?"
- "What happened when you entered the room?"
- "After you received the letter, then what happened?"
- "Please tell us what was said in this conversation."
- "How did he react when he found out that they would not extend the lease?"
- "Please describe the condition of my daughter when we picked her up from my ex-spouse."

Because open questions allow witnesses to respond in their own words but do not invite a long story (narrative) about an entire series of events, judges allow them. In their view, open questions pose less of a risk that

a witness will refer to improper evidence or digress into irrelevancies.

Closed Questions

Closed questions ask witnesses for specific pieces of information. They do not invite a witness to expand on an answer. Here are some examples:

- "What color was the car?"
- "On what day of the week did the meeting take place?"
- "After you told her that the tool sets were back ordered, how did she reply?"
- "What time was it when my ex-spouse brought my son home?"
- "How long was it until I was returned to regular job duties?"
- "What's the last thing the manager said before closing the door?"
- "Did the meeting start on time?"

Just like open questions, closed questions are one of your principal tools for direct examination. Sometimes you do not want witnesses to describe events in their own words. Instead, you want to focus the judge or jury's attention on a specific piece of information. You may want to do so either

because a witness has neglected to mention the information in response to an open question or because you want to emphasize particular testimony that a witness has already given.

Leading Questions

Leading questions suggest the answer you want a witness to give. They are basically statements in question form. Examples:

- "The car was red, wasn't it?"
- "Isn't it true that he never said anything about needing the manager's approval?"

Because they indicate your desired answers, leading questions violate the guiding principle of direct examination: that your job is to ask the questions, and your witnesses' job is to provide the information. If you ask leading questions of friendly witnesses, the witnesses are very likely to agree to whatever you say. So if your adversary objects, the judge will probably not allow you to ask leading questions during direct examination. (See Chapter 17 for information on objections.)

Despite the general policy forbidding leading questions during direct examination, they are permitted in a variety of special circumstances. The two most common arise when you elicit evidence of a witness's personal background or evidence that is "preliminary." Preliminary evidence is undisputed evidence that you want to run through quickly, in order to get to important testimony. Examples:

- During personal background questioning, you may ask, "You've been employed by the school district for over 15 years now, right?"

- Your adversary agrees that a meeting took place on August 31 but disputes what was said during the meeting. Before you ask your witness what was said during the meeting, you may ask, "A meeting took place on August 31, correct?"

- Your ex-spouse admits that he has done carpentry work for a Mr. Edwards and a few others, but claims that he does not earn enough to pay court-ordered child support. Before going into how much Edwards paid your ex-spouse, you may ask Edwards, "My ex-husband did carpentry work for you during June and July of this year, is that correct?"

- Your adversary admits that Dr. Phibes, an expert on the valuation of coin collections, examined your coin collection but disagrees with Phibes's opinion as to its value. You may properly ask Dr. Phibes, "Now, you examined my coin collection, right?"

- You call an auto mechanic to testify to the extent of the necessary repairs to your car following an accident. Your adversary admits that the mechanic repaired your car on June 22 and 23, but disagrees that all of the problems were caused by the accident. You may properly ask the mechanic, "You are the Exoff mechanic who repaired my car on June 22 and 23, right?"

You can also ask a leading question when you want to help a witness return to the place in the story where you left off if your direct examination has been disrupted by a somewhat lengthy court recess. For example, say that your witness testified that the traffic light in your direction was green when you entered the intersection. Following that answer, the court recesses for lunch. When you resume after lunch, you may begin by asking the witness, "Before lunch, you testified that the traffic light in my direction was green when I entered the intersection, correct?" Though the question is leading, you are not putting words in the witness's mouth. You are simply repeating evidence the witness has already given to get the witness (and the judge and jury) back on track following a break in the testimony.

You may also ask leading questions during your direct examination of a "hostile" witness. (See "Hostile Witnesses," below.)

Establish a Witness's Personal Knowledge

When you're planning the testimony you want to elicit on direct examination, remember that you must show that a witness is testifying from personal knowledge. (This rule doesn't apply to expert witnesses; see Chapter 19.) This means that you must show that a witness personally observed, heard, smelled, touched, or tasted whatever the witness is testifying about. Secondhand information may be good enough for TV talk shows and supermarket tabloids, but it won't work in court—a judge or jury cannot take it into account when arriving at a verdict.

! CAUTION

Make sure you understand other evidence rules. In addition to the requirement that a witness have personal knowledge, a variety of other evidence rules determine whether evidence is admissible. The most important of these rules are discussed in Chapter 16. Please be sure to read and understand that material before planning your testimony.

Usually, you do not have to make any special effort to show that a witness has personal knowledge; the testimony itself demonstrates it. For example, assume that you have brought suit against the owner of a dog that bit you on October 3. You call Jordan Miller as a witness to testify to the dog's attack on you. After the personal background questions, your direct examination of Miller continues as follows:

1 You:

Mr. Miller, where were you about four o'clock on the afternoon of October 3?

2 Witness:

I was outside my house, watering my front lawn.

3 You:

Did you see me that afternoon?

4 Witness:

Yes, I saw you walking your dog about two houses down from mine.

5 You:

Did anything happen to me as I was walking my dog?

6 Witness:

Yes. You were attacked by a German shepherd.

Transcript Analysis: With no need of complicated techniques, you have established that Miller has personal knowledge because he testified that he personally saw what happened to you.

Now let's see how the personal knowledge requirement works when you want a witness to testify to another person's statement. Jordan Miller is still testifying, and you want to ask him about what the dog owner said after his dog bit you. This portion of Miller's direct examination goes like this:

7 You:

Mr. Miller, what happened next?

8 Witness:

The German shepherd ran back across the street. Then a man came running over and said that he was very sorry for what his dog had done.

9 You:

How do you know this is what he said?

10 Witness:

I was standing only a few feet away from him; I could hear very clearly.

11 You:

Did he say anything else?

12 Witness:

Yes, he said that the dog got out of his yard through a hole in the fence that he hadn't had time to fix.

13 You:

Do you see the man who made those statements?

14 Witness:

Yes, he's sitting over there [indicating the defendant].

Transcript Analysis: Again, without any special effort, you have shown that Miller has personal knowledge of what the defendant said after the attack.

How to Identify People in the Courtroom

Pointing to a person in the courtroom while testifying is often the only way a witness can identify who made a statement or engaged in some other type of conduct. For example, in the dog-bite case testimony above, a witness points out your adversary as the person who made a certain statement. But be careful how you ask a witness to identify a person in the courtroom. It is improper to ask a leading question such as, "Is the defendant sitting over there the person who made the statement?" Instead, as in the example, ask a nonleading question: "Do you see the man who made those statements?"

Pointing isn't always the only way to identify someone. If a witness personally knows the person whose conduct you want the witness to talk about, you can simply ask, "Who made the statement?" and expect the witness to say something like, "It was Doris Defendant who said that."

If a witness points to a person in the courtroom, the court reporter cannot record the silent gesture. To make sure the record reflects the identification, say something like, "May the record show that the witness pointed to Doris Defendant."

Now let's look at an example in which a witness lacks personal knowledge. Assume that Miller's direct examination continues like this:

15 You:

Mr. Miller, do you know whether this dog has ever bitten other people?

16 Witness:

Yes, the dog bit three others before it bit you.

Transcript Analysis: In this example, you have not shown that Miller has personal knowledge of the dog's previous attacks. For all the judge can tell, Miller may know about three prior attacks only because other people have told him about them. Miller would then be testifying to secondhand information. So if your adversary objects, or perhaps even if there's no objection, the judge is likely to exclude the evidence in No. 16, meaning that the judge or jury could not consider that evidence in arriving at the verdict. (See Chapter 17 for more on objections.)

If you forget to show that a witness has personal knowledge, normally you can readily fix the problem. Here is how you could do so in the Miller example:

17 Judge:

Ms. Nolo, that last answer [No. 16] *is improper because you have not demonstrated that the witness has personal knowledge of previous attacks by the dog. I'm striking that answer from the record.*

18 You:

Sorry, Your Honor. Mr. Miller, let me ask you this. Did you ever personally see the dog bite other people?

19 Witness:

Yes. I've seen that same dog attack and bite three other people.

Here, with just one additional question, you have shown that Miller has personal knowledge of the prior attacks, and the testimony in No. 19 will be admissible (assuming, of course, that it does not run afoul of other evidentiary rules; see Chapter 16).

Special Personal Knowledge Rules for Conversations: Many judges apply a special personal knowledge rule for conversations. Before asking about what people said to each other (either in person or on the telephone), they want the witness to testify to three things:

- when the conversation took place
- where the conversation took place, and
- who was present during the conversation.

For example, assume that you own an apartment building and have brought suit to evict a tenant, Denise Beilenson, for keeping dogs in her apartment in violation of her lease. You have called Shelly Resnik as a witness to testify that she was present when Beilenson admitted to you that she was keeping three golden retrievers in her apartment and that she had no intention of getting rid of them. Your direct examination of Resnik might go as follows:

1 **You:**
Ms. Resnik, do you remember a conversation between me and Ms. Beilenson about dogs?

2 **Witness:**
Yes, I do.

3 **You:**
When did this conversation take place?

4 **Witness:**
If I remember right, it was on the 13th of April.

"Eileen Willis, come on down!"

5 You:

And where did the conversation take place?

6 Witness:

Down by the apartment's swimming pool.

7 You:

Was anyone else present during this conversation?

8 Witness:

No, just the two of you were talking. I was sitting a few feet away, but I didn't notice anyone else around.

9 You:

Now, please tell us what was said during this conversation.

Transcript Analysis: Having shown that the witness knows when the conversation took place (No. 4), where it took place (No. 6), and who was present (No. 8), you have satisfied the personal knowledge rule for conversations and properly proceeded to elicit what was said in No. 9. True, question No. 1 indicates to the witness that you want to hear testimony about a dog conversation, which to a stickler may seem leading and therefore improper. But few judges would deem it either leading or an improper question. The usual rule is that you can call a witness's attention to the subject matter of his or her testimony so long as you do not indicate your desired answer.

TIP

Don't worry if a witness doesn't remember exact details. The fact that a witness can't remember an exact date, time, or other background fact about a conversation (or other event) rarely defeats the personal knowledge requirement and prevents the admission of the conversation. If your witness cannot be specific, elicit a best estimate. Even testimony that "The conversation took place in early April," or that "It took place sometime in April," will usually be good enough to show personal knowledge.

Refresh a Witness's Recollection If Necessary

You should almost always rehearse a witness's testimony before trial. (See "Preparing for Direct Examination," above.) Nevertheless, even the best-prepared witness may suffer a lapse of memory while testifying. For example, in response to a question you know a witness can answer, the witness might respond, "I don't remember." If this happens, do not panic. It's perfectly proper to attempt to "refresh the witness's recollection" with a document that refers to the information the witness has forgotten.

You can use any helpful document as a refresher, such as the forgetful witness's deposition or an informal written statement. The document needn't have been personally prepared by the forgetful witness; you may refresh one witness's recollection with the statement of a different witness, a receipt, a police report, or any other document.

Assuming that you have handy a document that you think will refresh the flagging memory of your forgetful witness, here's how to do it:

Step 1: Ask the witness whether looking at the document might help refresh the witness's recollection.

Step 2: If the witness responds that looking at the document might help, mark it as an "exhibit," show it to your adversary, and then ask the judge for permission to approach the witness. When permission is granted, walk to the witness box and show the specific portion of the document that contains the information you hope will refresh the witness's recollection.

Step 3: Take the document away from the witness and return to the place where you are asking questions.

Step 4: Ask the witness if his or her memory is refreshed.

Step 5: If the answer is yes, go on and ask the question necessary to produce the testimony.

> ⚠ **CAUTION**
>
> **Your adversary may introduce the "refreshing" document into evidence.** In federal court and most state courts, you cannot offer the document you use to refresh a witness's recollection into evidence unless it's admissible for some other reason. (See Federal Rule of Evidence (FRE) 612.) However, your adversary is allowed to offer the document into evidence if the adversary chooses to do so. Therefore, be careful about the document you use to refresh recollection. If it contains information that your adversary wants to get before the judge or jury, the document may prove more helpful to your adversary than to you.

Here is an example of how the process works. You are examining Mr. Houston. He has unexpectedly forgotten information a building contractor told him about the type of wood the contractor was to use on the front of his house. Luckily, you have a document referring to the forgotten information, and proceed as follows:

1 You:
Mr. Houston, did the contractor say anything about the kind of wood he would use for the front of the house?

2 Witness:
Hmmm—I'm pretty sure he did, but I just can't remember.

3 You:
Do you think it might refresh your recollection if you looked at the estimate the contractor prepared? [Step 1]

4 Witness:
It might.

5 You:
Your Honor, I'm holding a written estimate marked Exhibit A. Counsel for the plaintiff has seen it. May I approach the witness for the purpose of refreshing his recollection? [Step 2] (See Chapter 15 for a discussion of marking and using exhibits.)

6 The Judge:
Go ahead.

7 You:
Okay, Mr. Houston, please look Exhibit A over, especially this section right here [pointing].

After waiting a few moments, you pick up the document and take it back with you to where you are asking questions. [Step 3]

8 You:
Now do you remember what kind of wood the contractor said he would use on the front of the house? [Step 4]

9 Witness:

Yes, I do.

10 You:

And what did he say? [Step 5]

11 Witness:

He said he would use cedar siding.

Offering Documents and Other Objects During Direct Examination

Tangible objects such as receipts, letters, business records, photographs, and computer printouts are often extremely important at trial. They convince a judge or jury of the accuracy of your testimony and that of your witnesses. They also add interest to your presentation of evidence (remember the old saying that "a picture is worth a thousand words") and provide hard evidence to support fallible human memory.

At trial, any tangible object that you want to introduce into evidence is called an "exhibit." Though presenting exhibits is not usually difficult, you generally have to follow a number of preliminary steps (called "laying a foundation") before your exhibits can be received into evidence. Different types of exhibits require different steps. For example, the foundation necessary to introduce a photograph into evidence is very different from that required to introduce a business record into evidence. For this reason, we've given exhibits a chapter of their own—Chapter 15. Because you will typically offer exhibits into evidence during direct examination, make sure that you understand the material in Chapter 15 before you plan direct examination testimony.

CAUTION

Remove the document before eliciting your desired testimony. When refreshing recollection, remember to remove whatever document you have shown the witness before asking whether the witness's memory has been refreshed (see No. 7). The reason is that under the evidence rule barring "hearsay," the witness cannot testify to what the document says. (See Chapter 16.) But if the witness testifies to an actual recollection as refreshed by the document, no hearsay is involved.

Hostile Witnesses

Subject to subpoena limitations, you can call and question any person who has information helpful to your case, even your adversary or someone else who is antagonistic to you. If you decide to call such a person as a witness, ask the judge for permission to treat the person as a "hostile witness." If a judge rules that a witness is hostile, you have the right to ask leading questions during direct examination. (See, for example, FRE 611, Texas Civil Rule of Evidence 611, and similar rules in almost all other states.)

For example, assume that you are involved in a child custody dispute with Jan, your ex-spouse. You are pretty sure that a coworker of Jan's has seen Jan drunk on at least two occasions in the presence of your young children. You want to call the coworker as a witness to help prove that Jan should not be awarded custody of the children. On the other hand, you know that Jan and the coworker are dating. The coworker is unwilling to meet with you informally, and you cannot afford to take the coworker's deposition. Moreover,

Approaching the Bench

according to Jan the coworker supports Jan's request for custody.

In this situation, if you do subpoena the coworker as a witness, ask the judge for permission to approach the bench before beginning the coworker's direct examination. Tell the judge that the coworker has been uncooperative, and ask for permission to treat the coworker as a hostile witness. The judge may grant immediate permission or delay a ruling until after the coworker begins testifying and the judge has a chance to evaluate whether the witness is antagonistic to you. When and if the judge rules that the witness is hostile, you may ask leading questions.

The advantage of leading questions is that you can limit the witness's testimony to the specific topics that support your claims.

They do not give an antagonistic witness an opportunity to launch into areas supporting your adversary that you don't want to cover. For example, here are some of the questions you might ask the coworker in the child custody case:

- "You have been dating Jan for about three months, correct?"
- "You and Jan took my children to a football game last October 9, right?"
- "And Jan got drunk at the game, right?"
- "Jan had so much to drink that you had to help Jan to the car?"
- "And my children were with you the entire time?"

Though of course you have no guarantee that a hostile witness like the coworker will answer honestly, leading questions at least allow you to control the subject matter of the testimony.

CAUTION

Other evidence rules are important too. A variety of other rules also affect whether direct examination questions are proper. For example, you should avoid questions that are "compound" or "vague" or that call for "hearsay" or "character evidence." These additional rules are described in Chapter 16.

The Judge's Role

It is important to recognize that judges have a good deal of discretion over what questions they will allow you to ask. For example, federal judges may exercise "reasonable control over the mode and order of interrogating witnesses and presenting evidence." (FRE 611(a).) No two judges interpret the term "reasonable" in exactly the same way. The same question that Judge A considers a proper "open" question, Judge B may consider an improper "narrative" question. Similarly, a judge will often allow much more deviation from strict rules of evidence in nonjury trials than in jury trials because the judge feels capable of ignoring any improper evidence you bring out through your questioning.

Pay attention to any instructions a judge gives you about how to question a witness. If you are uncertain about whether you can ask a certain kind of question, do not be afraid to ask your judge for permission to approach the bench and ask the judge how to elicit the information you want.

For example, let's examine how to ask a judge for help if your adversary makes an objection that confuses you. You have just concluded preliminary questioning and now want to ask your witness to testify to a conversation in which your adversary agreed to buy your car.

1 You:
Can you please tell the jury what was said during this conversation?

2 Opponent:
Objection, Your Honor. That calls for a narrative response.

3 Judge:
I'll sustain the objection.

4 You:
Your Honor, I'm a bit confused. May we approach the bench?

5 Judge:
Briefly. Both counsel please approach the bench.

6 You (at the bench):
Your Honor, I didn't think this question called for a narrative answer. I just want the witness to testify to what was said during this one conversation. I'm not quite sure what to do.

7 Judge:
Ms. Nolo, I sustained the objection because I think your question is too broad. Ask a narrower question; don't try to get the whole conversation with one question. Please resume your places and proceed.

8 You (back at the podium):
Let me ask you this. Tell us how the conversation got started.

9 Witness:

The first thing I remember is that you told the defendant that you were willing to reduce the price of the car by $500.

10 You:

And how did he reply?

Transcript Analysis: Here, the judge exercises discretion by sustaining a narrative objection to a question that many other judges would consider proper (No. 3). Rather than guess at the problem and getting yourself more confused, you ask for permission to approach the bench and then ask for help (No. 6). The judge makes a suggestion (No. 7), and you then begin to go step by step through the conversation (Nos. 8–10).

The Role of Objections in Enforcing Evidence Rules

A party who believes that the other party has violated a rule of evidence or procedure during trial can object. For example, if your adversary asks an improper leading question during direct examination, violates the personal knowledge rule, or commits some other evidentiary gaffe, or if an adverse witness improperly rambles on in response to a proper question, you may say "Objection" and succinctly state the reason for your objection. If the judge deems the objection valid ("sustains" the objection), the information cannot be considered by the judge or jury in arriving at its verdict. A judge can also rule that evidence is inadmissible, without waiting for a party to object. (Chapter 17 covers objections.)

Sample Direct Examination

Let's look at a sample direct examination transcript, followed by an analysis of the questioning techniques. This transcript has been shortened for illustrative purposes. A real direct examination is likely to be considerably longer.

This example is based on a negligence case (first described in Chapter 8) in which a building contractor named Sarah Adams allegedly made a careless left turn and struck you while you were in a crosswalk. Adams admits striking you with her truck but claims this occurred only because you suddenly ran out from between two parked cars a short distance north of the intersection.

After testifying yourself to what happened, you call Cynthia White as your next witness. Ms. White was at the intersection and saw the accident. In your direct examination, you want to emphasize that you were in the crosswalk and that Adams made the left turn carelessly because she was not paying attention to the road. You subpoenaed Ms. White even though she was very willing to come to court and describe what she saw. Then, under your local court's on-call procedure, you phoned her when the court broke for lunch and asked her to come to court at 1:30 p.m. to testify. Ms. White is escorted to the witness stand by the bailiff, placed under oath by the clerk, and seated. You go to the podium and begin asking questions. The direct examination goes as follows:

1 You:

Ms. White, please state your full name for the record.

2 Witness:

Cynthia White.

3 **You:**

Ms. White, are you employed?

4 **Witness:**

Not at the moment. I'm going to college.

5 **You:**

Which college do you attend?

6 **Witness:**

Vernal College in Atlantic Highlands. I'm working on a master's in psychology.

7 **You:**

So you've already completed your undergraduate work?

8 **Witness:**

Yes, about seven years ago. Then I went to work to earn some money so I could go back to school.

9 **You:**

Ms. White, were you at the intersection of Main and Elm at about 3 p.m. on the afternoon of March 31 of last year?

10 **Witness:**

Yes, I was.

11 **You:**

And did you see an automobile accident?

12 **Witness:**

Yes.

13 **You:**

Where were you when the accident occurred?

14 **Witness:**

I was in my car, stopped for a red light. I was heading south on Elm, and I was stopped just north of Main waiting for the light to change.

15 **You:**

Were any cars stopped in front of you?

16 **Witness:**

No, I was the first car in line. Actually, traffic was pretty light, and I don't know if anyone was behind me.

17 **You:**

Did you notice me at that intersection?

18 **Witness:**

Yes I did. I saw you step off the curb and begin to walk across Elm. The light was green for you.

19 **You:**

Is there any particular reason that you noticed me?

20 **Witness:**

I heard some young children shouting on the corner where you had been standing, so I looked over in your direction. That's when I saw you step off the curb.

21 **You:**

Did I walk into any particular area of the street?

22 **Witness:**

Yes, you were in the crosswalk.

23 **You:**

What happened after you saw me step off the curb into the crosswalk?

24 **Witness:**

I turned to look out my front window to see if the light had changed to green yet. That's when I saw her [pointing to the defendant Adams] heading east on Main and begin to make a left turn to go north on Elm.

25 You:

Let the record reflect the witness is pointing to the defendant, Sarah Adams. Then what happened?

26 Witness:

She sped up as she made the left turn. Then I suddenly realized that you were in the crosswalk, and I looked to see if you were in any danger. Just about then is when her truck ran into you.

27 You:

How long were you watching the truck before you saw it hit me?

28 Witness:

That's hard to say exactly. I'd say about five seconds.

29 You:

And can you estimate the truck's speed during the time it was making the left-hand turn?

30 Witness:

At least 30 to 35 m.p.h., much too fast.

31 You:

How long have you been driving?

32 Witness:

Over 15 years.

33 You:

Before her truck hit me, could you see where the defendant was looking while she made the left turn?

34 Witness:

Yes, I could see her. At least part of the time, she was looking back over her right shoulder out the back window of her pickup truck.

35 You:

Is there any reason you can remember that?

36 Witness:

Yes, seeing her look behind her like that is what made me think that you might be in danger, and that's why I turned back to see if you were still in the crosswalk.

37 You:

After the truck hit me, what happened?

38 Witness:

Well, I didn't have my cell phone with me so I pulled over to the curb and ran into a store to call an ambulance. Then I went out and stayed with you until the ambulance came.

39 You:

And what was the defendant doing?

40 Witness:

She pulled over to the opposite curb and just sat in the cab of her truck until the police came about ten minutes later.

41 You:

Thank you. No further questions at this time, Your Honor.

Transcript Analysis: You begin Cynthia White's testimony with a few personal background questions (Nos. 1–8). Because Ms. White is not employed, you quite properly ask a few questions about her college studies. These questions probably help her relax, and they tell the judge or jury a little bit about her.

Then you properly show that Ms. White is testifying from personal knowledge (Nos. 9–12). Note that No. 9 is a leading question because all the information is in the question, leaving the witness only to answer "yes." But a judge will probably allow you to ask this leading question, because it is preliminary: Adams does not dispute the fact that White was at Main and Elm and that an accident took place at that location.

Ms. White's testimony is in the form of a story. You begin by setting the scene before the accident (Nos. 13–18) and end by showing what happened immediately afterwards (Nos. 37–40). Within the story is certain crucial evidence that you want to emphasize. For example, you want the judge or jury to know that Ms. White had a particular reason to see you step into the crosswalk (No. 20) and to see the defendant looking back over her shoulder (No. 36). You also show that she observed the defendant's truck long enough to estimate its speed (Nos. 27–30). Though there is no minimum amount of time a witness must observe a truck to have sufficient personal knowledge to be able to estimate its speed, a judge will probably think that under ordinary circumstances five seconds is more than adequate. Also, you suggest that because Ms. White is an experienced driver, her estimate of speed is likely to be reliable (No. 32).

In eliciting Ms. White's story, you use a variety of types of questions. For example, Nos. 19 and 23 are open questions. They allow Ms. White to testify in her own words, but because they do not invite her to narrate an entire series of events, they are permissible.

By contrast, Nos. 27 and 29 are closed questions in which you ask for specific pieces of information. This is perfectly sensible: You need to have the witness testify to the speed of the truck (No. 30), and you have to show that she saw the truck long enough to be able to give an estimate (No.

28). Yet neither question is leading because you do not suggest how long Ms. White saw the truck or what its speed was.

Finally, look at Nos. 39 and 40. On the surface, you are just completing the story of what happened. But the fact that the defendant did not get out of her cab to check on your condition after the accident seems coldhearted. That information may make a judge or jury feel sympathetic towards you and hostile toward the defendant. While you cannot offer evidence on the ground that "it paints me in a sympathetic light," or because "it shows that my adversary is really a jerk," often you can get in this kind of emotional evidence during the course of telling the story.

TIP

Look at the witness you're questioning. Whether you stand at a podium or sit at the counsel table when asking questions, lay your outline in front of you. As each witness testifies, check off information to make sure you do not overlook important evidence. However, look at the witness who is testifying as much as possible. A judge or jury may lose interest in a witness's testimony if your face is buried in an outline and you are not paying attention to the testimony.

RESOURCE

Resources on Direct Examination. *Trial Advocacy in a Nutshell* by Paul Bergman (West Publishing Co.); Chapter 7 is a guide to direct examination.

Trying Cases to Win: Direct Examination, by Herbert Stern (Wiley & Sons), has numerous examples of direct examination. ●

Cross-Examination

Cross-examination is your opportunity to question any witness who testifies against you, including your adversary. Among nonlawyers, cross-examination is surely the most misunderstood phase of trial. For starters, forget about all those TV and movie dramas where a snarling cross-examiner shouts angry questions at a beleaguered witness from a distance of two inches. In fact, nothing will bring the wrath of a judge down upon a self-represented litigant (or a lawyer) quicker than overly argumentative cross-examination questions. Normally, you must cross-examine from a podium or counsel table, and the manner of questioning must show respect to the judge and the system of justice at all times. The fact that you believe a witness to be a damnable liar does not change this one bit.

A second popular misconception concerns how much helpful evidence you can realistically hope to elicit during cross-examination. Again, TV and movies create a false image, this time that lawyers routinely win cases during cross-examination by tricking witnesses into blurting out vital information. But in the real world, an adverse witness is unlikely to change major portions of his story just because you question his credibility. So while you'll want to do the best job you can on cross-examination, you'll probably win or lose on the strength and credibility of your testimony and that of your witnesses on direct examination. (See Chapter 12.)

Overview of Cross-Examination

Your adversary will probably conclude a witness's direct examination by saying, "No further questions at this time." The judge will then turn to you and say something like, "Ms. Nolo, you may cross-examine."

If you are at all uncertain about what you will ask on cross-examination, ask the judge for a few minutes to think about your questions. Lawyers are often granted this courtesy, and you should be entitled to no less. Use the time to look over the cross-examination outline in your trial notebook (see "Preparing for Cross-Examination," below). In general, you are best off asking no more than

"Look at him! He has malpractice written all over his face."

a few questions. Otherwise you may end up rehashing the entire direct examination, pointlessly giving your adversary's witness a chance to repeat damaging information.

Once you begin to cross-examine, behave exactly as you did (or will do, if you are the defendant) during direct examination. As with direct, all you are permitted to do during cross-examination is ask questions. You may not make speeches commenting on an adverse witness's testimony, argue with a witness, or approach the witness without the judge's permission.

> **TIP**
>
> **It's okay to read prepared questions during cross-examination.** On cross-examination it is usually effective to read prepared questions to an adverse witness. Unlike with direct examination of a friendly witness, a judge or jury won't dismiss the testimony you elicit as scripted.

After you finish cross-examination, your adversary may ask the court to ask additional questions on redirect examination. This gives the adversary a chance to bring out additional testimony in response to testimony you elicited during cross-examination, but is not to be used to rehash a witness's entire direct testimony. Following redirect, you will be allowed to ask questions on recross-examination, after which the judge will probably excuse the witness.

The Two Goals of Cross-Examination

You can pursue two goals during cross-examination. One line of questioning is affirmative: You seek to produce evidence from a witness called by your adversary that supports your version of events. This will be possible more often than you may think. Few witnesses are all good for one side and all bad for the other.

> **TIP**
>
> **Repeat helpful evidence from direct examination.** Do not be surprised if your adversary asks a witness to testify to some information during direct examination that is helpful to you. It is an oft-used tactic. Your adversary may hope that by "hiding" information that helps you in a long, direct examination, the judge or jury will overlook it. But to counter this tactic, you have the right to elicit the same helpful evidence during your cross-examination, even if it involves asking a witness to repeat exactly the same testimony already given on direct. Doing so emphasizes it for the judge or jury.

The second goal is to impeach adverse witnesses —that is, to cast doubt on their credibility. Using the impeachment techniques discussed in "Impeaching Adverse Witnesses," below, you try to give a judge or jury a reason to distrust the accuracy of the adverse witness's testimony.

> **TIP**
>
> **It's fine to pursue both goals.** You do not have to choose between goals one and two. During cross-examination of a single witness, you may try both to elicit information supporting your version of events and to impeach harmful evidence. When you do pursue both goals, as a general rule, seek the affirmative information first. An adverse witness may be far less cooperative after you have tried to impeach that person!

The Permissible Scope of Cross-Examination

The questions you ask during cross-examination must pertain to (be "within the scope" of) the topics that were explored on direct examination. Impeachment of a witness is allowed because you are attempting to weaken the credibility of direct examination testimony. But if you try to ask about a topic that supports your version of events, but wasn't addressed in your adversary's direct examination, your adversary may object that your questions are beyond the scope of the direct examination. In response, you may point out that the judge has discretion under evidence rules—for example, Federal Rule of Evidence 611—to interpret the scope of the direct examination broadly (and many judges do so).

Even if the judge sustains (agrees with) your adversary's objection, all is not lost. You can call the same witness to the stand again yourself after your adversary finishes presenting all of the evidence supporting the other side (rests his or her case), and ask the same questions that you were not allowed to ask on cross-examination. When you do call the witness again, ask the judge to rule that the witness is a "hostile witness." A judge's ruling that a witness is hostile to you gives you the right to ask leading questions even though technically you are conducting the witness's direct examination. (Hostile witnesses are discussed further in Chapter 12.) In fact, pointing out to the judge that it will be a waste of court (and witness) time for the same witness to return to court at a later time is often an effective argument for asking a judge to overrule (deny) your adversary's "beyond the scope" objection.

Should You Cross-Examine?

You have a right to cross-examine every witness who testifies against you, but you are by no means required to do so. Perhaps it makes sense to some people to climb a mountain just "because it is there," but cross-examining a witness just because the witness is sitting in the witness box is foolish.

If you don't reasonably expect to elicit information that helps prove your version of events, and you don't think that you can impeach the witness on an important point, don't cross-examine. When the judge invites you to cross-examine, just say, "No questions." That way the witness cannot take advantage of your cross-examination to retell the same story. And if you do not cross-examine, your adversary cannot conduct redirect examination, eliminating yet another chance for the witness to repeat a version of events that's different from yours.

Because adverse witnesses' stories are likely to sound better to a judge or jury the second or third time around, one of the worst things you can do on cross-examination is to conduct an aimless "fishing trip." You "fish" when you ask a question in the hope that a witness will give a response that is impeaching, but without factual support for that hope.

For example, assume that an adverse witness testifies that you ran a red light. You ask on cross-examination, "What were you doing when you saw me run the light?" You have no idea what the witness was doing, but hope that the witness will respond that he was memorizing the Gettysburg Address or was otherwise so preoccupied that he couldn't possibly know what color the light was. Unfortunately, in this situation a witness will almost invariably give an answer that solidifies the direct examination testimony. For example, the witness might answer, "Your question reminds me that I was studying the traffic at that intersection in meticulous detail as part of a government research safety project." If your only alternative is to fish, you are far better off saying, "No questions."

Although setting out any general rules about cross-examination is risky, here are some types of witnesses that should cause you to think twice (or even thrice) before cross-examining:

- Expert witnesses, who are likely to know much more about the subject of their testimony than you do and thus are especially likely to retell their story during cross-examination. (See Chapter 19 for more on this issue.)
- Witnesses who you think have even more damaging information than your adversary elicited during direct examination. Don't give them a second chance to hurt you.
- Witnesses with whom a judge or jury is likely to sympathize, such as children or elderly or infirm witnesses.

TIP

Offering impeachment evidence during direct examination. As any devotee of *Perry Mason* reruns knows, because of its dramatic effect, impeachment often takes place during cross-examination. However, cross-examination is not the only time you can offer impeaching evidence. Though it may be less dramatic, usually you can also introduce impeachment evidence when it is your turn to conduct direct examination.

For example, instead of asking a plaintiff's witness during cross-examination whether he had consumed three martinis a half hour before he supposedly saw you driving too fast, you can impeach the witness by later calling your own witness to testify that the plaintiff's witness was seen drinking martinis. The advantage of this choice is that the plaintiff's witness cannot undercut the force of the impeachment by immediately offering an explanation such as, "Yes, I did have three martinis, but I take medication that renders them as harmless as lemonade." The disadvantage is that you may lose the impeachment evidence altogether if you cannot produce your impeachment witness at trial.

Asking Questions on Cross-Examination

It's crucial not to allow an adverse witness to retell his or her entire story on cross-examination. While this may be fine advice, just like the adage "buy low, sell high," the key is in figuring out how to do so.

Ask Leading Questions

During cross-examination, the key to eliciting evidence without giving a witness a chance to retell a story is to ask leading questions. (Leading questions are explained in Chapter 12.) Because they call on witnesses to respond only by saying yes or no, leading questions do not give a witness a chance to rehash direct examination testimony.

Questions are leading when they suggest the desired answer. Leading questions are improper on direct examination when you're questioning your own witnesses, on the theory that a friendly witness will give the suggested answer even if it's not completely accurate. But leading questions are proper on cross-examination because there is little risk that an adverse witness will falsely agree with you. Here are some typical leading questions:

- "You never told me the date the inspector would come by to inspect the plumbing, did you?"
- "The first time that you saw the light, it was already red, correct?"
- "Isn't it true that you couldn't actually tell which person said 'Stop'?"

Because each of these questions is nothing more than an assertion of the answer you want the witness to give put in the form of a question, you can see why leading questions—especially short, unambiguous ones—typically limit the scope of a witness's answer. In each example, the only answer the witness is called on to give is "yes" or "no."

TIP

Stay in control during cross-examination. Increase the power of leading questions on cross-examination by asking them in a firm (but not nasty) voice that suggests that you expect nothing more than "yes" or "no" in response. And to further inhibit an adverse witness from straying from your script, keep your questions short.

For example, if you want an adverse witness to agree that "The wolf huffed and puffed until he blew the house down," break it up into two questions: "The wolf huffed and puffed, correct?" and "He continued to huff and puff until he blew the house down, isn't that right?"

Interrupt Nonresponsive Witnesses

Despite your best efforts, an adverse witness may attempt to give a narrative response to a leading question. For example, assume that the following dialogue takes place during your cross-examination:

You:

And then Jill came tumbling after, right?

Witness:

You could say that, but you've got to remember that Jill and her brother Jack had only one pail between them. I know for sure that Jack was carrying the pail ….

Here, even though your question calls for a yes or no answer, the witness launches into a retelling of his or her story. Fortunately, you have the power to stop the witness from pontificating. Quickly hold up your hand and say, "Excuse me." When the witness pauses, ask your next question. If the witness continues to talk, ask the judge to intervene by saying something like, "Your Honor, I object; the witness is not answering my question." Assuming that the judge agrees with (sustains) your objection, ask the judge to delete the answer from the record ("strike the answer") and to tell the jury (if there is one) to disregard the testimony the witness gave before you could stop the witness from talking. If the witness launches into diatribes on more than one occasion, you may also ask the judge to instruct the witness to stop making speeches and to answer only what you have asked. Most witnesses will be very cowed by a judicial reprimand.

Remember, however, that judges have a good deal of discretion when it comes to the scope of witnesses' answers. Occasionally, even if you ask a question that calls for a yes or no answer, a judge may allow a brief explanation if the judge believes it is necessary to allow a witness to answer accurately.

Use Exhibits If They Are Helpful

If your adversary offered exhibits (such as reports, photographs, or receipts) into evidence during direct examination, you may ask a witness to refer to those exhibits during your cross-examination. Once an exhibit is admitted into evidence, it is the property of the court, not of the party who offered it. For example, assume that during an adverse witness's direct examination, your adversary offers into evidence a photograph of his or her car to show the damage it sustained in an accident. You now want to use that photograph to call the judge or jury's attention to the open bottle of beer shown on the front seat. On cross-examination, you may show the photograph to the witness and ask about the object depicted on the front seat.

To do this, begin by retrieving the exhibit. Often, you will find it either in a shallow box on the counsel table or on the court clerk's desk. But it may be on the judge's bench, in which case you should ask the judge for "permission to have Exhibit 3." To show the exhibit to a witness, ask the judge for permission to approach the witness. (Check this procedure with the court clerk or watch what the other attorney does. Some judges prefer for the bailiff or clerk to transport an exhibit from wherever it is to the witness while you remain at the podium

or counsel table.) Then, ask the witness to refer to the exhibit and ask your question: "Ms. Spillenger, please look at Exhibit 3 and tell us if the object on the front seat depicted in that exhibit is an open bottle of beer."

TIP

Offering exhibits during cross-examination. Rules of evidence allow you to offer exhibits into evidence during cross-examination of adverse witnesses in the same way as you can during your testimony or direct examination of your witnesses. Whenever possible, however, offer exhibits into evidence only when you or your witnesses are testifying.

Eliciting Helpful Evidence

Affirmative questioning (questioning to bring out evidence that supports your version of events) during cross-examination can be very effective. A witness called by your adversary may well have some information that helps you, and focusing on that helpful information may lead a judge or jury to conclude that the witness hasn't hurt you.

For example, consider an incident from the well-publicized 1993 federal court criminal prosecution of the four Los Angeles police officers who were charged with using illegal force to arrest Rodney King. One of the defendants called a highway patrol officer, Melanie Singer, to testify that she was an eyewitness to the arrest and that King was acting in an aggressive, threatening manner toward the arresting officers. But on cross-examination by the prosecutor, Officer Singer cried on the stand as she testified that the defendant officers had kicked and struck King far too long and that she felt helpless to stop it. Without in any way attacking Officer Singer's credibility, the prosecution turned a defense witness into a witness who did not damage its case—and may have even helped.

How can you elicit evidence on cross-examination that supports your own case? As with direct examination, start by looking at the facts you're trying to prove. (Remember, even as a defendant you may have facts that you are trying to prove. See Chapter 9.) Then review the information you gathered before trial, whether through informal discussions, negotiations, or formal discovery, to identify information a witness has that supports those facts.

Let's take as an example a legal mal-practice claim. Say you're suing a lawyer for negligently failing to advise your stepmother that for you to inherit all of the stepmother's property in accord with a will the lawyer had previously drafted, she had to change the will to specifically disinherit a child she gave birth to after she made the will. You have presented all of your evidence and rested your case, and the lawyer's direct examination has just concluded. He testified that he prepared a will for your stepmother, that she came into the office to talk to him a couple of years after the will was executed, and that, while she did talk casually about her relatives, he is sure that she never said anything about having given birth to a child since signing her will.

You now have an opportunity to cross-examine the lawyer. From what you found out from the lawyer's answers to a brief set of interrogatories you sent him before trial, you know that estate planning is not the

lawyer's specialty and that he does only one or two wills per year. Also, the lawyer has a paralegal (an assistant) whom he relies on to take down most of the information from will clients. This information does not impeach any testimony the lawyer gave on direct examination, but you want to elicit it during cross-examination to support your assertion that the lawyer was careless. Your cross may go like this:

1 **You:**
Mr. Lawyer, preparing wills is not your legal specialty, is it?

2 **Witness (Defendant):**
Not my specialty, no.

3 **You:**
You probably don't do more than a will or two a year, right?

4 **Witness:**
Well, that's probably about right. But let me add that ….

5 **You:**
Excuse me. Your Honor, the witness has answered the question. I object to further testimony.

6 **Judge:**
Yes, that's right. Objection sustained.

7 **You:**
My stepmother came to see you a couple of years after she signed the will you prepared for her, right?

8 **Witness:**
Yes, I've testified that she did.

9 **You:**
And you didn't conduct her interview by yourself, did you?

10 Witness:

Not entirely, no.

11 You:

You asked your paralegal assistant to get most of the information from her, right?

12 Witness:

Most of it, but of course I talked to her too.

13 You:

And a paralegal is not an attorney, right?

14 Witness:

That's true.

Transcript Analysis: This cross-examination does not directly attack the lawyer's direct testimony that the stepmother said nothing to him about a child born after the will was made. Instead, you concentrate on information about the lawyer's experience and client interview procedures that support your contention that the lawyer was careless.

All of your questions are leading, which gives the witness no opportunity to retell his own story. And when the witness tries to explain an answer (No. 4), you quite properly and courteously stop his explanation by objecting that the witness has already answered your question. When the judge sustains your objection (No. 5), you promptly ask your next question. Because you stopped the lawyer quickly, you needn't ask the judge to strike any testimony from the record. (If the lawyer's answer to your questions contradict his interrogatory answers, you could impeach him with his contradictory interrogatory answers.)

You may also be able to base affirmative cross-examination on a witness's oral state-ment. For example, assume that you are seeking to regain custody of your children from your ex-spouse. Your ex-spouse calls one of your neighbors, Linda, as a witness to testify that you often have strangers staying overnight in your apartment. Another neighbor, Dick, has told you that in talking to Linda one day recently, Linda said a number of nice things about you—including that your apartment is always neat and clean and that she always feels comfortable asking you to watch her children for a few hours. On cross-examination of Linda you want to have her testify to this information because it is affirmative evidence for your custody. To do so, you might ask a series of questions such as:

- "Linda, whenever you've seen my apartment, it's always been neat and clean, right?"
- "In the last year, you've often asked me to watch your children for a few hours, correct?"
- "And you always feel comfortable asking me to watch your children, don't you?"

Here you do not impeach Linda's testimony that strangers often stay overnight at your apartment. Rather, you use Linda's oral statements to Dick as the basis of an affirmative cross-examination of Linda. (If Linda gives testimony that conflicts with what she told Dick, you may impeach her by later calling Dick as a witness.)

Note that these questions are within the scope of Linda's direct examination because they pertain to your fitness as a parent, the topic that Linda was asked about on direct.

Impeaching Adverse Witnesses

Your second cross-examination goal is to impeach an adverse witness and give a judge or jury some basis for doubting the witness's credibility. Despite the incredible variety of events that give rise to litigation, there are really only a few legally accepted impeachment methods that arise regularly. Most of them, such as raising the possibility that a witness is biased or prejudiced, will be familiar to you because they are based on the same logic you rely on in everyday life to evaluate what you hear and see.

Bias in Favor of Your Adversary

"Bias" refers to a witness's emotional or financial interest in favor of your opponent. If you can show bias, you hope the judge or jury will doubt the credibility of the witness's testimony.

An emotional interest can arise from such sources as family loyalty and friendship. For example, if you can use cross-examination to establish that Sarah is testifying on behalf of her childhood friend Hilary or that Adam is testifying on behalf of his cousin Kevin, the judge or jury may not believe (or may at least discount) Sarah's or Adam's testimony.

As you probably realize, a financial interest arises when a witness stands to gain financially if your adversary wins. For instance, one spouse or business partner may be testifying on behalf of the other in a situation where any financial gains resulting from the trial would be shared by both.

Whether the source of the bias is emotional or financial, the basis of impeachment is the same: The witness's

interest in the outcome arguably casts doubt on the accuracy of the witness's testimony. Of course, the judge or jury may believe a witness despite the witness's emotional or financial interest. But the possibility of bias will probably make the judge or jury more skeptical of the adverse witness's testimony.

Here's an example of how to impeach a witness on cross-examination based on bias. Assume that you are the homeowner in a breach of contract case and have sued the building contractor you hired to do a remodeling job. You claim that he failed to complete the job and that he used substandard workmanship. On direct examination, Wilkins, one of the contractor's employees, testifies that you orally agreed to give the contractor two additional months to complete the work. Wilkins also testifies that a couple of weeks before this conversation you agreed to wait at home so a building inspector could sign off on the rough plumbing and that your failure to do so caused a delay in the project. You dispute everything Wilkins says: You never agreed to a two-month extension, and you did not wait for the building inspector because neither Wilkins nor anyone else told you that the plumbing was supposed to be inspected. So in addition to testifying yourself on these points during your direct examination, you want to impeach Wilkins if you can.

When you took Wilkins's deposition before trial, you learned that he has had some discussions with the defendant about soon becoming a partner in the defendant's contracting business. Based on this information, you may cross-examine Wilkins in an effort to show that he has a potential financial interest in seeing the defendant win the case. You want the judge or jury to infer that because Wilkins has hopes of becoming the defendant's business partner, he wants both to remain on good terms with the defendant and to share ownership of a financially stable business. Here's how the cross-examination might go:

1 **You:**
> Mr. Wilkins, you've worked for the defendant for about nine years, right?

2 **Witness:**
> That's right.

3 **You:**
> And you and the defendant have discussed your becoming a partner in the business, right?

4 **Witness:**
> Well, there's nothing definite about that.

5 **You:**
> But you hope to become a partner, don't you?

6 **Witness:**
> We've talked about it, yes.

7 **You:**
> That means you would put money into the business?

8 **Witness:**
> Yes.

9 **You:**
> So you want this business to be worth as much as possible in case you become a partner, right?

10 **Witness:**
> I suppose so.

Transcript Analysis: In No. 4, Wilkins tries to downplay his potential interest in the business. However, in No. 5 you stick to your guns and ask whether Wilkins has a long-term interest in the business. No. 5 is a legally proper question; you have a right to press for an unequivocal answer. By contrast, you would be improperly argumentative if you asked this additional question: "And because you want the business to be worth as much as possible, you've lied on the stand, haven't you?" Such an attempt to put words in Wilkins's mouth is not a question, though if put in a less inflammatory way it is possibly material for your final argument. Note that your questions are leading and leave Wilkins no room to retell the story he told on direct examination.

Questioning to bring out bias can often be even shorter than this. Assume that instead of learning that Wilkins hopes to become a partner in the defendant's business, you've learned that Wilkins and the defendant are brothers. In that case, you might use just one question to show that Wilkins has an emotional stake in the outcome of the case, as follows:

1 **You:**
> Mr. Wilkins, you're the defendant's brother, right?

2 **Witness:**
> Yes.

TIP

Impeach using what you learned through discovery. By working backwards, you can see that if you want to impeach a witness as biased at trial, you should always try to find evidence of bias before trial, either through informal discussions with people who know a witness or through formal discovery tools, such as written interrogatories and depositions (though the latter may be costly). Discovery tools are discussed in Chapter 5.

Prejudice Against You

In legal terms, prejudice is the flip side of bias. Instead of showing that a witness is biased in favor of your adversary, you show that a witness might be prejudiced against you.

For example, assume that one of the witnesses who testifies against you in a traffic accident case is your former spouse, with whom you have argued bitterly concerning the custody of your children. If you bring out your former spouse's bitterness toward you during cross-examination, the judge or jury might disbelieve or at least partially discredit the former spouse's testimony.

To illustrate how this works, let's put the contractor's employee, Wilkins, back in the witness box. Now assume that you noticed that on a couple of occasions when he was working on your new addition, Wilkins appeared to have had too much to drink. You reported this fact to Wilkins's employer, the defendant. As a result of your complaint to the defendant, Wilkins was suspended for two weeks without pay. In this situation, after Wilkins testifies, you may cross-examine to show that he is prejudiced against you:

1 You:

Mr. Wilkins, I complained about you to your employer, didn't I?

2 Witness:

I remember that, yes.

3 You:

My complaint was that you had come to work having had too much to drink on a couple of occasions, right?

4 Witness:

That's what you said. But that's not the way it was.

5 You:

Your Honor, that last sentence is improper. I just asked him what my complaint was about. I did not ask him for his side of things.

6 Judge:

Yes, that's improper. I'll strike the second sentence.

If this is a jury trial, the judge might instruct the jury to disregard Wilkins's improper remark.

7 You:

So you know I made this complaint?

8 Witness:

Yes.

9 You:

And because of my complaint, you were suspended for two weeks without pay, correct?

10 Witness:

Yes, I was.

Transcript Analysis: Again, because all of your questions are leading and because they all focus on the specific topic of prejudice, you give Wilkins no chance to retell his story. When Wilkins does try to throw in information not called for by your question

(No. 4), you properly object. The judge strikes the improper testimony, meaning that the judge or jury must totally ignore that testimony when weighing the evidence and making a decision.

Prior Inconsistent Statements

One of the most widely used types of impeachment consists of proving that a witness's testimony at trial doesn't square with a statement the witness previously made. The theory behind this type of impeachment is that accurate tales do not change in the telling. Not surprisingly, lawyers call this "impeachment with a prior inconsistent statement."

You can use this cross-examination tool whether the witness made the previous statement under oath during a deposition, in a letter to her Aunt Agnes, or while playing tennis with a friend. If any statement previously made by a witness is inconsistent with the witness's in-court testimony, the previous statement is admissible for impeachment.

Oral Statements

Our old but long-suffering friend Wilkins can provide us with an example of this type of impeachment. Assume that on direct examination Wilkins testified that serious problems with your house's foundation required the contractor to demand an additional $20,000 to complete the remodeling job. You want to impeach Wilkins with a statement that he made to another construction worker, Alice Johnson. According to Ms. Johnson, after inspecting the foundation, Wilkins told her, "There's no problem with the foundation. It's in great condition." Your cross-examination bringing out Wilkins's prior inconsistent statement may go as follows:

1 You:
Mr. Wilkins, you testified that the reason for the demand of an additional $20,000 to complete the remodeling job was that you discovered a serious problem with the foundation, right?

2 Witness:
That's correct.

3 You:
Another person working on my job was named Alice Johnson, is that right?

4 Witness:
Yes, Alice was working on your job some of the time.

5 You:
And just after inspecting the foundation, you told Ms. Johnson that it was in great condition, didn't you?

6 Witness:
I did say something like that.

Transcript Analysis: This concludes your impeachment. You contrast Wilkins's testimony (No. 1) with his inconsistent prior statement (No. 5). You hope that the inconsistency will lead the judge or jury to conclude that Wilkins is untrustworthy.

What can you do if Wilkins denies making the statement to Alice Johnson? During the cross-examination of Wilkins, there is nothing you can do. However, after your adversary finishes presenting evidence (rests), you typically have a chance to present additional testimony to impeach your adversary's witnesses, even from witnesses who have previously testified for you. Here, if Wilkins denies making the statement to Alice Johnson, you could eventually call her as a witness to testify that Wilkins told her that the foundation was in great shape.

Written Statements

Now let's look at how you can cross-examine Wilkins if, instead of an oral statement, you have written evidence of a prior inconsistent statement. For example, assume again that during direct examination, Wilkins testifies that there were serious problems with the foundation of your house. But during his deposition, Wilkins admitted that his inspection revealed that your house's foundation was in very good condition.

To impeach Wilkins with his deposition statement, which is now in the form of a written transcript, mark the deposition as an exhibit, ask the judge for permission to approach Wilkins, and, when permission is granted, hand the exhibit to him. (See Chapter 15 for information on using exhibits.) Open the deposition transcript to the signature page and ask Wilkins to verify his signature. Then tell the judge and your adversary what page of the deposition the inconsistent statement appears on and read the prior inconsistent statement into the record. You do not need to give the witness a chance to deny making the prior statement or to explain why he has changed his story. The impeachment will go as follows:

1 **You:**
Mr. Wilkins, you testified that the reason for the demand of an additional $20,000 to complete the remodeling job was that

you discovered a serious problem with the foundation, right?

2 **Witness:**
That's correct.

You mark the deposition as an exhibit, ask the judge for permission to approach the witness, and, once permission is granted, you hand the deposition to Wilkins.

3 **You:**
All right, looking at your deposition, Exhibit 4, please examine it and tell us if this is the sworn deposition you gave in this case?

4 **Witness:**
Yes, it is.

5 **You:**
The signature on the last page, that's your signature?

6 **Witness:**
Yes.

7 **You:**
Your Honor, I'm reading page 23, lines 13–20 of Mr. Wilkins's deposition. "Question: What was your initial task in connection with my remodeling job? Answer: To inspect the foundation. Question: And what did that inspection reveal? Answer: That the foundation was in very good condition."

Transcript Analysis: Once you establish that the exhibit is the witness's deposition, you can read into the record any portion of the deposition that is inconsistent with the witness's testimony. And if the witness has given other direct testimony that is inconsistent with his deposition testimony, you can again impeach him without having to identify the deposition again.

Ability to Perceive

We have all seen movies or TV programs in which the key eyewitness turns out to be legally blind or someone who claims to overhear a crucial conversation is revealed to be almost deaf. In real life, chances are you will never be able to attack so decisively an adverse witness's ability to perceive.

But you may be able to cause a judge or juror to doubt a witness's ability to perceive what he or she claims to have seen or heard. Sometimes you will base your impeachment on adverse conditions in the outside world, such as when a witness claims to have overheard a whispered conversation while standing at a busy intersection. Other times, your best chance to impeach may be based on a witness's condition, such as when a nearsighted witness claims to have seen the color of a distant traffic light at dusk—or, if luck is really with you, ten minutes after leaving an optometrist's appointment at which his or her eyes were dilated.

Let's go back to the negligence case involving your claim that you were crossing Main Street in a crosswalk when you were struck by a truck driven by Sarah Adams, a building contractor. Assume that Adams, the defendant, calls a witness named Kris Knaplund, who testifies that she was coming out of a nearby shop when the accident occurred. Knaplund further testifies that after you were struck by the truck, you said, "Oh my God! Why didn't I use the crosswalk?" When you get a chance to testify later, you will deny making this statement. You will

testify that what you really said was, "Oh my God! Why didn't you see me in the crosswalk?" But before that, during cross-examination of Knaplund, you want to cast doubt on her ability to have overheard your statement accurately. Your cross-examination of Knaplund may go like this:

1 You:
Ms. Knaplund, you heard me say something after the accident?

2 Witness:
Yes.

3 You:
Isn't it true that what I really said was, "Oh my God! Why didn't you see me in the crosswalk?"

4 Witness:
No, that's not what I heard you say.

5 You:
You were just coming out of a shop when you heard me?

6 Witness:
That's right.

7 You:
The shop was a video game arcade?

8 Witness:
That's true.

9 You:
There were a number of noisy games being played at the time, right?

10 Witness:
Yes.

11 You:
Isn't it true that those machines and the people playing them are so loud that you

have to talk extra loud to be heard inside the arcade?

12 Witness:

Well, they're noisy, that's true.

13 You:

And isn't the arcade about 75 feet away from where I was hit by the truck?

14 Witness:

I wouldn't know, I'm not too good at estimating distances.

Transcript Analysis: Here, you begin by asking Knaplund directly (using a leading question) about your statement (No. 3). You do not expect her to suddenly admit that she made a mistake, but you have nothing to lose by having the judge or jury hear your side of things. Then you mention some outside factors that may cast doubt on Knaplund's ability to accurately hear what you said: just coming out of a noisy video game arcade (Nos. 5–12) and being some distance away from the scene (Nos. 13 and 14). Your cross-examination cannot prove that Knaplund was unable to hear your statement accurately. But, together with your own testimony, it can lead the judge or jury to doubt Knaplund's credibility.

Implausible Testimony

All of us carry around beliefs about how people usually behave and events usually occur. When we are told something that is at odds with these beliefs, we tend to doubt what we are told; we find it implausible. For example, if Jones tells you that he walked three blocks at 2 a.m. to return an overdue library book, you would probably doubt

him. Your own life experience suggests that people do not go out in the middle of the night to return a library book when the library is closed and the book would have to go into a drop box.

For the same reason, you should examine an adverse witness's story for its overall plausibility. Even if you have no other basis on which to try to impeach a witness, perhaps you can show that the witness's story is in some way implausible. This is far from an ironclad method of impeachment. What you consider implausible may seem quite normal to a judge or jury. A judge who grew up in a family of librarians, for example, might think it quite admirable to return a library book at 2 a.m.

To see how to conduct this type of cross-examination, return again to Knaplund's testimony in the negligence case. Assume that Knaplund gave a statement to the investigating police officer who came to the scene of the accident, but neglected to mention that, just after being struck, you said that you should have been in the crosswalk. You consider this implausible; if she really had heard you say this, surely she would have reported it to prevent the driver from being unfairly held responsible for the accident. Your cross-examination of Knaplund to emphasize the implausibility might go like this:

1 You:

Ms. Knaplund, you say that right after the accident I said, "Oh my God! Why didn't I use the crosswalk?"

2 Witness:

Yes, that's what I heard.

3 You:

A few minutes later a police officer came to the scene, right?

4 Witness:

That's correct.

5 You:

The officer was in uniform, correct?

6 Witness:

Yes.

7 You:

You knew that he was there to investigate the accident, right?

8 Witness:

That's true.

9 You:

You wanted to make sure that the police officer got accurate information about what happened, right?

10 Witness:

I guess so.

11 You:

But you never told him that I said something about wishing I had been in the crosswalk?

12 Witness:

No, I didn't.

Transcript Analysis: In this excerpt, you use leading questions to suggest that Knaplund's failure to mention what she heard you say is implausible. You hope that the implausibility will lead the judge or jury to discredit Knaplund's testimony.

Prior Convictions

In most court systems, you may impeach a witness by showing that the witness has been convicted of certain serious crimes. (For example, Federal Rule of Evidence 609 and California Evidence Code § 788 allow this.) However, in a civil case chances are that the witnesses you cross-examine will not have been convicted of a crime. Moreover, the rules are very strict and often confusing as to what kinds of convictions are admissible. If you find out that an adverse witness has been convicted of a crime, consult your legal coach or do some legal research to determine whether the conviction is admissible in evidence.

CAUTION

When implying wrongdoing, be sure you are right. You cannot ask a witness about a criminal conviction or otherwise imply wrongdoing on the part of a witness unless you have what the law calls a "good faith basis" to believe that your charge is accurate. At the least, you need to be able to point to a reliable source of information that justifies your question.

For example, assume that you have no evidence that an eyewitness had been using drugs. Nevertheless, you ask, "Had you been using any narcotic drugs just before you witnessed the accident?" If your adversary objects to the question, the judge may ask you to reveal your source. If you cannot identify a reliable source that the judge regards as a good faith basis for believing that the witness had used drugs, the judge will surely sustain the objection. And even allowing for your inexperience as a self-represented party, a judge may restrict your right to ask further questions.

Basing Questions on Evidence You Can Offer

One of the oldest cross-examination clichés is to "never ask a question to which you don't know the answer." This doesn't mean that you have to be 100% certain of how an adverse witness will answer your questions, because an adverse witness can always give an unexpected answer. What it does mean is that generally you should not ask a question unless you can offer evidence to contradict an unexpected answer. And this advice applies regardless of whether the information you seek on cross-examination supports your own fact or impeaches a witness.

Look back at some of the examples in this chapter. In one instance, you wanted to elicit helpful evidence from Linda that she has often asked you to take care of her children. Based on information you have from Dick, a friend of Linda's, you expect Linda to provide this evidence. But if Linda gives an unexpected answer, you can call Dick as a witness yourself to contradict her.

Similarly, in each of the impeachment illustrations, you could contradict an unexpected answer because your cross-examination questions were based on evidence that you could produce in court. Thus, you could impeach Wilkins with his statement to Alice Johnson because, if he gave an unexpected answer, you could later call Johnson as a witness and ask her what Wilkins told her. In addition, you could impeach Wilkins with his deposition testimony because you could contradict an unexpected answer with the deposition transcript.

Without any way to contradict an unexpected answer, your cross-examination may amount to a foolish "fishing trip." Without your own source of evidence to fall back on, your firm belief that an adverse witness is either lying or mistaken does you no good. To see this, assume that you have solid information that Knaplund was just leaving a noisy video arcade when she supposedly heard your "crosswalk" statement. Unless you can produce the person who provided you with this information as a witness, cross-examining Knaplund about where she was when she heard the statement is risky. If she answers that, no, she wasn't leaving the arcade but was standing outside the library, just ten feet from where you fell, you have no way to contradict her.

What to Do If Your Witness Is Impeached

If your adversary impeaches one of your witnesses—for example, with a prior inconsistent statement—talk to your witness during a recess (ask the judge for one, if necessary) or at lunch to see if the witness has a good explanation for the change of story. If your witness has an explanation that eliminates the negative impact of a prior inconsistent statement, you can let your witness give it during redirect examination, which takes place immediately after cross-examination. (See Chapter 12.)

For example, assume that in a case in which you are suing your employer for sexual harassment, Laura Rosas testifies for you on direct examination that she heard your employer tell you that you needed to go on a date with him if you expected a promotion. On cross-examination the employer's lawyer impeaches Rosas with a statement she previously made to an investigator from the Fair Employment Practices Department, in which Rosas said she could not remember your employer ever asking you for a date. Talking to Rosas at the recess that immediately follows her cross-examination, you learn that the reason she made that statement to the investigator was that your employer threatened to fire her if she gave the investigator any information. By bringing out this explanation during your redirect examination of Rosas, you hope to convince the judge or jury that Rosas's testimony during direct examination is credible. Your redirect may go as follows:

1 You:

Ms. Rosas, did you tell the Fair Employment Practices Department investigator something different than you told the court today?

2 Witness:

Yes, I did.

3 You:

And why is that?

4 Witness:

Because the day before the investigator came to the office, our employer said that he would fire me if I said that he had done anything wrong.

5 You:

Then why are you willing to testify against him today?

6 Witness:

I'm in court, and I'm going to tell the truth. If he fires me, I guess he's going to have another lawsuit on his hands.

Transcript Analysis: Note how your questions on redirect (especially Nos. 3 and 5) are open questions. Just as during direct examination, during redirect you cannot ask leading questions of your own witnesses. (See Chapter 12 for a discussion of the different types of questions.)

Preparing for Cross-Examination

Before trial, make an outline that briefly summarizes the testimony you expect an adverse witness to give on direct examination. Then in separate sections, list additional evidence a witness can provide that supports your version of events and evidence that impeaches the witness. You may even want to write down specific questions in each section because on cross-examination you are likely to be limiting your questions to only a few pieces of information. Finally, you may list any exhibits you plan to refer to or introduce during cross-examination, though probably you will only offer exhibits during your own testimony or direct examination of your own witnesses.

 TRIAL NOTEBOOK

Make sure to update your trial notebook. Devote a separate section of your trial notebook to cross-examination, and make a separate outline for each witness you will cross-examine. (See Chapter 18.)

Below is a form cross-examination outline that you may want to use.

Cross-Examination Outline

Witness:

Expected direct examination testimony:

Additional information that supports my version of events (List specific questions):

Impeachment (List specific questions):

Exhibits that I will refer to or introduce:

RESOURCE

Additional Resources on cross-examination. *The Art of Cross-Examination*, by Francis Wellman (Book Jungle), is regarded by many lawyers as the classic cross-examination work. Though some of Wellman's language is dated, the book (originally published in 1903) reviews the most common bases of cross-examination and is filled with colorful examples drawn from actual cases, including Abraham Lincoln's famous "almanac" cross-examination. (Lincoln impeached a witness who claimed to have seen an incident by moonlight by producing an almanac showing that there had been no moon that night.)

Trial Advocacy in a Nutshell, by Paul Bergman (West Publishing Co.), is an inexpensive review of trial techniques. Chapter 9 focuses on cross-examination and presents an approach for determining when you can contradict an unexpected answer.

Fundamentals of Trial Techniques, by Thomas Mauet (Little, Brown & Co.), reviews the common bases of cross-examination and provides a number of brief examples. ●

Closing Argument

Closing argument is your opportunity to tell the judge or jury why you should win. After repeatedly warning you not to argue when you deliver your opening statement, present evidence, or cross-examine witnesses, we can finally say, "Go for it."

During the trial, your story is presented one piece at a time, through testimony and tangible evidence. You have some control over the evidence and the order in which it comes out, but no opportunity to tie it all together. Closing argument gives you the valuable chance to help the judge or jury fit the pieces together—and convince them that the evidence presented at trial proves you should win.

Closing argument is also your chance to make a good last impression. But, contrary to what you may have seen in the movies, trials do not usually turn on dramatic closing arguments. Rather, most cases are won or lost because of the persuasiveness of the evidence presented. With that in mind, don't expect the judge or jurors to all nod their heads enthusiastically during your closing argument, and don't expect to (or feel you need to) give an award-winning performance. Just be yourself and try to follow the guidelines below.

> **CAUTION**
>
> **Don't be rude.** You are allowed to "argue" during closing argument, but not in the same sense as that word is often used in everyday life. In the courtroom context, permissible argument is telling the judge or jury how the evidence proves you should win. There are limits: Be persuasive, but don't yell, pound the table, or call your opponent names. You'll get a reprimand from the judge and alienate the jury, too.

When to Deliver Your Closing Argument

Closing arguments follow the presentation of all the evidence. That means they come after both you and your adversary have put all your witnesses on the stand and conducted direct and cross-examinations. Usually, the plaintiff gives closing argument first, then the defendant. The plaintiff can ask the judge to reserve (save) a small amount of time—for example, five minutes—for rebuttal argument, after the defendant's closing argument. This gives the plaintiff one last chance to try to refute the defendant's argument—the plaintiff gets the last word.

During jury trials, some judges instruct jurors as to their legal responsibilities in deciding a case before closing arguments, while others wait until after closing arguments. If yours is a jury trial, whether your closing argument comes before or after the jury instructions, you may use these instructions to prepare your argument, and you may refer explicitly to the language of the instructions during your closing argument. (For more on jury instructions, see Chapter 23.)

Preparing and Rehearsing Your Closing Argument

To decide what evidence to look for when you first investigate the legal claims and defenses involved in your trial, it helps to know what facts you will eventually have to prove or disprove in court. And to win your case, you must show the judge or jury how the evidence presented has actually proved or disproved those same facts. For this reason, some experts actually suggest you start writing the outline for your closing argument when you are in the very first stages of investigating your lawsuit. The good news is that you have already learned how to connect evidence to the legal elements you need to prove or disprove (some call this "marshaling evidence") in Chapters 8 and 9. And, if you look back to those chapters, you will see that the outlines you did then are really the first drafts of your closing argument.

It is also important to rehearse the closing argument you've prepared before your trial because you may not be allowed much time to prepare during trial. If your case is fairly complex, the judge may give you an hour or more, after you and your adversary have rested your cases, to get ready to deliver your closing argument. But in many cases, for example, those where less than $50,000 is at stake, your whole trial may last only a couple of hours. In these cases, especially if the court has lots of other cases on its calendar, you may be asked to go forward right after the close of evidence, and the judge may push you to finish up quickly. Even if the judge is pressed for time, you can likely get a five- to ten-minute recess to use the restroom. That is better than nothing; it may allow you to gather your thoughts and regain your composure.

Putting Together a Closing Argument

To convince the judge or jury to rule in your favor, the most important thing you can do is show how the evidence supports your case. Though you cannot be untruthful, you can and should emphasize those facts that are favorable to you and explain away those facts that hurt you. In addition, you can say why your witnesses were believable and your opponent's were not. And finally, you can review key pieces of evidence in an organized, persuasive way that is easy to follow and leads to the conclusion that your case is a winner. If you are the plaintiff, you will emphasize the evidence that establishes that you have met your legal burden of proof; if you are the defendant, it will show that, given the evidence, the plaintiff has failed to meet the requisite burden.

The main headings in the outline of your closing argument will be similar to the subheadings that follow here: introductory comments about your self-represented status, the legal and factual issues to be decided, evidence marshaling, the burden of proof, and the result you want. You will weave into the evidence-marshaling section of your argument the points you want to make about the believability of witnesses and exhibits. The core of your closing argument outline will be your list of the facts that satisfy the legal elements, with the key evidence that proves or disproves them underneath each element—the same core outline you did in Chapter 8 (if you are the plaintiff) or Chapter 9 (if you are the defendant).

TIP

Pointers for effective deliveries. "Rehearsing and Presenting Your Opening Statement," in Chapter 11, includes a variety of suggestions for effective courtroom speaking. You may want to refer to that section when preparing to deliver your closing argument.

Make Introductory Comments

Some judges and jurors may respect and even be extra sympathetic toward you if you very briefly acknowledge that in representing yourself, you have tried your best and hope you have not made too many mistakes. But you probably don't want to make too big a deal about this. It could backfire if the judge or jury doesn't find you genuine or thinks you are deliberately playing on their sympathies. As an introductory remark to a judge, you may try saying something like:

Your Honor, you have heard all the evidence. You have heard about how my roof leaked so badly last winter that water fell onto the electric stove while I was cooking. As my friend, Jane Keith, testified, it was so bad that one time when she was making breakfast, a piece of the ceiling plaster fell into our omelet.

I know I am not as familiar with court procedures as my opponent, but I have tried my best. I hope I have shown you why I had to get out of that apartment and proved to you that my landlord breached his duty to keep the apartment habitable. Now, to review the key pieces of evidence...

In fact, in some simpler cases, where the whole trial lasts only an hour or two, the introductory remark may be almost enough for your entire argument, especially if you add a sentence stating how you want the judge to rule. For example:

Based on the evidence, I ask that you find that I did not breach my rental contract as the defendant contends, and that I do not owe the defendant any money for the rent since I left or any back rent for the money I withheld during those last months when the roof was leaking.

TIP

Make closing argument to a judge shorter than to a jury. If you are arguing to a judge alone, you should prepare and deliver a much shorter closing argument than if you have a jury trial, for these reasons:

- Judges know the meaning of legal terms; you don't need to explain them.
- Judges are used to hearing testimony from witnesses, applying the law to various factual situations, and following along at trials.
- Judges can stop and ask you questions if they don't understand something; jurors cannot.

If you're addressing a jury, your introductory remarks may be something like:

Ladies and gentlemen, I have tried to present evidence to you today showing that the negligent driving of the defendant, Ms. Adams, caused the serious and painful leg injuries that I told you about. I know I made some errors during the trial. Frankly, as a nonlawyer I have felt somewhat like a fish out of water. Unfortunately, the high cost of hiring a lawyer left me no choice but to go it alone. Nonetheless...

And if your opponent's attorney was particularly stuffy or aggressive toward you, you may find it effective to add:

Probably it's clear that I don't have years of legal experience like my opponent's highly skilled lawyer, Anna Turney.

Identify the Issues to Be Resolved

You want to let the judge or jury know exactly which issues need to be determined—which questions of fact or law they must answer—in order to rule in your favor. This is especially important in longer, more complex cases. To determine which factual and legal questions remain to be determined by the judge or jury, you have to look at three things:

- the elements of the plaintiff's claims (remember, the plaintiff has to prove each element to win)
- rulings the judge made during trial, and
- stipulations you made with your opponent (if you and your adversary agreed on an issue, the judge or jury doesn't need to rule on it).

Though you will want to keep it much shorter in a judge trial, narrowing the issues can be helpful to a judge or jury, because they may not remember exactly what has been cleared up. Saying what remains to be decided can help avoid confusion and prevent wasting time and energy on questions that have already been resolved.

The example below is based on the negligence case in which you are suing Sarah Adams, a building contractor whose truck struck you as you crossed the street. In this version of the case, certain issues were resolved during trial, and you note that in your argument to the judge, as follows:

Your Honor, there are only two issues before you this afternoon: whether Ms. Adams breached her duty to drive with due care and whether she caused my injuries when her truck hit me. There is no question she owed me a duty: She stipulated that her truck struck me, so she owed a duty to me to use reasonable care. Also, there is no question about the amount of damages I suffered: The defendant stipulated that the doctor bills and employment records I introduced into evidence are accurate.

With a jury, you want to go into more detail:

Ladies and gentlemen, to prove the defendant was negligent and have you rule for me, I must establish all four of the legal elements of the negligence claim. Those are: one, that the defendant owed me, a pedestrian on a public street, the duty to drive carefully; two, that she breached that duty by driving carelessly; three, that her careless driving caused my injuries; and four, that I am out $100,000 because of money I had to pay for doctor bills, money I lost from being out of work, and money to compensate me for the pain I suffered from those injuries.

Element number one is not at issue. I was walking and she was driving on a public street, so she does not dispute that she has the duty that licensed drivers all have—to drive carefully. And element number four, damages, has been resolved as well: The defendant stipulated that the doctor bills and work records I introduced into evidence were accurate and that I, in fact, suffered a great deal of pain.

That leaves only two things for you to decide: element number two, whether or not Ms. Adams was driving carelessly, and element number three, whether she caused my injuries by hitting me with her truck.

Starting with element number two, did the defendant drive carelessly? Let's look at what the eyewitnesses who testified before you had to say about her driving. First, Cynthia White testified...

You can also use an exhibit to help show the judge or jury the issues to be decided. For example, if your case involves a dispute over a document like a contract, you may say:

We all admit the contract is valid, Your Honor. So this case really boils down to clause number two [holding up the contract and pointing to the clause]. All it says is the defendant, Louis Coombs, agrees to repair my roof. You have to decide what that means. My position is that it means Mr. Coombs was required to use the quality of wood that experts, such as Ed Barr who testified in this case, say is used by other roofers in the community. But the defendant thinks he had every right to use cheap plywood, even though the roof fell in this past winter, just because this clause doesn't specify a certain type of wood ....

Marshal the Evidence for Each Element You Must Prove

"Marshaling" evidence means connecting it up to the legal element it helps to prove or disprove. The outlines you prepared in Chapters 8 and 9 will help you do this. (You may want to skim those chapters again before reading on.) In those outlines of your legal claims (or those of your adversary), you listed facts that would be used to try to prove each element and items of evidence that would be used to prove these facts.

Using the negligence case discussed above, here's an outline of what the plaintiff must prove:

1. **Duty:** The defendant owed me the duty to drive carefully.
2. **Breach of duty:** She breached that duty by driving carelessly.
3. **Causation:** Her careless driving caused my injuries.
4. **Damages:** I am out $100,000 because of those injuries.

Element 1:

Defendant owed me a duty to drive carefully.

Fact to prove Element 1:

- Defendant is a licensed driver, driving down a public street. That creates a duty to me, as a pedestrian in the vicinity, to drive carefully.

Element 2:

Defendant breached that duty by driving carelessly.

Fact to prove Element 2:

- Defendant was looking down at her cell phone instead of at the road, and she was distracted by the call.

Evidence to prove this fact:

- Cynthia White's testimony that Defendant was holding a cell phone to her ear and looking down, instead of paying attention to the road.
- Defendant's cell phone records showing a call around the time of the accident.

Element 3:

Her careless driving caused my injuries.

Facts to prove Element 3:

- I was injured when her truck hit me.
- If she'd been paying attention, she wouldn't have hit me.

Evidence to prove these facts:

- Doctor's bills and my own testimony.
- Cynthia White's testimony.

Element 4:

I am out $100,000 because of those injuries.

Facts to prove Element 4:

- I paid $50,000 to doctors, lost $15,000 for four months of work, and suffered great pain.

Evidence to prove these facts:

- Doctor's bills.
- Employment records.
- My testimony about pain and suffering.

When preparing your closing argument outline, select the key evidence that supports your claims and the key evidence that refutes your opponent's claims and tell the judge or jury explicitly how the evidence proves or disproves those claims.

 TRIAL NOTEBOOK

Updating your trial notebook: One section in your trial notebook (see Chapter 18) should be devoted to your closing argument. Here you should keep:

- an outline of your intended closing argument

- blank paper for notes, and
- exact quotes—for example, explicit language from jury instructions.

Discuss Credibility

When weighing evidence, the judge or jury evaluates its credibility. As you know, you tried to show in direct examination that your witnesses were believable, and one of your main cross-examination goals was to attack the credibility of your adversary's witnesses. But in those earlier phases of trial, all you could do was bring out the evidence that supported or attacked the witnesses' credibility. You cannot, until closing argument, specifically tell the judge or jury why particular evidence should be discredited (because the witness was biased) or bolstered (because the witness was reliable). This type of information is an important ingredient to give the judge or jury as they move into final evaluations of evidence before making a decision.

A witness might appear less or more credible to the judge or jury because of a personal connection, or lack of one, to the parties. (See Chapter 13.) For example, the fact that an eyewitness to your car accident was a stranger to you before it occurred may make the witness believable; why lie for you if the witness didn't even know you? But if your opponent's chief eyewitness is his mother, the judge or jury may be more skeptical and conclude that she is biased in your adversary's favor.

There can be more than one reason why testimony is not credible. You will want to bring out these facts explicitly in closing argument. For example:

Your Honor, the witness, Ms. Speevack, said there were never any roaches in the defendant's apartments and that the roof had never leaked in the 20 years Mr. Shelley (the defendant) owned the property. But, Your Honor, let's remember that Ms. Speevack is Mr. Shelley's mother, and she quite understandably may see things in his favor.

What's more, she doesn't live in the building. And while she may have come around often to visit her son, she admitted on cross-examination that she did not conduct regular inspections of the apartments or talk to the tenants. As I testified, I don't ever remember her coming into my apartment ….

People also lose credibility when they make statements that are inconsistent. Once you have brought out the inconsistencies during trial, you can use them in closing argument. Here's an example:

Ladies and gentlemen, Cynthia White said this morning that she could see the defendant's truck perfectly clearly, that traffic was light and nothing was in front of her, and that she saw exactly what happened. But during a deposition that took place only three months after the accident, Ms. White said, under penalty of perjury, that there was a bus in front of her in the left-turn lane at the time of the accident. Now this accident did occur some three years ago. Clearly, memories fade, and Ms. White seems to have forgotten about a bus that she herself had said was right in front of her at the time. How faded are the other details that she now claims to remember perfectly?

Notice, in the previous example, you didn't accuse White of lying but of simply forgetting. That is often a better tactic than accusing people of lying on the witness

"… but I digress."

stand (which amounts to perjury, punishable as a crime). Judges and juries are reluctant to assume a witness is deliberately lying. By calling a witness a liar in your closing argument, you risk that the judge or jury will discount your version of what happened altogether rather than believe that an otherwise sympathetic person lied. But it isn't difficult to believe that a witness forgot or made a mistake, especially if the events the witness described happened a long time before. Forgetting is not a crime.

Every day we use our perceptions, experiences, and even prejudices to decide whether or not we find someone believable. Obviously, our prejudices are as different as we are. Nevertheless, it makes sense to try to put yourself in the position of judge or jury and try to determine which witness may seem the most credible. For example, a person who wears a business suit and speaks in an articulate way may appear more believable to certain judges or jurors than someone wearing sweatpants and a T-shirt who mumbles. Or, for instance, because some people don't believe anything used car salesmen say, if your key witness sells used cars for a living, you might try to bolster his credibility in your closing argument by saying:

Ladies and gentlemen, you may have heard people say that no one is as untrustworthy as a used car salesman. But remember, that is a stereotype, and in the case of Mr. Reback, a totally false stereotype. As you heard, Mr. Reback is working at the car dealer to put himself through school. He has finished three years and has only one to go to complete a degree in chemical engineering. He doesn't have a relationship with either myself or the plaintiff; he stands to gain

nothing from this case. He, like Cynthia White, just happened to be at the corner of Elm and Main when the accident occurred. Mr. Reback told you that he saw the plaintiff run out from between two parked cars, not in the crosswalk as Ms. White testified ….

You want to integrate points about a witness's credibility into your closing argument outline. The easiest way to do this is to put the point in right where you talk about that person's testimony. For instance, if you are the defendant, part of your outline might look like the one shown below.

Element 2:
Breach of duty to drive carefully.
Fact Plaintiff will try to prove:
I was careless.
Evidence to disprove this fact:
Testimony of Mr. Reback:
• Eyewitness.
• Testified he saw me driving carefully and not speeding.
• Saw Plaintiff run out from between parked cars; noticed Plaintiff NOT in crosswalk.
Reback is credible:
• "Used car salesman" is bad stereotype.
• Reback is in college; car sales is just part-time job, not career.
• Nothing to gain from lying…
My testimony
Under penalty of perjury I said:
• I was careful.
• Not distracted.
• I'm used to cell phone calls ….

Explain the Burden of Proof

Normally, the plaintiff has to prove each legal element of a claim by a measure lawyers call a "preponderance of the evidence." In other words, as the plaintiff, you do not have to prove the evidence beyond a reasonable doubt (as does the prosecutor in a criminal trial), but just by something more than 50%).

Judges know these terms, so you don't need to explain them during a judge trial, though you may want to mention the burden of proof. For example, you might say simply:

Your Honor, I recognize that I have the burden of proof in this case. But given all the evidence I have put forward, as to each of the legal elements of negligence, it seems I have clearly met that burden ….

To explain what this means to a jury or visualize it yourself, you may use the "scales of justice" metaphor. As the plaintiff, you can point out that if each side's evidence were piled on a scale, and the evidence tilts even a fraction of a feather weight toward you, then you have satisfied your burden. To make your explanation clear, you may want to hold your two hands in front of you as if each hand were one side of the scale and drop one hand ever so slightly lower.

Another way to explain the burden of proof to juries is to analogize it to a football field. If you are the plaintiff, you say:

Imagine I'm on a football field, ladies and gentlemen. Preponderance of the evidence does not mean I have to score a touchdown. I only have to make it past the 50-yard line.

You can never be certain whether an explanation will go over well, but be cautious about images you think are universal. Some of your jurors may not know much about sports, for example, so if you use the football analogy, you may want to use the scale analogy, too. In one recent case, an attorney was reprimanded for using an analogy to batting averages while cross-examining a witness because the judge didn't like or know much about baseball.

If you are the defendant, emphasize that the plaintiff has the burden of proof—that it's not up to you to prove what did not happen, but up to the plaintiff to prove what did. Focus on the legal elements where the plaintiff was weakest, pointing out how the plaintiff failed to prove those elements. Also, just as the plaintiff defines the legal term "preponderance of the evidence" for the jury, so too should you. But in your comments, you will stress that if the jury does not believe there is more weight on the plaintiff's side of the scale—that is, if they feel the evidence weighs equally for both sides—they must find in your favor. For example:

Ladies and gentlemen, as the judge will instruct you, the plaintiff has to prove four things: one, that I owed a legal duty to him to drive with reasonable care; two, that I breached that duty by driving carelessly; three, that my careless driving caused his injuries; and finally four, that he was damaged because of those injuries. Number one, I admitted. That is an agreement we all make when we get our very first driver's licenses. And I do not dispute that the plaintiff's doctor bills show he was treated for injuries and spent the money he claims he spent.

But ladies and gentlemen, that is only two elements out of four. The plaintiff has failed to prove number two—that I was driving carelessly—or number three—that his injuries were caused by my truck hitting him. He has not proven them at all, let alone by a preponderance of the evidence, as he must in order for you to find in his favor.

The plaintiff told you what the preponderance standard means. He said it meant that if you weighed the evidence and the scale tipped in his favor, he would win. But if you believe that he has not proven any one of the elements—and I will point out the severe weaknesses in his evidence as to my driving and as to what actually caused his injury—then you must find in my favor. Also, the scales must tip. If after hearing all the evidence you are not sure, you think that the evidence for both sides is more or less equal, then the plaintiff has failed to meet his legal burden of proof, and you must find for me.

Now let's look at the evidence more closely ....

After going through and showing why the plaintiff's evidence was weak and yours strong for each of the elements you dispute, you may conclude by saying:

At this point you may have some doubts. Part of you may think that the evidence shows I was careless, that Cynthia White is accurate when she says I was speeding. And part of you may believe that I was driving fine and that the plaintiff caused the accident by running out in the middle of the street, as I and Mr. Reback testified. You also may not be sure what really caused the plaintiff's injuries—the accident or a preexisting condition.

It's human to have some doubts. We all do. Nevertheless, the law still makes your decision clear, ladies and gentlemen. As the judge will instruct you, the plaintiff must prove all these things to you by a preponderance of the evidence. That means you must be more than 50% sure. The plaintiff told you this means he doesn't have to score a touchdown. Well, he is right. But he does have to get past the 50-yard line—and he's already gotten tackled by a few big players. I mean there are a lot of holes in his evidence. The most important one is that he did not prove that I was careless. As the plaintiff, he bears the burden of proving each element of his case to you. And if you are not more than 50% sure that he's proven all four, you must find that I am not responsible for his $50,000 in doctor bills or the other damages he has claimed.

Use Exhibits and Other Visual Aids

Visualizing the facts you or your adversary have put into evidence can help make your version of the story clearer for the judge or jury. For example, assume that you're the plaintiff in the negligence case mentioned earlier. During your direct examination of Cynthia White, you had her make a diagram of the accident scene at Elm and Main, where Ms. Adams's truck hit you. She marked the places where you, the truck, the parked cars, and the children playing on the street were located. You introduced the marked diagram into evidence. (See Chapter 15 for information on introducing exhibits.) It may be very helpful and effective for you to hold White's drawing up for the judge or jury when you are reviewing her testimony. For example, you may say:

Ladies and gentlemen, you may recall that when Cynthia White testified, she marked on this map [holding it up] *where all the key players in the accident were located.* [Pointing as you talk] *Here I was, here's where the defendant was, and here—this is where children were playing. You can see how easily the defendant might have been distracted by watching these children instead of the road ….*

Visual aids can help your argument, but there are some potential negatives in using them. You may feel clumsy carrying a bulky chart into court (you are already carrying a trial notebook); you may not be a great artist and might be concerned that your chart looks sloppy; you may not know where to set up your prop so that it can be clearly seen; and so on.

Judges may exclude visual aids they find misleading if they were not admitted into evidence during trial. For example, a map of Elm and Main Streets that your witness marked during trial is fine and likely helpful. But a judge may exclude a diagram that you did not introduce into evidence during the trial but drew up the night before your closing argument, especially if the judge feels your drawing misrepresents the evidence. Or the judge may view your diagram as an attempt on your part to introduce new evidence, which you cannot do in your closing argument. You can argue only from what is already in the record. (See "What Not to Say During Your Closing Argument," below.)

To decide whether to use a visual aid, think about what aspects of your case it will help explain and whether you can adequately explain them in words instead. For instance, to explain the legal concept of "preponderance of the evidence," you may do better orally explaining the analogy rather than drawing a football field with the yard lines clearly marked. The cons (bulky, judge may not allow it) may outweigh the pros (clear image of how much evidence it takes to meet the burden). But if your visual aid relates to specific factual evidence in your case and will help the judge or jury clarify a key point, it may help make your argument more concrete and believable.

Tell the Judge or Jury What You Want

One good way to finish your closing argument is by asking for an explicit result in the case. Even though some people feel awkward asking for money, it is important to let the judge or jury know exactly what you want them to decide. Otherwise, they might not know what to do. Here's an example:

Your Honor, you have heard all the evidence showing how flimsy the wood was that the defendant used to repair my roof. My family and I were terrified the night the roof caved in. It cost $10,000 to repair the structural damage to my home that was caused by the collapse. And I spent $20,000 more than I bargained for in the original contract just to get a solid roof over our heads—not to mention the countless hours it took to clean up the mess. Your Honor, please find that the defendant breached the contract by using the cheap plywood and order that he pay me the $30,000 I lost.

What Not to Say During Your Closing Argument

Now that you know what to include in your closing argument, here are some things to avoid.

Don't State Your Opinion

The basic principle is that you must argue from the evidence and show why it is or is not convincing. You must not interject what you believe unless you have presented some proof of the facts behind that belief to the judge or jury. For example, do *not* say:

Ms. Adams claims that the call she got on her cell phone before she hit me was not important. But look at her—she is shifty-eyed, and I just know she's a liar.

You should use facts that came out in trial that bolster a witness's credibility, but it is not appropriate to add your opinion about that witness's honesty or other good qualities. It doesn't matter to the judge that you like and trust your witnesses. Do *not* say something like:

I trust Ira; I've know him for years. If he says he saw me cross the street in the crosswalk, then that's exactly what happened.

And don't put your own credibility on the line except as to particular facts you testified about during the trial. To illustrate, you can say:

As I testified, I have been a building contractor in this community for 25 years. I value my reputation, and if I thought I was responsible for the plaintiff's roof falling in, I would have repaired it immediately. But that is not what caused the damage to his roof. As you heard from the inspector, the plaintiff let the large oak tree grow too close to the power lines, and during the storm…

But avoid saying something like:

I'm an honest man; I wouldn't have brought this to trial if I didn't think I had a good case.

Don't Argue From Evidence Unless It Was Presented at Trial

A key rule in making your closing argument is do not talk about evidence, even if it will help you win, unless it is in the trial record—meaning it was either testified to orally demonstrated by a document that was admitted into evidence. This is not the time to sneak in something that you forgot to cover during the trial.

 TIP

Take good notes during trial. It can be difficult to remember exactly what was said during your trial. So pay close attention and try these techniques.

- Keep your trial notebook open and check off issues on your outline that your adversary stipulates to (admits).
- Note bits of testimony that strike you as particularly helpful or damaging to your case. You can use them to support your case or try to explain them away, as necessary, during closing argument.
- Have a friend or relative come with you and take notes too, in case you miss

something. Although you could order a transcript of the trial record from the court reporter, it will be quite expensive and probably can't be done quickly enough for you to use in your closing argument.

While you must not misstate facts or argue what is not in the record, you can rely on logical inferences to show the judge or jury how particular evidence relates to the elements you must prove to support your legal claims. For example, assume you are the plaintiff in the car accident case and evidence was introduced that Ms. Adams got a call moments before she hit you. You can properly argue:

Ms. Adams got a call on her cell phone moments before she hit me. She was talking to someone in her office about the fact that her company messed up. They missed an important inspection. She said the job was an important one, potentially worth a lot of money. I ask you, is it possible that Ms. Adams's attention was not on the road when she hit me, but on the call she got? People who have just received important news, especially news that is likely to cost them a lot of money, are often distracted, even upset by such news. When someone is distracted, she has a harder time concentrating on traffic ....

Notice that while no evidence was presented that Adams was distracted, you are able to ask the judge or jury to draw the inference, based on their common knowledge, that people who receive important phone calls are involved in their conversations and less attentive to the road. Making such inferences is perfectly acceptable during closing argument, and it is important to make them

so you can help the judge or jury interpret the evidence in a way that is favorable to you.

Rebuttal Argument

If you are the plaintiff, and you decide to reserve a portion of your closing argument for rebuttal argument, your rebuttal should briefly state why particular things the defendant said in closing argument were wrong or misleading; you should not rehash things you already said or make brand-new points. If you do, your opponent may object, and the judge may rule that your comments are outside the scope of rebuttal.

Objections During Closing

Either you or your adversary can object during the other's closing argument. If you do not follow the rules—for example, you argue facts that are not part of the record—your adversary may well object. Also, a more experienced opponent may try to use technical objections to throw you off balance. Even though it might look bad for a lawyer to bully a self-represented party, some do. If you get an objection to some point in your closing argument, think through what is being said, remain calm, and stick up for yourself if you think the objection is wrong. (See Chapter 17 for more on objections.) Or try rephrasing your statement. Here are two examples of how to handle an objection:

EXAMPLE 1:

Plaintiff:

Therefore, Your Honor, since Ms. Adams admitted she got an important call on the cell phone moments before she hit me...

Defendant:

Objection, Your Honor. There is no evidence in the record that the call was important.

Plaintiff:

Your Honor, may I rephrase my statement?

Judge:

You may.

Plaintiff:

Since Ms. Adams admitted that moments before she hit me, she got a call on the cell phone reporting a missed inspection...

EXAMPLE 2:

Plaintiff:

Therefore, Your Honor, since Ms. Adams admitted she got an important call on the cell phone moments before she hit me...

Defendant:

Objection, Your Honor. There is no evidence in the record that the call was important.

Judge:

Plaintiff?

Plaintiff:

There certainly is, Your Honor. The defendant made that statement in this courtroom last Tuesday when I was cross-examining her.

Judge:

Overruled. You may proceed.

Should you object to your opponent's argument? Object only if you really feel strongly that your adversary is misstating evidence or arguing about evidence that

was not presented at trial and that the argument is prejudicing your case. It can be self-defeating to object at this stage because judges often allow people a lot of leeway when making closing arguments.

Sample Closing Argument and Outline

Now that you've gotten a sense of the various key parts of closing argument, let's take one all the way through. Below is a sample argument in a jury trial of the traffic accident case in which you have sued Sarah Adams for negligence. You were hit by Adams's truck as you crossed the street. Following that is a short analysis and sample outline of the argument. You will likely want to write out your intended argument in full (to the extent you can) before trial so that you can practice it and perhaps show it to your legal coach. Then, you can summarize it in outline form to use during your actual argument.

1 *Good afternoon. The evidence has come to a close and the task of deciding whose story you believe is in your hands, ladies and gentlemen. I have presented my evidence as well as I could—despite the fact that I am clearly not at home in the courtroom like the talented attorney representing my opponent.*

2 *You have heard lots of facts today, and you are very familiar now with what happened to me. As the judge instructed you, there are four legal elements I must show to prove that Ms. Adams was negligent. First, that she owed a duty to* *me as a pedestrian on a public street to drive attentively and follow the rules of the road. Second, that she breached her duty by driving carelessly. Third, that my injuries were caused by her truck hitting me. And last, that I lost $15,000 because of work I had to miss; I paid $50,000 in doctor bills; and it is fair to award me $35,000 to compensate me for the terrible pain I suffered as a result of her carelessness.*

3 *Let's take a look back to some of the key testimony that proves each of those four elements. First off, the judge instructed you that Ms. Adams had a duty to me to drive with due and reasonable care. She admits this, so the first element is proven.*

4 *Second, I must show that the defendant breached her duty of care to me by driving carelessly. This has also been proven. The evidence shows that the defendant was not driving safely. She let her mind and eyes wander, ladies and gentlemen, because she was distracted. What distracted her? A business call on her cell phone, which the telephone bills you saw show happened just moments before she slammed into me. A business call that, as she herself told you, reported a missed inspection on a big job. Now, the defendant told you this did not distract her at all, that inspections are missed all the time. But she may be forgetting exactly how much money was at stake in this job. Her own business records show it was a $10 million deal. She told you that the missed inspection could have caused delays both on this job and other ones. Ms. Adams is an entrepreneur who owns*

her own business. She is the one who is financially responsible if jobs are missed. And how many delays can occur before her reputation and business suffer? Isn't it likely that this phone call upset her and caused her to drive carelessly?

5 *You also heard from Cynthia White. She told you she was waiting for a bus at the Elm Street stop. She saw the whole thing. Ms. White is a schoolteacher. She didn't know me or the defendant. She has no reason to be anything but truthful with you. And she had a perfect view of the whole scene from the bus stop. Yes, she told the defendant at her deposition that a bus was in front of her in the left-turn lane, but she also told you she could see the crosswalk fine since it was off to the side of where she was. She told you that I was in the crosswalk when the defendant hit me and that she watched the defendant sit in her truck and wait for the police. After hitting me, she didn't even check to see if I was okay. Ms. White's testimony proves that I was in the crosswalk and that the defendant was negligent for not stopping for me.*

6 *I have also proven the third and fourth elements. The defendant's truck hitting me caused my injuries, and I have suffered a great deal—in physical pain, money paid for doctor bills, and lost wages. As I testified, when I saw her truck coming at me, I tried to get out of the way. But she hit me. I felt my leg snap as I fell to the ground. Dr. Duncan testified that he treated me that day for a broken leg. It took four months to heal, though as Dr. Duncan testified, my limp may* *never go away. During those months, I was in constant and excruciating pain. I had difficulty sleeping and, as I testified, I couldn't do even the most basic of household chores, like taking out the trash. I spent most of my time in bed and seeing doctors. I showed you the doctor bills.*

7 *Now, the judge has given you some important instructions on how you should weigh the evidence you've heard. She said I must prove my case to you by a preponderance of the evidence. Let me tell you what that means. It does not mean that I must prove my case beyond a reasonable doubt. That is only in criminal trials, like what you may have seen in the movies. A preponderance of the evidence means that if you imagine weighing the evidence on a scale, and my side weighs only a tiny bit more than the defendant's, then I have met my burden. That is all it takes. You don't have to be absolutely certain.*

8 *It is up to you, now. Deliberate fairly and honestly. Make the right decision, and hold the defendant responsible for the accident she caused. Please have her pay me back for the $50,000 I had to pay in doctor bills, the $15,000 I lost being out of work, and the $35,000 I have requested to compensate me for the painful injuries she caused me to suffer. Thank you.*

Transcript Analysis: This closing argument begins with some simple introductory comments, then moves right into the legal elements (No. 2). Noting that the jury is familiar with the evidence, you appropriately suggest that this closing argument will not simply rehash the evidence. Next, you are up front that you have to prove all four legal elements, and you begin immediately to show how you have done so. You first set out the elements (No. 2), then go back and connect the evidence to each one (Nos. 3, 4, 5, and 6).

If this argument had been to a judge alone, you would have done well to skip No. 2 and go right into the next sections. (You would also skip No. 7, of course.) Before a judge, make your arguments short, cut out as much as possible your explanations of the law, and hit only the key facts that prove each element.

Beginning in No. 3, you go element by element, emphasizing the key evidence that proves each.

In No. 4, you say that the defendant "let her mind and eyes wander." Evidence was presented that her eyes wandered (White saw her on the cell phone, looking down), but you really don't know where her mind was; only the defendant knows that. But it is proper to ask the jury to make an inference that because she was engaged in an important phone call, she was thinking about business rather than the road. The jurors, after all, are free to disagree.

Next comes some rebuttal of the defendant's testimony. Without saying she is a liar, you suggest that she may simply not remember the amount of money involved and how upset or distracted she really was.

Then, you summarize White's key testimony, along with some facts that bolster her credibility, such as her being a teacher and not knowing either party before the accident. You explain away the apparent contradiction in statements about her view being unobstructed, and you add that the defendant did not even come to see how you were, perhaps to make her look cold or insensitive.

Next (No. 6), you hit the elements of causation (your leg snapped when the truck hit you) and damages (the doctor bills and pain and suffering). And last, you discuss the burden of proof, stressing that the jury doesn't need to be absolutely certain, and ask for a specific result.

Here is one possible way you would make an outline for the sample closing argument above. As you read it, note how much of it could have been done before trial. There will, of course, be evidence that you first learn about during trial, points your adversary emphasized that you want to try to contradict or explain away, and other odds and ends you need to fill in during or just after the evidence has been presented. For that reason, it's a good idea to leave some room in your outline to add such items in.

I. Introduction

- Evidence finished; decision in your hands
- I tried but I'm not at home in the court-room
- You know what happened

II. Legal Elements

I must prove all 4

(Introduce 1st, then repeat w/evidence)

1. Defendant has duty to follow rules of road, drive carefully
2. She breached duty by driving carelessly
3. My injuries were caused by her truck hitting me

---

4. I was damaged (money on doctors, lost wages, pain and suffering) as a result of her carelessness

(Evidence clearly proves each element)

1. Duty:

- Public street and defendant has driver's license = she has a duty to be careful

2. Defendant was not driving safely; breached duty of care:

- Her mind and eyes wandered
- She was distracted by call on her cell phone
- Call moments before hit (telephone bills)
- Big job/missed inspection (Defendant admitted)
- Said missed inspections are common—not believable. This was big job, lots of money at stake
- Owns the business; she's responsible, might hurt her reputation and business

Cynthia White testimony

- White is credible—teacher, didn't know us
- White waiting for bus; saw whole thing
- Perfect view of scene—Yes, she said in depo that her view was blocked, but she meant her view of the street. Bus was in front, accident to side. So her view of the accident was clear
- She saw me in crosswalk when Defendant hit me
- She watched Defendant sit in cab of truck, wait for police, didn't even check if I was okay
- When I saw her truck, I tried to get out of way, but couldn't
- Leg broke on impact; I felt it

4. Damages:

- Pain, suffering, 4 months to heal

- You saw doctor bills at trial

- Lost work wages

III. Jury Instructions/Burden of Proof

Judge said I must prove case by "preponder-ance of the evidence"

- That does not mean beyond a reasonable doubt like criminal cases, just anything more than 50%

- Scales—if even a tiny bit more on my side, I meet burden

- "You don't have to be absolutely certain."

IV. Results

- Up to you, now

- "Hold Defendant responsible for the accident she caused"

- Make her pay $ 50,000 (doctor bills and costs), $ 35,000 (pain and suffering), $ 15,000 (lost work)

V. Thank you

RESOURCE

Resources on closing arguments.
Trial Advocacy in a Nutshell, by Paul Bergman (West Publishing Co.), is an easy-to-read, helpful, and inexpensive paperback about effective and persuasive trial techniques. Chapter 10 covers closing arguments.

The Trial Process: Law Tactics and Ethics, by J. Alexander Tanford (Lexis/Matthew Bender), is a textbook on trial practice that includes excerpts from many other leading books and dialogues of trial scenarios.

Art of Advocacy, by Lawrence J. Smith (Matthew Bender), includes an extensive, separate volume filled with examples of actual closing arguments, titled *Summation*. ●

Exhibits

Exhibits are the tangible objects that you present to a judge or jury during trial to help establish your case. Typical exhibits include documents such as letters, contracts, and receipts. Reports, such as those a child psychologist or a radiologist may prepare when testifying as an expert witness, are also exhibits. So too are photographs, X-rays, and all other physical objects. For example, if you sue someone for injuries you received as a result of being struck by a badly thrown boomerang, the boomerang can be an exhibit.

Under most circumstances, you are under no legal obligation to offer exhibits into evidence. You can present your entire case through oral testimony from you and your witnesses. But exhibits can dramatically add to the persuasiveness of your case in at least three ways:

- Just like the "show" part of "show and tell" in the first grade, tangible objects make your story more real and interesting.
- A little like shy first graders, you and your witnesses may testify more confidently—and therefore more credibly—when holding and talking about tangible objects.
- Exhibits have a longer shelf life than oral testimony. When it comes time to deliberate and arrive at a verdict, a judge or jury may forget oral testimony. But usually they have the opportunity to hold and examine an exhibit.

For an exhibit to officially become evidence that the judge or jury can consider when deciding your case, you must present it to the judge and demonstrate that it is authentic and trustworthy. You do this by "offering" (and providing), either through your own testimony or that of your witnesses, what lawyers refer to as "foundational testimony." If the judge decides that your foundational testimony meets evidence rule requirements, the judge will formally admit the exhibit into evidence. This chapter describes and illustrates the process for handling exhibits during trial and shows you how to elicit the necessary foundational testimony for many common types of exhibits.

Overview of Admitting Exhibits Into Evidence

The type of foundational evidence you need to offer in order to admit an exhibit into evidence varies greatly from one exhibit to another. Fortunately, the procedural steps are almost always the same. Here is an overview of those steps; you will read about each in more detail in the sections that follow.

Step 1: Mark your exhibit for identification and allow opposing counsel (or your adversary, if neither of you is represented by counsel) to examine it.

Step 2: Identify (authenticate) your exhibit by asking the judge for permission to approach the witness, handing the exhibit to the witness, and asking the witness to state what the exhibit is. (In some courts your judge may ask you to hand the exhibit to the bailiff, who will then pass it along to the witness.)

Step 3: Personally testify to or elicit from a witness any legally required foundational evidence.

Step 4:   Ask the judge to admit the exhibit into evidence.

TIP

You can offer exhibits into evidence during cross-examination. Though you will probably offer exhibits into evidence through your own testimony or that of your witnesses during direct examination, you can also offer an exhibit during cross-examination of an adverse witness. Apart from perhaps receiving more grudging responses to your questions, the process is identical.

As an alternative to this four-step process for admitting exhibits into evidence, ask your adversary before trial to stipulate (agree) to the admissibility of your exhibits. Stipulations to the admissibility of exhibits are common. Especially when the admissibility of exhibits is clear, attorneys (and self-represented parties) often stipulate to the admissibility of each other's exhibits.

If you and your adversary do reach a stipulation, put it in writing and sign it to prevent your adversary from suddenly denying the stipulation at trial, leaving you with no way to produce foundational evidence.

TIP

It doesn't matter which side admits an exhibit into evidence. If you are a defendant, you may find that by the time it is your turn to present evidence, the plaintiff has already offered an exhibit into evidence that you planned to offer. For example, if you are the tenant in a landlord-tenant case, the landlord may offer the lease and some canceled checks into evidence, two exhibits that you planned to offer. This won't affect your planned testimony.

Whether you or an adversary offers an exhibit into evidence, you may testify about the exhibit yourself, hand it to your witnesses and ask them questions about it, and make the same arguments about it that you would have made had you offered the exhibit into evidence. Perhaps you can even thank your adversary for offering the exhibit into evidence: It saves you the trouble of offering foundational testimony.

Then, either in a brief pretrial conference or when you are about to refer to the exhibit, inform the judge that you've reached a stipulation as to its admissibility. In the example above, you would say something like, "Your Honor, the defendant and I stipulate that the lease agreement of March 12, signed by me and Ms. Mason and consisting of three pages, may be admitted into evidence." The judge will almost certainly grant your request because it saves court time.

Step 1: Mark Your Exhibits and Show Them to Your Adversary

Marking an exhibit for identification consists of tagging an exhibit with a number or letter to distinguish it from others. You do not have to be testifying under oath when you mark an exhibit, so you can mark an exhibit either while you are presenting evidence yourself or while you are questioning a witness.

Traditionally, plaintiffs' exhibits are numbered and defendants' exhibits are lettered. But like the former practice of attaching only feminine names to hurricanes, this traditional system has been dropped by many courts. Read your local court rules or check with the court clerk in advance to find out what marking procedure your judge likes to follow.

In some courts, the court clerk does the actual marking of exhibits. Or the clerk may ask you to mark all your exhibits before trial starts. But usually, you'll mark an exhibit for identification and let your adversary examine it the very first time you or a witness refer to it. For instance, assume that you are the plaintiff in a breach of contract case. You have testified to the oral discussions leading up to the contract and you now want to offer the contract itself into evidence. Before you do, you must get it marked for identification like this:

"Your Honor, I have here a two-page document. It is headed 'Agreement' and dated December 8 of last year. I am showing it to defense counsel. May it be marked Plaintiff's Exhibit No. 1 for identification?"

When the judge gives you permission to mark the exhibit, you may write "Exh. 1" on the agreement itself with a pen. If an exhibit cannot be easily marked with a pen (for example, your exhibit is a boomerang or a hat), most court clerks provide small, gummed labels that you can attach to an exhibit and then mark. When you mark an exhibit, say no more than is necessary to identify it. For example, the statement above about the contract refers to objective characteristics of the exhibit: how many pages it consists of and its title and date. Do not try to gild the lily by turning the marking process into an argument. Never say anything like, "Your Honor, I want to mark this contract that proves that the defendant owes me $25,000."

Once an exhibit has been marked for identification, keep the record clear by mentioning its assigned number or letter whenever you talk about it in court. For example, when testifying on direct examination, you might say, "The first time I saw the lease, Exhibit 1, was when…"

TIP

Keep calm as you move about the courtroom during the marking process. Going through the marking process while you are testifying personally can be something of a logistical challenge. You may have to move back and forth between the witness box, the clerk's desk, your adversary at the counsel table, and your file folder containing the exhibit. Do not panic; with the judge's guidance you will probably glide about the courtroom with the grace of Fred Astaire or Ginger Rogers.

TIP

Make extra copies of written exhibits. When you mark an exhibit before showing it to a witness, hand extra copies that you have made before trial to opposing counsel and the judge. This speeds up the foundational process because a single piece of paper does not have to pass through four different pairs of hands. More importantly, you may impress the judge with the care you have put into your case, and the judge may give you the benefit of the doubt if a ruling on the admissibility of an exhibit could legitimately go either way.

Step 2: Identify (Authenticate) Your Exhibits

The next step is for you or a witness to identify (authenticate) an exhibit. Do this by offering brief testimony that tells the judge what the exhibit is and shows its connection to the case.

By way of illustration, assume again that you are the plaintiff in a breach of contract case and that you have just finished marking the contract for identification as "Exhibit 1." You are now testifying. Hold the exhibit and identify it as follows: "Exhibit 1 is the contract that the defendant and I signed on December 8 of last year." This testimony identifies the exhibit as the actual document that you and the defendant signed.

You can often add impact to authentication testimony by referring to the basis of your identification. With the contract, for example, you (or your witness, of course) could testify that, "I know that Exhibit 1 is the contract I signed because when I signed it, I noticed that the upper right-hand corner of the top page was torn, as you can see here."

You Don't Always Need the Real Thing

If you don't know the whereabouts of the actual physical object involved in your case, consider substituting a look-alike. When (as is often true) the precise appearance of the actual object is not significant, you can use a substitute that is similar in appearance if you make sure that everyone understands it is a substitute. (If, however, the exhibit is a document, you may be required to produce the original or explain why you can't. See "When Exhibits Are Required: The Best Evidence Rule," below.)

For example, assume that you are suing a defendant for carelessly throwing a boomerang in a shopping mall and striking you with it. You do not have the actual boomerang that struck you, but want to use an exhibit to add impact to your testimony. You know what the boomerang looked like and have gotten another one that is in all important respects identical to the one that struck you. To offer the substitute into evidence, simply identify it as "a boomerang that looks just like the one that hit me."

Step 3: Lay a Foundation

Once an exhibit is marked and identified, the judge can consider whether to admit it into evidence. Often, however, simply identifying an exhibit is not sufficient to admit it into evidence. In addition, you have to elicit testimony called "foundational evidence" that demonstrates that an exhibit meets evidence rules requirements. Not surprisingly, the process of eliciting this evidence is called "laying a foundation."

To complicate this task, foundational requirements are different for different types of exhibits. For example, the foundation needed to admit a business receipt is very different from the foundation needed to admit a photograph. And the foundation needed to admit a hospital record is different from either of them.

We do not have space in this book to describe the necessary foundation for every possible type of exhibit you may want to offer into evidence. We do, however, illustrate how to lay a foundation for many common types of exhibits. If we do not cover the type of exhibit you want to offer, consult one of the books listed at the end of this section for help.

> ⓘ **CAUTION**
>
> **Consider other rules of evidence before deciding that an exhibit is admissible.** Even if you lay a perfect foundation for an exhibit, other rules of evidence may bar the exhibit from being admitted into evidence. For example, you may provide foundational testimony for a letter, yet see the letter excluded because its contents are either irrelevant or inadmissible hearsay. Carefully study both this chapter and Chapter 16 before deciding that an exhibit is admissible.

When Identification Is Enough for Admissibility

Sometimes the testimony that identifies an exhibit also provides all the foundational evidence you need for the judge to admit it into evidence. Generally, identification evidence alone is a sufficient foundation when an exhibit is a physical object rather than a document, and you or a witness can identify it on the basis of your personal knowledge.

For example, assume again that you are testifying about how you came to be struck by the carelessly thrown boomerang. After you were hit, you picked up the boomerang and ran after the defendant. He got away, but his hat with his name in it fell off, and you picked it up. To illustrate and add impact to your oral testimony, you want to offer the boomerang and the hat into evidence. One at a time, you go through the process of marking both the boomerang and the hat for identification and showing each to opposing counsel. Next, you identify each of them with this testimony: "Exhibit 2 is the boomerang that hit me on the back of my head. Exhibit 3 is the hat that fell off the defendant's head when I chased him. I know these are the actual objects because after I was hit I picked up the boomerang and the hat and took them home with me."

In this situation, you have personal knowledge of both exhibits, and your identification evidence is the only foundation necessary for the judge to admit the boomerang and the hat into evidence. After giving the identification testimony above, you would ask the judge to admit both exhibits into evidence in this manner:

1 **You:**

Your Honor, now I'd like to offer the boomerang, Exhibit 2, and the hat, Exhibit 3, into evidence.

2 Judge (to opposing counsel):
Any objection?

3 Opposing Counsel:
None, Your Honor.

4 Judge:
Very well. Exhibits 2 and 3 are admitted into evidence.

Once the judge admits the exhibits into evidence, both you and your adversary can testify or ask questions concerning either of them.

> ⚠️ CAUTION
>
> **Exhibits stay in court.** When an exhibit is admitted into evidence, it becomes court property until it is released, usually after the verdict. Do not walk out of the court with "your" boomerang and hat at the end of the day, thinking you'll bring them back in the morning. Otherwise you, the boomerang, and the hat may end up spending the night together in the courthouse, courtesy of the bailiff.

When an Exhibit May Have Been Tampered With

With most exhibits, such as a contract, a business record, a photograph, or a boomerang, a witness with personal knowledge of the exhibit could likely readily detect any alterations in it. In such situations, you do not have to account for an exhibit's whereabouts prior to trial. But with other kinds of exhibits, if your adversary objects, the judge may refuse to admit an exhibit into evidence until you show that you have kept it secure so that it has not been tampered with. Such a situation may arise if you offer a liquid, a food, a drug, or a similar perishable item into evidence.

For example, assume that you claim that your adversary was driving under the influence of alcohol. You want to admit into evidence the open bottle of liquid you found on the front seat of his car along with the testimony of a laboratory technician who tested the liquid and determined that it was vodka. In this situation, before you can get the bottle of vodka admitted into evidence, you need to satisfy the judge that the liquid you had tested and are now offering into evidence is the same liquid you found in the car; lawyers call this "establishing a chain of custody."

To establish a chain of custody, both you and the laboratory technician must provide foundational testimony. You will need to testify to keeping the bottle and its contents in a secure place before and after it was tested, and then identify the bottle and its contents as the object that you delivered to the technician. The technician will have to identify the same bottle and contents as the one that the lab received from you, tested, and then either returned to you or brought to court. The judge will not admit the exhibit into evidence until both of you have testified.

As you can see, establishing a chain of custody can be complex. If you seek to admit an important exhibit for which a chain of custody is necessary, refer to one of the evidence treatises listed at the end of this section or consult with your legal coach if you are uncertain about how to do it.

Offering Foundations for Common Exhibits

This section examines the foundational requirements for the kinds of exhibits you are most likely to encounter.

Photographs

As suggested by the old expression that "a picture is worth a thousand words," photographs often make stories more convincing. But because a photograph is one step removed from whatever physical objects it depicts, you must lay a foundation beyond marking and identifying a photograph before you can offer it into evidence. When, as is usually the case, a photograph depicts an object that you or one of your witnesses can identify from personal knowledge, such as the interior of an apartment or a damaged car, the foundation for the photograph is quite simple. You offer testimony that the photograph is a "fair and accurate representation" of whatever it depicts.

For example, assume that you want to introduce into evidence a photograph of your living room, showing a portion of the ceiling that collapsed due to water damage. The witness who is testifying is a friend who has just concluded describing what the damaged portion of the ceiling looked like. You now offer foundational testimony for the photograph:

1 You:

Your Honor, I'm holding a photograph that has been marked Plaintiff's Exhibit 3 for identification and have shown it to defense counsel. May I approach the witness to show her the photograph?

2 Judge:

You may.

3 You:

Ms. Tobias, please look at the photograph, Exhibit 3, and tell me if you recognize what it shows.

4 Witness:

Yes, this looks like a picture of your living room ceiling, showing the part that collapsed.

5 You:

Does the photograph fairly and accurately depict the way the room looks since the ceiling collapsed?

6 Witness:

Yes, it does.

7 You:

Your Honor, I ask that the photograph be received in evidence.

8 Judge:

Any objection? Hearing none, it is received.

Here, the key foundational testimony comes in Nos. 5 and 6. By testifying from personal knowledge that the photograph fairly and accurately depicts what she saw, the witness links the photograph to the damaged ceiling. Technical details such as the kind of camera, lens, and film used to take the photograph are unnecessary. Note that a witness does not have to be absolutely certain of what a photograph depicts for the photo to be admissible as evidence. A qualified response like, "I'm pretty sure that's your ceiling" or "I'd say that's your ceiling" normally demonstrates sufficient personal knowledge for admissibility (see No. 4, above). On the other hand, if a witness says something like, "I'm guessing that's a picture of your ceiling," the judge will probably rule that the witness has not shown sufficient personal knowledge to admit the photo into evidence. If you are going to show a photo (or other exhibit) to a witness during trial, first show it to the witness during a pretrial rehearsal to make sure that the witness recognizes what it depicts.

> **CAUTION**
>
> **More foundation is needed if a camera reveals what no witness saw.** In very unusual circumstances, you may want to offer into evidence a photograph that depicts something that no witness actually saw. In one famous case, a photograph showed a stabbing taking place in the background; neither the photographer nor any other available witness had personally observed the stabbing. The photograph was admitted into evidence, but only after extensive foundational evidence about the camera, film type, and other details. In the unlikely event that you want to offer a photo that depicts something that neither you nor one of your witnesses can identify from personal knowledge, consult an experienced trial lawyer.

> **TIP**
>
> **Photographs don't have to be taken right away.** So long as you or a witness can testify that a photograph fairly and accurately depicts a scene as it existed when relevant events took place, it does not matter how long after those events a photograph is taken. So if you suddenly realize days, weeks, or even months after events took place that photographs will greatly help a

judge or jury understand your version of events, don't worry. As long as the physical condition of whatever you want to photograph has remained largely unchanged, you can take a photograph of it and offer the photograph into evidence.

For instance, you might want to show a photograph to demonstrate that an accident occurred because the view of an intersection is obscured by a large leafy tree, or that in a car crash your vehicle was hit in the right rear, or that part of your living room ceiling collapsed after heavy rains. So long as you or your witness can testify that the photos fairly and accurately depict conditions as they existed when the events occurred, you can successfully offer into evidence a photo taken long after the incident in question took place.

Diagrams

A diagram is an excellent way to illustrate some types of testimony. You and your witnesses may testify with far more clarity and confidence when you can point at and make markings on a visual representation of an event. You can efficiently use a diagram to help you or a witness explain such things as the path of a car before a collision, the floor plan of an apartment, or where on your child's body you saw bruises when he came home after a weekend visit with your ex-spouse. Be creative. A diagram is your chance to develop an exhibit on your own; you are not limited to tangible objects that existed when events giving rise to your dispute took place.

While you or a witness can draw a diagram directly on a courtroom blackboard (if there is one), a diagram becomes an exhibit that you can offer into evidence only if you or a witness draw it on a sheet of paper. To do this, obtain a large sheet of paper and vividly colored marking pens so the diagram you create will be clear to the judge or jury. You can prepare an entire diagram before trial and later testify to what it depicts. Or you can prepare a skeleton diagram before trial and complete it while you or a witness testify. Either way, a diagram does not have to be drawn to exact scale; it is enough for admissibility that a diagram fairly approximates whatever it depicts.

For example, assume that you are the plaintiff in a negligence case. You call Cynthia White to testify that a car driven by Defendant Sarah Adams made a left turn in an intersection and struck you in a crosswalk. During your pretrial rehearsal, you and White can prepare a skeleton diagram of the intersection that may look like the one shown below.

As White testifies, have her refer to the diagram. Begin by laying a foundation showing that the diagram fairly approximates the intersection where the accident took place. Based on this diagram, the testimony might look like this:

1 You:

Your Honor, the bailiff has pinned a diagram to the easel. May it be marked Plaintiff's Exhibit 1 for identification?

2 Judge:

It will be so marked.

3 You:

Ms. White, looking at Exhibit 1, do you recognize what it depicts?

4 Witness:

Yes, it is the intersection of Elm and Main Streets.

5 You:

How do you know that?

6 Witness:

Well, I know that intersection, and I drew this diagram of it when I met with you last night.

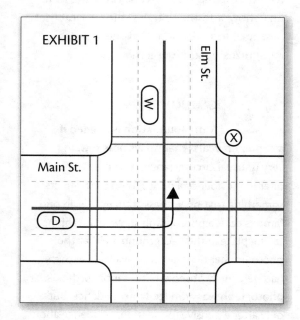

7 You:

Would you say it is a fair approximation of that intersection?

8 Witness:

Yes. Of course, it's not exactly to scale.

9 You:

Can you explain the markings on the diagram?

10 Witness:

It shows that Elm is a north-south street; Main runs east-west. Each street has two lanes of traffic in each direction. There's a left-turn lane for traffic going east on Main to turn north on Elm. There are crosswalks between all the corners.

11 You:

The crosswalks are the parallel lines at all corners?

12 Witness:

Yes.

13 You:

I see you put an "X" on the northeast corner of the intersection. What does the "X" stand for?

14 Witness:

That's where you were standing when I first saw you.

15 You:

And what about these two boxes, one marked with a "W" and one with a "D?"

16 Witness:

The one with a "W" is my car; that's where I was waiting for the light to turn green so that I could go south on Elm. The one with a "D" is the defendant's truck, at the place where I first saw it, going into the left-turn lane.

Transcript Analysis. This testimony lays the foundation to admit the diagram into evidence. Though it is not an exact depiction of the intersection, the diagram "fairly approximates" the scene of the accident (Nos. 7–8). Note that while No. 7 is a leading question asked on direct examination, judges generally allow leading questions to elicit foundational evidence. (Chapter 12 discusses different forms of questions and when each may be used.) The rest of the foundation simply explains the markings, giving you a chance to make White's testimony more vivid and real.

As a witness testifies, it is proper to ask the witness to make additional markings on the diagram. For example, assume that White testifies that the next time she saw you, you were in the crosswalk. To illustrate that testimony in a vivid way, ask her to walk over to the diagram and indicate your position:

23 You:

Where was I the next time you saw me?

24 Witness:

You were in the crosswalk.

25 You:

About how far from the curb?

26 Witness:

I'm not great at distances. I'd say about ten feet.

27 You:

Could you please mark "X-1" on the diagram to show where I was the next time you saw me?

28 Witness:

OK, right about here.

(The witness concludes her testimony about the diagram.)

55 You:

Your Honor, may the diagram be admitted into evidence?

56 Judge:

Any objection? All right, Exhibit 1 is admitted.

Transcript Analysis: You might have asked the judge to admit the diagram into evidence after No. 16, when the witness supplied foundational testimony for the skeleton diagram. But when you intend to ask a witness to make additional markings on a diagram (or when you personally will mark a diagram while testifying), it is proper to delay offering it into evidence until you are done.

> **TIP**
>
> **Keep a diagram simple.** When you use a diagram to illustrate a witness's story, include only major changes in location lest you have so many markings that the diagram becomes unintelligible. At all times, a judge or juror should easily be able to follow what's going on. If you can, rehearse any drawing that you or a witness will make in court in front of an audience and ask for suggestions as to how you can improve your presentation.

Letters and Faxes

To offer a letter or a fax transmission into evidence, you need to lay a foundation showing that the person or organization you claim wrote it actually did so. There are many ways to lay such a foundation. (See FRE 901.) For example, if you claim that Edelstein wrote a letter, here are some of the possibilities:

- Edelstein's own testimony that he wrote it
- the testimony of a witness who actually saw Edelstein write the letter
- if the letter is handwritten, the testimony of a witness who has personal knowledge of Edelstein's handwriting style
- if the letter is typed and signed, the testimony of a witness who is familiar with Edelstein's signature, or

- testimony that, based on the contents of the letter, it is unlikely that anyone other than Edelstein wrote it.

Here is a sample foundation for introducing a letter into evidence based on your personal familiarity with the writer's signature. Assume that you are involved in a breach of contract case, and you have testified that you talked to Edelstein about buying what he said was a valuable baseball card collection. You now want to offer into evidence a letter that you say was written by Edelstein and that contains what you claim are false statements about the collection. You are laying the foundation through your personal testimony:

1 **You:**
Two days later, I think it was on the 18th, I got this letter. May I mark it Exhibit 3?

2 **Judge:**
You may. What is the date?

3 **You:**
June 16.

4 **Judge:**
OK, a letter dated June 16 is marked Exhibit 3. Has defense counsel seen it?

5 **You:**
Yes, she has. This is the letter I received from Mr. Edelstein. I recognize the signature as Mr. Edelstein's because I've seen his signature on other letters that he sent me and we talked about. I'd like to offer Exhibit 3 into evidence.

6 **Judge:**
No objections? It is received.

By testifying from personal knowledge that you recognize the signature as

Edelstein's, you lay an adequate foundation to admit the letter into evidence.

If the document you want to offer into evidence is a fax transmission, you may have no handwriting to identify. However, just as with an old-fashioned letter, you have to offer foundational testimony connecting the fax to the person or organization who you claim produced it. Again, you may do this in a variety of ways. For example, if you claim that the fax was sent by your adversary, before trial you may send a request for admission asking your adversary to admit that he sent it. (See Chapter 5 for a discussion of requests for admission and other discovery devices.) In addition, you may testify that you had a conversation with or sent a fax of your own to the person whom you claim sent the fax and that the exhibit in court was sent in response to the conversation or your fax. Even a letterhead or similar logo on a fax is likely to be sufficient for a judge to admit it into evidence.

Business Records

As all of us know only too well, most business activities generate paperwork (And electronic records,too—see also "Computerized Business Records," below.) For example, if you are a manufacturer who shipped merchandise to a customer who has refused to pay for it, included in your paperwork will be the record of the unpaid bill and your delivery document (receipt). If you are a landlord, you probably have a rent book showing when the tenants paid and did not pay the rent. And if you are a parent seeking additional payments from your ex-spouse to cover your child's large medical expenses, you have medical bills.

At trial, exhibits such as these are generally referred to as "business records." The term is very broad; almost any document produced by any kind of organization, including non-profit corporations and community groups, is considered a business record. To have business records admitted into evidence, you must lay a foundation proving that they are likely to be accurate. The requirements are nearly identical in every state. (See, for example, FRE 803(6), New York Evidence Code § 803 (c)(5), California Evidence Code § 1271, and Texas Civil Rule of Evidence 803(6).) All provide that your foundation has to show three things:

- the document was made in the normal course of business
- the document was prepared around the time of the event to which it pertains, and
- the way the business makes and keeps records suggests that the document is trustworthy.

Business Records and the Hearsay Rule

Chapter 16 explains the hearsay rule, which excludes many out-of-court statements, and some of the important exceptions to the rule that make some types of hearsay statements admissible. A business record is hearsay when it is offered to prove that the transaction recorded by the record occurred. But if your case relies on a business record, you can relax: One of the most important hearsay exceptions is one that makes business records admissible upon a proper foundational showing.

For example, assume that you are a manufacturer of car stereos and that you delivered 100 radios to the defendant, a retailer who has refused to pay for them. You want to offer your company's unpaid invoice into evidence to prove that the defendant owes your company $10,000. If you are offering the invoice through your own testimony, your foundational evidence would look like this:

I have this Invoice No. 229 that has been marked as Exhibit 1 and shown to the defendant. Exhibit 1 is one of my company's invoices. It was prepared by my assistant manager, Steve Von Till; I recognize his initials in the lower right-hand corner of the invoice. Our company's business practice is to prepare an invoice for every order we receive the same day we receive it. Unpaid invoices are kept in a separate file folder by number. All payments received go to our bookkeeper, who stamps "Paid" on these invoices and puts them into a folder labeled "Paid Invoices." I took this invoice from the folder holding the unpaid bills, and it has not been stamped as paid. I ask for Exhibit 1 to be admitted into evidence.

This foundational evidence qualifies the invoice as an admissible business record. You did not prepare the invoice personally, but that is not necessary. Its trustworthiness comes from the routine practice of preparing and keeping invoices. You identify the invoice as a record of your business, establish that invoices are prepared right after orders are received, and explain your record-keeping system. This foundation suggests that the fact that the invoice has not been stamped "Paid" is a reliable indication that it

was not paid. Thus, the judge should admit the invoice into evidence.

Records from Someone Else's Business

You will have to lay much the same kind of foundation for a record that from someone else's business. Absent a stipulation, you may need someone familiar with the records of the other business to come to court and lay the proper foundation. For instance, assume that you are a parent seeking an award of additional money from your ex-spouse to pay for large medical expenses that your child recently incurred. You want to offer into evidence the sheaf of hospital bills you have received. The bills are business records of the hospital. If your ex-spouse will not stipulate to their admissibility, to admit them into evidence you will need to lay a foundation showing how and when the bills are prepared and maintained in the hospital's regular course of business.

To do this it is necessary to serve a document called a Subpoena Duces Tecum, available for free from the court clerk, on the hospital's custodian of records. A Subpoena Duces Tecum orders someone from the hospital's record-keeping staff to come to court on the date specified in the subpoena (that's the subpoena part) and bring along a copy of the hospital's bills (that's the duces tecum part). Then you will call the hospital employee as a witness and question the employee about the hospital's record-keeping procedures. (See Chapters 5 and 12 for additional information about subpoenas.)

TIP

Ask your adversary to stipulate to the admission of business records. Business records are often admitted into evidence by stipulation. Your adversary may well stipulate to the admissibility of business records, because there is often no doubt of their accuracy. (See "Overview of Admitting Exhibits Into Evidence," above, for a form of stipulation you might use.)

Computerized Business Records

Many businesses today store most of their records in computers. For example, if you are a manufacturer, employees probably regularly enter data into a computer reflecting merchandise delivered to, and payments received from, your customers. To prove at trial how much a customer owes, you will probably need to make a printout of the account and offer it as an exhibit.

TIP

Your court may have faster ways to admit business records. To save businesses the time and expense of sending employees to court, many states have adopted a shortcut procedure for admitting business records known as the Uniform Photographic Copies of Business and Public Records as Evidence Act. If your state has adopted this law, a business can comply with your Subpoena Duces Tecum asking for a business record by mailing records to the court along with an affidavit signed under penalty of perjury as to how the records are prepared and kept. The records are then admissible in evidence without your having to offer any further foundation. Most states have enacted the Uniform Photographic Copies of Business and Public Records as Evidence Act. Check in your state's evidence or civil procedure rules to find out whether your state is one of them.

Fortunately, evidence rules are flexible enough to permit admission of a business record consisting of a computer printout. As with any other business record, you will need to offer foundational evidence concerning how your business prepares and keeps records. Your foundation should include information about your business's computer system. Don't worry, you will not need to call an expert witness to explain the scientific theory and reliability of computers. Simply have a computer-literate employee explain how your records are entered and retrieved and testify that the computer from which the record was retrieved was in good working order. As long as your business has routine and reliable procedures for using and maintaining its computers, and the particular record was maintained according to those procedures, you should have no difficulty admitting the record into evidence.

Government Records

"Official records" is the legal system's label for reports and documents prepared by government officials and offices. For instance, if you are a tenant in a landlord-tenant case and your apartment is inspected by a county health inspector, the inspector's report is an official record. Likewise, if a police officer investigates an accident, the police officer's report is an official record.

Because record keeping by government offices is much like that of private businesses, the foundation you need to admit an official record into evidence is similar to that of business records. (See, for example, FRE

803(8), New York Evidence Code § 803(c)(7), California Evidence Code § 1280, and Texas Civil Rule of Evidence 803(8).) If anything, your judge will probably require less of a foundation for official records than for business records, based on a perception (reasonable or not) that official records are very likely to be accurate.

For example, assume that you are the defendant in an automobile accident case. To counter the plaintiff's claim that you drove on the wrong side of the road, you want to prove that your car left skid marks in your proper traffic lane. You know that soon after the accident, Officer Krupke arrived, examined the skid marks left by your car, and later prepared a report as to the location and length of the skid marks. After calling the police department and inquiring how to subpoena an officer, you served a Subpoena Duces Tecum on Officer Krupke by leaving it with the watch commander of Krupke's assigned police station. Krupke has come to court with the report, and you want the judge to admit this report into evidence as an official record. Your foundational evidence will look something like this:

1 You:

Officer Krupke, what is your occupation and assignment?

2 Krupke:

I'm a police officer for West Side City, assigned to routine traffic patrol.

3 You:

Did you investigate an accident in the 2100 block of Hillcrest Road on the afternoon of December 23?

4 Krupke:

Yes, I did.

5 You:

And what did you do?

6 Krupke:

After ascertaining that nobody was injured, I examined a set of skid marks that extended for approximately 50 feet behind the car you were in.

7 You:

Was there any reason you examined the skid marks?

8 Krupke:

It's routine investigation.

9 You:

Officer Krupke, did you prepare a report of your findings with regard to the skid marks following your investigation?

10 Krupke:

Yes, I did.

11 You:

When did you prepare it?

12 Krupke:

In line with department policy, I prepared the report before I went off duty, about three hours after I completed my investigation.

13 You:

How did you prepare that report?

14 Krupke:

From the notes about the skid marks that I made at the scene of the accident.

15 You:

Officer Krupke, the bailiff is handing you a document marked "Defendant's

Exhibit C for Identification." Is this the report you prepared in this case?

16 Krupke:

Yes it is. This is my signature.

17 You:

Your Honor, I offer the report into evidence as an official record.

18 Judge:

Yes, I'll admit it.

Transcript Analysis: This excerpt demonstrates that Officer Krupke, a government official, prepared the skid mark report as part of his official, routine duties. It was prepared in timely fashion, just a few hours after his investigation. In Nos. 15 and 16, Krupke identifies the exhibit as the report that he prepared. Thus, you have met all requirements for admissibility.

RESOURCE

Researching foundational requirements. If you plan to offer an exhibit into evidence but are uncertain about the foundation you have to lay, you'll have to do some research. One book that you may find especially useful is *Evidentiary Foundations* by Edward Imwinkelried (Matthew Bender). In a question-and-answer format, it illustrates foundational testimony for numerous kinds of exhibits.

Other books you may want to consult include:

McCormick on Evidence, by John Strong, ed. (West Publishing Co.), is a treatise widely used by lawyers and judges; Titles 8 and 9 review exhibits.

Evidence, by Ken Graham (Casenotes Publishing Co.), is a paperback "outline," which is a quick, relatively inexpensive refresher aimed at law students. You will find this and other evidence outlines in most law bookstores near law schools.

Researching evidence rules themselves is another way to find out about foundational requirements. The evidence rules governing trials in federal courts are found in the Federal Rules of Evidence (FRE). By way of example, Rule 803(6) lists the foundational requirements for business records, and Rule 901 lists foundations for authenticating documents. Many states have enacted the FRE almost in its entirety and collected it in a separate volume of laws. In a few states, evidence rules may be harder to find because they are included in a more general collection of civil laws; in these states you may have to ask a law librarian to help you find evidence rules. (See Chapter 23 for information on doing legal research.)

In addition to doing research, this is a good time to consult your legal coach, particularly if admission of an exhibit is crucial to your case. The brief time it should take an attorney to help you organize a sufficient foundation may be well worth the expense. (See Chapters 1 and 23 for more about legal coaches.)

Finally, if you find yourself uncertain in the middle of trial about what you need to do to lay a foundation, do not be afraid to ask the judge for help. Ask to approach the bench, and say something like, "Your Honor, I've got this repair estimate that I want to introduce into evidence, but I'm not quite sure what to do." Some judges may even respond by asking questions themselves to develop the necessary foundation.

Letting Jurors See Your Exhibits

If you review the mechanics for offering exhibits into evidence discussed above, you will realize that in a jury trial the jurors are frozen out of the process. An exhibit goes from your hand to the witness (sometimes via the bailiff) and then to the judge. Once an exhibit is admitted into evidence, the witness may give oral testimony concerning the exhibit, and then it is put in the custody of the court clerk.

Normally the judge allows the jurors to have all the exhibits with them when the case is complete and they deliberate. (See, for example, California Code of Civil Procedure § 612.) But that may be too late to influence them in your favor. If possible, you want to melt the jury freeze-out and allow the jurors to examine each exhibit as soon as the judge admits it into evidence.

Fortunately, a procedure does exist for showing an exhibit to a jury at the time it is admitted into evidence. (In some courts, this is called "publishing an exhibit.") Immediately after an exhibit is admitted into evidence, ask the judge for permission to show the exhibit to the jurors. Say something like, "Your Honor, may I hand Exhibit C, the photograph [business record, letter, and so on] to the jurors?" The judge, who probably wants to keep the trial moving, may respond by asking you to justify your request. If so, you can do two things to encourage the judge to rule in your favor:

- Explain why seeing the exhibit during the testimony will help the jury understand your evidence. For example, you may point out, "I'm going to be testifying

"Your Honor, after the trial will it be possible to purchase items from the exhibit table?"

about the damage to my car, and seeing the photo now will help the jury follow my testimony."

- If feasible, make enough copies of an exhibit to give to each juror. That will save time that otherwise will be wasted if testimony has to halt while a single page or photo wends its way among the jurors.

When Exhibits Are Required: The Best Evidence Rule

In most situations, you are not required to offer an exhibit into evidence. That is, though it may lack the storytelling impact of an exhibit, oral testimony describing an object is often admissible without the need of a physical backup. For example, when you testify that you were struck by a boomerang, you are not legally required to offer the boomerang into evidence. Similarly, you or a police officer may orally testify to the skid marks left after a car accident without offering the officer's police report into evidence.

But when you want to offer testimony about the contents of documents such as letters, business records, and photographs, a legal doctrine known as the "best evidence rule" restricts your right to rely on oral testimony. This rule is also known as the "original writing rule." (See FRE 1002, New York Evidence Code § 1002, California Evidence Code § 1500, Texas Civil Rule of Evidence 1002, and similar statutes in almost every state.) The rule states that you (or a witness) cannot orally testify to the contents of a document unless you produce the

document in court or prove to the judge that you have a valid reason for being unable to do so.

TIP

Offer at least a copy whenever possible. If you cannot produce an original document, try your best to locate and introduce into evidence a copy. To offer a copy of a document into evidence, follow the same foundational procedure as for any other exhibit, but make sure that you tell the judge that your document is a copy, not an original.

To see how the rule works, assume that you want to prove that Ihori wrote you a threatening note. Because of the best evidence rule, you cannot simply testify that, "I got a note from Ihori, and this is what it said…." You have to produce the note itself in court. If you cannot do so, you should offer a photocopy of the note, if you made one. If you do not have a copy, you can testify orally to what the note said if you lay a foundation showing the judge you have a valid excuse for not having the document. For example, you may testify that Ihori stole the note from you or that it was accidentally thrown out by your six-year-old child. The preference goes, in descending order, from originals, to copies, to oral testimony.

Objecting to Your Adversary's Exhibits

In addition to offering your own exhibits into evidence, you have the right to object to those your adversary tries to offer. (Of course, your adversary has the same right with respect to your exhibits.) An objection asks a judge to exclude (refuse to admit) an exhibit, which means that the judge or jury cannot consider the exhibit in reaching a verdict. (See Chapter 17.)

If the admissibility of an exhibit is challenged, the judge may have to halt the trial and conduct a short "mini-trial" on the spot to decide whether an exhibit is admissible. During the mini-trial, you and your adversary can present whatever evidence you have pertaining to the adequacy of the foundation. After listening to the evidence, the judge decides whether or not to admit the disputed exhibit into evidence. The main trial then continues.

For example, assume you offer foundational evidence that a letter was written by Edelstein, your adversary. But Edelstein objects to the admission of the letter into evidence and asks to offer foundational evidence of his own that he did not write it. The judge holds a short mini-trial, during which you offer your evidence supporting your contention that Edelstein wrote the letter, and Edelstein offers evidence that he did not. The judge's decision about the admissibility of the letter concludes the mini-trial, and the main trial resumes at once with or without the letter in evidence.

TIP

You can ask the judge to exclude the jury during the mini-trial. The judge can exclude or permit a jury to remain during a mini-trial. If you do not want the jurors listening to evidence about an exhibit that you hope the judge will exclude, ask the judge to exclude the jury during the mini-trial. However, do not ask to exclude a jury unless the danger of prejudice is very high; jurors resent being left out of things, and excluding them delays the trial.

Here are the most common reasons for objecting to the admissibility of an exhibit.

Insufficient Foundation

You can object to an adversary's exhibit on the ground that the adversary has not laid a sufficient foundation. For example, suppose that you are the tenant, Marjorie, in a landlord-tenant case. The owner calls the apartment manager as a witness and asks the manager to identify a photograph allegedly showing you throwing a rock through the manager's window. (You deny throwing the rock.) In response, the manager testifies, "That looks like Marjorie, but I really can't be sure." If the landlord attempts to offer the photo into evidence based on this foundation, ask the judge to exclude it on the ground that the manager lacks personal knowledge or that the foundation is insufficient.

You can also object by offering conflicting foundational evidence. For instance, assume that your adversary offers a computerized printout of a business record showing that you owe your adversary a lot of money. Your adversary offers evidence about her business's careful record-keeping procedures. However, your position is that the printout is wrong, and you have information from a former employee of your adversary's business who is willing to testify on your behalf about the business's sloppy record-keeping procedures that regularly get accounts mixed up.

You may object when the adversary offers the computer printout into evidence and ask the judge to listen to your evidence before making a decision about whether to admit the printout. Saying something like, "Objection, Your Honor. Lack of foundation. I'd like to call a witness to show that the printout is not trustworthy." Your objection may require the judge to conduct a mini-trial in which the only issue is the admissibility of the computer printout. If the testimony from the former employee convinces the judge that the adversary's printout is not trustworthy, the judge will exclude it from evidence. And because your adversary's whole case may be based on the contents of the printout, by excluding the printout you may win the whole trial!

TIP

You can attack the reliability of an exhibit after it is admitted into evidence. If your judge admits your adversary's exhibit into evidence over your objection, it means only that the exhibit is admissible in evidence, not that it is necessarily accurate. You can still offer your own evidence attacking the exhibit's reliability and argue (as part of your closing argument) that the exhibit is so untrustworthy that the judge or jury should not pay any attention to it when arriving at its decision.

Violations of Other Rules of Evidence

Even if an exhibit offered by your adversary satisfies all foundational requirements, you may still ask the judge to exclude it on the ground that it violates another rule of evidence, such as the hearsay rule or the rule of relevance. (See Chapter 16.) If you are uncertain about whether or not one of these other rules may bar an exhibit offered by your adversary, research the issue in a law library or talk to your legal coach. (See Chapter 23.)

The following examples may help you understand how to use evidence rules to object to your adversary's offered exhibits:

EXAMPLE 1: Hearsay. To prove that your carelessness caused an accident, your adversary offers into evidence a letter written by a person named Julie Even saying that you ran a red light. Object and ask the judge to exclude the letter as hearsay. The letter is made inadmissible by the hearsay rule even though your adversary properly marks, identifies, and lays a foundation showing that it was written by Even.

EXAMPLE 2: Unfair prejudice. A judge can exclude relevant evidence as "unfairly prejudicial" if its legitimate impact is outweighed by the likelihood that it will inflame the emotions of the judge or jury against you. For example, assume that your adversary claims that you carelessly ran a red light and collided with his car. He wants to offer into evidence photos of your car, one of which prominently shows a bumper sticker with the name of a musical rock group that many people claim promotes violent antisocial behavior. You may object that the photograph showing the bumper sticker is unfairly prejudicial. On the one hand, it has minimal relevance; your adversary has offered into evidence other photos of your car. On the other hand, it is likely to prejudice you in the eyes of the judge or jury as a fan of an outlaw rock group. The judge may decide to exclude the photo even though your adversary properly marks, identifies, and lays a foundation for the photo as a fair and accurate representation of your car.

> ! **CAUTION**
>
> **Only part of an exhibit may be admissible.** Whether you or your adversary offers an exhibit into evidence, be aware that only part of it may be admissible. For example, an admissible medical report may contain irrelevant material, or a police officer's report may contain the inadmissible hearsay statement of a bystander. In such situations, the improper matter must be "severed" from the exhibit. Depending on the type of exhibit and the extensiveness of the improper matter, severing may be accomplished by crossing or blocking it out, cutting it out with scissors, or preparing a new document without the improper matter.

Organizing Exhibits for Trial

To be thorough, refer to your exhibits in at least two different portions of your trial notebook. (See Chapter 18.)

In Chapter 12, we advised you to make outlines of your planned testimony and the direct examinations of your witnesses. In each outline of a witness's testimony, refer to any exhibit you plan to offer during the direct examination of that witness. For instance, assume that you want to offer a photograph of the intersection of Main and Elm Streets into evidence during your direct examination of Cynthia White. In your outline of her testimony, write down a simple reminder such as, "photo of intersection." Also, you may want to briefly note key foundational requirements: "Ask if the photo is a 'fair and accurate representation' of the intersection." (Normally, you offer exhibits when you and your witnesses testify. But if you plan to offer an exhibit during cross-examination of an adverse witness, note that fact in your cross-examination outline for that witness.)

It's also wise to keep a separate list of all of your exhibits in a separate section of your trial notebook. You can then check off the exhibits as each is admitted into evidence.

What about the exhibits themselves? Generally, keep all your exhibits together in the order in which you plan to introduce them into evidence so that you can easily lay your hands on them during trial. But usually it is unwise to keep them in your trial notebook because you should not make notebook holes in original documents. And some of your exhibits may be too bulky for a notebook—for example, a boomerang and a hat are not well suited to storage in a trial notebook. It is usually best to keep your exhibits in a folder or box, separate from your trial notebook. ●

Basic Rules of Evidence

The preceding chapters have explained many important evidence rules that apply to specific parts of the trial process. For example, you know that:

- During your *opening statement*, you cannot argue. (See Chapter 11.)
- During *direct examination*, you are generally limited to asking open and closed questions. During cross-examination, you may (and indeed should) ask leading questions. (See Chapters 12 and 13.)
- *Exhibits* are not admissible in evidence until you lay a proper foundation. For example, a photograph is not admissible unless a witness testifies that it is a fair and accurate representation of whatever it depicts. (See Chapter 15.)
- You may use any kind of document to *refresh a forgetful witness's recollection*. But you must show the document to your adversary, who may offer it into evidence. (See Chapter 12.)

By contrast, the evidence rules described in this chapter apply to *every* aspect of trial. They regulate information regardless of whether you are testifying personally, asking questions of your witnesses or those of your adversary, offering an exhibit into evidence, or making your opening statement or final argument.

Unfortunately, some of these rules run counter to common sense. They sometimes prevent you from offering the types of evidence that you probably rely on in everyday life. That makes it all the more important that you read this chapter carefully when you prepare for trial. If, after reading it, you are still not sure about whether important evidence that you or your adversary plans to

offer is admissible, consult one of the books listed at the end of the chapter or talk to your legal coach.

The Role of Objections in Enforcing Evidence Rules

Evidence rules are not self-enforcing. If one side offers legally improper evidence at trial, the evidence will normally be admitted—and can be considered by the judge or jury in arriving at a verdict—unless the other side objects. To keep out improper evidence, you must ask the judge to rule that the evidence is improper by making an objection, and the judge must uphold (sustain) the objection and exclude the evidence. On occasion, if evidence is blatantly inadmissible, a judge will exclude evidence without waiting for an objection. (Chapter 17 explains the objection process.)

Relevance

The most fundamental rule of evidence requires a logical connection between a piece of evidence you offer and the legal claim you are trying to prove or disprove. It's called the relevance rule. (See for example, FRE 401–402, California Evidence Code §§ 140 and 351, New York Code of Evidence §§ 401–402, and Texas Civil Rules of Evidence 401–402.)

To be relevant, evidence does not have to prove a certain point conclusively. Evidence is relevant if it makes a fact that a party is trying to prove a little more probable, or if it makes a fact that a party is trying to disprove a little less probable. For example, say you are attempting to prove that Melinda was speeding, and you offer evidence that at the time of the accident she was late for an important meeting. Your evidence is relevant. Melinda's being late by no means conclusively proves that she was speeding. But common sense tells you that sometimes people do speed when they are late for meetings. The evidence of lateness adds to the probability that Melinda was speeding.

Let's turn this example around and assume that you are Melinda, and you are attempting to prove that you were not speeding. You offer evidence that at the time your were driving, you had a valuable crystal vase on the back seat of your car. This evidence too is relevant. Again, common sense suggests that people sometimes drive more slowly when they are carrying expensive, breakable objects.

Judges have broad discretion to decide whether evidence is relevant. Whether your judge deems particular evidence relevant or not is often a close call that depends on the facts of a case, the importance of the issue to which the evidence pertains, other evidence already in the record, and the need to keep a trial moving efficiently. On the theory that, like snowflakes, no two trials are ever the same, legal precedent (prior court decisions about relevance) has almost nothing to do with whether evidence will be found relevant in your trial.

CAUTION

Not all relevant evidence is admissible. Evidence must be relevant to be admissible. But the converse is not true; relevant evidence is not always admissible. The rules you will read about in this chapter often exclude evidence even though it is relevant. For example, relevant evidence may be excluded because it is unfairly inflammatory or because it constitutes hearsay.

Perhaps the best way to demonstrate the meaning of relevance is with a few more examples, some of which are favorites of law professors:

- Lipkis is on trial for murder. The prosecution offers the murder weapon into evidence. Lipkis objects that the gun is irrelevant, because a police officer found it precisely halfway between Lipkis and a person standing next to Lipkis at the murder scene. *Ruling:* The gun is relevant. True, the gun evidence does not distinguish between Lipkis and the other person as the possible murderer. Nevertheless, evidence that the gun was found somewhere near Lipkis adds to the probability that he committed the murder. Again, evidence does not have to be conclusive to be relevant.

- In a divorce case, you are seeking custody of your young child. You testify that you recently heard your ex-spouse verbally abusing your child when you arrived to pick up your child. Your ex-spouse calls Shelley to testify that the day before the trial, she engaged in a short experiment at your ex-spouse's request. She will testify that she stood at the same spot where you were standing when you testified you heard the verbal abuse and that she was unable to hear a thing, even though your ex-spouse claims to have been yelling loudly. *Ruling:* Shelley's evidence is irrelevant. There is no logical connection between what two people can hear on two different occasions. Not only do people vary in their hearing ability, but also the external circumstances are likely to have been different. For example, it is unlikely that your ex-spouse used exactly the same tone of voice on both occasions, or that background noise from cars and other people was the same.

- You, Smith, have sued Jones, a coworker, for assaulting you. You offer evidence that about a week before the assault, Jones told a third coworker, "I'm going to get Smith the next chance I get." The defendant objects that the evidence is irrelevant because people often make threats that they do not carry out. *Ruling:* Your evidence is relevant. Evidence that the defendant made a threat against you increases the probability that the defendant later assaulted you.

- The plaintiff has sued you for negligence, claiming that your speeding was the cause of an accident on Third Street. You deny that you were speeding or otherwise negligent. To help prove that you were going too fast, the plaintiff offers testimony that about a week earlier, you were seen speeding on Ninth Street. *Ruling:* The plaintiff's evidence is irrelevant. There is no logical connection between how you drove at one time and location and how you drove at another time and location.

- You sue Universal Metals for fraud and breach of contract. You claim that Universal's personnel director, Sonny Ancher, induced you to leave another job by promising to hire you at an increase in salary and that he later reneged. Universal denies that any employment offer was made to you. To show that Ancher did violate an agreement with you, you offer evidence that a week after you filed the suit against Universal, Universal fired Ancher. *Ruling:* The evidence that Universal fired Ancher is irrelevant. Because Universal's decision to fire Ancher could have been based on so many different factors, there is no logical connection between your claim and his firing.

TIP

How to object to irrelevant evidence. To ask the judge to keep out irrelevant evidence offered by your adversary, simply say, "Objection, Your Honor; irrelevant." Do this as soon as you realize that your adversary's question seeks, or the adverse witness's answer refers to, irrelevant evidence. Do not make an argument as to why the evidence is irrelevant unless the judge asks you to do so. (See Chapter 17 for more on how to make objections.)

Excluding Relevant but Unfairly Prejudicial Evidence

If a judge believes that the relevance of a particular piece of evidence is outweighed by the risk that admitting the evidence will unfairly prejudice the other side, the judge can exclude the evidence. (See, for example, FRE 403, Cal. Evid. Code § 352, NY Code of Evid. § 403, and Texas Civ. Rule of Evid. 403.)

Evidence may be excluded as unfairly prejudicial when it is so likely to inflame the emotions of the judge or jury that the judge or jury will attach too much importance to it. For example, assume that you have been sued for fraud for supposedly intentionally concealing a dangerous condition in a house that you sold to the plaintiff, as a result of which the plaintiff suffered head injuries. Your defense is that no dangerous condition existed at the time of the sale. After testifying to her injuries, the plaintiff offers into evidence a series of photographs depicting her bloody head injuries before and during medical treatment. The photographs are of some relevance because they support the plaintiff's testimony about the extent of her injuries. But their relevance is slight because they do nothing to answer the question of whether the dangerous condition existed at the time of sale. And there is a risk that the photographs will inflame the passions of the jury against you and cause the jury to rule in favor of the plaintiff no matter what the condition of the house. So if you object, the judge may conclude that the risk that the photographs will be unfairly prejudicial outweighs their relevance and exclude them from evidence.

As is true with many rules of evidence, your judge is more likely to exclude evidence as unfairly prejudicial when your case is being heard by a jury rather than by the judge sitting without a jury. Judges tend to think that while jurors are likely to be unduly influenced by prejudicial evidence, judges are able to sort the relevant wheat from the prejudicial chaff. Nevertheless, even in a judge trial you should make the objection if you think the situation warrants it. Even if the judge overrules (denies) it, your objection may remind the judge that your adversary's evidence carries a risk of unfair prejudice.

> **TIP**
>
> **How to object to unfairly prejudicial evidence.** To ask a judge to exclude unfairly prejudicial evidence offered by your adversary, say, "Objection, Your Honor. The evidence is unfairly prejudicial." Object as soon as you realize that your adversary's question seeks, or the adverse witness's answer refers to, unfairly prejudicial evidence. Do not make an argument as to why the evidence is unfairly prejudicial unless the judge asks you to do so. (See Chapter 17 for more on making objections.)

If yours is a jury trial, also consider making a Motion in Limine to exclude unfairly prejudicial evidence before trial gets underway. (See Chapter 17.) The fact that you are a self-represented litigant may work in your favor, because the judge should realize that you may be unable to prevent a jury from hearing unfairly prejudicial evidence if you have to object on the spot when the evidence is offered at trial.

The Rule Against Opinions

If you are old enough to remember the character of Sergeant Joe Friday in the television show *Dragnet*, you may remember that he always asked witnesses for "just the facts." Sergeant Friday's warning sums up the opinion rule: Parties and witnesses are supposed to testify to specific factual observations, not to opinions. It is up to the judge or jury to decide what conclusions to draw from the witness's observations. (See FRE 701, Cal. Evid. Code § 800, NY Code of Evid. § 701, and Texas Civ. Rule of Evid. 701.)

Like the relevance rule, the opinion rule is impossible to define with precision. Your judge necessarily has wide discretion to decide what constitutes an improper opinion. To see why, let's take what may seem like a silly example. Ruth testifies, "I saw a car." Fact or opinion? It seems like a factual observation that would satisfy even Sergeant Friday. But if you stop to think about it, you will see that Ruth is giving an opinion. After all, she could have testified to greater factual detail: "I saw a large metal object with four round metallic objects covered with a black, rubbery material …." and left it to the judge or jury to conclude that what she saw was a car. But if a judge were to ban this kind of opinion, most types of information that people rely on every day to make sensible judgments would be forbidden, and a simple trial might last for weeks.

In practice, what the opinion rule really means is that witnesses can testify to opinions if these three things are true:

1. The witness has personal knowledge of the facts on which the opinion is based.
2. The opinion is of a commonsense type that people make every day.
3. The opinion does not consist of an unnecessary legal judgment that the judge or jury is supposed to make.

To illustrate, let's return to Ruth and the car. Ruth would probably not be allowed to testify that, "In my opinion, the blue car caused the accident." Even if she saw the events leading up to the accident, Ruth would be attempting to perform the job of the judge or jury. Also, a judgment of legal fault is not a commonsense, everyday opinion. It is reasonable to ask Ruth to testify to what she saw, and leave to the judge or jury the job of deciding who caused the accident.

Again, perhaps the best way to get a feel for the opinion rule is with concrete examples. A judge will normally allow a witness to give opinions such as the following:

- "When I saw him, Kebo was happy (or angry or sad)."
- "I watched Johnson for a half hour, and he seemed drunk."
- "Especially considering it was a rainy day, the car was going too fast."
- "In the couple of years that our families have been friends, Becky has always seemed more comfortable around her father than around her mother."

In each example, the opinions are likely to be admissible because they meet the three-part test set out above.

At the other extreme are a variety of opinions that witnesses cannot give because they combine observations with unnecessary legal judgments. A judge will probably not allow a witness to state opinions such as:

- "Philippe was driving carelessly."
- "It will be in Becky's best interests to live with her father."
- "Her former attorney committed legal malpractice."
- "I think the plaintiff should get a million dollars in damages."

In each example, it is reasonable to expect a witness to describe the behavior underlying the opinion and leave the legal judgment to the judge or jury.

CAUTION

Expert witnesses march to a different drummer. Expert witnesses are allowed to state opinions even if those opinions make legal judgments and are not based on personal knowledge. For example, a trained family counselor can testify to an opinion that a father should be granted custody of a minor child. (See Chapter 19 for more information on expert witnesses.)

TIP

How to object to improper opinions. To ask your judge to exclude an improper opinion offered by your adversary, say, "Objection Your Honor. The question calls for an improper opinion." Object as soon as you realize that your adversary's question seeks, or the adverse witness's answer refers to, an improper opinion. Do not make an argument as to why an opinion is improper unless the judge asks you to do so. (See Chapter 17 for more on making objections.)

Don't worry if the judge rules that the opinion you are testifying to or seeking from a witness is improper. You can almost always bring out the information you are after. You just need to testify, or elicit from a witness, the details on which the opinion was based. Consider this example in which you are questioning a woodsman:

1 You:
And what happened next?

2 Witness:
The wolf intended you to think that he was your grandma.

3 Adversary:
Object, and move to strike the testimony as to the wolf's intent as an improper opinion.

4 Judge:
Yes, the witness lacks personal knowledge as to the wolf's actual intent. Objection sustained.

Transcript Analysis: Here your witness's opinion (No. 2) is ruled inadmissible. But the ruling does not prevent you from offering evidence about the wolf's intent. You can continue by asking the witness to describe the behavior leading him to form this opinion:

5 You:
Please tell us exactly what you saw.

6 Witness:
Okay. When I arrived outside the cottage, I saw the wolf in bed dressed in a ladies' nightgown and cap, with the covers pulled all the way up to his chin.

7 You:
And what was the wolf doing?

8 Witness:
He was talking in a very soft voice, saying over and over how nice you were for coming to visit your dear sweet grandma.

9 You:
And then what happened?

10 **Witness:**

You said something about what big eyes your grandma had, and the wolf said in the same soft tone of voice that he had just gotten new contact lenses that made his eyes look a little funny.

11 **You:**

Yes, go on.

Transcript Analysis: This brief series of questions seeks the factual information underlying the witness's improper opinion about the wolf's intent. Compare the improper opinion (No. 2) with the factual information; doesn't the latter actually have more persuasive impact? Evidence rules aside, you are probably better off eliciting the details underlying the improper opinion.

Rules Excluding Evidence Based on Social Policies

This section describes rules that exclude specific types of evidence. These rules are based on social policies that are considered more important than the outcomes of specific trials.

Subsequent Remedial Measures

After a mishap occurs, the party allegedly responsible for it may want to make a change that will prevent the mishap from occurring again. For example, if a patron in a shop slips and falls on a slippery floor, the shop's owner may want to change to a different type of wax that is less slippery. However, the shop owner might be reluctant to change waxes if the patron could offer evidence of the change at trial to prove that the owner was negligent in the first place.

FRE 407 encourages changes that enhance public safety by providing that evidence of subsequent remedial measures is not admissible to prove negligence, culpable conduct, or a product defect. Thus, in the floor wax example, if the patron sued the shop owner for negligence for having a dangerously slippery floor, the patron could not offer evidence that the owner later changed to a different type of wax.

Judges interpret the term "subsequent remedial measures" broadly, so that almost any type of safety change made after a mishap occurs is likely to be inadmissible at trial. For example:

- Following an accident involving one of its truck drivers, a company fires the truck driver. Evidence of the firing is not admissible in a lawsuit against the company to prove that the truck driver's negligence caused the accident.
- A consumer sues an over-the-counter drug manufacturer, claiming that she became ill because the drug's warning label did not mention the danger of taking the drug and then eating grapefruit. The drug's manufacturer later changes the warning label to warn consumers not to eat grapefruit within 24 hours of taking the drug. Evidence of the changed warning label is not admissible to prove that the previous warning label was defective.
- A car buyer sues the car's manufacturer, claiming the reason that the buyer was involved in an accident was that the car's braking system was

defectively designed. Evidence that the manufacturer issued a recall notice advising purchasers to bring their cars to dealers to have the brakes inspected is inadmissible to prove that the brakes were defective.

Settlement Negotiations and Offers

When disputes occur, social policy favors parties resolving them amicably rather than going to trial. To further this policy, FRE 408 provides that neither settlement offers nor statements made during settlement negotiations are admissible at trial.

For example, assume that Toymaker Co. claims that Parts Co. breached a contract by shipping defective parts to Toymaker. Even before a lawsuit is filed, representatives from the two companies meet to try to resolve the dispute. At the meeting, the Parts Co. representative admits that "the colors on the parts we shipped to you were all wrong." The Parts Co. representative also offers to pay Toymaker Co. $35,000 to cover the losses it incurred because of the defective parts. If the negotiation efforts fail and the case goes to trial, Toymaker cannot offer evidence of the Parts Co. representative's admission or evidence that Parts Co. made a settlement offer. The social policy in favor of parties trying to work out disputes themselves outweighs whatever limited probative value the evidence might have. (Parts Co. might have admitted culpability and offered money to Toymaker even if Parts Co. didn't think it had done anything wrong, so that Toymaker would continue to do business with it in the future.)

For further discussion of settlement strategies, see Chapter 6.

Payment of Medical Expenses

A party may want to help an injured person cope with expenses caused by the injury, whether or not the party accepts legal liability for the person's injuries. Yet, the party may be reluctant to offset the expenses of an injury if a judge or jury could conclude that payment of medical expenses was itself an admission of liability. To encourage people to obey their humane impulses, FRE 409 provides that payment of medical or hospital expenses is not admissible to prove liability.

For example, following an auto accident, Driver A says to Driver B, "Go see Dr. Rex and have her send the bill to me. Also, if you have to miss work, I'll pay up to a week of your lost wages." Neither Driver A's statements, nor any payments that Driver A makes to Driver B, are admissible in evidence to prove that Driver A is legally liable to Driver B.

What if Driver A had said, "The collision was my fault. Go see Dr. Rex and have her send the bill to me?" The first sentence is an admission of liability that Driver B could offer into evidence at trial. However, FRE 409 would still exclude the second sentence.

Insurance Coverage

Under FRE 411, evidence that a party carries liability insurance is not admissible to prove that the party was negligent. One reason for the rule is that the relevance of insurance coverage is likely to be slight. Few people are likely to behave carelessly simply because they have insurance. A second reason is the social policy encouraging people to protect others by carrying liability insurance. People might be less likely to purchase insurance if judges and jurors were apt to find them liable because a big insurance company and not the party personally would have to pay any damages.

Character Evidence

Character evidence is evidence of past behavior that suggests that a person has a propensity to behave in a certain way (a "character trait"). In daily life, we commonly use what we know of people's past behavior to make judgments about their characters. For instance, we may think of a person as being careful, violent, honest, or nasty. And once we form an opinion about a person's character, we are likely to project it onto their specific conduct. For example, once we conclude that a person has a propensity to drive carefully, we may reason that the person was probably driving carefully on a particular occasion.

But for a variety of reasons, evidence rules contain a strong policy forbidding character evidence in civil trials. (See FRE 404, Cal. Evid. Code § 1101, NY Code of Evid. § 404, and Texas Civ. Rule of Evid. 404.) One reason is simply to save time. Trials would be much too long if parties were allowed to fight not only about how specific events took place but also about each other's character traits. Another reason is that character evidence is thought by our legal system to be of dubious value: People simply do not always behave in accordance with their character traits. And a third reason

is that evidence of character itself may be untrustworthy: Witnesses are not omniscient, and they may easily misjudge the character of you or your adversary.

Some examples may help you understand the type of information forbidden by the rule against character evidence:

- To prove that you were driving carefully before a traffic accident, you cannot ask a witness who has carpooled with you for 20 years to testify that in her opinion you are a safe driver. Similarly, you cannot offer evidence that you've never gotten a traffic ticket for a moving violation or that you've never before been involved in an accident. In each situation, you improperly ask the judge or jury to infer that because you have a propensity (a character trait) to drive safely, you were driving safely at the time of the accident involved in your trial.

- Although by way of introduction you are allowed to briefly question your witnesses about their personal backgrounds when conducting their direct examination (see Chapter 12), generally you cannot ask about a witness's good deeds, community activities, awards, and the like. As a judge is likely to view it, such evidence amounts to an improper attempt to prove that a witness is of upstanding moral character—and therefore is likely to tell the truth.

- To prove that a defendant assaulted you, you cannot offer evidence that the defendant has been involved in other fights. And you cannot call a witness who knows the defendant well to give an opinion that the defendant is violent. Again, such evidence improperly asks the judge or jury to infer that because the defendant has a propensity (a character trait) to be violent, the defendant assaulted you.

- Similarly, to prove that you struck the defendant only in self-defense, you cannot offer evidence that you have never instigated a fight or that in the opinion of a friend who knows you well, you are a peaceful person. This evidence, too, improperly asks the judge or jury to infer from evidence of your peaceful character that you were not the aggressor in the fight with the defendant.

- To prove that your landlord falsely promised to install a new central heating system in your apartment, you cannot offer evidence of a witness's opinion that your landlord is dishonest or that the landlord has made false promises to others.

Character Evidence May Be Admissible in Sexual Assault, Child Molestation, and Sexual Harassment Cases

Despite the general exclusion of character evidence in civil cases, special evidence rules in many jurisdictions allow character evidence when victims of child molestation, sexual assault, and sexual harassment sue their attackers for damages. Subject to judicial discretion, these rules allow victims to offer evidence of other similar acts that their attackers have committed. For example, assume that Darla sues Jeff, a former boyfriend, for sexually assaulting her. Under these rules, the judge would have discretion to allow Darla to call Bonnie as a witness to testify that Jeff also sexually assaulted her (Bonnie). An example of such a rule is Federal Rule of Evidence 415, which allows evidence of past acts of sexual assault and child molestation.

 TIP

How to object to improper character evidence. To object if your adversary tries to introduce favorable character evidence about himself or one of his witnesses, or unfavorable character evidence about you or one of your witnesses, say, "Objection, Your Honor. That's improper character evidence." Object as soon as you realize that your adversary's question seeks, or the adverse witness's answer refers to, improper character evidence, but do not make an argument as to why the evidence constitutes character evidence unless the judge asks you to do so. (See Chapter 17 for more on making objections.)

Hearsay

This section explains the hearsay rule. This rule potentially comes into play whenever parties offer evidence of out-of-court statements—that is, statements made outside the courtroom. Because the rule does not apply to many kinds of out-of-court statements, and because it is riddled with exceptions, out-of-court statements are often admissible in evidence. If an out-of-court statement is important evidence either for you or your adversary, study this section very carefully. If you are still not sure about the admissibility of an out-of-court statement, refer to the resources listed at the end of the chapter or consult your legal coach.

CAUTION

The hearsay rule applies to both oral and written out-of-court statements. Don't be fooled by the word "hearsay." The rule potentially applies to all out-of-court statements, whether they are made orally or written down in a letter, business record, or other document.

The Rule Against Hearsay

In our trial system, we do not think it fair to admit into evidence statements from witnesses who are not in court, where they can be seen and cross-examined. Hence we have adopted the hearsay rule, which under certain circumstances forbids a witness from testifying, "He said…" or "She said…." (For example, see FRE 802, Cal. Evid. Code § 1200, NY Code of Evid. § 802, and Texas Civ. Rule of Evid. 802.)

For example, assume that you, Ms. Nolo, are defending yourself against a claim that you were speeding. The plaintiff calls Andrea as a witness against you. Andrea testifies, "A couple of days after the accident I talked to Mark, who saw the whole thing. He said that he saw Ms. Nolo going at a speed of at least 75 m.p.h." The plaintiff offers Andrea's testimony about what Mark said to her to prove that you were speeding.

An objection to Andrea's testimony as hearsay should be quickly sustained by any judge. Our system of justice does not consider it fair for the plaintiff to use what Mark said as evidence against you. The reason is simple: Because Mark is not in court to testify personally, you cannot cross-examine him, and the judge or jury cannot observe his demeanor and credibility. Of course, the judge or jury can observe Andrea, and you can cross-examine her. But that will do you little good. She is not claiming to have seen the accident; all she can do is repeat what Mark said.

The hearsay rule can also prevent witnesses from testifying to their own out-of-court statements. For example, assume that you are testifying on your own behalf in a case in which you are seeking to limit visitation with your child, Summer, by your ex-spouse. To prove that your ex-spouse has been neglecting Summer during weekend visits, you testify that, "Last weekend I said to my neighbor Mr. Binder that my ex-spouse always returns Summer to me with torn and dirty clothes." Your testimony as to what you said to your neighbor is inadmissible hearsay. To avoid the hearsay problem, testify to the incident itself (that Summer always arrives home with torn and dirty clothes), and do not testify to your out-of-court statement to your neighbor.

When Out-of-Court Statements Are Not Hearsay

Despite the hearsay rule, witnesses can often properly testify to out-of-court statements, because they are not always hearsay. Confused? Don't worry, so are many lawyers. The hearsay rule makes out-of-court statements improper only if they are offered as evidence that what was said is true (or, as lawyers like to put it, if they are offered "for the truth of the matter asserted"). If an out-of-court statement is relevant regardless of whether or not it is true, the statement is "nonhearsay" and admissible.

When would you want to admit an out-of-court statement if no one cares whether it's true? Let's look at some examples. First, assume that you are trying to prove that Bob was alive on March 5. As evidence of this, you call Marisa as a witness to testify, "On March 6, I heard Bob say that all sports car drivers drive too fast." Here, you are not offering Marisa's testimony for the truth of Bob's statement, so there is no need to cross-examine Bob about the statement. Regardless of whether Bob's statement about sports car drivers is true or false, we know that people who say things on March 6 were alive on March 5. Thus, you are not offering Bob's statement for its truth—that is, to prove that all sports car drivers drive too fast—so it is fair to admit Marisa's testimony as nonhearsay.

Consider a more subtle example of a non-hearsay use of an out-of-court statement. Let's go back to the negligence case involving the building contractor, Sarah Adams, who made a careless left turn and struck a pedestrian in a crosswalk. Assume that you're the pedestrian, and you have evidence that moments before she hit you, Adams got a call on her cell phone from Holden, her assistant manager. In this phone call Holden told Adams, "There's a major problem on the Jennifer Drive job. It looks like it'll set us back a few weeks. You'd better get right over there." You can offer Holden's statement to Adams into evidence as nonhearsay to prove that Adams was not paying attention to the road. It doesn't matter whether there was really a major problem on the Jennifer Drive job. What matters is that Adams thought there was when she received the call, which is likely to have distracted and upset her and made it more likely that she would drive carelessly. Lawyers refer to this type of nonhearsay use as "effect on the hearer" or "state of mind" testimony. Holden's statement is admissible as nonhearsay because of its possible effect on Adams, the hearer of the statement.

Here's another example of nonhearsay. You are involved in a child custody dispute with your ex-spouse. A neighbor of your ex-spouse tells you that when your child, 11-year-old Margaret, recently had an overnight visit with your ex-spouse, in which your ex-spouse screamed at her and said, "You are the worst little brat in the whole world. You deserve to be locked in your room for a week." You can properly call the neighbor as a witness to testify to your ex-spouse's statement. You are not offering the statement because you think it's true—that Margaret is the worst brat in the world and deserves to be locked in her room for a week. Instead, what your ex-spouse said is itself some evidence that your ex-spouse is a poor parent who should not have custody of Margaret. Thus, the neighbor's testimony is nonhearsay.

"Prior inconsistent statements" are another common example of nonhearsay. Assume that you are involved in an auto accident trial, and one of your adversary's witnesses testifies that you were driving "at least 40 m.p.h." just prior to the accident. Yet according to the report prepared by the investigating police officer, this same witness told the officer, "I didn't really see what happened before the accident." You could offer into evidence the statement the witness made to the police officer, either by asking the witness about it on cross-examination or by calling the police officer to testify that the witness made this statement. Either way, the witness's statement to the police officer is not hearsay because the conflict between the two statements casts doubt on the witness's credibility. (California and a few other jurisdictions make prior inconsistent statements admissible as an exception to the hearsay rule, making such statements admissible both to cast doubt on credibility and for their truth. See Cal. Evid. Code Sec. 1235. Federal and most state courts have a hearsay exception only for prior inconsistent statements that were made under oath, as during a deposition.)

Consider a final example. Assume that Tobias sues you for assaulting him. You admit exchanging blows with Tobias, but claim that you acted in self-defense. To help prove that you did not assault Tobias, you will testify that about a week before your fight with Tobias, you got a letter from Pat in which Pat wrote, "Tobias beat up a friend of mine yesterday." You want to testify that this letter made you afraid of Tobias, and that therefore you would not have tried to assault him. Pat's letter is admissible as nonhearsay. You are not offering it as proof that Tobias in fact hit Pat's friend, but for its effect on the hearer (you). Because the person (you) whose demeanor the judge or jury needs to observe and who Tobias needs the opportunity to cross-examine is in court, it is fair for you to testify to the content of Pat's letter. Of course, Tobias can argue that Pat's letter made you want to get in the first blow. But this possibility affects how much credence (weight) the judge or jury attaches to Pat's letter, not the question of whether the letter has a valid nonhearsay use.

At this point, the difference between hearsay and nonhearsay may seem like a semantic distinction dreamed up by a gaggle of bored judges for the sole purpose of confusing you. But if you look back at the examples of nonhearsay, you will see that it really is fair to admit out-of-court statements when they are not offered for their truth. Only when an out-of-court statement is offered because the party offering it wants the judge or jury to believe it's true does the judge or jury need an opportunity to cross-examine the maker of the statement.

As you can see, you cannot tell merely by looking at an out-of-court statement whether or not it is hearsay. You have to know what the party offering the statement is trying to prove by using it. If it is offered for its truth, it is hearsay and inadmissible in evidence— unless a hearsay exception applies. (See below.) If it is offered for a relevant purpose other than its truth, it is nonhearsay and likely to be admissible. So whenever you want to offer evidence of what someone said out of court (whether the out-of-court statement is oral or written), always consider whether you can offer it for some purpose other than its truth.

TIP

How to object to hearsay. To object to a hearsay statement offered by your adversary, say something like, "Objection, Your Honor; hearsay." Make your objection as soon as you realize that your adversary's question seeks, or the adverse witness's answer refers to, hearsay evidence, but do not make an argument as to why the evidence constitutes hearsay unless the judge asks you to do so. (See Chapter 17 for more on making objections.)

Exceptions to the Hearsay Rule

Finding a relevant nonhearsay use for an out-of-court statement is one way of making it admissible. (See Section 2, above.) You can also successfully offer a hearsay statement into evidence (that is, you can offer it for its truth) if it qualifies under one of the many exceptions to the general rule barring hearsay. Usually, exceptions apply when statements have been made under conditions that make the statements more likely to be accurate.

This section briefly reviews the most commonly used of the at least 30 to 40 hearsay exceptions that are recognized by statutes and court opinions. (Some are so obscure that you could probably try cases for 25 years and not run up against them.) For the full panoply of common hearsay

exceptions, see FRE 803–804, Cal. Evid. Code §§ 1220–1350, NY Code of Evid. §§ 802-803, and Texas Civ. Rules of Evid. 802–803, or the comparable rules in your state.

Admissions

An "admission" is legal jargon for any out-of-court statement made by your adversary that you offer into evidence. The key word here is "adversary"; you can't offer your own statements or those of others as admissions. Despite the label of admission, your adversary's statement does not have to amount to a confession of wrongdoing for you to admit it into evidence. As long as your adversary made a statement—orally, in writing, during a deposition, or pulled behind a blimp during the Super Bowl—that is relevant to the dispute, you can offer it as an admission if you think it helps your case.

For example, assume that you are suing Mr. Citron, the previous owner of your house, for fraudulently concealing the fact that the house had a leaky roof. In a conversation before the sale, Citron told a real estate broker he had previously employed, "I've never done a thing about the leaky roof, so I'd better sell the house during the summer." You can offer Citron's out-of-court statement to the broker as an admission. For instance, you may conduct the following direct examination of the real estate broker:

1 **You:**
Did you speak with Mr. Citron on February 22?

2 **Witness:**
Yes, I did.

3 You:

Was anyone else present at this conversation?

4 Witness:

No, just the two of us.

5 You:

Do you remember where the conversation took place?

6 Witness:

I remember it was in the backyard because we were talking about how warm it was for April.

7 You:

What was the purpose of the conversation?

8 Witness:

The house had been on the market for some time, and my exclusive contract period to sell it had just expired. Mr. Citron asked me to come over, and he told me that he was going to try to sell the house himself.

9 You:

Do you remember Mr. Citron saying anything about the condition of the house?

10 Witness:

I do.

11 You:

And what did he say?

12 Witness:

He said that he had never taken care of the leaky roof, so he wanted to sell the house during the coming summer months.

13 You:

How did you respond?

14 Witness:

I told him that he had never told me about the leaky roof and that what he was talking about was illegal. He just said that I should take care of my business and he'd take care of his.

Transcript Analysis: The broker's testimony in Nos. 12 and 14 about what Citron told her is hearsay, but admissible in evidence as Citron's admission. Because Citron is your adversary and you are offering into evidence a statement he made, the hearsay rule does not exclude it. Also, if you look back at No. 14, you will see that the broker testifies not only to what Citron told her but also to what she told Citron. This is in line with the general rule of "completeness"—if statements made by one party to a conversation are admissible, then so are statements made by the other party.

TIP

How to respond to your adversary's objection that an admission is improper hearsay. When you testify or ask a witness to testify to a hearsay statement that qualifies as an admission, your adversary may object that it is hearsay. (Your adversary may be attempting to harass you or may not realize that the statement is an admission.)

To respond, say something like, "Your Honor, I am offering the statement as Citron's admission." Or, wait a moment before responding; the judge may recognize that the statement is an admission and overrule the objection immediately. (See Chapter 17 for more on objections.)

Admissions by Corporations and Other Organizations

If your adversary is a corporation or similar organization, you can probably offer into evidence a statement made by an employee or other representative of the organization as an admission. For a judge to admit such a statement, you typically have to show either that the organization specifically authorized the employee to make the statement or, more simply, that the employee's statement relates to his or her job duties with the organization.

For example, assume that you sue a supermarket for injuries you suffered as a result of slipping on a banana peel on the market's floor. To prove that the supermarket carelessly allowed the dangerous condition (the banana peel on the floor) to exist, you seek to offer into evidence a statement by the store manager, who came up to you right after you slipped and said, "I'm really sorry. I asked someone to clean up this peel hours ago." The manager's statement is admissible as an admission of the defendant supermarket because the statement relates to the manager's job duties.

Present Sense Impressions

A "present sense impression" is a statement that a person makes about an event while it is going on or right after it has taken place. The exception to the hearsay rule for present sense impressions is based on the theory that statements made about ongoing events are likely to be reliable. Offering present sense impressions into evidence is often a useful way of explaining to a judge or jury the meaning of conduct that may otherwise be ambiguous.

For example, assume that you are involved in a dispute with your landlord, Patrick, about substandard and illegal conditions in your apartment house. One day you ask Alison, who is doing some work in the apartment hallways, what she is doing. She replies, "Oh, Patrick asked me to remove the fire detection devices now that the inspection has taken place." Alison's statement explains what she is doing and is admissible as a present sense impression. Without the statement, you may have difficulty proving the significance of Alison's actions to the judge or jury.

The key to showing that hearsay statements qualify as present sense impressions is to show that they were made during or very shortly after an event. For instance, assume that you spoke with Alison three days after you saw her working in the hallway of your apartment house. You asked, "What were you doing the other day?" Alison replied, "I was removing the fire detection devices because we had already been inspected." Now Alison's statement probably does not qualify as a present sense impression because it was made three days after the event, not during or right afterwards.

Some states allow present sense impressions to be admitted into evidence as exceptions to the hearsay rule only if the event described by the statement was startling or exciting. (These statements are sometimes called "excited utterances.") The evidence rule drafters in these states believe that only when people are excited are they likely to blurt out the truth, and that otherwise a present sense impression may not be sufficiently reliable. For example, assume that you have evidence that Kevin opened a door and said, "Hi, Hilary. Nice to see you. Watch your step." Kevin's statement will probably not be admissible to prove that Hilary was at the door in those states that require the events described by present sense impressions to be exciting, unless, for example, Hilary is a long-lost relative who owes Kevin $30,000.

TIP

How to respond to an objection that a present sense impression is hearsay. When you testify or ask a witness to testify to a hearsay statement that qualifies for admission into evidence as a present sense impression, your adversary may object that it is hearsay. (Your adversary may be attempting to harass you or may not realize that the statement qualifies as a present sense impression.)

To respond, say, "Your Honor, I am offering the statement as the witness's present sense impression." Or, you may wait a moment before responding; the judge may recognize that the statement is admissible and overrule the objection immediately. (See Chapter 17 for more on objections.)

Declarations of State of Mind

Statements in which people describe their then-existing emotions, physical sensations, intents, plans, and the like are admissible as exceptions to the hearsay rule. Evidence rule drafters believe that such statements, called "declarations of state of mind," are likely to be reliable.

In the colorful 19th century U.S. Supreme Court case that created this rule of evidence, there was a question of the identity of a corpse found at Cripple Creek, Colorado. One party to the lawsuit, trying to prove the body was that of a man named Walters, offered into evidence Walters's statement that, "Next week I'm going to go meet my friend Hillmon at Cripple Creek." The Court ruled that the statement was admissible as nonhearsay, reasoning that people's declarations about their future plans (their intentions) are generally reliable and should not be barred by the hearsay rule.

The state of mind exception has many applications. Here are some examples of statements that describe present thoughts or feelings and so qualify as declarations of state of mind:

- You are trying to prove that Joe's arm was broken. The fact that Joe said, "Ouch! That really hurts!" when someone touched his arm is admissible. (Note that this statement would also qualify for admission as a present sense impression.)
- You are trying to prove that a salesperson made a false statement to induce you to buy a product. The fact that the salesperson told a friend, "I'll do anything to make a sale; I really need the money," is admissible.
- You are trying to prove that you didn't start a fight with Lenny. The fact that two days before the fight you wrote to a friend, "I'm scared to death of Lenny," is admissible.

TIP

How to respond to an objection that a declaration of state of mind is hearsay. When you testify or ask a witness to testify to a hearsay statement that qualifies for admission into evidence as a declaration of state of mind, your adversary may object that it is hearsay. (Your adversary may be attempting to harass you or may not realize that the statement qualifies under the state of mind exception.)

To respond, say, "Your Honor, I am offering the statement as a declaration of the witness's state of mind." Or, you may wait a moment before responding; the judge may recognize that the statement is admissible and overrule the objection immediately. (See Chapter 17 for more on objections.)

Statements Made to a Medical Practitioner

Statements made to a medical practitioner for purposes of treatment or diagnosis are admissible as an exception to the hearsay rule. Again, the drafters of evidence rules think such statements are likely to be reliable. After all, most patients don't want the doctor taking out their gallbladder when it's their right knee that hurts!

Here are some examples:

- Some months after an automobile accident, you go to a doctor for treatment. You tell the doctor or doctor's assistant, "My back has been hurting for the last six months." Your statement is admissible under this hearsay exception. You, the doctor, the doctor's assistant, or whoever else heard you say it can testify to your statement.

- You go to see a doctor not for treatment but just so the doctor can diagnose your condition and testify as

an expert witness on your behalf at trial. The statements you make to the doctor are still admissible under this exception because it covers statements made for purposes of treatment or diagnosis.

This exception may not cover everything said to a medical practitioner. A judge might admit into evidence some of what you've said and exclude the rest. For instance, assume you tell a doctor, "My back has been hurting ever since that idiot, the defendant, ran a red light and hit me." Your statement about your back pain is admissible. But the doctor really does not have to know what you think of the defendant and the color of the light in order to treat or diagnose you, so that part of your statement will not be admitted into evidence; it is inadmissible hearsay.

> **TIP**
>
> **How to respond to an objection that a medical declaration is hearsay.** When you testify or ask a witness to testify to a hearsay statement that qualifies for admission into evidence as a declaration of a medical condition, your adversary may object that it is hearsay. (Your adversary may be attempting to harass you or may not realize that the statement qualifies under the medical declarations exception.)
>
> To respond, say, "Your Honor, I am offering the statement as a declaration made to a medical practitioner for the purpose of treatment (or diagnosis)." Or, you may wait a moment before responding; the judge may recognize that the statement is admissible and overrule the objection immediately. (See Chapter 17 for more on objections.)

Business and Government Records

Written records reflecting regular business and government activities are admissible as hearsay exceptions. You must, however, lay foundations showing that the records are reliable. (See Chapter 15.)

Other Hearsay Exceptions

We have discussed only a few of the numerous hearsay exceptions. Some others carry colorful titles such as "dying declarations" and "ancient documents." Others carry no title at all; in some court systems, judges simply have discretion to admit into evidence hearsay statements that they consider trustworthy. Again, if either you or your opponent has important evidence that consists of an out-of-court statement, and you are uncertain about whether or not it is admissible, you should probably seek legal advice as to its admissibility.

If You're Confused, You're Not Alone

If you are feeling a bit perplexed, take heart from the fact that the sometimes subtle distinctions between inadmissible hearsay statements, admissible nonhearsay statements, and hearsay statements that are admissible under an exception to the hearsay rule are often as much a mystery to lawyers as they may be to you. Do not automatically assume that a lawyer for your adversary who makes what you think is an improper hearsay objection, or offers what you think is improper hearsay evidence, understands the hearsay rule any better than you do.

Remember that the touchstone of the hearsay rule is fairness. If you think it is fair for you to offer an out-of-court statement into evidence against your adversary or unfair for your adversary to offer an out-of-court statement into evidence against you, consider offering or objecting to the statement even if you are not sure of the correct legal analysis. Whatever a state's specific evidence rules, an overall policy of modern evidence law is to depend on a judge's discretion to ensure a fair trial for both sides, in which the truth has a chance to emerge. Especially in a judge trial, a judge may discount technical concerns and make a ruling based on the trustworthiness of an out-of-court statement.

RESOURCE

Resources on Evidence. *Wigmore on Evidence*, by John Wigmore (Little Brown & Co.), is a multivolume treatise that has been revised by other authors since Wigmore's death in 1943. Deemed to be the greatest treatise ever written on any legal subject, it masterfully explores the history of and policies behind most modern rules of evidence, and its updates have case citations from every state. You should probably refer to the treatise only if you already have a basic understanding of evidence principles.

McCormick on Evidence, by John Strong, ed. (West Publishing Co.), an evidence text, is widely used by lawyers and judges.

Weinstein's Evidence Manual, by Jack Weinstein and Margaret Berger (Matthew Bender), sets forth and explains the text of each of the Federal Rules of Evidence.

Evidence, by Ken Graham (Casenotes Publishing Co.), and *Evidence*, by Steven Emanuel (Emanuel Law Outlines), are evidence outlines designed as quick refreshers for law students. They are usually available in law bookstores near law schools. ●

Making and Responding to Objections

An objection is a request to a judge to rule that an adversary's statement or offer of evidence is improper under the rules of evidence. If the judge grants the request (sustains the objection), the improper evidence or statement will be excluded. Neither the judge nor a jury may then consider it when arriving at its verdict. This chapter shows you how to make and respond to objections. It also includes a list of common objections, which you can take with you into the courtroom and use during the trial.

You can make an objection at any point during a trial. For example, you can object to a statement made by your adversary during an opening statement or closing argument, to a question asked by your adversary during direct or cross-examination, or to an adverse witness's answer.

Nonetheless, in general you will be wise to follow a practice of many experienced attorneys: Do not object just because you believe that a technical evidence rule violation has occurred. Save your objections for evidence that you really want to exclude. Even if a judge sustains your objection, often your adversary can get the evidence admitted anyway simply by rephrasing an improper question or answer. Also, as a party representing yourself, you are likely to come off second best if you turn your trial into a war of objections against your adversary's lawyer. So unless you think that the evidence your adversary is attempting to offer is important and should be excluded from evidence altogether, an objection may serve only to slow down your trial and incur the wrath of the judge or jury. Hollywood images notwithstanding, attorneys often manage to try entire cases with few or no objections.

CAUTION

Evidence rules are covered in other chapters. This chapter focuses on the procedures for making and responding to objections. Please refer to other chapters for discussions of the evidence rules on which objections are based.

Overview of Objections

Many people believe that a judge plays a role similar to that of a football referee—that is, making sure that the "game" of trial is played according to the rules, in this case rules of evidence. If so, it may seem strange to you that you have to object at all. After all, referees call penalties on their own whenever a rule is violated; they do not wait for one team to object to something the other team has done.

But at trial, it's your responsibility to object to important impermissible evidence or statements. If you fail to object, you waive (give up) the objection, and the judge or jury may consider the impermissible information along with the rest of the evidence in arriving at its verdict.

Unfortunately, this system really works well only when both sides are represented by skilled trial lawyers. It may be less satisfactory when one side is self-represented and doesn't (and can't reasonably be expected to) have in-depth knowledge of evidence rules. Fortunately, many judges understand this unfairness and will exclude obviously improper evidence on their own. But others will not, perhaps believing that being at a disadvantage serves you right for not hiring a lawyer. (Of course, many lawyers aren't exactly experts on the rules of evidence either.)

Typically, objections are made orally and refer to the rule of evidence that a party believes has been violated. For example, if your adversary asks a witness to testify to an out-of-court statement, you might say, "Objection, Your Honor; hearsay."

Normally, a judge makes an immediate ruling in response to an objection. If the judge thinks that the objection is erroneous —that is, that the offered evidence or statement is proper—the judge will overrule (deny) the objection. If the judge thinks that the objection is correct, the judge will sustain (uphold) it.

Objections Made Before Trial: Motions in Limine

A Motion in Limine (rhymes with "Jiminy") is Latin legal jargon for an objection you make before trial starts. You may choose to make a Motion in Limine when you believe that important evidence your adversary plans to offer during trial is not admissible. However, you are not required to make a Motion in Limine; you always have the option of waiting until your adversary offers the evidence at trial and making your objection at that time.

Why bother to make a Motion in Limine if you can object during trial? Two good reasons. First, you can plan more effectively if you know before your trial starts whether a judge will allow your adversary to offer a particular item of important evidence.

Second, if you wait to object until your adversary offers evidence, the jury may well hear some or all of it before you can object. Even if the judge sustains your objection, excludes the evidence, and instructs the

jury to disregard it, some jurors may still be influenced by it. Far better to exclude evidence in advance. This explains why Motions in Limine are primarily made only in jury trials. In judge-tried cases, the judge will hear about the disputed evidence anyway in order to rule on its admissibility.

To make a Motion in Limine, typically all you have to do is notify your adversary and the court clerk, or the judge during a pretrial conference, that you want to make a Motion in Limine. If the judge agrees to hear the motion (the judge might refuse and ask you to raise the point during trial), the judge will conduct a short hearing on your objection before trial starts. During the hearing, orally tell the judge what evidence the adversary plans to offer and why you think it's improper. Your adversary will, of course, have a chance to respond to your argument.

 CAUTION

Check your local court rules. Read your local court rules carefully for procedures that you must follow to make a Motion in Limine. For example, you may have to give your adversary ten days' notice (perhaps in writing) of your intention to make a motion. And some judges may require you to submit your Motion in Limine in writing. (For general information on pretrial motions, see Chapter 7.)

The judge may rule on your Motion in Limine on the spot or may postpone a decision by asking you to renew your objection when the evidence is actually offered. By delaying a ruling, the judge has a chance to evaluate how important or prejudicial the evidence is. Nevertheless, even if the judge postpones a ruling, your motion will not be wasted effort. The fact that you have brought the judge's attention to the problematic evidence early and in an organized way is likely to encourage the judge to think more seriously about excluding the evidence than if you first raise the point during trial.

Motions in Limine made by attorneys are sometimes submitted in the form of written arguments that lawyers call "briefs" (though their long-winded complexity often makes them just the opposite). Like an oral motion, a brief identifies the evidence that the lawyer seeks to have excluded and the grounds for objection. In addition, a written brief may include references (citations) to supporting legal authorities such as statutes and cases.

You, too, may find it sensible to do a little research and to present a written brief in support of your Motion in Limine. The sample below illustrates what a simple written brief in support of a Motion in Limine may consist of. (As with other sample documents in this book, this one is for illustration purposes only. The motion you file could look very different, depending on your state's law and rules of procedure.)

Using a Motion in Limine Affirmatively

In theory, you can also use a Motion in Limine to ask a judge for an advance ruling that evidence you plan to offer is admissible. But generally you should not do this. The motion may act as a red flag that admissibility of the evidence is in doubt. Put the burden on your adversary to object if the adversary thinks it's warranted.

Making Objections During Trial

As with so many things in life, success at making objections depends not only on what you say but also on how and when you say it. Or in the words attributed to Albert Einstein, "God is in the details." Follow these procedures:

Stand Up

When you make or respond to objections, stand up as a sign of respect to the court. You can begin speaking as you rise.

Speak Only to the Judge

Always state your objection directly to the judge rather than to opposing counsel or your adversary. If you want to talk directly to your adversary, ask the judge for permission to go "off the record."

State Your Objection Succinctly

To object, it is normally sufficient to refer briefly to the reason (legal basis) for the objection. For example, you might say, "Objection, Your Honor; hearsay," or "Objection, Your Honor; irrelevant."

When you object to only a portion of a statement, a question, or an answer, specify the portion to which you object. For example, if your adversary asks a proper question and the witness refers to an improper hearsay statement while answering, you may say something like, "Objection to the portion of the answer in which the witness referred to what Mr. Moore said; hearsay." If the judge sustains your objection, you should also ask the judge

Sample Motion in Limine

1   Fred Nolo
     [Street Address]
2   [City, State, Zip Code]
     [Phone Number]
3
4   Plaintiff in Pro Per

5

6

7   THE _____ COURT OF _____ COUNTY

8   STATE OF _____

9

10   Fred Nolo,   )
)   Case No. 12345
11   Plaintiff,   )
)   PLAINTIFF'S MOTION IN LIMINE
12   v.   )
)
13   Sarah Adams,   )
)
14   Defendant.   )
     _____)
15

16

17   Plaintiff Nolo submits this Motion in Limine for an order excluding from evidence Plaintiff's three-

18   year-old conviction for reckless driving.

19   Statement of the Case

20   Plaintiff Nolo has filed suit against Defendant Binder for careless driving resulting in both personal

21   injuries to Plaintiff and property damage to Plaintiff's car. Defendant claims that Plaintiff's careless

22   driving caused the accident. As part of the Defendant's proof that Plaintiff drove carelessly, Defendant

23   has indicated that she intends to offer into evidence a record of Plaintiff's three-year-old conviction for

24   reckless driving.

25   Argument

26   Plaintiff's conviction cannot properly be admitted into evidence. This is a civil case governed by the

27   laws of the State of California, and California Evidence Code § 1101 provides that character evidence

28

                                             -1-

Sample Motion in Limine (continued)

1   is not admissible in a civil case to prove conduct. Plaintiff's prior conviction would be character

2   evidence, as its only purpose is to prove that Plaintiff has a propensity to drive carelessly and therefore

3   was driving carelessly when Plaintiff collided with Defendant Binder. Therefore, the conviction should

4   not be admitted into evidence.

5

6

7   Respectively submitted,

8   *Fred Nolo*

                       Fred Nolo, Plaintiff in Pro Per

9

10

11

12

13

14

15

16

17

18

19

20

21

22

23

24

25

26

27

28

to delete (strike) the improper testimony from the record. (See "Ask to Strike Improper Evidence," below.)

Object Promptly

If your adversary's question calls for improper evidence, object immediately after the question—before the answer if you can. If you wait until after the witness answers to object, the judge or jury may hear improper information. More importantly, the judge may refuse to sustain your objection because it is untimely or because by waiting you are deemed to have waived the objection. Similarly, if a question is proper but an adverse witness throws improper evidence into the answer, object immediately after (or even during) the answer and before another question is asked.

> **TIP**
>
> **Don't be overly polite—interrupt to object when necessary.** If an adverse witness's improper answer is longer than a sentence or two, you do not have to wait until the witness is done talking but can interrupt the answer to object to improper evidence. Try not to "talk over" the witness; the judge and especially the court reporter are likely to become quite testy if you and a witness are both talking at once. Instead, say "Excuse me" and perhaps hold up your hand to stop the witness in mid-answer, then make your objection.

Consider this example of a late objection during your adversary's direct examination of a witness:

1 **Adversary:**

What's the next thing that happened?

2 **Witness:**

Well, just like she had done many times before, Ms. Nolo [you] *began drinking a bottle of beer.*

3 **Adversary:**

How much beer did Ms. Nolo drink this time?

4 **You:**

Objection to the testimony that I had done this many times before. That's irrelevant.

This ground for objection is discussed in Chapter 16.

5 **Judge:**

I agree with your objection, Ms. Nolo. But you should have made that objection before counsel asked the next question. I'll overrule the objection as untimely.

Transcript Analysis: In this example, opposing counsel's question (No. 1) is proper, but the answer that introduces prior drinking (No. 2) refers to evidence that you think is improper. Your objection should have come immediately after the answer, before your adversary asked another question.

A judge has discretion about how rigidly to enforce the rule that you must object as soon as the ground for objection appears, and a more sympathetic judge may treat you more leniently. Consider this example:

1 **Adversary:**

What did the person standing next to you say?

2 **Witness:**

He said that the blue car ran the red light.

3 **You:**

Objection; hearsay.

This ground of objection is discussed in Chapter 16.

4 **Judge:**

Mr. Nolo, you really should have objected before the witness answered, as it was apparent that the question called for hearsay. But I'll overlook that this time and sustain the objection. The answer is stricken, and I instruct the jury to disregard it.

Don't Argue the Merits of Your Objection

Do not include in your objection an argument about why the judge should sustain it. Here's an example of how *not* to object to a witness's answer:

Your Honor, I object to that entire answer as irrelevant. This is a case about what happened on April 24. The witness is talking about things that took place three months earlier, and that has nothing to do with what we're talking about now.

This is called arguing an objection, and it is improper. State an objection concisely: "Objection; irrelevant." A judge who wants an explanation will ask for one. In that case, an explanation like the one above would be proper.

Ask to Strike Improper Evidence

Ask the judge to strike any improper testimony given or statements made before your objection was made and sustained. By striking (removing) improper evidence or statements from the official record, the judge indicates that the evidence can't be considered by the judge or jury when arriving at a decision.

Requests to strike improper testimony are necessary because, as you've seen, it's not always possible to object before objectionable testimony is given. For example, if the opposing attorney asks a proper question but the witness gives improper testimony while answering, you cannot possibly object until the improper testimony has already been given.

A judge who sustains your objection to testimony that has already been given may strike the answer without being asked. However, if the judge neglects to do this, it's up to you to request that the improper testimony be stricken by saying something like, "Your Honor, I also move to strike the answer."

If there is a jury, you should also ask the judge to instruct the jury to disregard the stricken testimony. Unless the judge instructs the jury to disregard it, the jury can properly consider even stricken testimony when arriving at a decision.

TIP

You can't unring a bell. Whenever possible, try to keep a jury from hearing improper evidence in the first place. Just like telling someone not to think about pink elephants may make the person think of nothing else, so a judge's instruction to disregard stricken evidence is easier said than done. Or as lawyers are fond of saying, you can't unring a bell. This human weakness is a primary reason to consider making a Motion in Limine before trial.

Here is an example of how to follow up an objection with a motion to strike testimony:

1   **Adversary:**

After the blue car completed making the left turn, what happened?

2   **Witness:**

It started swerving back and forth, like the driver had had too much to drink.

3   **You:**

Objection to "too much to drink," Your Honor. Lack of personal knowledge and an improper opinion.

(The first ground of objection is discussed in Chapter 12 and the second in Chapter 16.)

4   **Judge:**

Objection sustained.

5   **You:**

I move to strike the testimony and ask that you instruct the jury to disregard it.

6   **Judge:**

The motion to strike is granted. Jurors, the witness's remark about drinking was improper, and I instruct you to disregard it.

Transcript Analysis: Here, you properly specify the portion of the answer to which you object (No. 3). At your request, the judge strikes that portion and instructs the jury to disregard it.

TIP

Don't thank a judge for sustaining your objection. Like a baseball umpire calling a strike, a judge is doing the job—not doing you a favor—by sustaining your objection. Many toadying lawyers ignore this advice and thank the judge early and often; most judges hate it.

CAUTION

You may be unable to object to deposition testimony. The judge may give your adversary permission to read a portion of a witness's deposition into the trial record. Often, you can only object to deposition testimony at trial if you objected to it during the deposition. See Chapter 5.

Object Only When Absolutely Necessary

As mentioned at the beginning of this chapter, if evidence to which you object is unimportant, or if your adversary can get around your objection by simply rephrasing a question or an answer, your repeated objections may succeed only in depriving you of whatever empathy the judge or jury may feel toward you. Use this chapter to learn the mechanics of objecting, but remember that your goal is to object as infrequently as possible, especially in a judge trial.

Responding to Your Adversary's Objections

Of course, you are not the only one playing the game called trial. The opposing attorney (or your self-represented adversary) can object to a statement you make, a question you ask, or testimony you or one of your witnesses gives. That means you also need to understand how to respond to objections.

Harassment by Your Adversary's Lawyer

As radio therapists remind us regularly, you can control only your own behavior. Your sensible reluctance to make objections may not be reciprocated by your adversary. Particularly in a jury trial, the adversary's attorney may try to take advantage of your "new kid in court" status by sending a barrage of objections your way, no doubt trying to intimidate you. If this happens, your best bet is to ask the judge for permission to approach the bench or to have a conference in chambers (the judge's office). Ask the judge for the court reporter to be present and to take down what's said so that the official record will show that you sought the judge's help. Tell the judge that the attorney is using the rules of evidence improperly to try to harass and intimidate you and to prevent you from getting a fair trial. Ask the judge to warn the attorney that repeatedly trying to invoke technicalities to thwart the larger purpose of achieving a fair trial won't be tolerated.

In addition, during your final argument, you may use your adversary's unfair tactics to try to gain the judge or jury's understanding. Point out that while you are not familiar with all the technical rules of evidence, you have done your best to present your case fairly and honestly and, unlike your adversary, did not try to hide behind a smoke screen of objections.

TIP

Abusive lawyering is less likely to occur during a judge trial. Compared to jury trials, in which judges tend to enforce evidence rules more strictly, in judge trials, a judge is less likely to put up with numerous technical objections. A judge may even regard repeated objections as interfering with the judge's authority to decide what evidence to listen to. It's another reason why, as a self-represented party, you are usually better off with a judge than a jury trial. (See Chapter 10.)

Making a Counterargument

The first rule in responding to an objection is to wait: Do not immediately follow an adversary's objection by arguing why the judge should overrule it. Instead, wait for the judge to either make a ruling or ask you to respond. In most cases, a judge will rule without asking for your position. Here's an example of the procedure you should follow:

1 You:
And after you saw the two cars collide, what happened?

2 Witness:
I remember this person standing right next to me said, "My God, that red car went right through the stoplight."

3 Adversary:
Objection; hearsay.

4 Judge:
Ms. Nolo, any response?

5 You:
Yes, Your Honor. I think that what the witness heard this person say is

admissible as a present sense impression made in response to a startling event. The person saw two cars collide, so that's an exciting event, and he made a statement about what he saw right away.

(See Chapter 16 for a discussion of this evidence rule.)

6 Judge:

All right, I'll overrule the objection and allow the testimony.

7 You:

Thank you, Your Honor.

8 Judge:

What's that, Ms. Nolo? Didn't you read the earlier section of this book telling you not to thank the judge after a favorable ruling?

9 You:

Oh right, sorry. I'll move on. Now, after…

Transcript Analysis: In this excerpt, you properly wait for the judge to ask you to respond (No. 4) before telling the judge why you think the evidence should be admitted (No. 5). (And, in case you missed it again, do not thank the judge for doing his or her job.)

TIP

If you believe that a judge's ruling is clearly wrong, ask the judge to reconsider. When a judge follows the typical practice of making a ruling without giving you a chance to respond to your adversary's objection, you may ask for an opportunity to change the judge's mind if you are confident that you have a sound legal reason for thinking that the judge wrongly sustained the adversary's objection. Because the judge has already made a ruling, you first have to ask the judge for permission to talk about it.

For example, if the judge has sustained your adversary's objection that your evidence is irrelevant, you may say something like, "Your Honor, might I speak briefly as to why I think the evidence is relevant?" If the judge denies permission, that ends the matter. You have no right to argue evidence rulings. If the judge grants permission, you may then try to persuade the judge to change the ruling. And, unlike baseball umpires, judges sometimes do reverse their rulings when an argument sheds additional light on the purpose of evidence. Nevertheless, it's just plain dumb to repeatedly challenge a judge's rulings. Save your fire for when it really counts.

Laying a Better Foundation

When your adversary objects, it will probably often be on the ground that you have failed to lay a sufficient foundation for evidence to be admissible. (See Chapters 5 and 12 for additional discussions of laying a foundation.) If the judge is uncertain about whether a foundation is sufficient or simply wants to hear more foundational testimony to see what you are driving at, the judge may delay a ruling on the objection and let you lay a further foundation.

For example, assume that after your adversary objects to the out-of-court statement about the red car going through the stoplight (No. 5 above), the following dialogue takes place:

6 Judge:

Well, you may be right that the statement qualifies as a present sense impression, Ms. Nolo. But before I make that ruling,

I'd like to hear additional foundational testimony.

(See Chapter 16 for more information about this hearsay exception.)

7   You:

What would that be, Your Honor?

8   Judge:

Well, it's really not my job to tell you the rules. But as you're representing yourself, I'll tell you that, before I rule, I want to be satisfied that the person's statement really was blurted out in the excitement of the moment, which this state requires for a present sense impression to be admissible. Can you ask some questions that might satisfy me about that?

9   You:

I'll try, Your Honor. [Turning to witness] Mr. Grady, how far away from you was this person standing?

10   Witness:

Oh, not more than a few feet. He was as close to the collision as I was.

11   You:

How long had he been standing there, if you know?

12   Witness:

Well, we both came out of the store the same time, so he'd been there the same amount of time as me, about 30 seconds.

13   You:

And how long after the cars collided did you hear him say that the red car ran the stoplight?

14   Adversary:

Objection, Your Honor; leading.

15   Judge:

Overruled. The witness has already testified to what the person said [see No. 2 in the previous section]; Ms. Nolo is simply seeking to establish the time framework. Please refrain from meaningless objections.

16   Witness:

I'd say just a second or two. It was right away.

17   You:

That's all the questions I can think of, Your Honor.

18   Judge:

Let me ask one or two. What tone of voice did this person use?

19   Witness:

He really shouted. He made my ears hurt.

20   Judge:

And where did he go after he said this?

21   Witness:

I'm not really sure. I ran over to see if the drivers were okay, and I didn't see him again.

22   Judge:

Well, the issue is a close one, but on balance I think that there's enough of a foundation to admit this as an exception to the hearsay rule on the ground that it qualifies as a present sense impression. The objection is overruled. Ms. Nolo, you may resume questioning.

TIP

There's no harm in asking. As we have emphasized throughout this book, a judge is a human being who, within the limits set by the adversary system, may be willing to help you cope with the nuances of technical evidentiary rules. So if you are not sure of what foundation the judge has in mind, do not be too embarrassed to ask. The judge, you hope, wants to have the benefit of considering all proper evidence before making a decision and may suggest the kind of foundational testimony you need to elicit.

Checklist of Common Objections

Making objections is obviously a demanding task. In about the same tiny interval that it takes the average cab driver to honk a horn when a light changes from red to green, you have to decide not only whether to object but also what objection to make. The following checklist of common objections should help, especially if yours is a jury trial where it often makes sense to object to inadmissible evidence.

Objections to the Form of Questions

An objection to the form of a question—for example, on the ground that it is leading—asserts that a question is improper. However, an objection to form does not challenge the admissibility of the information the questioner is trying to elicit. So even if the judge sustains the objection, the questioner can ordinarily elicit the information simply by rephrasing the question.

Object with caution when it comes to form-of-question objections: Do not make them unless a question is so poorly phrased that you are not sure of what the witness

will say in response, or your adversary is attempting to browbeat a reluctant witness into giving your adversary's desired testimony.

Here are common objections to the form of a question:

"Objection; the question is vague [or ambiguous or unintelligible]."

You may object on this ground when you are unsure what a question means. Questions should be clear enough so that you can reasonably determine in advance what information a witness is being asked to give.

If your adversary makes this objection to you—that your question is vague or unintelligible—and the judge sustains it, think about the specific information you are after and rephrase your question.

"Objection; the question is compound."

You can object on this ground when opposing counsel combines two questions into one, leaving you unsure which part the witness will answer. For example, say your adversary asks a witness, "What time did he arrive, and what did he do when he got there?" But again, especially if there is no jury and the question is not otherwise improper, you are probably better off not making this kind of technical objection.

If the judge sustains an objection by adversary that your question is compound, break up the single question into two different questions.

"Objection; the question calls for a narrative response."

You can object on this ground when opposing counsel's direct examination question asks a witness to narrate a series of events. (See Chapter 12 for a discussion of narrative questions.) Also, if an adverse witness starts into a lengthy narrative response to a proper narrow question, stop the witness in mid-answer and state, "Objection. The witness is narrating."

If the judge sustains an objection by your adversary that your question calls for a narrative response, ask a question with a more limited scope.

"Objection; the question is repetitive (or has been asked and answered)."

An opposing attorney may try to take advantage of you by trying to hit the judge or jury over the head repeatedly with the same information. This is improper because it wastes time and artificially boosts the importance of evidence. You may object on this ground when opposing counsel persists in asking questions about information a witness has already given.

If the judge sustains an objection by your adversary that your question has been asked and answered, move on to a new topic.

"Objection; counsel is misquoting the witness."

You may object on this ground when opposing counsel misstates testimony that has already been given. This problem typically arises during cross-examination, when the proper use of leading questions allows your adversary to refer to evidence in a question. (See Chapter 13.)

For example, assume that a witness who testified for you stated that "the red car was going at least 60 m.p.h." On cross-examination, opposing counsel asks, "Now,

you said that the red car was going pretty fast, right?" This question misquotes the witness's actual testimony: The witness said "at least 60 m.p.h.," not "pretty fast."

If the judge sustains an objection by your adversary that your question misquotes a witness, rephrase your question if you are able to recall the witness's actual testimony. If you cannot recall the actual testimony and want to refer to it, you may ask the judge to ask the court reporter to read back the previous testimony. However, the judge may not grant your request, especially if considerable time has elapsed since the answer was given. A third possibility is not to refer to the previous testimony in your question, but to ask the witness to repeat what was said earlier.

"Objection; the question is leading."

Consider objecting on this ground when opposing counsel asks an improper leading question during direct examination, especially if the witness seems reluctant to give your adversary's desired answer unless verbally bullied into doing so. This can be an important objection, because under some circumstances your judge may not allow your adversary to rephrase so as to elicit the evidence with a proper question. If the judge believes that your adversary is overtly trying to put words in the witness's mouth, the judge may not only sustain your objection but also forbid any testimony on the same subject from that witness.

If the judge sustains an objection by your adversary that your question is leading, rephrase it in a way that does not suggest your desired answer. Or, if the judge allows you to respond to the objection, perhaps point out that your leading question is proper because the information you seek to elicit is background or preliminary. (See Chapter 12 for a discussion of when leading questions are proper during direct examination.)

"Objection; the question is argumentative."

You can object on this ground when opposing counsel cross-examines your witness in a hostile or angry way or asks a question before you or your witness has completed the answer to a previous question. (In movies and TV shows, this practice is often referred to as "badgering the witness.")

For example, assume that opposing counsel asks you or your witness, "So, you're willing to perjure yourself?" or "You couldn't possibly have done what you've said you did, could you?" These questions do not ask a witness to provide evidence. Instead, they amount to your adversary making an argument in question form.

If the judge sustains an objection by your adversary that your question is argumentative, rephrase the question so as to elicit evidence rather than state your point of view.

"Objection; the question assumes facts not in evidence."

You can object on this ground when opposing counsel surreptitiously tries to insert new evidence into the record while asking for other information.

For example, assume that you are a tenant in an eviction case and that there has been no evidence admitted about complaints from other tenants concerning your supposedly loud stereo. The landlord's attorney asks you this question: "Ms. Nolo, even after numerous other tenants complained to you about your loud stereo, didn't you say to the landlord that she had no right to tell you how to live your life?" Here, the question asks only about a statement you may have made to the landlord. The material about other tenants' alleged complaints is improperly inserted into the trial without giving you a chance to deny that there were any such complaints. As you may guess, this ground of objection is more important in a jury than a judge trial because you can expect a judge to disregard this sort of unsubstantiated remark.

If the judge sustains an objection by your adversary that your question assumes facts not in evidence, make the portion of the question that assumes facts into a separate question. If you were the landlord in the cross-examination sample above, for instance, you could properly have asked, "Didn't you receive complaints from other tenants about playing your stereo too loudly?"

Objections to the Content of Testimony

Unlike form objections, content objections assert your belief that the information opposing counsel seeks is inadmissible no matter what type of question is asked. Because most of these grounds for objection have already been discussed in earlier chapters, we discuss them here only briefly.

"Objection; lack of personal knowledge."

You may object on this ground when an adverse witness has not personally seen, heard, or otherwise acquired firsthand information about what the witness is testifying about. Clues that a witness lacks personal knowledge are in introductory phrases like, "It later came to my attention that…," "I later found out that…," "I'd guess that what happened is…," and "My best estimate is…."

If the judge sustains an objection by your adversary that your witness lacks personal knowledge, ask the judge for permission to ask additional questions to lay a foundation showing that the witness is testifying from personal knowledge. (See Chapter 12 for a discussion of the requirement of personal knowledge.)

"Objection; speculation (or improper opinion)."

You can object on this ground when an adverse witness testifies to matters that are hypothetical, beyond the witness's powers of observation, or contain impermissible legal judgments. Often, a lack of personal knowledge objection is equally correct in these situations.

Here are some examples of improper speculative testimony:

- A witness testifies, "Nelson intended to mislead me into buying the defective car." Instead, the witness must testify to Nelson's words and deeds, leaving it to the judge or jury to determine what Nelson intended.
- A witness gives an improper opinion, such as, "If there had been any truth to the rumor, I would have known about it." In most circumstances, a witness can testify only to what did happen and what he or she does know.
- A witness testifies to a legal judgment, such as, "Bryant was negligent." Again, a witness has to describe

factual circumstances and leave it to the judge or jury to determine their legal consequences.

If the judge sustains an objection by your adversary that your question is speculative or calls for an improper opinion, ask questions that elicit factual details about which the witness has personal knowledge. (For more examples and an explanation of the opinion rule, see Chapter 16.)

"Objection; hearsay."

Object on this ground when an adverse witness testifies to hearsay, which is an out-of-court statement offered for its truth.

If the judge sustains an objection by your adversary that your question calls for hearsay, consider whether you can respond that the statement is admissible as an exception to the hearsay rule or as nonhearsay. (See Chapter 16 for a discussion of the hearsay rule.)

"Objection; irrelevant."

Object on this ground when you believe that the adversary's evidence has no logical connection to the claims that either party is trying to prove or disprove.

If the judge sustains an objection by your adversary that the information you seek is irrelevant, move on to a new topic. (See Chapter 16 for a discussion of the relevance rule.)

"Objection; the value (or probative value) of this evidence is outweighed by the unfair prejudice it will cause."

Object on this ground when you recognize that the adversary's evidence is relevant, but think that its slight relevance is outweighed by the likelihood of unfair prejudice to you.

For example, assume that an adverse witness is describing your car as the one involved in an automobile accident. The witness is about to mention that, among a number of things she remembers about your car, it had a bumper sticker identifying you as a fan of a rock group that many people believe promotes antisocial behavior. You may object on this ground to prevent the witness from mentioning the bumper sticker. It has slight relevance to prove the identity of your car, and is likely to cause you to suffer unfair prejudice.

💡 **TIP**

Make a Motion in Limine. Unfairly prejudicial evidence typically consists of gruesome photographs, improper character evidence, and the like. Often, you will know or suspect that your adversary plans to offer such evidence before trial, so, in a jury trial, you should strongly consider making a Motion in Limine.

If the judge sustains an objection by your adversary that the probative value of your evidence is outweighed by its likely prejudicial effect, move on to a new topic. (Chapter 16 covers the unfair prejudice rule.)

"Objection; lack of foundation."

Object on this ground when opposing counsel has failed to elicit a proper foundation for evidence. This is a catch-all objection, because all evidence, whether it is oral or written, must be supported by some type of foundation. For instance, if a witness lacks personal knowledge or if there is insufficient evidence to show that a business record is reliable or that a photograph fairly and accurately represents what a witness actually saw, you may object based on lack of foundation. This can also be an important objection because your adversary may be unable to supply the missing foundational evidence—which means the evidence won't be admitted at all. (See Chapters 12 and 15 for more about foundational requirements.)

Because it is a catch-all, you may be uncertain about what's missing if the judge sustains an objection by your adversary that your evidence lacks foundation. If so, you may need to ask the judge for help. Say something like, "Your Honor, I'm not really sure what foundational evidence is missing. Might you or opposing counsel tell me what evidence I need to introduce to lay a proper foundation?" If the judge sympathetically accedes to your request, ask additional foundational questions. (Note that, as suggested above, you ask the judge to ask opposing counsel to tell you what foundation is missing; don't ask opposing counsel directly.)

"Objection; cumulative."

Object on this ground when your adversary calls a number of witnesses to testify to the same point. For example, you may object if your adversary is a home buyer who bought a house from you, claims that you concealed the fact that it had a leaky roof, and attempts to call five witnesses to testify that, on one particular day, the roof leaked.

If the judge sustains an objection by your adversary that your evidence is cumulative, move on to a new topic. Alternatively, you might ask the adversary to stipulate (agree) that if your additional witness were called and sworn, they would all testify that, for example, "On September 22, the roof leaked."

"Objection; improper character evidence."

Object on this ground when your adversary offers character evidence. Character evidence suggests that you have a propensity to engage in conduct associated with a particular character trait, and it is almost never admissible in civil cases. (See Chapter 16 for a discussion of character evidence.)

If the judge sustains an objection by your adversary that your question seeks improper character evidence, move on to a new topic.

RESOURCE

Resources on objections.
Transcript Exercises for Learning Evidence, by Paul Bergman (West Publishing Co.), consists of brief explanations of many of the rules of evidence and 19 sample transcripts in a variety of civil and criminal case examples. Various questions, answers, and judicial rulings within the transcripts are numbered; your task is to decide the legal propriety of each numbered transcript portion. An appendix gives the correct responses.

The following books discuss trial advocacy generally but have specific explanations and examples of the objections process:

Trial Advocacy in a Nutshell by Paul Bergman (West Publishing Co.).

Fundamentals of Trial Techniques by Thomas Mauet (Little, Brown & Co.).

Trial by Roger Haydock and John Sonsteng (West Publishing Co.).

Common Objections

Objections to the Form of Questions

a. "Objection; the question is vague (or ambiguous or unintelligible)."

b. "Objection; the question is compound."

c. "Objection; the question calls for a narrative response."

d. "Objection; the question is repetitive (or has been asked and answered)."

e. "Objection; counsel is misquoting the witness."

f. "Objection; the question is leading."

g. "Objection; the question is argumentative."

h. "Objection; the question assumes facts not in evidence."

Objections to the Content of Testimony

a. "Objection; lack of personal knowledge."

b. "Objection; speculation (or improper opinion)."

c. "Objection; hearsay."

d. "Objection; irrelevant."

e. "Objection; the value (or probative value) of this evidence is outweighed by the unfair prejudice it will cause."

f. "Objection; lack of foundation."

g. "Objection; cumulative."

h. "Objection; improper character evidence."

TRIAL NOTEBOOK

Make a copy of the list of common objections. Place it in your trial notebook so you can refer to it throughout trial. (See Chapter 18.) ●

Organizing a Trial Notebook

Organizing key documents and trial preparation outlines into a trial notebook can help you present your case effectively and persuasively. At trial, you want to make sure that you introduce all your planned evidence and exhibits and that you tie them to the facts you are trying to prove or disprove. By making a trial notebook, you will have the documents that can help you do this close at hand. For example, you can refer to a direct examination outline when you question a witness and to your closing argument outline when you present your final argument.

This chapter reviews the documents that you are likely to need in your trial notebook and suggests a way to organize them efficiently.

Setting Up Your Notebook

A typical trial notebook is an ordinary three-ring binder in which documents are grouped and separated by index tabs. Be sure to buy a set of index tabs that are easy to write on or otherwise customize, and put a good supply of blank three-hole paper into the binder. You may also want to have a three-hole punch handy in case you need to punch holes in documents you want to have in the notebook.

CAUTION

Never punch holes in materials you will offer as evidence. Never alter originals of documents that you plan to offer into evidence. Keep them in a manila envelope or accordion file separate from your trial notebook. (You may have to keep larger exhibits, such as a piece of defective machinery or an article of clothing, in a bag or a box.) However, you may place copies of each original in the notebook to give to the judge, opposing counsel, and the jury.

Now let's look at what you should place into your trial notebook.

Index Tab 1: Legal Pleadings

The pleadings (the complaint and the answer) should be in your notebook because they form the legal backdrop of the trial. Unless a judge allows you or your adversary to slightly change the theory set forth in a complaint or answer to match the evidence presented at trial (this is called "conforming a pleading according to proof"), the pleadings control such matters as which facts each party can prove or disprove and the relevance of evidence. You can punch holes in your copies of the pleadings because the originals will already be in the court's file.

Your judge may issue a pretrial order (which you, your adversary, or the judge will prepare) following a conference with you and your adversary. (See Chapter 7.) A pretrial order is essentially a trial plan that supersedes the pleadings and identifies the facts each party may prove or disprove, as well as each party's witnesses and exhibits. (See FRCP 16.) If your judge issues a pretrial order, include it in this section of your notebook.

> **TIP**
>
> **You probably don't need to include pretrial motion documents in your notebook.** Usually, issues that give rise to pretrial motions are disposed of before the start of trial. (Motions in Limine are a common exception; see Chapter 17.) You will probably not have to refer to the pretrial motion papers during trial, so you needn't include them in the notebook.

Index Tab 2: Discovery Materials

Discovery is the formal process parties use to uncover evidence before trial. As a self-represented party, the discovery devices you are most likely to encounter are depositions, interrogatories, and requests for admission. (See Chapter 5.)

If you use formal discovery procedures, you might want to include the information you get, inserting it "as is" into your notebook. In most cases, however, even a short deposition or a single set of interrogatory answers is likely to be too unwieldy for you to refer to quickly in the middle of trial. Instead, make summaries of the important information in your adversary's responses and put the summaries in your notebook. Include in the summary a reference to the specific page or interrogatory number where the important information appears in the original.

For example, a portion of your summary of a deposition you took of a witness named Prager might look like the one shown below.

Summary of Prager Deposition

....

9. Jack fell down and broke his crown and Jill came tumbling after. (p. 24, lines 11–22)
10. Jack waited two days before going to see a dentist to repair his broken crown. (p. 25, lines 25–28)

A portion of your summary of the answers you received in response to written interrogatories might look like this:

Summary of Berkowitz Co. Answers to Interrogatories

....

5. The person at Berkowitz Co. who inspected the car stereos before they were shipped is Stella Ong. (answer to Interrog. 4)
6. Ong's inspection consists of testing the AM/FM switch on each radio. (answer to Interrog. 5)

If you prepare summaries, you can keep the original discovery documents in your case file—which you also need to bring to court with you. Then, if you need information from a discovery document during trial (perhaps to impeach a witness with a prior inconsistent statement; see Chapter 13), you can refer to the summary in your notebook to find the exact whereabouts of the information.

Index Tab 3: Legal Claim Outline

Whether you are a plaintiff or a defendant, you should prepare a legal claim outline. (See Chapters 8 and 9.) This outline is not tied to the testimony of any single witness but rather lists the elements of the claim you are seeking to prove or disprove, identifies the fact satisfying each element, and lists the important evidence from all your witnesses tending to prove or disprove each fact. As the outline organizes important evidence according to facts, you want it near at hand to serve as a road map to the testimony you bring out and the arguments you make.

Index Tab 4: Opening Statement Outline

An opening statement outline summarizes the information you will present to the judge or jury during opening statement. (See Chapter 11.) You do not want to read your opening statement to the judge or jury, but you can use the outline as a roadmap, to remind you of the points you want to make when you speak.

Index Tab 5: Direct Examination Outlines

Direct examination outlines identify, by witness, the important evidence you plan to elicit, selected specific questions you plan to ask, and any exhibits you plan to offer. (See Chapter 12.) Though you don't want

to script a witness's direct examination, you can refer to an outline during questioning to make sure you elicit the witness's story in chronological sequence and do not overlook any evidence or exhibits you want to raise for each witness.

For example, let's say you own a small shopping center and that you have brought suit to evict a tenant, The Broccoli Shop, owned by Elvin Goodman, for nonpayment of rent. One witness you plan to call is your on-site property manager, Brice Catlin. A direct examination outline for Catlin is shown below.

Direct Examination Outline

Witness: Brice Catlin

Background Information:

Married with three children; has been manager of the shopping center for six years; responsible for all matters related to leases, maintenance, and security for the center.

Important Evidence:

- Broccoli Shop became a tenant about 15 months ago.
- Terms of lease: Rent due on 1st of each month; $1,500 per month.
- Six months ago: Broccoli Shop started paying rent two weeks late.
- April 14: last rent payment received from Goodman.
- May 1: No rent paid.
- May 3: Brice talks to Goodman, and Goodman says he's busy opening another store but will pay rent within three days.

- May 8: Brice again talks to Goodman. He says bookkeeper was supposed to send check, he'll see to it immediately.
- No further contact with Goodman.
- May 23: Brice serves eviction notice on Goodman.

Important Questions:

- When I bring out the foundation for the lease, remember to ask Brice how he knows it's Goodman's signature on the lease (Brice saw him sign it.)
- Show that rent book is admissible as a business record. Be sure to ask what the rent book is, and about our business practice of what the bookkeeper uses the rent book for. Then ask, "Does the rent book indicate any payments from Mr. Goodman after April 14?"—answer "No."

Exhibits:

- Lease agreement will be Exhibit 1.
- Rent book will be Exhibit 2.
- Eviction notice will be Exhibit 3.

CAUTION

Make a more detailed outline for an expert witness. Your outline for an expert's direct examination can follow this format, but it should be far more detailed. For example, you should list the background information that qualifies the witness as an expert and identify not only the expert's opinion but also the reasons for it. (See Chapter 19.)

Index Tab 6: Cross-Examination Outlines

Cross-examination outlines identify, for each adverse witness, the witness's expected direct examination testimony, evidence you plan to elicit to support your version of events, evidence you plan to elicit that impeaches the witness, and (occasionally) exhibits you plan to offer. (See Chapter 13.) Because you may want to be sure to ask leading questions that elicit very specific information, you may write down your questions and read them to an adverse witness during cross-examination.

For example, let's say that you're a plaintiff in a negligence case. You claim that due to Defendant Sarah Adams's careless driving, you were struck by her truck while you were in a crosswalk. Adams claims that she was driving carefully and that she unavoidably struck you when you suddenly ran out from between two parked cars some distance away from the crosswalk. You are planning to cross-examine Kris Knaplund, who will testify for Adams that after the accident you said that you should have been in the crosswalk. Based on information you gathered before trial, the cross-examination outline you put in your trial notebook and use as the basis for questioning Knaplund might look like the one shown below.

Cross-Examination Outline

Witness: Kris Knaplund

Summary of expected testimony:

Knaplund will testify that she heard me say that I should have been in the crosswalk.

Additional information that supports my version of events: None.

Questions I have for impeaching her:

- "Ms. Knaplund, isn't it true that you were coming out of a video game arcade when you heard me say something after the accident?"

- "The arcade was noisy, wasn't it?"

- "Several arcade games were being played near you, correct?"

- "Those games are so loud that you have to talk extra loud to be heard inside the arcade, right?"

- "And where you were standing is about 75 feet away from where I was hit by the truck, right?"

Index Tab 7: Closing Argument Outline

A closing argument outline summarizes the introductory remarks you plan to make and lists the elements and facts you seek to prove or disprove, important items of evidence, burden of proof, exact language of important jury instructions (in a jury trial), and results you want the judge or jury to reach. (A sample outline is in Chapter 14.) As in your opening statement, you do not want to read your argument to the judge or jury. However, referring to the outline from time to time as you speak will ensure that you do not overlook important evidence or arguments. You can also ask the judge for a few moments to review your outline before you make your argument.

Index Tab 8: Jury Trial Documents

In a jury trial, you'll need a blank chart on which to write down information about prospective jurors as it emerges during voir dire questioning. (See "Keep Track of Jurors" in Chapter 10.) You can review this information when deciding whether you will challenge any jurors. For use during the questioning process, you may also want to make a list of topics or, if your judge asks all the questions but allows you to submit questions you want asked, a list of specific questions. (See Chapter 10.) You should also insert a copy of the jury instructions that the judge will read to the jurors (which the judge will do either at the beginning of trial or just before the jury begins deliberating).

Index Tab 9: Miscellaneous Documents

Depending on the complexity of your case and your judgment concerning what documents may prove important, you may want to have a "Miscellaneous" section of your trial notebook in which you put documents such as the following:

- A list of all the exhibits that you plan to introduce. Keep this list at the top of this section so that you can easily check off the items as the judge admits them into evidence. If you have made extra copies of exhibits to hand to opposing counsel, the judge, or the jury, place them immediately beneath the list. If you have copies of numerous exhibits, you may want to create a separate "Exhibits" section in your notebook.

- A copy of any rules of evidence that may be important if your adversary or you are likely to object to the admissibility of important evidence during trial. Having the text of the controlling rule of evidence in front of you will strengthen your argument. For example, assume that your trial is in federal court and you want to offer an important business record into evidence. Your adversary has indicated an intention to object to the exhibit as hearsay. (See Chapters 15 and 16.) You may want to make a copy of FRE 803(6), which specifies the foundational requirements for business records, and put it in this section of your notebook.

TIP

Have all evidence rules with you during trial. In most jurisdictions, you can buy a book that compiles the court system's rules of evidence. If the rules are part of a larger collection of rules that is too expensive, perhaps you can photocopy the section on evidence. Either way, you should have the evidence rules with you during trial. You should also make a copy of any rule that is likely to be the focus of argument and put it in your trial notebook.

- If you or your adversary submit a Motion in Limine (a pretrial request to the judge to exclude evidence), insert the motion and any written response into this section. (See Chapter 17.) Especially if the judge has "reserved" (postponed) a ruling on the motion until the evidence is actually offered, having the written motion in front of you during trial can help you present a stronger argument.
- A copy of the list of common objections from Chapter 17.
- A copy of any written stipulations.
- A list of the names, addresses, phone, and fax numbers of your legal coach (if you have one who has agreed to be on standby to help you during trial) and your witnesses. If your witnesses are late to court, you or the judge may want to contact them immediately, sometimes with the sheriff's help!
- The names and addresses of a few good restaurants within easy walking distance of the courthouse. ●

Expert Witnesses

Experts are witnesses who have acquired specialized knowledge through education, training, or other experience. Experts usually testify to help judges and jurors understand evidence and arrive at their verdicts. (See FRE 702; nearly all states' rules are identical.) Experts commonly appear in trials; as daily affairs have become more complex, parties have increasingly had to turn to expert testimony to prove their claims.

If proving your claim or disproving your opponent's claim requires a judge or jury to understand the significance of scientific, specialized, or technical information, you may have to hire an expert witness. However, an expert witness is likely to be very expensive. This chapter helps you recognize when you really need an expert witness, tells you how to find the right expert, and explains how to work efficiently with and elicit testimony from an expert witness.

CAUTION

The final decision rests with the judge or jury. A judge or juror is free to disregard an expert's opinion. Evidence rules make experts' opinions admissible in evidence; the rules do not make the opinions binding on judges and jurors. It's up to you to find an expert who is well-qualified and likely to be convincing.

Who Are Expert Witnesses?

As you might expect, given the variety of situations that end up in court, a wide spectrum of professional people offer their services as expert witnesses. One recent legal journal contained expert witness advertisements not only by doctors, lawyers, and accountants but also by experts in alarm system failures, architectural engineering, tree-growth problems, accident reconstruction, escalator maintenance, corporate histories, ladders and other household devices, railroad accidents, bicycles, skydiving, and many other subjects.

A person does not need an advanced professional or scientific degree to qualify as an expert. As long as expert testimony would assist the average judge or juror, any person who has special knowledge, experience, or skill in that subject can qualify as an expert. (See FRE 702.) For example, if your case involves the cause of rutabaga crop failure, a farmer who has grown rutabagas for many years would likely qualify as an expert. Or if your case involves defective house paint, an experienced painter may qualify as an expert. (See "Questioning Your Expert Witness at Trial," below, for a discussion of how to qualify a witness as an expert.)

Do You Need an Expert Witness?

One of the first things you must determine is whether the subject matter of the claim you are trying to prove (or, if you are a defendant, disprove) requires expert testimony. The test is this: If understanding the subject matter of a claim requires specialized knowledge that is beyond the everyday experience of the average judge or juror, you will probably need an expert.

For example, assume that you have sued an accountant for negligently (carelessly) preparing an analysis of a financial statement for you. To prevail, you must prove that the accountant's preparation fell below the professional standards to which accountants are held. The average judge or jury doesn't know what those standards are. So you'll need another accountant, in the role of an expert witness, to describe the professional standards that govern accountants and to explain how the accountant you sued negligently deviated from those standards. The defendant is likely to counter with another accounting expert in an effort to show that professional standards were met.

Here are some other types of claims that would probably require expert testimony:

- To prove your claim that injuries you suffered as the result of an accident are likely to be permanent, you need a medical expert.
- To prove your claim that a new home you purchased was built on improperly compacted landfill, you probably need an expert in soil engineering.
- To prove your claim that a piece of jewelry sold to you as a valuable "flawless" diamond is actually an inexpensive imitation, you probably need an expert in gemology.
- To prove your claim that you were injured because a lawn mower you purchased was defectively manufactured, you probably need an expert in lawn mower design and safety.
- To prove your claim that a series of psychological tests administered to your child demonstrates that your ex-spouse is not taking proper care of the child, you probably need an expert in child psychology.

What each of these examples has in common is that the average judge or juror cannot evaluate the truth of the claim without an expert's help. You will have to hire an expert with the proper qualifications prior to trial, demonstrate to the judge that your witness is sufficiently qualified to give expert testimony, and then elicit the expert's testimony so as to convince the judge or jury that your claim is true.

By contrast, let's look at a few examples where expert testimony is *not* necessary:

- You claim that your opponent drove negligently by driving 50 m.p.h. in a residential area.
- You claim that a landlord's failure to fix problems in your apartment rendered it uninhabitable and so excused your obligation to pay rent.
- You claim that a witness who testified against you should not be believed because he is biased and has made inconsistent statements.
- You claim that a developer intentionally made false statements about the number of home sites in a tract of land to induce you to purchase one of the sites.

In these types of situations, a judge would not permit you to use an expert witness because the subjects are within the understanding of the average judge or jury. The legal system expects and trusts judges and juries to decide the truth of such claims based on their commonsense and everyday experiences.

If you can't tell whether the subject matter of the claim you are making requires expert testimony, consult one of the reference works listed at the end of the chapter. Also, you may want to seek the advice of a legal coach well before trial. (See Chapters 1 and 23 for more on legal coaches.) If you need an expert, it will take time to find and hire the right one and to allow the expert to become familiar with your case in order to testify clearly and persuasively.

Judges Are Not Experts

A savvy or sympathetic judge cannot take the place of an expert witness, even if the judge is very knowledgeable about a subject ordinarily thought of as reserved for experts.

For example, assume that you will offer evidence of your medical condition. Based on the fact that your judge was a doctor before becoming a judge, you may think that you do not need a medical expert to testify about how your medical condition will affect your future activities. Or, you may be suing your former lawyer for legal malpractice for omitting an important clause from a contract. Based on the fact that your judge was recently a practicing lawyer in the same field, you may think it unnecessary to call a legal expert to testify that omission of the clause was legal malpractice.

Think again: The rule is that a judge's personal knowledge is no substitute for expert testimony. The law regards all judges as having no more than everyday knowledge regardless of their actual personal backgrounds. If the subject matter of your claim is beyond the understanding of the average judge or jury, you must produce a qualified expert witness no matter what your judge's background.

! **CAUTION**

You must notify your adversary and the court well before trial that you will call an expert witness. Check your local court rules on deadlines for advising your adversary and the court that you intend to call an expert and disclosing the expert's identity. If you fail to meet the deadline, the judge may not permit your expert to testify. For example, in federal court you must name your expert before the judge makes the final pretrial order. (See FRCP 16.)

Special Rules for Expert Witnesses

The rules of evidence reward experts—who, after all, have pleased their parents by developing special skills and knowledge—by bestowing on them three general advantages not shared by lay (nonexpert) witnesses.

Personal Knowledge Is Unnecessary for Experts

Unlike lay witnesses, experts are not required to testify from personal knowledge. (See FRE 703.) Evidence rules allow an expert to gain information secondhand and then give the judge or jury an opinion about the significance of that information. An expert's review of documents and discussions with you and other people can substitute for the expert's lack of personal knowledge about what actually happened. For example, even though a medical expert does not know how you got hurt and never treated you, evidence rules allow the expert to examine your medical records and testify that your injuries are permanent. Similarly, even though a legal expert has no firsthand knowledge about what took place between you and a lawyer who once represented you, evidence rules allow the expert to testify that you were the victim of legal malpractice based on the expert's analysis of the lawyer's actions.

Experts Can Give Opinions That Nonexperts Cannot

Unlike ordinary witnesses, experts can provide opinions about the meaning of scientific, technical, or specialized evidence, even if that opinion refers directly to the legal issue the judge or jury has to decide. (See FRE 704.)

For example, a lawyer who qualifies as an expert witness can testify to the opinion that the attorney you have sued for legal malpractice deviated from professional standards, even though this is exactly the issue the judge or jury has to decide. Similarly, an expert child psychologist can give an opinion that it would be in the best interests of your children for them to remain with you rather than go to live with your former spouse, and a medical expert can give an opinion that an injury will cause lifetime discomfort. In each instance, the expert can render an opinion based on specialized knowledge that an ordinary witness would be unable to give.

Experts May Be Allowed to Testify to Otherwise Inadmissible Evidence

Because experts do not have to testify from personal knowledge, to form their opinions they often rely on information in reports and on statements made to them by the party who hired them and others. As long as the information is of a type that other experts in the same field reasonably rely on, a judge may allow an expert to testify to that information, even if it would not otherwise be admissible under the rules of evidence. The judge has to decide whether the probative value of the inadmissible information outweighs the risk of unfair prejudice. (See FRE 703.)

Scientific Evidence

For many years, judges admitted scientific evidence if the evidence was based on principles that were "generally accepted" by the scientific community.

In federal court, however, judges must now make sure that scientific evidence admitted at trial is not only relevant but reliable. Under a 1993 U.S. Supreme Court ruling, judges cannot admit scientific evidence just because it is based on generally accepted scientific principles. Judges must make their own decisions about the scientific validity of evidence. *Daubert v. Merrell Dow Pharmaceuticals Inc.*, 509 U.S. 579 (1993). This rule applies to all expert testimony, whether it is based on scientific principles, technical knowledge, or any other form of specialized knowledge. *Kunho Tire Co. v. Carmichael*, 526 U.S. 137 (1999). (See Chapter 23 for information on how to locate cases.)

For example, assume that in a lawsuit against your ex-spouse you have hired a child psychologist as an expert to testify that in the expert's opinion you should have sole custody of your minor children. In arriving at this opinion, the expert may have spoken to the children's teachers, read evaluations prepared by school personnel, and consulted books written by other child psychologists. Much of this information would not itself be admissible under the rules of evidence. For instance, the hearsay rule would normally bar the expert from testifying to the teacher's out-of-court statements and to statements in a book. (See Chapter 16.) But if experts in the field of child psychology reasonably rely on such information, and if the judge decides that the probative value of the information outweighs the risk of unfair prejudice, your expert can refer to it while testifying.

In formulating this rule, the drafters of modern rules of evidence have shown uncharacteristic humility. They have reasoned that if courts need expert testimony to dispense justice, there is no sense telling experts what information they may or may not use to arrive at an opinion.

TIP

Your own expert can tell the judge what experts in the same field rely on. How does a judge, who after all is not an expert, know whether information is "of a type reasonably relied upon by experts in the particular field?" From your expert, of course. So when your child psychologist expert testifies to the information on which his opinion is based, ask, "Mr. Expert, do child psychologists commonly rely on information from teachers and from books written by other child psychologists in forming their opinions?"

The rule that lets experts themselves determine what information they can rely on has commonsense limits. A judge may rule that the expert's reliance on certain information is unreasonable no matter what the expert says and forbid the expert from testifying to the information or relying on it in forming an opinion. For instance, assume that your child psychologist expert testifies that, "in forming my opinion I consulted the children's astrological chart, because we child psychologists commonly rely on astrological readings." A judge would undoubtedly forbid the expert from testifying to or relying on such information.

Pretrial Disclosures

If you intend to call an expert witness at trial, you'll probably have to provide your opponent with a variety of extensive "disclosures." The purpose of the disclosure requirement is to make sure that parties have a chance to prepare responses to expert testimony and to encourage settlements by airing expert opinions in advance of trial.

Here are the pretrial disclosures you'll have to make under Federal Rule of Civil Procedure 26(a)(2) and similar state rules for each expert you may call as a witness at trial:

- the expert's identity, and
- a written report prepared and signed by the expert that describes:
  - each opinion that the expert is prepared to give
  - the bases of each opinion
  - any exhibits the expert plans to use
  - the expert's qualifications, including all publications that the expert has written in the past ten years

- how much you are paying for the expert's knowledge, analysis, and testimony, and
- a list of all cases in which the expert has testified as an expert at trial or in a deposition during the past four years.

You will have to make these disclosures at least 90 days before the start of trial, though judges have the power to give you more or less time.

Finding and Hiring an Expert Witness

The expert you hire should have good credentials that your adversary cannot easily impugn, be knowledgeable about the specific subject matter of your case, be able to communicate specialized knowledge in language that a judge or jury will understand, and employ a credible manner of testifying in response both to your friendly direct examination and your adversary's challenging cross-examination. This section describes how to find and hire such a person.

Two Kinds of Experts

In the world of trial there are "consulting experts" and "testifying experts." You'll have to consider whether a case is so complex and involves so much money that you want to hire each type of expert. (The same person can serve in both functions.)

Consulting experts. You can use a consulting expert to help you evaluate the strength of your case, to decide what evidence to look for before trial starts, and for other planning and strategy tasks. Having the assistance of a consulting expert can be especially valuable because you do not have to disclose to your adversary what you have said to the expert and what advice the expert has given you. This information is your "work product," and the work product privilege shields the expert's work from the inquisitive eyes of your adversary. For example, your adversary can't depose a consulting expert and ask what case strategies the expert advised you to follow. In fact, often you need not even disclose to your adversary that you have retained a consulting expert.

Testifying expert. No such shields exist for a testifying expert. Pretrial discovery rules require you to disclose the identity of a testifying expert in advance of trial, and to provide your adversary with a summary of the testimony you expect the expert to give, as well as other information about the expert. At a deposition, the adversary can ask your testifying expert to disclose conversations and information exchanges between you and your expert. You can designate a consulting expert to serve as a testifying expert, but when you do that the work product privilege ceases to exist and the discovery rules relating to testifying experts kick in.

When to Look for an Expert

If you need an expert witness, the best time to hire one is well before trial, when you are still looking for evidence to prove your claim or disprove your opponent's claim. Your expert can coach you as to what evidence to gather and will also have more time to conduct whatever tests or research are necessary to formulate a reliable opinion.

Using an Expert to Enhance Your Settlement Position

Another reason to hire an expert as soon as possible is that the overwhelming percentage of cases do not go to trial; most are settled. Before you hire an expert, an adversary's attorney may try to take advantage of your limited trial skills by making you a "lowball" offer. But having a credible expert in your corner well before trial strengthens your case no matter how rough your trial skills. This, in turn, is likely to induce your adversary to eventually make you a better settlement offer. See Chapter 6 for more information on settlement.

Paying an Expert

Expert witnesses can be and almost always are compensated for their testimony. In most states, statutes prohibit ordinary witnesses from being paid to testify, allowing them only a small fee as reimbursement for the expense of traveling to and from the courthouse. But the legal system regards an expert's specialized knowledge and training as a personal asset for which the expert can charge whatever the market will bear.

Most experts charge an hourly fee—often hundreds of dollars per hour—for time spent reviewing a file, conducting necessary tests, preparing a written report, preparing for trial, and testifying. The expert may also charge you for out-of-pocket expenses incurred for materials and travel. Win or lose, you have to pay the expert—usually up front.

The potential for profit has spawned an army of experts who peddle their services for substantial sums. If you need to hire an expert witness, you'll need to be a smart consumer. Make sure that your fee arrangement is in writing. And if one expert quotes you a fee that you think is too high, look for one with good credentials who will provide the help you need for less.

Where to Look for an Expert

If you need an expert, you can start by checking the listings and advertisements in magazines aimed at trial lawyers. For example, the magazine *Trial*, published monthly by the American Trial Lawyers Association and available in most law libraries, lists experts according to subject matter. Many state and county bar associations (lawyers' organizations) also publish magazines or newsletters in which local experts advertise their services. Universities and local branches of professional associations (for example, the American Medical Association) are also possible sources of expert witnesses.

Many experts list their services by specialty in national "expert witness registries." Most of these registries are now available online.

 RESOURCE

Where to find expert witness registries. Expert Resources Inc., 800-383-4857, www.expert resources.com.

The Legal Expert Network, 800-597-5371, www.expertnetwork.com, will send you experts' credentials and charge you only if you select one of its experts to review your case.

National Forensic Center, 800-526-5177, www. national-experts.com, publishes the *National Directory of Expert Witnesses* annually, a book listing over 2000 experts by specialty all across the country. You can order this publication and use a free expert search online.

Court-Appointed Expert Witnesses

If you need the services of an expert but can't afford to hire one, consider making a written pretrial motion to request a judge to appoint the court's own expert. (See Chapter 7.) In most court systems, a judge has the power to appoint experts in appropriate circumstances and pay them out of an expert witness fund. (See FRE 706.) A judge may even order your opponent (especially if it is a large corporation or the government) to pay all or most of the court-appointed expert's fees.

However, judges rarely use their power to appoint experts. If you do make a request, stress the public's interest in the issue involved in your case. For example, in one case in which a self-represented litigant challenged a government swine flu vaccination program, a trial court appointed (at government expense) a panel of three experts to investigate and testify because of the importance to the public and the complexity of the medical issues. (*Gates v. United States*, 707 F.2d 1141 (10th Cir. 1983).) Another court appointed an expert on behalf of a self-represented prisoner who claimed that forced exposure to secondhand smoke inside prison constituted cruel and unusual punishment, because the prisoner was indigent and could not find an expert who would testify without being paid. (*McKinney v. Anderson*, 924 F.2d 1500 (9th Cir. 1991).) (See Chapter 23 for information on how to find and use cases such as these.)

Choosing the Right Expert

The expert you hire must be able to render an opinion that backs your claim and must be able to give convincing reasons in support of the opinion. When you do find an expert you are interested in hiring, here are some of the steps you can take to make sure you spend your money wisely.

When you contact a potential expert, ask for a résumé or "curriculum vitae" (CV) that includes the expert's personal background, education, job history, publications, and honors. If you contact more than one expert, compare their CVs before deciding whom to hire. Try to gauge whether a judge or jury will be impressed with your expert's credentials.

Ask for a list of cases (the more recent the better) in which the person has been hired as an expert, and the names and phone numbers of the attorneys involved. Then check those references to make sure that the expert gets a good recommendation from the attorneys and parties who hired the expert. If, however, a person has excellent credentials, but hasn't been hired as an expert before, do not automatically dismiss the person; everyone has to start somewhere.

Try to get as close a fit as possible between an expert's area of expertise and the facts of your case. For example, say you're involved in a legal malpractice case against the lawyer who failed to advise your stepmother that she had to change her will to accomplish her stated wish to disinherit a child born after the will was signed. You need a legal expert who will give an opinion that the estate planning lawyer's failure to give the advice constituted legal malpractice. Look for a lawyer who specializes in estate planning (will drafting and related matters)

The Loser's Obligation to Pay Expert Witness Fees

The judge normally awards the winner of a lawsuit "costs of suit" in addition to any other relief to which the winning party is entitled. One of the costs that the judge may award is the fee paid to an expert witness. Keep written records of your expert's charges and, if you win the case, ask the judge to order your opponent to reimburse you.

Of course, a judge's ability to order payment of expert witness fees is a double-edged sword. If your opponent uses an expert witness and you lose, your opponent will surely ask the judge to order you to pay. Be ready to give the judge reasons for denying your adversary's request or limiting how much you have to pay. These reasons might include:

- **Lack of necessity.** Argue that your adversary's claim could have been proved without an expert. You may also be able to argue that your adversary, knowing you were not represented by a lawyer, needlessly hired an expert just to run up costs and try to force you to give up your right to a trial.
- **Too many experts.** If your adversary called two or three experts who gave similar testimony, ask the court to award your adversary costs for only one expert. Most judges resent cumulative testimony, so this argument may be convincing.
- **Excessive fees.** If your adversary's expert's fee is based on what you think is an excessive hourly rate, or if the expert put in an excessive number of hours (especially compared to the amount of money at stake in the lawsuit), ask the court to order payment of only a portion of the fee. One way you can demonstrate that a fee is excessive is to point out to the judge that the expert who testified (or offered to testify) for you charged a much lower fee.

and is knowledgeable about the ethical rules of that aspect of legal practice. Do not hire as your expert a lawyer who has only general legal expertise.

Before you agree to hire an expert, make sure that the expert takes the time to analyze your legal position thoroughly before forming an opinion. (You may have to pay for the expert's time to conduct this analysis.) Give the expert whatever information the expert requests in order to formulate an opinion. You don't want to hire an expert who will jump at the chance to deliver whatever opinion you are willing to pay for. Nor do you want to invest time and money in an expert who is unwilling to render a favorable opinion.

 CAUTION

Tell your expert the truth. Reveal all relevant information—good or bad—to your expert. Never try to hide bad information in order to get a favorable opinion from an expert. If you do and later at trial your adversary reveals the negative information to your expert, the embarrassed expert may change his or her opinion and do irreparable harm to your case.

If time and finances permit, talk to more than one expert before hiring one. If the first expert you contact is unwilling to render a favorable opinion, of course you'll need to seek another opinion. Many areas of expertise involve judgment. Even if one expert disagrees with your position, a second expert may honestly make a favorable assessment.

But even if the first expert you talk to renders a favorable opinion, you may want to talk to others before deciding whom to hire. You want an expert who not only has a favorable opinion but who is also knowledgeable, convincing, and easy to work with. Remember that you will pay well for the expert's help, so there is absolutely no reason to be intimidated by the "expert" label. No matter how good an expert looks on paper or how strongly an expert is recommended, your expert has to testify in a way that gives a judge or jury confidence in the correctness of the expert's opinions. If the expert cannot explain an opinion clearly and credibly to you, the expert probably will also be unconvincing in front of a judge or jury. It is your case, and you should hire only a person who is well qualified and can explain the meaning of evidence in clear, everyday terms.

Find out whether your expert has, in the past, represented more than one point of view. Generally, you want to avoid experts whose opinion is the same in every case— for example, that doctors are negligent or that custody of children should be awarded to fathers. Your adversary is likely to bring this fact out at trial, leading a judge or jury to disbelieve your expert on the grounds of bias. Far better for your expert to testify about experiences working for different litigants and offering opinions that reflect the unique circumstances of each case.

Questioning Your Expert Witness at Trial

There are two major phases of your expert's direct examination. First, you must elicit foundational testimony to qualify the witness as an expert. Then you move on to elicit testimony about the expert's opinion in your case and the reasons justifying it.

Laying a Foundation

Before a witness can give expert testimony, you have to offer foundational evidence showing that the witness is qualified as an expert in the field to which the testimony relates. (For a refresher on the concept of evidentiary foundations, see Chapters 12 and 15.) That means that you must begin the direct examination with questions about the expert witness's background. The idea is to demonstrate that the witness really does have specialized "knowledge, skill, experience, training, or education" in the field of claimed expertise. Only after the judge rules that your witness qualifies as an expert can you go on to bring out the testimony that helps to prove your case.

 TIP

Make your expert seem as knowledgeable as possible. Though the purpose of foundational questions is to show that your witness possesses the necessary qualifications to give expert testimony, your questions have a secondary purpose: to show a judge or juror what an outstanding, credible expert your witness is. The more your expert comes across as a star, the more convincing the expert's testimony is likely to be.

So even if the judge tries to hurry you along or your opponent offers to save time by stipulating (agreeing) that your witness is an expert, you should politely resist, especially if you are in a jury trial and your expert has a very distinguished background. For example, you might reply to the judge by saying something like, "I appreciate the offer to stipulate. I promise that I will not waste the court's time. But I need to bring out a few more facts about Ms. Expert's background to show the jury how well-qualified she is."

Obviously the specific foundational questions you ask will depend on your witness's field of expertise. If your expert has testified previously, you should ask the expert what topics to cover to highlight the necessary qualifications to give expert testimony. Your foundational questions of an expert are likely to cover the following general topics:

- **Education.** This is particularly important for experts like doctors, lawyers, and others who need advanced degrees to enter their profession. Ask about college and any graduate school degrees. It's also a good approach to ask about special courses the expert might have taken after completing formal training. For example, a tax attorney may just have completed a two-week course in "Tax Planning for Estate Planners," and a police officer expert may have taken a special police academy course in "Accident Reconstruction."

- **Professional experience.** For example, what is your expert lawyer's specialty, what does your expert doctor's practice consist of, or what is your expert farmer's experience with the growing of rutabagas? Your questions should elicit a description of whatever it is that constitutes the expert's professional life or specialized knowledge and the length of time the expert has been at it. Also elicit evidence about any licenses your expert holds, such as a doctor's license to practice internal medicine.

- **Professional organizations.** Ask about any professional organizations of which the expert is a member. For example, a doctor may be a member of the American Medical Association and the College of Orthopedic Surgeons. If your expert is an elected officer of such an organization or needed special qualifications to qualify for admittance to the organization, be sure to bring that out and have the expert explain what it means.

- **Teaching experience.** Highlight any courses taught by your expert, either in colleges or in special training courses.

- **Publications.** Inquire about any books or articles that your expert has written.

- **Experience as an expert witness.** Finally, you might ask how many times your expert has been previously qualified to give expert testimony.

To see how these factors combine into foundational testimony, let's go back to one of the sample cases used throughout this book: a legal malpractice claim against an attorney. You're suing the lawyer for failing to advise your stepmother that she needed to change her will in order to accomplish her stated wish to disinherit her child who was born after the will was signed. To prove that the defendant attorney committed malpractice, you may need to call another attorney as an expert witness to explain how the defendant's conduct violated professional standards. The foundational testimony that qualifies your witness to give expert testimony might go as follows:

1 You:

What is your name and occupation?

2 Expert:

My name is Anna Turney, and I am a lawyer and a part-time law teacher.

3 You:

How long have you been doing these things?

4 Expert:

I've been a lawyer for ten years and a part-time law teacher for the past four years.

5 You:

What is your educational background?

6 Expert:

I graduated with a Bachelor of Arts degree from the University of Chicago 13 years ago, then went to law school at UCLA. I graduated with a law degree, known as a Doctor of Jurisprudence, ten years ago, passed the California Bar Exam, and entered the practice of law.

7 You:

Are you licensed to practice law?

8 Expert:

Yes, I'm licensed by our State Bar. I'm also admitted to practice before the federal courts of our state.

9 You:

Can you briefly describe your practice experience?

10 Expert:

Yes, I began practice with Hoffman, Upham and Downey, a local law firm that specializes in estate planning. Five years ago I left the private practice of law to go to work for the Enforcement Division of the State Bar, which disciplines lawyers who violate the rules of the profession. I've been there ever since. I also teach a course in professional ethics every other semester at the Milwaukee Law School.

11 You:

Have you ever written about legal ethics?

12 Expert:

Yes, I've written three articles on ethical duties of lawyers. Two of these have been published in our state magazine for lawyers, The Bar Journal, *and the other in a local county bar journal.*

13 You:

How much of your work deals with professional standards for estate planning lawyers?

14 Expert:

Well, one of my articles dealt specifically with that topic, and, because that was my practice specialty, I regularly discuss the ethical responsibilities of estate planners in my professional ethics course. Working at the State Bar, I'd estimate that about 20% of the discipline cases that I investigate and prosecute involve estate planning lawyers.

15 You:

Can you give me any idea how many of these cases you handle in an average month?

16 Expert:

Well, if you mean estate planning discipline cases, I'd say about ten per month. This is about how many I investigate; of course, I don't necessarily prosecute that many.

17 You:

Have you ever previously testified as an expert witness involving legal malpractice by an estate planning attorney?

18 Expert:

Yes, on two occasions within the past three years. In addition, I was hired in connection with two other cases, but the cases settled before I testified.

19 You:

Your Honor, I request that Ms. Turney be accepted as an expert witness.

20 Judge:

Defense counsel, do you have any foundational questions you would like to ask the witness?

21 Adversary:

None, Your Honor.

22 Judge:

Very well, I rule that the witness is quali-fied to give expert testimony. Mr. Nolo, you may proceed with your questioning.

Transcript Analysis: This testimony establishes that the witness is qualified to give expert testimony in your legal mal-practice case. Your witness has five years of experience enforcing professional rules of conduct, teaches a course on professional ethics, and has written articles about lawyers' ethical duties (Nos. 10 and 12). Moreover, throughout her career she has been concerned with estate planning matters. In private practice she was an estate planning attorney (No. 10), both her articles and her teaching have focused on ethical rules in the estate planning context (No. 14), and she regularly investigates and prosecutes disciplinary cases involving estate planners (No. 16). Finally, she has twice qualified as an expert witness in similar matters (No. 18).

Note that many of your foundational questions, especially Nos. 5, 9, and 13, ask the expert to provide a narrative of her background. These questions encourage the expert to describe her background fully in her own words, letting her display her expertise and bolster her credibility in the eyes of the judge or jury. As you may remember from Chapter 12, judges usually do not allow you to ask narrative questions during direct examination. But they often make an exception for experts because they trust experts to keep their answers within legal bounds.

 CAUTION

The adversary may be saving an attack for cross-examination. Your adversary's response in No. 21 indicates only that the adversary has no questions pertaining to Turney's qualifications as an expert. During cross-examination, your adversary may nevertheless attack Turney's credibility—for example, by showing that Turney always testifies on the side of plaintiffs who are suing their former attorneys.

Eliciting the Expert's Testimony

Once your witness has qualified as an expert, you may elicit testimony in any order you choose. Unlike with ordinary witnesses, who usually describe events in chronological order, there is no standard format for expert testimony. Your main task is to bring out the expert's opinion and the reasons supporting that opinion in whatever way seems most credible. Remember, when testifying to the reasons for an opinion, the expert can refer to information that is not itself admissible in evidence.

 TIP

Elicit the reasons for your expert's opinion. You aren't required to ask your expert the reasons for his or her opinion (see FRE 705 and similar rules in most states), but it is almost always far more convincing to elicit your expert's opinion and then ask for the reasons behind that opinion.

When planning the direct examination, get help from your expert. Ask the expert to tell you all the reasons that support the expert's opinion. Then ask for the expert's advice as to how much of this information you should be sure to bring out during the expert's direct examination.

Here is an example of a format you may want to follow to elicit an expert's opinion and the reasons for it. Assume that you have already finished foundational questioning, and that the judge has ruled that your

witness is qualified to give expert testimony. In the case of the legal expert in the legal malpractice case, your questioning would go as follows:

1 You:
Ms. Turney, do you have an opinion as to whether the defendant committed legal malpractice?

2 Expert:
Yes, Ms. Nolo, I do.

3 You:
And what is that opinion?

4 Expert:
My opinion is that the defendant breached the professional standard of care and committed legal malpractice.

5 You:
Can you please tell the judge how you arrived at this opinion?

Transcript Analysis: It is generally a good idea to ask the expert whether he or she has been able to arrive at an opinion (No. 1) before eliciting the opinion (No. 3). You can then go on to elicit the reasons underlying the opinion with a broad, narrative-type question (No. 5). Again, judges typically allow such questions of experts because they trust experts to stay on point.

The reasons supporting an expert's opinion will, of course, depend on the kind of expert a person is. An engineering expert may rely primarily on a stress test of a piece of metal, a medical expert on a physical examination of you and your medical history, an accident reconstruction expert on an inspection of the accident site and the condition of the cars, and a child psychology expert on the results of psychological testing and conversations with the child's parents, teachers, and other counselors.

The following suggestions should help you maximize the credibility of your expert's testimony:

- **Ask the expert to explain his or her field of expertise.** If the expert's field of expertise is likely to be unfamiliar to a judge or jury, ask the expert to explain it briefly. For instance, because many people know that a radiologist takes and interprets X-rays, you may not have to ask your expert radiologist a question like, What is it that radiologists do? But a judge or jury may not be familiar with more unusual fields of expertise such as linguistics or ceramic coatings. Therefore, you might ask your linguistics expert questions such as, "What is linguistics?" and "What kinds of things do linguists do?"

- **Ask the expert to explain any tests that were performed.** Have the expert explain what the tests were, why they were administered, how they work, and what the results mean. Any working models, charts, photographs, slides, or other materials your expert can bring to court to illustrate how the tests were performed will almost certainly bolster the expert's credibility.

- **Have the expert read from a treatise.** If your expert consulted an authoritative textbook or treatise that supports the expert's opinion, consider asking the expert to read a clear, brief portion to the judge or jury. (See FRE 803(18), which is a hearsay exception that allows an expert to read information from a reliable treatise to a judge or jury.) Before the expert does so, ask why the expert consulted it and what makes it authoritative. Then mark the book as an exhibit, have the expert testify that it is authoritative, and ask the expert to read the supportive portion to the judge or jury.

- **Have the expert explain reports.** If your expert prepared a written report before trial, have the expert explain how and when it was prepared. Then mark the report as an exhibit, have the witness authenticate it, and offer it into evidence. (See Chapter 15 for information on exhibits.) This is especially important when an expert is a professional with an advanced degree, because the judge or jury will probably expect such an expert to document an opinion in writing.

- **Have the expert describe discussions with others.** If your expert based any opinion in part on statements from other people, ask who the expert talked to, why, what they said, and how their statements influenced the expert's opinion. Ordinarily, testimony about the out-of-court statements of other people constitute inadmissible hearsay. (See Chapter 16.) But remember, experts may be allowed to refer to hearsay and other inadmissible evidence so long as it is of a type that experts in the particular field reasonably rely on.

- **Have the expert use everyday language.** Ask the expert to translate technical jargon into plain English. Almost every field of expertise has its own jargon, and experts tend to use it automatically without realizing that an ordinary judge or jury might not have the faintest idea what the expert is talking about. Up to a point this can sound like impressive "insider talk," but its impact will be lost if the judge or jury has no idea what it means. A good general rule is that if your expert had to explain a term to you, you should ask the expert to explain it to the judge or jury.

For example, a stock market expert might refer to "convertible subordinated debentures," a term that would baffle most judges or jurors. Here's how you could ask your expert to explain this term:

1 **You:**

Ms. Expert, you used the term "convertible subordinated debenture." What exactly is a convertible subordinated debenture?

2 **Expert:**

A convertible subordinated debenture is a bond that a corporation issues to a person from whom it borrows money. The bond is paid back with interest or, if the lender chooses, is convertible into stock in the corporation, usually at a price set out in the bond. Obviously, the lender will take advantage of the convertible feature only if the price of the stock on the open market is higher than the price set out in the bond, so that the lender stands to make a profit by acquiring the stock.

3 **You:**

Thank you. Now let me ask you…

- **Let the expert testify in his or her own words.** You want the expert to impress the judge or jury with his or her expertise, so ask narrative and open questions frequently. Broad questions allow experts to testify convincingly in their own words.

 TRIAL NOTEBOOK

Make a direct examination outline. Make an outline of the expert's testimony just as you do any other witness's testimony and include it in the "Direct Examination Outlines" section of your trial notebook. Include the important personal background information that qualifies the person as an expert, the expert's opinion, and the reasons supporting it. You might also want to include any specialized jargon that you want your expert to explain, as well as exhibits you plan to offer while the expert is testifying. (See Chapter 18.)

Hypothetical Questions

Experts used to almost always testify in response to hypothetical questions. Lawyers asked experts to assume that certain facts were true and then asked them to state what their opinion would be given those facts. Today, there is no need to use hypothetical questions with experts, and we generally recommend against it. You can get trapped in a "Twilight Zone" between not putting enough information into a hypothetical to support your expert's opinion and putting in so much information that the judge rules that you have improperly launched into your closing argument.

However, many attorneys (especially those whose legal education predated modern evidence rules) still use hypothetical questions, and they are still permitted. If your adversary uses a hypothetical question, make sure that the "assumed" facts in it accurately reflect testimony. If the facts are not accurate, you should object to the question. For example, if your adversary's hypothetical question misstates a witness's actual testimony, state your objection by saying that, "The question is misleading because it does not accurately reflect the evidence before the court." (See Chapter 17 for more on objections.)

Cross-Examining Your Opponent's Expert Witness

If cross-examination of an expert was sold like a pack of cigarettes, it too would carry a warning label ("Caution: Cross-examining an expert witness may be hazardous to your health"). Unless you have as much expertise in the subject area as the expert you are questioning, cross-examination is likely to give the opposing expert the chance to restate and even elaborate on his or her opinions.

In many cases, the smartest choice is to decline the invitation to cross-examine an expert witness. You can instead rely on your own expert as well as your other evidence to convince a judge or jury that your claims are accurate.

But if you cannot pay for your own expert testimony and the judge refuses to appoint an expert for you, you may have no choice other than to try to undermine your adversary's expert. In that situation, you may want to at least hire an expert for some pretrial consultation. Tell your expert consultant what you expect the opponent's expert to say, and ask what areas of weakness you might probe during cross-examination. Even if you come up with no more than four or five good questions, you may give the judge or jury some reason to question the expert's testimony.

Seek your consulting expert's help in wording your questions, and write down the questions exactly as you expect to ask them in your cross-examination outline. When you cross-examine an expert, the exact words you use are often more important than when you cross-examine ordinary witnesses.

If you do want to cross-examine your adversary's expert, here are some possible approaches. You may be able to use them during cross-examination without giving an adverse expert the opportunity to rehash all of his or her opinions, as follows:

- **Demonstrate weaknesses in the expert's qualifications.** Perhaps the expert testified impressively about being a member of numerous professional organizations. If you show that any attorney, electrical engineer, accountant, or other expert can join those organizations merely by paying a membership fee, the impressiveness may evaporate. For example, any lawyer willing to pay the required fee can join the American Bar Association—no special qualifications are required.

- **Show that the expert lacks certain expected qualifications.** For instance, medical experts are often "board certified" in particular medical specialties such as surgery or radiology, meaning that they have passed tests conducted by a national board of experts in their field. If you ask your adversary's medical expert if he or she is board certified and the answer is no, you may undercut the expert's credibility.

TIP

You may attack a qualified expert's background. You may attack an opposing expert's qualifications on cross-examination even though the judge has ruled that the witness is qualified to give expert testimony. Your questions are relevant to the credibility of the expert's opinions.

- **Ask the witness about fees.** If you know from pretrial discussions or answers to your formal discovery requests that your opponent's expert is receiving what the average judge or juror will think is a large fee, ask how much the expert is being paid. The judge or jury may conclude that the expert is slanting the testimony in favor of the hand that feeds him or her.
- **Show that the witness is biased.** If you know that the expert always testifies on behalf of one position, ask the expert how often he or she testifies and then how often the testimony is for the same position. For example, assume that your opponent has called an expert legal witness to testify that

your former lawyer, whom you have sued for legal malpractice, was not negligent. You may learn through discovery that this expert has testified in 20 other legal malpractice cases and has always testified that there was no legal malpractice. When you bring out this background, you suggest that the expert is slanting the testimony (is biased) to favor a certain ideological position rather than to provide the truth in each case.

- **Contradict the expert with a reliable published opinion.** If you know that the expert's opinion is at odds with a passage in a treatise or textbook that the expert regards as reliable, show the book to the expert, ask the expert to admit that experts in the same field generally regard that treatise or textbook as "authoritative," and then read into the record the conflicting opinion.

Cross-examining an expert based on a passage in a treatise that is at odds with an expert's opinion is also an inexpensive way for you to introduce expert evidence favorable to your side. Although it requires you to find an authoritative book that takes a position at odds with that of an expert, this may not be so difficult if you have hired an expert to help you prepare for trial.

For example, assume that the adversary's expert, an economist, testifies that he can predict with reasonable accuracy the future rate of inflation by tracking the consumer price index for the past five years. You have located a book that you are told is generally regarded as authoritative that says that "anyone who says that he can predict the rate of inflation is an idiot." On cross-examination, mark the book as an exhibit, show it to the expert, and ask him to authenticate it as one that experts in the field regard as "generally authoritative." Then read the quoted language into the record.

You may also use widely respected books and articles to demonstrate that the information on which the expert's opinion is based is less than complete. For example, assume that an expert testifies that an important factor in her conclusion is "the results of test A," which she conducted. You have an authoritative treatise that states that "the best test is test B." By reading this conflicting passage into the record, you may lead the judge or jury to question the expert's methodology and, by extension, her opinion.

TIP

You can use formal discovery to prepare for the testimony of your adversary's expert witness. Federal Rule of Civil Procedure 26(b)(4) is typical of rules that provide for pretrial discovery of the identity of your adversary's expert and the expert's qualifications and opinions. Under this rule, you can send a written interrogatory (question) to your adversary asking whether your adversary intends to call an expert witness and, if so, the expert's name and address. In a separate interrogatory, you can also ask your adversary to summarize the expert's likely testimony. Finally, if you need additional information, you can take the expert's deposition. Doing so is likely to be costly, however. (For more information on depositions and interrogatories, see Chapter 5.)

TRIAL NOTEBOOK

Make a cross-examination outline. Include an outline of the evidence you expect to elicit from your adversary's expert in the "Cross-Examination Outlines" section of your trial notebook. This outline may be quite short. For example, you might limit it to the fee your adversary is paying for the expert's testimony and to reminders to probe for one or two weaknesses in the expert's qualifications. (See Chapter 18.)

RESOURCE

Resources on expert witnesses. *Federal Rules of Evidence in a Nutshell,* by Michael Graham (West Publishing Co.), reviews evidence principles. The book is organized according to the Federal Rules of Evidence with an emphasis on their practical application.

Evidentiary Foundations, by Ed Imwinkelreid (Matthew Bender), contains numerous sample foundational transcripts, including how to qualify an expert.

McCormick on Evidence, by John Strong, ed. (West Publishing Co.), is a basic treatise on evidence, frequently used by judges and attorneys.

Weinstein's Evidence Manual, Student Edition, by Jack Weinstein and Margaret Berger (Matthew Bender), is another well-regarded work organized according to the Federal Rules of Evidence.

Expert Witnesses and the Federal Rules of Evidence, by James McElhaney, 28 *Mercer Law Review* 463 (1977), an article written shortly after the Federal Rules of Evidence were enacted, explains the provisions concerning expert witnesses. ●

When Your Trial Ends: Judgments and Appeals

After both you and your adversary rest (have finished presenting) your cases and the trial ends, the judge or jury will render a verdict—make a final decision stating who wins and who loses. If your case is tried before a jury, the verdict will be announced at the close of the jury's deliberations. But if your trial is before a judge alone, the judge may take the case "under submission" or "under advisement." That means the judge will think the matter over for anywhere from a day or two to several months and then let you know the final decision in writing.

Even when you find out the decision in your case, that may not be the last word. This chapter looks at three things that can happen after a verdict is rendered:

- The judge can overturn the jury verdict, in some circumstances.
- The decision can be appealed and reconsidered by a higher court at the request of a party.
- If you win the trial and your adversary doesn't appeal, you still have the sometimes time-consuming task of "collecting your judgment"—getting your adversary to pay you the money the judge or jury awarded you.

This chapter gives you a general picture of what you may encounter at and after the close of your trial; it is not a guide on how to actually make posttrial motions or appeal a verdict against you. Where possible, we have tried to refer you to other resources for further guidance on posttrial proceedings.

"After careful deliberations, Your Honor, we'd rather not get involved."

How Final Decisions Are Made at the End of Trial

In many jury trials, the jury is instructed to decide who wins and how much money that person is entitled to; the jury doesn't have to state the reasons for the decision. Some juries, however, are requested to return what is called a "special verdict." This means the jury must state whether it finds particular facts to be true, in response to specific questions in the jury instructions. For example, in some states, each party to a personal injury action can be found partly responsible for the injury under a theory called "comparative negligence." In such states, a jury may be asked to render a special verdict in which it decides which party was responsible for what percentage of the harm.

Remember that jury verdicts in civil trials do not have to be unanimous. In most states, only three-fourths of the jurors have to agree in order to render a verdict. This means that if a jury panel consists of 12 jurors, nine jurors must agree to reach a verdict.

At the end of a judge trial, the judge may rule from the bench and orally declare a winner. Or a judge may rule later, in a document stating who won and how much the winner was awarded. Sometimes when a judge writes a decision, called a "judgment," "order," or "final order," it is a one-liner. (A sample is shown below.)

Other times, judges write longer opinions, which include the legal and factual reasons for their decisions. These documents are sometimes called "opinions" or "findings of fact and conclusions of law." A judge can also state findings (legal and factual reasons for the decision) orally, from the bench.

The final decision or judgment in a case is often written up by the court's clerk. But sometimes, especially if the judge rules from the bench at the close of trial, the judge may ask you or your adversary to write up the findings and the judgment (who wins and what the loser is ordered to pay). The process is similar to the one sometimes followed with a court order on a pretrial motion. (See Chapter 4.)

If the judge asks you to write up the decision or findings, ask the court clerk for a sample or form from another case. Ask also for an explanation of what you have to prepare and how you should prepare it, who must get copies, and any other advice about the process. For example, in some courts, a party who prepares an order is expected to send a draft (sometimes called a proposed order) to the judge and the other party. Then, if the draft correctly reflects the judge's decision and there are no objections, the judge will sign the document.

Lawyers often jump at the opportunity to write the findings at the end of a case. Even though it takes work, the writer can sometimes interpret what the judge said in a way that is favorable to the writer's side. Because appellate courts don't hear evidence themselves, if your case is appealed to a higher court, that court will rely on these findings to determine the facts the trial judge found to be true. And once a decision becomes part of the written record of the trial court, it is likely to take on a life of its own and be difficult to change.

For all these reasons, if you are asked to draft the judge's decision or specific findings,

Sample Judgment

```
 1    SARAH ADAMS
      [Street Address]
 2    [City, State, Zip Code]
      [Phone Number]
 3
      Defendant in Pro Per
 4

 5

 6

 7              THE _____ COURT OF _____ COUNTY

 8                    STATE OF _____

 9

10    Nolo Pedestrian,                    )
                                          )   Case No. 12345
11                     Plaintiff,         )
                                          )   JUDGMENT
12        v.                              )
                                          )
13    Sarah Adams,                        )
                                          )
14                     Defendant.         )
      _____)
15

16

17        Judgment for Defendant, Sarah Adams.

18

19    Date: _____        _____
                                          Victor Michaels, Judge
20

21

22

23

24

25

26

27

28
```

or if you are reviewing a document drafted by your adversary, pay attention to detail. And, if possible, have your legal coach or someone else whose legal savvy you trust read the document to see if it is open to interpretations you have not seen.

After the judgment is signed by the judge, it will be "entered"—which means it becomes part of the final, permanent court record. Only when a judgment is entered into the court records is it considered final. You may not file an appeal until the judgment is final. Also, if you want to appeal, you may have to file a Notice of Appeal within a certain number of days after the judgment is entered. (See "Filing a Notice of Appeal," below.)

> **TIP**
>
> **Make sure you are notified of the judgment.** To be sure that you are properly notified when the judgment is entered in your case, ask the clerk whether you will receive a Notice of Entry of Judgment. You may want to give the clerk a self-addressed, stamped envelope in order to be sure you get a copy.

Requesting a New Trial or Change in the Verdict

After a judge trial, the loser—be it you or your adversary—can ask the trial court judge to modify the judgment or vacate it (withdraw it altogether and order a new trial). Because you are asking the very judge who made a decision to change the decision, such a request is often unsuccessful—unless it asks merely to correct a typographical or mathematical error. But if you have a good

reason to be unsatisfied with the judgment, such a motion may be worth a try, if only because it is generally simpler and less expensive to prepare, file, and argue than an appeal.

Mathematical Errors in Judgments

One request that is usually successful is a motion to modify the judgment if a party has found a mathematical error in the computation of the judgment amount. If you review the judgment and find such an error, ask whether the clerk can fix it without any formal proceedings. If not, you may have to make a motion asking the court to change the judgment to reflect the correct amount. (For reference, see FRCP 60(a) on correcting clerical errors in federal court.)

If you do have to bring a motion, the judge will likely make a decision without a hearing, based on written papers that you and your adversary submit. (See Chapter 7 for more on making motions.)

Other Reasons to Modify or Vacate Judgments

You can also ask the court to modify or vacate its judgment if you can show that the judge made errors of law or there was serious misconduct on the part of your adversary or the judge. (See, for example, FRCP 59 and similar state rules.) Although you're unlikely to succeed, your written request (motion) could convince the judge to reconsider a decision, especially if you persuasively explain your reasons and clearly support them with citations to relevant, binding legal authorities. (See Chapter 23 for information on legal research.)

Examples of the types of errors for which a court may change a judgment are:

- The judge excluded highly important, relevant, and admissible evidence—for example, keeping out computer records that were essential to your case as hearsay when they clearly fell within the business records exception as you argued at trial. (See Chapter 16.)

- The judge allowed your adversary to introduce highly prejudicial, irrelevant evidence despite your objections.

- Your adversary engaged in serious misconduct by making one-sided (ex parte) contact with the judge during trial, which prejudiced your case.

You can also request a new trial if you discover new and extremely helpful evidence after the judgment is entered and you can show very good reasons why this evidence was not available at the time of trial. Failing to prepare because you were on vacation is not a good reason, but finding out your adversary lied about critical evidence during discovery would be. Your request might also be granted if something happens after the trial that you certainly would have wanted to introduce evidence about. For example, say you sue your roofer, Monica Doherty, for using inferior quality wood when repairing your roof. Two weeks after trial, five other houses on your block, also repaired by Doherty, collapse due to the same problem of inferior quality wood. You may be able to get a new trial to introduce this new evidence.

Overturning or Changing Jury Decisions

Judges have the power to overturn or modify a jury's verdict, but they rarely exercise it. You may, however, try to convince the judge to overturn the jury's verdict or change the amount of damages that the jury awarded. To do this, you make a written request (motion) for something called a Judgment Notwithstanding the Verdict, known by its abbreviation, "JNOV." (See FRCP 50(b).)

A motion for JNOV in effect says to the judge: "No reasonable jury could reasonably have concluded what the jury in this case did. And because the jury verdict was so preposterous, you, as a judge of reason, should overturn its outrageous verdict—or at least change the ridiculously unfair amount of damages it awarded."

Here's an example of a situation in which a judge might lower the amount of a jury's verdict. Assume that you are Sarah Adams, a building contractor who was sued by a pedestrian. The plaintiff alleged that you negligently struck him as he crossed the street. You defended yourself, but the plaintiff was represented by a lawyer.

The plaintiff, a firefighter, was a community hero. Because of the injuries, he was confined to a desk job and unable to work on the front lines—and the jury clearly sympathized. Even though the jury found that you were only partly responsible for the injuries and that the plaintiff's own carelessness was a significant cause of the injuries, the jury still awarded the plaintiff a million dollars in damages.

You may be successful in arguing to the judge that the damages should be reduced because, however unfortunate his injuries are, the plaintiff is partly responsible for injuring himself.

Judges very rarely order new trials. A judge might order one if a juror admits some wrongdoing—for example, if one or more jurors say they did not follow the judge's instructions, were coerced to vote in a certain way and do not in their hearts and good consciences support the verdict, or had one-sided contacts with your adversary outside the courtroom during the trial that prejudiced your case. Judges also order new trials in the event of a mistrial (a trial that ends before the full proceeding is completed because of some prejudicial conduct or error).

If you decide to make a posttrial motion to change the judgment or request a new trial, remember that you probably won't win. In all likelihood, you will have to appeal if you are not satisfied with the trial court judgment.

 RESOURCE

Researching posttrial motions. To find information at a law library (see Chapter 23), ask the librarian to point you to reference books on "civil practice" in your state. Look for a section on posttrial motions or in the index under these or similar headings:

- "Motion for a New Trial"
- "New Trial"
- "Judgment—Amendments to," or
- "Judgment—Vacating."

Appeals

If you lose your trial, you may have grounds for an appeal. Appeals, however, are often complex; you may be wise to have an attorney represent you even if you successfully conducted the trial yourself.

Though explaining the appeals process in detail is far beyond the scope of this book, here is a brief overview.

What Appellate Courts Do

An appeal is a request to a higher court to review and overturn the decision of a lower court. If appealed, your trial court verdict will be reviewed by an appeals (appellate) court. Appeals of federal trial court (district court) decisions are heard by the U.S. Court of Appeals; in state court systems, appellate courts go by various names.

If either party is dissatisfied after the first appeal, that party can appeal to the highest court in the state or federal system, sometimes known as the "court of last resort." For the federal courts, this is the U.S. Supreme Court; most states also call their highest court Supreme Court of the state. These courts accept only a few of the appeals submitted to them. If they don't accept your appeal, you are stuck with the decision of the lower appeals court.

Appellate courts generally resist overruling trial judges on appeal. Normally, a higher court can overturn the decision of a lower court only if the lower court made a significant error of law.

Appellate courts will not conduct a new trial or look at new evidence. Instead of putting witnesses on the stand and conducting a new trial for the appellate court, you will need to present a "brief"—a written argument setting out the mistakes the trial court made and the laws that support your positions. To write a brief, you will almost certainly have to look at how other courts have decided similar legal problems and apply their reasoning to your case. (For more on researching case law, see Chapter 24.)

An appellate court will review the official record (a transcript of the testimony plus exhibits) of the trial court, focusing on the legal errors you claim were made. It's up to you and your adversary to bring important portions of the trial transcript and exhibits to the appellate court's attention. Appellate courts will not scour the record of the trial court looking for injustices or mistakes that you neglect to identify.

Should You Appeal?

In deciding whether to appeal your case, consider:

- the monetary costs—for filing fees, transcripts, other court fees, consulting a lawyer, and missing work
- the costs in time—doing legal research, writing a brief, and preparing for oral argument
- the emotional stress on you and your family, and
- your chances of succeeding.

You may also consider your desire for justice if you feel it was unfairly denied at trial. You may benefit psychologically by taking the case as far as you can because it's important to you to get fair treatment and respect. This may be especially true, for example, in lawsuits involving unlawful discrimination or similar civil rights claims.

But before you appeal for these reasons, consider that you may feel far worse if you again lose after spending more time, money, and energy to appeal.

Before committing yourself to taking an appeal, carefully review the procedural rules you'll need to follow and the paperwork you'll have to prepare. Next, draft a realistic timeline, estimating how long it will take, and a budget outlining how much it will cost. Then consult your legal coach or, if you don't have one, an appellate attorney, to get an assessment of your chances for success. Armed with this information, you will be much better able to make a satisfying decision.

TIP

Find an attorney who specializes in appeals. Ask the lawyer who serves as your coach about experience with appellate practice. An attorney who handles nothing but appeals may be better suited than a trial lawyer to evaluate your appeal prospects and advise you or handle the appeal for you if you decide to proceed. Your present legal coach may be able to refer you to an appellate lawyer, or you can use the process outlined in Chapter 23 to find an appellate specialist.

Filing a Notice of Appeal

There are strict time limits for filing appeals. You will probably have to file a Notice of Appeal very soon (ten to 30 days) after you receive notice that judgment has been entered—typically called a Notice of Entry of Final Judgment. The Notice of Appeal is a very brief, simple document that merely tells your adversary and the court that you plan to bring an appeal. Later, if you change your mind, you can withdraw your Notice of Appeal without penalty. But if you don't file it by the deadline, your right to appeal will likely be lost forever (waived).

CAUTION

You may have very little time to appeal. Even before your case is decided, find out the deadline for filing a Notice of Appeal. If you think you may possibly consider appealing, do not wait until the case is over; start work immediately. Usually a court clerk, your legal coach, or a law librarian can show you the procedural rules on appeals in your court system. Also, find out when the court clerk will be sending the Notice of Entry of Judgment, in case it gets delayed in the mail.

The Appeals Process

Appealing a case involves preparing documents and making an oral argument before an appellate court. Appellate courts have their own sets of rules that differ from the rules in trial courts. This section outlines the basic process of an appeal. For further details, consult a book on appellate procedure for your court.

Making and Preserving a Record

Because appellate courts do not hear evidence—they review the written record from the trial court—the trial record is all-important. The official trial record consists of:

- what is said and taken down by the court reporter during court proceedings

- exhibits that get admitted into evidence, and
- documents that are filed with the court.

TIP

Make a good record at trial. To make a complete record during trial, you must articulate clearly and make sure all the witnesses do as well. Also, if someone gestures or makes remarks that are not clear, clarify them "for the record."

For example, assume your witness in the faulty roof case, your neighbor Marla Kristy, testifies that her roof (repaired by Doherty Roofers, the same roofing company as the one that repaired your roof) also caved in during the heavy storms. As she is testifying, Ms. Kristy holds up a photograph of her collapsed roof (that you had previously marked as Exhibit A and asked the judge to accept into evidence). You ask, "Now, Ms. Kristy, how did you know that Doherty Roofers used inferior grade wood?" She replies, "I could see that the wood was a lighter color there [pointing to the bottom left corner of the photo where the roof fell in] than the rest of the roof." Unless you stop and say aloud, "Let the record reflect that the witness is pointing to the bottom left corner of the photograph of her house, Exhibit A," an appellate court will not necessarily know from reading the record that the witness was pointing to a photo.

Getting Necessary Documents

If you appeal, you will have to order a trial court transcript from the court reporter. (See Chapter 2 for more on court reporters). Transcripts are usually quite costly. But the court of appeal must have the official record from the lower court to review what happened at the trial court, and you must prepare and assemble that record for them. To do that, you may need to attach other documents to your appellate brief, such as:

- all or relevant parts of the trial court transcript, especially anything you refer to in your written papers
- copies of exhibits
- a copy of your Notice of Appeal (and Proof of Service of that notice), and
- a copy of the trial court's judgment.

Writing a Brief

Once you decide to appeal a case and file a Notice of Appeal, you will get a briefing schedule and hearing dates from the appellate court. To make sure you don't miss any deadlines, you may want to make a list of important dates, like the one shown below.

IMPORTANT DEADLINES

Event	Date
Judgment entered	
Deadline for filing Notice of Appeal	
Deadline for filing Appellant's Opening Brief	
Deadline for filing Respondent's Brief	
Deadline for filing Appellant's Reply Brief	
Oral Argument	

The person who brings an appeal (the "appellant" or "petitioner") usually files an opening brief, the other side (the "appellee" or "respondent") files a response, and then the appellant can file a response to that (often called a "reply brief").

Appellate courts have extensive and often picky requirements for most every aspect of appellate practice; written briefs are no exception. The appellate rules often limit the number of pages and specify the type of paper and binding, color of binding cover, margin size, and print type you must use. Because of these rules and because the law can be complex, drafting an appellate brief can be difficult even for an experienced attorney. You may have to do extensive legal research to understand and make appropriate references to necessary statutes, court cases, administrative regulations, and sometimes even your state or the federal constitution. It may be wise to hire a lawyer for your appeal.

RESOURCE

Resources on appeals. For more information on appeals, an easy-to-read, inexpensive source is *Appellate Advocacy in a Nutshell* by Alan D. Hornstein (West Publishing Co.). This book reviews the appellate process and appellate courts and discusses the content of oral appellate arguments and written appellate briefs.

If you decide to write your own brief, ask a librarian for some references to appellate brief-writing resource books. One helpful resource is the *Handbook of Appellate Advocacy*, prepared by the UCLA Moot Court Honors Program (West Publishing Co.). Though geared for law students writing briefs for hypothetical arguments (called "moot court"), this will give you an idea of what you must do.

Making an Oral Argument

After all the briefs are in, you and your adversary may have the opportunity to appear before the appellate court to argue the appeal. It is common practice, however, for courts to decide many appeals on the papers alone. If you do appear in person, you will normally have a limited amount of time—from two to five minutes in some state appellate courts and up to 30 minutes in some federal courts—to make arguments about why you should be granted the appeal or your adversary denied the appeal. Because you and your adversary will have submitted your arguments in writing ahead of time, the appeals court will know what the issues are, and the judges may have specific questions for you or your adversary.

 TIP

Watch appellate court arguments before it's your turn. If you are going to argue before an appellate court, make an effort to observe that court in action before the date of your hearing. This is one of the best ways to find out what you are facing. Also, reference books you consulted when writing your appellate brief may have helpful suggestions for oral argument.

What to Do If Your Adversary Appeals

Even if you win, remember that your adversary may appeal or may threaten to appeal. Don't party too hard quite yet and, whatever you do, don't throw out any of your files, papers, or notes as you will need them if you do face an appeal.

Don't be intimidated if your adversary threatens to appeal. First, if your adversary appeals but does not have valid grounds to bring an appeal, you may be able to request reimbursement for the attorneys' fees you incur defending yourself. Be aware that this also cuts the other way; if you file a frivolous appeal (one without validity), you may have to pay your adversary's fees. Second, an experienced attorney may cynically threaten to appeal to get you to settle for less money than the full amount of the judgment. And third, it is common practice to file a Notice of Appeal to preserve the right to appeal even though no appeal may ever be filed.

If you receive a Notice of Appeal from your adversary, consult your legal coach, assess the pros and cons of continuing the process, and stand your ground unless there is a good reason to give in now. Remember, you won at trial, so the odds are strongly in your favor now.

Collecting and Paying Judgments

After the trial ends and you are notified of the court's decision, you will have to take specific action to collect your judgment if you won and to pay the judgment if you lost.

If You Won

Just because you won your trial and the judge told your adversary to pay you $50,000, don't expect to find a check in your mailbox next week. Unfortunately, enforcing or collecting a judgment (getting the dollars in your hands) can sometimes be as difficult, if not more difficult, than winning at trial. This is especially true if you won by default (your adversary did not appear in court and the judge ruled in your favor after you showed enough evidence to prove your claim).

CAUTION

Your opponent can still stall. Appeals and posttrial motions usually have the effect of putting a judgment on hold, sometimes called "staying" the judgment. If your opponent appeals or makes a posttrial motion, you will have to wait until it is resolved to collect your judgment.

It's important to understand that, generally, neither the judge nor the court clerk will help you collect a judgment. In some cases, however, you can ask the court to intervene. If your adversary intentionally disobeys the court's order—for example, by refusing to pay a judgment even though you have evidence that the adversary clearly has sufficient funds to pay—you can bring a motion requesting the court to compel your adversary to come to court and explain the failure to comply with the court's order.

If the court concludes that the person deliberately disregarded the court's order, it is likely that the judge will find such a person in contempt of court (in violation of the court order) and impose sanctions, usually a monetary fine on top of the judgment. This often happens, for example, when a parent refuses to pay alimony or child support.

Enforcing Nonmonetary Judgments

If the court judgment ordered the losing party to do something other than pay you money, special rules apply when you try to enforce (get the loser to comply with) the judgment. For example, a judgment may require a losing party to fix your roof, reinstate your employment, not come near you (a restraining order), or not build a second story that will block your view. These are all examples of what lawyers call "injunctive relief" as opposed to "monetary relief." Your best bet is to consult reference books on injunctive relief in your court system.

RESOURCE

For some basic information on injunctive relief, see *Injunctions in a Nutshell*, by John F. Dobbyn (West Publishing Co.), an inexpensive paperback that describes the different types of injunctions and the elements courts consider when deciding whether to grant or enforce them.

Common sense usually suggests that you wait until the appeal period has ended before you push your adversary to pay the judgment. If you have still not been paid by a reasonable time after the deadline for filing a Notice of Appeal, you may begin the process of collecting your judgment.

First try writing a demand letter to your adversary. Sending a copy to your legal coach—and noting that you are doing so at the bottom of your demand letter with a "cc"—may provoke your adversary into responding. A sample is shown below.

Sample Demand Letter

[William Nolo's address]
[City, State]
November 16, 20XX

Sarah Adams
[Address]
[City, State]

Re: *Nolo v. Adams*, Case No. _____

Dear Ms. Adams:

As you know, the court entered a judgment against you on May 27 in the sum of $80,000. It is November 16, and I still have not received payment from you. If you do not send the full payment to me within two weeks, I will have no choice but to begin enforcement proceedings against you.

Sincerely,

William Nolo

William Nolo

cc: Victor Rosenberg, Esq.

As with every document you send or receive in connection with your lawsuit, save a copy of this letter, mark the date and time you sent it, and keep it organized along with other important papers relating to your case. If one demand letter doesn't work, you may want to follow it up with another sent by registered mail, return receipt requested.

If you do not succeed by simply asking for your judgment, you will have to take steps to enforce it. If it's a money judgment, you will want to research and use one of the powerful legal remedies available to enforce judgments, such as attaching bank accounts, garnishing wages, or requesting that the sheriff (or federal marshal, in federal cases) seize your adversary's assets.

RESOURCE

Resources on enforcing judgments. Explaining how to follow through on specific enforcement proceedings in your state is beyond the scope of this book, but information may be available from:

- The sheriff's or marshal's office where your opponent lives, does business, or owns property.
- Your law library, which will have continuing education and practice books for lawyers that explain the steps necessary to collect judgments in your state. (Ask a librarian or look in the index under "collection of judgments," "judgments," "enforcement of judgments," or "debt collection.") (See Chapter 23.)
- Your legal coach or your coach's secretary or paralegal, who may be able to advise you and provide specific forms you need for enforcement proceedings.
- The Internet, including www.nolo.com.

If You Lost

Even at this stage of the game, you still have some options. First, you can pay immediately and be finished with the whole matter. If you feel you did your best, had your day in court, and lost after a relatively fair fight, it may be time to put the matter behind you.

Second, you can try to negotiate with your adversary. If you do not have the money to pay the judgment, for example, you might suggest that your opponent accept a lesser amount in exchange for a cashier's check payment in full now of that lesser amount. Your adversary may decide that it's more costly and time-consuming to fight with you and deal with a lengthy collections process than to accept less money now and be done with it all.

Or, you could ask your adversary to accept a monthly payment plan, something workable within your budget. You may want to remind your adversary that it will be impossible to collect anything on the judgment if you are forced into filing for bankruptcy. An honest offer of a realistic payment plan will be much better for everyone in the long run than promising the full sum and not delivering.

If you and your adversary agree to settle the matter now for an amount or arrangement other than what was decided in court, be sure to get everything in writing. Your settlement agreement is in effect a new contract that, if breached, can give rise to another lawsuit to enforce its terms.

Also, check your local rules to see if you are required to file any new agreements with the court. Because these settlements can change the terms of the judge's order (for example, less money for cash up front or a payment plan over time), they are sometimes called "substituted judgments."

TIP

The court may order time payments. In some courts, if your adversary will not agree voluntarily to accept a payment plan from you, you have the right to go to court and ask the judge to order the other side to accept such payments.

Finally, you may not own any collectible assets; you may be what is called "judgment proof." This means that you have little or no property or income that a creditor can legally take to collect a judgment, now or in the foreseeable future. Generally, property that is necessary for basic living—such as food, clothing, and limited allowances for things like medical care, transportation, and housing—cannot be seized by creditors. It is said to be "exempt."

Exactly what property is exempt depends on your state's law. One good resource to help you determine whether you are judgment proof is *Solve Your Money Troubles: Get Debt Collectors Off Your Back & Regain Financial Freedom*, by Robin Leonard and John Lamb (Nolo). It contains every state's list of exemptions and a worksheet to help you figure out how much property you can protect. ●

Representing Yourself in Divorce Court

I f you are getting divorced, need child support or alimony, seek a change in child custody, or want the court to protect you from an abusive spouse, chances are you will have to deal with a special court—known in many states as family court. Though family court proceedings are similar in many respects to the general civil court proceedings explained in the rest of this book, they also differ in some key areas. For example:

- Judges alone decide family law matters.
- Important issues are often resolved in short hearings, where you have only a few minutes to ask for specific outcomes and explain why you deserve them.
- Mediation—both voluntary and required—is used more frequently than in other courts.
- Judges tend to be paternalistic; they will commonly intervene if they believe that one of the parties isn't getting a fair deal. And if children are involved, judges often attempt to act more like the biblical Solomon than "the legal referee" described in other parts of this book. (See "Solomon's Custody Decision," below.)
- Unlike most other civil cases, family court cases often don't end for many years. For example, divorced spouses may have to come back to family court even after a divorce is final to enforce or modify court custody or support orders.

SKIP AHEAD

The first two sections of this chapter provide background material. If you have already filed for divorce and understand the key legal issues involved, please skip to "Filing for Divorce," below, where we deal with the specifics of the divorce process.

Solomon's Custody Decision

As recounted in the Bible, Solomon, a king and judge, was approached by two women both claiming to be a child's mother. When Solomon proposed cutting the baby in half, so that each "mother" could get her half, one mother cried out, "No!" Rather than see the baby cut in half, she would let the other woman have it. Solomon determined that this woman, the one who would give up her own child rather than see it harmed, was the real mother and, accordingly, gave her the baby.

Today's fathers and mothers who end up in family court have much to learn from Solomon's wisdom. Just as was true of Solomon, most modern family court judges are highly sympathetic to the position of the parent who appears most concerned with the child's well-being. And these judges are far less sympathetic to a parent who places the parent's own needs ahead of a child's or approaches the proceedings with a win-at-any-cost attitude.

This chapter is designed to give readers who face family court hearings an idea of what to expect. The first two sections provide some background material designed to be especially helpful to people who know little about family law and divorce procedures. The next several sections explain in more detail how divorce cases get filed and processed through the courts. The final section alerts readers to the most common traps for the unwary self-represented party in divorce court and suggests ways to avoid them.

RESOURCE

Nolo resources to help you through your divorce. Throughout this chapter we suggest additional resources that may be helpful if you are doing your own divorce. Here are several books published by Nolo that may be of help.

Divorce and Money: How to Make the Best Financial Decisions During Divorce, by Violet Woodhouse with Dale Fetherling, guides you through the process of divorce and helps you make decisions about key financial issues, such as dividing real estate, investments, taxes and debt, setting alimony and child support, and negotiating a settlement.

Building a Parenting Agreement That Works: How to Put Your Kids First When Your Marriage Doesn't Last, by Mimi Lyster, presents a step-by-step method for creating workable agreements on child custody and visitation rights and sets out a variety of solutions for common trouble spots.

Divorce Without Court: A Guide to Mediation and Collaborative Divorce, by Katherine E. Stoner, explains the process of divorce mediation step by step, from choosing a mediator to finalizing your agreement. It also includes tips on how to communicate your position effectively and handle common mediation roadblocks.

Nolo's Essential Guide to Divorce, by Emily Doskow, is a comprehensive guide to the legal landscape of divorce, with an emphasis on taking the high road for the benefit of your children and your sanity. The book demystifies the divorce process for everyone, whether the divorce is uncontested or an all-out battle.

Formulate a Divorce Game Plan

Each year a million and a half American couples file for divorce. In a number of states, both spouses represent themselves in more than 50% of all divorces; in over 80%, at least one spouse does. These statistics underline a fundamental point: Doing your own divorce is feasible. But that is not the same thing as saying it's easy. Nor does it mean that people who represent themselves in divorce proceedings always get what they want or need from the court.

Before starting your own divorce case, you should gather enough information to be able to:

- file the right papers in the right court
- appear in court (or where allowed, process papers by mail) to get these papers approved by the judge, and
- have the resulting court orders (granting a divorce and awarding child custody and support, for example) officially entered in the court record.

To do this paperwork in an informed manner—so that you will fully understand your legal rights and attain the objectives you desire and are entitled to—you will need to:

- learn some basic legal terminology

- understand and possibly research the divorce laws in your state
- have a clear, realistic picture of your own needs and wants
- have as clear and realistic a picture as possible of your spouse's needs and wants, and
- understand what the family court is legally authorized to do.

In short, you need to create a family court "game plan." This is important for a couple of reasons. First, by going into the divorce process with a clear, well-informed plan, you have a better shot at getting what you want from the court and saving yourself time, money, and stress. Second, you will be prepared to take corrective action promptly if you, your spouse, or the court misses a critical step in the process.

Research Your State's Rules

Family courts follow state laws. While broadly similar throughout America, laws can differ in important ways from state to state. For instance:

- Each state has its own requirements for how long you must live in the state before filing for divorce. (Six months is typical.)
- Many, but not all, states make you wait for a period between when the divorce is preliminarily granted by the court and when it becomes final. (Three to six months is common.)
- Each state sets legal requirements for getting a divorce. In some, to get a no-fault divorce, you and your spouse must agree to divorce or you must actually separate for some continuous period of time, such as one year.

But in many others, all it takes is a statement by one spouse that the marriage suffers from irreconcilable differences. In these states it is of no legal consequence that the other spouse may not want a divorce. See "The Legal Divorce," below.

- Each state has its own rules about how much child support should be paid and when alimony (spousal support) is appropriate.
- Each state has its own rules that define marital property and how it should be divided. (Some states use "community property" rules, while most states use a system called "equitable distribution." See "Property and Debt Division," below, for explanations of these terms.)

In addition, every state and county (and sometimes even individual courts) have different procedural rules governing the divorce process. Procedural rules govern the facts and claims (allegations) you must include in your divorce papers, the hearings required before a divorce (or a temporary custody order, support order, or restraining order) can be granted, and how trials are conducted. Although the paperwork to get a divorce is similar in every state, no state's rules or forms will work in any other state.

Fortunately, there are some good starting places for getting the information you'll need. Do-it-yourself divorce books are available in many states (though a few states don't allow or strongly discourage self-representation). However, chances are that you will have to supplement those books with additional information from a law library, website, or lawyer. (See Chapter 23 for more on finding a lawyer and using a law library or doing legal research online.)

Consult a Legal Coach

As discussed in Chapter 23, some lawyers are willing to advise you without handling your whole divorce. If you find such a lawyer, it may well be worth getting at least an hour or two of advice as early as possible in your case. Often, after asking you a series of basic questions, an experienced family lawyer can tell you:

- whether you are eligible to file for divorce in your state or county (or whether you'll have to wait and for how long)
- whether you have the correct forms (and possibly whether you have completed them correctly) or at least where you can obtain the correct forms and get help completing them
- what a judge has the power to decide, how likely you are to achieve the result you desire, and whether you have a relatively simple case (one that you can realistically handle on your own) or one that is likely to prove much more complicated
- whether important "holes" exist in a tentative agreement that you and your spouse have made, and
- how long the divorce process is likely to take.

CAUTION

It can be tough to find a good legal coach. Unfortunately, many lawyers are not willing to advise self-represented parties in a piecemeal fashion (possibly because they fear

a malpractice suit later, if things don't go well). And others who pretend they are open to legal coaching will primarily be interested in trying to get you to hire them to handle the entire case. We believe many more lawyers will be open to coaching in the future. In the meantime, if you absolutely can't find a lawyer sincerely open to coaching you but you need more information, consider meeting with a family lawyer for a consultation, so you can ask as many questions as possible. We don't suggest that readers should attempt to take advantage of lawyers—some of whom offer the first hour of advice free. Better to pay for the lawyer's time (or if it's free, to keep an open mind as to whether you may ultimately decide to hire the lawyer). If you receive free help but don't ultimately hire the lawyer, it is a good idea to write a polite thank-you letter explaining that although you've decided to represent yourself, you will recommend the lawyer to others in the future. That way, if your case turns dicey and you really do need help, the lawyer is far more likely to return your phone call.

Get Help If Your Spouse Is Playing Nasty

While a majority of divorces—especially those involving short marriages and modest amounts of property—can often be done yourself, you may need to get competent help if your spouse does (or seriously threatens to do) any of the following:

- physically abuses, mentally harasses, or otherwise hurts you or your kids
- takes your kids away from you without a court order
- cancels health insurance for you or your kids
- hides or sells your marital property, or

- denies your right to live in the family home without a court order.

If you are a victim of one of these types of domestic abuse, you should be able to get help and a lawyer referral from a battered women's shelter or a domestic violence support group. Not only is it likely that a lawyer recommended by such an organization will be at least reasonably sensitive to your needs but the lawyer may also offer to help you for free or a reduced fee if you cannot afford to pay more.

Assistance for Domestic Abuse Victims

For emergency assistance in your area, look in your local or area phone book under the headings "social services," "rape crisis," "domestic violence," "victim services," and "mental health services" to find local helping groups. Or, enter one of these terms along with your city name in an Internet search engine such as Google (at www.google. com) or Yahoo! (at www.yahoo.com) to find resources online. For example, if you type the phrase "rape crisis, Chicago" into the search bar at www.google.com, you will get numerous entries for local centers and hotlines that may provide help. You may also get help from your local sheriff, courthouse, or prosecutor's office (ask to speak to a specialist in domestic violence).

If Necessary, Get a Temporary Restraining Order (TRO)

Often, dealing with a spouse who engages in abusive conduct involves two steps:

- First and most important, if you fear for your own or your children's safety, get out of harm's way.
- Second, go to court to obtain a "temporary restraining order." Often called a TRO or "protective order," a restraining order is a piece of paper signed by a judge ordering the person doing the illegal or threatening behavior to stop. Judges may issue restraining orders before, during, or after divorce proceedings.

A judge may also use a restraining order to tell a spouse to:

- stay away from you or your kids or visit them only in certain places, at certain times, or under supervision (sometimes called a "monitored visit")
- move out of the family home
- not sell, mortgage, or otherwise "encumber" (use as collateral or security for a debt) marital property, or
- not cancel medical, life, or other insurance.

These last two orders are standard restraining orders that are automatically placed on both parties in most states as soon as divorce papers are filed by one party and delivered to the other.

Once a restraining order is issued, courts expect it to be followed. If a party nevertheless does something a restraining order prohibits (or does not do what it requires), a judge may follow up by issuing an arrest warrant. The police will then attempt to find and bring the violator into court, where the judge may reprimand, fine, or even jail that person for "contempt of court" (disobeying a court order). In addition, although police should assist any spouse in trouble regardless of whether there is a restraining order, law enforcement personnel often respond more quickly (and do so without questioning the victim) when a person needing help has a restraining order.

Usually hearings for restraining orders occur only after the responding spouse receives notice of your motion (petition) and a time is set for your spouse to appear and be heard. However, it is sometimes possible to obtain a restraining order without giving your spouse the advance written notice usually required by court rules. This single party ("ex parte" in legal lingo) procedure is typically reserved for true emergencies—for example, when you have good reason to fear your spouse may hurt you or abduct your kids. Even so, some courts require you to make at least some attempt to notify your spouse of your request for a restraining order (12- to 24-hour advance notice by telephone is common), while others dispense with the notice requirement altogether.

Any ruling or order a judge issues at a single party hearing is called an emergency or "ex parte" order. This type of order is usually issued only for a short period so that the other spouse can be given a prompt opportunity to respond and be heard in court.

In the following dialogue, Mae Jules will ask Judge Duncan for an ex parte temporary restraining order. Just as the clerk is getting ready to call a scheduled custody hearing, Mae runs into the courtroom, accompanied by a volunteer from the Southside Women's Shelter. The two women approach the bailiff. Mae tells the bailiff that she called the court clerk earlier in the day and was told to come in to request a TRO. The bailiff gives Mae

and her supporter permission to approach the courtroom clerk's desk, which is located in front of and below the judge's bench.

1 Clerk to Mae:
What do you want?

2 Petitioner Mae Jules:
I called this morning. Someone in the clerk's office downstairs said I should just come to this courtroom. I want a restraining order against my—

3 Clerk (in a loud whisper to the judge):
Oh yeah, this is the ex parte request the clerk's office alerted us to on your voice mail. I called her back and told her to come in after lunch. [To Mae] You have your paperwork?

4 Petitioner (nods):
Yes, here.

5 Clerk:
Please hand it to the bailiff to give to Judge Duncan.

Procedural Note: Just above, note how the clerk asks rather brusquely, "What do you want?" and then whispers to the judge so that all can hear. Though surely not the most tactful approach, such behavior is typical of many courtrooms and likely not meant to be rude. Clerks are busy and trying to keep things moving. And ex parte hearings—even those where a divorcing spouse faces a truly scary situation—must be squeezed into an already overloaded calendar. So try not to let comments of court personnel throw you off balance. Just answer questions as calmly and thoroughly as possible.

Mae hands the bailiff a copy of her forms. Judge Duncan takes a quick look and says softly to the clerk, "This is as good a time as any. I'll take it in chambers." The clerk then announces to the people in the courtroom, "We will be taking a ten-minute recess." To Mae, Judge Duncan says, not unkindly, "Follow me." Mae and the judge go to the judge's office behind the courtroom. The judge sits behind her desk and motions to Mae to sit on a couch near the bookshelf. Their discussion goes as follows.

6 **Judge:**

Let me take a minute to look over these papers. [Pauses.] You obviously want a restraining order against your husband. Let's see what your affidavit says is the main reason. [Reading.]

"Repeatedly over the past few months my husband has threatened to kill me if I divorce him. I have marked the dates and exact language he used on the attached calendar pages. I've asked him to move out, but he won't. I am really scared for my life, I want him out, and I want him to stay away from me. I also don't want him to be able to see the kids alone, at least not until he calms down. I'm afraid he will kidnap them, or maybe even hurt them. He has directly threatened to take them from me, and he has hit me in front of them. I've also marked those occasions on the attached calendar. I fear he may hit them if he takes them alone and they say anything he doesn't like.

7 **Judge:**

Fine, your written statement is very clear. Now I need to ask, do you have any evidence to back what you say?

8 **Petitioner:**

Excuse me, Your Honor. I am not sure what you mean.

9 **Judge:**

Do you have any witnesses who can testify about your husband's past abuse of you, photos of a black eye or other injuries, or other proof, such as a medical report?

10 **Petitioner:**

Yes. I'm gathering them. My babysitter is willing to sign a statement that she once saw my husband hit me in front of the kids, and she's also heard him yell really nasty things at the children. And the counselor I saw at the woman's shelter, whom I brought with me today, saw my bruises last week.

11 **Judge:**

OK, but you did not notify your husband of this hearing?

12 **Petitioner:**

That's correct. I did not notify him because I was in a big hurry and because I was afraid he would hurt me for getting the courts involved.

13 **Judge:**

OK, I'm going to try to call him right now. Do you know his work number? [Mae gives the judge her husband's work number, and the judge tries but cannot reach him.] All right, what I'm going to do, based on your affidavit and our discussion, is to issue a temporary restraining order stating that your husband must at all times stay over 100 yards away from you and the children.

My clerk will also set a hearing date, as soon as possible, probably later this week, during which your husband will have the opportunity to come in and have his say. At that time, you will want to present your proof, such as a written declaration of the babysitter or, better yet, have her come to court. Also, I will listen to anything the counselor from the women's shelter has to say, so please ask her to attend. The purpose of this hearing is for me to decide if the temporary restraining order should be made permanent and if it is necessary to set up a procedure for your husband to see the kids with formal supervision.

14 Petitioner:

Thank you, Your Honor. What about the kids?

15 Judge:

I will also order him to temporarily refrain from visiting the children until he comes into court for a hearing. After that, I may also order a home evaluation by the Children's Protection Agency. Then I will decide to grant unsupervised or supervised visitation, as the circumstances warrant.

16 Petitioner:

Thank you.

17 Judge:

You must also give notice of the hearing on whether to extend the temporary restraining order to your husband. Talk to the Clerk's Office or the woman's shelter, if you need help.

Procedural Notes: Mae does several important things in her presentation set out above:

- She asks the judge to explain terms she doesn't understand rather than trying to answer when she's not clear.
- Her papers say clearly what she wants, and she provides backup documentation.
- She sticks to the facts. Judges don't want to hear spouses name call or attack each other, unless what is said specifically relates to why the person needs a restraining order. Note that Mae wrote in her papers that she fears her husband might attack her or the children if she files for divorce— certainly a relevant and specific "fact," properly brought to the judge's attention.

Although most judges recognize that it can be difficult to "prepare" when asking for a restraining order in an emotionally charged and physically dangerous situation, judges are nevertheless more apt to grant relief to those people who clearly explain and, if possible, document what happened. Notice that in Mae's conversation with the judge, even though she had not yet written down the statements of the babysitter and counselor, she clearly tells the judge who these people are and exactly what they will be able to testify to. In addition, the fact that Mae had kept or reconstructed a record of when she was hit is obviously of interest to the judge.

Different judges have different styles. Some will act as Judge Duncan did, by hearing all TRO requests informally in chambers, while others may conduct the hearing in the courtroom. In addition, some judges will immediately try to contact the opposing spouse by phone, as Judge Duncan did, while others will simply grant an emergency order that lasts for a few days and schedule a prompt court hearing to allow the other spouse to respond.

Do Some Planning Ahead of Time

Before you file for divorce, or if possible even before you separate, it's wise to gather key financial information. To do this, you will usually need to:

- make a list of everything you and your spouse own (assets) and owe (debts)
- make a current monthly budget of your income and expenses, and, if possible, a second budget projecting income and expenses after separation, and
- gather copies of important financial documents such as bank records, lists of investments (including retirement plans), and joint tax returns for the several years prior to separation.

RESOURCE

Divorce and Money: How to Make the Best Financial Decisions During Divorce, by Violet Woodhouse with Dale Fetherling (Nolo), can help you with these and other tasks. You can also get oriented to the big picture by reading *Nolo's Essential Guide to Divorce,* by Emily Doskow (Nolo).

Parents who want to increase their chances of getting joint or shared custody, or at least generous visitation rights, should plan ahead by polishing their "parenting

resume." For example, a parent who has been less active in parenting, but wants to play a bigger role in the future, might take a parenting class or develop a better track record of participating in parenting tasks such as taking children to the doctor, participating in religious training, or involving themselves in school or after-school activities, such as attending PTA meetings, coaching a sports team, or leading a scout troop.

Learn How Mediation Can Help You

One reason for the large number of people representing themselves in divorces is that separating spouses understand that they can sensibly make most divorce-related decisions themselves without turning them over to a judge. Some couples negotiate entirely on their own, while many others turn to mediation as an excellent process for working out disagreements.

Divorce Mediation in General

Divorce mediation involves the parties sitting down with a mediator—a neutral third party—and working out a plan to which both parties can agree. (Mediation in general is covered in Chapter 6.) The idea is for the spouses to work through an orderly process designed to help them find mutually agreeable solutions to important questions, such as who will get what kind of custody or visitation rights and how to divide the marital property. Divorcing spouses can participate in mediation by jointly choosing and paying for a private mediator and attending one or more mediation sessions. Or, if they live in one of the approximately 35 states that either offer or require court-sponsored mediation for issues related to child custody and visitation, they may be eligible for free mediation assistance. (For more on court-ordered mediation, see below.)

Solving problems through mediation is fundamentally different from fighting over problems in court. For starters, mediation is less formal. It takes place in an office or conference room, and the strict rules of evidence and procedure used in the court-room don't apply. Instead, spouses speak for themselves in ordinary English. Where spouses want and can afford to have lawyers involved, the lawyers may attend mediation sessions, but typically only to give advice to their client.

The crux of the mediation process is that parties are encouraged to work together to resolve their disputes. Mediators try to help spouses do this by getting each to articulate his or her true needs, as opposed to making exaggerated demands. Mediation is a huge contrast to how disputes are settled in court, where a judge (often listening almost exclusively to lawyers) imposes a decision on the parties, usually creating a "winner" and a "loser."

Couples who make their own agreements, with or without a mediator's help, usually file them or bring them to court. Often, by agreement of the parties, one spouse appears in court (with the other not contesting), and the judge confirms the couple's decisions unless they are grossly unfair to one spouse or do not adequately provide for the couple's children.

RESOURCE

Resources on divorce mediation.
Divorce Without Court: A Guide to Mediation & Collaborative Divorce, by Katherine E. Stoner (Nolo), explains the process of divorce mediation step by step, from choosing a mediator to finalizing your agreement. It also includes tips on how to communicate your position effectively and handle common mediation roadblocks.

Mediate, Don't Litigate: Strategies for Successful Mediation, by Peter Lovenheim and Lisa Guerin (Nolo), available as a download at www.nolo.com, is an excellent resource for people who want to understand the mediation process and resolve their disputes, and includes an extensive chapter on strategies for mediating divorce and child custody disputes.

A Guide to Divorce Mediation: How to Reach a Fair, Legal Settlement at a Fraction of the Cost, by Gary Friedman (Workman), is a clear explantion of the process by an experienced mediator, and includes transcripts from actual mediations.

Building a Parenting Agreement That Works: How to Put Your Kids First When Your Marriage Doesn't Last, by Mimi Lyster (Nolo), is an informative resource for people who wish to negotiate joint-parenting issues, with or without the help of a mediator. This book identifies all of the major issues typically involved in figuring out custody and visitation and sets out a variety of solutions for each (many of which have been identified by the author in the course of actual mediations).

The Complete Guide to Mediation: The Cutting-Edge Approach to Family Law Practice, by Forrest S. Mosten (ABA), is a detailed exploration of the lawyer's role in mediation. As well as providing useful information and resources, this book will help readers learn what qualities and services they may want to seek in a mediator and lawyer if they hire one.

The Divorce Mediation Handbook: Everything You Need to Know, by Paula James (Jossey-Bass), an informative book written by a divorce mediator and family lawyer, includes chapters on choosing a mediator, pros and cons of mediation, conferring with attorneys, the mediation process, protecting children, and dividing financial assets.

Once you understand how divorce mediation can help you and your spouse, you may want to find a private mediator in your community. For a referral, contact any local community-based mediation program, your family court, or a local bar association. It's also a good idea to do some planning before the mediation so you are as clear as possible on the following issues:

- what you want

- what your spouse wants
- how far apart you are (if you dispute dollar figures) and what is your acceptable compromise range
- whether there are any other ways to resolve the dispute, and
- how a court would likely resolve the dispute.

Consider creating a chart, such as the example provided below, to highlight the main areas of dispute between you and your spouse. Some lawyers write legal memos, or "briefs," to set out their positions for the mediator ahead of time, but—especially in a court-ordered mediation—the mediator may not have time to read anything significant before you sit down. The mediator may, however, be willing to take a quick look at a chart you make. Making such a chart will help you clarify your own wants, needs,

Main Areas of Dispute

Issue	Likely Court Disposition	Husband's Most Recent Offer	Wife's Most Recent Offer	Difference Between Current Offers
Family Home	Defer sale of house until the children reach age 18, then split the proceeds 50-50 after all costs are paid	Husband will buy out Wife's interest for $300,000	Wife will sell her interest to Husband for $500,000	$200,000
Wife's Car	Assign a value of $10,000	Should be valued at $11,000	Should be valued at $9,000	$2,000
Husband's Car	Assign a value of $20,000	Should be valued at $15,000	Should be valued at $25,000	$10,000
Spousal Support	Open-ended order for guideline spousal support of Husband paying Wife $800 per month	Husband will pay Wife $500 per month for three years	Husband will pay Wife $1,000 per month for seven years or a lump sum now of $30,000	$500 per month and four years in term length

and possibilities and may also help prepare you to focus the mediation in a helpful manner, as is illustrated in the example above. Also, even if your case is not resolved at the mediation and you have to go to court, planning for and going through the mediation may help resolve some issues and bring you and your spouse closer to settlement on the issues that remain.

After you've made the chart, practice (in front of a trusted friend or family member) stating your positions on why your value should be accepted rather than the other side's. Focus on reasons based on data. Doing this will help you whether you end up negotiating a point directly with your ex, or presenting your position to a mediator or judge.

Court-Ordered Mediation

Some courts require that the parties attend a mediation session before they may proceed with litigation in a contested divorce case. Mediations required by the courts may differ from private mediation in several ways. Court-ordered mediations tend to be more hurried, and the mediator, usually a lawyer serving on a mediation panel, is assigned randomly to your case. Especially in large urban areas, mediators may have to handle several cases in each morning or afternoon session.

By contrast, private mediations tend to be less rushed; a private mediator of your and your spouse's choosing will likely have only your case scheduled for a particular time slot. Also, some court mediations take place in the courthouse, under less than ideal conditions (though some courts have created more pleasant offices for court-connected

mediators). In contrast, private mediators often use more comfortable office spaces, without the adversarial courtroom ambiance as the backdrop. Lastly, court mediators often view their jobs as to push parties into settlement—the clear goal being to use the required mediation to limit the number of cases that ever get to the already overloaded courtrooms. Thus, the focus may be on whatever "compromise" is possible, whereas the ideal goal of private mediation is to help both parties meet their needs through (sometimes creative) win-win solutions.

The example below illustrates a single-issue mediation in which Husband and Wife dispute the amount of spousal support that Husband should pay wife. For ease of calculation, let's assume that Husband believes he should pay Wife $500 per month in spousal support, and Wife believes he should pay $1,000 per month. The mediator gathers both parties in the small court-assigned room and begins the following dialogue:

1 Mediator:

Thank you for waiting. I have six mediations scheduled this morning. Wow. (Both parties nod and say nothing.) I'm going to meet with each of you individually, once or maybe more than once, and then I'll call you back in here together. Who wants to go first?

2 Husband:

I'd like to go first.

3 Wife:

That's fine with me. I'll go grab a coffee.

4 Mediator:

Don't go too far. I'll be just a short while with him, then I'll call you in. If you're not here, I'll take one of my other cases, and you two will have to wait until I'm done with that one.

In a private session with Husband, the mediator asks two minutes of questions about Husband's work, how much he makes, and how much Wife makes. The mediator plugs some numbers into his laptop and then says the following.

5 **Mediator:**

Here's the deal. The judge will look at what you both earn and order that you pay between $700 and $800. You say she's asking for $1,000. If I can get her down to $750, I suggest you take it. Your $500 is unreasonable given her income. You can always come back in and move to lower the number if she starts earning a lot more.

The mediator then sends Husband out and calls Wife in.

6 **Mediator:**

Okay, your husband told me what you both earn, and you've got to come down on this $1,000. A judge will never order him to pay that much. Now I think I may be able to get him up to $750 per month. If I can, will you take that?

7 **Wife:**

Did he tell you that up until two years ago he was making twice what he's making now, and that with one phone call he could triple his salary? We've been married more than ten years. This is a long-term marriage. If I were disabled today, before trial, you and I both know he'd have to pay support for my entire life.

8 **Mediator:**

He didn't tell me about his earning potential. And you're right that the judge will probably look at what you both earn now and your earning potential. By the way, how about you? Are you earning all you are capable of earning?

Procedural Note: Notice that Wife sticks to the facts and does not get caught up in feeling slighted that the mediator listened first to Husband and apparently accepted Husband's version of events. Wife brought out her own points clearly and calmly, and the mediator was then able to see her side of the story as well. It is critical to try not to take things personally. This mediator is rushed and has been somewhat rude, but that's not necessarily unusual given court caseloads. Knowing what facts a judge will consider to be relevant will help you as a party to bring out what is important and leave the emotions aside.

9 **Wife:**

I'm working three-quarter time. I've just started a new credential program, so I'm back in school part time.

10 **Mediator:**

Well, as I said, how about you split the difference right down the middle. $750 and we'll be done with this. The judge won't be happy if you two come in so close and waste court time because you're unwilling to compromise.

11 **Wife:**

I don't believe the support should be lower than $1,000 per month. I would, however, be open to taking a lump sum if he pays it now. Let's say $30,000—his

$500 figure, but for a limited time of what would be five years, but all paid now.

Procedural Note: Again, Wife does not allow the mediator's pushing to throw her, and she's prepared well enough to know when and where to bring up other possible ways of resolving the dispute.

12 Mediator:

Great idea. I take it your earnings may go up when you finish your credential program in—what did you say, three years?—so you could use the money up front while you're earning less. He pays more but takes less of a risk that the court will order either the higher amount or for a longer number of years.

They meet in joint session and end up agreeing to a lump sum based on her higher figure, but for a limited time of only three years and discounted to the present value.

Procedural Note: In a private mediation session, the mediator probably would have taken more time to explore each party's needs and would have discovered that Wife was back in school, needed more money now, and expected her earnings to go up in three years. The lump-sum payment is a win-win solution. Husband's needs are met because the amount of support he must pay is capped and he gets, in essence, the lower rate he wants to pay, but he does have to pay the money up front. As noted above, in the rushed setting of a court mediation, it was only because Wife was prepared and assertive that the information necessary for such a win-win solution even came out. You can see that the mediator's goals were clearly

to get to a compromise figure as quickly as possible, so that the mediator could get on to the next case.

Understanding the Basics of Family Law

In addition to having to cope with emotional issues, divorcing couples almost always have to make one or more big decisions regarding property division, child custody, visitation, and child or spousal support. To make educated decisions, mediate, or go to court about any of these issues, you must know your rights and obligations under the law. This section provides a basic overview of key family law issues to help get you started. Because family law is governed by state law (as opposed to federal law), you will need to research your own state's laws for more information.

 SKIP AHEAD

This section explains several legal issues in detail. If you feel comfortably grounded in the basics of divorce law or if legal issues are not a big deal in your case (perhaps because you have no children and have already divided your property), you may want to skip ahead to "Filing for Divorce," below.

The Legal Divorce

This section explains several different types of divorces that may be available under your state's laws.

Ending a Marriage by Legal Separation or Annulment

Some couples want to end their relationship but stay legally married for religious or financial reasons. For example, a spouse who is ill may want to stay married to continue using the other spouse's health insurance. Such couples may obtain what's called "a legal separation," which keeps the marriage intact but allows the family court to make orders dividing property and awarding custody and support. Other couples may seek a legal decree called an "annulment" or "nullity of marriage" that says, in effect, the marriage never existed. Annulments are usually only awarded when the marriage was induced by fraud or because of an unknown physical or mental condition that made the marriage unviable from the start.

No-Fault Divorce

Every state now allows divorce on a "no-fault" basis, although a few states allow it only for couples who meet certain qualifications (for example, having been separated for at least one year). This means that if one or both spouses want a divorce, they can get it on the basis of "incompatibility" or "irreconcilable differences," with no legal battle over who was at fault for the breakdown of the marriage. If there is to be a dispute, it will be about property, spousal support, or child-related issues—not about whether the divorce itself should be granted. But fault can come into play in some states when the court is deciding financial or custody issues.

Fault-Based Divorce

Before the advent of the no-fault divorce, state laws typically required one spouse to prove that the other was insane, in prison for an extended period, or legally at fault for the breakdown of the marriage before a divorce could be granted. Such laws commonly found "at fault" a spouse who:

- committed adultery
- inflicted emotional or physical pain on the other spouse, or
- deserted the other spouse (left the family home without consent for some prescribed amount of time).

If one spouse proved severe mistreatment by the other (for example, that the other spouse committed adultery), judges had the power when dividing property to favor the innocent spouse over the spouse at fault. Although most states no longer consider fault in deciding whether to allow a divorce or how to divide property, some states still consider fault in determining the amount (if any) of spousal or child support and the extent of custody or visitation rights to award. And some states do still allow divorces based on fault grounds.

Uncontested Divorce

Depending on a couple's attitudes and practical situation (for example, whether they have kids or significant property), divorce proceedings can be almost as easy as getting a driver's license; or, they can be long, painful, and complex. For the "easy" cases, where spouses agree on all major decisions (typically in shorter marriages with no kids and relatively small amounts of property or debt), many states now offer streamlined divorce procedures. Under these simplified procedures, an uncontested divorce may even be handled entirely by mail. And when the person who files the initial divorce papers (the petitioner) has to make a court appearance, little more is involved than briefly confirming that the information he or she included in the divorce papers (typically called a divorce "petition" or "complaint") is correct. "How Uncontested Divorces Work," below, explains in more detail how a typical uncontested divorce proceeds.

Contested Divorce

A divorce becomes contested if, after one spouse files a divorce petition, the other spouse files papers (usually called a "response" or "answer") opposing one or more of the first spouse's requests. Filing such a response puts the court on notice that the spouses are not in full agreement about what should happen in the divorce.

Divorces tend to be contested when some or all of the following factors are present:
- emotions are running high
- valuable property is involved
- there are minor children, and one or both spouses has strong doubts about the ability of the other spouse to be a good parent, or
- the spouses disagree about the amount of child or spousal support that should be awarded.

Contested divorces may involve many pretrial procedures and court appearances. These are explained in more detail in "How Contested Divorces Work," below.

Contested Divorces Can Turn Into Uncontested Divorces and Vice Versa

Fortunately, many divorces that start out contested later become uncontested—thereby avoiding the need for a court battle. This typically occurs when the parties reach agreement through negotiation or with the help of a mediator. But, if you are representing yourself in a divorce, one thing about the contested divorce process is clear. If a divorce starts out contested, it will almost always be much more complicated procedurally than if you and your spouse resolve any disputes before you file the first papers. Unfortunately, sometimes tempers and passions heat as a divorce unfolds. Details that surface can make people who were not angry become angry. If you begin your divorce amicably but later sense that the tide is turning, listen to your gut and get help if you need it.

Whether contested or uncontested, a divorce technically comes to an end when a court's final judgment or divorce decree is signed and entered into the court record, and the time to appeal has passed. But, unlike many other civil proceedings, spouses may come back into court and relitigate some key issues even after a divorce is final. Most often, this is to seek a modification in the divorce judgment's provisions regarding child support or child custody and visitation, but occasionally the issue of spousal support can also be relitigated. Modifications are discussed in more detail below.

Property and Debt Division

Unless spouses have already divided debts and property, as is common when there is a long delay between separation and divorce, spouses need to make decisions about who will own what items of property and who will pay which debts. As part of thinking about how to do this, it is wise to understand your state's basic legal rules so you can determine:

- what property belongs to each spouse separately (usually called "separate property"), and
- what property the two of you own together (often called "marital property" or, in some states, "community property").

In many marriages where spouses don't own or owe a great deal, doing this is mercifully simple. But complications commonly arise when significant property is involved. For example, deciding who owns a family business, real estate, an investment portfolio, or even pensions can often be tricky.

Taking the time to understand who legally owns what can provide these benefits:

- In negotiation, you can make a clearer presentation of facts to support why you should get the property you want.
- In mediation, you will be able to make proposals that are clearly reasonable and not risk sabotaging the process by making unreasonable demands.
- In court, you can ask the judge for what you are entitled to, without annoying the judge with overreaching demands.

The final reason why you need to understand property law may strike you as odd: If, in an effort to get your divorce over with, you want to allow your spouse to keep more than he or she is entitled to under law (perhaps to minimize conflict, keep relations amicable, or just get on with your life), you may have to justify your decision to a judge. If you are able to persuade the judge that you are making an educated decision, the judge is much more apt to grant your request on the spot than if the judge feels you are "selling yourself short" out of ignorance. Some judges who feel a self-represented spouse is getting seriously shortchanged will even require the spouse to consult with an attorney before proceeding further.

CAUTION

If you incurred a debt, you're still on the hook. A divorce judgment may, and usually does, divide both property and debts. But, when it comes to debts, there is an important catch: Even if the court assigns a certain debt to your spouse to pay, if you were responsible for paying the debt when it was incurred (for example, your spouse purchased a TV with your joint credit card), the creditor still has the legal right to go after you if your spouse violates the court order and doesn't pay. You, of course, have the legal right to rely on the divorce court's order and seek reimbursement from your spouse, but doing this won't help much if your spouse has disappeared or doesn't have money or other property to give you.

RESOURCE

Finding your state's property division rules. Chapter 23 will help you find the key property or debt division rules for your state. But before heading into the thicket of

Divorce and Bankruptcy

Divorces all too often coincide with money troubles. As a result, many divorcing couples also find themselves considering bankruptcy. If this describes you and your spouse, you will want to learn how federal bankruptcy laws and your state's divorce laws interact. For example, although most debts are "discharged" or wiped out in a Chapter 7 bankruptcy, this is not true for child or spousal support debts, which still must be paid after bankruptcy. Therefore, if you think bankruptcy is a real possibility for your spouse, don't agree to a divorce decree unless it clearly identifies payments as child or spousal support, thereby protecting against the possibility that the payments could be discharged in a later bankruptcy. To start your research, consult the following resources:

- *Divorce & Money: How to Make the Best Financial Decisions During Divorce*, by Violet Woodhouse with Dale Fetherling (Nolo), includes a section explaining the different types of bankruptcies and the basic interaction between bankruptcy and divorce.
- *Solve Your Money Troubles: Get Debt Collectors off Your Back & Regain Financial Freedom*, by Robin Leonard and John Lamb (Nolo), explains bankruptcy and nonbankruptcy alternatives for resolving financial difficulties and helps you decide which type of bankruptcy may be best for your situation.

Bankruptcy is discussed in more detail in Chapter 22.

legal research, it will help if you take a look at a self-help law book on divorce to gain a clear understanding of some basic rules. *Divorce and Money: How to Make the Best Financial Decisions During Divorce*, by Violet Woodhouse with Dale Fetherling (Nolo), will help you to understand the value of your house, investments, pensions, and other property and debts. This book also capably deals with the many tax issues that accompany divorce.

Spousal Support (Alimony)

Spousal support (also called "alimony" or "maintenance") is money one spouse pays to the other following a divorce or separation. Once awarded routinely, spousal support is now typically ordered only in certain situations, including:

- long marriages—especially where one spouse pursued a successful career while the other raised children
- where one spouse's earning power is significantly higher than the other's, or
- where one spouse is ill or disabled and without significant financial resources and the other has a decent job or other income.

When spousal support is awarded, one spouse is usually ordered to make monthly installment payments to the other for a set number of years (though in some cases, judges order one lump-sum payment). If the marriage lasted for many years, the payer spouse may have to pay spousal support indefinitely or at least until the recipient spouse gets remarried (one reason a lump-sum payment up front may be preferable).

How Much Money Will You Have to Pay?

In most states, judges determine how much, if any, spousal support to award by referring to published financial schedules or guidelines, unless the spouses signed a valid prenuptial agreement establishing the amount in advance. You should be able to locate these financial schedules in a law library, your court's Clerk's Office, or by consulting a lawyer. In addition, judges may consider factors such as:

- the length of the marriage
- each spouse's earning power
- each spouse's age, health, financial needs, and the standard of living to which each is accustomed
- the payer spouse's ability to pay and the recipient spouse's ability to become self-supporting, and
- how much property each party will receive under the property division.

CAUTION

Tax considerations are important when spouses are trying to negotiate spousal support. Spousal support is tax deductible to the payer spouse and taxable to the recipient spouse. For more information on divorce-related tax issues, see *Divorce and Money: How to Make the Best Financial Decisions During Divorce* by Violet Woodhouse with Dale Fetherling (Nolo). The IRS also provides several helpful publications for free on its website, at www.irs.gov, including: Publication 503, *Tax Information on Selling Your Home;* Publication 504, *Tax Information for Divorced or Separated Individuals;* and Publication 523, *Child and Dependent Care Expenses.*

Child Custody and Visitation

Parenting after a divorce obviously involves making many important decisions. Who will physically take care of the children, where, and when? Who will decide whether and what type of education and medical treatment they get? Who will pay for which of the children's needs?

Detailed Parenting Agreements Often Work Best

Court orders dealing with child custody are very brief, often stating no more than who has custody during what time intervals. When spouses get along well, leaving these details vague is usually not a problem. But experts have found that where tensions between the spouses are running high, everyone is usually better off creating a detailed written parenting plan. The idea is that disagreements have less opportunity to fester when both parents and children know exactly what to expect.

For example, a detailed agreement might specify the exact time a spouse must pick up and drop off a child. And, especially if the couple is attempting joint physical custody, it would list which holidays and birthdays kids will spend with each parent. It might also include a clear delineation of what, if any, visitation rights grandparents and other significant adults will have. An additional advantage of spelling out details is that if a dispute arises, the couple (and, if necessary, a judge) can look to the agreement to help resolve it. It may also help if tensions arise later and it's harder to communicate.

As with dividing property, many divorcing couples work out their own parenting agreements. For couples who can do this, the family court may only get involved to approve the couple's agreement. But for those who cannot agree, or where one spouse does not abide by an agreement or court order, a couple may make repeated trips to family court to ask a judge to fine-tune their child-rearing decision making.

RESOURCE

Resources on child custody. *Building a Parenting Agreement That Works: How to Put Your Kids First When Your Marriage Doesn't Last,* by Mimi E. Lyster (Nolo), identifies the important issues that divorcing parents are likely to face and suggests practical solutions for each. The book also explains how to negotiate a comprehensive parenting agreement and how mediation can help if negotiations break down. And it includes a number of useful forms and worksheets.

Child Custody Made Simple: Understanding the Laws of Child Custody and Child Support, by Webster Watnik (Single Parent Press), provides a good overview of the laws governing child custody decisions.

The term "custody" doesn't just refer to whether minor children will live primarily at Mom's house or Dad's house. In addition to physical control over the children, custody governs which parent has the legal authority to make critical parenting decisions, such as which school kids will attend and which religion they will practice. Up until 25 years ago, judges almost always awarded the mother custody and the father visitation rights. The current trend is more often towards "joint" or "shared" custody arrangements. Although mothers still get primary physical custody more often than fathers, joint custody means decision-making authority is shared.

When judges decide custody and visitation issues, they try to determine what arrangement is in the "best interests of the child," considering factors such as:

- The age and sex of the child and the child's relationship with the parent, stepparents, and siblings. Not surprisingly, judges try to keep siblings together.
- The fitness (mental and physical health) of each parent, including any history of verbal or physical abuse and alcohol or drug problems. In addition, most judges will carefully consider who is really the primary caretaker, who is the more nurturing parent, and possibly who has better judgment.
- The familiarity of the children with an existing family home, school, or community. (Courts seek to disrupt kids' lives as little as possible.)
- The child's preference. (This is a far more important consideration for kids over the age of ten than it is for younger children).

Child Support

Child support is money that one parent (usually the noncustodial parent or the parent with the higher income) pays to the other parent (usually the custodial parent or the parent with the lower income). The trend toward joint custody arrangements sometimes makes it less clear which parent (if either) will have to pay child support.

Federal law requires every state to publish written guidelines for how child support is calculated in that state, often called child support "formulas" or "schedules." Typically, these guidelines are based on a combination of each parent's ability to pay, which parent has physical custody most of the time, and the needs of the children. Guidelines are important, even for couples who make their own child support agreements, because judges probably won't approve an agreement unless it provides at least the minimum amount of child support set forth in that state's schedules. In short, finding out how much child support you should receive or will have to pay under your state's guidelines is key legal information that you should get early on in the divorce process—either by doing the legal research or by asking the clerk of your family court.

Child support orders issued by the court typically specify how many years the payer spouse has to pay child support. If no time period is specified, payments usually continue until the child reaches 18 years of age (or, in a few states, gets through college). Child support payments may not be claimed as tax deductions by the payer spouse, nor are they considered taxable income to the payee spouse. But as with other aspects of divorce, there are significant tax ramifications to the paying of child support and custody— for instance, who may claim the child as a dependent. If there is no written agreement on this issue, the general rule is that the custodial parent gets to claim the child as a dependent. However, if a noncustodial parent pays for more than 50% of the child's support and can produce a written waiver of exemption from the custodial parent, the noncustodial parent can claim the exemption instead.

CAUTION

Child support survives bankruptcy. Neither past-owed child support (arrears), nor future child support obligations may be canceled (discharged) in a bankruptcy proceeding. This means that if a parent owing child support is unable to pay it—if, for example, the parent loses a job—that parent would be wise to ask the family court for an order at least temporarily reducing the support obligation instead of letting it pile up, thereby creating a debt that must eventually be paid off.

What Happens If Child Support Isn't Paid?

All states have an easy method for garnishing wages if a wage earner fails to meet child support obligations. In fact, in many states child support is automatically paid out of a person's wages before the payer even gets a paycheck. However, if the person owing support is not employed or is self-employed, there may be collection problems if payment isn't made voluntarily. When this occurs, the person owed support can ask for a court hearing (often with the help of the district attorney's child support enforcement division) to request that the judge enforce it. Often this means the judge will first verbally order the nonpaying spouse to pay up. If that doesn't work, the judge can hold the nonpaying spouse in contempt of court—and issue a fine or even a jail sentence.

Filing for Divorce

From a formal legal point of view, divorce proceedings begin when one spouse files a document called a "complaint" or "petition," depending on the state. The person who files this document (the "plaintiff" or "petitioner") then arranges to have it served on (delivered to) the other spouse (the "defendant" or "respondent").

Nonlawyer Help is Usually Available for Divorce Paperwork

In addition to other resources identified in this book, legal typing services (often called independent paralegals) can be a huge help to people filing their own divorce papers. They assist self-represented parties with preparing divorce papers for a reasonable fee, often in the range of $100 to $300. Because typing services are not owned or operated by lawyers, their personnel may not give you legal advice. But, because they are very familiar with the paperwork involved in the typical divorce (many are former legal secretaries), they can make your job much easier. Remember, however, that it is your divorce and therefore your responsibility to carefully check any forms, advice, or information you receive from a typing service.

Creating a Divorce Petition or Complaint

Though states vary as to exactly what language you must include in a divorce petition, most require the following three things:

(1) A statement of facts (often called "allegations"). This is a statement that one or both spouses reside within the state, the dates of the marriage and separation, the names and birth dates of any minor children, and lists of property owned and debts owed.

(2) The grounds for divorce. This is often a short sentence saying that the couple no longer wants to be married because they have "irreconcilable differences." Here the exact terminology differs from state to state. For example, in Hawaii and several other states, the spouses must say their marriage is "irretrievably broken." But the requirements are usually the same in the states that allow no-fault divorces: The petitioning spouse states that the spouses can no longer live together and want to end their marriage. In the few states where fault is still taken into account in some divorces, the petitioning spouse will typically describe the "wrong" committed (such as desertion, mental cruelty, or adultery) as the grounds for divorce.

(3) A statement describing what the petitioner/plaintiff wants (sometimes called the "prayer for relief"). The prayer usually appears near the end of the petition and includes a request that:

- the marriage end
- the marital property and debts be divided
- the petitioning spouse be awarded custody of any minor children (or both spouses be awarded joint custody)
- the petitioning spouse be awarded a specified monthly sum for child support (assuming that the spouse will have primary physical custody)

- if appropriate, spousal support be awarded
- if applicable and desired, the wife's maiden name (or both spouses' former names, if combined after marriage) be restored, and
- if the petitioning spouse has a lower income, the other spouse pay all attorneys' fees and court costs.

In some states, a petitioner must type or neatly print all of this information in narrative form. Other states use preprinted forms; the petitioner need only check the appropriate box and insert requested information in specified blanks.

Summary Divorce for Short Marriages

Many states offer a streamlined procedure for couples who have been married a short time (usually, less than five years) and don't have children or own property. These summary procedures use fewer (and simpler) forms and allow the parties to petition together to end their marriage. If you think you might qualify for a summary procedure, check with your local court clerk to find out the requirements in your state and get the appropriate forms.

Filing and Serving the Petition or Complaint

Once the filing spouse completes the required divorce papers or forms, filing and serving them on the other spouse usually involves the following:

- Taking or mailing the filled-in forms (with the appropriate number of copies) to the appropriate Clerk's Office in the county where one of the parties lives. In some states, this is the main trial court, where many other types of lawsuits are handled, while in others, it is a separate family court.
- Paying the filing fee (often from $25 to $150, depending on the state, and sometimes significantly more).
- Obtaining a stamped (confirmed) copy from the clerk, by hand or return mail. The confirmed copy will typically have a case number (sometimes called a "cause number") on the front page. All future documents filed with the court as part of the divorce proceedings should use that same number.
- Serving the documents on the nonfiling spouse. Each state has its own technical service rules that the filing spouse should check (with a clerk, legal coach, or through legal research) before making service. It is important to complete this step correctly: Serving divorce papers on the nonfiling spouse is what gives the family court authority (jurisdiction) to decide the case. (See Chapters 3 and 5 for general service requirements.)

What happens next depends, most importantly, on whether the divorce is contested or uncontested. Procedurally, this will turn on whether the nonfiling spouse files responsive papers. Your state's divorce law requirements will also play a part in determining your next steps.

SKIP AHEAD

Is your divorce contested or uncontested? If you and your spouse have reached agreement on all the important issues that affect your divorce—or your spouse is simply no longer in the picture and everything has already been taken care of—your divorce is uncontested and you can proceed to "How Uncontested Divorces Work," below.

If you don't know whether or not your divorce is likely to be contested, reread "Understanding the Basics of Family Law," above, and, depending on what you conclude, proceed to "How Uncontested Divorces Work" or skip ahead to "How Contested Divorces Work."

If you file for divorce now without reaching agreement with your spouse on all major issues, your divorce will be contested, unless your spouse decides not to respond in court. For now, you should assume that the divorce will be contested, but read both sections below.

How Uncontested Divorces Work

The vast majority of divorces in the United States are uncontested.

Why Divorces Are Uncontested

Perhaps the most common reason a divorce is uncontested is that there is nothing to fight about—no minor children, no valuable property, few debts, and no claim for spousal support. Another reason is that spouses often live separately for a long period of time (several years is common) before one of them decides to make it official by filing for divorce. During this separation period,

passions have time to cool and the spouses work out agreements on all significant issues, such as child custody and support and the division of property. Still another reason for more divorces being uncontested is the increasing use of mediation to help divorcing spouses resolve disputes.

Typical Uncontested Divorce Procedure

Because there is nothing to fight about, uncontested divorces are usually very simple to handle in court. Here are the steps to be taken in most states:

Step 1: One of the spouses (the plaintiff or petitioner) files a petition or complaint with the court containing required facts. In some states, both spouses can file one petition as co-petitioners.

Step 2: When one spouse files, the divorce petition is delivered to (served on) the other spouse. If the other spouse is cooperative and willing to acknowledge receiving the papers, this process can be quite informal (first-class mail or personal delivery by the filing spouse). If the other spouse does not cooperate, a process server must formally serve the papers on the other spouse. When a spouse can't be located, service can often be accomplished by publishing notice of the action in a newspaper.

Step 3: Typically, the other spouse does not file responsive papers with the court. If responsive papers are filed, they do not identify any areas of disagreement.

Step 4: If responsive papers are filed and there are some areas of disagreement, the spouses (or if they are represented, their lawyers) engage in informal negotiation or mediation to quickly resolve them before the case goes any further.

Step 5: Once spouses reach agreement—with or without a mediator—they put their agreement in writing and file it with the court.

Step 6: Once the court is informed that the divorce is (or has become) uncontested, it either issues a divorce decree on the basis of written documents, with no court hearing required, or schedules a hearing before the judge with one or both spouses attending. (An example of a hearing on an uncontested divorce petition is set out below.)

Step 7: In some states, the divorce is effective immediately. In others, there is a waiting period before it becomes final.

Below is an example of an uncontested divorce hearing. In this hearing, both spouses are present. But if no responsive papers are filed, it is also possible (likely in some states) that only the petitioning spouse will be in court. In this hypothetical case, the parties originally disagreed about property division but managed to reach agreement and put it into a formal document (called a "marital settlement agreement") that they filed with the court before the hearing. In cases in which there is little or no property or one spouse is missing, there will be no written agreement of this type.

CAUTION

Research your own court's procedures. Because the facts of any particular case and the rules and customs of each court will differ, this transcript is only an illustration. As we stress throughout this chapter, to effectively handle your own case you should do additional research and preparation, including, if possible, sitting in on similar hearings in front of the judge who will hear your case. Fortunately, many family courts assign all family court cases to one or a few judges, so it shouldn't be too hard to figure out who your judge will be.

Entering the packed, noisy courtroom, we wait for Judge Jackie Equitable to take the bench as people constantly come in and out. In last-minute conferences with their clients and each other, lawyers hauling big briefcases huddle with their clients in the spectators' seats or chat with each other near the front of the courtroom. When the judge enters, the clerk or bailiff asks everyone to stand—at which point things quiet down. After the bailiff (or perhaps the judge herself) says, "Be seated," the low buzzing of whispers continues. Judge Equitable spends a few minutes sipping coffee and looking through a stack of papers. The judge's clerk, sitting at a desk in front (or to the side) of the judge's bench, also sifts through stacks of files, stapling and marking documents. Occasionally, the clerk hands a file to the judge, making a few whispered remarks. (See Chapter 2 for more on the layout of a courtroom.) Finally, after what seems like a long time but is probably only a few minutes, the clerk calls, "Superior Court, now in session. The Honorable Jackie Equitable presiding. Come to order." To the judge, the clerk whispers, "First up, Peter Parto v. Rita Parto—uncontested."

1 Clerk:

Next case, Parto.

2 Judge:

Are the parties present and ready to proceed?

3 **Petitioner (standing):**
I am.

4 **Respondent (standing):**
I am also.

5 **Judge:**
Please approach the bench. (Peter and Rita get up from their seats in the spectator section of the courtroom and walk up to the judge's slightly elevated bench.)

Procedural Note: In this hearing, the judge requests that the parties stand before the bench. Although many judges handle uncontested proceedings this way, proceedings are more formal in other courtrooms, with the judge asking the petitioning party, in this case Peter, to present the case from the witness box.

6 **Judge (nodding toward Peter):**
You are?

7 **Petitioner:**
Peter Parto, and I am the petitioner in this case.

8 **Judge (nodding toward Rita):**
And you are the respondent, Rita Parto?

9 **Respondent:**
Yes, Your Honor.

10 **Judge:**
Are all the facts stated in this petition and the response true?

11 **Petitioner:**
Yes, Your Honor.

12 **Respondent:**
Yes.

13 **Judge:**
And, at the time this petition was filed, you both had resided in this state for six months?

14 **Petitioner:**
Yes.

15 **Respondent:**
Yes.

16 **Judge: (nodding to Peter Parto):**
You were married on December 7, 1995, and separated on July 4 of this year?

17 **Petitioner and Respondent:**
Yes.

18 **Judge:**
During the course of your marriage, irreconcilable differences developed, leading to the breakdown of the marriage, and there's no hope you'll get back together?

19 **Petitioner:**
That's right.

20 **Respondent:**
Yes.

21 **Judge:**
Do you have children?

22 **Petitioner and Respondent:**
No.

23 **Judge (flipping through papers):**
I see here you have filed a marital settlement agreement with regard to property division, which you both have signed. Petitioner, is this your true and correct signature?

24 **Petitioner:**
Yes.

25 Judge:

And have you signed voluntarily?

26 Petitioner:

Yes.

27 Judge:

Respondent, is this your true and correct signature?

28 Respondent:

Yes, and I signed voluntarily also.

29 Judge (after glancing at the agreement):

You are aware that under the laws of this state, your property probably would be divided somewhat differently than you have agreed in this writing?

30 Respondent and Petitioner:

Yes.

31 Judge:

And you both wish that this agreement be made part of the proposed dissolution decree you have submitted?

32 Respondent and Petitioner:

Yes.

Procedural Notes: Note that the judge questioned the parties' decision to make a different property division than the 50-50 division called for under that state's law. Though this judge did not pursue the matter beyond verifying that the parties are aware of a difference, many family law judges would question the parties further. Specifically, the judge might encourage the party who agreed to take less than what would be provided for under the law to rethink this issue or, possibly, see a lawyer before the case proceeds further. Occasionally, a judge might even try to unilaterally decide to divide the property as he or she sees fit, regardless of what the parties say they want. If this occurs, one or both parties may want to ask the judge to delay the case so they can get some legal advice.

33 Judge:

Do either of you have anything further to say at this time?

34 Respondent:

Yes, Your Honor. I would request that the court's order also restore my former name, Rita Singla.

35 Judge:

So ordered. The proposed order for dissolution of marriage is granted.

36 Clerk:

Next case.

Procedural Note: Except for Rita's request for her name to be changed, most of what occurred in the dialogue above was the judge asking all questions necessary to qualify the parties for a divorce and the parties answering "yes" or "no." However, as noted above, if this case were heard in another courtroom, it might have proceeded very differently. For instance, the judge might have said little more than, "You may proceed." At that point, the petitioner must make an oral presentation that includes all key information the judge needs to hear in order to grant a divorce.

For instance, if Peter Parto were in such a court as a self-represented party on a default divorce, he might begin by saying something like the following:

"Good morning, Your Honor. Rita Parto and I were married on December 7, 1995,

and we separated on July 4 of this year. We have not lived together as husband and wife since that time. I am seeking a divorce because we have reached irreconcilable differences that have destroyed all that was good in our marriage and has led to its irretrievable breakdown. Therefore, I am here today to request a divorce."

RESOURCE

Find a do-it-yourself divorce book for your state. Because you can't count on a judge to be as helpful as Judge Equitable, you will want to obtain good information and practice your presentation.

The following books show you how to handle your own divorce without a lawyer, including sorting out debts, taxes, division of property, child support, child custody and visitation, and provide the forms required to get a divorce in the state the book cover:

- *How to Do Your Own Divorce in California* by Ed Sherman (Nolo Occidental), and
- *How to Do Your Own Divorce in Texas* by Ed Sherman (Nolo Occidental).

For general information and a guide to resources in all 50 states, see *Nolo's Essential Guide to Divorce* by Emily Doskow (Nolo).

How Contested Divorces Work

If an uncontested divorce is usually simple, a contested divorce can be nightmarishly complex. The court procedures are often complicated, time-consuming, and, if lawyers are involved, expensive. Divorce cases can be complicated further if the parties try to use the courts to punish each other (as is often the case).

What follows is a brief outline of the typical procedures in a contested divorce case. But remember, all states have their own slightly different laws and procedures. If you are involved in a contested divorce case without legal help, you will need to do additional legal research. You will also want to master the information about representing yourself in a contested court action discussed throughout the rest of this book.

Getting a Lawyer

The first big question in a contested divorce is whether to hire a lawyer. As we stressed earlier, divorcing parties are almost always better off if they mediate their disputes rather than fight them out in the courtroom. However, if feelings are running extremely high, there is a history of abuse, or one spouse is far more powerful or knowledgeable about business or financial affairs than the other, mediation may not be advisable, at least at first. What then? The traditional solution is to turn to the legal profession.

If one spouse hires a lawyer, the other spouse may feel the need to hire one, too. Once two lawyers are in on a case, the divorce is obviously beyond the scope of this book. But it is also possible for one spouse to hire a lawyer (typically the spouse who files the divorce) and the other spouse to continue to self-represent.

Filing a Divorce Petition or Complaint

One of the spouses (the "petitioner" or "plaintiff") files a document called a "petition" or "complaint" with the court. See "Filing for Divorce," above, for what you should typically include in a divorce petition.

Serving the Petition or Complaint

The spouse who files the petition or complaint serves the papers on (delivers them to) the other spouse. See "Filing for Divorce," above, for how to do this.

Filing a Response or Answer

The spouse who is served with the papers (the "defendant" or "respondent") prepares a written "response" or "answer" to clearly set out what that spouse wants the judge to do and how this differs from what the petitioner/plaintiff requested in the petition or complaint.

Obtaining Temporary Orders

If your spouse moves out and leaves you without enough money to provide food and shelter for your kids, you can go to court for a temporary order before the divorce is completed—or, in some instances, even before the initial divorce papers (the petition or complaint) are filed. Especially when the trust level between the spouses is low, one or both of the spouses will typically want the court to intervene immediately and issue certain orders to be in effect pending the final divorce decree. If one spouse has committed or threatened physical abuse or has threatened to abscond with the children, the other spouse can seek a temporary restraining order, as described above. But even if this type of emergency relief isn't necessary, a spouse may want the court to:

- temporarily establish who has custody of the children and when the other parent may visit
- temporarily require child or spousal support payments
- issue orders freezing or preventing the sale of assets, or
- award temporary possession of the family home or car to one of the spouses.

Unless you obtain an emergency order, the actual process of getting a temporary order, including the paperwork you must complete and file and how to prepare for the hearing, is similar to that of filing other motions (requests for court orders). To succeed, you must typically prepare, file, and serve on your spouse all of the following:

- **A Request for an Order to Show Cause (OSC) and the OSC itself.** An Order to Show Cause is a legal form or short, typed legal document that sets out what you are asking for—in this case a temporary order—and tells (orders) your spouse to come to court at a specific time and explain (show cause) why the court should not grant your request.
- **A supporting declaration.** This is your written statement under penalty of perjury that sets forth facts necessary to legally justify the issuance of the temporary order. Although a judge may issue a temporary order on the basis of your declaration alone, you are also entitled to submit declarations of other people who have firsthand knowledge of the facts. (You'll find more on declarations in Chapter 7.)

- **A Proposed Temporary Order granting you the relief requested in your application.** It's "proposed" because the court hasn't signed it yet.
- **A Proof of Service.** This document provides the court with proof that your spouse has been properly served with the papers described just above. (See the sample Proof of Service in Chapter 3.) If you haven't filed this document by the time of the court hearing, the hearing will likely be postponed.

Your next step is to attend the court hearing at which the judge will determine whether the temporary order should be granted (this is often called an "Order to Show Cause" hearing). The judge may listen to testimony from you, your spouse, and possibly other witnesses, or may only accept written evidence, such as medical bills, rent receipts, expense budgets, or declarations submitted by you or persons with knowledge of the facts. Either way, the judge will:

- review your requests (or those of your spouse if it's your spouse requesting the order) and the underlying facts
- possibly ask you some questions, and
- ask for your spouse's side of the story, if your spouse is present.

Then the judge will likely make a ruling, usually either issuing the requested temporary order, denying your request, or continuing the hearing to another day. If you previously obtained an emergency restraining order without your spouse being present (an "ex parte order"), the judge may simply continue that order in effect or modify it slightly.

When you request a temporary order, make sure to cover all key details, because the order may remain in effect for a year or two, depending on how long it takes to complete the divorce procedure. Although a judge can modify or terminate the order if circumstances change, it is no fun to have to return to court.

CAUTION

Temporary orders are just that. Temporary orders may be modified later, so don't count on them for the long term. For example, if you are receiving a certain sum for support, do not budget for the future expecting to receive that sum down the road. Even so-called permanent orders for things like spousal and child support may be modified in some circumstances.

Below is an example of a hearing on an OSC for an order setting temporary child custody and visitation. Mark Daniels has come to court to request temporary custody of his son. During the course of the hearing, visitation issues also come up when Mark accuses his spouse, Diane, of not allowing him to see their son. Responding to Mark's concerns, the judge also makes a temporary ruling on when visits will occur.

1 **Clerk:**
Next case, Daniels.

2 **Judge:**
Is Mr. Daniels present?

3 **Mark Daniels:**
Yes, Your Honor.

4 **Judge:**
Ms. Daniels?

5 **Diane Daniels:**
Also here, Your Honor.

6 **Judge:**

You may be seated. [Mark and Diane walk to and take seats at the respective counsel tables. (See Chapter 2 for an explanation of where litigants sit.) Shuffling through papers, the judge continues.] *Mr. Daniels, let's see, you want custody of your son?*

7 **Mark:**

Yes, my wife, Diane, and I are trying to work out our divorce. We have been going to mediation, and we've decided most of the property issues. But the mediator told us it could be a while before we finish, and even longer before the divorce is final. I want custody of our boy, at least for the present, while we're trying to work things out.

8 **Judge:**

Go on.

9 **Mark:**

My son, Roger, is now living with his mother, who asked me to leave the house months ago—which I did. But she is not letting me see him regularly. [Mark shakes his head.] *She's so damn difficult—*

10 **Judge:**

Watch your language in my courtroom, Mr. Daniels. And please stick to the facts.

11 **Mark:**

Excuse me, Your Honor. It's just that, every time I go to pick Roger up, he's hungry. I've spoken with my wife's day-care provider, and she says Diane brings little Roger in at 7 a.m. and doesn't pick him up until after 6 p.m. I work freelance, mostly from home.

I could spend much more time with him. He wouldn't need to be in day-care more than six hours a day if I had him. I feel this neglect has been going on long enough. I have to step in and do something now. I can't wait while we hash things out in mediation. Who knows if we'll ever agree? Also, my wife says she has been "busy" lately, so the past few mediation sessions have been delayed. Meanwhile, my son's most precious years are rushing by. I am here today asking for you to grant me primary custody of Roger—at least until we can work out an agreement that's fair to both of us.

12 **Judge (to Diane):**

Do you have anything to say?

13 **Diane:**

Yes, yes, Your Honor. I sure do. (Diane stands and gathers some papers in front of her.) *I'm just astounded at Mark's claims. It's absurd for him to say Roger goes hungry.*

14 **Judge:**

Mrs. Daniels, it will help me if you will state the facts and keep the value judgments to yourself.

15 **Diane:**

I'll do my best, Your Honor. The point is, Mark never fed Roger when he lived with us. I've always been the one who took care of all Roger's physical needs. He's a growing healthy boy, and I'm responsible for that. And Roger probably does say he's hungry when Mark picks him up because he knows his father will buy him ice cream or some other junk food, which I don't usually allow.

As to the day care, forgive me if I say I'm in shock. First off, Mark and I picked the day-care provider together. He knows it's a good place. Second, I need to work long days to provide for Roger and pay the entire mortgage, now, on my own. I'm working extra to try to keep Roger and me in a home fit for a child—with a backyard, friendly neighbors, the whole package.

Also, it is true Mark works "freelance," but his idea that he has a regular six-hour workday with plenty of time for Roger just isn't accurate. What he really has are long periods when he's not doing much, then crunches when ten projects hit at once and he works around the clock. What will he do with Roger then? He'll call me.

16 Judge:

Is it true that you are not letting him visit your son regularly?

17 Diane:

Well, no. Not really. There have been a few times lately when I've said Mark can't take Roger. But that was because he didn't tell me ahead of time, or because Roger was involved in something else at the time—like taking a nap. One time when I said no, Mark had shown up unexpectedly when we had planned to visit Roger's grandmother. Another time, I'd bought tickets for the circus before he asked to visit with Roger. Mark cannot just come over to play whenever he feels like it; he doesn't live with us anymore. He's got to make arrangements with me in advance and stick to his promises.

18 Judge:

Mr. Daniels, do you have any proof other than your own testimony that Diane Daniels is not adequately caring for your son?

19 Mark:

Proof?

20 Judge:

Yes. Medical records? Testimony of other witnesses who also believe he is not being properly fed?

21 Mark:

No, Your Honor. But I know I can do better for the child. I will be there more for him—

22 Judge:

Without documentation, and based on the fact that Roger is currently living in the family home he is used to, I am denying your custody request, Mr. Daniels. Temporarily, and until this court enters an order stating otherwise, Ms. Diane Daniels will have primary custody over Roger Daniels, and Mark Daniels will have the following visitation rights. Mr. Daniels will take the boy every other weekend—beginning this coming Friday, January 15. He will come to your house, Ms. Daniels, and pick Roger up at 6 p.m. every other Friday evening, and return him to your home by 7 p.m. the following Sunday. You will have Roger ready to go, and will not refuse Mr. Daniels the right to have Roger for those weekends. As for you two, Mr. and Ms. Daniels, I strongly urge you to go back to your mediator ASAP to work out a custody arrangement that both of you can live with—but more important, one that puts Roger's interests to stay close to both of you without lots of tension first and foremost. Mr. Daniels, if you continue to truly believe your wife is not properly caring for your son, get some evidence together and file it with my clerk.

Engaging in Discovery/Disclosure

As with other lawsuits, family law cases provide a means for the parties to obtain information from each other through formal legal tools such as depositions, interrogatories, requests for admission, and subpoenas. (See Chapter 5 for more on discovery.) In addition, many states automatically require divorcing couples to exchange disclosure statements detailing their income, property, and debts, as well as their knowledge about property-related transactions made during the marriage that may affect the rights of the other spouse in the divorce.

Home Investigations

If child custody and visitation issues are in dispute, you or your spouse may have to undergo a court-ordered home study or investigation, in which a counselor checks out your parenting situation and submits a written report for the court.

Pretrial Hearings

One or more pretrial hearings may be necessary when one party feels the other is not abiding by proper procedures. For instance, one party may ask the court to enforce a discovery request to which the other side has failed to respond.

Informal Negotiation

As the divorce proceeds, offers and counteroffers are likely to fly back and forth between the spouses regarding one or more issues. For example, one spouse might propose to keep the house and several investments in exchange for the other gaining full ownership of a small family-owned business. This type of informal negotiating can be emotionally draining, as it requires the spouses to pay constant attention to a process that frequently causes one or both of them a fair amount of pain.

Mediation

Frequently, courts encourage divorcing spouses to mediate their differences rather than submit them to the court for settlement. In many states, if the spouses can't agree on child custody or visitation issues, the court will require them to participate in court-ordered mediation.

Settlement Conferences

Depending on the state and sometimes the individual court, the court may order a settlement conference, at which the judge will meet with the spouses and try to narrow contested issues and look for areas of agreement. Judges can quite forcefully urge compromise in these settlement conferences and, in situations in which one party refuses to go along, may even indicate how they plan to rule on a particular issue if the parties don't settle it first. Sometimes the judge's intended ruling is seen as being in neither spouse's best interest and therefore encourages settlement, occasionally as late as the day of the trial.

Trial

Although most divorce-related disputes are settled before trial, occasionally a formal court trial is held. However, especially in divorce cases, many courts are experimenting with informal procedures. Still, most of the information in Chapters 9 through 18 of this book applies to divorce trials.

Judgment

A marriage eventually ends when the judge issues a decree or judgment of divorce. In some states, the judgment or decree is final on the date it is issued, while in others (where it is often called an "interlocutory decree") it is not final until a period of time passes during which the divorcing spouses have the opportunity to change their minds.

 CAUTION

You may have to prepare the final decree. In many states, after the judge issues a divorce decree orally, it's up to the parties to prepare the necessary paperwork to ensure that the decree is written and entered into the court's docket. A self-help divorce book designed for use in your state should show you how to do this.

Appeals

If a contested trial is held, either or both parties can appeal. Normally, appeals succeed only if the trial judge has made a clear legal mistake—for example, ordered child support in an amount below the minimum allowed in your state. Appeals claiming the judge made a poor decision based on the facts of the case—for example, ordered one spouse to have primary child custody over the objection of the other—are almost never successful.

Now that we've covered the basic procedures in a divorce, below we provide an example of a stipulated judgment in an uncontested divorce. Again, as with other examples in this book, this sample judgment is provided as an illustration only; be sure to follow the appropriate procedures and forms required by your local court.

Procedural Note: Individual judgments may also include separate paragraphs on any number of additional matters, including taxes, reimbursement and release of liability claims, spousal support if applicable, and, if there are children, provisions regarding custody, visitation, child support, vacation, holidays, and the like. (In some jurisdictions, it is common to have separate parenting agreements; in others these provisions become part of a central judgment.) The judgment will likely conclude with some sort of space for the parties and judge to sign, such as the "Acknowledgment" that appears at the end of the document.

Sample Stipulated Judgment

1	Harry H. Husband
	[Street Address]
2	[City, State, Zip Code]
	[Phone Number]
3	
	Petitioner in Pro Per
4	

7	Petitioner: Harry H. Husband,	)	Marriage of Husband and Wife
8	Plaintiff,	)	
		)	Case No. 12345
9	v.	)	
		)	STIPULATED JUDGMENT
10	Respondent: Wilma W. Wife,	)	
		)	
11	Defendant.	)	
		)	

14   This proceeding was heard as an uncontested matter, before the Honorable Judge Judicio, on this

15 1st day of May 20XX. The court acquired jurisdiction on September 1, 20XX, when Respondent was

16 served with process.

17   The court orders, good cause appearing, that the judgment of dissolution is entered. Marital status

18 is terminated, and the parties are returned to the status of unmarried persons on this 1st day of May

19 20XX. Wife's former name is restored: Wilma Wilde.

20   The court makes the following further orders:

21   I. DIVISION OF COMMUNITY OF PROPERTY

22 A. Petitioner is awarded the following property as his sole and separate property:

23   1. _____ automobile [year, make, and model], license number

24   _____, with a value of approximately $_____

25   at the date of separation;

26   2. Fifty percent of funds in [bank name] Account # _____ with a balance of

27   approximately $_____ at the date of separation;

Sample Stipulated Judgment (continued)

1   3. Fifty percent of the funds in_____ Retirement Fund/Acct. No.

2   _____, valued at approximately $_____

3   at the date of separation;

4   4. Household furnishings, furniture, and appliances in Petitioner's possession.

5   B. Respondent is awarded the following property as her sole and separate property:

6   1. _____ automobile [year, make, and model], license number

7   _____, with a value of approximately $_____

8   at the date of separation;

9   2. Fifty percent of funds in [bank name] Account # _____ with a balance of

10   approximately $_____ at the date of separation;

11   3. Fifty percent of the funds in_____ Retirement Fund/Acct. No.

12   _____, valued at approximately $_____

13   at the date of separation;

14   4. Household furnishings, furniture, and appliances in Respondent's possession.

15   C. The community residence located at 16 Maple Drive, in Big City, and legally described as: Lot

16   _____ of Tract _____, City of Big City, per map recorded in Book _____,

17   pages _____ to _____ ("the residence") shall be divided as follows:

18   1. Each party is awarded an undivided one-half interest in the residence, and the residence shall

19   be held by Respondent and Petitioner as Tenants-in-Common.

20   2. Respondent is awarded exclusive use and possession of the residence for a period of five years

21   from the date of separation.

22   3. During said period, Respondent shall be solely liable for the payment of the following

23   expenses related to the real property: mortgage payments, property taxes, homeowners

24   insurance, and ordinary maintenance, so long as the amortized monthly total of said

25   payments do not exceed the fair rental value of the real property.

26   4. All capital improvements and repairs shall be shared equally by the parties. Except in an

27   emergency, the parties shall agree in writing prior to any improvements or repairs being made

28   to the real property.

Sample Stipulated Judgment (continued)

5. Both parties are restrained and prohibited from encumbering said real property without the prior written consent of the other party.

6. At the end of the five years in which Respondent has exclusive possession, Respondent shall have the right to buy Petitioner's interest in the house at its then-current fair market value (FMV). The FMV will be determined by averaging the value of appraisal from two local, certified real estate appraisers, one chosen by each party. If Respondent does not wish to buy the home, Petitioner may buy Respondent's interest using the same valuation method. If neither wishes to buy, the home shall be sold and the net proceeds divided equally between the parties.

II. CONFIRMATION OF SEPARATE PROPERTY

A. In addition to that property awarded Petitioner as his sole and separate property in this Judgment, Petitioner is confirmed the following as his sole and separate property:

1. Any and all earnings or acquisitions received after the parties' date of separation;

2. Monies in separate property fund or gift account ([bank name] Account # _____).

B. In addition to that property awarded Respondent as her sole and separate property in this Judgment, Respondent is confirmed the following as her sole and separate property:

1. Any and all earnings or acquisitions received after the parties' date of separation;

2. Lake cabin, located at 1 Water Drive, in Blue Lake City.

III. ASSETS OF THE MINOR CHILDREN

[If there were funds in the names of minor children, the bank account names and numbers would be listed here.]

IV. OBLIGATIONS

The following debts are assigned to Petitioner to assume full responsibility for payment thereof:

[list debts—including name of creditor, account number, and amount owing at separation]

The following debts are assigned to Respondent to assume full responsibility for payment thereof:

[list debts—including name of creditor, account number, and amount owing at separation]

Respondent and Petitioner are ordered to be solely and separately liable for all liabilities incurred after the date of separation and shall hold the other harmless therefrom.

Sample Stipulated Judgment (continued)

1   The parties are ordered to cooperate with each other so that existing charge accounts can be

2   established on the separate credit of the party desiring to maintain said account or establish a new

3   account.

4   The parties acknowledge that, although an obligation is assigned to one party as part of the

5   division of community property, if the party to whom the obligation was assigned defaults upon

6   payment of the obligation, the creditor may have a cause of action against the other party. Nothing in

7   this clause shall be construed to give any third-party creditor additional rights that they may not have

8   absent this Judgment.

9   *[Include separate paragraphs on any other relevant matters here. (See Procedural Note at the end of*

10   *this sample document.)]*

11   ACKNOWLEDGMENT

12   Each party agrees and acknowledges that each has read the foregoing instrument in full,

13   understands the terms thereof, and finds it to be fair, just, and equitable in all respects.

14

15   IT IS SO STIPULATED:

16
     Date: _____   _____

17   Harry H. Husband
                                              Petitioner
18

19   Date: _____   _____
                                              Wilma W. Wife
20   Respondent

21

22   IT IS SO ORDERED:

23
     Date: _____   _____

24   The Honorable _____
                                              Judge of the Superior Court
25

26

27

28

-4-

Modification of Support, Custody, and Visitation

Though provisions regarding the care and support of children of the marriage are usually written into court orders (or marital settlement agreements), they are not set in stone. If circumstances change significantly, you may go back to the judge and ask that the support, custody, or visitation order be modified or enforced in one or more of its particulars. For example, divorced people may go back into court and request that child support be modified if:

- either parent's income decreases substantially (for example, a parent loses a job)
- either parent's financial needs substantially increase (for instance, if either has a baby)
- either parent receives a large inheritance or gift, thereby either increasing their ability to provide support or decreasing their need to receive it
- a change occurs in one parent's life that bears on the parent's ability to care for the children, or
- the needs of the children change (for example, a teenager may want to go to school near Dad's, rather than Mom's, house)

Some courts handle modification requests in public court just like other motions. Other judges handle such requests—as well as requests to change or enforce support payments—informally in the judge's chambers (office).

In the following dialogue, Molly Patricks, who recently lost her job, wants her former husband to pay more child support based on her reduced income. Molly filed with the family court and paid the sheriff's office to serve (deliver to her ex-husband) an Order to Show Cause (OSC) ordering her ex-husband to appear in court if he wished to say why the court should not modify the child and spousal support payments (see above for more on OSCs). The OSC contained the date, time, and location of the court hearing along with Molly's supporting documentation—which consisted of an income and expense declaration:

1 **Judge Wilbur Washington:** *Patricks?*

2 **Molly Patricks:** *Present, Your Honor.*

3 **Judge:** *Is the Respondent present?*

4 **Molly:** *No.*

5 **Judge:** *Do you expect him to be here today?*

6 **Molly:** *I have no idea. It's already 10:30 a.m.; my papers say the hearing will be in this courtroom at 9 a.m.*

7 **Judge:** *Indeed.* [The judge flips through a file, mumbling, checking to see the paperwork is in order.] *Ms. Patricks, I see your modification request here is based on the fact that you lost your job?*

8 **Molly:** *Yes.*

9   Judge:

Do you have a letter from your employer verifying that you no longer work there?

10   Molly:

No, Your Honor, but I have here a pay stub that indicates it is final payment for the last period.

Procedural Note: Molly did not have the exact document the judge was requesting, so she wisely admits as much. But she also sensibly tells the judge she has other evidence that establishes the same point.

11   Judge:

Hand it to the bailiff, please. (Molly hands the pay stub to the bailiff, who hands it to Judge Washington.) *And are you looking for another job?*

12   Molly:

Yes, actively. I have clippings here from want ads for positions I have applied to, including a list of the salaries offered. Unfortunately, all pay less than what I made at my former job. I hope to find another job soon, but I am not sure how long it will take, and I'm pretty sure that even when I do, the pay will be significantly less, because several companies in my industry, like the one I worked for, are relocating out of state where wages are lower.

13   Judge:

And your declaration here estimating the Respondent's income is based on what facts?

14   Molly:

What he was making at the time we divorced, two years ago, as he entered

on his income statement. Plus I added a small cost of living increase, which I am sure he has received. I didn't put anything in for a real raise, which I'm pretty sure he's also gotten since then.

15   Judge:

Okay; I'm just going to run some numbers. (The judge does some work at a laptop computer on his desk while everyone waits. After a few minutes he looks up.) *Respondent having been duly notified and not appearing to contest the OSC, modification from $800 monthly to $1,200 monthly is hereby granted.*

Procedural Note: The last bit of legal gobbledegook translates into English as follows: "The father was given proper notice of this hearing. He didn't show up or file any responsive papers, so I'm going to assume he doesn't want to argue over the request to increase child support, and in any event the request is reasonable in light of our state's support guidelines. Therefore, I'll give Ms. Patricks what she has requested."

In this next dialogue, Suzie has asked her ex-husband Tom to change their prior visitation agreement from half of every weekend for each parent, to every other weekend with each parent. Because Tom refused, Suzie has brought the matter to the family court. As was noted above, even if issues of custody, support, and visitation were decided and a court ruled on them, family courts still have jurisdiction over such matters until children reach the age of majority.

1   Judge:

Johnson v. Smith?

2 Suzie:

Yes, Your Honor.

3 Tom:

Yes, Your Honor.

Both Suzie and Tom approach the bench and stand at the respective counsel tables.

4 Judge:

I'm reading your papers, Ms. Johnson, and I can see you wish to have your children spend every Friday night and Saturday with you and every Saturday night and Sunday with your husband, I mean your ex-husband.

5 Suzie:

No, Your Honor. That is the present arrangement. I'm requesting that be changed so the children spend every other weekend with me, and every other weekend with their father.

Note that Suzie calmly directed the judge to what she wanted, and did not get flustered that the judge did not know what she wanted.

6 Judge:

How long has the present arrangement been in place?

7 Suzie:

Two years, Your Honor.

8 Judge:

And why do you want this change?

9 Suzie:

Several reasons. The children are carted around so much. I think it would be better for them to settle in, one place or the other, and have more quality time.

10 Judge:

Are you saying the time is not quality time now?

11 Suzie:

Well, not exactly, Your Honor. It's just that they are packing and unpacking each weekend, and well, every Saturday night both Joey and Jimmy come home late, and they are tired and cranky —wired too, probably because of all that junk food he feeds them. I have to spend hours calming them down, then they need to sleep in Sunday, so we really don't have time to do things as a family.

12 Judge [to Tom]:

What do you think of this?

13 Tom:

It's absurd. They sleep fine at my apartment. And they don't eat any more junk food than any other kids. And that's none of her business anyway. It's my home. Besides, I think Suzie's just jealous because my new girlfriend moved in with me.

14 Judge:

Let's stick to the facts, both of you. Look, Ms. Johnson, I'm not inclined to rock the boat here. You haven't given me any real reason to change things that have been set for two years, especially when Mr. Smith is opposed to your request.

15 Suzie:

Your Honor, there is an additional reason that the change I am seeking is in the best interests of the children. The change is necessary to facilitate the children's ability to visit with and continue to have a meaningful relationship with their only living grandparents, my parents.

Notice how Suzie sticks to her requests. She got off track a bit on the junk food, and realized though this was an important issue to her, it was not moving the judge at all. She refocused her arguments on the children, remaining calm but not giving up, and using the key phrase, "Best interests of the children."

16 Judge [to Suzie]:
Explain.

17 Suzie:
Well, you will see in the Declarations attached to my Petition for Visitation Modification, the Declaration of my father, Mr. Robert Johnson, and my mother Mrs. Betty Johnson, that both are fully mentally competent and both have participated actively in the care of Jimmy and Joey since their birth. They further state that this year, they moved about a five hours' drive from our home, to Spring City. With the distance, Your Honor, I simply don't have the time to drive the kids there and back to visit their grandparents under our current arrangement. If I had the whole weekend, every other weekend, I could take them.

Notice that Suzie not only had the facts, but had her parents each prepare a Declaration, so the judge had legally substantial evidence of the facts Suzie relies on for her argument about visiting the grandparents.

18 Judge:
I imagine you cannot go yourself alone either to help them out, given the distance and the fact that you have the children every Saturday evening.

19 Suzie:
Yes, that's right. It's difficult to help them under the current arrangement.

Here, though Suzie might be sensing the judge may be coming around to her point of view, she is wise to continue answering just what the judge is asking about, and not digress.

20 Tom:
Your Honor, that is BS. She just hates my girlfriend. She's not going to drive to Spring City every weekend, even for her parents.

21 Judge:
Watch your language in my courtroom, Mr. Smith. Are you accusing Mr. and Mrs. Johnson of lying?

Note that a party may fast lose ground with the judge by using profanity in the courtroom. Stick to the facts and remain as calm and polite as possible.

22 Tom:
No.

23 Judge
Do you have any evidence or reasons why an every-other-weekend arrangement would be detrimental to the children?

24 Tom
No.

25 Judge:

Is there any reason you know of why it would not be in the children's best interest to have the opportunity to have more time with their extended family?

26 Tom:

No.

27 Judge:

Well then, because Ms. Johnson submitted declarations to support her request, and based on the compelling interest of a child spending time with his extended family, particularly the importance of a relationship with grandparents, I am inclined to grant Ms. Johnson's request.

In addition to having an argument that the judge finds persuasive enough to change a visitation order, Suzie was wise to have declarations from her parents to support her position.

28 Judge:

You may stay in the courtroom until the Clerk has prepared a Minute Order and you each will be given a copy.

Tom and Suzie leave the bench and return to wait in the courtroom. ●

Representing Yourself in Bankruptcy Court

Bankruptcy allows debtors to embark on a "fresh start" by shedding existing debts. While big business bankruptcies tend to be complex and dominated by lawyers, it is not unusual for individuals who file for bankruptcy to represent themselves because:

- many bankruptcy procedures are routine, and
- debtors and creditors who are individuals or small businesses often can't afford to hire an attorney.

This chapter provides an overview of common courtroom procedures in personal liquidation bankruptcy cases. These cases are often called "Chapter 7s" because they are covered by Chapter 7 of the Federal Bankruptcy Code—the federal laws that govern bankruptcy procedures nationwide. However, if you plan to represent yourself in a Chapter 7 bankruptcy, you should also consult at least one of the more specialized resources listed in "Getting Help Beyond This Book," below.

Because this chapter is intended as an overview, if you are or may be representing yourself in a bankruptcy case, you should be aware that:

- This chapter assumes that you have already filed a bankruptcy petition. If you are in debt and thinking about whether to file, or if you need more information to know if you are eligible to file (and, if so, which kind of bankruptcy to pursue), consult one of the resources listed below.
- This chapter describes the procedures in Chapter 7 (liquidation) bankruptcy cases only. Because of legal changes some people who could have filed

bankruptcy under Chapter 7 in previous years now have to file under Chapter 13 instead (a personal reorganization bankruptcy). A debtor who goes through a Chapter 13 typically has to pay back debts according to a court-approved schedule. To learn more about Chapter 13 bankruptcies, consult one of the resources listed below.

 TIP

The Federal Bankruptcy Code is codified in Title 11 of the United States Code. Throughout this chapter, you will see references to specific sections of this code that you can look up online or in a law library cited as "11 U.S.C. § X," with "X" being the number of the appropriate section of the code. You will also see references to the Federal Rules of Bankruptcy Procedure—federal procedural rules that govern bankruptcy proceedings in federal courts, much like the Federal Rules of Evidence or the Federal Rules of Civil Procedure. For more on researching the law, see "Getting Help Beyond This Book," below, and Chapter 23.

The Chapter 7 Bankruptcy Process

A Chapter 7 bankruptcy starts when a debtor pays the filing fees and files a document called a "petition." Debtors have to satisfy a "means test" (an income limit) and attend an approved credit counseling program before filing a Chapter 7. Debtors must also file detailed financial information under oath in what are called "schedules." Schedules list and value a debtor's property, income, debts, and creditors.

After a filing, each case is assigned to a bankruptcy trustee. The trustee's main job is to liquidate (sell) the debtor's "nonexempt" (nonessential) property and distribute the net proceeds to creditors. To find out what property the debtor has (called property of the bankruptcy "estate"), the trustee reviews the debtor's schedules and conducts an investigatory examination called the "Meeting of Creditors," described in "Meeting of Creditors," below.

Who Is the "U.S. Trustee?"

Each Chapter 7 bankruptcy is assigned to a trustee (sometimes called the "bankruptcy trustee" or "Chapter 7 trustee"). The trustee's main function is to find and sell property and distribute it to creditors. Chapter 7 trustees are appointed by a Department of Justice employee called the "United States Trustee." There are some 21 U.S. Trustees nationwide, whose regions are composed of various federal districts. The U.S. Trustee monitors the Chapter 7 trustees and helps ensure that bankruptcy rules and procedures are complied with by reviewing court papers and bringing errors to the attention of the court. Local bankruptcy rules often require parties to serve the Chapter 7 trustee and the U.S. Trustee, as well as each other, with copies of any court documents.

All creditors listed by a debtor are automatically notified by the court of a bankruptcy filing and told when the "Meeting of Creditors" will be held. Additionally, creditors may learn about the bankruptcy from the debtor—or by word of mouth. Regardless of how creditors learn that a debtor filed for bankruptcy, the "automatic stay" currently requires most creditors to immediately cease all efforts to collect from the debtor. However, some creditors can continue collection efforts without violating the automatic stay.

If the trustee determines that nonexempt property is available to be sold for the benefit of creditors, the creditors are notified and sent "Proof of Claim" forms to file with the bankruptcy court. If the trustee finds no evidence of such property, the case is labeled a "no asset" case, and the creditors need not file a Proof of Claim. Creditors must therefore read such notices carefully and be sure to comply with any listed claims deadlines.

No-Asset Cases Can Turn Into Asset Cases

The trustee may first discover the presence of assets to be sold for the benefit of creditors after having made an initial determination that no such assets existed. When this happens, the trustee's office will send out a second notice advising creditors to file a Proof of Claim. Thus, creditors must carefully review *every* notice they receive from the trustee's office and the bankruptcy court: They should not assume that, just because they receive a "no-asset" notice, they will never get a piece of the pie.

Debtors have many duties while their bankruptcies are pending. (11 U.S.C. § 521.) Debtors attend the Meeting of Creditors (often called the "341(a) hearing"), at which time the trustee and sometimes creditors question the debtor under oath. Debtors must also make decisions with respect to any "secured" property they may have and put their decisions in writing in a document called a "Statement of Intention." (The terms "secured" and "unsecured" are defined in "Secured and Unsecured Debts," below. Both debtors and creditors who fail to take appropriate actions with respect to secured property may lose important rights. Self-represented parties therefore need to understand these concepts.

Typically, a Chapter 7 bankruptcy resulted in a debtor's discharge within three to six months after the case was filed. The changes that took effect in October 2005 can lengthen this time period, because the court and the trustee have greater powers than in the past to examine debts and declare them not dischargeable—meaning that a debtor remains liable for debts even after a bankruptcy discharge is final.

These changes also extend the time that most debtors who have already gone through bankruptcy have to wait before they are eligible to file again. Anyone with a previous bankruptcy who plans to file again should check the resources listed in "Getting Help Beyond This Book," below.

Secured and Unsecured Debts

A "secured debt" is an obligation guaranteed by specific property, often called "collateral" or "security." A debt may be voluntarily secured, such as with a home or car loan, or involuntarily secured, such as through a tax lien or a mechanics lien. The holder of a secured debt is a "secured creditor." A secured creditor has a "lien" on property (a legal right to collect a debt by "foreclosing on" or "repossessing" the underlying collateral or security). A Chapter 7 bankruptcy ordinarily does not wipe out property liens. So, unless liens are specifically wiped out in bankruptcy by court order or by agreement, secured creditors will typically be able to repossess their property once the debtor's case is closed (through a discharge or dismissal) or earlier with the bankruptcy court's permission.

By contrast, an "unsecured debt" is one that is linked only to a debtor's promise to repay and not to any specific item of property. While outside of bankruptcy a creditor can sue to collect an unsecured debt, bankruptcy's automatic stay bars such collection efforts. So the usual effect of a bankruptcy is to force unsecured creditors to wait in line for a percentage of whatever property a trustee can collect. Unsecured creditors don't get paid until after the government, lawyers, secured creditors, and other so-called priority claimants get their shares.)

Surviving as a Self-Represented Party in the Clique-ish World of Bankruptcy Court

Though bankruptcy is a familiar concept to most people, bankruptcy court processes are a mystery to just about everyone who is not a "regular." The same bankruptcy lawyers tend to appear in the same courtrooms over and over. They usually know each other, the judges, the trustees, and the courtroom staff personally. Even lawyers who don't handle bankruptcy cases often may feel like fish out of water in bankruptcy court. So you're not alone if you feel like an outsider.

It is particularly important to get on the judge's good side early, because the same judge usually handles a case from start to finish. To demonstrate that you are an exception to the negative stereotype of unprepared laypersons who waste a court's time, be sure to dress conservatively, answer the judge and trustee honestly and succinctly, and speak courteously to everyone, especially court staff. Come to court on time. And last but most important, be prepared. Even something as simple as having extra copies of important documents will make you stand out positively.

Meeting of Creditors (341(a) Hearing)

The first hearing in many Chapter 7 cases is the Meeting of Creditors. You may see this referred to as a "341(a) hearing," after the Bankruptcy Code section that governs it (11 U.S.C. § 341(a)). A debtor must appear in person at a 341(a) hearing and answer the trustee's (and possibly creditors') questions, under oath. The hearing may take place in a courtroom or a government office. The following is a summary of key factors in a 341(a) hearing.

Purpose of a Meeting of Creditors: The Meeting of Creditors is often a trustee's only opportunity to question a debtor under oath about his or her financial information. Creditors who attend the hearing may also question the debtor. Most 341(a) hearings take place within 20 to 90 days after filing.

Procedures: The trustee places the debtor under oath, reviews the debtor's bankruptcy schedules, and poses a series of questions to the debtor. (See Federal Rule of Bankruptcy Procedure 2003.)

Debtor's Position: As the debtor, you should honestly answer questions about what you wrote in your schedules. You may need to justify how you arrived at property valuations, explain apparent inconsistencies in your schedules, and correct any mistakes.

Creditor's Position: As a creditor, your goal is to determine the condition, whereabouts, and value of property in which you hold a security interest, as well as find out whether the debtor has any nonexempt property that may be sold for your benefit and that of other creditors.

Trustee's Role: The trustee's main goal is to determine the existence and value of nonexempt assets.

Judge's Role: A judge is not present at 341(a) hearings.

The trustee may ask the debtor how the debtor calculated the value of an asset, and may ask about possible unlisted assets. For example, a trustee may ask whether a debtor expects a tax refund or an inheritance. A trustee may also continue to investigate after a 341(a) hearing, using discovery devices similar to those discussed in Chapter 5.

Will the Trustee Investigate After a 341(a) Hearing?

If a trustee's initial review reveals that a debtor has little or no nonexempt property, the trustee will not likely investigate further. However, if the trustee or a creditor suspects that the debtor has unlisted nonexempt property, has overvalued exempt property, or has unlawfully transferred property, the trustee may investigate further. Informally, the trustee may interview creditors or witnesses, research public records, or ask the debtor (who is required to cooperate) to provide further information or documentation. If necessary, the trustee may engage in more formal investigation, such as demanding documents or taking depositions. Even before a formal "adversary proceeding" is filed (the name for a bankruptcy-related lawsuit), Federal Rule of Bankruptcy Procedure 2004 conveys broad investigatory powers on trustees and creditors to question parties under oath.

The trustee may also use the 341(a) hearing to find out whether the debtor sold or gave away assets that should be available for the benefit of creditors. For example, 11 U.S.C. § 547 allows the trustee to sue to recover what is known as a "preference"—the payment or transfer of more than $600 worth of property in the 90 days before filing or in the year before filing it to an "insider," meaning a relative, friend, or partner. And a trustee has the power under 11 U.S.C. § 548 to sue to recover property that was sold or given away to defraud creditors.

Relief from Stay Hearing

The filing of a petition in bankruptcy has one immediate effect—an automatic stay. Governed by 11 U.S.C. § 362, the automatic stay serves as a legal "stop sign" that says, "Creditors, stop all collection efforts immediately!" The automatic stay gives a trustee a breather from having to fight off creditors, while providing time to assess what property exists and to whom it belongs.

A stay prohibits most creditors from taking action against a debtor or the debtor's property. For example, creditors may not make harassing phone calls, send collection letters, file civil lawsuits against a debtor (or continue litigating a lawsuit that was initiated before the filing), seize money in the debtor's bank account, garnish the debtor's wages, or record liens against the debtor's property. Actions such as these violate the stay, and creditors who take them may be held in contempt and fined. (See 11 U.S.C. § 362(h).)

As with most legal rules, however, there are exceptions. And the legal changes that went into effect in October 2005 enlarge the categories of creditors who can proceed with collections despite the automatic stay. The law specifies which proceedings may continue, including criminal prosecutions against the debtor, certain family court actions (such as alimony or child support modifications), certain landlord-tenant disputes, and some tax-related proceedings (such as IRS audits). (11 U.S.C. § 362(b).)

A creditor seeking to lift a stay typically must file a motion that includes some or all of the following documents:

- a Notice of Motion and motion to lift the stay,
- a declaration in support of the motion,
- possibly some other documentary evidence,
- a Memorandum of Points and Authorities (or "brief") in support of the motion, and
- a Proposed Order granting the motion.

A party opposing the motion will likely have to file a written opposition along with a declaration and possibly other supporting evidence, though local rules may permit those opposing the motion to do so orally, at the hearing. The following is a summary of key factors in a hearing to get relief from a stay.

Purpose of Relief from Stay Hearing: A relief from stay hearing is the court proceeding in which a judge will rule on a creditor's request to lift the automatic stay.

Procedures: A creditor files a Motion for Relief from Stay and notifies interested parties. Relief from Stay hearings are governed by 11 U.S.C. § 362 and Federal Rules of Bankruptcy Procedure 4001 and 9014, as well as applicable local rules.

Debtor's Position: As the debtor, your goal is to convince the judge not to lift a stay so that you can keep property or prevent a creditor from taking legal action against you.

You may prevail if you can refute a creditor's contention that you have no equity in listed property (frequently the basis for filing a motion to lift the stay), or if you can prove that the creditor's property interests will not be negatively affected by continuing the stay.

Creditor's Position: As a creditor, your goal is to convince the judge that a debtor has little or no equity in property and that it would not interfere with the bankruptcy to allow you to proceed to collect your debt, repossess your property, or pursue other legal action against the debtor. In addition or as an alternate theory, you may try to show that the stay is negatively affecting your property interests.

Trustee's Role: The trustee will likely object if lifting the stay would cut into nonexempt estate assets. But if the trustee has no economic interest in the creditor's property or claim, the trustee will likely not object.

Judge's Role: The judge decides whether to lift a stay in whole or in part. For example, a judge may allow a creditor to collect some, but not all, of the property at issue.

In a relief from stay dispute, 11 U.S.C. § 362(g) states that the moving party (creditor) must prove the debtor's equity (or lack thereof) in the subject property. After that, the debtor has the burden of proving all other issues, the most important of these being whether property available for other creditors is affected (causing "harm to the estate") and whether the protesting creditor's property is "adequately protected." The concepts of harm to the estate and adequate protection are explained below:

- **Harm to the bankruptcy estate.** The court may allow a creditor to proceed despite the automatic stay if the creditor's proposed action will not affect the property of the bankruptcy estate. For example, the bankruptcy court may grant relief from a stay to a nonfiling spouse who wants to resolve a child custody dispute because the family court's ruling would neither bring in nor take money away from the bankruptcy estate. Thus, no other creditor's interests would be harmed by allowing the custody proceeding to go forward. A bankruptcy court may also lift a stay for a creditor to collect a personal injury lawsuit judgment, but only from insurance proceeds and not from the debtor directly, because those insurance proceeds would not have been available for distribution to other creditors—so there is no effect on the estate.

- **Adequate protection.** To illustrate this concept, assume that before filing for bankruptcy the debtor bought a car and, some time later, stopped making car payments. The creditor was poised to repossess the car when the debtor filed for bankruptcy. Every day the car sits, it depreciates in value and risks being damaged. In such a case, the court may allow the creditor relief from a stay, unless the debtor could prove that the creditor is being adequately protected. Adequate protection in such an example might consist of maintaining sufficient car insurance and making some monthly payments to offset depreciation.

TIP

Obtaining "relief from stay" forms. Many of the documents filed in relief from stay motions have been simplified for routine cases with fill-in-the-blank forms. You can obtain these from your bankruptcy court Clerk's Office or in the *Collier* book series, under Section 362. (*Collier's* is discussed and cited below).

Objection to Exemption Hearing

To obtain a fresh start and begin to rebuild a sound financial life, people need clothes, food, shelter, tools, and other essentials. Accordingly, both federal and state laws "exempt" certain property, meaning they classify it as essential and thus beyond the reach of creditors. For a debtor's property to be exempted, however, the following conditions must be met:

- There must be an applicable state or federal exemption law. (11 U.S.C. § 522 governs federal exemptions.) In some states, a debtor must use state exemption rules, while in other states the debtor may opt for either state or federal exemptions. In some states, married couples who file jointly for bankruptcy may "double" certain exemptions.

- A debtor must expressly "claim" property as exempt by listing it in the bankruptcy schedule designed for this purpose (Schedule C). Property not claimed as exempt may be seized and sold by the trustee.

A creditor who wishes to object to such exemptions may do so in an objection hearing. The following is a summary of key factors in such a hearing.

Purpose of an Objection to Exemption Hearing: A creditor objects to exemptions that a debtor has claimed, and a judge decides whether to grant or deny the debtor's exemption claim.

Procedures: The trustee or a creditor disputes an exemption by filing an Objection to Exemption. This proceeding is governed by Federal Rules of Bankruptcy Procedure 4003(b) and 9014.

Debtor's Position: As the debtor, your goal is to support your claim that certain property should be deemed exempt. For example, if a creditor or trustee argues that you overvalued an asset, you may need to justify how you calculated the property's value and show that it's within the legal exemption limit.

Creditor's Position: As a creditor, your goal is to prove that property is nonexempt. If the trustee has objected to a claim of exemption, which is most often the case, you will usually be observing rather than playing a main role in the proceedings.

Trustee's Role: The trustee, typically the objecting party, must prove that an exemption is improper. Often, a trustee does this either by proving that the debtor incorrectly claimed nonexempt property as exempt, or by showing that there is equity in property over and above the exemption limit that should be liquidated for the benefit of all creditors.

"I don't give a damn what Judge Wapner said."

Judge's Role: The judge rules on whether or not the property is exempt.

Unless the court grants an extension per Federal Rule of Bankruptcy Procedure 4003(b), exemption objections must be filed within 30 days of the filing of a petition or within 30 days of an amendment that affects that exemption. (See 11 U.S.C. § 522(l) and *Taylor v. Freeland and Kronz,* 503 US 638 (1992).) Exemption objections must generally be served (by mail or delivery) to the trustee, the debtor, the debtor's counsel (if the debtor has one), and probably to the U.S. Trustee, but check your local rules to be certain. The burden of proof in an exemption objection proceeding is on the objecting party to show why exemption is not proper. (Federal Rule of Bankruptcy Procedure 4003(c).) If no one objects to a debtor's exemption claim within the specified time period, an exemption claim will be upheld, even if it is legally invalid.

Your Chances for Settlement May Decrease Over Time

Though debtors may negotiate and "settle" with a trustee, time may be of the essence. Early on in a case, to avoid the time, cost, and hassle of having to appraise and sell certain property, a trustee may be willing to accept a reasonably discounted payment. However, it is less likely that a trustee will settle after taking the time to have property appraised and even less likely after preparing an objection and appearing in court.

Discharge of Debt Hearing

All debts are not alike in the eyes of bankruptcy law. Some are "dischargeable" while others are not. To be dischargeable, a debt must, at a minimum, be listed on a debtor's schedule, either originally or by amendment. After bankruptcy, a debtor is no longer obligated to pay discharged debts.

Under federal bankruptcy law, some debts almost always survive bankruptcy. Debts in this category include child support and alimony payments, court fees, court judgments in certain drunk driving cases, court-ordered restitution, many tax debts, and most student loans.

To raise the issue of whether or not a particular debt is dischargeable, the moving party—whether debtor or creditor—must file a separate lawsuit in the bankruptcy court (called an "adversary proceeding"). Federal Rule of Bankruptcy Procedure 7001 lists the issues that must be handled by way of adversary proceedings. The Bankruptcy Rules in these cases are similar to the Federal Rules of Civil Procedure in civil cases, and bankruptcy litigation concerning whether a debt is dischargeable (either under 11 U.S.C. § 523 or 11 U.S.C. § 727) tends to resemble other types of civil lawsuits. The following is a summary of key issues when objecting to the discharge of debts.

Purpose of Discharge of Debts Hearing: Litigation under 11 U.S.C. § 523 determines whether a particular debt is dischargeable (wiped out). (By contrast, in litigation under 11 U.S.C. § 727, the debtor may be denied a discharge altogether, meaning no debts will be wiped out, and the debtor will remain obligated to pay all of the creditors.)

Procedures: To contest whether a debt is dischargeable, the creditor whose debt is affected files a complaint to start an "adversary proceeding" (bankruptcy lawsuit). Adversary proceedings are governed by Federal Rules of Bankruptcy Procedure 7001–7087.

Debtor's Position: As the debtor, your goal is to get a debt discharged. For example, you may try to dispute a creditor's claim that you committed fraud by showing that you honestly intended to pay for what you purchased.

Creditor's Position: As a creditor, your goal is to prove why a debt should not be discharged. You try to persuade the court that your claim fits into one of the categories listed as nondischargeable under 11 U.S.C. § 523(a), and offer admissible evidence to support your claim.

Trustee's Role: Ordinarily, a trustee has no role in a discharge of debt action because this lawsuit is brought by one particular creditor concerning only that creditor's claim against the debtor.

Judge's Role: The judge decides whether or not a debt is dischargeable.

Reaffirmation of Debt Hearing

To "reaffirm" a prebankruptcy debt means that a debtor agrees to repay a discharged debt. Though reaffirmation defeats a major purpose of bankruptcy, it may allow debtors to remain on good terms with an important creditor, such as a family doctor or a local merchant, or to retain a necessary item of nonexempt property.

Debtors must know the risks and benefits and understand their alternatives before agreeing to reaffirm. Here are some general guidelines for debtors:

- Reaffirm a debt only if you are able to repay and really need an asset.
- Do not reaffirm a debt for an amount greater than property's current value. Negotiate for a lower amount before agreeing to reaffirm.

The following is a summary of key issues in a hearing to reaffirm debt:

Purpose of a Reaffirmation of Debt Hearing: Reaffirmation hearings are conducted to determine whether to allow an agreement between a debtor and a creditor to repay a debt despite a discharge.

Procedures: Under 11 U.S.C. § 524(d), judges are required to conduct reaffirmation hearings for self-represented debtors who want to reaffirm a debt. The reaffirmation hearing may be scheduled separately or may be part of a discharge hearing that closes a case.

Debtor's Position: As the debtor, you want to convince the judge that you are able to pay the debt and understand that you have the right not to pay it, but that repaying this particular debt is in your best interests.

Creditor's Position: As a creditor, if you attend a reaffirmation hearing, your primary concern will be to refute any suggestion that you coerced a debtor into signing a reaffirmation agreement—so that the judge will approve the agreement (and you will get paid).

Trustee's Role: The trustee is not likely to attend this hearing.

Judge's Role: The judge's primary concern is that allowing the debtor to reaffirm will not defeat the purpose of the bankruptcy, that is, for the debtor to be able to make a fresh start.

Getting Help Beyond This Book

The resources below provide further information on topics of concern to parties involved in personal bankruptcy cases. (See also Chapter 23 for information on law libraries and doing legal research in general.)

Help Filing and Amending Bankruptcy Forms

You can obtain all the necessary forms to file for bankruptcy from your nearest bankruptcy court or by downloading them from the Federal Judiciary website, at www.uscourts.gov/bankform. These forms are also provided in *How to File for Chapter 7 Bankruptcy,* by Stephen Elias, Albin Renauer, and Robin Leonard (Nolo), which also includes step-by-step instructions on how to amend your bankruptcy schedules if you filed already but need to change some information you listed. If you know or think you want to file for Chapter 13 bankruptcy (instead of Chapter 7), consult *Chapter 13 Bankruptcy: Repay Your Debts* by Stephen Elias and Robin Leonard (Nolo).

Help Managing Debt and Deciding Whether to File for Bankruptcy

To help you consider the pros and cons of bankruptcy and alternative strategies for debt management, consult *Solve Your Money Troubles: Get Debt Collectors Off Your Back & Regain Financial Freedom,* by Robin Leonard and John Lamb (Nolo). You may also want to visit the website of Myvesta (formerly the Debt Counselors of America), a nonprofit money management and counseling organization, at www.myvesta.org.

Where to Start Bankruptcy Research in a Law Library

Two resources that will help you begin your bankruptcy research are the laws and rules themselves and a good reference book that explains them. The basic laws and rules you will need for most bankruptcy court procedures are the relevant sections of the Federal Bankruptcy Code (11 U.S.C. §§ 101 and following), the Federal Rules of Bankruptcy Procedure, and your own district's local bankruptcy rules. You may also need to consult bankruptcy court cases, state law (for example, as to whether certain property is exempt), and other federal law or rules (such as the Federal Rules of Evidence).

You can usually locate all of these rules in a public law library at or near your bankruptcy court, on your bankruptcy court's website (if it has one), or from your bankruptcy court's Clerk's Office. If you cannot find your local bankruptcy rules, ask your judge's courtroom clerk for a copy. Local rules are critical, especially in contested hearings and adversary proceedings. Also, ask your bankruptcy court's Clerk's Office staff or your judge's courtroom clerk for a copy of what are sometimes called the "local local rules"—guidelines issued by your particular courthouse or judge.

For reliable reference books that explain bankruptcy law, you may want to start with one of the multivolume treatises that bankruptcy lawyers often consult:

- *Collier on Bankruptcy* (and *Collier Bankruptcy Practice Guide*), which includes thorough information on local court rules, published by Matthew Bender, or
- *Norton Bankruptcy Law and Practice,* published by Clark Boardman Callaghan.

Both of these books are organized by federal bankruptcy code section number. They also include detailed subject matter indexes, if you know the name but not the section number of the proceeding that you wish to research.

Where to Start Bankruptcy Research Online

In addition to library resources, there is a great deal of helpful information on bankruptcy law on the Internet. The following websites are among the best places to start your research online:

- **http://thomas.loc.gov**
  This official site of legislative information from the Library of Congress provides summaries, full texts, status information, and more on all recent federal legislation.
- **www.abiworld.org**
  This site of the American Bankruptcy Institute provides news updates and commentary on bankruptcy legislation and court decisions, plus general bankruptcy information for consumers.
- **www.clla.org**
  This site of the Commercial Law League of America provides information and news on bankruptcy and credit issues.
- **www.law.cornell.edu/topics/bankruptcy. html**
  This site of the Legal Information Institute at Cornell University Law School provides an overview of bankruptcy law, the text of the Federal Bankruptcy Code, court decisions, and links to other bankruptcy sites.
- **www.uscourts.gov/bankform**
  This site provides official bankruptcy court forms from the Federal Judiciary.
- **www.findlaw.com**
  This is a useful site to check for each state's statutes and cases, as well as numerous links to helpful bankruptcy resources. (Findlaw.com also provides a legal dictionary at http://dictionary. lp.findlaw.com.)

Bankruptcy Court Procedures Not Covered in This Chapter

The list of issues during a Chapter 7 bankruptcy case that may require additional court appearances is potentially endless. The following are among the most common:

- A creditor must respond to the trustee's objection to claims. ("The Chapter 7 Bankruptcy Process," above, discusses when creditors need to file a Proof of Claim; Bankruptcy Code § 502 and Federal Rule of Bankruptcy Procedure 3007 set forth the procedures by which to raise objections to claims.)

- A debtor wants to request relief—for example, to avoid a lien under 11 U.S.C. § 522. (There are several procedures by which debtors can eliminate ("avoid") or reduce the amount of certain liens on some exempt property. *How to File for Chapter 7 Bankruptcy*, by Stephen Elias, Albin Renauer, and Robin Leonard (Nolo), explains these procedures and includes instructions for filing a routine motion to avoid a lien.)

- A debtor has failed to comply with his or her duties under 11 U.S.C. § 521.

- A debtor or third party is holding property of the estate, and the trustee files a "turnover motion" (see 11 U.S.C. §§ 542 and 543).

- A debtor, creditor, or third party has been sued by the trustee to return estate property that was unlawfully transferred away. ("The Chapter 7 Bankruptcy Process," above, explains the trustee's power to avoid preferences under 11 U.S.C. §§ 547 and fraudulent conveyances under 11 U.S.C. § 548.)

If you must appear in a bankruptcy court proceeding that is not described in this book, your best bet is to consult the subject matter index (or if you know the applicable code section number, look up the corresponding section) in *Collier on Bankruptcy*, published by Matthew Bender (described above in "Where to Start Bankruptcy Research in a Law Library"). For each new proceeding, try to first get a clear grasp of the "bottom line." In other words, learn the main purpose of the new hearing, the basic procedures you must follow, and what each of the parties' positions and goals will be. Next, determine what you risk—what is personally at stake for you. Then decide whether this seems like a proceeding in which you will be able to effectively represent yourself. If you do proceed to court and then find yourself in over your head, you can politely ask the judge for a continuance in order to hire counsel.

Help Beyond the Book:
People, Places, and Publications

In law as in life, there is always more information to be had. For any number of reasons, you may want to learn more about matters not covered or not detailed in this book. Some of those areas you may want or need to research are outlined in "What You May Want to Research," below. If your case is not too complex, you may not need to conduct extensive legal research, but you may need to look up a few points online or talk with someone who can answer basic questions. "Sources of Information" notes some of the people who can be helpful resources and how to find them, and introduces basic legal research tools. "Getting Help From a Lawyer" discusses working with a lawyer to help you represent yourself.

Resolving Legal Research Questions

When you have legal questions, it often helps to keep this three-step process in mind:

1. Try to find a resource person who can give you an answer or direct you to the place where you can find it.
2. Next, look for reference materials (sometimes called "secondary sources") that explain and summarize the area of law your question involves.
3. If you still need more details, you may go on into researching the law itself (what are called "primary sources"), looking first into a pertinent statute and then, if needed, reading court decisions that clarify and interpret the statute or statutes.

If you need to do further legal research, we recommend you consult a comprehensive legal research guide, such as *Legal Research: How to Find and Understand the Law,* by Stephen Elias and Susan Levinkind (Nolo), an easy-to-read book that provides step-by-step instruction on how to find legal information; or *Legal Research for Beginners*, by Sonja Larsen and John Bourdeau (Barrons), a general legal research guide that emphasizes computerized research methods.

What You May Want to Research

Normally, the information you'll need to research to try your own case in court will fall into four areas:

- the substantive law governing the legal claims and defenses involved in your case
- rules of evidence
- rules of civil procedure, and
- local rules.

The Substantive Law of Your Case

"Substantive" law is the term for rules that govern the heart of your dispute, like particular laws about a contract or tort (civil wrong or personal injury) lawsuit. The term "substantive" law is used in contrast to "procedural" law, which deals with the rules that govern how your case moves through the court system.

Substantive law can be classified into certain discrete subjects—for example, contracts, torts, wills, property, tax, immigration, and bankruptcy. But keep in mind that your case may involve more than one subject.

For example, if you are involved in a divorce and child custody battle, naturally you'll need to deal with family laws covering divorce, alimony, child custody, child support, and division of marital property. But in dividing your property, you may also deal with federal and state tax laws and state property laws.

The same is true if your case deals with a car accident. You claim that your adversary was negligent in that he made an unsafe lane change and sideswiped your car. To find laws relating to what lane a car must be in when making a turn, you will look at your state's traffic laws (perhaps grouped together in a section, title, chapter, or code under "vehicle" or "traffic"). Laws relating to the standard elements of a negligence claim may be in state laws under a general "civil" category, perhaps grouped under the heading "negligence" or "torts" and supplemented by the decisions of judges (case law).

Both your state and the federal govern-ment enact laws that may affect your case. Some areas of law are unique to the federal system, such as bankruptcy, copyright, and patent law. Other areas of law are typically state court subjects—for example, torts (personal injury), contracts, family law (divorce, child custody, guardianship), and wills. Your case may involve both federal and state laws. For instance, divorce cases may involve state family law and federal income tax law, and claims of civil rights violations may be made under federal and state civil rights laws.

Elements of the Claims in Your Case

Probably your most important substantive research task is to learn the legal elements of each of the legal claims (sometimes called "causes of action") or defenses in your case. (See Chapters 8 and 9.) You need to know these elements to prepare for trial, present relevant evidence during trial, and make persuasive legal arguments to the judge or jury at the close of trial.

One good place to look for lists of elements is in standard jury instructions (instructions the judge reads to the jury at the close of trial). These instructions identify the elements that a jury has to find for a plaintiff to win a particular legal claim. Judges use the same elements in deciding cases without a jury.

RESOURCE

Resources on jury instructions. Many states have books that set out complete jury instructions for common kinds of lawsuits. For example, federal jury instructions are published in a book called *Modern Federal Jury Instructions*, by Leonard Sand (Matthew Bender). Michigan has a book called *Michigan Standard Jury Instructions* (Institute of Continuing Legal Education). New York has *New York Pattern Jury Instructions, Civil*, Committee on Pattern Jury Instructions (West Group). And in California, there's the *California Jury Instructions, Civil: Book of Approved Jury Instructions (BAJI)*, Committee on Standard Jury Instructions (West Publishing Co.). Ask a law librarian where to find the published jury instructions in your state. You can also enter key terms for the jury instructions you wish to find into an Internet search engine, as many jury instructions are now available online.

Understanding the Elements

Once you've found the elements of each of the claims in your case, you've got to figure out what they mean—so you may need to do some more research. For example, assume that you bring a breach of contract action against a painter who agreed to paint your roof and then stopped midway through the job. You want to recover both the deposit you gave the painter originally and the difference between the amount of money you were going to pay this painter and the sum you ended up having to pay another painter to complete the job. You know (from Chapter 8) that a claim for breach of contract usually consists of four elements:

1. **Formation:** You and the defendant had a legally binding contract.
2. **Performance:** You performed as required—under the contract.
3. **Breach:** The defendant failed to perform as required under the contract.
4. **Damages:** The defendant's failure to perform caused you economic loss.

But you may need to do some legal research to find out what the abstract legal jargon of the elements means in English. For instance, what constitutes a "legally binding contract" (the first element)? What if you had only spoken with the painter and neither of you had anything in writing? When he walked off the job, he was angry and said something like, "I'm outta here. Just try to sue me; we don't even have a contract. You'll never be able to prove anything."

One question you may ask is, "Can an oral contract be valid?" For the answer, you may first try asking a reliable resource person or you can go to a law library and look up the answer. (First ask a law librarian to direct you to some resources about oral contracts. This will typically save you lots of time.) You may consult a treatise (reference book) about contract law, such as *Contracts in a Nutshell,* by Gordon Schaber and Claude Rohwer (West Publishing Co.) or a legal encyclopedia. (More below on legal reference books.) In this example, you will find that you do not need a written contract or other document to form a valid contract for painting a house; an oral contract is sufficient so long as it can be proved. (Of course, you may have more trouble proving the terms of an oral contract than a written contract.)

The Rules of Evidence

After you understand the substantive law affecting your case, you will want to be sure you are up to speed on evidence rules. These rules govern how you present and respond to testimony, the exhibits you and your adversary refer to, and what you attempt to introduce into evidence—or attempt to keep out.

Chapter 16 explains the most frequently encountered rules of evidence and refers to particular rules from the Federal Rules of Evidence (FRE). The FRE is a good starting place for research because its rules have been adopted or used as a guideline in over half the states. But you may want to read a particular rule of evidence in your state or find out how courts in your state have interpreted some aspect of a particular rule of evidence. Ask a law librarian to show you where to find the evidence rules for your state or where the library keeps the FRE if your case is in federal court.

The Rules of Civil Procedure

Procedural rules govern the process of conducting litigation before, during, and after trial. Rules of civil procedure control such things as how many days you have to file a response to your adversary's complaint, the deadline for requesting a jury trial, how many interrogatories you can ask the other side during discovery, and dozens of other details.

Procedural rules for civil cases may be grouped together in a particular chapter, title, or section of general state laws under the heading "civil procedure." Some states have conveniently separated books of rules called "codes." In those, you will find a separate "code of civil procedure." In other states, you will likely have to use the general index to the statutes to find the rules you need. In the federal court system, they are in the Federal Rules of Civil Procedure (FRCP). Before you begin looking around, you may want to ask a law librarian how to find the rules of civil procedure that apply to your case.

Local Rules

Local court rules also affect procedure, and they can be critical to the task of effectively trying your case. Local rules can govern many details—for instance, how many copies of legal documents you must submit or the type of paper you must use. These sound like picky little details, and they are. But they are details that you must follow. Even different counties within the same state can have different rules. For example, one area's local rules may allow ten days to reply to a motion, while another's allow two weeks. So

as early on as possible in the process, search your state or court's website or go to the court clerk or law clerk where your case is pending (or the courthouse law library) and ask for a copy of all local Rules of Court.

Sources of Information

Many people faced with a legal research task are tempted to begin by poring over stacks of books or the pages of websites. For the novice, this too frequently results in floundering for hours through material that doesn't relate to your case. Fortunately, there are better ways to get the information you need. One, simply enough, is to just ask someone; another is to consult a book that explains and organizes the substantive law. Finally, you may want to look up the law itself—the actual statute (sometimes called a piece of "legislation") or written decision of a court—which you can do in a law library or online. This section discusses all these sources of information.

People

You may not *always* get a right answer or even an answer at all, but *often* you can get quick and helpful information by asking someone who regularly deals with legal documents. The most likely candidates for help with your case are court clerks, law librarians, self-help law centers, or a lawyer who agrees to consult with you (see "Getting Help From a Lawyer," below).

Court Clerks

Clerks at the court where your case is pending can sometimes be very helpful, especially when it comes to procedural details. For example, court clerks can help you greatly by locating for you or telling you where to obtain copies of documents such as:

- local court rules
- state or federal court rules
- legal forms (pleadings, motions, or court orders), or
- jury instructions.

You may encounter resistance or even outright hostility from court clerks, some of whom still view self-represented parties as people who will waste their and the court's time. For example, a clerk may refuse to answer your questions, saying something like, "I'm not allowed to give legal advice." But asking how to get forms and copies of court rules is not seeking legal advice. Be polite, state up front that you are not asking for legal advice, and be sure to express how much you appreciate the help; these few steps often make the difference between getting help from clerks or not. And, remember, you have nothing to lose by asking.

Court-Sponsored Self-Help Law Centers

Because self-representation has become so much more common, many courts have set up self-help law centers—especially in areas such as family law where parties very often represent themselves. Some of these centers have offices in courthouses where you can go in and get forms, ask questions, and do research; others are online resources. Ask the court clerk for information about how to contact such a center if there is one available to help in your area, or enter terms such as "self-help law center and courts" into an internet search engine to find one online. Here are a few online sites for Centers in selected states.

- Virtual Self-Help Law Center, Contra Costa County, California: www.cc-courthelp.org
- California Courts Self-Help: www.courtinfo.ca.gov/selfhelp
- Florida State Courts Self-Help: www.flcourts.org/gen_public/family/forms_rules/index.shtml
- Clark County, Nevada, Family Law Self-Help: www.co.clark.nv.us/district_court/self_help_center.htm
- Colorado courts, self-help: www.courts.state.co.us/chs/court/forms/selfhelpcenter.htm
- Alaska Court Family Law Self-Help Center: www.state.ak.us/courts/selfhelp.htm
- Illinois (Southern Illinois University): www.law.siu.edu/selfhelp/

RESOURCE

If you are representing yourself in a divorce case, *Nolo's Essential Guide to Divorce*, by Emily Doskow (Nolo), has a complete listing of state court websites where you can get information about divorce and the courts.

Law Librarians

All sorts of legal information, including legal forms, reference books explaining particular areas of law, rules of evidence and procedure, court cases, statutes, and more are available at law libraries. Law librarians, who usually have extensive legal training, can be most helpful in pointing you to these and other resources.

Do not ask or expect a law librarian to do your research for you, and don't ask for legal advice. They can't and won't provide these services. But they will help you find what you need and, often, explain how to use the research tools you've found. Many law libraries also have online resources in addition to information on site.

Finding a Law Library

In some states, finding a well-stocked law library that is open to the public is no problem; the principal courthouse in every metropolitan area will almost always have a public law library. But in other places, courthouse libraries are nonexistent or inadequate, and the only decent law libraries open to the public are located at publicly funded law schools. Some private law schools also open their law libraries to the public, at least for limited hours.

For simple legal research tasks, a public library can also be a fine place to start. Many public libraries have small but helpful legal sections where you can find your state's statutes as well as county and local ordinances. Another possibility is to ask for permission to use some of the resources in the law office library of a local lawyer if you are using a lawyer's services for any part of your case.

Lawyers

Consulting a lawyer may be helpful, and doing so does not necessarily mean turning over control of your entire case. You may want advice on what is sometimes called an "unbundled" basis—similar to ordering à la carte from a restaurant menu. "Getting Help From a Lawyer," below, provides details about how to find and work with a lawyer in this way.

Books and Other Publications

Books that summarize and explain court cases, statutes, and other rules of law (including law summary books often called "treatises") can be your most important legal research tools. They are a good place to start your research because they can help you get a picture of where you are going—and maybe give you an answer, or at least point you to a resource in which you will find an answer. By streamlining your research, they can cut down on time and frustration.

 CAUTION

Publications about the law are not the last word. If you find a useful explanation in an encyclopedia, treatise, or article, keep in mind that the conclusions expressed are not the law itself but the analysis of the authors, and a judge does not have to follow what they say. Also, the author may be mistaken or information in the article may be outdated. If you want to use the specific laws that the author cites to support your position, look them up yourself.

Secondary Sources or Books that Explain the Law and Legal Terms

It often helps save time and frustration to begin researching online or with a hard copy of one or more of the following types of resources discussed in this chapter:

- Law dictionary
- Subject-specific treatise
- Form book
- Legal encyclopedia
- Law journal
- Lawyer's practice guide

Legal Dictionaries

Just like any other specialized aspect of our society, law has its own jargon. When you are representing yourself, it is very important for you to become fluent (or at least comfortable) with a lot of new terms. You probably have already increased your legal vocabulary a great deal by reading and consulting the Glossary in this book, but a good legal dictionary will be most helpful.

Obviously, you need to look up words you don't know. But it can even pay to look up words you think you know, because they may have different connotations or even meanings in a legal context. Take the word "discovery," for example: To nonlawyers, a discovery is a find, as in, "The explorers discovered buried treasure." But in law, "discovery" is the pretrial process of gathering information, usually from your opponent. Another example is "hearsay," an important word you need to understand. Nonlawyers typically define hearsay as unsubstantiated talk or rumors. For example, someone said, "Loretta told me there were going to be mass layoffs next month, but I don't believe her; it's just hearsay." In legal language, "hearsay" means, "an out-of-court statement offered in court for the truth of that statement." It's similar to the nonlegal meaning, but not identical. (Chapter 16 explains the hearsay rule.)

Readable Dictionaries

The best known legal dictionary, *Black's Law Dictionary* (West Publishing Co.), has long frustrated even people in the legal profession with its confusing language and convoluted definitions. However, the tome has recently been revised and, beginning with the seventh edition, has garnered good reviews for its clearer language. In addition to *Black's*, you may want to take a look at one or more of these dictionaries, some of which make a point of putting the law into plain language:

- *Law Dictionary* by Stephen Gifis (Barrons)
- *Dictionary of Legal Terms* by Stephen Gifis (Barrons)
- *Law Dictionary for Nonlawyers* by Daniel Oran (Delmar Thomson Learning)
- *Legal Thesaurus-Dictionary* by William Statsky (West Publishing Co.)
- *Dictionary of American Legal Usage* by David Melinkoff (West Publishing Co.), and
- *Ballentine's Law Dictionary* by Jack Handler (Delmar Thomson Learning).

Finally, you may want to check out Nolo's free online legal glossary at www.nolo.com.

Treatises on Particular Subjects

Treatises have been written on almost every conceivable legal subject. Because they summarize whole areas of law, they can be useful research tools. But because the great majority are written for lawyers or law students, you may have to wade through a lot of legal jargon to get valuable information. Ask your law librarian or legal coach to recommend a treatise about the area your case involves—for example, torts or contracts.

The Nutshell series, published by the West Publishing Company, is a series of paperback treatises written in more down-to-earth language. The Nutshell series—for example, *Contracts in a Nutshell*—cover a wide range of legal subjects, including trial advocacy, civil rights, community property, constitutional law, environmental law, workers' compensation and employee protection laws, and a lot more. To find out whether there's a Nutshell for the subject you are interested in, check the first few pages in any Nutshell book for a list, in alphabetical order, of all the other Nutshell books. Also listed are West Publishing's major law textbooks and "hornbooks" (longer, usually hardbound treatises).

Plain-English Law Books

Only a few publishers, such as Nolo, gear their books especially toward nonlawyers. Nolo publishes books, software, and downloadable products on a very wide variety of subjects, including landlord-tenant law, wills, divorce, bankruptcy, tax, buying and selling property, employment law, and many more. For a list of all of Nolo's books and software, visit Nolo's website at www.nolo.com.

Also, Southern Illinois University Press publishes a series of books edited by the American Civil Liberties Union (ACLU). These explain many civil rights—for example, the rights of crime victims, employees, gay and lesbian people, Native Americans, and women—and the right to government information.

Form Books

Form books are collections of model legal documents. Most include fill-in-the-blank documents that you can copy and fill out. Form books can help you enormously when you have to prepare any legal paperwork, such as initial pleadings (complaint and answer) or discovery tools (such as interrogatories, pretrial motions, and stipulations). With a form in front of you, you don't have to reinvent the wheel, although you may have to change the model forms a bit to fit the circumstances of your case.

Form books also usually explain the procedural background for each form. They can provide helpful explanations of the laws you will have to follow as well as instructions for completing the forms, and they refer you to other resources should you need further information.

Some states provide their own fill-in-the-blank forms that you must use for specific purposes. These are available for free or for a small fee at local courts. Ask the court clerk or a law librarian, or check one of the online resources such as a self-help law center website, discussed above for help in locating court-approved forms. A list of form books can also be found in *Legal Research: How to Find and Understand the Law*, by Stephen Elias and Susan Levinkind (Nolo).

Legal Encyclopedias

Legal encyclopedias, like regular encyclopedias, contain detailed explanations of various topics, organized alphabetically by topic. There is a detailed index at the end of the last volume, which you can use to find the topic you want. Encyclopedias can give you a great deal of general background information about a particular subject and can often refer you to state and federal statutes and cases. That makes them a good place to start if you just want to get a general understanding of the legal principles that govern your dispute.

There are both national and state-specific encyclopedias. The two main national law encyclopedias are *American Jurisprudence* (Am. Jur.) and *Corpus Juris*. They include broadly based discussions on the laws of all 50 states. Both are now in their second series, so you'll find citations to "Am. Jur. 2d." and "C.J.S." (*Corpus Juris Secundum*). Many of the larger states have their own encyclopedias as well. Here are a few examples:

- *Pennsylvania Law Encyclopedia*
- *New York Jurisprudence 2d*
- *Encyclopedia of Georgia Law*
- *Florida Jurisprudence*
- *California Jurisprudence 3d*

Check a law library or online legal research site to find a legal encyclopedia for your state.

Journals and Law Reviews

Many legal organizations publish journals (magazines) that contain articles covering current legal issues. For example, in a journal published by a state bar association you might find a review of recent changes in your court's local rules or an analysis of a recent court opinion.

Law schools also produce journals, called "law reviews," that consist of scholarly articles written by law students, law professors, and practicing attorneys. Though law reviews are notorious for their complex and confusing language, they sometimes cover timely topics and can provide leads to relevant state or federal laws.

To locate relevant articles, you can use the *Index to Legal Periodicals,* the *Current Law Index,* or a computerized index called LEGALTRAC, found in many law libraries. (Ask a law librarian for help finding these.)

Lawyers' Practice Guides

Books written for practicing lawyers can be helpful resources for finding instructions, practical suggestions, and forms for specific areas of state and federal law practice.

These publications cover a huge variety of subjects, such as negligence, copyright, bankruptcy, mechanics' liens, tax law, and many more. There are specific guides on pretrial, trial, and post-trial tactics, and practice guides on pretrial motions, discovery, direct and cross-examination, opening statement, closing argument, appeals, and more. They are available in many states, and some publishers gear their materials specifically toward lawyers in particular states. For example, the Practicing Law Institute (PLI) gears some materials toward New York lawyers, while the Rutter Group and the Continuing Education of the Bar (CEB) are geared toward California lawyers. Check a law library near you or one of the online legal resource sites noted in this chapter.

The Law Itself

The law consists of constitutional provisions, statutes, court cases, ordinances, and administrative regulations.

State and Federal Legislation

Legislation is the word for the rules enacted by federal and state legislatures. These rules are sometimes called statutes, acts, or laws.

State statutes are grouped by subject matter. Most sets of statutes take up many volumes, but they are divided into "codes," "chapters," or "titles," which are in turn divided in sections and subsections. Federal laws are published in the "United States Code."

As are some other statute books, the U.S. Code is divided into titles and sections. Each statute has a particular number, called a citation or cite. Once you've found a citation to a statute from a treatise or article, you can easily find the statute. For example, imagine that an encyclopedia mentions a statute called the "Civil Rights Act of 1964" and gives the citation "42 U.S.C.A., Sections 2000 a–h." To find this statute, you would look in Title 42 in the United States Code Annotated (U.S.C.A.) and then find the volume of that title containing Section 2000, Subsections a through h.

Statute books typically include a subject index in the last volume, where you can look for references to relevant laws. When using an index, try to think of several possible headings for the subject you are researching. To do this, review headings in a treatise or encyclopedia or ask a librarian. If you don't find anything under the first logical heading, keep searching, or look in a legal dictionary to find related words or phrases. For example, if you don't know the name or citation to the federal law that forbids racial discrimination, you might first look in the index under "civil rights." If that doesn't work, you might try "discrimination" or "racial discrimination."

Legal subjects overlap, so you may find what you need under more than one heading. For example, a law regarding an exception to the hearsay rule may be listed under "evidence," "hearsay," "hearsay rule, exceptions to," and under the specific name of the exception itself—for instance, "business records."

When you look up statutes, try to use an "annotated" version of the statute books. Annotated versions contain the actual language of an official statute, along with short summaries of the significant court cases (including their legal citation for easy reference; see below) that discuss the statute and references to other resource books and articles.

Once you have found a relevant statute, here are some suggestions for reading and making sense of it:

- Make sure you understand all the terms. Refer to a legal dictionary to look up words in the statute. In longer statutes, the first parts often define terms used in other parts of the law.
- Always check to see if the law is current. Laws are often revised and sometimes repealed (removed from the books). So, after you find a statute in the main section of your state's hardbound statute book, be sure to look in the paper-bound supplement or update, called a "pocket part," usually located inside the back cover of the book. Pocket parts contain the changes that have been made to a law or its wording since the publication of the hardbound volume. Some pocket parts are also annotated with references—for example, citations to recent cases discussing a statute.

Local Ordinances

Cities and counties pass a wide variety of ordinances—rules that, subject to state and federal laws, have the force and effect of law. They can have a great impact on your daily life and business. Among other things, they can affect:

- parking and driving
- health and safety standards in rental properties
- new building requirements, and
- zoning (restrictions on how land can be used).

Local governments vary as to how they organize and publish their ordinances, so you may have to check with a law librarian for help finding what you need. You can find many local ordinances online, and public libraries often have local ordinances. Sometimes you can also obtain copies of local ordinances from a city office, such as a police or motor vehicles department for traffic concerns or a planning department for zoning and building rules. If you know the specific subject of the ordinance you are looking for, you can probably get a copy by calling the city or county clerk's office, or the city or county attorney. They will usually send you a copy free or for a small photocopying fee.

Court Cases

In cases that come before appellate courts, appellate judges review the record and decisions of trial courts. They interpret the meaning of statutes, constitutional provisions, and other court cases, making what's known as the "common law" (judge-made law). Sometimes, appellate courts write decisions (called opinions, case law, or cases), in which they summarize the facts that the trial judge or jury found to be true and set forth the appellate court judges' legal reasoning and "holding" (rule).

Appellate court cases are collected and published in hardbound volumes called "reporters," "reports," or "case reports." There are many separate reporters for different courts and geographical areas. For example, a case from the New York Court of Appeals may be published in a series of state reporters called *New York Appeals* and also in a regional reporter series called the *Northeastern Reporter,* which includes cases from several states. Federal cases are published according to the court that decided them. For example, decisions by the U.S. Courts of Appeal are collected in the *Federal Reporter.*

Recent cases, not yet included in a hardbound reporter, are located in softbound supplements. And cases decided in the last few days or weeks may often only be available from the appellate court itself or a computer reporting service. If you want to look up a new case you just read about in the newspaper, for example, ask the librarian to assist you; it won't be in the hardbound books yet.

Cases, like statutes, have citations that let you look them up easily. Let's say you want to read the famous school desegregation case *Brown v. Board of Education.* Consulting an encyclopedia or legal dictionary, you learn that its citation is "347 U.S. 483 (1954)." The first number means the case is located in volume 347. The letters in the middle (U.S.) are the abbreviation for *United States-Reports,* the case reporter series where the *Brown* case is published. The last number tells you the case begins at page 483. The names reflect the parties to the lawsuit, and the date

at the end is when the U.S. Supreme Court decided the case. If you have a case citation, a law librarian will always be able to help you find the book in which the case appears.

State Constitutions and the U.S. Constitution

The U.S. Constitution is the supreme law of the land, which means all local, state, and federal laws must comply with it. State constitutions have the same authority over state laws, but state constitutions must also comply with the U.S. Constitution. Courts decide whether or not laws comply with constitutional provisions. Courts also interpret what constitutional provisions mean, just like they interpret statutes.

The research you do is not likely to involve constitutional law. Most of what you need will be found in reference materials, statutes, and court cases. Because constitutional law is often complex, if your case involves a constitutional issue—for example, if you want to challenge a law that you feel is unconstitutional—you probably should consult a lawyer for assistance.

Once court cases are published, they are usually not removed from the books even if later courts conclude that the decision is no longer correct. Thus, you always need to check that a case you rely on is still "good law," meaning that it has not been "overruled" by a later case. A series of case histories called *Shepard's Citations for Cases* reports the status of published cases. Ask a law librarian how to use *Shepard's* to verify that any case you intend to rely on is still good law. *Shepard's* can also help you find more recent cases that discuss (but don't overrule) the case you're interested in.

The Numbering System for Case Reporters

Case reporters are published in numbered volumes. After a series accumulates years of numbered volumes, the publisher starts over with another series. So you may find a cite to "2d" or "3d" series for some reporters. For example, "*York v. Story*, 324 F.2d 450 (1963)" is at volume 324 of the *Federal Reporter*, Second Series, beginning on page 450.

In addition to the full text of the court's opinions, reporters include "headnotes," short summaries of the legal issues in a case. Headnotes are numbered in the order in which the issues are discussed in a case. They can be quite useful, both for a quick look at what a case is about and as a table of contents to help you locate issues that interest you.

Headnotes are not written by the judge who wrote the opinion but by the editors of the reporter. They can be inaccurate and are not "law," so don't quote them to support your position when making an argument to a judge. You must rely on the decision of the court itself.

What Rules Judges Must Follow

How will you know which of the rules you may find in your research the judge will have to follow? Primary authorities (statutes, cases, administrative regulations, and local rules and ordinances) can be "mandatory," which means that a court has to follow them. But they can also be just "persuasive," which means a court can consider them but does not have to follow them. For example, a state court in New York may find it helpful and convincing that a California court recently decided the same legal question now before the New York court. But the New York court does not have to follow the California court's decision.

A judge must, however, follow the decisions of higher courts in the same state. For example, a Los Angeles trial judge must follow a decision of the California Supreme Court (the highest state court in California), but a trial judge in Alabama doesn't have to.

When researching cases, it is best to find an appellate court case from your own state (or from your circuit in the federal court system); that way the case is binding on your trial judge. But if all you can find is an out-of-state case that is nonetheless right on point and very helpful to your case, you may try to convince your judge that its reasoning is persuasive.

Similar rules apply to statutes. Statutes are mandatory if they were enacted by the legislature in the state where your case will be tried.

Administrative Regulations

Administrative regulations ("regs") are enacted by federal, state, and local agencies. For example, the federal Equal Employment Opportunity Commission, a state Veterans' Board, and a local school board all make their own rules. Administrative regs govern agencies' policies and procedures, such as how they conduct hearings and the reasons they will grant or withhold benefits.

You'll need to research agency regulations if you are presenting your case at a hearing before an administrative agency. Although the hearing may resemble a trial, in reality it is quite different. For example, most agencies do not follow the rules of evidence, and you have no right to a jury. Lawyers may be excluded, and you may not be able to subpoena witnesses or documents or even have witnesses testify. Some hearings are not open to the public.

Law on the Internet

As noted above, there are many online law library and legal research resources. You can often find background information and even specific laws such as statutes, rules, regulations, and case decisions that affect your case.

Getting an Overview

Getting an overview of the legal topic that concerns you may well be the most productive way to begin your research. Nolo's website, www.nolo.com, is a great place to start when looking for background information. The site features a huge collection of free articles on dozens of topics, including employment rights, consumer and insurance issues, real estate problems, debt and credit

pickles, and family and neighbor disputes. Many of the articles contain links to other websites that will help further your research. You can also find answers to many frequently asked questions (FAQs) on Nolo's site.

You may want to search for background information by entering keywords for the topic you want to research into either a general online search engine such as a Google (www.google.com) or Yahoo! (www.yahoo.com), or on a legal website such as one of those listed below. And, note that in the bankruptcy and family law chapters of this book, there are resources for more information in those particular areas.

- **Nolo:** www.nolo.com
- **FindLaw:** www.findlaw.com
- **All Law:** www.allaw.com
- **National Federation of Paralegal Associations:** www.paralegals.org, and click on "Legal Resources"
- **LawGuru:** www.lawguru.com
- **The Legal Information Institute:** www.law.cornell.edu

Federal Codes, Rules, and Regulations

There's a wealth of federal law online. You can access the United States Code, the Federal Rules of Civil Procedure, and the Federal Code of Regulations through Nolo's website, at www.nolo.com/statute/index.cfm. Click on "Federal Laws" to locate what you need. For the Federal Rules of Civil Procedure or the Federal Rules of Evidence, visit the Legal Information Institute at www.law.cornell.edu/rules/frcp or /fre, respectively. Another good source for information on federal (and state) law is the Washburn University School of Law website at www.washlaw.edu.

State Statutes

Most states have made their statutes available online. You can access them by visiting Nolo's website, at www.nolo.com/statute/index.cfm. Click on "State Laws" and then choose your state to search or browse the statutes.

Local Laws

It is often possible to find local ordinances on the Web. One online resource is www.municode.com. Another is the Municipal Codes Online website maintained by the Seattle Public Library at www.spl.org/?pageID-collection_municodes. First, select your state. Then select your city or town from the list that appears on your state's page. Click there and search your municipality's website for the law you need.

If that doesn't turn up anything, try finding your city or county's official website by entering the city or county name plus the word "government" into a search engine such as Google (www.google.com) or Yahoo! (www.yahoo.com). Or, find your city's website at www.FirstGov.gov/Agencies/Local_Government/Cities.shtml.

Court Forms

Many courts have developed forms for documents that are routinely filed in court, and many of these forms are now available online. To see whether your court publishes its forms online, try searching online by typing the name of the court plus the words "court forms" into a search engine such as Google or Yahoo! Or, you can look on the forms section of the FindLaw website, at http://forms.lp.findlaw.com.

Court Rules

With increasing frequency, federal, state, and local courts are making their local rules available online. But these postings are still spotty—for example, your state may publish its Supreme Court rules on the Web, but not its trial court rules.

Your court's rules may be accessible on your court's website, if it has one. Enter the name of the court in a search engine, such as Google or Yahoo!, or call the court clerk and ask whether the court has a website and, if so, whether the court's rules are posted there.

You can also check www.llrx.com/courtrules or www.uscourts.gov/rules. If you don't find the rules you need, you can turn back to traditional sources: In this case, a visit to the law library or court clerk's office.

Case Law

Finding cases on the Internet can be tricky. If you're looking for a recent U.S. Supreme Court case, you'll probably have no trouble. Wander into the wider world of federal and state case law, however, and you may come up empty-handed—or you'll have to pay a fee for what you want. If you must do case research, you can try the Web, but your best bet may be the books in a law library.

Federal cases. You may be able to find federal cases online. FindLaw, at www.findlaw.com, contains cases decided by the U.S. Supreme Court and federal appellate courts (called Federal Circuit Courts of Appeal) within the past four or five years, some bankruptcy opinions, and very recent tax court cases. The Legal Information Institute, at www.law.cornell.edu/index.html, provides access to some U.S. District Court cases and some bankruptcy opinions. VersusLaw, at www.versuslaw.com, also has some U.S. District Court cases and some bankruptcy opinions that you can research at a flat cost (of between about $14 and $40 per month) for unlimited use. If you can't find something on one of these websites, your best bet is Westlaw or Lexis. (See "Using Lexis and Westlaw to Do Legal Research Online," below, for more information.)

Using Lexis and Westlaw to Do Legal Research Online

Lexis and Westlaw are the chief electronic legal databases that contain the full text of many of the law resources found in major law libraries, including almost all reported cases from state and federal courts, all federal statutes, the statutes of most states, federal regulations, law review articles, commonly used treatises, and practice manuals.

Although Westlaw and Lexis databases are available over the Internet, subscriptions are pricey. However, both offer some fee-based services to nonsubscribers that are helpful and reasonably priced (between $9 and $10 per document). To find out more about these services, visit Westlaw at www. westlaw.com and Lexis at www.lexis.com.

State cases. If the case is recent (within the last few years), you may be able to find it for free on the Internet. A good place to start is FindLaw, at www.findlaw.com. If the case is older, you can still find it online, but you will probably have to pay a private company for access to its database. VersusLaw (described above) maintains an excellent library of older state court cases that you can research for a modest fee. You can also get state cases online through the Lexis and Westlaw databases. (See below.)

Getting Help From a Lawyer

This section explains how to locate and work with a lawyer or paralegal as a sort of "coach," on an unbundled or à la carte basis. Note: this type of arrangement also may be called by other terms such as "limited scope representation," "discrete task representation," "segregated task representation," "legal coaching," and other terminology. Whatever it's called, what it means is that the lawyer doesn't represent you, but assists you with specific tasks that you believe you would do better with a lawyer's help and gives you advice when needed.

Lawyers have traditionally represented clients in full-service capacities, so you may encounter hostility or have difficulties finding a lawyer willing to work on an unbundled basis. A lawyer will often need reassurances that you know you may not "win," that you are aware of the risks in representing yourself, and that you are taking full responsibility for your own representation and are willing to sign a waiver so the lawyer will not be held responsible should something go wrong. (See "Sample Legal Coach Agreement," below.)

RESOURCE

Resources on lawyer-client dealings.
Finding the Right Lawyer, by Jay Foonberg
(ABA), is a detailed guide to finding and hiring
a lawyer, from the ABA Section of Law Practice
Management.

*The Lawsuit Survival Guide: A Client's
Companion to Litigation*, by Joseph Matthews
(Nolo), guides readers who are represented by
lawyers through the civil litigation process from
start to finish. It includes information on how to
find the right lawyer for your case.

What Services Might You Seek on a Piecemeal Basis?

Even though you are representing yourself, a
lawyer or legal coach can help you in several
important ways. For example, you might
ask an attorney to help you do any of the
following:

- learn what laws apply in your case,
  and assess whether you have a solid
  claim or defense
- strategize about a potential settlement
  and write a demand letter to your
  opponent urging settlement
- explore alternatives to litigation—like
  mediation or arbitration—and help
  you prepare for a mediation or
  arbitration hearing
- assist you in completing legal forms
  and drafting legal documents, filing
  them with the court, and serving them
  on the appropriate parties
- review and advise you about
  documents you receive from your
  opponent and the court

- conduct or plan for discovery and
  factual investigation of your claims, or
  help you with witness interviews and
  document searches
- help you practice responding to
  likely questions a judge might pose
  in a court hearing, or an opponent
  or opposing counsel might pose in a
  deposition
- help you determine if you need to
  consult an expert, and help you locate
  and prepare to meet with an expert if
  you do need one
- be "on call" should you get thrown
  for a loop during trial, and step in
  and take over should you feel you
  are unable to continue representing
  yourself, and
- help you collect a judgment if you
  win, or advise with respect to a
  possible appeal if you lose.

Finding a Lawyer Who Will Provide Unbundled Legal Services

Finding a lawyer who is open to working
with you as a self-represented client isn't
impossible, but it is likely to require some
searching. You want a lawyer who has trial
experience and is familiar with the specific
legal issues involved in your case. You also
want someone you are comfortable with—
someone who understands and respects
your decision to represent yourself and
agrees to take on a role that's different from
the traditional lawyer's role. You may need
to interview a number of different lawyers
before you find the right person.

You'll start trying to find a legal coach the same way you would try to find a full service lawyer, by seeking referrals from:

- friends or family
- small businesses
- another local professional such as an accountant or financial advisor who works with individuals or small businesses and may be familiar with local lawyers
- legal and other community organizations

- paralegals and paralegal services
- Martindale-Hubbell's lawyer directory,
- state or local bar association referral services or
- online legal directories such as Nolo's directory at http://lawyers.nolo.com, which includes detailed profiles that include the advertiser's philosophy about helping self-represented clients.

You may need to get creative and contact a lawyer who is on a bar association committee that deals with delivery of legal services,

---

Finding a Lawyer: An Example

You are a homeowner who bought a house from Colleen Larky. Colleen told you that the roof was in very good condition. You have just discovered that she lied. The roof, patched in several hard-to-see places, must be replaced before the winter. Also, your neighbor, Craig Jamner, just told you that he is planning to build a guest house on part of your garden near his house, which he claims belongs to him. Craig said that he had allowed Colleen to plant rose bushes there while he wasn't using the land, but that she knew he would eventually want it back.

You want a lawyer to tell you whether you would have a good lawsuit against Colleen for misrepresenting these important facts and to serve as a legal coach to help you prepare and try the case should you decide to do so.

To find some initial referrals, you ask friends and family. All you come up with is that your Uncle Pat was very happy with a lawyer who recently wrote his will. You call the lawyer and say that you were referred by Pat. You explain (briefly) what your case involves and that you

understand that this area is not the lawyer's specialty. You politely ask for the name of one or more good lawyers in your community who regularly handle property disputes. You get two names.

Then you phone several businesses in your area: a title insurance company, a real estate brokerage firm, and a lumber yard, and ask who they use. The title insurance company says, "None of your business," but the other two supply you with names of lawyers they recommend.

Next, you look in *Martindale-Hubbell*, a nationwide directory of lawyers, under your city's listing. You find one attorney who has written an article on property law and belongs to the local real estate lawyers' groups and two others who are part of the real estate group as well.

After looking at your list of names, you notice that one lawyer on your list was referred by two of your sources. It is sensible to start your interviews with that lawyer.

or a lawyer in your state who has authored a book or article on unbundled legal services, and ask that person for a recommendation or resource.

You can also ask lawyers who refuse to take on coaching themselves whether they know of others in their field who might accept discrete task representation work. Be polite and explain that you will keep them in mind for referrals when you or someone you know needs full-service legal representation.

There are many helpful web resources to learn more about working with lawyers on an unbundled basis, including www. unbundledlaw.org and www.abanet.org/ legalservices/delivery/delunbund.html.

Working With a Lawyer

In some respects, working with a lawyer on a piecemeal basis is a lot like working with a full-service lawyer—the more proactive, prepared, and thorough you are, the more effective the services you will receive. Here are some guidelines to keep in mind.

First, take the time to interview prospective lawyers. Your purpose here is to make certain that the lawyer is in fact open to providing unbundled services, and you want to ensure that you feel comfortable with the lawyer.

Second, expect that the lawyer will ask you to sign an agreement making it clear that the lawyer is merely advising you, and that you are representing yourself. There's a sample shown below.

Third, don't expect something for nothing. Many lawyers provide initial consultations for free or minimal fees, but because you are requesting an unconventional relationship,

you should expect to pay for each of the discrete services you obtain. (Time that the lawyer spends just reading background documents and listening to the basics of your case is a lawyering "service"—so be sure to prepare for meetings as well as possible. For example, in an initial meeting, give a brief overview and show the lawyer key documents and then let the lawyer request further detail if needed.)

Next, confirm how you will be billed should you decide to go forward with this lawyer (fixed fee for a project or task, hourly fee for time the lawyer spends, or contingency fee based on your potential recovery.) The lawyer may also request a retainer (a deposit or advance the lawyer keeps in a trust account and draws down on to pay your fees and costs.) Most lawyers will also charge for costs, which include things like copying costs or court filing fees.

Finally, ask about your coach's accessibility and about what is the best time to contact your lawyer—and also about how and whether in writing or by phone. And be sure anything you put in writing remains confidential. Write "Confidential and Privileged" at the top of anything you write, and do not discuss confidential matters with anyone other than the lawyer. There's more on privileged information in Chapters 5 and 6.

You can see that self-representation does not necessarily mean going it completely alone. And, it certainly does not mean "winging it" or doing without the information necessary to competently represent yourself. There are lots of resources that can help you—people, books, websites, and more. If you make use of them and get the help you need, you should do fine.

Sample Legal Coach Agreement

Legal Coach Agreement

William Nolo, a pro per litigant ("Nolo"), and Anna Turney, an attorney in the state of _____ ("Lawyer"), agree as follows:

Lawyer will serve as Nolo's legal coach to advise Nolo on the negligence action he has filed against Sarah Adams.

1. Nolo is representing himself in the case *Nolo v. Adams*. Lawyer is not representing Nolo, but merely advising Nolo on an as-needed basis if and when Nolo seeks Lawyer's advice.

2. Nolo takes responsibility for all decisions made in litigating the case and for all results that stem from the case.

3. Lawyer will keep all communications made by Nolo to Lawyer in connection with this case confidential.

4. Nolo will pay for Lawyer's advice at the rate of $225 per hour. This advice may include, but is not limited to, matters such as helping Nolo research the legal issues involved in his case, reviewing pleadings that Nolo has prepared or received in connection with the case, and assisting Nolo in developing and implementing a litigation strategy.

5. Nolo may also arrange, through Lawyer, for assistance from Lawyer's office personnel, such as a paralegal at the rate of $90 per hour and a legal secretary at the rate of $30 per hour.

6. Nolo will pay Lawyer a $300 retainer. Lawyer will bill Nolo monthly.

7. Nolo will have reasonable access to Lawyer's office services as needed, including the conference room and library.

Date: _____   _____
                            William Nolo

Date: _____   _____
                            Anna Turney

What You Should Know About Lawyers' Fees

When you interview a potential legal coach, ask about all fees and costs—including the initial interview. It obviously defeats your purpose if you have to spend more to consult a legal coach than you would to hire a lawyer to handle your entire case. Typically, lawyers use hourly, fixed, or contingency fee arrangements. Most likely, someone serving as your legal coach will charge you by the hour.

Hourly rates for lawyers who do personal legal-services work typically run from $100 to $250 per hour. Certain experts and big-firm lawyers charge even more. It is important to find out exactly how the lawyer will calculate the bill. For example, some lawyers who charge by the hour bill in minimum increments of 15 minutes (quarter hour), and others bill in increments of six minutes (tenth of an hour). That means that a five-minute phone conversation for which you are billed the minimum amount could cost you different amounts, depending on how the lawyer figures the bill.

Although getting good value for your money is key, this doesn't mean that you should always look for the lowest hourly fee. You can often benefit by hiring a more experienced attorney, even if the attorney's hourly rates are high, because the lawyer may take less time to review and advise you on particulars of your case.

Many lawyers routinely ask clients to pay a "retainer"—a deposit or advance fee—that is kept in a trust account and used as services are provided. Your legal coach may ask for a retainer in order to see that you are serious and have the money to pay. However, you shouldn't be expected to come up with a large amount of money, because you do not plan on running up high legal bills. A fee of more than $500 is excessive, especially before you know whether the legal coach relationship is really working out.

There are a couple of specific types of fees that you should know about:

Contingency Fees. When representing people in personal injury cases, lawyers often take a percentage of the final judgment—often one-third, but varying depending on factors such as whether a case settles before trial—as their fee. Because you will try your own case, you will probably not use a contingency fee arrangement. If your coach suggests one, do not agree to give too high a percentage, since you will be doing most of the work.

Fixed Fees. A fixed fee is a set fee for a particular project. For example, a lawyer may charge $500 to write your will. It is unlikely that an attorney will suggest a fixed fee to coach you through your whole case, because the lawyer will have little idea of the amount of work involved. But the lawyer may suggest fixed fees for particular services along the way. For example, you may find a lawyer willing to charge you no more than a specific sum of money to review and edit your complaint or to help you respond to your opponent's interrogatories.

Keeping Legal Bills in Check

Working with a competent, supportive lawyer will likely be well worth the expense. But there are approaches you can use to keep the bills down and get the most for your money:

- **Prepare before you talk to your coach.** To save time and thus money, prepare for all sessions, including the initial interview and phone calls.

- **List your questions before you meet.** If possible, get questions to the lawyer in writing before meetings. That allows the lawyer time to look up answers and saves you an additional meeting. It also helps focus the conversation so there's less of a chance of digressing into unrelated topics.

- **Consolidate questions.** Hourly charges are usually divided into parts of an hour, so you may be charged for more time than you actually spend. For example, if your legal coach bills in 15-minute intervals and you only talk for five minutes, you may still be charged for the whole 15. If that is your coach's practice, it pays to gather your questions and ask them all at once, rather than calling every time you have a question.

- **Try to answer questions on your own.** Remember that you are hiring a legal coach, not a full-service lawyer. That means you need to do as much as you can by yourself and only turn to the coach when you are really stuck. By reading this book all the way through and consulting a nearby law library, you can answer many of your questions on your own. And those you cannot answer completely you can often narrow down.

- **Beware of other costs.** Whatever the formal fee arrangement, there may be incidental costs, such as photocopy and fax charges. If so, you might cut down on these by picking up or delivering documents yourself, or making your own copies.

- **Review lawyer bills carefully.** A lawyer who bills at $200 an hour who spends six minutes talking with you might charge you $20 or "0.1" on the bill. If that were transposed by accident as 1.0 (one hour) when the data is entered, you could end up paying $200.

Glossary

This glossary provides brief definitions of many of the terms that appear in this book. For a list of recommended legal dictionaries, see Chapter 23.

Action

Another word for a lawsuit. ("I began this negligence action last fall after the defendant, Ms. Adams, struck me while I was crossing the street at Elm and Main.")

Admission

An out-of-court statement by your adversary, which you can offer into evidence as an exception to the hearsay rule.

Affidavit

A written statement of facts made under oath. (See also "Declaration.")

Affirmative defense

A claim made by a defendant in an answer that acts as a bar to a claim in a complaint. (One common affirmative defense is that the plaintiff should not win because the "statute of limitations" (time limit within which to sue) has expired.)

Alimony (also called "spousal support" or "maintenance")

Money that one spouse pays to support the other (usually, but not always, monthly) following a divorce or separation.

Allegation

A statement by a party in a pleading saying what that party's position is and what that party intends to prove.

Annulment (also called a "nullity of marriage")

A legal decree that says, in effect, that the marriage never existed.

Answer

A defendant's response to a plaintiff's complaint. It often both denies allegations made by the plaintiff and asserts affirmative defenses.

Appeal

A request to a higher court to review the legal decision made by a lower court.

Appellant

The party who brings an appeal to an appellate court.

Appellate court

A higher court that reviews the decision of a lower court. ("The appellate court reviewed and overturned the decision of the trial court.")

Appellee

The party who responds to an appeal brought by an appellant.

Arbitration

A procedure for resolving disputes by an impartial third party (the "arbitrator") without a formal court trial.

Argument

A persuasive presentation of the law and facts of a case or particular issue within a case to the judge or jury.

At Issue Memorandum

A document stating that all parties have been served, that the parties disagree (or are "at issue") over one or more points to be resolved at trial, and how much time the parties estimate will be required for trial.

Authenticate

Identify. You "authenticate" an exhibit by offering testimony that tells the judge what the exhibit is and its connection to the case.

Bailiff

A court official, classified as a peace officer and often dressed in uniform. The bailiff performs a wide variety of duties, such as maintaining order in the courtroom, escorting witnesses in and out of court, and handing exhibits to witnesses who are testifying.

Battery

A legal claim of an uninvited touching. If someone hits you, you may have a claim of battery against that person.

Bench

The seat where a judge sits in the courtroom during a trial or hearing. Sometimes the word "bench" is used in place of the word "judge"—for example, someone might say she wants a "bench trial," meaning a trial by a judge without a jury.

Best evidence rule

A rule that restricts a witness from orally testifying to the contents of a document unless the document is produced in court or there is a valid reason why it can't be produced.

Breach

A failure or violation of a legal obligation.

Breach of contract

A legal claim that one party failed to perform as required under a valid agreement with the other party. ("The roofer breached our contract by using substandard supplies when he repaired my roof.")

Brief

A legal document written by a party to convince a judge to rule in favor of that party on one or more issues in the case.

Burden of proof

The requirement that a party convince the judge or jury that his or her claim is correct. In most civil cases, the plaintiff has the burden of proving a claim by a "preponderance of the evidence," which means something more than 50%.

Business records exception

An exception to the hearsay rule that allows a business document to be admitted into evidence if a proper foundation is laid to show it is reliable.

Caption

A heading on all pleadings submitted to the court. It states basic information such as the parties' names, court, and case number.

Case

Lawsuit. "Case" also refers to a written decision by a judge, found in books called case reporters or reporters. A party's case or "case-in-chief" also refers to the evidence that party submits in support of his or her position.

Case number (also called "cause number")

Number assigned by the clerk's office to identify a particular case. Often the case number is stamped or printed on the front (or "caption") page of the initial pleading when it is first filed. That same case number should appear on the front page of all other documents filed as part of the case.

Cause of action

See "Legal claim."

Challenge for cause

A way to get a juror dismissed from your case in which you state a reason (such as bias or a personal relationship to one of the parties) why the juror is objectionable.

Chambers (also called "judge's chambers")

A judge's private office, often located adjacent to the judge's courtroom.

Child custody

Physical control over the children and legal authority to make critical parenting decisions.

Child support

Money that one parent (usually the noncustodial parent or the parent with the higher income) pays to the other parent (usually the custodial parent or the parent with the lower income).

Child support formulas

Written guidelines (or "schedules")—typically based on a combination of the parents' ability to pay and the needs of the children—that set forth how child support is calculated in each state.

Citizenship

Allegiance to the government of the United States and to the state in which a person resides.

Circumstantial evidence

Evidence that proves a fact by means of an inference. For example, from the evidence that a person was seen running away from the scene of a crime, a judge or jury may infer that the person committed the crime.

Civil

Noncriminal. Civil lawsuits are generally between two private parties; criminal actions involve government enforcement of the criminal laws.

Claim

See "Legal claim."

Claim for relief

See "Legal claim."

Clear and convincing evidence

The burden of proof in a few types of civil cases, such as cases involving fraud. "Clear and convincing" is a higher standard than a "preponderance of the evidence," the standard typical in most civil cases, but not as high as "beyond a reasonable doubt," the standard in criminal cases.

Clerk's Office

The administrative office in a courthouse where legal documents are filed, stored, and made available to the public.

Closing argument (also called "final argument")

A persuasive presentation of your side of the case to the judge or jury at the conclusion of the evidence.

Common law

Judge-made law, resulting from appellate court decisions. Common law is often contrasted with "statutory law," which is enacted by legislatures.

Community property

A method used by about ten states to determine who owns property acquired during marriage and to divide property and debts upon divorce.

Compensatory damages

Money that is meant to compensate or make up for the losses the plaintiff suffered.

Complaint

The initial pleading, which sets out the plaintiff's legal claims and starts a lawsuit. Sometimes called a "petition."

Concurrent jurisdiction

When two courts (often one state and one federal) both have power to hear a case.

Conformed copy

Copy of a document filed with the court that bears the court's stamp and date.

Consideration

Something of value that is given in exchange for a promise in order to form a legally binding contract.

Contempt of court

Behavior, in or outside of court, that obstructs court administration, violates or resists a court order, or otherwise disrupts or shows disregard for the administration of justice. It is punishable by fine or imprisonment.

Contested divorce

A divorce is contested if, after one spouse files for divorce, the other spouse opposes some aspect of what the moving spouse requests in his or her initial pleading.

Contingent fee

A method of compensating a lawyer for legal services in which the lawyer receives a percentage of the money a client is awarded at the close of a trial or by settlement.

Continuance

A delay. A party who wants the court to postpone a deadline requests a continuance.

Contract

A legally valid agreement to do (or not do) something, such as an employment contract or contract of sale for real estate.

Costs (also called "costs of suit" or "court costs")

Expenses of trial other than attorneys' fees, such as fees and costs for filing legal documents, witness travel, court reporters, and expert witnesses. Sometimes, the party who wins a lawsuit can recover costs from the opposing party.

Counsel

Attorneys or lawyers (also called counselors). To counsel means to advise.

Counterclaim

A legal claim by a defendant against a plaintiff.

Court clerk

A court employee who assists a judge with the many administrative tasks of moving cases through the court system. For example, the court clerk may prepare and maintain the judge's calendar, retrieve case files from the main Clerk's Office, administer oaths to witnesses during trial, and prepare orders and judgments.

Court reporter

A person who records every word that is said during official court proceedings and depositions and prepares a written transcript of those proceedings.

Cross-claim (also called a "cross-complaint")

A claim filed against a third party who was not a party to the original lawsuit.

Cross-examination

A party's opportunity to ask questions of the adversary's witnesses—including the adversary if he or she testified on direct examination.

Damages

Money sought by a party who has suffered some legal wrong.

Declaration

A signed statement of facts personally known to the "declarant," the person signing the statement. (See also "Affidavit.")

Default

A party's failure to do what is required—for example, a defendant's failure to respond to the complaint.

Default judgment

A court order for judgment against the defendant to pay the amount requested by the plaintiff, because the defendant failed to answer and defend against a properly filed lawsuit.

Defendant

A party who is being sued. Sometimes called a respondent.

Demurrer

Another name, used in some court systems, for a Motion to Dismiss a Complaint for failure to state a legally valid claim.

Deponent

A person whose deposition is being taken.

Deposition

A discovery (formal pretrial investigation) tool in which a party (or his or her lawyer) asks a series of oral questions of another party or witness. The questions are answered under oath and taken down by a court reporter.

Directed verdict

A ruling by a judge, typically at the close of the plaintiff's evidence in a jury trial, that awards judgment to the defendant.

Direct examination

The initial questioning of a witness by the party who called that witness.

Discovery

Formal investigation that parties conduct before trial in order to obtain information from each other about the case to prepare for settlement or trial. The primary discovery tools in most cases are depositions and interrogatories.

Dismiss a case

When a judge dismisses a case, the judge essentially throws the case out of court, so that the moving party must refile initial pleading papers.

Diversity jurisdiction

Federal court jurisdiction based on the parties to a lawsuit being citizens of different states.

Divorce

The legal ending of a marriage.

Divorce papers

Initial pleadings (typically called a "petition" or "complaint") filed with the court to start divorce proceedings.

Docket

The term is used in two ways:

1. A formal record of all the legal documents that have been filed and the court proceedings and orders in a particular case.
2. A calendar or list of all the proceedings on a court's schedule.

Doe Defendants

Fictitious defendants that a plaintiff names in a complaint when the plaintiff is not aware of the identities of the people or organizations that caused the harm.

Elements (also called "legal elements")

Component parts of legal claims. To win, a plaintiff must prove all of the elements of a claim.

Emergency order

An emergency procedure (reserved for urgent cases, such as where you fear your spouse will hurt you or abduct your children) whereby a party may sometimes obtain a court order without giving the other party the advance written notice usually required by court rules.

Encumber property

To mortgage or otherwise use property as collateral or security for a debt.

Equitable distribution

A method the majority of states follow to distribute marital property equitably (fairly) upon divorce.

Equitable relief

A court order that a party perform an act (such as cut down a tree), rather than (or in addition to) paying money damages.

Evidence

Information presented to a judge or jury, including testimony of witnesses and documents.

Exhaustion of remedies

A legal doctrine that courts use to stay (postpone) proceedings until plaintiffs have tried other means of seeking relief—for example, by complaining to an administrative agency.

Excited utterance

An out-of-court statement made about a startling event while the speaker is experiencing that event. Such statements are admissible in evidence under an exception to the hearsay rule.

Exhibit

A tangible object that a party presents to the judge or jury during trial to help establish his or her case.

Ex parte

One-sided. A contact with the judge by one party outside the presence of the other party is considered an "ex parte contact" and is generally forbidden.

Expert witness

A person who testifies based on his or her special knowledge or training.

Fair market value

The price an item—such as a home, a business, artwork, or jewelry—would get if sold today (as opposed to the original purchase price).

Family courts

Civil courts that typically have jurisdiction over matters such as divorce, child support and custody, spousal support, paternity, and domestic abuse.

Fast track

A system certain courts have adopted to help streamline the administration and litigation of lawsuits.

Fault-based divorce

Laws requiring that a spouse filing for divorce prove that the other spouse was legally at fault for the breakdown of the marriage—for example, alleging the other spouse committed adultery or left the family home.

Federal question jurisdiction

Federal court jurisdiction based on federal rules and statutes.

Former name

Maiden name.

Forum non conveniens

A claim that a case has been filed in an inconvenient court and should for that reason be moved to a different court.

Forum shopping

Trying to have a case heard in an advantageous court.

Foundation

A basis for the admission of testimony or exhibits into evidence.

Fraud

Intentional deception causing legal injury.

FRCP

Federal Rules of Civil Procedure.

FRE

Federal Rules of Evidence.

Freeze

To close, as in to "freeze" joint bank accounts and open new ones alone following a separation or divorce.

Frivolous motion

A motion that is made without legally valid grounds, such as a motion that is designed to harass an opponent or delay proceedings.

"Full Faith and Credit Clause"

A constitutional requirement that court judgments (and other official rules) of one state be honored by all other states.

Hearsay

An out-of-court statement offered in court to prove the truth of what that statement asserts.

Hostile witness (also called "adverse witness")

A witness so hostile to the party who called him or her that the party can ask the witness leading questions.

Impanel (or "empanel")

The act of assembling a panel of prospective jurors for jury selection.

Impeach

Discredit. To impeach a witness's credibility is to cast doubt on that person's believability.

Inadmissible

When evidence offered by a party is ruled inadmissible by the judge, it is not allowed to become a part of the court record.

Injunction or injunctive relief

A form of equitable relief, such as an order that the defendant stay away from the plaintiff.

In rem jurisdiction

A court's power to decide issues concerning property located in the court's geographical area.

Interrogatories

A set of written questions submitted by one party to another party to answer under oath as part of the pretrial investigation of a lawsuit.

Irreconcilable differences (also referred to as "irretrievably broken")

Terminology spouses must use in some states to say that they feel certain they cannot get back together and that they want a divorce. (The exact term differs from state to state, but the idea is the same.)

Irrelevant

Not related to. Evidence that is irrelevant to the claims at issue in a lawsuit is not admissible in trial.

Joint (or "shared") custody

An arrangement whereby both parents share either or both the physical custody of the children (living with them some or all of the time) and the legal authority to make parenting decisions.

Judge

A public officer who presides over court hearings and trials.

Judge pro tem

A temporary or substitute judge, often a lawyer, who temporarily fills in for a regular judge. Parties can refuse to have their case heard by a judge pro tem.

Judgment

A final court ruling resolving the claims at issue in a lawsuit and determining the rights and obligations of the parties.

Judgment Notwithstanding the Verdict (JNOV)

A decision by the judge to overturn a jury's verdict because, as a matter of law, the jury's decision was unreasonable. This procedure is like a directed verdict but comes at the end of the case.

Judgment proof

A party who doesn't have money or other property to pay a court judgment is considered "judgment proof."

Judicial arbitration or mediation

Court-ordered alternative dispute resolution following the filing of a complaint and answer.

Jurisdiction

The scope of a court's authority. Often the term refers to the geographic area where a court has power.

Juror

A person selected to serve on a jury.

Jury

A group of people selected to apply the law, as given by the judge, to the facts they find to be true, to decide the outcome of a case.

Jury instructions

Legal rules given by the judge to the jury.

Jury selection

See "Voir dire."

Law clerk

An assistant to a judge, typically a recent law school graduate, who helps the judge with things such as researching issues and drafting court opinions or decisions.

Lawsuit

A legal case initiated in court.

Leading question

A question asked of a witness at trial that suggests the answer. It's really just a statement phrased as a question.

Legal claim (also called a "claim for relief" or "cause of action")

A statement of the legal wrong (such as negligence or breach of contract) for which the plaintiff seeks legal relief.

Legal separation

A legal decree that keeps a marriage intact but allows the family court to make orders separating property and awarding custody and support.

Litigant

A party to a lawsuit.

Litigation

The process of resolving a dispute through a lawsuit in court.

Litigator

An attorney whose practice involves handling lawsuits.

Local rules

Rules adopted by specific courts or specific regions that regulate case administration and litigation. Local rules sometimes modify state and federal rules, and it is critical to understand them to effectively present a case in court.

Magistrate

A court official who acts as a judge in certain (often lower level) court proceedings.

Malicious prosecution

A claim that a lawsuit was filed without sufficient justification or for an improper purpose.

Malpractice

Professional negligence; failing to use the type of care a professional should reasonably use in a given situation.

Marital property

Most property acquired by a couple during marriage. (Marital property may be "community property" in states that use that system of property classification).

Marshal

A law officer who is empowered to enforce certain court rulings and orders. The federal government has U.S. Marshals, and some states also have marshals, similar to sheriffs.

Mediation

An out-of-court dispute resolution procedure in which parties use a neutral third party (a mediator) to help them reach an agreement or settlement.

Memorandum of Points and Authorities

A document that cites (refers to) legal authorities, such as statutes and court cases, and explains how those authorities support the position advocated by the party who wrote the memorandum.

Minimum contacts

Sufficient connections to a state to give jurisdiction to the courts of that state.

Mistrial

A trial that the judge ends before the full proceeding has been completed because a prejudicial error or wrong has occurred.

Modifications

Changes a court makes to previous court orders.

Monitored visit

Court requirement that a parent (or other related adult) only visit his or her children under supervision, sometimes also only in certain places or at certain times.

Motion

A request to the court for an order or ruling. Some motions are made orally, others in writing. Depending on the ruling sought, a motion can be made before, during, or after trial.

Motion for a Continuance

See "Continuance."

Motion for Summary Judgment

See "Summary Judgment."

Motion in Limine

A request for a court order to exclude irrelevant or prejudicial evidence from being presented at trial, typically made shortly before a jury trial begins.

Movant

The party making or bringing a motion.

Moving Party

See "Movant."

Negligence

A legal claim that alleges a failure to use "ordinary and reasonable care" in a given situation.

No-fault divorce

Most states now allow divorce if either or both spouses want a divorce, on the basis of incompatibility, with no legal battle over who was at fault for the breakdown of the marriage.

Nondischargeable debts

Debts, such as child and spousal support, that are not wiped out by a bankruptcy.

Nonsuit (also called "dismissal")

The court's dismissal of a lawsuit that a plaintiff began but did not pursue.

Notice

Notification. To give someone notice of a hearing is to let them know when and where it will take place and give them other basic information.

Notice of Motion

A document that notifies an adversary about when and where a hearing on a motion will be held, what the reason for the motion is, and what supporting documentation will be relied on in making the motion.

Objection

A party's request, made during trial, asking the court to prevent certain testimony or exhibits submitted by the other side from being admitted into evidence.

Offer of judgment

A written settlement offer that can impose costs on a party who refuses it.

Opening statement

A statement made by an attorney or self-represented party at the beginning of a trial (before the evidence is introduced) to preview the evidence and set the stage for the trial.

Order

A ruling or decision by a judge. A court order can be made orally or in writing.

Order to Show Cause (OSC)

A legal document that sets forth the legal relief one party is asking for and tells the other party to come to court at a specific time and explain why the court should not grant the moving party's request.

Overrule

Deny. When the judge overrules an objection the judge denies the objection, and the evidence objected to is allowed.

Pain and suffering

Inconvenience and discomfort resulting from injuries for which damages can be sought in a lawsuit.

Party

A person or entity who has brought a lawsuit, or one who is defending against or responding to a lawsuit.

Paternity

A court action to recognize a man as the legal father of a child.

Percipient witness

A witness who perceived the facts he or she testifies about. A percipient witness is an ordinary witness (as opposed to an "expert witness" who, because of special knowledge or training, may testify about things he or she did not actually observe).

Peremptory challenge

An opportunity for a party to challenge (dismiss or excuse) a potential juror during jury selection without having to give a reason. Each party gets a limited number of peremptory challenges.

Perjury

The crime of lying while under oath—while testifying during trial, in a sworn affidavit or declaration, in a deposition, or in written interrogatories.

Personal jurisdiction

A court's power over a party to a lawsuit.

Personal property

All property that isn't real estate ("real property").

Petitioner

A person who brings a petition (in some court systems, another word for a complaint) before the court.

Plaintiff

The person who initiates a lawsuit. Sometimes called a "petitioner."

Pleadings

Legal documents filed in court that set forth the legal claims and defenses of the parties to a lawsuit

Points and Authorities

See "Memorandum of Points and Authorities."

Prayer for relief

The concluding portion of a complaint, where the plaintiff specifies what he or she wants from the court.

Prejudice

Bias or discrimination.

Prejudicial error

A wrong that occurs during trial that seriously impairs a party's ability to have a fair trial.

Prenuptial (or "antenuptial") agreement

An agreement establishing in advance the amount a spouse will have to pay in the event the couple later divorces.

Preponderance of the evidence

The burden of proof in most civil lawsuits—amounting to something more than 50%.

Present sense impression

A statement made about an event while, or just after, the event occurs. Such statements are admissible in evidence under an exception to the hearsay rule.

Pretrial conference

A meeting of the parties, before trial, to resolve and narrow the disputed issues, identify undisputed facts, and sometimes try to settle the case. Pretrial conferences may be conducted by a judge in court or by the parties themselves out of court.

Pretrial memorandum (or "Joint Pretrial Memorandum")

A document prepared before a pretrial conference in which a party identifies undisputed and disputed facts, legal issues, witnesses expected to testify, and other basic information to facilitate the pretrial conference. Some courts require parties to meet and prepare this document together (then called a "Joint Pretrial Memorandum").

Pretrial motion

A request to the court made before trial for an order or ruling. Typical pretrial motions include a Motion for Continuance, Motion to Dismiss for Failure to State a Claim, Motion for Default Judgment, and Motion for Summary Judgment.

Pretrial order

A document prepared after a pretrial conference and signed by the judge. It sets out the agreed-upon facts and the remaining factual and legal issues to be resolved at trial, the anticipated witness list, exhibits the parties will introduce, and other decisions made during the pretrial conference.

Privileged

Confidential. Information that is confidential because of a particular legal rule, such as information revealed during a private doctor-patient examination or lawyer-client meeting.

Privileges

Legal rules and principles that keep certain information confidential and out of court or discovery. Some common privileges include communications made to a spouse, doctor, lawyer, psychotherapist, or member of the clergy.

Probative

Tending to prove or disprove some contested issue. This term is usually used to describe evidence.

Pro bono

Legal services performed pro bono are done for free or at a reduced fee (from the Latin meaning "for the good").

Procedural law

Laws or rules that govern how a case is administered and tried in court. (Contrast rules of "substantive law," which define the rights and duties of parties.)

Process server

A person, such as a sheriff, who is legally authorized to serve (deliver) legal papers to a party in the case.

Promissory note

A written agreement by a borrower of money to repay a loan at a definite time.

Proof of Service

A document, often attached to a pleading, motion, or brief, that states on whom such papers were served and how and when the service was made. A Proof of Service must often be filed with the court.

Pro per (also called "pro se")

Someone who represents him- or herself in court without a lawyer.

Proposed order

A party's draft of a court order that it presents to the court along with a request for the order it seeks ("proposed" because the court hasn't signed it yet).

Pro se

See "Pro per."

Protective Order

A ruling by the court that limits or disallows a party's discovery requests. A party might seek a Protective Order, for example, if the other side's interrogatories ask for confidential, privileged information. The Protective Order would allow the party not to answer the objectionable questions.

Punitive damages

Damages meant to punish the person who committed a wrong, not simply to compensate the person who was wronged. Punitive damages are allowed only in certain circumstances—for example, when the defendant's conduct is shown to have been malicious.

Real property

Land or real estate, as opposed to "personal property" (such as money, cars, and stereos).

Rebuttal evidence

Evidence offered to contradict evidence presented by the adversary.

Recess

A break in a hearing or trial.

Record

The official written transcript of court proceedings and depositions. When something goes "on the record," it appears in the official transcript. If some aspect of the case is "off the record," such as a brief procedural question at the judge's bench, it will not appear in the official transcript.

Recross examination

Additional cross-examination of witnesses called by an adversary on redirect examination.

Redact

To delete or cover up part of a document because it refers to inadmissible evidence.

Redirect examination

Additional direct examination of a witness by the party who called that witness. It takes place just after that witness has been cross-examined by the adversary.

Release

The abandonment of a claim against a party, often in exchange for a promise or offer by the other party.

Relevancy

A connection or applicability to the issues in the case. Relevant evidence is evidence that helps to prove or disprove some fact in connection with the case.

Relief

The benefit, compensation, or redress sought in connection with a legal claim.

Remedy

The relief a party seeks in a case. Remedies for a typical tort (personal injury) claim, for example, are compensatory damages and monetary relief for pain and suffering.

Reply

A plaintiff's answer or responsive pleading to a defendant's counterclaim.

Request for Admission (or "Request to Admit")

A discovery tool in which a party asks an adversary to admit that certain facts are true. If the adversary admits the facts or fails to respond in a timely manner, they will be deemed true for the purposes of trial.

Request for Production of Documents (or "Request to Produce")

A discovery tool in which a party asks an adversary to produce (deliver or make available) specific documents.

Residency

Living in a particular state with the intention of remaining there.

Residency requirement for divorce

Each state has its own requirements for how long you must live in the state before filing for divorce (for example, six months is typical).

Respondent

The name for the defendant (responding party) in cases where the plaintiff is called a "petitioner." Also, the party who responds to an appeal (the appellee) is often called a respondent.

Response (or responsive pleading)

A general term for a legal document in which a party responds to an adversary's pleading, motion, or brief.

Restraining Order (also called a "Protective Order" or "TRO")

A court order to stop certain illegal or threatening behavior. A Restraining Order may also require a person to stay away from a spouse or children, move out of a family home, or refrain from selling property or canceling insurance.

Sanctions

Penalties, often fines, imposed by a judge for improper conduct during litigation.

Separate property

Certain property that a married person may keep separately to spend, give, or will away without the consent of the other spouse.

Service of process

The delivery of legal documents, such as initial pleadings, to an opposing party.

Settlement conference

A meeting of the parties, with or without the judge present, to discuss settlement of a lawsuit. Many courts require the parties to have at least one settlement conference, called a mandatory settlement conference (MSC), before trial.

Small claims courts

Courts with informal procedures, often limited to cases involving a maximum of $5,000.

Statutes

Laws enacted by legislatures.

Statute of frauds

A law requiring certain contracts to be in writing—for example, contracts to buy or sell real property. Most other contracts can be oral.

Statute of limitations

The legal time limit in which a lawsuit can be filed for a particular legal claim.

Stipulation

An agreement between parties. For example, you and your adversary may stipulate (agree) to the admissibility of certain testimony or an exhibit.

Strike

Delete testimony from the official court record.

Subject matter jurisdiction

The power of a court to hear certain kinds of cases.

Subpoena (or "subpena")

A court order compelling someone to appear in court.

Subpoena Duces Tecum

A court order compelling someone to appear in court and bring along with them certain tangible objects or documents.

Substantive law

Rules defining the rights and duties of parties (as opposed to procedural laws, which govern the litigation process).

Summary judgment

A final decision by the judge resolving the claims in a lawsuit before trial, based on affidavits and written evidence. A summary judgment is issued when the parties have no issues of fact to litigate, only legal questions.

Summons

A notice, typically served along with a complaint, informing the defendant that a lawsuit has been initiated and notifying the defendant of where and when he or she must respond.

Supporting declarations

Written statements under oath setting out facts that justify the issuance of a court order.

Sustain

Uphold. When a judge sustains an objection, it is upheld, and the evidence objected to is not allowed in.

Tentative ruling

A preliminary decision of a judge in a hearing or trial, based on the papers submitted and typically issued sometime before the scheduled court proceeding.

Testify

To give testimony under oath.

Testimony

Evidence given by a witness under oath, in court, or in a deposition.

Tort

A legal claim of civil wrong (other than a breach of contract), often referred to as a personal injury.

Transcript

A written record of a court proceeding or deposition.

Treatise

A legal reference book, usually covering an entire legal subject.

Trial

The in-court examination and resolution of issues between litigants.

Trial notebook

A notebook or binder set up to help you organize your case.

Uncontested divorce

A divorce is uncontested if both parties want the divorce and have agreed upon questions of property division, support, or child custody. Simplified court procedures are available for uncontested divorces.

Venue

The geographic area in which a court has authority to hear a case.

Verdict

The jury's final decision in a lawsuit.

Verified pleadings

Pleadings signed under oath.

Voir dire

The process of questioning and selecting a jury.

Waiting period

A period of time that many states require spouses to wait between when a divorce is granted by the court and when it becomes final (often three to six months).

Witness

A person who testifies in court.

Index